## PRAISE FOR *EIS PEIRASMÓN*

"Elmetti has written an important book which forces readers to grapple with the meaning of the biblical text rather than focus on what scholars have proposed. He clarifies the meaning and role of temptation in the Lord's Prayer in the context of seminal Old and New Testament texts. Clearly written, this book is a thought-provoking pleasure to read!"

—Eckhard J. Schnabel, Gordon-Conwell Theological Seminary

"A very thorough investigation that takes as its starting point the theological difficulty—within the church itself—of making sense of the traditional translation of the Lord's Prayer. The study answers the question whether God can lead into temptation by applying a whole arsenal of accepted exegetical methods. The result is well argued and surprising: an endorsement of God's grace in the time of *peirasmós*."

—David J. Trobisch, New Testament scholar

"Elmetti problematizes the range of ways in which *eis peirasmón* in the Lord's Prayer has been understood by scholars, and for that, he deserves our commendation. He then goes on to offer a fresh and quite distinctive understanding of this challenging phrase that warrants careful scrutiny."

—John Nolland, retired New Testament scholar

"Elmetti's book is an innovative and thought-provoking search for the meaning of the sixth petition of the Lord's Prayer, which audaciously moves to and fro from Semitic and Greek philology to theology, and discusses the Scriptures and the church fathers, as well as the religious poetry of Dead Sea Scrolls."

—Eibert Tigchelaar, Katholieke Universiteit Leuven

# Eis Peirasmón

# Eis Peirasmón

On the Quest for the Lost Message of Redemption
and Damnation Contained in the Lord's Prayer

FEDERICO ELMETTI

RESOURCE *Publications* • Eugene, Oregon

EIS PEIRASMÓN
On the Quest for the Lost Message of Redemption and Damnation Contained in the Lord's Prayer

Copyright © 2022 Federico Elmetti. All rights reserved. Except for brief quotations in critical publications or reviews, no part of this book may be reproduced in any manner without prior written permission from the publisher. Write: Permissions, Wipf and Stock Publishers, 199 W. 8th Ave., Suite 3, Eugene, OR 97401.

Resource Publications
An Imprint of Wipf and Stock Publishers
199 W. 8th Ave., Suite 3
Eugene, OR 97401

www.wipfandstock.com

PAPERBACK ISBN: 978-1-6667-4947-2
HARDCOVER ISBN: 978-1-6667-4948-9
EBOOK ISBN: 978-1-6667-4949-6

03/02/23

*To my parents, who taught me reason,
and to my wife, who taught me faith.*

*"Sic et Pater meus caelestis faciet vobis
si non remiseritis unusquisque fratri suo
de cordibus vestris."*
(MATT 18:35 VUL)

# Contents

| | | |
|---|---|---|
| Preface | | xi |
| Abbreviations | | xv |
| Introduction | | xix |
| 1 | God Does Not Lead Us into Temptation | 1 |
| 2 | The Sermon on the Mount | 4 |
| 3 | *Eisphérō* | 7 |
| 4 | To Lead or to Allow to Go? | 11 |
| 5 | The Lord's Prayer in Different Idioms | 18 |
| 6 | Causative vs. Permissive | 23 |
| 7 | The Permissive Construct in Biblical Greek | 27 |
| 8 | Can God Lead Man Astray? | 35 |
| 9 | The Permissive Sensitivity in the Old Testament | 48 |
| 10 | The Causative Form of "to Enter" in the Old Testament | 60 |
| 11 | The Theory of the Divine "Cardiodynamic" | 68 |
| 12 | Divine Justice and Free Will: the Choice between Good and Evil | 77 |
| 13 | God and the Necessary Evil: the Examples of Noah and Lot | 94 |
| 14 | The Relationship between God and Satan: the Example of Job | 105 |
| 15 | Critique of the Church Fathers | 121 |
| 16 | The Concept of Temptation in the Old Testament | 156 |
| 17 | The Concept of Temptation According to the Evangelists | 172 |
| 18 | The Big Misunderstanding | 194 |
| 19 | Lead Us Not into *Peirasmós* | 213 |
| 20 | But Deliver Us from Evil | 223 |
| 21 | Is It *Ponērós* or *Ponērón*? | 240 |
| 22 | The Dead Sea Scrolls and the Extra-Biblical Tradition | 251 |
| 23 | The Active Interpretation | 271 |
| 24 | The Eschatological Interpretation and the Unsolved Problem | 278 |

| | | |
|---|---|---|
| 25 | The Lord's Prayer in the *Gethsēmaní* and the Problem of Trivialization | 299 |
| 26 | *Agnus Dei* | 320 |
| 27 | The Meaning of *Peirasmós* in the Sixth Petition | 328 |
| 28 | The Meaning of the Sixth Petition | 345 |
| 29 | The Secretary of Divine Mercy | 357 |
| 30 | The Lord's Prayer, Corrected | 367 |
| Appendix | | 373 |
| Bibliography | | 379 |

# Preface

"Are you a believer?"

The point-blank question posed to me by my eight-grade teacher left me bewildered. There and then, as a teenager whose only contact with religion was the Sunday Mass I attended more out of habit than conviction, I honestly did not know what to answer. My relationship with faith was not high on my list of priorities, but probably not to make a bad impression, I sketched a not-too-convinced "Yes, I am."

"You must have read the Bible then."

I was stunned. No, of course I had not read the Bible. I admitted that no, I had not read it.

"Then how can you call yourself a believer if you have never read the Bible?"

Since I had no good answer to such a simple question, I quietly returned to my desk.

Many years later, an adult and with family in tow, I was sitting in the pews of our parish church. I still remember the moment when, in the middle of the Sunday homily, Fr. Bill—now bishop Byrne in Pittsburgh, Massachusetts—commenting on the Lord's Prayer, pointed out how this prayer is so rich in meaning that hundreds of pages could be written—and indeed have been written—for each of its verses. I thought he was exaggerating. But those words, for some obscure reason, stuck with me. Strange—because I tend to forget the content of a homily the exact instant it ends.

I would not understand the reason until a few years later when, wandering through the news from my home country—Italy, I was struck by an article announcing that finally, after much waiting and much debate, the new Italian text of the Lord's Prayer had been approved by the Italian Bishops' Conference in which the translation of the sixth petition, "lead us not into temptation," had been officially changed to "do not abandon us to temptation."

This fact intrigued me. What had prompted the church to change the best-known prayer among the Italian faithful—the very first one that I learned as a child? I began to read a little, here and there, about the reasons for such a choice, and I knew right away that, in doing so, I was getting myself into an alley from which I would never get out, at least not until I had found a satisfactory answer to the question.

Thus began three years of intense work. I set about reading everything that had been written on the interpretation of this verse of the Lord's Prayer over the past decades. Suddenly, it became clear to me how right bishop Byrne was. I discovered how the debate among academics was anything but recent and anything but mild. I discovered that interpretations of all sorts and kinds—that would make the sixth petition say anything and everything—have been circulating even since the days of the earliest Christian communities. Each of them supported by complex theological and exegetical reasoning.

I must confess that, amid that jumble of such authoritative and at the same time conflicting comments, I have several times been tempted to throw in the towel. If emeritus scholars and theologians had debated for centuries on the correct interpretation of the petition without ever reaching a universally agreed conclusion, what chance did I have of finding a solution to the dilemma? The very idea seemed naive to me and, frankly speaking, quite arrogant.

Until I set out to read the text of the Lord's Prayer in its original language (never did I expect my liberal studies of ancient Greek to come in handy in life). And immediately I had the feeling that all those commentaries, all those learned disquisitions, all those sophisticated interpretations contained something profoundly incorrect, as far as they tried to make the Lord's Prayer say not what the Lord's Prayer was trying to say, but what that particular scholar, no matter how authoritative, wanted the Lord's Prayer to say.

At that time, I still had no idea what the correct solution was, but one thing was clear to me: if a solution existed, it could not be any of those proposed to date.

I began to study and especially began to read the Bible. It was a deeply humbling experience. As I was reading, I began to realize how little I knew about my religion. I began to understand how shaky the foundations of my faith were. I began to understand how right my eight-grade teacher was: "How can you call yourself a believer if you have never read the Bible?"

As I was reading, I began to understand things that—I must admit—I should have understood many years before. I felt embarrassed to realize that I had never really grasped the meaning of expressions heard from the pulpit a million times, such as "Christ died for us," or "Christ saved us from our sins." I realized that even the rite of Mass, which I had attended every Sunday since I was a child, was something profoundly different from what I had always thought it was!

And as I was reading the Bible, frantically jumping from one passage in one book to another passage in another book related to it, trying to tie up the loose ends and put together the tiny pieces of a very intricate puzzle, I came to realize how impossible it was to be able to decode the sixth petition of the Lord's Prayer without understanding who Jesus was and why he did what the Gospels tell us he did.

And to understand all this, it requires diving into the meanders of the original texts—the Hebrew of the Old Testament and the Greek of the New Testament—and recognizing how one reverberates in the other. Hence, the decision to present the reader, when necessary, with the original passages in Hebrew and Greek, in order to play it straight, without linguistic tricks that may alter their meaning.

But no fear: no knowledge from the Greek or Hebrew language is needed to tackle this book. Every technical/grammatical detail, even the most arduous, is explained and eviscerated in such a way that the reader will have a chance to appreciate the complexity of any interpretative nuances. In this book, the reader will be exposed to hundreds of passages in Scripture, which are not simply referenced quickly but fully presented and carefully analyzed in their context (too often, biblical quotes are taken out of context to make them say whatever one wants them to say). I believe this is the most intellectually honest way of proceeding, which is also the only way I know of to show respect for the reader.

It may sound odd, but this book was not written *after* I had pondered and found my personal solution to the sixth petition dilemma. It was written *while*. In fact, this book was the means by which I arrived at the solution I arrived at. More than once I found myself in the position of not knowing, given the conclusions I had come to in the previous chapter, what the conclusions I would come to in the next chapter would be.

This book was written as a continuous discovery—really like a puzzle that takes shape bit by bit and whose final figure you can guess, but not fully understand, at least until the last piece is applied. And the final figure was a surprising discovery for me as well. Surprising, but also revealing.

Because once we understand the true meaning of the sixth petition and realize that it does not mean what we have always thought it meant, it is no longer possible to recite the Lord's Prayer in the same way we were taught as children.

No matter which translation we may decide to adopt.

# Abbreviations

## BOOKS

| | |
|---|---|
| Gen | Genesis |
| Exod | Exodus |
| Lev | Leviticus |
| Num | Numbers |
| Deut | Deuteronomy |
| Josh | Joshua |
| Judg | Judges |
| 1 Sam | Samuel (First Book) |
| 2 Sam | Samuel (Second Book) |
| 1 Kgs | Kings (First Book) |
| 2 Kgs | Kings (Second Book) |
| Isa | Isaiah |
| Jer | Jeremiah |
| Ezek | Ezekiel |
| Hos | Hosea |
| Joel | Joel |
| Amos | Amos |
| Obad | Obadiah |
| Jonah | Jonah |
| Mic | Micah |
| Nah | Nahum |
| Hab | Habakkuk |
| Zeph | Zephaniah |
| Hag | Haggai |
| Zech | Zechariah |
| Mal | Malachi |
| Ps (*pl.*: Pss) | Psalm |
| Job | Job |

## ABBREVIATIONS

| | |
|---|---|
| Prov | Proverbs |
| Ruth | Ruth |
| Song | Song of Songs |
| Eccl | Ecclesiastes (Qoheleth) |
| Lam | Lamentations |
| Esth | Esther |
| Dan | Daniel |
| Ezra | Ezra |
| Neh | Nehemiah |
| 1 Chr | Chronicles (First Book) |
| 2 Chr | Chronicles (Second Book) |
| Bar | Baruch |
| Jdt | Judith |
| 1 Macc | Maccabees (First Book) |
| 2 Macc | Maccabees (Second Book) |
| 3 Macc | Maccabees (Third Book) |
| 4 Macc | Maccabees (Fourth Book) |
| Sir | Sirach (Ecclesiasticus) |
| Tob | Tobit |
| Wis | Wisdom of Solomon |
| Matt | Matthew |
| Mark | Mark |
| Luke | Luke |
| John | John |
| Acts | Acts of Apostles |
| Rom | Romans |
| 1 Cor | Corinthians (First Letter) |
| 2 Cor | Corinthians (Second Letter) |
| Gal | Galatians |
| Eph | Ephesians |
| Phil | Philippians |
| Col | Colossians |
| 1 Thess | Thessalonians (First Letter) |
| 2 Thess | Thessalonians (Second Letter) |
| 1 Tim | Timothy (First Letter) |
| 2 Tim | Timothy (Second Letter) |
| Titus | Titus |
| Phlm | Philemon |
| Heb | Hebrews |
| Jas | James |
| 1 Pet | Peter (First Letter) |

| | |
|---|---|
| 2 Pet | Peter (Second Letter) |
| 1 John | John (First Letter) |
| 2 John | John (Second Letter) |
| 3 John | John (Third Letter) |
| Jude | Jude |
| Rev | Revelations |

## BIBLE TRANSLATIONS

| | |
|---|---|
| AB | Amplified Bible |
| AFV | A Faithful Version |
| AKJV | American King James Version |
| ASV | American Standard Version |
| BSB | Berean Study Bible |
| CEV | Contemporary English Version |
| CPDV | Catholic Public Domain Version |
| CSB | Christian Standard Bible |
| DBT | Darby Bible Translation |
| DRB | Douay-Rheims Bible |
| ERV | English Revised Version |
| ESV | English Standard Version |
| GNT | Good News Translation |
| HCSB | Holman Christian Standard Bible |
| ISV | International Standard Version |
| KJV | King James Version |
| LSV | Literal Standard Version |
| NAB | New American Bible |
| NASB | New American Standard Bible |
| NET | New English Translation |
| NHEB | New Heart English Bible |
| NIV | New International Version |
| NKJV | New King James Version |
| NLV | New Living Translation |
| NRSV | New Revised Standard Version |
| SLT | Smith's Literal Translation |
| VUL | Vulgate |
| WBT | Webster's Bible Translation |
| WEB | World English Bible |
| YLT | Young's Literal Translation |

# Introduction

"This translation is . . ."

Pope Francis, born Jorge Mario Bergoglio, sitting in a purple armchair with floral embroidery—the crucifix framed in the corner but clearly visible behind him—cannot hide a grimace of disappointment. He hesitates, searches for the most appropriate adjective, and finally falls back on a diplomatic "not good."

"Not a good translation."

He is referring to the controversial passage in the Lord's Prayer, the prayer taught to us directly by Jesus Christ, in which the Father is asked not to lead us into temptation. When asked by the interviewer,[1] Fr. Marco Pozza, how it is possible to imagine a God who willingly leads us into temptation, Pope Francis admits that the problem lies entirely in the translation, which does not do justice to the true message of Christ.

It is theologically wrong to think that Jesus could have taught us to ask the Father not to do something that contradicts the infinitely merciful nature of God. Leading into temptation is something that is only in the chords of the devil. This is his (the devil's) main occupation, Pope Francis explains. It is its distinctive feature. It is the very reason for his existence: trying to bring us down, by whatever means and at whatever time. Even thinking of associating this kind of activity to God, the merciful Father, would have a vague taste of blasphemy.

The debate about "lead us not into temptation" is hardly recent. Pope Francis certainly did not raise it. It animated the first Christian communities from the beginning, so much so that most of the church fathers tried to explain its deep meaning. The discussion among bishops, theologians, academics, and biblical scholars intensified after the Second Vatican Council (1969), which had replaced, in liturgical celebrations, the Latin of St. Jerome's Vulgate[2] ("*ne nos inducas in tentationem*") with the vernacular.

In the year 2000, under the pontificate of Pope John Paul II, a small commission of five expert biblical scholars was charged with developing a new Italian translation that would overcome the "scandal" of a God who would lead us into temptation. After

---

1. The interview was broadcasted on December 6, 2017, for the program "Padre Nostro" (TV2000it).

2. The so-called Vulgate, the Latin translation of the Bible by St. Jerome, dates to the fourth century and was officially adopted by the Catholic Church in the sixteenth century.

a long and meticulous study, the commission decided that the most accurate Italian translation should be "*non abbandonarci alla tentazione.*"[3] The proposal received formal approval from the Italian Episcopal Conference (CEI) in 2002. The Holy See (under the pontificate of Pope Benedict XVI) approved the translation in 2007. But, at the time of Pope Francis's interview with Don Pozza in 2017, it had not yet come into force, due to an interminable work of revision of the Roman Missal (the one that regulates liturgical celebrations).

In his 2007 book, Pope Benedict XVI devotes an entire chapter[4] to the correct interpretation of the Lord's Prayer, and, regarding the critical passage, he admits that "the way this petition is phrased is shocking for many people: God certainly does not lead us into temptation."[5] Therefore, what we are really asking of the Father is not to "set too wide the boundaries within which"[6] we may be tempted, that is, not to let Satan tempt us beyond the limits of our possibility of endurance.

Although apparently disconcerting, Pope Benedict XVI explains, the language of the Lord's Prayer should not sound scandalous, but rather be interpreted considering the words of St. Cyprian of Carthage (third century), who recalled how "the adversary [Satan] can do nothing against us without God's prior authorization."[7] And God certainly does not have our destruction in his plans. Instead, he cares about our moral fortification. This fortification can pass only through a process—even a very painful one—of temptation, which humbles our pride and makes us rediscover our faith. Using a wartime comparison, St. Cyprian reminds us that "it is not in times of peace that one sees the man who is trained in the tactics of war."[8] On the contrary, to be able to call oneself an expert in battle, "one must have proved oneself a proud fighter against the enemy."[9]

St. Cyprian's position, which Pope Benedict XVI takes up in his analysis, well represents the solution that most of the church fathers found to the age-old question of the interpretation of this passage of the Lord's Prayer.

Tertullian, between the second and third centuries, had arrived at the same conclusion in his *De oratione*,[10] when he explained, "*ne nos inducas in tentationem, id est, ne nos patiaris induci ab eo utique qui temptat.*"[11] Even in the *Codex Bobbiensis*, one of the oldest Latin manuscripts of the New Testament, there is a gloss that makes it

---

3. "Do not abandon us to temptation."
4. Benedict XVI, *Jesus of Nazareth*, 128–68.
5. Benedict XVI, *Jesus of Nazareth*, 160.
6. Benedict XVI, *Jesus of Nazareth*, 163.
7. Cyprian, *De oratione dominica*, 25.
8. Cyprian, *De oratione dominica*, 25.
9. Cyprian, *De oratione dominica*, 25.
10. *On prayer.*
11. "Do not lead us into temptation, that is, do not suffer us to be led into temptation, obviously by the one who tempts" (Tertullian, *De oratione*, 8).

clear that the incriminated passage should be understood as *"ne passus fueris induci nos in tentationem."*[12] Marcion of Sinope, a bishop and theologian, although expelled from the early church because he was accused of heresy (he claimed that the God announced by Christ was fundamentally different from the God of the Old Testament), had come to the same conclusion.[13] Also St. Chromatius of Aquileia, St. Jerome of Stridon, St. Ambrose, and St. Augustine (fourth century) all converged on the same solution with minor lexical differences.

And so? If the issue had already been discussed and resolved within the church of the first centuries, why do we continue to talk about it? Probably because, as Pope Benedict XVI well says, the expression "lead us not into temptation" sounds disconcerting and, despite all the possible turns of phrase and explanations and glosses to make it more acceptable, it still upsets the faithful who pronounce it, just as, most likely, it upset the faithful of the first communities of Christians.

And upon this red thread that goes from the church fathers up to Pope Benedict XVI, the sharp words of Pope Francis pounce. With the frankness and simplicity that distinguish him and that have made him extremely popular among the faithful and not only, he does not evade the interviewer's question. The reasoning is dry, linear. Since it is not God, but the devil, who leads us into temptation, there is only one possibility. That verse of the Lord's Prayer is mistranslated and should be changed to a more correct "do not let us fall into temptation," or "do not abandon us to temptation."

Probably weighing in here are the Argentine origins of Pope Francis, who has been accustomed since his childhood to reciting the Spanish translation of the Lord's Prayer in the form *"no nos dejes caer en la tentación,"*[14] clearly a much more acceptable expression than "lead us not into temptation."

In fact, recently France has officially abandoned the Vulgate translation and veered to alternative formulations that would reconcile the Lord's Prayer with the authentic message of Christ.[15] Following France, in 2020, right after Easter, the Italian Episcopal Conference officially published the new Italian Missal with the new translation ("do not abandon us to temptation").[16]

With one slight problem: there is not much in the original Greek text of the Gospels that may legitimize such translations. The Greek text is clear, and it says, "lead us not." Not "do not let us fall." Not "do not abandon us." Just "lead us not."

So what? So, we are back to square one, faced with an apparent paradox that shakes the foundations of the Christian doctrine. Either we accept the original Greek

12. "Do not suffer us to be led into temptation."
13. Harnack, *Marcion*, 207.
14. "Do not let us fall into temptation."
15. On December 3, 2017, France officially changed the French translation of the Lord's Prayer agreed upon during the Second Vatican Council, replacing the expression "do not submit us to temptation" with "do not let us enter into temptation."
16. Liturgical use in the Italian Mass did not officially begin until November 29, 2020.

## INTRODUCTION

text as the expression of the word of God—of the *lógos* revealed to people through the work of the Holy Spirit—at the risk, however, of pronouncing a blasphemous invocation, or we look for free interpretations that better suit the doctrine of faith, but that wreak havoc on the original text of the Gospels, with the inevitable risk of relativizing them and thus depriving them of their transcendent nature.

But is it thinkable that the Vulgate, which has been considered the reference text of the Catholic Church for centuries, is wrong? Is it thinkable that the English translation of the Lord's Prayer, as we have always known it, and which was modeled on the Vulgate, is wrong? Is it thinkable that it is necessary to correct the words of Christ, which sound scandalous to our ears? Is there no other possibility? Is there no third way?

This essay is an ambitious and reckless attempt to rethink the Lord's Prayer from the beginning, and with it to come closer, if possible, to the authentic message of Christ.

Let us begin.

# 1

# God Does Not Lead Us into Temptation

Let us begin with a fundamentally inescapable principle. The same one from which both Pope Benedict XVI and Pope Francis derive their arguments: God does not lead us into temptation. Period. And he does not, simply because there is already someone who does it: Satan. The act of leading into temptation implies ruthless malice: rejoicing in people's ruinous fall into sin. And anything that contains malice cannot derive from God, who is pure good. Therefore, God has nothing to do with temptation, understood as induction to sin. That is satanic territory, in which not even God enters.

At the basis of this argument are the powerful words that appear in the first chapter of the epistle of James. Let us read the original text: "μηδεὶς πειραζόμενος λεγέτω ὅτι Ἀπὸ θεοῦ πειράζομαι· ὁ γὰρ θεὸς ἀπείραστός ἐστιν κακῶν, πειράζει δὲ αὐτὸς οὐδένα"[1] (Jas 1:13).

The verse is divided into two parts. The first warns anyone in the condition of being tempted against saying they are tempted by God. The *incipit* is peremptory. *Mēdeìs legétō*: "let no one say," "let no one venture to say." The term *peirazómenos* is a passive participle derived from the verb *peirázō* (πειράζω), indicating the act of tempting. *Mēdeìs peirazómenos legétō* should therefore be understood as, "let no one, tempted, say," "let no one, in the moment of temptation, say," "let no one, when tempted, dare to say." What should not we say? *Apò theoû peirázomai*: I am tempted by God! The second part of the verse explains why. God is *apeírastos* (ἀπείραστος), literally "untemptable."[2] Impervious to temptation, we might say. *Apeírastos* goes hand in hand with *kakôn* (κακῶν), which represents evil, malice. James is telling us that God

---

1. "*Mēdeìs peirazómenos legétō hóti Apò theoû peirázomai; ho gàr theòs apéirastós estin kakôn, peirázei dè autòs oudéna*" = "Let no one say when tempted, 'I am tempted by God,' for God cannot be tempted with evil neither tempts anyone."

2. From the root of the verb πειράζω with the addition of the privative alpha. It appears only once in the entire New Testament.

is incorruptible, refractory to any evil temptation. Finally, while it is not possible to tempt God, on the other hand, God himself *peirázei oudéna*, that is, "tempts no one."

Crystal clear. Definitive. God has nothing to do with temptation, he cannot be tempted, he does not lead anyone into temptation, and let no one dare to say otherwise.

Given this background, how is it even possible to imagine that Christ could have uttered words like "Father, lead us not into temptation"? This is exactly what James is enjoining us never to say! And, although there is no consensus among biblical scholars on the exact identification of the historical figure of James, it is absolutely plausible to think that he was a deep connoisseur of the words and teachings of Jesus—a Jew belonging to those very first Christian communities of the first half of the first century who had had direct contact with Jesus himself or with the closest disciples of Jesus.[3] Somebody with a certain culture, a good knowledge of the Greek language, and—it is legitimate to think—a perfect mastery of the Lord's Prayer. Not only. James must have been a well-known and respected personality of the time, since his short letter, composed of only five chapters, began to circulate widely within those first Christian communities, until it officially became part of the canonical letters of the New Testament (third century). In the opening of the letter, the author, who calls himself simply "James, servant of God and of the Lord Jesus Christ," seems to know that he needs no other epithet to be recognized by the reader.

Things do not add up. If it is true, as it is true, that God does not tempt anyone, how could Jesus Christ, the self-proclaimed Son of God, have used that very expression that James, a profound connoisseur of Jesus, categorically forbids? And what is more, how could he have used that very expression in the prayer that he himself taught and handed down to people as the prototype of the invocation to God the Father? How is it possible to make coexist the "lead us not into temptation" pronounced by Christ with James's admonition to never say we are tempted by God? How could James write such a letter and at the same time recite the Lord's Prayer without feeling embarrassed? The only plausible answer is that in this letter James was trying to unravel the confusion that we imagine had spread even among the first Christian communities. And in James's mind, it was clear that Jesus never intended to teach us to ask the Father not to lead us into temptation.

But what did Jesus mean by those words then? Did he really mean, "do not abandon us to temptation," or "do not let us fall into temptation," or "do not allow us to be led into temptation by the Evil One more than we can bear"? That may be. But if this is what he meant, why did he not simply say that?

Now, the only reasonable answer to this observation would seem to be the imperfection of the Greek text handed down by the evangelists Matthew and Luke. We

---

3. There are five James's mentioned in the New Testament. Two of the twelve Apostles: James of Zebedee, also called James the Greater, and James of Alphaeus, called the Lesser. Then there is James, father of the Apostle Judas, and James, son of Alphaeus, disciple of Jesus. Finally, we find James the Just, also known as "the brother of the Lord," head of the church in Jerusalem after the death of Jesus until 62 AD and to whom the authorship of the epistle of James in the New Testament is generally attributed.

would have then to assume that what Jesus said (most likely in Aramaic and certainly not in Greek) is something slightly different. In other words, the Greek text would not exactly match the words spoken by Jesus. So, here is the question. Are we willing to sacrifice so easily the sacredness of the original texts of the Gospels, understood as the revealed *lógos*, on the altar of an alleged theological coherence?

Is another, equally reasonable, explanation possible that preserves Christ's word as it is handed down in the Gospels? Perhaps, Christ never explicitly said "do not abandon us to temptation," or "do not let us fall into temptation," or "do not allow us to be led into temptation," simply because *none* of this was what he meant.

# 2

# The Sermon on the Mount

Picture the scene.

Jesus has just begun his preaching, but his miracles have already attracted literally thousands of people to him—an overflowing crowd, from his closest disciples, who follow him everywhere and hang on his every word, to the simply curious, eager to see and hear the one who proclaims himself to be the true Messiah, sent to earth by God to save humanity.

"And seeing the multitudes . . ." So begins chapter 5 of Matthew's Gospel, which introduces the long so-called "Sermon on the Mount." Jesus sees the flood of people waiting for him, wanting to listen to his teachings, and decides that the only suitable place to be able to address the crowds is to climb a mountain, most likely in such a way that the slope would give everyone a chance to see him and, more importantly, to hear him. When his disciples catch up with him, Jesus begins, "Blessed are the poor in spirit." And here Matthew seems to suspend the story of the events related to Jesus' life, slows down the narrative, and dilates the time to summarize the highest teachings of Jesus in a long sermon that will occupy the three central chapters of his Gospel. Matthew will mention four other great sermons of Jesus, but the Sermon on the Mount is the first and the one that undoubtedly lays the foundations of Christian doctrine.

We do not know if Jesus really said all that Matthew reports in a single speech, or if for descriptive simplicity Matthew decided to condense the *summa* of Christ's thought right here, at the beginning of his Gospel, as a fundamental starting point, essential for every believer. In any case, it is plausible that Jesus simply did not speak off the cuff, but that in some way the themes he touched on were inspired by the context, by his contact with the crowd, by talking with them, by listening to their questions, their concerns, by looking at their faces thirsting for truth. It is plausible to think that in front of a spiritually disoriented crowd, asking the teacher for explanations about the Law, Moses, the prophets, and the commandments, Jesus decided to reveal to them the true meaning of Scripture and, above all, their practical implications in daily life.

What emerges is one of the most revolutionary speeches ever delivered in the history of humankind, almost scandalous for the modernity of the message, which suddenly overturns the scale of values, displaces common sense, reveals to the people the new face of a God who had not been understood or imagined until then.

Amidst the general excitement mixed with bewilderment, Jesus speaks of the last, the afflicted, the meek, the persecuted who will inherit the kingdom of heaven. He flogs the hypocrisy of scribes and Pharisees, he does not get lost in lofty theological disquisitions, he faces concrete themes, even delicate and thorny ones, such as murder, adultery, divorce. He exhorts to turn the other cheek, to love one's enemy, for "if you love those who love you, what merit do you have?"[1] (Matt 5:46). He urges people to repudiate hypocrisy in every minimal daily action. Almsgiving and good works? They must be done in secret. Prayer? In the privacy of your room. "Pray to your Father in secret; and your Father, who sees in secret, will reward you" (Matt 6:6). And here comes the most interesting part.

Picture the scene. A crowd accustomed to the strict and obtuse respect of the Mosaic law contained in Scripture, suddenly hears from the Son of God that, if they want to enter the kingdom of heaven, they must first of all repudiate the hypocrisy of praying in public with useless and convoluted words, for the sole purpose of impressing those present. "But then how should we pray?" We are almost able to imagine the comments of the crowd. And Jesus' explanation is one of disarming simplicity. To be heard by the Father, you do not need empty high-sounding words and long ramblings. Direct, simple, dry words are enough, "because your Father knows what you need even before you ask him" (Matt 6:8). And so, at the request of those present to teach them what the correct words to use when praying are, the Son of God amazes them by declaiming what will become the Lord's Prayer, an invocation to God the Father, containing seven short petitions, without frills, that unite heaven and earth, and that concretely show how the transcendent God is actually very close to the practical needs of the immanent. Just as the very body of Christ represents the ineffable union between the transcendent and immanent nature of a God who was not afraid to become man, there is nothing scandalous in asking the Father to help us not only to reach spiritual perfection, but also to provide for our daily needs, to give us food to survive, to preserve us from all that could cause us harm and suffering, both physical and moral. Christ's human and divine natures coexist in him as two complementary forces—one necessary to the other—sometimes in harmonious symbiosis (as in the episode of the transfiguration on Mount Tabor), sometimes in dramatic antithesis (as in the agony in the garden on the Mount of Olives). It is therefore reasonable that his prayer to the Father contains within itself both elements, divine and earthly, even if

---

1. Unless otherwise indicated, all Scripture references are taken from the King James Version (KJV).

in an obvious hierarchical scale (the first part of the Lord's Prayer pertains to heaven, the second part to earth).

It is precisely in this second part that the sixth petition is inserted. This is one of the most controversial verses, which has sparked endless debates, and which precisely prompted Pope Francis to speak of "not a good translation" of the Gospels. Let us start then from the original Greek text: "μὴ εἰσενέγκῃς ἡμᾶς εἰς πειρασμόν"[2] (Matt 6:13; Luke 11:4).

*Mḕ* (μὴ) is a particle that introduces the negative imperative associated with the verb *eisenénkēis* (εἰσενέγκῃς), which indicates the action of "leading into" and has as its object the personal pronoun *hēmâs* (ἡμᾶς) in the first-person plural. The expression *mḕ eisenénkēis hēmâs* is therefore generally translated as "lead us not." The place where we ask the Father not to lead us into is defined by the expression *eis peirasmón* (εἰς πειρασμόν), which is generally translated as "into temptation." All very straightforward. So how is it possible that a period with such a trivial grammatical construct can give rise to so much controversy? How is it possible not to have "a good translation" of such a simple sentence?

There must be an underlying misunderstanding. And the misunderstanding must hide in that verb, *eisenénkēis*, which cannot (should not) be translated as "to lead." The correct interpretation must be different. Otherwise, we would find ourselves in a logical absurdity: a God who is pure goodness and who voluntarily pushes us to evil. So, let us try to understand exactly where this misunderstanding lies.

After all—as we all know—it is in the details that the devil hides.

---

2. "*mḕ eisenénkēis hēmâs eis peirasmón*" = "lead us not into temptation."

# 3

# *Eisphérō*

Let us start with a fundamental question. Is it possible to assume that the meaning of *mḕ eisenénkēis hēmâs* is not "lead us not," but rather "do not abandon us," or "do not let us fall,"[1] or similar variants? In our opinion, the answer is very simple. No, it cannot. At least, if we want to remain faithful to the Greek text. Below, we will try to explain why.

From a grammatical point of view, *eisenénkēis* is a particular conjugation[2] of the verb *eisphérō* (εἰσφέρω). The verb *eisphérō* is derived, in turn, from the combination of the verb *phérō* (φέρω) with the particle *eis* (εἰς), which describes a motion *into* something. The verb *phérō* is one of the most common verbs in the Greek language. Browsing through any dictionary of ancient Greek, one may find that this verb can generally be translated as "to take," with all the meanings, figurative and otherwise, that this term can have in the English language. The verb *eisphérō* does not differ substantially from the original meaning of the verb *phérō*. Simply, the preposition *eis* reinforces the idea of a movement into something. "To take into." Therefore, "to introduce." "To lead into," in fact. Not "to leave," nor "to abandon." After all, there is a big difference between letting someone fall into a ravine, for example, and throwing them into it on purpose. Between abandoning a person in distress and causing a person to be in distress.

But to eliminate even the slightest doubt, we will analyze below all the occurrences of the verb *eisphérō* within the New Testament and try to grasp the different nuances.

Beyond the sixth petition of the Lord's Prayer, identically reported by both Matthew and Luke, *eisphérō* is used only six other times. Three in the Gospel of Luke, one

---

1. The long-accepted and widespread version of the Lord's Prayer in Spain, Portugal, and Latin America contains this convoluted formula.

2. Aorist subjunctive (second-person singular).

# Eis Peirasmón

in the first letter to Timothy, one in the letter to the Hebrews, and one in the Acts of the Apostles. Let us begin.

What better way to understand the true meaning of a term than to analyze its use by the same author in other contexts? Luke gives us this possibility in a brief passage in chapter 5 of his Gospel, where, in the span of a couple of sentences, he succeeds in condensing the verb *eisphérō* twice and the verb *phérō* once. This is the episode in which Jesus heals a paralytic. Let us read: "And, behold, men brought [*phérō*] in a bed a man which was taken with a palsy: and they sought means to bring him in [*eisphérō*], and to lay him before him. And when they could not find by what way they might bring him in [*eisphérō*] because of the multitude, they went upon the housetop, and let him down through the tiling with his couch into the midst before Jesus" (Luke 5:18–19).

The verb *phérō* is used by Luke at the beginning of verse 18 to indicate the generic act of transportation (over a palsy). Then, immediately afterward wanting to indicate in a more specific way the transportation into a place, Luke chooses the verb *eisphérō*, which contains the idea of a movement into a specific place—in this case, the house where Jesus was preaching, literally stormed by the crowd. And then again, when he has to describe that, because of the crowd, there was no way to enter through the main door, Luke chooses the verb *eisphérō*, which seems to unequivocally indicate transportation into a place.

And it is a curious coincidence—but perhaps it is not—that the first time the term *eisphérō* appears in Luke's Gospel, it would be just impossible, even if we wanted to, to translate this verb with softer expressions, such as "to abandon," or "to allow," or "to let." In fact, the object of the transportation is a paralytic, who, by definition, cannot move alone. A paralytic cannot be "let in." He must be transported! The responsibility of the movement inside the house is to be charged—without possibility of denial—100 percent to those who are transporting him on a palsy. Any other translation that in some way would suggest that the movement inside the house by the paralytic is the work of the paralytic himself would obviously sound ridiculous.

And it is a curious coincidence—but perhaps it is not—that when Luke, six chapters later, gives his version of the Lord's Prayer and must render, in Greek, the image of the (figurative) movement of people toward temptation, he uses exactly the same verb *eisphérō* used twice in the episode of the paralytic.

We better then keep in mind the image of this paralytic brought on a crib by force inside a house after a hole in the roof had been made. Because this is exactly what the verb *eisphérō* means: the transportation of something or someone, even with the use of brute force, inside a particular place. The movement suggested by the verb *eisphérō* does not seem to be a spontaneous movement, but a movement induced and caused by the one who performs the action of transportation, to whom the movement itself must be charged. And so, when Luke and Matthew report the incriminated verse of the Lord's Prayer in which God is asked to "lead us not into temptation," and both use exactly the verb *eisphérō*, they seem to be painting the picture of a God who would take us, as those men do with the paralytic, and carry us into temptation, without us being able to do much about it.

And if this image is correct, how is it possible to think of toning down the text of the Lord's Prayer with expressions such as "do not abandon us," or "do not let us fall"? All these interpretations tend to minimize divine responsibility. It would not be God who pushes us into temptation. It would be we who fall into temptation (created by the Evil One). We would be simply asking God to give us the strength not to sin, not to turn away while we fall, but to intervene before it is too late. This is inevitably incompatible with the image, suggested by the verb *eisphérō*, of a God who would seem instead to participate actively in the act of making us fall into temptation—in our physical transportation within the temptation itself.

Let us continue with the other examples. The fourth and last occurrence of the verb *eisphérō* in Luke's Gospel (after the episode of the paralytic and the Lord's Prayer) is found in chapter 12 when Jesus, surrounded by thousands of people, "insomuch that they trode one upon another" (Luke 12:1), harangues the crowd and, among the many themes touched upon, explains, "And when they bring you [*eisphérō*] unto the synagogues, and unto magistrates, and powers, take ye no thought how or what thing ye shall answer, or what ye shall say: For the Holy Ghost shall teach you in the same hour what ye ought to say" (Luke 12:11–12).

In this context, the verb *eisphérō* is used to indicate transportation not necessarily into something, but to and before something/someone. Luke, unlike in the text of the Lord's Prayer, chooses not the preposition *eis* (which usually indicates a movement into something), but the preposition *epí* (ἐπί), which renders the image of a movement *up to* a certain place, without necessarily entering it.

This passage from Luke makes the meaning of *eisphérō* even clearer. Here, Jesus alludes to the future persecutions that the disciples will have to endure when they are arrested and brought *before* the authorities and confirms the fact that this verb renders the idea of a coercive transportation, even against the very will of the one being transported. At the same time, the scientific use of the preposition *epí* to indicate a movement that stops right before something/someone—as an antithesis to the verse of the Lord's Prayer where the movement is instead rendered with the preposition *eis*—confirms the image of a God who, according to the original texts of Luke and Matthew, would not only bring us before the temptation (exposing us to it), but would also push us right into it by making us sin. The classic translation "lead us not into temptation," in the light of what has been observed up to this point, seems even too benevolent, where instead the original sense of the Greek text would seem to be closer to "do not push us into temptation." Let us continue.

In chapter 6 of his first letter to Timothy, St. Paul utters the famous phrase, "For we brought [*eisphérō*] nothing into this world, and it is certain we can carry nothing out" (1 Tim 6:7). The image of "bringing into the world" is rendered by the verb *eisphérō*, followed by the preposition *eis*: *eis tòn kósmon* (εἰς τὸν κόσμον), that is, into the world. By contrast, the image of "carrying out" is rendered by the use of the verb *ekphérō* (ἐκφέρω), obtained by the union of the verb *phérō* with the preposition *ek* (ἐκ). The preposition *ek* usually indicates a movement not only "away from," but precisely "out of." Here then, by antithesis, if *ekphérō* indicates the action of bringing out, *eisphérō* must necessarily indicate the action of bringing into, confirming the meaning discussed so far.

The verb *eisphérō* also appears in the letter to the Hebrews, used to describe the gory image of a high priest who, as an offering for sins, brings the blood of animals into the sanctuary, while their carcasses are burned outside the camp (Heb 13:11). Again, the verb *eisphérō* indicates the act of bringing in. And not coincidentally, the place into where the motion occurs, *tà hágia* (τὰ ἅγια), that is, "the sanctuary," takes the preposition *eis*. Further confirmation that the *mḕ eisenénkēis hēmâs eis peirasmón* that appears in the Gospels of Luke and Matthew may indicate our transportation (by God) *into* the temptation.

The last occurrence of the verb *eisphérō* in the New Testament is found in chapter 17 of the Acts of the Apostles, which speaks of the first preaching of St. Paul in Athens, Greece, where the cult of the gods was still widespread, and people looked with distrust at a preacher who came from afar to speak to them of one all-powerful God who had sent his Son to earth to save humanity. It was on one such occasion that, intrigued by Paul's words, a group of Stoic and Epicurean philosophers invite him to come with them to the Areopagus, near the Acropolis: "May we know what this new doctrine, whereof thou speakest, is? For thou bringest [*eisphérō*] certain strange things to our ears: we would know therefore what these things mean" (Acts 17:19–20). That "bringest to our ears" is rendered by the verb *eisphérō* followed by the preposition *eis*: *eis tàs akoàs* (εἰς τὰς ἀκοὰς), that is, "into our ears." This confirms how the combination of the verb *eisphérō* with the preposition *eis* indicates the act of bringing in, which becomes even a "put in," "throw in." In any case, the image is clear, and suggests to us that translations along the line of "to abandon," or "to leave" are probably too tenuous.

In the light of this brief digression, we could already conclude that, if Luke and Matthew, when reporting the text of the Lord's Prayer in Greek, had wanted to imply that Christ meant "to abandon," or "to let fall," they would probably not have used an expression such as *eisenénkēis hēmâs eis peirasmón*, with the redundancy of that *eis*, which instead would seem to indicate the intention of the Father to lead us, to put us, to drive us, to push us right into temptation.

In fact, there is a small detail that we have not yet spoken of, and which is systematically and culpably ignored. It is a subtle lexical choice that could help us make a breach in the mystery of the Lord's Prayer. In Greek, when one has to indicate the action of leading a person somewhere, usually one does not use the verb *phérō*, which is more appropriate to the transportation of things or animals, but the more common verb *ágō* (ἄγω).

Why do Luke and Matthew both tack on *eisphérō* instead?

# 4

# To Lead or to Allow to Go?

Let us go back for a moment to the passage just quoted from the Acts of the Apostles, in chapter 17, where it says that Stoic and Epicurean philosophers led St. Paul to the Areopagus. Let us read: "ἐπὶ τὸν Ἄρειον Πάγον ἤγαγον"[1] (Acts 17:19). *Ḗgagon* (ἤγαγον) is the aorist of the verb *ágō*: they led him. In fact, *ágō* also describes the act of transferring someone from one place to another, just like *phérō*. *Ágō*, however, does not necessarily indicate coercive transportation. In most cases, it indicates the generic act of "leading," "accompanying," "directing," "guiding." As in the episode of St. Paul, who is not forcibly led, but simply accompanied.

We need only think that the verb *ágō* appears sixty-five times in the New Testament. In sixty cases, the object of the movement is a person and in only five cases it is an animal (four times a donkey, one time a sheep). Never does the object of the movement turn out to be a thing. Moreover, only in a few cases—but they are the minority—does the verb *ágō* describe a forced, coercive movement, against the will of the person being led.[2]

On the other hand, the verb *phérō* also appears in abundance in the New Testament (sixty times). But only in 20 percent of these cases, the object of the movement is a person. In the remaining 80 percent, it is things (forty-four cases) or animals (four cases). This is not a coincidence. As mentioned, the verb *phérō* contains the idea of transportation by physical force. There is the idea of a weight that weighs down, like a burden, on the body, on the arms of the person who is carrying. So much so that, figuratively speaking, the verb *phérō* can also describe the act of "bearing," therefore "suffering." It is a verb necessarily better suited to describe the physical/mechanical transportation of objects, than the transportation of people.

---

1. "*epì tòn Áreion Págon ḗgagon*" = "they led him to the Areopagus."
2. See, for example, Luke 23:1: "They led him before Pilate."

# Eis Peirasmón

Nevertheless, it is not exceptional to find the verb *phérō* associated with human beings (in the New Testament, as noted, it occurs in twelve out of sixty instances). However—and this is the most interesting side for our discussion—whenever the object is a person, the motion indicated by the verb *phérō* always turns out to be coercive, either against the will of the one being led or because of his or her psychophysical disability.

Let us briefly look at all these examples, because they will help us shed light on the meaning of the verb *phérō* and, consequently, of the verb *eisphérō* used in the Lord's Prayer of Matthew and Luke.

In Matt 17:17 and Mark 9:19–20, Jesus asks that a little boy who was possessed be brought to him. In Mark 1:32, it is told how people began to bring all the sick and possessed to Jesus for him to heal them. In Mark 2:3, the episode of the paralytic brought on a crib inside a house is recounted (see also Luke 5:19). In Mark 7:32, it is recounted that they brought a deaf-mute to Jesus. In Mark 8:22, they brought him a blind man. In Acts 5:16, it is told how people from the villages around Jerusalem brought the sick and the possessed to the Apostles for healing. In Mark 15:22, Jesus himself is led to Golgotha. In all these episodes, a state of psychophysical subjection on the part of the one being carried/led clearly emerges with respect to the one carrying/leading. Sick, demonized, paralytic, deaf, blind, mute. Flagellated and dying (in the case of Jesus). All people who are not able to move independently or of their own free will, and who depend entirely on the one who takes charge of their transportation. And it is precisely for this reason that, in all these examples, *phérō* is preferred to a more generic *ágō*: to render the idea of forced transportation.

And again in Acts 27, Luke tells how the ship on which St. Paul was embarked was swept away by the winds of a hurricane near the coast of Crete: "And when the ship was caught, and could not bear up into the wind, we were driven [*phérō*] helplessly.[3] And running under a certain island which is called Clauda, we had much work to come by the boat: Which when they had taken up, they used helps, undergirding the ship; and, fearing lest they should fall into the quicksands, strake sail, and so were driven [*phérō*]" (Acts 27:15–17).

That "being driven," drifting at the mercy of the storm, is rendered, twice, by the passive form of the verb *phérō*. This gives the idea, with great descriptive power, of a group of people who are dragged through the waves by the winds—completely powerless. The movement is dictated by a superior force (the hurricane) and there is literally nothing the sailors can do to control the ship's course. They are not simply "led." They are actually "carried about" on the sea, at the mercy of the storm.

Finally, in the last chapter of John's Gospel, Jesus utters the famous phrase, "Verily, verily, I say unto thee, When thou wast young, thou girdedst thyself, and walkedst whither thou wouldest: but when thou shalt be old, thou shalt stretch forth thy hands, and another shall gird thee, and carry [*phérō*] thee whither thou wouldest not" (John

---

3. The KJV has "we let her drive."

21:18). These are among the last words spoken by Jesus.[4] In this passage, he addresses Simon Peter directly. He asks him three times, "Peter, do you love me?" He wants to be sure that Peter will have the strength to follow him to the end, even to the most difficult test. And at the third affirmative answer, Jesus ideally passes the baton to him on earth. But in doing so, he foreshadows that he will have to suffer many sufferings, following in his footsteps in every way, until he dies on the cross. That phrase ("another shall gird thee, and carry thee whither thou wouldest not") is pronounced to allude to the kind of (violent) death that Peter will die. Now, the expression "carry thee whither thou wouldest not" (that is, to die on the cross) is rendered with the verb *phérō*, which once again confirms the idea of a movement that takes place independently, if not against the will of the one being transported.

At this point, for the sake of completeness, we will go on to examine various other compounds of the verb *phérō* within the New Testament, in order to corroborate our thesis. There is, for example, the verb *prosphérō* (προσφέρω), obtained by the addition of the preposition *prós* (πρός), which indicates a motion to a generic place (toward). *Prosphérō* and *eisphérō* are largely overlapping verbs, the only difference being that the former generally indicates a motion *toward* a place, while the latter indicates a motion *into* a place. The verb *prosphérō* appears forty-three times in the New Testament with the meaning of "to carry." In thirty-one cases, the object is a thing, an offering, a sacrifice, gifts, coins, and so forth. Only in twelve cases is it referred to people. But of these twelve cases, eight involve human beings with obvious disabilities (epileptics, paralytics, the possessed, the deaf and mute, and so forth.). Three cases appear in the famous episode in which children are brought to Jesus, but the apostles object and are reprimanded for it (Matt 19:13; Mark 10:13; Luke 18:15). The last case we find applies to Jesus himself, led by Pilate into a state of arrest (Luke 23:14). All these further examples confirm, without exception, that even the compound *prosphérō*, in the few cases in which it refers to human beings, always indicates a state of subjection between the one who leads and the one who is led. Illuminating is the use of the verb *prosphérō* to indicate the fact that children were being led to Jesus. This episode is recounted by both Mark, Matthew, and Luke. They all agree that the correct verb to use is a compound of *phérō*, to give the idea that adults were carrying them (probably in their arms). A child is a weak creature—powerless by definition—who goes where the adults lead him without any possibility of opposing them.

Of opposite meaning, the verb *apophérō*, obtained by the addition of the preposition *apó* (ἀπό), which indicates a generic motion *from* a place (away from), is used only five times in the New Testament, four of which refer to a person. In Mark 15:1, it is told how the high priests had Jesus bound and had him "carried away" by handing him over to Pilate. Again, the act of carrying indicates a forced movement of a person deprived of freedom. In Luke 16:22, it is told how the beggar Lazarus died and "was carried by the angels into Abraham's bosom." Here, transportation refers to a dead

---

4. Jesus, at this point in the narrative, has already risen and appeared several times to the disciples.

person. In Rev 17:3 and Rev 21:10, St. John recounts in his apocalyptic vision how an angel carried him away first into the desert and then up a high mountain. John is completely at the mercy of the angel and is transported by him wherever he wants without being able to resist.

We have already had occasion to analyze (1 Tim 6:7) the verb *ekphérō*, obtained by the addition of the preposition *ek* indicating a motion *out of* a place. It is used seven times within the New Testament, four of which refer to a person. In chapter 5 of the Acts of the Apostles, it is told how a man named Ananias, after being reprimanded by Peter for having kept for himself part of the proceeds from the sale of his property, fell dead on the spot. Then, the young men that were present, seized with fear, wrapped up Ananias's body and took it out (*ekphérō*) to be buried (Acts 5:5–6). The same fate befell his wife. Peter admonished her, "behold, the feet of them which have buried thy husband are at the door, and shall carry [*ekphérō*] thee out" (Acts 5:9). At those words, the wife also fell dead on the spot, was carried away (*ekphérō*), and was buried beside her husband. Three times the verb *ekphérō* is used to indicate the carrying away of a body of a dead person. Again in the same chapter, it is told how, as more and more men and women followed the Apostles, they brought forth even "the sick into the streets, and laid them on beds and couches, that at the least the shadow of Peter passing by might overshadow some of them" (Acts 5:15). The theme is always the same: transportation of the sick, and so forth.

There are two other compounds of *phérō* that appear in the New Testament with the generic meaning of carrying/leading. These are *anaphérō* and *periphérō*.

The verb *anaphérō*, obtained by the addition of the preposition *aná* (ἀνά) indicating an *upward* motion, is used ten times within the New Testament, four of which refer to a person. In two of these instances, the verb *anaphérō* takes on the meaning of "to bring upward," that is, "to bring toward God," that is, "to offer in sacrifice." In Heb 7:27, it is said that Christ offered himself for our sins. In Jas 2:21, it is recalled how Abraham offered his son Isaac on the altar. The verb *anaphérō* is thus associated with human beings only because those same human beings (Isaac and Jesus) were immolated as a sacrificial offering. In Luke 24:51, we are told of the assumption of Jesus, who was literally "taken up into heaven" by his Father, rendering the image of a God who takes his Son by weight and draws him to himself in heaven. In Matt 17:1 and Mark 9:2, the famous episode of Jesus' transfiguration is recounted. The two evangelists both explain that "Jesus taketh Peter, James, and John his brother, and bringeth them up into an high mountain apart." The verb used to render the movement to the top of Mount Tabor is *anaphérō*. It is plausible that the lexical choice of both evangelists wanted to render the idea of the three disciples who, disoriented and probably frightened, obey without a word the peremptory direction of Jesus to follow him to the top of the mountain. What they will see after a while is something that will instill terror in their hearts (Matt 17:7; Mark 9:6). In any case, we can say with certainty that we are not in the presence of a voluntary movement of the disciples toward the summit of the mountain, a movement assisted by Jesus. On the contrary, the movement is imposed by Jesus, who has decided to reveal at that moment, for the first time and only to the three of them, the glory of his divine nature—a movement from which Peter, John and James have no possibility to escape.

Finally, the verb *periphérō*, obtained by the addition of the preposition *perí* (περί) indicating a movement *around*, is used five times in the New Testament, three of which refer to a person. In Mark 6:55, it is told how people, when they learned of the presence of Jesus, ran to him bringing around him on cribs all the sick. In his letter to the Ephesians, St. Paul reminds us, "we henceforth be no more children, tossed to and fro, and carried about with every wind of doctrine" (Eph 4:14). Similarly, in the letter to the Hebrews, St. Paul repeats, "Be not carried about with divers and strange doctrines" (Heb 13:9). Being "tossed to and fro" and being "carried about" is rendered in both cases by the verb *periphérō*, which closely resembles the image of Paul's ship cast adrift by the hurricane (Acts 27:15–17). We are in the presence of an involuntary motion, which is entirely dictated by a superior force ("every wind of doctrine," "divers and strange doctrines ") to which it is hard to resist.

After analyzing all the occurrences of the verb *phérō* and its compounds within the New Testament, one must necessarily conclude that the use of this verb, in the few instances in which it is associated with human beings, describes:

1. a coercive movement, totally imposed and dictated by the one leading;
2. a movement from which it is not possible to escape;
3. a movement with an *asymmetrical* relationship of forces, whereby the one being led is in a state of psychophysical subjection to the one leading;
4. a movement that is to be attributed entirely to the one who leads and that could not happen otherwise by the sole will of the one being led.

All this should not be surprising. If the verb *phérō* (and compounds) is commonly associated with the carrying of inanimate objects, the verb *phérō* associated with a human being suggests that that human being is being led as if it were a thing. And if all these features just listed are present without exception whatsoever in every single example we just cited, why should the two occurrences of the verb *eisphérō* that appear within the Lord's Prayer of Matthew and Luke be an exception?

And why—this question cannot be avoided—despite having a more standard *ágō*, do both evangelists Matthew and Luke agree on the need to render the Aramaic expression used by Jesus with a rarer *eisphérō*?

Indeed, it is good to reiterate a concept. Within the semantic field of "leading a person," that is, of making someone move from point A to point B, *ágō* and *phérō* are by no means synonymous. They are not interchangeable.

While it is true that the verb *phérō* associated with a person could always be replaced by the verb *ágō* without the general meaning being lost, the opposite is not true. Using the verb *phérō* instead of *ágō* in some contexts would result in a total distortion of the meaning. Consider the sentence "They transported my father to the hospital." From the use of the verb "to transport" (instead of a simple "to take") the listener understands that most likely my father was in no condition to go to the hospital alone, being in a precarious, if not serious, state of health. In any case, even the simple expression "They took my father to the hospital" would not change the overall meaning, only making it less precise. On the other hand, if we think of the sentence "I took my wife to the movies," it would sound grotesque to replace the verb "to take" with the verb "to transport." The listener would probably think that my wife came unwillingly and that I forced her to see a terrible movie! In other words, when we carry someone, we are also leading them; when we lead someone, we are not necessarily carrying them.

A similar argument applies to the specific lexical choice made by Matthew and Luke. It is not possible to reduce the meaning of *eisphérō* to a generic "to lead into." Certainly not before we understand that what Matthew and Luke really want to tell us is that God is not simply leading us, but precisely carrying us inside, that is, introducing us into temptation. As one introduces a key into the lock. As if we were a simple powerless instrument in his hands.

We started out trying to figure out if there was any room to tone down that "lead us not into temptation," perhaps replacing it with a softer "let us not fall" or "do not abandon us," and we discovered instead that this translation might actually be even too mild, even more tenuous than the rough and powerful image that emerges from the original Greek text.

Letting someone go somewhere implies that that someone is fully responsible and conscious of his/her movement. The movement is neither determined nor imposed, but simply "unhindered" by the one who "lets." There is no plane of subordination between the two. There is no pressure, neither physical nor psychological, from the one who allows the movement, who, if he wanted, could prevent it, but does not. At the same time, there is no coercion so that the one who moves could of his own free will interrupt the movement itself but does not do so. In the case of "letting," there is no need for any relationship between who, independently, moves and who, voluntarily, decides not to intervene. The same considerations apply to translations along the lines of "to abandon." If, however, "to let fall into temptation" implies a non-action on the part of one who could have prevented the movement (toward evil) before the movement itself occurs, "to abandon" indicates a more devious attitude, as far as one does not run to the aid of one who, after the movement has already taken place, finds himself immersed in evil.

In conclusion, both translations ("to let" or "to abandon") violate all the semantic features of the verbs *phérō*/*eisphérō* listed above. Far from faithfully reproducing the sense of the Greek text, they venture into semantic fields not immediately deducible from the original writings, thus opening a dangerous chasm in the process of translation and interpretation of the Gospels. If a "free translation" for this verse of the Lord's Prayer is considered acceptable on the sole basis of supposed motivations of theological consistency, nothing then, in principle, prevents altering other passages of the Gospels on the sole basis of personal sensibility or theological maturity achieved in a particular historical context.

How is it possible that for two thousand years "lead us not into temptation" was considered acceptable and now it appears so out of tune? Should not the Gospels, the written representation of the revealed divine *lógos*, be above time?

# 5

# The Lord's Prayer in Different Idioms

We will digress now to briefly analyze how the verb *eisphérō*, which appears in the Lord's Prayer, is translated in the main idioms. It is an interesting exercise and certainly useful in understanding how different linguistic sensibilities have tried to solve the problem of interpreting this Greek verb. Let us begin, for obvious reasons, with Latin.

First, it should be noted that the Greek verb *phérō* also exists in Latin (*fero*), with the exact same meaning: "to take," both literally and figuratively. Also in Latin, *fero* is mainly associated with the transportation of things and inanimate beings. The Latin verb *fero*, being the closest to the Greek verb *phérō* from a philological and semantic point of view, would be the best candidate for a translation that is as close as possible to the original text. Consequently, the Latin verb *infero* (composed of *fero* with the addition of the preposition *in*) would be the exact analogue of *eisphérō* (composed of *phérō* with the addition of the preposition *eis*).

It is interesting to note that one of the greatest theologians of the church, St. Augustine, in the second book of his *De sermone Domini in monte*,[1] admits, "*Sexta petitio est: Et ne nos inferas in tentationem. Nonnulli codices habent inducas, quod tantundem valere arbitror; nam ex uno graeco quod dictum est utrumque translatum est.*"[2] According to St. Augustine, the most widespread version in Latin at that time used the verb *infero*. However, even the form with the verb *induco* could be found in some codices instead of *infero*, so that, he concludes, the two Latin verbs *infero* and *induco* in this case must necessarily have the same meaning, since they represent the translation of the same Greek verb *eisphérō*. In the same period (second half of the fourth century) in which St. Augustine wrote these ideas, St. Jerome finished drafting what would

---

1. *The Lord's sermon on the mount.*

2. "The sixth petition says: 'And do not bring us into temptation.' Some codices have 'lead,' which I believe has the same meaning, since both versions are translations of the same Greek verb" (Augustine, *De sermone Domini in monte*, 2.9.30).

become the official Latin translation of the Bible, the so-called Vulgate. And in the Vulgate, St. Jerome, instead of using *infero*, which would be the perfect Latin equivalent of the Greek verb *eisphérō*, prefers to turn to the verb *induco*. *Induco* is a compound of the verb *duco* with the addition of the preposition *in*. The Latin verb *duco*, which can be considered the equivalent of the Greek *ágō*, indicates a generic "leading" from one place to another and is usually utilized when the object of the movement is a human being. St. Jerome, probably sensing as anomalous (and certainly rough) the use of the verb *infero* associated with people, prefers a plainer *induco*. And so, the official Latin translation will become "*ne nos inducas in tentationem.*" As a result, the Latin translation of the Vulgate makes a very small semantic leap—almost imperceptible—compared to the Greek original, in that it moves from the more specific "to carry into" (*eisphérō*) to a more generic "to lead into" (*induco*). Imperceptible, but fundamental in our opinion, because from that moment onward it will make the coercive nuance, so peculiar of the verb *eisphérō* present in the original Greek text, disappear forever.

This explains how the English translation, directly derived from the Latin text of the Vulgate, uses the verb "to lead," which belongs to the same semantic field as the Greek *ágō* and the Latin *duco*. In English, the physical transportation of an object is usually described by the verbs "to carry," "to bring" or "to take."[3] All these verbs can be traced back to the same semantic field defined by the Greek verb *phérō*. Nevertheless, the verb "to lead" is the one used in the English translation of the Lord's Prayer, which states, "*lead us not into temptation.*"

Similarly, the German translation uses the verb *führen*,[4] from the ancient High German root *fuoren* ("to set in motion," "to lead"), certainly closer to the Greek verb *ágō* than to the verb *phérō*. Here is the German text: "*führe uns nicht in Versuchung*" ("lead us not into temptation").

It is interesting to see the evolution of the translation of the Lord's Prayer in French. During the Second Vatican Council (1962–1965), the following version was approved: "*ne nous soumets pas à la tentation*" ("do not submit us to the temptation"). It is interesting because it differs significantly from all other translations (Latin, English, German) to the extent that it suggests that God would not simply lead us toward temptation but would actually subject us to it. A much stronger image, almost violent, and certainly much closer to the original Greek text, where *eisphérō*, as we have seen, seems to indicate the act of forcing someone into something. But later, after much controversy and theological debate, in December 2017, more than fifty years after the Second Vatican Council, the French Catholic Church decided to revise this translation by sweetening it as follows: "*ne nous laisse pas entrer en tentation*" ("let us not enter into temptation"). This is a total reversal of the semantic fields we have been discussing, whereby the

---

3. In principle, "to carry" is used to indicate physical transportation; "to bring" is used when the movement is toward the one who is speaking (from there to here); "to take" is used when the movement is in the opposite direction (from here to there).

4. Hence, for example, the epithet *führer* (commander) associated with Adolf Hitler.

movement toward temptation is implicitly attributed to humans, when previously it had been clearly attributed to God himself. And it is precisely this overturning of semantic fields that Pope Francis refers to, explicitly inviting us to take this new French version as a model for adjusting what he considers to be "not a good translation."

Throughout the Hispanic context ranging from Latin America to Europe (Spain and Portugal), the official translation of the Lord's Prayer has long adopted the formula "let us not fall into temptation" ("*no nos dejes caer en la tentación*" in Spanish; "*não nos deixes cair em tentação*" in Portuguese). From this point of view, the more recent French version aligns with the Hispanic version, where we simply ask God to intervene before we can fall into temptation, implying that the movement toward temptation is the sole responsibility of the human being.

The Italian translation, directly derived from the Latin text of the Vulgate, uses the same verb (*indurre*), which belongs to the same semantic field of the Greek *ágō* and the Latin *duco*: "*non ci indurre in tentazione*" ("induce us not into temptation"). It should be noted that in Italian the verb *indurre* ("to induce") has developed a mainly negative sense, when associated with human beings. In fact, in most cases, when Italians use the expression "to induce someone to," they do it to indicate the act of convincing someone to do something inappropriate, to commit an error. Inducing someone to commit a crime. Inducing someone to sin, and so forth. This is why "*indurre in tentazione*" in Italian sounds even more out of tune and unacceptable than a simple "to lead into temptation" or "to lead toward temptation," as far as "to induce" implies malice on the part of the one who leads, with an implicit satisfaction in seeing the one being led fall. Malice, of course, is incompatible with the infinitely merciful nature of God. This is precisely the reason why recently (November 29, 2020) the Italian translation was changed as follows: "*non abbandonarci alla tentazione*" ("do not abandon us to temptation").

We will summarize below the different semantic field choices for the translation of the verb *eisphérō* in the major idioms.

| Idiom | Semantic field of "to carry" (*phérō*) | Semantic field of "to lead" (*ágō*) | Semantic field of "to let" |
|---|---|---|---|
| Latin | | *Induco* | |
| English | | To lead | |
| German | | Führen | |
| French | *Soumettre*[5] | | *Laisser entrer* |
| Spanish | | | *Dejar caer* |
| Portuguese | | | *Deixar cair* |
| Italian | | *Indurre*[6] | *Abbandonare* |

5. Only until December 2017.
6. Only until November 28, 2020.

It should be noted that the only translation that fitted faithfully into the semantic field of the Greek text (the French "*soumettre*") has recently been abandoned, leaving only translations that, for various reasons, deviate from the sense that emerges from the original texts of the Gospels.

If we extend the horizon to the various idioms spoken in the rest of the world, we realize that most have either borrowed the translation of the Vulgate ("lead us not into temptation") or have adopted the more nuanced permissive form ("do not let us fall into temptation"). Only a small group of idioms has maintained the literal sense of the Greek texts, and it happens to be precisely those Balkan languages that developed geographically around the Greek archipelago from which they were clearly influenced.[7] It is interesting to note the use of the verb *vvesti* (Ввести) in the Russian translation, which gives the idea of "introducing," of "putting in." Another curious exception is found in the Basque language, an idiom with no apparent ties to any other language spoken in the world, which renders the sixth petition in the Lord's Prayer with the verb *eraman*, which means "to carry," thus fully capturing the original sense of the Greek verb *eisphérō*. A full table containing the translations of the sixth petition in the main idioms can be found in Appendix.

In any case, if on the one hand the semantic leap from "to introduce" to "to lead" is so minimal that it may be considered acceptable if not, in some cases, reasonable according to different linguistic sensibilities, the semantic leap from "to introduce" / "to lead" to "to let" / "to abandon" (as seen in Hispanic languages and now also in French and Italian) may be too big to be justifiable from an exegetical point of view.

We say, "it may," because it is tremendously more complicated than this. And, upon closer inspection, the translations that have opted for the permissive construct, in addition to a theological argument,[8] also claim a purely linguistic justification. Such justification is rooted not in the Greek text but in a grammar technicality found in Semitic languages, including Hebrew—usually utilized by Pharisees and the doctors of the Law—and Aramaic, the language commonly spoken in the region of Galilee in the first century—the main language used by Jesus in his preaching.[9]

In Semitic languages, it is common to use a verbal stem, so-called *causative*, which in some cases, as the supporters of this thesis claim, may admit a permissive nuance. Such permissive nuance should precisely apply to the translation of the Lord's Prayer, they say. This interpretation would be justified by the Aramaic substratum, which would allow us to completely bypass the Greek text.

---

7. Albanian, Bosnian, Bulgarian, Croatian, Macedonian, Slovenian, Serbian.

8. God does not tempt us, but simply *allows* us to be tempted by the devil.

9. That Jesus commonly spoke a particular Aramaic dialect is beyond dispute (see Mark 5:41; 7:34; 14:36; 15:34; Matt 27:46). Jesus obviously also knew Hebrew (see Luke 4:16–21), the idiom in which the Old Testament is written.

Let us try to understand more. But, to do so, we will have to dive into Aramaic. After all, this is the language that Jesus spoke on a daily basis. The language he likely used to teach the Lord's Prayer to his disciples.

Ready?

# 6

# Causative vs. Permissive

First of all, let us clarify what is meant by the causative form of a verb. As the word itself says, the causative form emphasizes the *causal* link between the doer of the action and the action itself, so the effect of the action is to be attributed, directly or indirectly, to the person who causes it. In English, in order to build a causative form, an explicit construct is usually needed, such as "to cause somebody to do something." Now, "causing somebody to do something" may result, according to the different contexts, into "getting somebody to do something," or "making somebody do something," or "having somebody do something," or even "letting somebody do something." All of these represent examples of explicit causative constructs in English, but all of them have slightly different nuances of meaning.[1]

The structure of the causative construct changes depending on whether the basic action is described by a transitive or intransitive verb. If we are in the presence of a transitive verb, the causal construct expands into a "three-way" predicate. If we take, for example, the transitive verb "to learn," and we think of the sentence "the student learns Latin," we can build the causative construct as "the *teacher* causes the *student* to learn *Latin*," or " the teacher makes the student learn Latin," or even better, "the teacher teaches the student Latin." In the latter case, the causative form of the verb "to learn" is rendered simply by another verb, "to teach," which bears an implicit causative meaning. "To teach" can thus be considered the causative of "to learn." The causative construct indicates that the teacher is the cause of the student learning Latin. The causal sequence of events is clear: the teacher teaches, and the student learns. Which implies that the student would not learn if the teacher did not teach.

On the other hand, if we are in the presence of an intransitive verb, the causal construct expands into a simple "two-way" predicate, consisting only of subject and

---

1. "Getting" or "making" imply "forcing" somebody to do something; "having" means "convincing" somebody to do something; "letting" implies either "granting a permission" or "not opposing" an action.

object. Let us take, for example, the intransitive verb "to go." If we think of the sentence "the boy goes to school," we can construct its causative form using a two-way construct such as "the *parents* cause the *boy* to go to school," or " the parents make the boy go to school," or even better, "the parents take the boy to school." In the latter case, the causative form of the verb "to go" is rendered simply by another verb, "to take," which bears an implicit causative meaning. "To take" can thus be considered the causative of "to go."

Now, one of the biggest difficulties in the exact translation of a causative form lies in the interpretation of the connection/relationship between the cause and the effect. To cause someone to do something is a very general concept that does not specify *how* this happens. Returning to the example of the parents who cause the student to go to school, depending on the context, it can be understood as the action of the parents convincing the child to go to school despite his unwillingness, or as the action of dragging him by the ear, or simply as the action of accompanying the child to school. In each case, the parents are the cause of the fact that the student goes to school, but the contexts are completely different. And in the absence of further details, given only the causative construct, it is virtually impossible to understand how the one doing the action causes the action to be done. And, more importantly, whether the one who suffers the action, does so unwillingly or willingly. Precisely this indeterminacy about how the cause produces the effect necessarily exposes the use of the causative form to the most varied interpretations.

To add further confusion to the matter, even verbs that do not carry *per se* any implicit causative meaning may be used in a causative sense to imply an *indirect* intervention of the person causing the action. For instance, if we take the famous example "*Caesar pontem fecit*,"[2] it is clear that it was not Caesar who built the bridge with his own hands, but he *had* his men do it. The verb *facere* ("to make"), which in general does not carry any causative sense, is here used with a causative nuance that we could call "indirect." Caesar is the indirect cause (the bridge would not have been built if Caesar had not given the order), but his men are the direct cause (they are the ones who materially built the bridge). The most pedantic translation might be something like "Caesar had a bridge built" or "Caesar gave the order to build a bridge." But the truth is that, in any case, no one would have any doubts about the real meaning of the phrase. No one would think that Caesar started to build the bridge with his bare hands. While on the one hand this example leaves no room for ambiguity, unfortunately it is not always so obvious to distinguish the cases in which a verb may be understood with an implicit indirect causative nuance.

Finally, the causative construct can sometimes also allow for permissive interpretations. That is, the one who causes the action does not do it with a direct intervention aimed at pushing someone to do something, but he/she does it by giving his/her permission for the action to be done, or at least by not opposing it. If we think

2. Caesar made a bridge.

of the phrase "the parents, after their son finished his homework, let him go out with his friends," it obviously means that they allowed him to go with them, not that they forced him. The parents are certainly the cause of their son going out with his friends, but only in the sense that they endorsed an action under particular conditions (the fact that he finished his homework), an action that under other circumstances they probably would not have allowed.

We can see then how the range of interpretations available in the presence of a causative construct is wide:

1. a *direct* causative (the example of the parents dragging their child to school) implies a material intervention in order for the action to be performed and places the responsibility for the action entirely on the subject of the causative construct;

2. an *indirect* causative (the example of Caesar having a bridge built) implies a chain of causal successions with the intervention of third parties in the middle facilitating the action and thus distributing the responsibility for the action among different subjects;

3. a *permissive* causative (the example of parents letting their child go out with friends) implies a permission or a renunciation of intervention, which pours the responsibility for the action almost entirely onto the object of the causative form.

At this point, it should be clear that all the discussion about the translation of the Greek verb *eisphérō* into the different idioms is reduced to the dilemma between the causative ("lead us not") and permissive ("let us not fall/go") interpretation of the expression used by Jesus. If we think about it, the verbs "to introduce" or "to lead into" are nothing but the direct causative form of the verb "to enter." In fact, "to introduce" means "to cause something/somebody to enter."

Which of the two interpretations (causative vs. permissive) makes more sense from a theological point of view, and which one is more justifiable from an exegetical point of view? Even better: is it possible to find a point of balance on a translation that is able to bring out the correct theological message while maintaining the maximum exegetical adherence to the original texts of the Gospels? In order to answer these questions without falling into the brawl of the debate between scholars—often spoiled by personal bias rather than driven by objective analysis—it will be necessary to maintain an attitude as rigorous as possible from the analytical point of view, which is, in our opinion, the only possible criterion for proceeding on such a delicate terrain. We will try to advance slowly—very slowly—clearing the field, as far as possible, from subjective interpretations and logically weak arguments.

We first observe that both Hebrew, the language mainly used in the Old Testament and used by the doctors of the Law, and Aramaic, the language spoken daily by Jesus and the masses, make abundant use of causative expressions. In these two idioms, however, the causative is an actual verbal form (not a construct), that is, it is grammatically a different conjugation of the same verb.[3] This is a key point to keep in mind. In these two Semitic languages, the base verb and its corresponding causative form are *not* two distinct verbs (think of the example "to learn" / "to teach," or "to go" / "to take," "to enter" / "to introduce"). They are simply the same verb morphologically modulated on two different semantic fields. Borrowing a daring mathematical analogy, we could say that the causative stem is a sort of *first derivative* of the base verb.

If we assume that *eisphérō* is the Greek equivalent chosen by Matthew and Luke to render the causative form of an Aramaic verb pronounced by Jesus, we can try to do the reverse—in a sort of back-translation, and from the causative form ("integrating," just to continue with the mathematical analogy) derive the basic Aramaic verb. For what has been said earlier, *eisphérō*, which means "to bring in," "to carry inside," has an intrinsic direct causative meaning, whose base verb must be close to "to go inside," that is, "to enter." In Hebrew, the verb commonly used to indicate the action of "going in" is *bô'* (בּוֹא), while in Aramaic it is *'ălăl* (עֲלַל). Therefore, it is likely that, when Jesus declaimed the Lord's Prayer in Aramaic and uttered the famous verse "lead us not into temptation," he used the causative form of *'ălăl*.[4]

Once this aspect is clarified, we can move on to discuss what the best translation of the Aramaic causative expression should be. Obviously, those who advocate translations such as "do not let us fall/enter into temptation" are opting for the permissive interpretation. On the other hand, those who prefer translations such as "lead us not into temptation" are opting for the direct causative interpretation.

Which of the two makes more sense and why?

To answer this question, the only way to proceed is to weigh the pros and cons. The permissive interpretation has the undoubted advantage of resolving the theological paradox of a God who would seem to push us to sin. And this is no small thing. On the other hand, however, it seems to deviate substantially from the original Greek text, which represents, in the absence of written Aramaic texts, the most authentic interpretation of Christ's message. Those who support this thesis must necessarily explain why both Matthew and Luke seem instead to be pushing the reader toward a direct causative—rather than permissive—interpretation. We will attempt to demonstrate below how, in our opinion, a permissive interpretation, while fascinating, needs to be rejected, since it is not logically sustainable nor has any credible exegetical foundation.

---

3. In Hebrew, the causative stem is called *hiphil*. In Aramaic, it is called *haphel*.

4. See, for example, Heller, "Die Sechste Bitte des Vaterunser," 85–93; Carmignac, *Recherches*, 237–304.

# 7

# The Permissive Construct in Biblical Greek

One of the main arguments of the supporters of the permissive interpretation of the sixth petition of the Lord's Prayer[1] is that in Greek neither Matthew nor Luke opted for an explicit permissive construct simply because there was no need for it. Greek, they say, while not having, like Aramaic and Hebrew, a specific causative conjugation, frequently uses verbs with an implicit causative sense that may have sometimes a permissive nuance. The case of the Lord's Prayer would not be an exception. Indeed, the reader of the time would have easily grasped the permissive sense, albeit implicit, because such a practice was in common use in the Greek language. There is a whole series of examples that proponents of the permissive thesis usually point out, which would show how the New Testament Greek makes abundant use of implicit causatives. Well, let us look at them one by one.

In Matt 5:45, it is said that the heavenly Father "maketh his sun to rise on the evil and on the good." The verb used is *anatéllō* (ἀνατέλλω), which technically is an intransitive verb meaning "to grow," "to rise." The use in this case of the intransitive verb associated with an object ("God rises the sun"), clearly indicates the causative function of the verb. A direct causative, though. God is the cause of the fact that the sun rises. Without intermediaries, and above all without permissive nuances. The sun does not ask God's permission to move, but it is dragged through the heavens by the divine power.

In Matt 2:16, it is told of when Herod, once he realized he had been deceived by the Magi, "sent forth to kill all the children of Bethlehem." The construct used contains the verb *apostéllō* (ἀποστέλλω), meaning "to send forth," followed by the infinitive of the verb *anairéō* (ἀναιρέω), meaning "to kill." Far from proving anything,

---

1. See, for instance, Carmignac, *Recherches*, 237–304; Jeremias, *The Lord's Prayer*, 27; Fitzmyer, "And Lead Us Not into Temptation," 259–273; Charlesworth, "The Beth Essentiae and the Permissive Hipel (Aphel)," 67–78.

this example tells us two things. First, when the Greek language wants to make a causative construct explicit, it has every means of doing so, without resorting to ambiguous implicit expressions. Second, the causative construct under consideration here is clearly an indirect one. Herod is not the one who materially kills the children, but the one who orders their death. Again, no permissive overtones can be found here. No one is asking Herod's permission to carry out the slaughter, but it is the king himself who gives the cruel order.

In Matt 3:11, John the Baptist admonishes those present by announcing to them the coming of Jesus who "shall baptize you with the Holy Ghost, and with fire." It is argued that this expression should be interpreted in a causative sense because it is not Jesus who physically baptizes each human being. This is obviously true. However, we are in the presence of an indirect causative, not a permissive one. It is not we who ask Jesus' permission to be baptized by him, but it is he himself who baptizes us (directly or indirectly) through the Holy Spirit.

In Luke 24:20, it is recorded how "the chief priests and our rulers delivered him to be condemned to death, and have crucified him." Of course, we know that the high priests did not crucify Jesus materially with their hands (it was the Roman soldiers). So, the expression is to be understood again with an indirect causative sense: "they had him crucified." The high priests are morally responsible for the crucifixion of Jesus. Without their intervention and their insistent request, Pilate would have never indulged their thirst for vengeance. But they are not the material executors. Again, we find a total absence of any permissive nuance. The high priests are not asking permission to crucify Jesus (they have no legal authority to do so), but they are asking that Pilate execute a death sentence in their place (indirect causative). The responsibility of the high priests in the death of Jesus is clear in Luke's mind, which is why he says, they "crucified him," without any need to sweeten its meaning with an improbable permissive construct.

In John 19:1, we are told how "Pilate therefore took Jesus, and scourged him." A short and brutal opening for chapter 19 of his Gospel. The use of these direct causative verbs ("he took him," "he scourged him") is part of a precise descriptive style, which would have been lost if John had opted for pedantic indirect causative constructions such as "Pilate had Jesus taken and scourged." Obviously, this is the ultimate meaning of the expression (Pilate literally went down in history for not getting his hands dirty), but John's sentence is clear and needs no explanation whatsoever. Pilate is the one who causes the scourging of Jesus with his own order. If the high priests have the moral responsibility of the scourging and death of Jesus, Pilate has the material responsibility. Period. It does not matter how thoroughly he washed his hands. It is obvious that the soldiers who take and scourge Jesus do not do it of their own free will (nor are they asking permission, but they are carrying out an order). Those who would have wanted to kill Jesus with their own hands but did not have the legal authority to do so, were the elders and high priests and not the Roman soldiers.[2] The soldiers act only by Pilate's order, and it could not be otherwise. The only one who has the power of life and death is the Roman governor, who thus administers justice, whether we like it or not. The fact that Pilate, had it been for him, would not have condemned Jesus, is irrelevant, and does not diminish his material responsibility. Responsibility that is clear in the mind of John, who says, "he scourged him," without any need to sweeten its meaning with an improbable permissive construct ("Pilate let Jesus be crucified").

In Mark 6:16, Herod pronounces the phrase, "It is John, whom I beheaded: he is risen from the dead." It refers to the famous episode of the beheading of John the Baptist, ordered by Herod himself to keep a promise made to Salome, the daughter of Herodias with whom Herod himself had an illicit love affair.[3] This is a grammatical example analogous to the passage in John seen above. According to Mark's account, it is Herod who ordered one of his soldiers to go to the cell where John the Baptist is imprisoned, to cut off his head and bring it to him on a plate.[4] The fact that Herod himself did not want to kill John the Baptist (of whom he was in some way an admirer, even though he had him imprisoned), but simply fulfilled a promise made to Herodias's daughter, is, again, irrelevant. This is a another example of indirect causative with no permissive nuance. Salome does not ask Herod for permission to be able to cut off John the Baptist's head, but she does ask that the king give the infamous order. Likewise, Herod does not let John the Baptist have his head cut off. And he does not do so simply because no one would ever dream of committing such a heinous crime if Herod himself had not given the order first. The cruel sentence comes directly from the king who, as in the case of Pilate, has the power of life and death. Herod's responsibility in the death of the Baptist is clear in Mark's mind, which is why he makes Herod say, "It is John, whom I beheaded," without any need to sweeten its meaning with an improbable permissive construct ("It is John, whom I let be beheaded").

Before continuing with our analysis, it will be good to clarify one concept. The fact that some scholars glimpse the theoretical possibility of translating all these examples with a permissive convoluted construct (the high priests let Jesus be crucified, Pilate let Jesus be scourged, Herod let John the Baptist's head be cut off) does not reduce by one iota the actual responsibility of the subjects in question. And, above all, it cannot justify the permissive interpretation of a direct causative in every context in which one wants in some way to diminish the responsibility of the one who is the cause of the action. It is somehow permissible, for example, to say that Pilate allowed Jesus to be scourged only and exclusively to the extent that we are aware that it was Pilate who ordered his death. Similarly, it is somehow licit to say that Herod allowed

---

2. See, for example, John 18:31: "Pilate said, 'Take him and judge him according to your own laws.' 'But we have no right to condemn anyone to death,' they objected."

3. Herodias was the wife of Herod's brother (Herod Philip).

4. "And immediately the king ordered John's head to be brought in. He sent an assassin, who went and beheaded him in prison" (Mark 6:27).

## Eis Peirasmón

John to be beheaded only and exclusively to the extent that we are aware that it was Herod who ordered his death, and so forth. This way of talking is simply a form of *euphemism*. If, however, the permissive construct served to get across the message that Pilate and Herod were somehow innocent of the deaths of Jesus and John, such an expression would be to be immediately rejected as misleading.

To recap. So far, all the examples shown, which are no more than a handful, fall into the realm of direct or indirect causation, and there is, as seen and argued, no reason or need to understand them in a permissive sense, simply because no one is asking permission to anyone to do anything. On the other hand, however, there are multiple instances where, when the permissive sense is to be made explicit in the New Testament Greek, an explicit permissive construct is used (imagine that!). That is, the verbs "to allow," or "to let" are used. Exactly as in English. After all, in Greek there is a wide choice of synonyms we can draw on. The most common are *epitrépō* (ἐπιτρέπω), *aphíēmi* (ἀφίημι), *eáō* (ἐάω), and *dídōmi* (δίδωμι). All quite simple and straightforward. Without resorting to ambiguous implied meanings.

For example, when Jesus invites his disciples to leave everything behind and follow him, one of them sketches out, "Lord, suffer me first to go and bury my father" (Matt 8:21). To which Jesus responds with the famous phrase, "Follow me; and let the dead bury their dead" (Matt 8:22). In a couple of verses, two *explicit* permissive constructs: the first introduced by the imperative of the verb *epitrépō* and the second by the imperative of the verb *aphíēmi*, both followed by an infinitive construct. Matthew, the same evangelist who reports the text of the Lord's Prayer that we all know, is therefore fully aware of the explicit permissive construct and does not seem to have any preclusion to use it, if necessary. And since that disciple addressed Jesus almost certainly in Aramaic, it is significant that Matthew does not think for a moment about rendering the permissive sense with a direct causative expression, which would sound like "Lord, lead me first to bury my father." It would make no sense. The disciple does not need Jesus to go bury his father. He only needs his verbal permission. The action of going to bury does not take place on Jesus' instructions (Jesus is not the cause of the action), but derives from a determination of the disciple, independent of and even against Jesus' own will. It would not make sense for Matthew to render the Aramaic permissive expression with, for example, the Greek verb *phérō* or even *ágō*. If he had done so, he would have completely distorted the general sense of the disciple's request.

Again, in chapter 8 of Luke's Gospel we come across a strange episode: "And there was there an herd of many swine feeding on the mountain: and they besought him that he would suffer them to enter into them. And he suffered them" (Luke 8:32). Even Luke, the other evangelist who reports the text of the Lord's Prayer, when he has to describe a clear permissive context, makes it explicit without too many problems. The expression "to suffer to enter" is rendered, again, with the verb *epitrépō* followed by the infinitive of the verb *eisérchomai* (εἰσέρχομαι), which means "to enter." Let us read the original passage in Greek: "ἵνα ἐπιτρέψῃ αὐτοῖς εἰς ἐκείνους εἰσελθεῖν"[5] (Luke 8:32).

The reader may have already grasped the importance of this passage for the correct interpretation of the sixth petition of the Lord's Prayer. *Eiselthein* is the aorist infinitive of the verb *eisérchomai*, which is a compound of the verb *érchomai* (ἔρχομαι), meaning "to go," with the addition of the preposition *eis*. Just as the verb *eisphérō* used in the Lord's Prayer is a compound of the verb *phérō* with the same preposition *eis*. And *eisphérō* ("to lead in") is precisely the causative of the verb *eisérchomai* ("to enter"). Both verbs, finally, are followed by the place where the motion end into, which is introduced by the preposition *eis*. In the case of the Lord's Prayer the place is figurative ("into temptation"), while in the present case the place is the physical body of the pigs. If in both cases the meaning is permissive, why did Luke not opt in this episode for the same expression used in the Lord's Prayer? The answer is obvious. The demons do not need Jesus to physically put them inside the pigs. They only need his permission to enter them. The action of entering the pigs does not occur on Jesus' instructions or orders (Jesus is not the direct cause of the action), but results from a perverse determination of the demons to which Jesus simply gives his assent ("Jesus consented"). The exquisitely permissive sense is clear in Luke's mind, and as such, he depicts it by means of an explicit permissive construct. Had he opted for a direct causative construct with the use of *eisphérō* ("they begged Jesus to introduce them into those animals"), he would have completely distorted the sense of the passage.

It is impossible at this point not to cite another illuminating example that appears in Matthew's Gospel. Jesus is verbally flogging the scribes and Pharisees, denouncing their hypocrisy. Not only do they do nothing to enter the kingdom of heaven, but they do not allow those who would like to enter, to enter. It is worth reading the original Greek text: "ὑμεῖς γὰρ οὐκ εἰσέρχεσθε, οὐδὲ τοὺς εἰσερχομένους ἀφίετε εἰσελθεῖν"[6] (Matt 23:13).

This example is even more pertinent to the "lead us not into temptation" of the Lord's Prayer. It is a negative permissive construct in relation to the action of entering. We might call it a *prohibitive* construct, which instead of encouraging, impedes movement. Exactly what the Lord's Prayer, according to the thesis of those who advocate a permissive interpretation of the sixth petition, should have meant in the Aramaic version. We would be asking God the Father to prevent us from falling into temptation. But, as it happens, once transposed into Greek, the permissive negative (prohibitive) construct is rendered by Matthew explicitly with the use of the verb *aphíēmi* followed by an infinitive. It does not occur to Matthew to render the Aramaic expression used by Jesus in this context with an improbable *eisphérō*, which would instead sound like, "For you do not enter, nor bring in those who want to enter." And he does not do so

---

5. "*hína epitrépsēi autoîs eis ekeínous eiselthein*" = "that he would allow them to enter them."

6. "*humeîs gàr ouk eisérchesthe, oudè toùs eiserchoménous aphíete eiselthein*" = "for you do not enter, nor do you allow those who wish to enter."

because the prohibitive sense would have been totally lost, and the meaning of Jesus' words would have been completely distorted. Those who want to enter the kingdom of heaven do not need the Pharisees and scribes to bring them in by force, they only need that they do not hinder them. With their hypocrisy, the scribes and Pharisees, even if they wanted to, would not be able to bring anyone into the kingdom of heaven! The least they can do is to step aside and not divert from the right path those who are walking to enter it.

And then there is the famous episode in which Jesus takes back his disciples who were preventing people from letting their children come near so that Jesus could touch them. This fact is reported by all three synoptic evangelists (Matthew, Mark, and Luke), and all three agree on Jesus' exact words, "Let the children come to me." In Greek: "Ἄφετε τὰ παιδία ( . . . ) ἐλθεῖν πρός με"[7] (Matt 19:14); "Ἄφετε τὰ παιδία ἔρχεσθαι πρός με"[8] (Mark 10:14; Luke 18:16).

Again, the idea of "not preventing" a movement is rendered explicitly with a permissive construct introduced by the imperative of the verb *aphíēmi* followed by an infinitive. None of the three evangelists opt for a direct causative construct with the use of the verb *phérō*, which would sound like, "Bring the children to me." And for a simple reason. The children do not need the disciples to be brought closer to Jesus (there are already their parents trying to do that). Just like those who want to enter the kingdom of heaven in the case of the scribes and Pharisees, the children just need the disciples not to hinder their motion toward Jesus. That is, this is a clear permissive (or if you will, not prohibitive) expression: "Do not hinder little children from coming to me," and as such is reported by all three evangelists.

The same arguments could be repeated identically for the passage in Acts of the Apostles where Luke says, "Who in times past suffered all nations to walk in their own ways" (Acts 14:16), and not "Who in times past *led* all nations to walk in their own ways." In Acts 16:7, Luke says, "After they were come to Mysia, they assayed to go into Bithynia: but the Spirit suffered them not," and not "but the Spirit did not *lead* them in," just to emphasize the prohibitive sense. In Acts 19:30, Luke explicitly says, "And when Paul would have entered in unto the people, the disciples suffered him not," and not "the disciples did not *lead* him in." In Acts 23:32, Luke explicitly says, "On the morrow they left the horsemen to go with him, and returned to the castle," and not "they *led* the horsemen with him." Finally, in Acts 27:32, Luke explicitly says, "Then the soldiers cut off the ropes of the boat, and let her fall off," and not "and they *threw* her off." In all these examples, Luke opts for an explicit permissive construct introduced by the verb *eáō* followed by the infinitive.

Is there any need to continue?[9]

---

7. "*Áphete tà paidía ( . . . ) entheîn prós me*" = "Let the children ( . . . ) come to me."

8. "*Áphete tà paidía érchesthai prós me*" = "Let the children come to me."

9. Other examples of explicit permissive constructs can be found in Matt 5:40; Mark 1:34; 5:37; 11:6; Luke 8:51; 9:60; John 11:44; 18:8.

In order not to bore the reader too much, we will cite only one last example from the New Testament. It is an especially important passage—we would say almost indispensable—one of the most critical in terms of the subject matter. It would be wrong not to quote it here, keeping in mind that we will in any case return to this at length later. This is Paul's famous phrase on temptation, found in the first letter to the Corinthians and taken up and quoted by practically every single theologian and scholar who has ventured a possible explanation of the sixth petition of the Lord's Prayer. Let us read it in the original Greek text: "πιστὸς δὲ ὁ θεός, ὃς οὐκ ἐάσει ὑμᾶς πειρασθῆναι ὑπὲρ ὃ δύνασθε"[10] (1 Cor 10:13).

God is faithful and will not allow you to be tempted beyond what you can bear. There will be a way to elaborate on its theological meaning later. What is important for us now is to underline how St. Paul, when he wants to clarify the fact that God does not play at deceiving people but allows them to face only those temptations that they are able to bear, uses an explicit permissive construct, introduced by the future of the verb *eáō* followed by an infinitive (passive). And he does not venture into an improbable and ambiguous "and he will not tempt you beyond what you can bear," which could legitimately introduce doubt that God does in fact tempt people, in blatant contrast to what is asserted in the epistle of James. And why does Paul use a permissive and not a direct causative construct? The answer is obvious. God does not need to cause Satan to tempt us (he has the freedom to do it anyway), but he has the possibility, if he wants, to limit his action. Paul's phrase means, "God will not allow (the devil) to tempt you above your ability to resist."

We set out trying to unearth examples of implicit permissive senses found in the New Testament Greek and found *not even one*. In contrast, we found countless examples of explicit permissive constructs. This proves that, when Aramaic expressions used by Jesus are perceived by the evangelists with a permissive (and not causative) sense, they are rendered in Greek with an explicit permissive (and not causative) construct. It follows, in a very straightforward way in our view, that the use of a direct causative (*mḕ eisenénkeis*), instead of an explicit permissive construct, in the sixth petition of the Lord's Prayer means that Jesus did not use an Aramaic expression with a permissive sense when he declaimed the prayer. In other words, Jesus did not mean at all to say, "do not allow us to enter into temptation," or similar variants. In fact, if he had said all that, Matthew and Luke would probably have used an expression such as "μὴ ἀφῇς ἡμᾶς εἰσελθεῖν εἰς πειρασμόν."[11]

Pure speculation? Well, then, let us read the opening of chapter 23 of the book of Sirach: "Lord, father and master of my life, do not abandon me to their will, do not

---

10. "*pistòs dè ho theós, hòs ouk eásei hymâs peirasthênai hypèr hò dýnasthe*" = "God is faithful and will not allow you to be tempted beyond what you can [bear]."

11. "*mḕ aphêis hemâs eiseltheîn eis peirasmón*" = "do not allow us to enter into temptation" (cf. Matt 19:14; Mark 10:14; Luke 18:16).

let me fall because of them" (Sir 23:1).[12] To understand to whom this prayer is referring when it speaks of "them," it is necessary to read the conclusion of the previous chapter: "Who will set a guard over my mouth, over my lips a prudent seal, lest I fall through them and my tongue be my ruin?" (Sir 22:27). The one who is invoking the Lord is asking for his strength to keep his lips in check, that is, so that no unseemly words come out of his mouth that could cause him to fall into sin. That "them" refers to the lips, the mouth, the tongue. What is the exact prayer? Do not let me fall (into the temptation of speaking scandalous words). Isn't this exactly what the supporters of the permissive interpretation of the sixth petition of the Lord's Prayer propose? Do not let us fall (into temptation). And guess how this invocation is rendered in the Greek text of Sirach? With a direct causative form as in the Lord's Prayer? No, of course not. It is rendered with an explicit prohibitive form, identical to the one we proposed, with the use of the verb *aphíēmi* followed by the aorist infinitive of the verb *píptō* (πίπτω), which means "to fall": "μὴ ἀφῇς με πεσεῖν ἐν αὐτοῖς"[13] (Sir 23:1).

It did not occur to the translator of Sirach to use causative expressions such as "do not cast me," "do not throw me," "do not push me" into sin. Why? Because God in this case is not perceived as the cause, either directly or indirectly, of the fact that sinful expressions may come out of people's mouth. The cause of this is specified in that *en autoîs* ("because of them"): it is the lips themselves! God, in this case, is perceived as an external entity, completely independent and not responsible for the words that come out of the mouth of those who utter the prayer. No causative sense, then. God can only do two things: either turn away and let those lips continue to commit sin (permissive attitude) or give people the strength to control them (prohibitive attitude). The prayer consists precisely in asking God the Father not to opt for the permissive attitude.

This, in our opinion, is a powerful indication that, when Matthew and Luke decide to use a direct causative verb instead of an explicit permissive construct in the sixth petition of the Lord's Prayer, they are clearly indicating to us that God is perceived as the active protagonist, the main and sole cause, of our movement within the *peirasmós*. But what did Jesus mean by *mḕ eisenénkēis eis peirasmón*, then? Well, to try to grasp the true meaning of these words, it is necessary to dig deeper. Much deeper.

---

12. The book of Sirach (also known as The Wisdom of Ben Sira or Ecclesiasticus) was originally composed in Hebrew at the beginning of the second century BC and completed around 175 BC. The Hebrew text was then translated into Greek by the author's grandson after 117 BC. The book of Sirach was accepted as canonical and introduced into the Catholic Bible. Jews and Protestants, on the contrary, rejected it as apocryphal. The original Hebrew text was considered lost until the end of the nineteenth century AD when, between 1896 and 1900, several incomplete manuscripts were discovered in Masada, Egypt, near Cairo, and then later in 1931 and 1956 in the so-called Dead Sea Scrolls found in Qumran. Around 70 percent of the book is currently available in the original Hebrew language.

13. "*mḕ aphêis me peseîn en autoîs*" = "do not let me fall because of them."

# 8

# Can God Lead Man Astray?

There is one last case within the New Testament that is interesting to discuss. Interesting because the one who is the cause of the action is not a person, but God himself, just as in the Lord's Prayer. Even more interesting because it is Jesus Christ who speaks these words, just as in the Lord's Prayer. And from the words of Jesus, it would sound that God is associated with actions that at first glance would not seem appropriate to an infinitely merciful God. Just as in that "lead us not into temptation," which sounds so out of tune in the Lord's Prayer. It is worth reading the original Greek text: "Τετύφλωκεν αὐτῶν τοὺς ὀφθαλμοὺς καὶ ἐπώρωσεν αὐτῶν τὴν καρδίαν"[1] (John 12:40).

Jesus speaks these seemingly brutal words ("He blinded their eyes and hardened their heart") as he is trying to explain to his disciples why so many people, despite having seen his miracles, still do not believe. And he cites here a passage from the Old Testament in which God gives Isaiah the following order, of apparently obscure meaning: "Make the heart of this people fat, and make their ears heavy, and shut their eyes; lest they see with their eyes, and hear with their ears, and understand with their heart, and convert, and be healed" (Isa 6:10).

The Hebrew text contains three verbs, one after the other, in the causative (*hiphil*) form: *shāmăn* (שָׁמַן), meaning "to be fat," *kāvăd* (כָּבֵד), meaning "to be hard," and *shāʿăʿ* (שָׁעַע), meaning "to be blind." The causative stem transforms the meaning of the basic verbs to "to make fat," "to make hard," and "to make blind," respectively. Before trying to see whether these causatives can be interpreted in a permissive sense, let us better understand the context. After reading chapter 6 of the book of Isaiah, we discover that in this vision, the prophet sees the Lord seated on a high throne, surrounded by hosts of Seraphim glorifying him. Isaiah is seized with sudden fear at the sight of God because he realizes that he is a sinner amid a people of sinners. At that

---

1. "*Tetýphlōken autôn toùs ophtalmoùs kaì epṓrōsen autôn tền kardían*" = "He blinded their eyes and hardened their hearts."

point, one of the Seraphim grabs a burning coal from the altar and places it on Isaiah's lips. At that very moment, his sins are forgiven. Here then Isaiah hears the voice of the Lord himself asking in a sibylline manner, "Whom shall I send, and who will go for us?" To which, Isaiah, not yet knowing exactly what God has in mind, volunteers. "Here am I; send me," he replies (Isa 6:8). It is at this point that God gives Isaiah that specific command to harden the hearts of his people, to make them hard of hearing, and to blind their eyes.

Is it possible, in light of the context just described, to interpret the causative forms of *shāmăn*, *kāvăd*, and *shā'ă'* in a permissive sense? There is no reason to do so. God is angry with his people and is giving Isaiah a specific order. He is not telling him to let their hearts harden, or to allow their ears to close or their eyes to blind. Simply because all these things do not happen by themselves but require an external cause (hence the causative form). God, of course, could do all of this on his own, but in this case, he decides to use Isaiah as the instrument of his (mysterious) will. And the fact that the action described sounds somewhat out of tune to our ears or is even difficult for our sensibilities to accept (why would God want to harden the hearts of his people?) is not a good reason to try to alter or sweeten its meaning.

The following principle should apply: if the meaning of Scripture is apparently antithetical to the reader's sensibility, the reader should try to see if there is something wrong with his/her sensibility before trying to alter the meaning of Scripture.

And the meaning is clear. God, like it or not, wants to make the chances of his people being converted minimal.[2] And for this reason, he calls Isaiah to weigh down their hearts, harden their ears, and blind their eyes. Let us return to the expression used by Jesus in the Gospel of John: "(God) blinded their eyes and hardened their heart." Those who support the thesis that the sixth petition of the Lord's Prayer should be understood in a permissive sense, usually cite, among others, this very passage to show how it is not possible that Jesus said this. God does not blind or harden anyone's heart, they claim. At most, he allows this to happen. Unfortunately, this is exactly one of those cases in which we try to alter the meaning of Scripture, simply because the obvious meaning of Scripture is antithetical to our sensibility. This way of proceeding, in addition to being fallacious, is dangerous, because it exposes us to enormous logical-linguistic misunderstandings. From the Old Testament context to which Jesus makes clear reference, we know that there is no room for permissive interpretations. It is God who gives the order to Isaiah. God does not allow, but orders from the height of his omnipotence.

So, while we are at it, let us take the subject head on and try to treat it in the most direct way possible. It is a thorny subject because, digging into it, we will find ourselves having to answer extremely uncomfortable questions. Why does evil exist in the world? Is God the cause of evil in the world? And if not, why does God allow

---

2. We will have the opportunity later to elaborate and eviscerate this concept in order to fully understand it.

evil in the world? But let us go step by step and first try to understand why God might want to harden the hearts of people, according to what seems to emerge from the passage from the book of Isaiah just analyzed. To do this, we need to read another passage from the book of Isaiah, found in chapter 63, which echoes the one just read in chapter 6: "O Lord, why hast thou made us to err from thy ways, and hardened our heart from thy fear? Return for thy servants' sake, the tribes of thine inheritance?" (Isa 63:17).

The Hebrew text contains two verbs, one after the other, in the causative (*hiphil*) form: *tāʿâ* (תָּעָה), meaning "to go astray," and *qāshăh* (קָשַׁח), meaning "to be hard." The causative stem transforms the meaning of the basic verbs into "to lead astray" and "to make hard," respectively. This is one of the other examples that proponents of the permissive thesis of the sixth petition of the Lord's Prayer usually quote. Since it is not possible to think that God leads people astray or hardens their hearts, some translations opt for a permissive construct.[3] The context is always the same. God is angry with the people of Israel, who do not listen and obey his words, and therefore God turns away from them by "blinding their eyes and hardening their hearts."

We will try to demonstrate below how the correct interpretation, in our opinion, is that God may cause people to stray from the right path to the same extent that he may harden his heart. Even better: the fact that people stray from the right path is a direct consequence of the fact that their heart has been hardened. And like it or not, the cause of this is God himself. And this is why the Hebrew text, rightly, uses the causative form to indicate that relationship of cause-effect between the intervention of God, who intervened to alter his people's heart, and the fact that his people have deviated from the right path.

But why would God want such a thing? St. Paul explains it to us in his letter to the Romans:

> And not only this; but when Rebecca also had conceived by one, even by our father Isaac; (For the children being not yet born, neither having done any good or evil, that the purpose of God according to election might stand, not of works, but of him that calleth;) It was said unto her, The elder shall serve the younger. As it is written, Jacob have I loved, but Esau have I hated. What shall we say then? Is there unrighteousness with God? God forbid. For he saith to Moses, I will have mercy on whom I will have mercy, and I will have compassion on whom I will have compassion. So then it is not of him that willeth, nor of him that runneth, but of God that sheweth mercy. For the scripture saith unto Pharaoh, Even for this same purpose have I raised thee up, that I might shew my power in thee, and that my name might be declared throughout all the earth. Therefore hath he mercy on whom he will have mercy, and whom he will he hardeneth. Thou wilt say then unto me, Why doth he yet find fault? For who hath resisted his will? Nay but, O man, who art thou that repliest against

---

3. See NLT and GNT.

God? Shall the thing formed say to him that formed it, Why hast thou made me thus? Hath not the potter power over the clay, of the same lump to make one vessel unto honour, and another unto dishonour? (Rom 9:10–21)

Definitive. Let us read it again slowly, if necessary. St. Paul, appropriately quoting several passages from the Old Testament, destroys with perfect lucidity and in a couple of lines the permissive thesis. He begins by recounting what happened to Rebecca, Isaac's wife, even before her two sons Jacob and Esau were born. It had been prophesied that the elder (Esau) would be subject to the younger (Jacob) against the natural right of succession. Why? Because this is what God had decided in his unfathomable plan. Period. Whether we like it or not. Who are we, humble mortals, to decide what is appropriate for God to do or not to do? Do we dare to say that God is ungrateful, just because he decided to favor Jacob over Esau? Just because he decided to harden the hearts of some and not others? Do we claim to know God's mysterious plans and want to change them? Do we really have the courage to understand how and why divine Providence manifests itself? St. Paul gives another example, that of Pharaoh, who was first raised to the highest honors and then destroyed. Why? Simple: so "that I might shew my power in thee, and that my name might be declared throughout all the earth." Isn't that reason enough? It would be better to rest our souls, says Paul, because the God of the Old Testament (which is also the same as the God of the New Testament) is a God who acts according to his will and his logic, which transcend human reasoning: "hath he mercy on whom he will have mercy, and whom he will he hardeneth." This would be enough to dismiss as superfluous all those disquisitions on the fact that God cannot act in the world to produce something that, in the eyes of people, may seem "evil," and that God can at the most allow evil, but not encourage or produce it.

Let us be careful. This is a crucial passage, which might shock even the most devout ears. The fact that God is pure love and infinitely merciful is not inconsistent with the fact that God himself can cause evil to occur in the world (in a causative, not permissive, sense!), if that evil turns out to be necessary for the fulfillment of his inscrutable providential plan for humanity.

And to bring further evidence to the skeptical readers who shake their head and rightly doubt, following the intuition of St. Paul, let us analyze the many biblical passages that tell how God hardened Pharaoh's heart. Everyone knows the story. God, through Moses, admonishes Pharaoh to let his people go free. Penalty: multiple calamities would befall the kingdom of Egypt. But God hardens Pharaoh's heart and makes him insensitive to the divine fear. As a result, after having promised to send the people of Israel free, Pharaoh always goes back on his word and prevents Moses and his people from leaving. And each time, punctually, a different calamity befalls Egypt. For ten times Pharaoh sees with his own eyes the power of God that wreaks havoc on his land and his people, but for ten times he decides to go against the will of God because his heart is so hard that he succumbs to his own pride. For example, we read from the book of Exodus: "And the Lord said unto Moses, When thou goest to return into Egypt, see that thou do all those wonders before Pharaoh, which I have put in thine hand: but I will harden his heart, that he shall not let the people go" (Exod 4:21).

Note that in this case the verb used in the Hebrew text for "to harden" is *hāzăq* (חָזַק), which means "to be strong, hard," conjugated not in the causative *hiphil* form, but in the *piel* form. The *piel* stem is one of the most versatile in the Hebrew language and can express simple, intensive, resultative, causative meanings, depending on the context. In this context, it has a causative meaning and indicates the action of "making hard." There are no examples of permissive interpretations of the same verb in the *piel* form. At best, it can indicate the action of making strong; at worst, precisely that of hardening. Any interpretation that attempts to make God say, "But I will let his heart be hardened" is arbitrary and has no exegetical, theological, or logical foundation. It would not make sense, according to a purely human logic, that Pharaoh could continue (once, twice, even ten times!) to commit the same unforgivable mistake of disobeying God's orders. One after the other, he and his people are hit by evil plagues, in a crescendo of destruction and death, until all the firstborns are killed, including Pharaoh's son. As they say, "to err is human, but to persist is diabolical." In this case the devil has nothing to do with it, but it cannot be anything else but a divine work that Pharaoh for ten times falls into the same error. If God had not intervened personally and had simply let Pharaoh's heart harden, Pharaoh would probably have given up after a couple of calamities, at most. Which, unfortunately for Pharaoh, was not within the divine plans. God confused Pharaoh's mind, hardened his heart, made him insensitive to divine fear, and consequently threw him into the ruin of his pride.

And similar examples are found in abundance in the Old Testament.[4] In fact, in the Old Testament there is no permissive nuance in relation to God's action. God is all-powerful, and as such disposes of people and the world. At his pleasure and according to his plans. Whether people like it or not. Period.

Let us look at another example related to the fact that God may want to harden the hearts of people. It is found in the book of Joshua: "For it was of the Lord to harden their hearts, that they should come against Israel in battle, that he might destroy them utterly, and that they might have no favour, but that he might destroy them, as the Lord commanded Moses" (Josh 11:20).

Again, we are confronted with a God who acts personally to obstinate these nations to war against Israel. Why? Because the Lord's plan has for these nations, unfortunately for them, is to be annihilated in war. Quite simple. Ruthless? Unfair? And who are we to argue about the divine plan?

The fact that the permissive sense is absent and completely flattened on the causative one for all that concerns the work of God in the Old Testament is clear if we read, for example, the passage in the book of Ezekiel where God announces that (just to stay

---

4. See, for example, Exod 7:3; 9:12, 34; 10:1, 20, 27; 11:10; 14:4, 8, 17; Deut 2:30.

on the subject) his wrath will come down violently on Pharaoh and his people. Let us read the whole passage because it is worth it.

> Thus saith the Lord God; I will therefore spread out my net over thee with a company of many people; and they shall bring thee up in my net. Then will I leave thee upon the land, I will cast thee forth upon the open field, and will cause all the fowls of the heaven to remain upon thee, and I will fill the beasts of the whole earth with thee. And I will lay thy flesh upon the mountains and fill the valleys with thy height. I will also water with thy blood the land wherein thou swimmest, even to the mountains; and the rivers shall be full of thee. And when I shall put thee out, I will cover the heaven, and make the stars thereof dark; I will cover the sun with a cloud, and the moon shall not give her light. All the bright lights of heaven will I make dark over thee, and set darkness upon thy land, saith the Lord God. I will also vex the hearts of many people, when I shall bring thy destruction among the nations, into the countries which thou hast not known. Yea, I will make many people amazed at thee, and their kings shall be horribly afraid for thee, when I shall brandish my sword before them; and they shall tremble at every moment, every man for his own life, in the day of thy fall. For thus saith the Lord God; The sword of the king of Babylon shall come upon thee. By the swords of the mighty will I cause thy multitude to fall, the terrible of the nations, all of them: and they shall spoil the pomp of Egypt, and all the multitude thereof shall be destroyed. I will destroy also all the beasts thereof from beside the great waters; neither shall the foot of man trouble them any more, nor the hoofs of beasts trouble them. Then will I make their waters deep, and cause their rivers to run like oil, saith the Lord God. When I shall make the land of Egypt desolate, and the country shall be destitute of that whereof it was full, when I shall smite all them that dwell therein, then shall they know that I am the Lord. (Ezek 32:3–15)

Not exactly the sweetened image of a mild and good-natured God. The Old Testament is full of similar episodes, in which divine wrath explodes in all its omnipotence and hurls itself balefully at peoples who do not please the Lord. Trying to explain all these passages in the light of the permissive sense (that is, God does not directly inflict evil on people, but simply allows evil to befall people by removing his saving protection) is objectively a desperate exercise. And above all, it is a futile exercise. For in the Old Testament sensibility, there is nothing in this divine behavior that is in any way inconsistent with his infinitely merciful nature.

Being infinitely merciful cannot translate into being unjust. And if God is immensely just, it means that he will have to reward the God-fearing and punish the proud. Pharaoh is the emblem of pride par excellence. And against the pride of Pharaoh the wrath of divine justice is abated. There is no need to sweeten anything. The terrible punishment inflicted on Pharaoh and his people, far from being a sign of an imperfect mercy, is instead the logical conclusion of a perfect divine justice. Like it or not, the God of the Old Testament (which is the same as the God of the New Testament) is a God who is characterized primarily by his mercy and his justice, which translate into the exaltation of the humble and the destruction of the powerful and the proud. Such characteristics of God, mercy and justice, reverberate in the *Magnificat*, the famous prayer declaimed by the Virgin Mary in front of her cousin St. Elizabeth, shortly after receiving the announcement by the angel Gabriel:

> And Mary said, My soul doth magnify the Lord, And my spirit hath rejoiced in God my Savior. For he hath regarded the low estate of his handmaiden: for, behold, from henceforth all generations shall call me blessed. For he that is mighty hath done to me great things; and holy is his name. And his mercy is on them that fear him from generation to generation. He hath shewed strength with his arm; he hath scattered the proud in the imagination of their hearts. He hath put down the mighty from their seats, and exalted them of low degree. He hath filled the hungry with good things; and the rich he hath sent empty away. He hath helped his servant Israel, in remembrance of his mercy; As he spake to our fathers, to Abraham, and to his seed forever. (Luke 1:46-55)

Trying to manipulate the *Magnificat* by introducing a permissive meaning into Mary's words would be as wicked as it is useless. Mary resumes magnificently—it is the case to say—those fundamental characteristics of mercy and justice of the God of Abraham and Jacob that result in the physical destruction of the proud and in the elevation of the humble. The God Mary knows at that moment is obviously the God described in the Old Testament and she refers to him. Likewise, there is no reason to reinterpret the Old Testament in the light of an improbable permissive sense. God is fully aware of the evil he is ordering to befall the nations he intends to punish, and this is the ultimate manifestation of his infinite justice. Psalm 92(91)[5] explains this concept perfectly:

> A brutish man knoweth not; neither doth a fool understand this. When the wicked spring as the grass, and when all the workers of iniquity do flourish; it is that they shall be destroyed forever: But thou, Lord, art most high for evermore. For, lo, thine enemies, O Lord, for, lo, thine enemies shall perish; all the workers of iniquity shall be scattered. But my horn shalt thou exalt like the horn of an unicorn: I shall be anointed with fresh oil. Mine eye also shall see my desire on mine enemies, and mine ears shall hear my desire of the wicked that rise up against me. The righteous shall flourish like the palm tree: he shall grow like a cedar in Lebanon. Those that be planted in the house of the Lord shall flourish in the courts of our God. They shall still bring forth fruit in old age; they shall be fat and flourishing; To shew that the Lord is upright: he is my rock, and there is no unrighteousness in him. (Ps 92(91):6-15(7-16))

---

5. From now on, we will use the Masoretic numbering of the psalms (in parentheses the Greek numbering of the Septuagint, if it differs).

In God there is no unrighteousness: the righteous is lifted, the sinner is destroyed forever. Does the evil that the proud receive come from God? Yes, without a doubt, and without any permissive interpretation. We could cite Isaiah again: "Therefore is the anger of the Lord kindled against his people, and he hath stretched forth his hand against them, and hath smitten them: and the hills did tremble, and their carcasses were torn in the midst of the streets. For all this his anger is not turned away, but his hand is stretched out still" (Isa 5:25). Or Jeremiah: "Therefore thus saith the Lord God; Behold, mine anger and my fury shall be poured out upon this place, upon man, and upon beast, and upon the trees of the field, and upon the fruit of the ground; and it shall burn, and shall not be quenched" (Jer 7:20). Or the book of Lamentations: "He hath cut off in his fierce anger all the horn of Israel: he hath drawn back his right hand from before the enemy, and he burned against Jacob like a flaming fire, which devoureth round about" (Lam 2:3).

The examples are too many and would bore the reader. Suffice it to mention here Deuteronomy chapters 7 and 28, which contain a summary of the typical divine attitude. Those who follow the divine laws and obey God will be filled with blessings; on the contrary, God will bring down all kinds of evil on the heads of the wicked and proud.

However, supporters of the permissive thesis may argue that God does not cause evil, but rather allows evil to befall people simply by *removing his protection*. For example, let us read the passage in chapter 31 of Deuteronomy in which God says, "Then my anger shall be kindled against them in that day, and I will forsake them, and I will hide my face from them, and they shall be devoured, and many evils and troubles shall befall them; so that they will say in that day, Are not these evils come upon us, because our God is not among us? And I will surely hide my face in that day for all the evils which they shall have wrought, in that they are turned unto other gods" (Deut 31:17–18).

True. The removal of his protection against enemies is one of the ways in which God can bring down evil on people, as a punishment for their behavior. However, trying to convey the idea that God is not responsible for that evil (God only allows it, but does not cause it) is just a useless rhetorical exercise.

Let us make an even clearer example to dispel any doubt, since this is a crucial point of our reasoning. Let us take the example of the Roman emperors who, at the end of the fights in the Colosseum, decided whether or not to spare the lives of the gladiators who had participated in the games.[6] With a single hand gesture, they had the power to keep the ferocious beasts inside their cages. But, if for any reason, the fight was not to their liking, they had the power, with a simple thumbs-down, to remove the bolts and unleash the ferocity of the hungry beasts against the poor men. Would we really have the courage to say that the emperor was not the direct cause of the death of the slaves mauled by the beasts, but that he simply allowed the beasts to pounce on them by having the bolts of the cages removed? As if that opening of the cages was

6. The fact that the veracity of this practice has not been historically established is irrelevant here.

a minor thing, ordered incidentally? Which, by the way, resulted in the gruesome execution of the slaves amidst the cries of the delirious crowd. Could we really say that the death of the slaves was simply due to the fact that the emperor *let* the beasts pounce on them? Obviously not. If the emperor had not given the order, none of this would have happened. The beasts would have remained in their cages, and the slaves would have survived. The removal of protection, far from being something negligible, is exactly the cause of the evil falling on those poor people. The removal of the bolts ordered by the emperor, as well as the removal of the protection on his own people by God, are exactly the direct intervention (causative, not permissive!) that determines the death of the slaves, as well as the destruction of the chosen people of God.

Let us read the passage found in the book of Exodus where God speaks to Moses: "And said, If thou wilt diligently hearken to the voice of the Lord thy God, and wilt do that which is right in his sight, and wilt give ear to his commandments, and keep all his statutes, I will put none of these diseases upon thee, which I have brought upon the Egyptians: for I am the Lord that healeth thee" (Exod 15:26).

The Hebrew term used to refer to God's action of inflicting calamity on the Egyptian people is the verb *sûm* (שׂוּם), which means "to put," "to place," "to impose." It is used twice in this passage in Exodus, and in both cases in the base form (*qal*). The *qal* stem indicates a simple, objective action, without any nuance of meaning. Thus, even if we wanted to, it is grammatically impossible in this case to use the trick of the causative stem to introduce a permissive sense to the passage. God is the one who, literally, will put (inflict) on the heads of his people the same calamities he put (inflicted) on the heads of the Egyptians, if they do not do what he says. All very straightforward. God is the direct cause of the calamities that have befallen the Egyptians, just as he will be the direct cause of the calamities that will befall his own people, if they disobey his orders. Without too many rhetorical flourishes.

But the final verse that sets the matter is found in the book of Isaiah in chapter 45. God reveals himself to his people with these words: "I form the light, and create darkness: I make good, and create evil: I the Lord do all these things"[7] (Isa 45:7).

I make good and create evil. The Hebrew verbs used to render the idea of "making" (good) and "creating" (evil) are respectively ʻ*āsâ* (עָשָׂה) and *bārāʼ* (בְּרָא), both conjugated in the *qal* form, without any sort of ambiguity. "To make" and "to create" are neutral, clear, objective verbs, without subtext, without nuance. The term "good" is rendered by the term *shālôm* (שָׁלוֹם), probably the best-known word in the Hebrew language, used in the daily greeting, which means "peace," "prosperity," "happiness." Evil, on the other hand, is rendered by the term *răʻ* (רַע), the exact opposite of *shālôm* and the most generic possible term in the Hebrew language for anything that causes pain, destruction, unhappiness. God, in his omnipotence, is creator of both.

---

7. The KJV has "peace" instead of "good." We believe the antithesis between "good" and "evil" (the same as between "light" and "darkness") should be maintained.

Now, unless we start arguing with the crystalline words of God himself, who defines himself as the creator of good and evil,[8] I would say that we can also begin to consider as highly unlikely the permissive hypothesis, designed specifically to justify in some way the evil that comes from God. Because there is really nothing to justify. God's actions, by definition, do not need to be justified. They just need to be accepted, whether they seem right or not. And never mind if they do not seem right to us. The problem is ours, not God's. What appears as "evil" in the eyes of people is nothing more than a simple instrument, one of many, used by God to fulfill the providential plan that God has for humanity.

Beware, though. This does not mean that God is the origin of *moral* evil. Throughout the Old Testament God is primarily responsible for the physical and material evil inflicted from time to time on humanity, usually as a form of punishment. And this kind of evil, God claims with pride, is the highest expression of his justice. On the contrary, God is never responsible for moral evil. The one who incites the perpetration of moral evil is Satan, the devil, the serpent who appears in chapter 3 of the book of Genesis.

But then—the supporters of the permissive thesis argue back—how do we explain the expressions we find in a couple of psalms, specifically Psalm 119(118) and Psalm 141(140)? Well, then, let us analyze them both, one by one.

Let us start with Psalm 119(118): "With my whole heart have I sought thee: O do not lead me astray[9] from thy commandments" (Ps 119(118):10). The Hebrew term used to convey the idea of deviating from the right path is the verb *shāgâ* (שָׁגָה), which means "to go astray." Again, the verb is used in the causative *hiphil* form and thus means "to lead astray."

Similarly, Psalm 141(140) reads: "Incline not my heart to any evil thing" (Ps 141(140):4). The Hebrew term used to convey the idea of inclining is the verb *nātâ* (נָטָה), which means "to extend." Again, the verb is used in the causative *hiphil* form and thus means "to incline" or "to bend."

These two passages just presented echo Isa 63:17 ("O Lord, why hast thou made us to err from thy ways, and hardened our heart from thy fear?") and Sir 22:27 ("Who will set a guard over my mouth, over my lips a prudent seal, lest I fall through them and my tongue be my ruin?"). In the Greek version of the Septuagint,[10] the expressions used to translate "do not lead me astray" and "do not incline" are *mè apósēi* (μὴ ἀπώσῃ) and *mè enklínēis* (μὴ ἐκκλίνῃς), respectively, which are immediately relatable by grammatical construct to the *mè eisenénkēis* (μὴ εἰσενέγκῃς) of the Lord's Prayer—totally causative, non-permissive verbs.

---

8. It would be illogical to translate two grammatically identical expressions differently just because it suits us: one with a direct causative value ("I make good") and one with a permissive value ("I allow evil").

9. The KJV has "let me not wander."

10. The Septuagint (LXX) is the earliest extant koine Greek translation of the Old Testament from the original Hebrew (third and second century BC).

It should be clear by now that the permissive interpretation of the sixth petition of the Lord's Prayer is essentially based on the following syllogism:

1. Since God cannot lead people astray from his precepts, nor incline their heart to evil, the only possible interpretation of the causative *hiphil* forms found in the original Hebrew texts must be the permissive one ("do not let me depart from your precepts" and "do not let my heart incline toward any evil thing").

2. The Greek translation of both passages in the Septuagint version, however, does not "reproduce" the permissive sense, and limits itself to a literal translation of the Hebrew text ("do not lead me astray from your precepts" and "do not incline my heart to any evil thing").

3. Given these two premises, we must conclude that the sixth petition of the Lord's Prayer is also merely a literal translation of the Hebrew causal construct, which should instead be interpreted in a permissive sense.

*Et voilà*. Very fascinating reasoning, which seems to save goats and cabbages (theology and exegesis). Unfortunately, as we will now show, it is a fallacious reasoning, based on fallacious premises. And since it is a syllogistic type of reasoning, we would only need to refute one of the two premises. Below, we will refute both. Let us begin.

The idea that "God cannot lead people astray from his precepts, nor incline their heart to evil" is simply wrong. It is more the result of our modern sensibility than of empirical evidence. We have already explained extensively and demonstrated with abundant examples how God not only can, but in some cases decides to harden the hearts of people by inclining them to perform actions against the divine will itself (think of the example of Pharaoh above all). Actions that will turn against them and will be for them a source of pain and destruction. So yes: God can incline the heart of people to evil to the extent that he may make them insensitive to his teachings, thus diverting them from his precepts. And all this is part of the inscrutable plan that God has for us and for humanity. The idea of a good-natured God, who does not get his hands dirty and who passively suffers the evil that spreads in the world before his eyes and for which he is not responsible, is, again, fascinating, but it does not find empirical support in Scripture. It represents what most of us would like God to be. But not what he is, at least according to what emerges from the Old Testament.

It is worth repeating that applying improbable interpretations to the texts of Scripture, just because those texts seem "wrong" to us, is as common an error as it is theologically devastating. And we should always ask ourselves if there is a better explanation than altering the meaning of the sacred texts. And in this case, there is. We will devote the following chapter to the philosophical-theological explanation of the idea of a God who decides to harden the heart of people.

And now for the second premise. Let us focus on the passage in Psalm 119(118). The Greek translation of the Septuagint reads: "μὴ ἀπώσῃ με ἀπὸ τῶν ἐντολῶν σου"[11] (Ps 119(118):10). The Greek verb chosen to denote the action of "diverting" is (the aorist subjunctive of) *apōthéō* (ἀπωθέω). It is interesting to note that this Greek verb is generally used sparingly within Scripture (it appears only six times in the New Testament). To render a similar concept, Greek generally uses the more common *planáō* (πλανάω), which means "to lead astray" and which appears about forty times in the New Testament. Why such a particular choice of translation? Actually, *apōthéō* and *planáō* are not exactly synonymous. The verb *planáō* derives from the Greek word *plános* (πλάνος), which indicates the action of "wandering aimlessly," a movement without a precise direction, which slowly drifts away from the main road. The verb *planáō* therefore indicates the action of leading someone away from the right path. Isn't this exactly what the Hebrew text is saying? The verb *apōthéō*, on the other hand, comes from the combination of the preposition *apó* (ἀπό), which indicates the action of moving away from a place, and the verb *ōthéō* (ὠθέω), which indicates the action of pushing. The verb *apōthéō* therefore means "to drive away," "to push away with a shove." It is a much rougher verb than *planáō*. Why then, despite having a more neutral *planáō*, does the Septuagint decide to switch to *apōthéō*?

Doesn't it remind you of the very particular lexical choice of Matthew and Luke when, in order to render the sixth petition of the Lord's Prayer, despite having a more neutral *eiságō* ("to lead") at their disposal, they decide to veer toward a rougher *eisphérō* ("to bring")?

These lexical subtleties are precisely the key to refuting the second premise as well. The thesis is that the Greek version (both of the psalms and of the Lord's Prayer) is a simple literal translation of the Hebrew text, whereby

1. the translator decided to maintain a neutral position that does not make explicit the permissive sense, aware of the fact that
2. the reader would have perceived and grasped it in any case.

Both hypotheses do not hold up. We have already seen that if the Septuagint, as well as Matthew and Luke, had wanted to maintain a neutral, detached position, without introducing any personal interpretations, they would have had at their disposal very trivial lexical choices. The fact that they venture into extremely specific terms shows that their translation does not want to be neutral at all, but rather wants to pass a very clear idea. Which is? That the passages of the psalms, as well as of the Lord's Prayer, must be understood with a strong direct causative sense, and not permissive.

How could the readers of the time have easily grasped the permissive sense from the Greek text, if the Greek translators instead do everything possible to choose specific verbs that have absolutely nothing permissive about them?

---

11. "*mḕ apṓsēi me apò tôn entolôn sou*"= "Do not lead me astray from your precepts."

Let us take a practical example. If we were climbing on a rock face and we wanted to remind the climber above us not to let us fall into the void, would we say, "Please, don't throw us down!"? Of course not. Unless we were joking with our climbing partner.

So why would the Septuagint, Matthew, and Luke, in a context that could not be more serious (the translation of the revealed *lógos*), instead say "push off" instead of "let go," or "lead into" instead of "let go in"? An objectively confusing, ambiguous, and misleading language, if Christ's words had really intended to have a permissive meaning. Wasn't it Jesus himself who, just before reciting the Lord's Prayer in the famous Sermon on the Mount, admonished the crowds so that their speech would be "yes yes, no no" (Matt 5:37)? It would be a curious and unfortunate coincidence if, right after Christ harangued the disciples on the need to use simple and clear words, Matthew himself, who was in the crowd, started to translate Christ's words in an ambiguous way. Especially because, as we have seen, he had all the grammatical tools to be able to make explicit in Greek a hypothetical permissive meaning.

Regarding the second passage in Psalm 141(140) ("Incline not my heart to any evil thing") we only note for now that the concept of "inclining" is different from the concept of "throwing in." To incline someone to evil means to make him *more likely* to do evil, not to force him to do evil. It is a subtle difference, we admit it, but a fundamental one. We will see extensively in the next chapter how there is reason to think that God very often works exactly this way with people, and we will try to explore all the possible reasons for such behavior, which is then the only intellectually honest way to proceed, rather than trying to deny the evidence.

At this point, we hope to have succeeded in convincing the reader—even the most skeptical one—of the logical-theological inconsistency of the permissive interpretation of the sixth petition of the Lord's Prayer. But, in any case, we must recognize that it is not a great step forward, since all our arguments cannot in any way be used to justify the idea of a God who leads us into temptation.[12] The problem remains, and it's not small.

But before taking this dilemma head on, as promised, it will be good to clarify what it means from a theological point of view that God may decide to harden the heart of people, and thus to be an active part in the ability of people to resist the temptation of sin. Does this mean that the evil done by people is not people's responsibility, but rather a divine one? And what meaning, then, can sin have? And how can all this be reconciled with free will—the free choice between good and evil—which is the basis of the Catechism of the Catholic Church? All legitimate questions, which we will try to unravel in the following chapters.

---

12. We have already made it clear that not God, but Satan, is to be held responsible for *moral* evil in the world.

# 9

# The Permissive Sensitivity in the Old Testament

Let us go back to the starting point. Is it God who hardens the hearts of people, or is it people who are obstinate in their pride, and God simply lets them be? In the previous chapter we listed an innumerable series of examples that testify without any doubt that God can (and declares himself to) be in many cases the main architect of such obstinacy. Yet, there are those who still do not want to give up and quote, for example, Exod 8:15 where it is said, "when Pharaoh saw that there was respite, he hardened his heart, and hearkened not unto them." Or Exod 8:32 and Exod 9:34, where again it is said that it was Pharaoh who hardened his own heart. And finally, in the first book of Samuel, the priests and soothsayers advise the Philistines not to defy the God of Israel: "Wherefore then do ye harden your hearts, as the Egyptians and Pharaoh hardened their hearts?" (1 Sam 6:6).

In these four examples (which are however a minority compared to the total) it would seem to be understood that it was not God, but Pharaoh himself who hardened his heart. And so? How do we explain the apparent contradiction? Who hardens what? The supporters of the permissive thesis immediately conclude that all the other examples in which God seems to harden Pharaoh's heart must be interpreted in the opposite way. They speak of a hypothetical permissive sensitivity that had not yet matured at that time (even when God lets something happen, he is said to have caused it).[1] The permissive sensitivity would instead emerge as the centuries passed, especially in the transition from the Old to the New Testament. A fascinating thesis, again, but one that does not stand up. The definitive words of St. Paul,[2] a man of the first century, would be enough to disprove such a thesis. But there are clear examples

---

1. See, for example, Fitzmyer, "And Lead Us Not into Temptation," 259–273.

2. "Therefore hath he mercy on whom he will have mercy, and whom he will he hardeneth" (Rom 9:18).

where, when the Hebrew text wants to associate God with a clear permissive sense, it does so without too much trouble. And especially, without using causative forms.

Because (surprise!) even Semitic languages do use explicit permissive constructs when necessary, having at their disposal verbs that precisely indicate the action of "letting" and "allowing." Let us look at some of them.

Let us take perhaps one of the best known and most dramatic passages in the Old Testament: the final plague that the Lord decides to inflict on the Egyptian people in order to convince Pharaoh to let the people of Israel go free. God has announced that he will send his Destroying Angel to kill all the firstborn, including Pharaoh's own little son. In order for his angel to spare the Israelites, they will have to sprinkle the lintel and side posts of their doors with the blood of a sacrificed lamb, so that when "the Lord will pass through to smite the Egyptians; and when he seeth the blood upon the lintel, and on the two side posts, the Lord will pass over the door, and will not suffer the destroyer to come in unto your houses to smite you" (Exod 12:23).

This very gesture of "passing over" is what gives the Passover its name.[3] In order that his people might be spared, it is said that the Lord did not allow the Destroying Angel to enter their homes. So, the meaning of the passage is *prohibitive*, which is exactly what we would have Jesus say in the sixth petition of the Lord's Prayer ("do not allow us to enter into temptation"). And how is this expression rendered in Hebrew? Let us read the original text (from right to left): "וְלֹא יִתֵּן הַמַּשְׁחִית לָבֹא אֶל־בָּתֵּיכֶם"[4] (Exod 12:23). *Wəlō'* (וְלֹא) is a negative conjunction ("and not"); *yittēn* (יִתֵּן) is the imperfect of the verb *nāthăn* (נָתַן), which indicates the action of "giving," or "putting," and in some cases, as in this one, of "allowing." The verb *nāthăn* is thus used to introduce an *explicit* permissive construction with the use of the infinitive; *hămmăshḥîth* (הַמַּשְׁחִית) denotes the Destroying Angel and *lāvō'* (לָבֹא) is the infinitive of the verb to enter *bô'* (בּוֹא); *'el-băttêkhĕm* (אֶל־בָּתֵּיכֶם) translates the motion into a place ("into your houses"). The entire expression can be translated as "and will not allow the Destroyer to enter your houses." Why does the Hebrew text not use the causative form of the verb *bô'* to express the same concept? Is it not true that the readers of the time would have immediately percieved that the *hiphil* form was not to be understood in a causative sense but rather in a permissive sense? Isn't it also true that the permissive sensibility at that time was not yet developed? Evidently, the answer to both questions must be no. If Moses, who pronounces these words, had used a causative expression ("and he will not *bring* the Destroyer into your houses"), the prohibitive sense would have been lost. Instead, Moses wants to emphasize the supernatural protection that God will grant to his people. The Destroyer will come, but God will not allow him to enter. The image is not of a God who does not bring the Destroying Angel into their homes, but rather of a God who opposes his entry. Clearly, the Destroying Angel acts

---

3. From the verb *pāsăh* (פָּסַח), which means "to pass."
4. "*wəlō' yittēn hămmăshḥîth lāvō' 'el-băttêkhĕm*" = "and will not suffer the Destroyer to come in unto your houses to smite you."

## Eis Peirasmón

on behalf of God, but Moses' expression is meant to paint a picture of the Destroyer on the one hand, and the people of Israel protected by God on the other. The Destroyer does not seem to have the power to distinguish between Egyptians and Israelites. If it were up to him, he would exterminate all the firstborn. It is only because of the protection offered by God that the Destroyer will pass over. And how does the Septuagint translate this expression? With a direct causative? No, it does not. It translates it with an explicit permissive construct introduced by the verb *aphíēmi*.[5] This proves that the Greek translation of the Septuagint can perfectly recognize and render the permissive sense of Scripture when this is evident.

Let us take this other passage, found in the book of Numbers: "And Balaam rose up in the morning, and said unto the princes of Balak, Get you into your land: for the Lord refuseth to give me leave to go with you" (Num 22:13).

The context is post-exodus. The people of Israel, protected by the Lord, camp in the steppes of Moab, beyond the Jordan, close to Jericho. Balak, king of Moab, frightened by how numerous the Israelites are, sends a delegation of leaders to the soothsayer Balaam, asking him to curse the people of Israel. Only in this way will he have any chance of driving them out of his land. At that point, God intervenes and orders Balaam not to follow the leaders sent by Balak nor to curse the Israelites. The next morning, Balaam has no choice but to inform the leaders that God has not allowed him to go with them. We are thus faced, as in the previous example, with a God who stands in the way (prohibitive function). The action of not allowing someone to go somewhere is again rendered with an explicit prohibitive construction through the use of the verb *nāthăn* followed by the infinitive of the verb *hālăk* (הָלַךְ), which means "to go," "to walk." No shadow of *hiphil* causative forms of the verb "to go," for God did not refuse to *lead* Balaam to the land of Balak. And he did not do so simply because God is completely unrelated to the movement, he does not participate in it, and he does not cause it. The only thing that God cares about is not allowing Balaam to move from his land to go and curse the people of Israel. God intervenes to prevent a movement that is independent of him and not pleasing to him. And isn't this exactly what we would like God to do in the sixth petition of the Lord's Prayer? To oppose our entering into temptation, to intervene to prevent our falling into sin. Such movement would be independent of God and opposed by God. And if this is true, why then would Christ have used an ambiguous causative construct, having at his disposal a clearer explicit permissive construct, as demonstrated by this passage in Num 22:13? The Septuagint faithfully translates the explicit permissive sense with the use of the verb *aphíēmi*.[6]

---

5. "καὶ οὐκ ἀφήσει τὸν ὀλεθρεύοντα εἰσελθεῖν εἰς τὰς οἰκίας ὑμῶν [*kaì ouk aphḗsei tòn olethreúonta eiseltheîn eis tás oikías hymôn*]" = "and will not allow the Destroyer to enter your houses."

6. "οὐκ ἀφίησίν με ὁ θεὸς πορεύεσθαι μεθ' ὑμῶν [*ouk aphíēsín me ho theòs poreúesthai meth' hymôn*]" = "God did not allow me to go with you."

Let us look at another interesting example. It is found in chapter 20 of the book of Genesis. Abraham has just settled with his family, incognito, in Gerar. In order not to let it be known that Sarah is his wife, Abraham declares before Abimelech, king of Gerar, that Sarah is his sister. Sarah plays along and confirms that Abraham is her brother. At that point, King Abimelech, enamored of Sarah and believing her to be unmarried, sends for her to take her to his chambers and spend a night of love with her. But just before approaching her, God intervenes and reveals to the king that Sarah is married to Abraham. Abimelech, overcome with fear, tries to justify himself. God, knowing that the king's intentions are not sinful, reassures him with these words: "I know that thou didst this in the integrity of thy heart; for I also withheld thee from sinning against me: therefore suffered I thee not to touch her" (Gen 20:6).

Once again, we are faced with a God who stands in the way (prohibitive function) and does not allow someone to do anything improper. Also in this case, the Hebrew expression is rendered with an explicit prohibitive construction through the use of the verb *nāthăn* followed by the infinitive of the verb *nāgă'* (נגע), which means "to touch." No shadow of *hiphil* causative forms of the verb "to touch" here, for God did not urge King Abimelech to lie with Sarah. And he did not do so simply because, had he done so, he would have forced the king to commit a mortal sin against God himself. God is completely uninvolved in the king's willingness to lie with Sarah, and he does not incentivize him in any way, knowing his good faith. It would not make sense. God is faithful (*pistós*, as St. Paul would say), he does not play tricks, and he does not rejoice to see people fall into sin. God intervenes to prevent an act independent of him and not pleasing to him. The Septuagint faithfully translates the explicit permissive sense with the use of the verb *aphíēmi*.[7] This example is relevant because it touches on one of the most delicate issues we are about to discuss: the relationship between God and sin.

Another example that shows how God can personally decide to intervene and prevent events that are independent of and unwelcome to him is found a little further on, in book 31 of Genesis. Jacob is harassed by his father-in-law Laban, father of both his wives. Lia, the elder sister, was Jacob's first wife, given to him in marriage by her father under false pretenses (Jacob thought she was Rachel). Rachel, the younger sister, is then given in marriage to Jacob in place of Leah, but Jacob, in return, will have to work for Laban seven years. When Jacob realizes that Laban has bad intentions toward him, on divine advice, he takes Leah and Rachel and announces to them that they will have to leave secretly and return to the land of his fathers: "And ye know that with all my power I have served your father. And your father hath deceived me, and changed my wages ten times; but God suffered him not to hurt me" (Gen 31:6–7).

Jacob emphasizes here how God kept his protection over him so that Laban could not harm him in all the years he worked for him. The Hebrew prohibitive expression is again rendered by the verb *nāthăn* followed by the infinitive construct. God has

---

7. "οὐκ ἀφῆκά σε ἅψασθαι αὐτῆς [*ouk aphêká se hápsasthai autês*]" = "I did not allow you to touch her."

nothing to do with his father-in-law's evil intentions, and therefore no causative form is used. The Septuagint faithfully follows the original text and adopt an explicit prohibitive construct with the use of the verb *dídōmi* (δίδωμι), one of the many synonyms that can be used in Greek to indicate the action of "allowing," "letting."[8]

In chapter 18 of the book of Deuteronomy, God turns to the people of Israel and announces that he is going to expel from the Promised Land those nations that follow idols and sorcerers. On the contrary, "as for thee, the Lord thy God hath not suffered thee so to do" (Deut 18:14).

That is, "O people of Israel, God has not allowed you to follow idols and sorcerers." God's prohibitive action is again evident. God is not the cause of other people indulging in idolatry, but he obviously has the power to prevent it from happening, as in the case of the people of Israel. Since the sense of the passage is permissive, the Hebrew text once again employs an explicit permissive construct with the verb *nāthăn*. The Septuagint translates in perfect harmony with the Hebrew original by the verb *dídōmi*.[9]

In chapter 9 of the book of Job, Job himself complains about all the terrible torments he is receiving, which afflict him relentlessly, and referring to God declares, "He will not suffer me to take my breath, but filleth me with bitterness" (Job 9:18). Since the action of "taking one's breath" is independent of God (breathing is a mechanical-physiological phenomenon that does not need a divine order to occur), the Hebrew text does not use causative expressions, but rather an explicit prohibitive construct through the use of the verb *nāthăn*. The Septuagint translates accordingly with an identical construct, introduced by the verb *eáō*.[10]

All these examples seem to demonstrate that the permissive sensibility regarding God's action in the world was already well developed even in the Old Testament context.

Several passages from the book of Psalms give us confirmation of this. The book of Psalms is particularly relevant to our arguments because it represents a collection of songs and prayers with specific invocations addressed to God to make or not to make certain things happen. Exactly as in the sixth petition of the Lord's Prayer in which God is asked not to "lead us into temptation." There are several passages that we would like to briefly quote.

In Psalm 121(120), also called the Song of Ascensions, it is said that the Lord "will not suffer thy foot to be moved" (Ps 121(120):3). Similarly, in Ps 55(54):22(23), it is said that the Lord "shall never suffer the righteous to be moved." In Ps 105(104):14, the greatness of the Lord is proclaimed because "he suffered no man to do them wrong."

---

8. "οὐκ ἔδωκεν αὐτῷ ὁ θεὸς κακοποιῆσαί με [*ouk édōken autôi ho theòs kakopoiêsaí me*] = "God did not allow him to harm me."

9. "σοὶ δὲ οὐχ οὕτως ἔδωκεν κύριος ὁ θεός σου [*soì dè ouch hoútōs édōken kýrios ho theós sou*] = "To thee, however, not so hath the Lord thy God permitted."

10. "οὐκ ἐᾷ γάρ με ἀναπνεῦσαι [*ouk eâi gár me anapneûsai*] = "For he does not let me take a breath."

In Ps 16(15):10, King David glorifies the Lord saying, "thou wilt not leave my soul in hell; neither wilt thou suffer thine Holy One to see corruption." All of these passages are rendered in Hebrew with an explicit prohibitive construct through the use of the verbs *nāthăn* or *yānăh* (יָנַח), which are translated in the Greek of the Septuagint with the verbs *dídōmi* and *aphíēmi*, respectively. No surprises so far.

There are, however, two other passages within the book of Psalms that are worth mentioning at this point, which are translated permissively in various editions of the Bible, even though there is no explicit permissive construct in either the original Hebrew texts or the Septuagint translation.

The first is found in Ps 30(29):1(2), where David thanks the Lord because he delivered him and did not cause his enemies to rejoice over him. The Hebrew verb indicating the action of "rejoicing" is *sāmăh* (שָׂמַח) and is conjugated in the *piel* (not *hiphil*) form. The *piel* form can be very versatile in general, but in this context, it indicates a clear causative sense, that is, "to make one rejoice." The Greek of the Septuagint remains faithful to the Hebrew text and uses the verb *euphráinō* (εὐφράινω) causatively.[11] The original Hebrew and Greek texts opt for a causative sense ("to make rejoice"), while many modern versions of the Bible veer toward permissive constructs.[12] This is one of those cases where a translation with a permissive construct does not change the general sense of the expression much, as far as it emphasizes the fact that God protected David from his enemies, as opposed to a Hebrew text that instead emphasizes the fact that God did not give them the strength necessary to defeat him. They are, on closer inspection, two sides of the same coin. Would this be a demonstration that a true permissive sensibility had not yet developed in the Old Testament context? Of course not. We have seen numerous examples that prove otherwise. And this specific example alone demonstrates that the true meaning of David's words is a dispassionate thanksgiving to the Lord for favoring him, and not his enemies, in battle, knowing full well that the Lord could easily have decided and willed otherwise. David is aware that the merit of the victories of the people of Israel over the other armies is only due to the favor he met with the Lord. Favor that could cease at any moment if this were to fall within the unfathomable divine plans. A translation in a permissive sense does not alter its meaning by much, but it is not necessary. Nothing more.

The second passage is found in Psalm 37(36) where it is said, "The wicked watcheth the righteous, and seeketh to slay him. The Lord will not leave him in his hand, nor condemn him when he is judged" (Ps 37(36):32–33). The Hebrew text uses the causative form (*hiphil*) of the verb *rāshă'* (רָשַׁע) to indicate the act of "condemning," while the Septuagint chooses the verb *katadikázō* (καταδικάζω).[13] The Latin Vulgate

---

11. "οὐκ ηὔφρανας τοὺς ἐχθρούς μου ἐπ' ἐμέ [*ouk ēúphranas toùs echthroús mou ep' emé*] = "He did not make the enemies rejoice over me."

12. See, for example, NIV, NLT, ESV, NKJV, NASB.

13. "οὐδὲ μὴ καταδικάσηται αὐτόν, ὅταν κρίνηται αὐτῷ [*oudè mḕ katadikásētai autón, hótan krínētai autôi*]" = "Nor will he condemn him when he is judged."

also traces the causative (and not permissive) expressions of both the Hebrew and Greek texts through the verb *damnare*.[14] Nevertheless, most modern translations of the Bible[15] "correct" the original texts by introducing an explicit permissive construct. This is one of those cases where, when it is said that God condemns somebody, what it actually means is that God lets somebody be condemned. In fact, they argue, it is not God who condemns, but the wicked who seeks to put to death the righteous by blaming him and bringing him to trial unjustly. This interpretation, fascinating as it is, contrasts irreparably with the reality of the facts. There are, unfortunately, numerous examples of righteous people unjustly put to death in the Bible, without God intervening to prevent it. Think of the story of Naboth, told in chapter 21 of the first book of Kings. Since he had disrespected Ahab, king of Samaria, by refusing to sell him a vineyard near the king's palace, Naboth was the victim of a plot hatched by Jezebel, the king's wife. Two false witnesses were brought who, in front of the elders and leaders, swore that they had heard Naboth curse God and the king. As a result, Naboth was sentenced to death and stoned to death. How do we put it then? Does or does God let a righteous person be put to death unjustly? Well, say the proponents of the permissive view, this verse found in Psalm 37(36) is only a theoretical rule, which may not always come true in practice.

We clearly see in this example how our insistence on having the sacred texts say what we think the sacred texts *should* say leads us to having to introduce assumptions that are difficult to prove. In this particular case, the sacred texts clearly say that "God will not condemn the righteous," but because it is convenient for us to think of a God who prevents the wicked from condemning the righteous, we assume that the correct interpretation of the passage is that "God will not *let* the righteous be condemned by the wicked," assuming that the *hiphil* form can be interpreted in a permissive sense. But, since there are examples that prove otherwise, we further assume that this interpretation applies only in a general sense and not in an absolute sense. A chase of arbitrary assumptions that need other arbitrary assumptions to stand. This is obviously not a rigorous method of approaching biblical exegesis.

If one only thinks about it, there is a much simpler explanation that does not jibe with the original text. The Hebrew verb *rāshă'* literally means "to pass a sentence of condemnation." So do the Greek *katadikázō* and the Latin *damnare*. The sacred texts literally read, "The Lord will not abandon him to their hand, nor will he judge him guilty, in case he is put on trial." Could it be that all the ancient texts failed to grasp the permissive sense of the biblical passage? Obviously, they did not. It is simply saying that, even in the case in which ungodly people succeed in bringing to trial and unjustly condemning a righteous person, that person will remain innocent before God. A sentence of condemnation by ungodly people will not result in a sentence of

---

14. "*nec damnabit eum cum judicabitur illi*" = "Nor will he condemn him when he is judged."
15. See, for example, NIV, NLT, ESV, BSB, NASB, AB, CSB, GNT, NAB, NET, NRSV.

condemnation by God, who knows everything and knows how to distinguish without doubt a righteous heart from an ungodly one. Very trivial.

So far, we have dealt with examples in which the main actor of the permissive (or prohibitive) action is God himself. In the Old Testament, however, there is no shortage of passages in which the explicit permissive construct refers to human behavior as well. Let us look at some of them briefly.

In chapter 21 of the second book of Samuel, it is recounted how Rizpah, daughter of Aiah and concubine of King Saul, after her two sons had been hanged, watched over their bodies for days and days and "suffered neither the birds of the air to rest on them by day, nor the beasts of the field by night" (2 Sam 21:10).

The love of a mother for her children, who in a heroic effort protects their lifeless bodies from birds and wild beasts, dramatically represents a prohibitive action. The mother opposes with all her strength to something terrible that hangs over her like a nightmare. The mother has nothing to do with the insistent will of the beasts to rage on the bodies of her two children and obviously she is not the cause of it. Therefore, it would have made no sense to use a causative form. The Hebrew text opts for the use of the usual verb *nāthăn*, followed by two infinitive constructs. The Septuagint translates in perfect agreement with the use of the verb *dídōmi*.[16]

In the books of Job and Ecclesiastes, we find two short—but illuminating—passages. In chapter 31 of the book of Job, Job is listing all the good works he has done in his life and all the temptations he has never given in to: "If I rejoice at the destruction of him that hated me, or lifted up myself when evil found him: Neither have I suffered my mouth to sin by wishing a curse to his soul?" (Job 31:29–30).

Job, despite all the torments and anguish he is receiving, claims that he has never cursed his enemy and has never allowed his tongue to commit sin. He is emphasizing how the rational part of his being has always had the better of the instinctive part, to the extent that reason and instinct (soul and flesh) are continually in opposition. On the one hand, there is the impulsive force that tends to sin, and on the other the rational soul that opposes it with a clear prohibitive action. For this reason, the Hebrew text renders the expression once again with the verb *nāthăn*.

In the book of Ecclesiastes, we find a similar passage: "Suffer not thy mouth to cause thy flesh to sin; neither say thou before the angel, that it was an error: wherefore should God be angry at thy voice, and destroy the work of thine hands?" (Eccl 5:6).

What a coincidence! A permissive expression and a causative expression in the same sentence! What is being said? That the rational part of the human being must prevent the mouth (the tongue) from driving the body to sin. There are three actors in play: the rational soul, the tongue, and the flesh. The first operates a prohibitive action on the second, which in turn operates a direct causative action on the third. Why?

16. "οὐκ ἔδωκε τὰ πετεινὰ τοῦ οὐρανοῦ καταπαῦσαι ἐπ' αὐτοὺς ἡμέρας καὶ τὰ θηρία τοῦ ἀγροῦ νυκτός [ouk édōke tà peteinà toû ouranoû katapaûsai ep' autoùs hēméras kaì tà thēría toû agroú nyktós]" = "He did not allow the birds of the air to perch on them by day and the wild beasts by night."

Because, as mentioned, reason does not cause the body to have sinful instincts, but, on the contrary, can oppose them. On the other hand, the tongue, which represents the instinctive impulse, can indeed cause the flesh to sin. The Hebrew text has such a developed sensitivity that it is able to distinguish exactly between these two actions. The first is rendered with an explicit prohibitive construct through the use of the verb *nāthăn*, while the second is rendered by the causative (*hiphil*) form of the verb *hātā'* (חָטָא), which means "to sin." The Septuagint faithfully translates the explicit prohibitive expression by the verb *dídōmi* and the causative expression through the implicitly causative verb *examartánō* (ἐξαμαρτάνω), which means "to cause to sin."[17]

Let us consider another example. Remember the story of Jacob who had fled with his two wives Leah and Rachel and their entire family in secret from his father-in-law Laban to escape his evil intentions? Well, the story continues with Laban who, once he realizes that Jacob has fled with all his possessions, decides to pursue him. He reaches him after seven days of walking in the mountains of Gilead, where Jacob had set up his tents. At that point, coming face to face with Jacob, Laban apostrophizes him in this way: "Wherefore didst thou flee away secretly, and steal away from me; and didst not tell me, that I might have sent thee away with mirth, and with songs, with tabret, and with harp? And hast not suffered me to kiss my sons and my daughters? thou hast now done foolishly in so doing" (Gen 31:27–28).

Laban complains that Jacob did not even let him kiss his daughters before he left. The prohibitive construct is rendered through the verb *nātăsh* (נָטַשׁ), which means "to abandon," "to leave," and thus also "to allow."

And—just to continue in the furrow of tensions between father-in-law and son-in-law—in chapter 24 of the first book of Samuel it is narrated how King Saul, returned from a battle against the Philistines, is warned that David, husband of his youngest daughter Michal and his rival to the throne, is staying in the desert of En Gedi. Saul considers his son-in-law David a real enemy to be eliminated. Saul gathers three thousand people throughout Israel and sets out in search of David. At a certain point, Saul needs to fulfill his physical needs and enters a cave, where, by chance, David is staying with his men. The latter, not believing their eyes, consider the opportunity to eliminate the hated Saul and would have already attacked the unsuspecting king if David had not intervened to stop them in time. Let us read: "So David stayed his servants with these words, and suffered them not to rise against Saul. But Saul rose up out of the cave, and went on his way" (1 Sam 24:7).

David intervenes to oppose an action that is about to take place—an action that is independent of him. For this reason, the Hebrew text renders the passage once again with an explicit prohibitive construct through the verb *nāthăn*. The Septuagint faithfully translates with the use of the verb *dídōmi*.[18]

---

17. "μὴ δῷς τὸ στόμα σου τοῦ ἐξαμαρτῆσαι τὴν σάρκα σου [*mè dôis tò stóma sou toû examartêsai tèn sárka sou*]" = "Do not let your mouth cause your body to sin."

18. "οὐκ ἔδωκεν αὐτοῖς ἀναστάντας θανατῶσαι τὸν Σαουλ [*ouk édōken autoîs anastántas*

Having seen all these examples, let us slowly try to get back to the point that is most important to us, which is the use of causative forms with verbs of movement ("to go," "to enter," "to fall"). Can these, at least, be interpreted in a permissive sense? Is it possible to interpret "lead us not into temptation" as "do not let us fall into temptation"? Is it possible that, at least for these verbs, a permissive sensibility had not yet developed in the Old Testament context? Let us look at a few examples.

When the rivalry between David and Saul was yet to emerge and David was a simple young boy who had distinguished himself by valiantly slaying the Philistine giant Goliath, King Saul asks for enlightenment about who that boy is and, full of esteem for his heroic action, takes him with him and "would let him go no more home to his father's house" (1 Sam 18:2).

The prohibitive action on Saul's part is rendered in the Hebrew text again by the verb *nāthăn*. The Greek text is no exception and uses an explicit permissive construct by means of the verb *aphíēmi*.[19]

In the book of Judges, in chapter 15, we find another incident between son-in-law and father-in-law. It involves Samson who, having returned from harvesting the fields, would like to visit his wife in her room, but "her father would not suffer him to go in" (Jdt 15:1). This example is very fitting for our arguments because it shows an explicit prohibitive construct referring to the action of "entering," an action rendered by the verb *bô'*, which represents the Hebrew counterpart of the Aramaic verb that, as we have seen, Christ is supposed to have used (in the causative *hiphil* stem) when he declaimed the sixth petition of the Lord's Prayer. If indeed the causative *hiphil* stem of the verb *bô'* was perceived in a permissive sense by the reader of the time, why then was it not used in this context? Why, instead of using a faster and more streamlined verbal form, did they opt for an explicit prohibitive construct through the usual verb *nāthăn* followed by the infinitive of the verb *bô'*? Simply because the author did not mean to say, "her father did not *introduce* him," but precisely "her father did not allow him to enter," emphasizing the fact that the father opposes an action that is independent of him and that he does not agree with.

In chapter 27 of Deuteronomy, we find an interesting passage: "Cursed be he that maketh the blind to wander out of the way" (Deut 27:18). The Hebrew text uses the causative (*hiphil*) form of the verb *shāgâ* (שָׁגָה), which indicates—in the base *qal* form—the action of going astray. The causative form means "to lead astray." This is the same verb we have already encountered in Psalm 119(118):10 where it says, "With my whole heart have I sought thee: O let me not wander from thy commandments." Some[20] would like to give a permissive interpretation of this passage, "Cursed is he who allows the blind to go astray." Unfortunately, this interpretation not only does

---

*thanatôsai tòn Saoul]"* = "He did not allow them to pounce on Saul and kill him."

19. "οὐκ ἀφῆκεν αὐτὸν ἐπιστρέψαι εἰς τὸν οἶκον τοῦ πατρὸς αὐτοῦ [*ouk aphêken autòn epistrépsai eis tòn oîkon toû patròs autoû*]" = "He did not allow him to return to his father's house."

20. See, for example, BSB.

not fully represent the meaning of the Hebrew text, but it is also plain wrong. Here we are cursing not those who, although they could run to the aid of a visually impaired person who is going astray, are disinterested and do not do so, but those who, by their own evil nature, take advantage of the disability of the visually impaired to throw them culpably off the road. The act of cursing, rendered by the verb ' ārăr (אָרַר), is a terrible and solemn act, which is a reaction to an act that is grossly unjust and contrary to morality. Clearly, a sin of omission (not running to the aid of a blind man), while generally unpleasant, does not immediately fall into this category. It is precisely the force of that "cursed be!" that makes us understand the purely causative sense of the passage. So again, we have the demonstration that the Old Testament sensibility in distinguishing between permissive and causative expressions was already well developed and mature.

Let us take again the example of Pharaoh who, persisting in his pride, refused ten times to let the people of Israel go free. The expression "to let go" appears thirty-one times in the book of Exodus, referring to Pharaoh not letting the people of Israel go free. In none of them does the Hebrew text use *hiphil* forms of verbs of movement. Instead, it uses either explicit permissive constructs through the use of the verb *nāthăn*[21], or directly the verb *shālăh* (שָׁלַח), which already in its base *qal* form contains an implicit permissive sense, and which means "to release."[22] Similarly, the concept of whether or not to allow someone to go is rendered with the verb *shālăh* in various other Old Testament passages.[23]

Countless are the examples of explicit permissive forms relating to verbs of movement in the Old Testament. In Num 20:21, we are told of the time when "Edom refused to allow Israel to pass through its borders" (the verb *nāthăn* is used in Hebrew and the verb *dídōmi* in the Septuagint). In Num 21:23, Sihon, king of the Amorites, "would not suffer Israel to pass through his border" (*nāthăn* in Hebrew, *dídōmi* in the Septuagint). In Judg 3:28, the Israelites, led by the Lord, seized the fords of the Jordan and "suffered not a man to pass over" (*nāthăn* in Hebrew, *aphíēmi* in the Septuagint). In Judg 1:34, "the Amorites forced the children of Dan into the mountain: for they would not suffer them to come down to the valley" (*nāthăn* in Hebrew, *aphíēmi* in the Septuagint). In 2 Chr 20:10, the Israelites turn to God for help in confronting "children of Ammon and Moab and mount Seir, whom thou wouldest not let Israel invade" (*nāthăn* in Hebrew, *dídōmi* in the Septuagint). Finally, in Josh 10:19, Joshua orders his men to show no mercy to their enemies: "pursue after your enemies, and smite the hindmost of them; suffer them not to enter into their cities" (*nāthăn* in Hebrew, *aphíēmi* in the Septuagint). All these verses describe the prohibitive action

---

21. See Exod 3:19.

22. See Exod 3:20; 4:21, 23; 5:1–2; 6:11; 7:2, 14, 16; 8:1–2, 8, 20–21, 28, 32; 9:1, 7, 13, 17, 28, 35; 10:3–4, 10, 20, 27; 11:1, 10; 13:15.

23. See Gen 24:54; 32:26; Exod 4:23, 26; 21:26; Judg 19:25; 1 Sam 6:6.

of preventing someone from going somewhere, and all of them indiscriminately are rendered by means of an explicit prohibitive construct.

There is only one example, found in chapter 2 of the book of Deuteronomy (Deut 2:30), which recounts the same episode just encountered in Num 21:23 and which uses the causative form of the verb ʿāvăr (עָבַר), meaning "to pass through," that conveys the idea of Sihon, king of the Amorites, who does not want to let the people of Israel pass through his borders. Could this finally be the proof that the *hiphil* stem can have permissive value? After all, both passages (Num 21:23 and Deut 2:30) say essentially the same thing: the king opposed the Israelites' request to pass through his territories. And in one case (Num 21:23) the explicit permissive form is preferred, in the other (Deut 2:30) the causative form is. Are the two forms therefore interchangeable? Does this show that a true permissive sensibility had not yet matured within the Old Testament? In our opinion, it does not, for three specific reasons:

1. Even if indeed these two passages were superimposable and the causative (*hiphil*) stem found in Deut 2:30 had a purely permissive sense, it would still be difficult from a logical point of view to derive a general rule from an exception (there are dozens and dozens of examples in which *hiphil* forms of the verb ʿāvăr appear in the Old Testament and all with a clear causative, not permissive, sense).

2. The fact that the same incident is once told in the permissive form and once in the causative form does not mean that the two forms are interchangeable. The same fact can be narrated from two slightly different points of view, without having to conclude that the two points of view are identical just because the fact narrated is the same.[24]

3. The expression used in Deut 2:30 is not exactly superimposable on the one used in Num 21:23. In fact, the Israelites pronounce these exact words, "Sihon was not *willing* to let us pass." That "being willing" is rendered by the Hebrew verb ʾāvâ (אָבָה), which means "to want," "to be willing to do something." It thus indicates a volitional disposition to a specific action. The Septuagint skips the problem by translating with a simple infinitive construct, introduced by the verb *thélō* (θέλω) which means "to want," "to desire."[25] The *hiphil* form is used in order to underline how the king did not want to move a finger in order to allow the Israelites to pass through his kingdom. Refusing to give the order to open the borders to the Israelites, he did not want to be the cause of the Israelites themselves trampling on his soil. Nothing more than that.

---

24. We have already encountered a similar example in Ps 30(29):1(2).

25. "οὐκ ἠθέλησε Σηὼν βασιλεὺς Ἐσεβὼν παρελθεῖν ἡμᾶς δι' αὐτοῦ [*ouk ēthélēse Sēṑn basileùs Esebṑn parelthein hēmâs di' autoû*]" = "Sihon, king of Heshbon, did not want us to pass through his territories."

# 10

# The Causative Form of "to Enter" in the Old Testament

We hope, at this point, to have convinced the reader that a permissive interpretation of the Hebrew *hiphil* verbal form is not only unnecessary, but downright incorrect from a logical point of view. All the examples of causative forms seen so far in the Old Testament do not need permissive explanations. And the reason is simple. The causative stem in Semitic languages, by definition, indicates just that: the cause-and-effect relationship between the subject causing the action and the action itself. It clearly indicates whose responsibility the action should be. It is obvious that if an action takes place independently of the will of the subject (even if this subject does not intervene to prevent it, even though in theory he or she has the power to do so), this subject cannot be blamed for the action itself. And so, the use of a causative form in these cases would be logically incorrect.

In fact, one will not find a single example within the Old Testament where the *hiphil* stem is used to indicate the fact that someone simply *lets* an action happen, without doing anything about it, perhaps turning away, without intervening. The *hiphil* stem *always* indicates a direct (or at most indirect) intervention by the one who makes the action happen. When there is no obvious cause-effect relationship between subject and action, Semitic languages typically use an explicit permissive construct without any problems.

In particular (and here we come to the point that matters most to us), if we focus our analysis on the Hebrew verb *bô'* (בּוֹא), or its Aramaic equivalent *'ălăl* (עֲלַל),[1] the same verb that Christ most likely used when he proclaimed the sixth petition of the Lord's Prayer, we will discover the following facts:

---

1. Both translate the action of entering a place.

1. The verb *bô'* appears more than 470 times conjugated in the Hebrew causative *hiphil* form within the Old Testament; by contrast, the Aramaic equivalent *'ălăl* conjugated in the Aramaic causative *haphel* form appears only in the book of Daniel (five times).

2. In 58 percent of the cases, these verbs are associated with inanimate objects (or in rare cases with animals), and undoubtedly indicate the causative idea of carrying/transporting, without any permissive nuance.

3. In 20 percent of the cases, the object is a human being and the one who transports/leads is God himself, one of his angels, or his Spirit. In none of these cases is even the slightest permissive nuance detectable.

4. In the remaining 22 percent of cases, the object is a human being and the one who transports/leads is another human being. According to our analysis, in only a couple of these cases a permissive nuance may be detected, even if not necessary (Ezek 44:7; Dan 6:18).

5. For all of the approximately 200 cases in which the *hiphil* form of the verb *bô'* (or the *haphel* form of the verb *'ălăl*) is associated with the transportation of humans, the Septuagint translates with the verb *ágō* (ἄγω)—or compounds—in 87 percent of cases, with other verbs of movement in 9 percent of cases, and with the verb *phérō* (φέρω)—or compounds—only in eight cases (4 percent!), where the transportation is clearly of a forced and coerced kind.

This impressive series of cold statistical data would be enough to eliminate once and for all the possibility that Christ intended to infuse a permissive sense into the sixth petition of the Lord's Prayer. Even assuming that the hypothesis of Jesus' use of the *haphel* form of the verb *'ălăl* to indicate the action of leading into temptation is correct, it would be quite arduous, if not entirely impossible, on the basis of these percentages, to try to defend a permissive interpretation of the same causative form.

Since this is the tombstone that, in our opinion, definitively closes the debate, let us analyze in detail those only passages that may be interpreted in a permissive sense (Ezek 44:7; Dan 6:18) and all eight instances in which the Septuagint translates the *hiphil* form of the verb *bô'* with the verb *phérō* (φέρω) or compounds, to confirm our hypothesis.

In chapter 44 of the book of Ezekiel, the prophet has a vision in which the Lord brings him before the Temple in Jerusalem and instructs him as to who may and who may not enter it. God is angry that unworthy people inhabit his Temple and addresses Ezekiel with these words: "And thou shalt say to the rebellious, even to the house of Israel, Thus saith the Lord God; O ye house of Israel, let it suffice you of all your abominations, In that ye have brought into my sanctuary strangers, uncircumcised in heart, and uncircumcised in flesh, to be in my sanctuary, to pollute it, even my house, when ye offer my bread, the fat and the blood, and they have broken my covenant because of all your abominations" (Ezek 44:6–7).

God is blaming the people of Israel, a rebellious people that turned away from his commandments, for having introduced inside the Temple "strangers, uncircumcised in heart, and uncircumcised in flesh," that is, idolaters of extremely low moral standing. In some translations of the Bible,[2] this passage is softened by the use of a permissive construct. The question, as futile as it may be, closes immediately, in our opinion, by underlining the following point. Here, God is blaming the Israelites not for not having prevented these people from entering the Temple, but precisely for having *voluntarily* introduced them into the Temple, thus shamelessly rebelling against the dictates of the Lord. God has clearly identified who is the cause of the fact that his Temple has been made "a den of thieves," as in Luke 19:46. They are the Israelites, who are totally to blame. Causative meaning rendered by a causative form. Period.

In chapter 6 of the book of Daniel, we find the famous story of Daniel, who is thrown into the lion's den by King Darius because of the guilt of having prayed to his God. The governors and the traps of the kingdom had convinced the king to issue a decree that anyone who made supplications to any god or person other than the king himself would be thrown to the fierce beasts. The decree had been conceived and written by the traps to frame and get rid of Daniel, who had been discovered praying in the darkness of his room. King Darius, unable to contravene the edict he himself had issued, reluctantly condemns Daniel. After throwing him into the lion's den, he returns to his palace and, in the grip of conscience, "passed the night fasting: neither were instruments of musick brought before him: and his sleep went from him" (Dan 6:18).

The king's decision that no entertainment or food be brought before him is rendered by the *haphel* form of the Aramaic verb ʿ *ălăl*.[3] Some translations[4] adopt permissive reformulations. This is one of those cases where the permissive rendering of a causative form is a simple euphemistic expression. The fact that various entertainments (musical instruments, concubines or whoever) were brought to the king to enliven his evenings was not the initiative of the servants, but a specific order from the king. The king is not opposing an action that is independent of him. He is giving an order contrary to the usual. Just as the king is the cause of the fact that usually various entertainments brighten his evenings, on this particular night he is the cause of the fact that no entertainment is required. The Aramaic text thus perceives this context as a case of indirect causation (the king does not materially bring, but rather has the entertainments brought by means of his servants). And as such, the Aramaic text uses a *haphel* causative form. Nothing unusual here.

At this point, it is very interesting to go and take a look at those exceptional cases in which the Septuagint feels the need to translate the *hiphil* form of the verb

2. ESV, CEV, GNT, NAB, NRSV.
3. The book of Daniel is one of the few passages in the Bible written in Aramaic.
4. See, for example, CEV.

*bô'*, when associated with the movement of human beings, not with a simple *ágō* but with a rarer *phérō*. Just as in the sixth petition of the Lord's Prayer. Let us look at them one by one and try to understand the reason for such a particular stylistic choice. The *incipit* of the first book of Kings reads, "Now king David was old and stricken in years; and they covered him with clothes, but he got no heat. Wherefore his servants said unto him, Let there be sought for my lord the king a young virgin: and let her stand before the king, and let her cherish him, and let her lie in thy bosom, that my lord the king may get heat. So they sought for a fair damsel throughout all the coasts of Israel, and found Abishag a Shunammite, and brought her to the king. And the damsel was very fair, and cherished the king, and ministered to him: but the king knew her not" (1 Kgs 1:1–4).

The action of leading the young girl to King David is rendered in the Greek text by the verb *phérō*. The reason is twofold:

1. it indicates a coercive movement against the will of the one being led (one can well imagine that the young girl was not happy to be taken away from her home to go and "warm up" an old king);

2. it indicates a movement that the one being led cannot oppose (imagine a poor female creature, in a historical context where women enjoyed minimal if any rights, opposing the will of a great king).

In the second book of Chronicles, chapter 25 tells of the deeds of King Amaziah who reigned over Jerusalem for twenty-nine years. In one of the war actions undertaken by the king it is narrated that "Amaziah strengthened himself, and led forth his people, and went to the valley of salt, and smote of the children of Seir ten thousand. And other ten thousand left alive did the children of Judah carry away captive, and brought them unto the top of the Rock, and cast them down from the top of the rock, that they all were broken in pieces" (2 Chr 25:11–12).

The action of leading the prisoners of war to the top of the Rock is rendered in the Greek text by the verb *phérō*. The reason is twofold:

1. it indicates a coercive movement against the will of the one being led (one can well imagine that the prisoners were not very happy to be sent to die a violent death);

2. it indicates a movement to which the one being led cannot oppose (they were indeed prisoners).

In the second book of Chronicles, chapter 36 tells of a tormented succession to the throne of Jerusalem. After the people of the country had proclaimed Jehoahaz, son of Josiah, king in place of his father, when he was only twenty-three years old, he reigned only for three months. He was ousted by the king of Egypt and replaced by his brother Jehoiakim. Jehoiakim was only twenty-five years old at that time and reigned over Jerusalem for eleven years, after which he was overthrown by Nebuchadnezzar, king of Babylon. Instead of Jehoiakim, his son Jehoiachin became king. Jehoiachin was only eight years old at that time and reigned over Jerusalem for three months and ten days, after which he too was deposed by the same Nebuchadnezzar: "And when the year was expired, king Nebuchadnezzar sent, and brought him to Babylon, with the goodly vessels of the house of the Lord, and made Zedekiah his brother king over Judah and Jerusalem" (2 Chr 36:10).

The action of Jehoiachin's deportation to Babylon by King Nebuchadnezzar is rendered in the Greek text by the verb *eisphérō*. The reason is twofold:

1. it indicates a coercive movement against the will of the one being led (one can well imagine that Jehoiachin was not happy to be ousted after reigning for only three months and ten days);
2. it indicates a movement to which the one who is led cannot oppose (Jehoiachin is taken prisoner by the king Nebuchadnezzar).

In the book of Ezra, chapter 8, it is narrated how the priest Ezra, with the blessing of King Artaxerxes, gathered some of the leaders of Israel, so that they could leave with him for Jerusalem. After they had camped for three days by the canal flowing to Ahava, Ezra made a survey of the people and the priests and found no Levites:

> Then sent I for Eliezer, for Ariel, for Shemaiah, and for Elnathan, and for Jarib, and for Elnathan, and for Nathan, and for Zechariah, and for Meshullam, chief men; also for Joiarib, and for Elnathan, men of understanding. And I sent them with commandment unto Iddo the chief at the place Casiphia, and I told them what they should say unto Iddo, and to his brethren the Nethinims, at the place Casiphia, that they should bring unto us ministers for the house of our God. And by the good hand of our God upon us they brought us a man of understanding, of the sons of Mahli, the son of Levi, the son of Israel; and Sherebiah, with his sons and his brethren, eighteen. (Ezra 8:16–18)

The action of bringing ministers for the temple of God is rendered in the Greek text twice with the verb *phérō*. The reason is twofold:

1. it indicates a movement that would not occur of one's own free will (the occupation of the Levites was not among the most attractive: they owned no property, lived off the alms of the faithful, and devoted their lives to the service of the religious functions that took place in the Temple);
2. it indicates a movement that the one being led cannot oppose (the order comes directly from Ezra, who works on behalf of the great king Artaxerxes).

In the *incipit* of chapter 11 of the book of Nehemiah it is said: "And the rulers of the people dwelt at Jerusalem: the rest of the people also cast lots, to bring one of ten to dwell in Jerusalem the holy city, and nine parts to dwell in other cities" (Neh 11:1). The action of having a tenth of the population move to Jerusalem to populate the holy city is rendered in the Greek text once again with the verb *phérō*. The reason is twofold:

1. it indicates a coercive movement against the will of the one being led (most of the Israelites were generally shepherds and preferred to live in the country than at Jerusalem);
2. it indicates a movement that the one being led cannot oppose (once the drawing of lots has taken place, the one being chosen must move to Jerusalem).

In the next chapter of the book of Nehemiah, another episode is recounted that is similar to the one narrated in Ezra 8:17: "And at the dedication of the wall of Jerusalem they sought the Levites out of all their places, to bring them to Jerusalem" (Neh 12:27). The action of bringing the Levites to Jerusalem is rendered in the Greek text with the verb *phérō*, whose use is related to the same reasons described for Ezra 8:17.

Finally, Solomon's Song of Songs, a *sui generis* book within the Old Testament since it celebrates the intimate love between two lovers, opens with the beloved's invitation to the king to kiss her and cover her with tenderness and take her to his chambers: "Let him kiss me with the kisses of his mouth: for thy love is better than wine. Because of the savor of thy good ointments thy name is as ointment poured forth, therefore do the virgins love thee. Draw me, we will run after thee: the king hath brought me into his chambers: we will be glad and rejoice in thee, we will remember thy love more than wine: the upright love thee" (Song 1:2–4). The action of introducing the young lover into the king's chambers is rendered in the Greek text with the verb *eisphérō*. The reason is twofold:

1. it indicates the total abandonment of the lover to the will of the beloved;
2. it describes the physical transportation of the young lover by the king, who takes her in his arms and transports her into the intimacy of his room.

We thus have the ultimate proof, certified by the Septuagint, that the Greek translation of the *hiphil* form of the Hebrew verb *bô'*, in the rare cases when it adopts the verb *phérō* (or *eisphérō*) to denote the movement of human beings, indicates the most extreme form of direct causative. That is, given the spectrum of all possible nuances of the *hiphil* form—from the more attenuated permissive to the more pronounced causative—the verb *phérō* (or *eisphérō*) is at the opposite extreme of the permissive nuance, representing in fact the most dramatic form of direct causative.

We have tried to summarize all the concepts set forth so far in the following chart.[5]

---

5. The percentages that appear in the chart are for illustrative purposes only.

# Eis Peirasmón

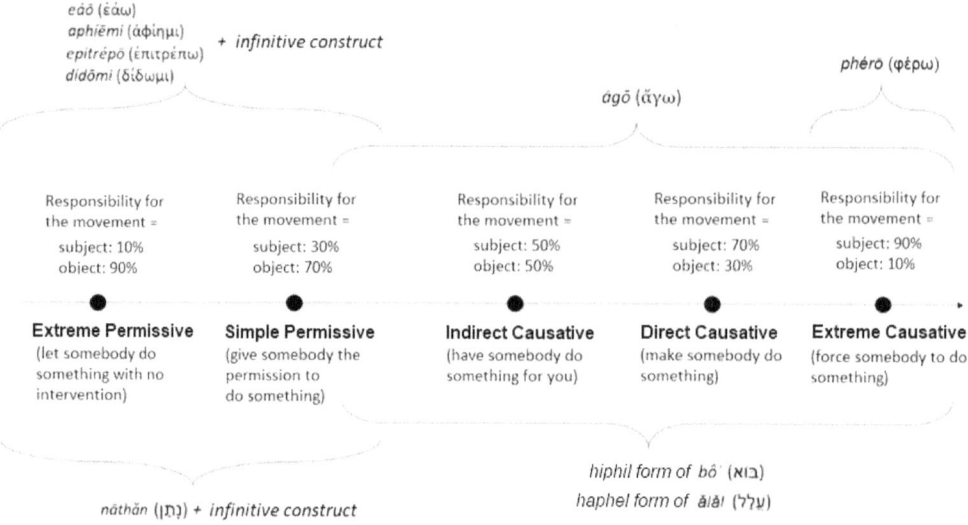

As imperfect as a simple chart can be for illustrating complex concepts, it becomes clear how the thesis of the permissive interpretation of the sixth petition of the Lord's Prayer fits within what we have called "Extreme Permissive" in the chart, that is, the action of letting someone do something (even though this something may have unpleasant consequences for him) without intervening and turning away ("let us not fall into temptation"). On the other hand, the causative (*hiphil*) form of the verb *bô'* essentially covers the same semantic field that the verb *ágō* defines in Greek, that is, all possible shades of causative, from the most tenuous (indirect) to what we have called "Extreme Causative" in the chart, with a very small, exceptional overlap with the most tenuous shades of permissive (what we have called "Simple Permissive" in the chart). If there is no possible overlap between the causative (*hiphil*) form of the verb *bô'* and the "Extreme Permissive" nuance proposed for the sixth petition of the Lord's Prayer, even more jarring is the semantic distance if we consider that both Matthew and Luke decide to translate the *hiphil* of the verb *bô'* not with the verb *ágō* but with the verb *eisphérō*, which, as seen, is commonly used only to render the most extreme forms of direct causative.

We must conclude that it is impossible that the evangelists decided to use a verb like *eisphérō*, which is used only to render the most extreme forms of direct causative, to translate the most extreme form of permissive causative.

Unless we affirm that the evangelists did not understand much of what Christ meant when he recited the Lord's Prayer, the conclusion can only be one. With the use of that *eisphérō*, Matthew and Luke are literally screaming to us that the correct interpretation of the causative form used by Jesus must be the extremely causative one ("do not lead us into," "do not introduce us into," "do not bring us into," "do not carry us into"), and certainly not the extremely permissive one ("let us not fall into").

But what should the Lord not lead us into? Do we really think that God can lead us to fall into temptation? Is it really God who hardens the heart of a person, or is it that person who persists in rejecting God? Questions that remain unanswered and that we are going to address in the following chapters.

# 11

# The Theory of the Divine "Cardiodynamic"

*Quos Deus vult perdere, prius dementat.*[1]

This phrase, mistakenly attributed to Euripides and made famous since the seventeenth century, has deep roots in antiquity. The same concept appears for the first time in Sophocles's *Antigone* (441 BC): "Evil appears as good in the minds of those whom God leads to destruction."[2] But Sophocles himself is keen to point out that this was already a "famous saying"[3] in his time. The term Sophocles uses for "destruction" is *átē* (ἄτη), which in Greek mythology usually indicates a reckless action performed by a hero—an action that leads him to death or ruin. By the same name, Ate, the Greeks called the goddess of deception, illusion, ruin, and madness. In the Greek imaginary, the goddess Ate was sent by Zeus to those who performed wicked actions dictated by their arrogance and pride, called *hýbris* (ὕβρις), to confuse their minds and make them inclined to perform even more wicked actions in the eyes of the gods. A vicious circle that usually ended with a final act of defiance to the gods. At that point intervened *Nemesis* (Νέμεσις), the Greek goddess of divine wrath, which dispensed the necessary punishment, said *tísis* (τίσις), to the unfortunate.

Doesn't all this remind us in some ways of the story of Pharaoh told in the book of Exodus? With due caution and distinctions, Sophocles and Greek mythology in general may help us understand and make sense of the Old Testament workings of God in the world. As pointed out earlier, God cannot be the creator of moral evil. For if God judges people, among other things, by their moral character, how can their moral character be predefined and predetermined by God? We would come to the illogical conclusion that God is judging himself. At the same time, we have seen numerous

---

1. Those whom God wants to lose, he first deprives of reason.
2. "τὸ κακὸν δοκεῖν ποτ' ἐσθλὸν τῷδ' ἔμμεν' ὅτῳ φρένας θεὸς ἄγει πρὸς ἄταν [*tò kakòn dokeîn pot' esthlòn tôid' émmen' hótōi phrénas theòs ágei pròs átan*]" (Sophocles, *Antigone*, 620–623).
3. "κλεινὸν ἔπος [*kleinòn épos*]."

examples where God intervenes to harden the hearts of those he wishes to abandon to ruin, much like Zeus sent the goddess Ate to confuse the minds (*dementare*) of those who committed acts of *hýbris* against him.

In the book of Lamentations, traditionally attributed to the prophet Jeremiah, one implores nefarious fate for enemies and sinners: "Give them hardness[4] of heart, thy curse unto them. Persecute and destroy them in anger from under the heavens of the Lord" (Lam 3:65–66).

Unfortunately for those who try to plead an unlikely permissive thesis, no stem that might give rise to interpretation (*piel* or *hiphil*) is used in this passage. The imperative "give them" is rendered with the imperfect of the verb *nāthăn*, the same verb that, followed by an infinitive, (ironically!) usually introduces the explicit permissive construct. Here, however, the verb *nāthăn* is followed not by an infinitive but by a simple object and is conjugated in the base *qal* form. It therefore means "to give." And what is God asked to give to the wicked? Hardness and stubbornness of heart. The exact term used in the Hebrew text, a *hapax legomenon* in the Bible, is *məghinnâ* (מְגִנָּה), indicating a covering. The image is that of a God who, according to the plea, should place a heavy blanket upon the hearts of the wicked to make them hard, obstinate, blind. It is a very plastic image offered by the Hebrew text, whereby the heart of sinners is almost "suffocated," "bound," "tightened," and made incapable of doing good. And God is the one who imposes this "suffocating blanket."

There is another episode, also recounted by the prophet Jeremiah, in chapter 24 of the book of the Bible that bears his name, which is illuminating in this regard. The Lord shows Jeremiah two baskets of figs: one full of tasty early figs, one full of figs gone bad. The good figs, the Lord explains, are the people of Judah, whom God had previously sent into exile in the land of the Chaldeans, but whom he now wants to bring back to himself. The Lord says, "And I will give them an heart to know me, that I am the Lord" (Jer 24:7).

The action of "giving them" is again rendered by the verb *nāthăn*. And in this case the sense is positive, not negative. God can grant a person a heart capable of knowing him, just as he has the power to give him a heart that we might call "hard of understanding." Again, it would not be honest to translate the positive action of giving in a causative sense ("I will give them a good heart") and the same action, but in the negative form, in a permissive sense ("I will let them have a hard heart").

Chapter 14 of the book of Ezekiel is one of the richest and most profound in this sense, and it outlines exactly the contours of our discussion. God is angry with the people of Israel for indulging in idolatry. Some elders of Israel, probably fearing divine punishment, go to the prophet Ezekiel to question him and thus learn more about what God has in store for them. God considers this attempt by the elders a blatant affront. His anger is aroused, and he promises that he will not let them question him through the prophet. He warns Ezekiel himself with these words: "If the prophet be

---

4. The KJV has "sorrow."

deceived when he hath spoken a thing, I the Lord have deceived that prophet, and I will stretch out my hand upon him, and will destroy him from the midst of my people Israel" (Ezek 14:9).

Let us pay attention here. Not only is God threatening Ezekiel with blotting him out from the people of Israel if he allows himself to be persuaded by the elders to make a prophecy for them. He is also telling him plainly that, should he allow himself to be persuaded, it is because it was the Lord himself who arranged for him to be persuaded. That is, he is somehow taking responsibility for the future ruin of the prophet himself. But why does God feel the need to emphasize this concept? Isn't it counterintuitive for God to cause (causatively!) someone to perform an action that is not pleasing to him and then punish him for performing that very action? Isn't this reminiscent of that vicious cycle of *hýbris*, *átē*, *némesis*, and *tísis* that we discussed earlier for Greek mythology? It is the same question that St. Paul runs into in his letter to the Romans and that we have already had the opportunity to analyze, "Why doth he yet find fault? For who hath resisted his will?" (Rom 9:19). That is, why does God get angry with human behavior if it is he himself who causes it? St. Paul's answer is disarming, "O man, who art thou that repliest against God?" (Rom 9:20). Disarming, but unsatisfying. Unsatisfying as far as we would like to try to find meaning in divine justice, even if that meaning still eludes us.

Poor Job, who tries to find a meaning to the tribulations that afflict him, gets angry and asks the same questions and reaches more or less the same conclusion as St. Paul. He cannot help but notice that it is neither possible nor useful to discuss divine omnipotence, because "with him is strength and wisdom: the deceived and the deceiver are his" (Job 12:16).

Everything that happens in the world is in some way attributable to God, who is endowed with infinite wisdom and power. God has the ability to imagine how the plan he has in store for humanity should develop in history, and at the same time he has the ability to put it into practice. In this sense, everything belongs to him: he who is led astray, as well as he who goes astray. The evil and sin that people commit, this is the bitter conclusion reached by Job, are only pieces, instruments that God uses to bring his plan to completion.

On the other hand, in the famous Psalm 95(94), the Lord addresses a plea directly to his people: "Harden not your heart, as in the provocation, and as in the day of temptation in the wilderness" (Ps 95(94):8). God is pleading with them not to make the same mistake—not to harden their hearts as their fathers had done. So, it is clear in this case that it was not God who hardened their hearts, but it was the people of Israel who abandoned God of their own free will. Or, in chapter 28 of the book of Proverbs, it is recorded that "he that hardeneth his heart shall fall into mischief" (Prov 28:14). This passage is echoed by the book of Sirach: "Do not go astray to avoid falling" (Sir 2:7).

In all these passages there is no shadow of divine intervention. The responsibility for sin falls entirely on people. Is there, then, a contradiction between a God who says, claims, and reiterates that he is responsible for the fact that the hearts of people harden and become refractory to his teachings, and the same human beings who seem instead to be primarily responsible for the fact that their hearts turn away from God? How are the two views reconciled?

Zechariah, in chapter 7 of the book of the Bible that bears his name, offers us a glimpse to explain this apparent paradox. The prophet recalls, "But they refused to hearken, and pulled away the shoulder, and stopped their ears, that they should not hear. Yea, they made their hearts as an adamant stone, lest they should hear the law, and the words which the Lord of hosts hath sent in his Spirit by the former prophets: therefore came a great wrath from the Lord of hosts" (Zech 7:11–12).

Once again, we are faced with human beings who willingly plug their ears and harden their hearts so as not to hear the words of the Lord. But how does the Lord speak to them? What specifically are people opposing? Zechariah explains it to us: "the words which the Lord of hosts hath sent in his Spirit." The Holy Spirit is the intermediary between God and people, the one who conveys the divine message to them. Here lies the key to understanding how God works in the hearts of people. The answer to our question lies in the action of the Holy Spirit, one of the three persons of the Holy Trinity, perhaps the least understood and most mysterious. For if we do not understand how the Holy Spirit works, we cannot understand all these Old Testament passages.

Let us begin with an enlightening passage found in chapter 36 of the book of Ezekiel: "A new heart also will I give you, and a new spirit will I put within you: and I will take away the stony heart out of your flesh, and I will give you an heart of flesh. And I will put my spirit within you, and cause you to walk in my statutes, and ye shall keep my judgments, and do them" (Ezek 36:26–27). The Holy Spirit is the one who materially has the ability to soften the hearts of people, to change them from stone to flesh. What does "softening" mean? It means to make them *more inclined* and receptive to divine teachings. It is important to clarify this concept to be able to continue in our argumentation. The way God may harden the heart of a person is *by removing* from that person his Holy Spirit. A heart not even remotely touched by the Holy Spirit is a hard heart, as inert as stone, which knows no morals, and therefore dangerously inclined and prone to evil. The further the Holy Spirit is from a person's heart, the more hardened that heart will be. Vice versa, the more a heart is filled with the Holy Spirit, the purer it is and the more naturally refractory to sin. So much so that when by exceptional divine grace, a person's heart is completely invaded by the Holy Spirit, that heart will be virtually incapable of sinning. This, for example, is the essence of the dogma of faith of the immaculate conception of Mary. The Catholic Church has affirmed that from the very moment of conception, that is, even before she was given birth from her mother's womb, Mary was devoid of sin, and in particular devoid of original sin. Why? Because she had obtained a special grace from God[5] by which the Holy Spirit, that is, God himself,[6] dwelt in her.

Another example, perhaps less well known, shows this clearly to us. Before the Annunciation of the angel Gabriel to Mary, the same angel had announced to Zechariah the birth of a son to whom they were to name John and who would later become John the Baptist, cousin and precursor of Jesus himself. The words of the angel to Zechariah, who in disbelief does not understand how his wife Elizabeth, old and sterile, could have any chance of conceiving a son, are illuminating: "For he shall be great in the sight of the Lord, and shall drink neither wine nor strong drink; and he shall be filled with the Holy Ghost, even from his mother's womb" (Luke 1:15). This prophecy of the angel Gabriel will be fulfilled when, later on, Elizabeth is already six months pregnant, and she receives the visit of Mary who is already holding Jesus, who has just been conceived, in her womb: "And it came to pass, that, when Elisabeth heard the salutation of Mary, the babe leaped in her womb; and Elisabeth was filled with the Holy Ghost" (Luke 1:41).

It is on the basis of the combination of these two passages from the Gospel of Luke that St. Thomas Aquinas will come to the conclusion that John the Baptist, although conceived with the stain of original sin, at the moment when he is sanctified by Jesus himself with the grace of the Holy Spirit in the sixth month of gestation, will be born from his mother's womb devoid of original sin. A sort of immaculate birth, the one proposed by St. Thomas, which, however, will never become dogma of faith for the Catholic Church. It matters little for our reasoning. The point is to understand the dynamic with which God opens himself to human sin. Since God is the antithesis of sin, in the place where the Holy Spirit dwells, that is, God himself, there can be no shadow of sin. It follows that the further the Holy Spirit dwells from our hearts, the more prone we will be to sin.

The gift of the Holy Spirit is a particular grace that one receives from God, which can be the consequence of an act of unconditional love on the part of God himself (blessing, sanctification) or the consequence of incessant prayer on the part of the human being, to which God agrees to respond positively. On the other hand, as God grants this grace, God has the faculty to remove it at a time and in a way that suits him, according to the plan that God has for us or, obviously, for specific demerits of our own. This is one of the most terrible and dreaded conditions, that of the removal of the Holy Spirit from the heart of people.

In the chapter 8 of the first book of Kings, Solomon thanks the Lord for remaining faithful to the people of Israel and implores him to remain always by their side: "The Lord our God be with us, as he was with our fathers: let him not leave us, nor forsake us: That he may incline our hearts unto him, to walk in all his ways, and to keep his commandments, and his statutes, and his judgments, which he commanded

---

5. "Fear not, Mary: for thou hast found favour with God" (Luke 1:30).
6. "*Ave Maria, gratia plena, Dominus tecum*" (Luke 1:28).

our fathers" (1 Kgs 8:57–58). What Solomon is asking of God is to never remove from the people of Israel his grace. On the contrary, he is asking him to send his Holy Spirit to soften their hearts, to incline them toward good and toward God himself.

We begin to understand the meaning of all those expressions that sounded so ambiguous or at least out of tune with our sensibilities. Do you remember Psalm 141(140) in which the Lord was asked "not to incline our hearts to any evil thing"? Most modern translations of the Bible, in order not to risk appearing heretical, sweeten the text with a permissive construct.[7] Now we are in the privileged condition of clearly understanding what is meant in that psalm, though. The Lord is being asked not to remove his Holy Spirit from our hearts, which otherwise would harden like arid soil and would thus be *inclined* to fall into sin. Do you remember the passage in Isa 63:17 in which the Israelites bitterly wondered why God had led them astray from his path by hardening their hearts? Now those words are finally clear, without the need for permissive interpretations ("why hast thou made us to err from thy ways, and hardened our heart from thy fear?").

The theory of divine "cardiodynamics" (this is how we could call it) that is revealed in the Old Testament is based on these fundamental concepts:

1. The heart is the physical seat of human propensity to follow divine dictates.
2. The heart, irreparably stained by original sin, is a substratum *per se* arid and inclined to evil.
3. Like the soil of the field, the heart constantly needs to be watered so that it may produce good fruit.
4. What irrigates the heart of person is the Holy Spirit, who is sent by God on the basis of a particular grace.
5. When God grants people's heart the grace of being inundated with the Holy Spirit, that heart will become inclined to good and refractory to sin.
6. The more the Holy Spirit pervades the heart of a person, the more that person will be inclined to good and refractory to sin.
7. God, who is one with the Holy Spirit, is by definition *apeírastos*, that is, perfectly immune to temptation (Jas 1:13).
8. When the Holy Spirit is removed from the heart of a person (because God himself removes him or because the person rejects him), that heart will return to its natural state of dryness and hardness, and that person will again be dangerously inclined to deviate from the right path.

Once we understand this dynamic, we will no longer be afraid to causally translate some key Old Testament passages. Most importantly, all the pieces of the puzzle will fit together meekly without the need for unnecessary permissive forcing. Every

7. NIV, NLT, ESV, CSB, CEV, ISV, NAB.

single "problematic" passage in the Old Testament is immediately resolved, and what emerges is the image of a God who works in the world in a coherent way. Let us read in this regard a passage from the book of Sirach: "Sensuality and lust shall not take hold of me; do not abandon me to shameful desires" (Sir 23:6).

Unfortunately, the original Hebrew text of this verse has not been preserved. We do, however, have the Greek translation that guides us: "ψυχῇ ἀναιδεῖ μὴ παραδῷς με."[8]

The action of abandoning is rendered by the verb *paradídōmi* (παραδίδωμι). However, the verb "to abandon" does not fully render the meaning of the Greek text. *Paradídōmi* is the same verb used countless times in the Gospels to indicate the betrayal of Jesus,[9] which, as we know, takes the form of Judas delivering him into the hands of his tormentors. This is the meaning of the expression used by the Septuagint. We ask the Lord not to deliver us into the clutches of shameful desires. One understands then that the meaning of that *mḕ paradôis me* has little of the permissive ("do not abandon us to") and much of the causative ("do not deliver us into the hands of"). After all, Judas does not abandon Jesus into the hands of the high priests, but delivers him, leading the guards into the garden on the Mount of Olives, kissing Jesus, and having him arrested (what can be more causative than that?). And how would the Lord deliver us into the shame of our impure desires? The answer is always the same: by turning away from our heart the grace of the Holy Spirit, making it arid, hard, inert, and almost unable to distinguish good from evil. The adjective used to indicate shameful desires is *anaidés* (ἀναιδής) which indicates something that is in antithesis with *aidṓs* (αἰδώς), that is, the sense of modesty. *Anaideia* was the Greek goddess of shamelessness, effrontery, and lack of pity. Not surprisingly, in Greek mythology *Anaideia* was the companion of *Hybris*, the goddess of insolence and arrogance. When the Holy Spirit dwells far from our hearts, our obfuscated minds become prey to the most abject instincts, fed by our *hýbris*. This is the most dangerous condition for us because we are one step away from the divine *némesis*.

In the second book of Kings, in chapter 21, God is so angry with Manasseh, king of Judah, for the abominations he has committed and the rampant idolatry into which he has led his people, that he threatens, "And I will forsake the remnant of mine inheritance, and deliver them into the hand of their enemies; and they shall become a prey and a spoil to all their enemies" (2 Kgs 21:14). The action of abandoning a person to his destiny of ruin and destruction is rendered in the Hebrew text by the verb *nātăsh* (נָטַשׁ), which means "to abandon," "to leave," "to reject far from oneself." The threat of being abandoned by God is, as seen, the most terrible and frightening for people, because the immediate and inevitable consequence is their physical and moral destruction.[10] For this reason, in Psalm 27(26) we implore the Lord in this way: "Hide

---

8. "*psychêi anaideî mḕ paradôis me*" = "To a depraved soul do not deliver me."

9. See, for example, Matt 26:21: "Verily I say unto you, that one of you shall betray [*paradídōmi*] me."

10. Again, the divine nemesis, that is, the fact that God will deliver them into the hands of their enemies, is rendered in the Septuagint with the verb *paradídōmi*.

not thy face far from me; put not thy servant away in anger: thou hast been my help; leave me not, neither forsake me, O God of my salvation" (Ps 27(26):9).

The action of repelling in the Hebrew text is rendered by the *hiphil* form of the verb *nātâ* (נָטָה), which means "to extend," "to incline," "to bend." This is the same verb we encountered in Psalm 141(140):4 ("Incline not my heart to any evil thing"). Here the idea is that of bending away from oneself, that is, of repelling. But the dynamic is always the same. How does God incline our hearts to sin? By removing his face from us, by withdrawing the saving action of the Holy Spirit from our heart. The hardening of people's heart is a consequence of the removal of God from people. They are two sides of the same coin. This is why the Lord is asked not to leave us or forsake us. The verbs used in the Hebrew text are two synonyms: the verb *nātāsh*, already encountered in the previous example, and the verb '*āzăv* (עָזַב).[11]

We are able to finally understand why there are multiple biblical passages in which divine responsibility for the hardening of the human heart is evident, but at the same time there are instances in which people are solely responsible for the hardening of their hearts. The answer is very trivial. There is no contradiction, because the two things can coexist and are not mutually exclusive. If, however, on the one hand we are accustomed to the idea of human beings who, because of their fragility, close their hearts to divine dictates, yield to the temptation of moral evil, reject God, and persist in their *hýbris*, it is much more difficult for our modern sensibility to accept the fact that God, for his part, may also be the author of the fact that our hearts dry up. Everything, however, is logically part of the concept of divine justice, which, being divine, very often reveals itself to be inscrutable. This is clearly shown to us by the passage in Psalm 81(80) which reads, "But my people would not hearken to my voice; and Israel would none of me. So I gave them up unto their own hearts' lust: and they walked in their own counsels" (Ps 81(80):11–12(12–13)). The Hebrew term used here to indicate the fact that God removed the people of Israel from himself is the verb *shālăh* (שָׁלַח), the same used to indicate the promise, always unfulfilled by Pharaoh, to release the Israelites. The verb *shālăh* translates the action of "sending" and therefore of "sending away," of "pushing away." The image offered by the Hebrew text is extraordinarily strong. God does not want to deal with them anymore and not only decides to abandon them to the hardness of their hearts, but pushes them away, having lost all hope of converting them to himself.

There are many reasons why God may decide to reject us and abandon us to the obstinacy of our hearts. The main one is to make us understand how wretched the life of a human being is, who has lost the relationship with God and, consequently, his saving protection. To make us taste the ruin and with it grant us the grace of humility, which is the first step, essential, indispensable, to undertake a true movement of total

---

11. The verb '*āzăv* is also used in the famous *incipit* of Psalm 22(21), which will then be the same words pronounced by Jesus on the cross: "*Eloì, Eloì, lemà sabachthàni?*" = "My God, my God, why have you forsaken me?" (Mark 15:34; Matt 27:46).

conversion to God. Unfortunately, if a person's withered heart gets lost in the spiral of the vicious circle of sin, which withers the heart even more, making it more and more inclined to sin—in a mad and accelerated race toward the ravine of ruin—at that point God has no choice but to exercise his divine justice, which translates into a terrible punishment. This also clarifies, incidentally, the obscure words of Jesus when he teaches, "And whosoever speaketh a word against the Son of man, it shall be forgiven him: but whosoever speaketh against the Holy Ghost, it shall not be forgiven him, neither in this world, neither in the world to come" (Matt 12:32).

There is only one sin, Jesus explains, that cannot be forgiven, and that is the sin against the Holy Spirit. What does it mean to sin against the Holy Spirit? It means rejecting him from our hearts and rejecting his saving grace. It means to stubbornly wallow in moral evil unrepentantly. It means putting God, who is infinitely merciful, with his back against the wall. It means voluntarily placing oneself outside of his grace. And outside of divine grace there can be no forgiveness. There is instead only eternal punishment.[12]

Someone may object: is God punishing himself then? The answer is: no, he is not. For there is a particularly important variable of this "theory," of which we have not yet spoken: free will.

---

12. "There shall be weeping and gnashing of teeth" (Luke 13:28).

# 12

# Divine Justice and Free Will: the Choice between Good and Evil

Let us start from an immovable principle. However much God may decide to harden human heart—making it arid by removing his face from it—the ultimate choice between good and evil is always and only the responsibility of human beings, to whom God grants the luxury of free will. Only by introducing this variable is it possible to explain satisfactorily how divine justice operates.

It is important to reiterate this because it represents a pivotal element in our reasoning. In all the occasions in which in the Bible we implore God "not to lead us astray" or "not to incline us" to evil, we are not asking God not to force us to sin (this would be a blasphemous idea, but before that it would not make sense from a logical point of view). Instead, we are asking him not to make our hearts *more inclined* to sin, that is, weaker in the face of temptation. This God can do, he has done it on various occasions, and he has even claimed it. However, when it comes to the choice between doing or not doing evil, God stands aside and observes. The choice between good and evil is the exclusive prerogative of human beings, endowed with free will. It is an immense freedom but also an immense responsibility. In fact, it is on the basis of our choice that God will judge us.

And the choice between good and evil is the work of the rational part of a person. If the heart represents the flesh, *sárx* (σάρξ) in Greek, that is, the impulsive part, the spirit, *pneûma* (πνεῦμα) in Greek, represents the rational part, which has dominion over instinct. In a person in a state of complete grace, whose heart is pervaded by the Holy Spirit, heart and mind, flesh and spirit, *sárx* and *pneûma* are in perfect harmony. The impulse of the heart will always be projected toward the good, and the rational effort to choose good over evil will be non-existent. On the contrary, the more a person's heart is hardened and inclined to sin, the more his/her mind will have to strive to overcome temptation and still choose good. So much so that in a completely hardened heart, the effort needed to resist temptation becomes infinite, with the probability of success close to zero.

Let us go back, for example, to that passage in the book of Jeremiah seen earlier, in which the Lord was showing the prophet two baskets of figs. The good figs represent the people of Judah in exile, to whom God decides to grant the grace of a new heart ("I will give them an heart to know me"). The verse ends with these words: "They shall be my people, and I will be their God: for they shall return unto me with their whole heart" (Jer 24:7).

The Lord foretells the total and unconditional conversion of the people of Israel. But it is important to note that this conversion is caused by the Lord only to the extent that he has granted them a heart inclined to recognize and follow the divine dictates. However, the act of conversion is a particular choice of the people of Israel. Chapter 15 of the book of Sirach perfectly explains the concepts just set forth. In verse 11 we read: "Do not say, 'I rebelled because of the Lord,' for what he hates, you must not do" (Sir 15:11).

The verb used in Greek to translate the action of rebelling is *aphístēmi* (ἀφίστημι), which indicates a motion of separation (from God). Fortunately, for this verse of Sirach, the original Hebrew text has been found[1] (from right to left): אל תאמר מאל פשעי כי את אשר שנא לא עשה.[2]

First of all, the Hebrew text does not use a verb to denote the action of rebellion but rather its corresponding noun, *pĕshă'* (פֶּשַׁע),[3] which means "rebellion against God," and thus "sin." Therefore, the term פשעי means "my sin." The Hebrew text then uses the prefix *m-* (-מ) associated with the term *'ĕl* (אֵל), which means God, to indicate a motion *from* the place where sin would come, that is, from God. The expression מאל פשעי therefore means, "My sin (is) from God."[4] The second part of the verse, on the other hand, does not call for not doing what he detests, but instead explains why sins cannot be said to come from God: God himself could never be the cause of what he detests. The negation *lō'* (לא) is the strongest negation in Hebrew, which remains valid in all times and circumstances. The expression לא עשה cannot be a negative imperative ("you shall not do!"). In fact, in biblical Hebrew, the negative imperative is always constructed with the imperfect conjugation of the verb. And the imperfect conjugation requires a prefix, which does not appear in the Hebrew text.[5] The verb עשה is thus simply the third-person singular of the base *qal* form of the verb *'āsâ*

---

1. From now on, we will leverage Beentjes, *The Book of Ben Sira in Hebrew*.

2. "*' l t' mr m' l psh' y ky ' t ' shr shn' l' ' sh*" = "Do not say, 'My sin came from the Lord,' for he never produces what he detests."

3. *Pĕshă'* comes from the root verb *pāshă'* (פָּשַׁע), which means "to rebel."

4. In Hebrew, the verb "to be" is almost always implied.

5. As a counterproof, the negative imperative "do not say" that appears at the beginning of the verse contains the prefix *t-* (-ת), which denotes the imperfect of the verb *'ămăr* (אָמַר), "to say."

(עָשָׂה), which means "to make," "to create," "to produce." We can conclude that a more correct translation of the passage might be as follows: "Do not say, 'My sin came from the Lord,' for he never produces what he detests."

This passage from the book of Sirach is teaching us not to blame God for our poor choices. It is teaching us that the cause of sin is never God, but rather the weakness and inability of our rational side to rein in the sinful instincts of our (hardened) heart. And it is logical that God cannot be the cause of human sin because sin is what he detests most of all. Since people sin, even though they know very well that this is an abomination in the eyes of God, the responsibility for sin, that is, for choosing evil instead of good, rests entirely on people's shoulders. The following verse is even more enlightening: "Do not say, 'He has led me astray,' for he has no need of a sinner" (Sir 15:12).

Does this sound familiar? Sure. It seems to echo the words of Isaiah, "O Lord, why hast thou made us to err from thy ways" (Isa 63:17). Or of Ps 119(118):10: "O let me not wander from thy commandments." How is this possible? The book of Sirach is teaching us never to say that it is the Lord who leads us astray, when in two other passages in the Bible these very words are explicitly pronounced! Have we perhaps found an inconsistency in the sacred texts? And if so, how do we resolve it? The supporters of the permissive thesis use this apparent contradiction to explain that both the passages in Isaiah and Psalm 119(118) should not be taken literally, because otherwise we would commit the heresy of saying that God leads us astray, which, as Sirach teaches, is wrong. Instead, we should interpret these passages in a permissive sense: he does not lead us astray, but he only *allows* us to be led astray. This is a fascinating thesis that would seem to have a reason to exist if we had only the text translated into Greek as a yardstick. The verb used in the Greek translation of the Sirach passage to indicate the action of misdirection is *planáō* (πλανάω), which is the exact same verb used in the translation of the passage of Isaiah. If one compares these two passages in Greek, the contradiction is evident, if not jarring, so an explanation is necessary. And the permissive explanation appears to be a reasonable way out.

Fortunately, however, these verses of chapter 15 of the book of Sirach were found at the end of the nineteenth century in their original Hebrew form, which allows us to fully understand the meaning of the passage, which does not transpire from the Greek translation. Let us compare the passages in question in Hebrew. As already seen, the verbs used in Isa 63:17 and in Ps 119(118):10 are respectively *tāʿâ* (תָּעָה) and *shāgâ* (שָׁגָה), two synonyms indicating the action of wandering aimlessly away from the main road. Conjugated in the causative form, they indicate the action of leading someone astray. In contrast, the Hebrew verb used in the Sirach passage is *tql* (תקל), a term that does not appear in any other book of the Bible,[6] and which is synonymous with the more commonly used *kāshal* (כָּשַׁל). Both verbs, *tql* and *kāshal*, indicate the action of staggering, losing one's balance, stumbling, and thus falling. For this reason,

---

6. The Aramaic noun *təqāl* (תְּקָל) appears three times in a couple of verses of the book of Daniel and indicates a unit of weight.

the causative form in which the verb *tql* is conjugated in the Sirach verse in question, *hithqîl* (הִתְקִיל), takes on the meaning of "making one stumble," "making one fall." The correct translation of Sir 15:12 is as follows: "Do not say, 'He caused me to stumble,' for he has no need of a sinner."

Unfortunately, the Greek translation in this case does not do justice to the extremely specific image offered by the original Hebrew text, and unwittingly introduces confusion, giving rise to apparent contradictions in the sacred texts.[7] The passage in the original Hebrew, on the other hand, is clear, and sweeps away any permissive conjecture. The direct causative interpretation for both the verses of Isa 63:13 and Ps 119(118):10, and of Sir 15:12 is the correct one, and the three expressions do not contradict each other. Let us see why.

Is it correct to say that the Lord can lead someone astray? Yes, it is! To the extent that he can harden our hearts, which inevitably leads us to stray from the main road (that of respecting the divine dictates), to wander without reference points. And when a person wanders far from the right path, the path becomes bumpy, with a *greater probability* of stumbling, since it is difficult for our mind, which responds to a hardened heart, to recognize good from evil. When it is said in the Bible that God has led a person astray, it means that he has made that person go along paths strewn with stumbling blocks, that he has placed that person in the condition of having a greater probability of falling (into the trap of sin). It is a statistical matter. Nothing more, nothing less.

Is it fair to say that the Lord may cause us to stumble? No, it is not! No matter how arduous he may make the path for us, never will he trip us up to make us fall into sin (as Pope Francis rightly points out). Why? The passage in Sirach tells us clearly, "because he has no need of a sinner." And what would be the point of a God tripping us up? None. God is *pistós*, faithful, as St. Paul says. He does not play tricks. He does not deceive. While it is certainly true that he can harden our hearts, making us generally more prone to fall into temptation, the choice that people face when confronted with a stumbling block is their total responsibility. If they choose good, they will have overcome the stumbling block. If they choose evil, they will have stumbled and fallen into sin. But God does not enter this choice. He does not want to enter. And he certainly does not cheer for us to fall.

It is necessary at this point to slow down and dwell on this metaphor of stumbling into the trap of temptation with the consequent fall into sin. It is a fundamental concept that we will take up in the following chapters and that is worth explaining in full.

There is a passage in Paul's letter to the Romans that we would like to present. It is full of important concepts. It is worth reading it slowly.

---

7. A Greek translation more faithful to the Hebrew text could have been obtained by the verb *ptaíō* (πταίω), which in the transitive form indicates the action of tripping.

## DIVINE JUSTICE AND FREE WILL: THE CHOICE BETWEEN GOOD AND EVIL

> I say then, Hath God cast away his people? God forbid. For I also am an Israelite, of the seed of Abraham, of the tribe of Benjamin. God hath not cast away his people which he foreknew. Wot ye not what the scripture saith of Elias? how he maketh intercession to God against Israel saying, Lord, they have killed thy prophets, and digged down thine altars; and I am left alone, and they seek my life. But what saith the answer of God unto him? I have reserved to myself seven thousand men, who have not bowed the knee to the image of Baal. Even so then at this present time also there is a remnant according to the election by grace. And if by grace, then is it no more of works: otherwise grace is no more grace. But if it be of works, then it is no more grace: otherwise work is no more work. What then? Israel hath not obtained that which he seeketh for; but the election hath obtained it, and the rest were blinded. (According as it is written, God hath given them the spirit of slumber, eyes that they should not see, and ears that they should not hear;) unto this day. And David saith, Let their table be made a snare, and a trap, and a stumbling block, and a recompence unto them: Let their eyes be darkened, that they may not see, and bow down their back always. I say then, Have they stumbled that they should fall? God forbid: but rather through their fall salvation is come unto the Gentiles, for to provoke them to jealousy. (Rom 11:1–11)

As we have already seen, St. Paul is a firm believer in what he calls "election by grace."[8] God decides who to harden according to the inscrutable plan that God has in store for humanity, and not based on the works of each person. The grace of receiving a heart filled with Holy Spirit is precisely a grace, that is, a blessing that God grants to a person, regardless of the merits of that person, "otherwise grace is no more grace." And then he quotes passages from the Old Testament that testify to what we have already amply demonstrated, namely that God has the power to harden the hearts, darken the eyes, and cover the ears of anyone, if he deems it necessary for the fulfillment of his plan. For example, the Israelites. They did not get what they were looking for, because their hearts were hardened. St. Paul quotes a little freely from verses 22–23(23–24) of Psalm 69(68) in which the psalmist (perhaps David) wishes his enemies that their table will become a trap for them. That is to say that, once their guard is down, while they are relaxing and enjoying themselves, they will be suddenly attacked and destroyed, thus receiving a just reward for their evil deeds. St. Paul makes this invocation his own and reuses it in a different context, where the snare and the stumbling block represent the temptations that cause people to fall into sin. The terms Paul uses to refer to a trap, a net for hunting animals, are *pagís* (παγίς) and *théra* (θήρα). The stumbling block, on the other hand, is rendered by the term *skándalon* (σκάνδαλον), which literally indicates the physical mechanism by which a trap succeeds in catching prey. We have confirmation that the metaphor of the trap, of the obstacle, of the stumbling block to indicate the temptation that causes one to fall

---

8. "ἐκλογὴ χάριτος [*eklogè cháritos*]."

into sin (just as a prey falls into the hunter's net) was a widely known image in biblical imagery. St. Paul concludes on a hopeful note. The fact that the hard-hearted Israelites repeatedly stumbled did not prevent them in the end from converting and returning to the right path. On the contrary. Their unfortunate example aroused a movement of conversion even among the pagans. This is how the inscrutable divine Providence works. The Israelites were led astray by the Lord and used as an instrument of conversion for other nations.

As far as the Old Testament is concerned, chapter 4 of the book of Proverbs is entirely dedicated to the advice that a father gives to his son to keep the right path. The passage is steeped in the same concepts, the same images, the same metaphors that we have discussed so far. Let us look at some passages.

> Hear, O my son, and receive my sayings; and the years of thy life shall be many. I have taught thee in the way of wisdom; I have led thee in right paths. When thou goest, thy steps shall not be straightened; and when thou runnest, thou shalt not stumble. Take fast hold of instruction; let her not go: keep her; for she is thy life. Enter not into the path of the wicked, and go not in the way of evil men. Avoid it, pass not by it, turn from it, and pass away. For they sleep not, except they have done mischief; and their sleep is taken away, unless they cause some to fall. For they eat the bread of wickedness, and drink the wine of violence. But the path of the just is as the shining light, that shineth more and more unto the perfect day. The way of the wicked is as darkness: they know not at what they stumble. My son, attend to my words; incline thine ear unto my sayings. Let them not depart from thine eyes; keep them in the midst of thine heart. For they are life unto those that find them, and health to all their flesh. Keep thy heart with all diligence; for out of it are the issues of life. Put away from thee a froward mouth, and perverse lips put far from thee. Let thine eyes look right on, and let thine eyelids look straight before thee. Ponder the path of thy feet, and let all thy ways be established. Turn not to the right hand nor to the left: remove thy foot from evil. (Prov 4:10–27)

Once again, we come across the image of the straight path that is like "the shining light" that allows those who walk on it not to fall—not to stumble. There is only one recipe to stay on this path: keep your heart, mouth, and eyes—the impulses of the flesh, of the *sárx*—at bay. And who should keep watch? Obviously, the rational part, our spirit, the *pneûma*. If, however, our hardened heart leads us to deviate from the "path of the just" and to proceed by "the way of the wicked," at that point everything becomes more complicated. Our mind, enveloped in darkness, no longer sees clearly. It has immense difficulty in distinguishing between good and evil. Our feet waver, our steps are hindered, and we find ourselves in the potential condition of falling at the slightest stumbling block that we encounter on the way.

It becomes even clearer to us from this passage how the fact of deviating from the right path does not in itself constitute an offense against God. To deviate from the right path means to expose oneself to temptation much more frequently than if we were to follow the main road, but it is not itself a sin. In fact, temptation is represented by the metaphor of the stumbling block, the trap, the obstacle that one encounters on the path of the ungodly, while sin is represented by the action of falling into the trap itself, by the act of stumbling. As long as one deviates, one has *not yet* committed sin. This is why there is no scandal in thinking of a God who, for several reasons (to temper us, for the good of others, to make us know the virtue of humility, because he has lost patience with us, and so on), can push us off the main road. Falling, however, after stumbling into temptation, is the prerogative and exclusive choice of human free will. It will never be God who pushes our foot so that we stumble into the obstacle of temptation (see Sir 15:12: "Do not say, 'He made me stumble,' for he has no need of a sinner.").

Then there is chapter 59 of the book of Isaiah, in which the prophet lists to the people of Israel their faults and the reasons why the Lord has hidden his face from them. They are unrepentant sinners, their hands are stained with blood, and only lies come out of their mouths. They have completely lost sight of the right path and are groping in the darkness of their iniquity. Isaiah says, "We grope for the wall like the blind, and we grope as if we had no eyes: we stumble at noon day as in the night; we are in desolate places as dead men" (Isa 59:10).

Isaiah's words are very harsh, and to indicate the image of a people that stumbles into sin he uses the verb *kāshăl*. The same verb is also used by the prophet Jeremiah in chapter 18 of the book that takes his name: "Because my people hath forgotten me, they have burned incense to vanity, and they have stumbled in their ways from the ancient paths, to walk in paths, in a way not cast up" (Jer 18:15). The metaphor is always the same. The road of the wicked is not level but paved with stumbling stones. The same image, described with the same verb *kāshăl*, is also taken up by Malachi, who recalls how sinners not only stumble in sin, but by their perverse example cause others to stumble: "But ye are departed out of the way; ye have caused many to stumble at the law; ye have corrupted the covenant of Levi, saith the Lord of hosts" (Mal 2:8).

There are many other passages in the Bible where the verb *kāshăl* is used and where the main actor is God himself. That is, God himself becomes a stumbling block for people. In all these cases, however, the stumbling stone does not refer to a moral fall (into sin) but to a physical fall (into destruction). This is in line with the fact that, if God is never ultimately responsible for moral evil, he may be responsible for the physical evil that befalls a person, usually *as a punishment* for the evil committed. This is one of the fundamental concepts underlying our argument, and we will do well to keep it in mind. Let us read Isaiah: "And he shall be for a sanctuary; but for a stone of stumbling and for a rock of offence to both the houses of Israel, for a gin and for a snare to the inhabitants of Jerusalem. And many among them shall stumble, and fall, and be broken, and be snared, and be taken" (Isa 8:14–15).

Here we have a summary of all the key terms encountered so far. In particular, the "stone of stumbling and rock of offence" is an expression that will be used several times in the New Testament. The Hebrew text uses this redundancy expressly to emphasize the idea of the ruinous fall. There is a similar emphatic redundancy in the expression "for a gin [net] and for a snare," all terms that we have already encountered before. If, however, in the examples we have seen so far, obstacles, stumbling blocks, traps, and nets were metaphors for the moral temptation that leads one to fall into sin, here they are instead a metaphor for the *némesis* that inflicts the *tísis*, that is, the divine punishment that falls upon the wicked and destroys them. Just as God can be sanctuary and refuge for the righteous, those same stones that make up the temple of God can be the ruin and destruction for the wicked, who smash against them.[9] Jeremiah could not be clearer when he reports, "Therefore thus saith the Lord, Behold, I will lay stumbling blocks before this people, and the fathers and the sons together shall fall upon them; the neighbor and his friend shall perish" (Jer 6:21).

To the one whom God wants to punish, he will place stones of stumbling on the path. However, since God does not produce moral evil, but at most physical evil, the fall due to the stumbling will not produce moral death (sin) but physical death ("shall perish"). Jeremiah himself, further on in chapter 18, uses more or less the same image to indicate the divine punishment invoked against enemies: "Yet, Lord, thou knowest all their counsel against me to slay me: forgive not their iniquity, neither blot out their sin from thy sight, but let them be overthrown before thee; deal thus with them in the time of thine anger" (Jer 18:23).

The words of the prophet Ezekiel are on the same wavelength: "Again, When a righteous man doth turn from his righteousness, and commit iniquity, and I lay a stumbling-block before him, he shall die: because thou hast not given him warning, he shall die in his sin, and his righteousness which he hath done shall not be remembered; but his blood will I require at thine hand" (Ezek 3:20).

God is the one who materially inflicts death on the sinners, placing before them a stumbling block on which they will smash. This is the kind of death one should fear most: out of divine grace. For all good works done previously "shall not be remembered."

We began with a simple verse from Sirach (Sir 15:12), which seemed to contradict other passages of Scripture, and instead it opened up vast horizons for us on the concept of deviation from the main road, temptation, fall, sin, and divine punishment. It is worthwhile at this point to continue reading the entire passage of Sirach that follows that verse. It will help us set some firm points. Let us start again from the Greek translation of Sirach, and then refine it on the basis of the original Hebrew text: "The Lord hates every abomination, which is not wanted by those who fear God. He created man from the beginning and left him at the mercy of his free will. If thou wilt, thou shalt keep the commandments; to keep the faith is a matter of good will. He has set fire

---

9. See Isa 28:16; Rom 9:33; 1 Pet 2:8.

and water in front of you; wherever you wish you shall stretch out your hand. Life and death stand before men; to each shall be given what he pleases. For great is the wisdom of the Lord; he is all-powerful and sees all things. His eyes on those who fear him, he knows every action of men. He has not commanded anyone to be ungodly, nor given anyone permission to sin" (Sir 15:13–20).

Crystal clear. In a handful of verses, the idea of free will granted to all people by God since Adam's creation is theorized. According to free will, a person has, in every moment of his life, the possibility, the burden and the responsibility to choose between good and evil, between "fire and water," between "life and death." The choice to observe the divine commandments is always and only determined by human willpower ("if thou wilt"). The conclusion is masterful. Neither God has ever commanded man to sin, let alone given him permission to do so. The Greek term used in verse 14 for free will is *diaboúlion* (διαβούλιον), which indicates what one deliberately decides to do. The original Hebrew is even more specific and uses the term *yētsĕr* (יֵצֶר), which appears only a handful of times in the entire Old Testament. The noun *yētsĕr* is derived from the same root as the verb *yātsăr* (יָצַר), which means "to give form," "to shape." The *yētsĕr* indicates the intellectual structure of people—their *forma mentis*, their intrinsic nature, their way of thinking, their way of seeing things, their way of conceiving the surrounding reality, their imagination, their instinct, their inclination, their emotions, their desires, their will. Their free will, precisely. *Yētsĕr* is a term of enormous semantic significance, probably untranslatable, that contains all these things together.

Another passage from the book of Sirach, found in chapter 27, tries to explain it to us even better. Let us read the translation of the original Hebrew text preserved in Manuscript A: "The fruit is the result of the way the tree is cultivated; similarly, the reasoning ability is an expression of the individual *forma mentis*" (Sir 27:6).

What we have translated as "reasoning ability" is the Hebrew term *hĕshbôn* (חֶשְׁבּוֹן), which indicates the rational part of an individual.[10] As the quality of the fruit is a consequence of the goodness of the cultivation technique (Matt 7:16–20; Luke 6:43–45), so our *yētsĕr*, that is, our intellectual structure, our *forma mentis*, defines our ability to reason, discern, understand, which in Greek is defined with the term *lógos* (λόγος). The Hebrew noun *yētsĕr* is in this case translated with *enthýmēma* (ἐνθύμημα), which indicates what our heart is inclined toward: "the *lógos* is an expression of the inclination of man's heart."

The following verse (Sir 15:15) reiterates how free will stands at the beginning of every human choice. *Eàn théleis* (ἐὰν θέλῃς): "If thou wilt." Observing and maintaining the divine dictates is a precise will of human beings. The conclusion of the verse then seems redundant, in the way it repeats exactly the concept expressed in the first part: "keeping the faith is a matter of good will." Nothing wrong with this, if it were not for the fact that, if we analyze the original Hebrew text, the expression used is

---

10. It derives from the same root as the verb *hāshăv* (חָשַׁב) which means "to think," "to consider," "to calculate," "to judge," "to estimate," that is, every activity pertaining to the rational part of a person.

different, and in this case refers not to the good will of a person, but to the will of God. The original meaning of the passage is the following (depending on which manuscript we consider): "If thou wilt, thou shalt keep the commandments and the intelligence to do his will" (Sir 15:15 MS. A); "If thou wilt, thou shalt keep the commandments and the faith to do God's will" (Sir 15:15 MS. B).

Manuscript A contains the term *bînâ* (בִּינָה), which indicates the intellectual capacity to understand. Manuscript B, on the other hand, contains the term *'ĕmûnâ* (אֱמוּנָה), which suggests the concept of firm conviction, that is, faith. The two versions are obviously not at odds, but rather complete each other. To accomplish the divine will, we need both faith and reason. Finally, the divine will is rendered by the term *rātsôn* (רָצוֹן), which indicates the satisfaction and delight that God takes in human behavior that is to his liking. This is what in Greek is called *eudokía* (εὐδοκία), composed of the prefix *eu*, which indicates something good, and the verb *dokéō* (δοκέω), which means "to consider," "to judge." The *eudokía* is what God considers good and has purchased his favor. Doing the will of God coincides with doing what pleases him.[11]

Two chapters later, we find confirmation of the idea of a God who infuses *lógos*—reason—into human beings so that they themselves can discern good from evil: "Free will, tongue, eyes, ears, and heart he gave them so that they might reason. He filled them with knowledge and intelligence and showed them good and evil" (Sir 17:6–7).

Free will, indicated again by the term *diaboúlion*, represents the rational part, and is given to human beings along with the tongue, eyes, ears, and heart, which represent the sensory, emotional, instinctive part, the *sárx*, so that he can consider, ponder, judge, reason (διανοέομαι) in a complex and complete way. Not only that. God has infused all people with intelligence, cognitive ability, wisdom, *sýnesis* (σύνεσις), which enables people to acquire a store of knowledge, *epistḗmē* (ἐπιστήμη), useful for discerning good from evil. It follows that, if we choose evil, the fault can only be ours. In fact, God has provided each of us with all the necessary means to understand what should be avoided at all costs.

As mentioned, people's *forma mentis* is indicated by the Hebrew term *yētsĕr*, which comes from the root verb *yātsăr*, meaning "to shape." It is the same verb used in Gen 2:7 when it says that "God formed [*yātsăr*] man from the dust of the ground, and

---

11. Incidentally, it is interesting to note that the term *eudokía* also appears in the Angel's announcement of Jesus' birth to the shepherds of Bethlehem: "Glory to God in the highest and peace on earth to people of good will" (Luke 2:14). Very often, this exclamation, which is recited daily in churches throughout the world, is mistakenly perceived as a blessing for all those who possess good will, that is, who are animated by benevolent intentions. However, as mentioned, *eudokía* is a concept that refers primarily to the way God judges human behavior, and not so much to human intentions themselves. The meaning of the passage is: "Glory to God in the highest, and on earth peace to the people who enjoy God's favor" (see Luke 1:30: "And the angel said unto her, Fear not, Mary: for thou hast found favour with God"). Being the object of divine favor is—before being a human merit—a grace granted by God. And in fact, among the changes to the Roman Missal published in 2020 by the Italian Episcopal Conference (CEI), this verse of the Gloria has been reformulated as follows: "Glory to God in the highest, and on earth peace to people *loved by the Lord*."

breathed into his nostrils the breath of life; and man became a living soul." This is no accident. *Yātsăr* is the verb of artists, artisans, potters, who work with clay and shape their works with their hands. The *yētsĕr* is thus the intellectual structure that God has fashioned for a person. It is no coincidence that the image of the potter is precisely the one used by St. Paul in the letters to the Romans that we have been analyzing, in which the Apostle theorizes the idea of a God who deals with people the way it pleases him most—without people having any say in the matter, just as a potter does with his clay vessel.

We find the exact same metaphor of the potter in chapter 18 of the book of Jeremiah, in which God himself tells the prophet to go down into the potter's workshop, where he would make him hear his voice. Jeremiah obeys and finds the potter working at the potter's wheel. Observing him, he realizes that if "the vessel that he made of clay was marred in the hand of the potter: so he made it again another vessel, as seemed good to the potter to make it" (Jer 18:4). At that point God makes his voice heard, which could not be clearer: "O house of Israel, cannot I do with you as this potter? saith the Lord. Behold, as the clay is in the potter's hand, so are ye in mine hand, O house of Israel" (Jer 18:6).

What does this mean in practice? It means, for example, that if some people are the object of divine punishment for their evil behavior, but the same people decide to convert, at that point God may decide to revoke his punishment. On the contrary, if some people, object of God's benevolence, decide to deviate from his dictates, at that point God may decide to revoke his favor and inflict on them the just punishment. The Lord invites Jeremiah to warn the people of Israel that if they do not improve their perverse conduct, he will send a calamity against them. However, God predicts to Jeremiah that the Israelites will not listen to his voice: "And they said, There is no hope: but we will walk after our own devices, and we will every one do according to the stubbornness of his evil heart" (Jer 18:12).

The stubbornness of the wicked heart is rendered by the noun *shərîrûth* (שְׁרִירוּת), which indicates the hardness of the Israelites' soul. This term is derived from the root verb *shārăr* (שָׁרַר), which means "to twist," "to screw." When the heart of people is screwed in on itself, hard and arid, twisted like a rope or like a wrung-out cloth, it becomes refractory to the word of the Lord. It hears it but does not listen to it. With the logical ruin that follows.

Such a metaphor—that of the potter—is also taken up in the book of Sirach chapter 33: "As the clay in the hands of the potter who shapes it to his liking, so people in the hands of him who created them, to pay them according to his justice" (Sir 33:13).

So, here we come to the point: divine justice. What is it and how does it manifest itself? Let us begin with the following fact: "Pride is hateful to the Lord and to men; injustice is an abomination to one and to another" (Sir 10:7).

These are the two sins at the top of the list, the sins that God himself does not tolerate: pride, *hýbris*[12] on the one hand, and injustice, *adikía* (ἀδικία) on the other. However, if we analyze the original Hebrew text, we realize that what the Septuagint translates as a generic *adikía*, represents instead a specific form of injustice, which is that perpetrated using violence and oppression. The exact term is ʽ*ōshĕq* (עֹשֶׁק), which is derived from the verb root ʽ*āshăq* (עָשַׁק), indicating a violent, extortionate, insolent action. The insolent violence, expressed by the term ʽ*ōshĕq* (what today we would probably call "bullying" or "mafia" behavior), is a direct consequence of pride. When we consider ourselves superior to the moral law and to the divine law, we may commit any atrocity. What God abhors the most is the *hýbris* and the reckless act in defiance of any moral restraint, which derives from *hýbris* and is fed by it.

Later, in chapter 10 of Sirach, the same concept is taken up and expanded:

> The principle of human pride is to turn away from the Lord, to keep one's heart far from the one who created it. For the principle of pride is sin; whoever indulges in it spreads abomination around him. That is why the Lord makes his chastisements unbelievable, and scourges him until he is finished. The Lord has pulled down the throne of the mighty, and in their place has made the humble to sit. The Lord has uprooted the roots of the nations; in their place he has planted the humble. The Lord has upset the regions of the nations, and destroyed them from the foundations of the earth. He has uprooted them and annihilated them; He has made their remembrance disappear from the earth. Pride is not made for men, nor arrogance for those born of women. (Sir 10:12–18)

If pride, *hyperēphanía* (ὑπερηφανία), as the Septuagint understands it, that is, that sense of superiority over God and people, feeds on sin and produces sin, in an endless vicious circle, the ultimate consequence of pride is divine wrath, which does not tolerate such behavior and punishes it in the harshest way possible. As we have already seen, this is one of the characteristics of divine justice—the just punishment, the *ekdíkēsis* (ἐκδίκησις), proportionate to the gravity of the sin. The *ekdíkēsis* is manifested in all its power in what the Septuagint calls *epagōgḗ* (ἐπαγωγή), that is, the calamity, the scourge, the physical destruction and annihilation of the unrepentant sinner. Pharaoh and his plagues are just one of many examples of divine justice in action, destroying the proud and raising up the humble. The Hebrew term for the category of the "humble" is ʽ*ānî* (עָנִי), which is derived from the root verb ʽ*ānâ* (עָנָה), indicating the action of exerting a force from above downward to compress and oppress someone or something. The original Hebrew text speaks not only of the "humble" as a moral category opposed to the "proud," but also and above all of the poor, the afflicted, those who find themselves in a situation of physical and psychological oppression. In

---

12. The Septuagint uses the term *hyperēphanía* (ὑπερηφανία), which indicates the showing off beyond measure.

## DIVINE JUSTICE AND FREE WILL: THE CHOICE BETWEEN GOOD AND EVIL

other words, the last of the last. These are the ones to whom God promises "the throne of the mighty."[13]

That the fate of the wicked is the *epagōgḗ* is repeated several times within the book of Sirach. Chapter 5 warns against procrastinating in asking forgiveness from the Lord: "Do not wait to turn to the Lord, and do not put it off from day to day, for the Lord's wrath will suddenly break out, and at the time of punishment you will be destroyed. Trust not in unjust riches, for they shall not profit thee in the day of trouble" (Sir 5:7–8).

We find in these two verses a summary of the dynamic of divine justice in three moves.

1. People must not abuse the Lord's patience. Although he is slow to anger,[14] his wrath can be unleashed at any time, suddenly. It is what the Septuagint calls *orgḗ* (ὀργή), that is, that motion of indignation which grows, swells in the face of the impudence of human action, and finally explodes into a violent rage. The corresponding Hebrew term is *zāʿām* (זַעַם), which literally reproduces the image of "foaming at the mouth." In other cases, the Hebrew term used is ʿ*ĕvrâ* (עֶבְרָה), indicating an explosion, an outburst. In other cases, the Hebrew term used is *hārôn* (חָרוֹן), which reproduces the image of scorching heat. God's reaction in front of sin without conversion is a "foaming of fiery and explosive anger," similar to the pressure that silently accumulates for centuries inside a volcano and then erupts in all its destructive force.

2. Wrath produces punishment, *ekdíkēsis*. It is what in Hebrew is indicated by the term *nāqăm* (נָקָם), that is, revenge. Obviously, God does not take vengeance in the human sense of the term,[15] but he avenges sin itself. He avenges the humble, the oppressed who are distressed by sin, sending the just punishment for the evil done by the wicked.[16]

3. And righteous chastisement produces *epagōgḗ*, which, as seen, translates the concept of calamity. The corresponding Hebrew terms can be ʾ*êd* (אֵיד), *tsārâ* (צָרָה), and *rāʿâ* (רָעָה), which indicate anything that produces affliction, oppression, tribulation, suffering, and the synonyms *shôd* (שֹׁד) and *shĕvār* (שֶׁבֶר), indicating material and physical destruction.

ʿ*ĕvrâ*, *nāqăm*, *tsārâ*. *Orgḗ*, *ekdíkēsis*, *epagōgḗ*. Wrath, chastisement, calamity. These are the three basic passages of how divine justice develops.

---

13. See Matt 5:3: "Blessed are the poor in spirit: for theirs is the kingdom of heaven."
14. See Ps 103(102):8: "The Lord is merciful and gracious, slow to anger, and plenteous in mercy."
15. See Deut 32:35: "To me belongeth vengeance and recompence."
16. *Ekdíkēsis* contains the root noun *díkē* (δίκη), which implies the concept of justice.

In a passage from Psalm 78(77) we find an accumulation of all these terms: "He cast upon them the fierceness of his anger [*hārôn*], wrath [*'ĕvrâ*], and indignation [*zā'ām*], and trouble [*tsārâ*], by sending evil angels among them" (Ps 78(77):49).

And what trouble can the Lord inflict as a just punishment for the wicked? The book of Sirach explains it again in chapter 40: "death, blood, strife, sword, destruction [*shôd*], ruin [*shĕvār*], calamity [*rā'â*], scourges. These evils were created for the wicked; because of them there was also the Flood" (Sir 40:9–10).

"These evils were created," and the one who created them can only be God himself. This is the profound meaning of the passage in Isa 45:7 ("I make good, and I create evil"). God is the creator of evil, as far as this evil represents the physical destruction inflicted as a just punishment on ungodly humanity. It would be impossible to enumerate all the examples of disastrous punishment that God inflicts on people found in the Old Testament. Let us look at just a few.

In Sir 23:11, it is explained how the scourge of God will never depart from the dwelling place of an ungodly man, and "his house will be filled with misfortune [*epagōgḗ*]." In Zech 7:14, God threatens to scatter the people who do not heed his words "among all the nations whom they knew not. Thus the land was desolate after them, that no man passed through nor returned." In Jer 24:9–10, God threatens them along the same lines: "And I will deliver them to be removed into all the kingdoms of the earth for their hurt, to be a reproach and a proverb, a taunt and a curse, in all places whither I shall drive them. And I will send the sword, the famine, and the pestilence, among them, till they be consumed from off the land that I gave unto them and to their fathers." In 2 Kings 21:13, God promises to annihilate Jerusalem, "as a man wipeth a dish, wiping it, and turning it upside down." In Ezek 5:12, God warns, "A third part of thee shall die with the pestilence, and with famine shall they be consumed in the midst of thee: and a third part shall fall by the sword round about thee; and I will scatter a third part into all the winds, and I will draw out a sword after them." In Ezek 14:8, God promises to take away his favor from those who follow abominable practices of idolatry: "I will set my face against that man, and will make him a sign and a proverb, and I will cut him off from the midst of my people; and ye shall know that I am the Lord." In Jer 15:3, the Lord admonishes his people of Israel: "I will appoint over them four kinds, saith the Lord: the sword to slay, and the dogs to tear, and the fowls of the heaven, and the beasts of the earth, to devour and destroy."

It is precisely for this reason that, in Heb 10:31, St. Paul, after quoting the passage in Deuteronomy in which God declares, "To me belongeth vengeance and recompence" (Deut 32:35), concludes, "It is a fearful thing to fall into the hands of the living God."[17]

It is fearful to fall into the hands of the living God. These are New Testament words. They cannot be reduced to some sort of archaic way of understanding the divinity. Very often we tend to forget (or it is convenient not to think about it) that

---

17. "φοβερὸν τὸ ἐμπεσεῖν εἰς χεῖρας θεοῦ ζῶντος [*phoberòn tò empeseîn eis cheîras theoû zôntos*]."

the God of the New Testament is the same as the God of the Old. Christ did not come to change people's perception of God in the Old Testament, but rather to make it even more evident. The body of Christ himself is the fulfillment of the prophecies contained in the books of the Old Testament. There is not a single "fearful" trait of the Old Testament God that Christ comes to correct or blunt or sweeten. It is fearful to come upon the divine wrath.

It is no accident that one of the distinctive traits of the righteous is being "God-fearing." The fear of God, of his just punishment, is a virtue that dwells in the soul of the humble. It follows all too clearly that God is much more than just "love." Thinking that God, because he is infinitely merciful, cannot produce evil (that is, suffering) is to lose sight of a fundamental aspect of his character. The fact that God is slow to anger, is forgiving and merciful,[18] that is, is always waiting, until the last moment, a glimmer of repentance by the wicked to desist from his punitive intentions and run to the prodigal son after forgetting in an instant all the sins he has done, does not mean that he cannot, in the face of insolent and unrepentant sin, act accordingly, inflicting a just and terrible punishment. Let us take a look at the words contained in the book of Amos, "Can a bird fall in a snare upon the earth, where no gin is for him? shall one take up a snare from the earth, and have taken nothing at all? Shall a trumpet be blown in the city, and the people not be afraid? shall there be evil in a city, and the Lord hath not done it?" (Amos 3:5–6).

The Lord is in control of history. And if this is true, he is also in control of the physical evil that befalls humanity. If we do not keep these simple, yet fundamental concepts in mind, we will never be able to fully understand the profound meaning of the words of the Lord's Prayer.

Before concluding this long digression on the character of divine justice, we would like to introduce one last concept, a small piece of the big puzzle, but necessary for the complete understanding of the puzzle itself. If the evil inflicted on the wicked by God is somehow "digestible," as far as it represents the just punishment for the abominations committed by them, what do we make of the evil, the calamities that afflict the innocent? What sense do they have? And do they also come from God? These are very delicate questions, which it will be good to approach slowly. To introduce the discussion, let us start with a handful of examples.

We have already seen how, in Exodus chapter 12, the last calamity God inflicts on Pharaoh is also the most terrible: the death of all the firstborn in the land of Egypt, including Pharaoh's own little son: "And Pharaoh rose up in the night, he, and all his servants, and all the Egyptians; and there was a great cry in Egypt; for there was not a house where there was not one dead" (Exod 12:30). If, from the point of view of Pharaoh, who had disobeyed the Lord's orders ten times, such a chastisement can also be considered proportionate to his *hýbris*, what about all those poor little boys cut down at an early age, in what can be considered a real "slaughter of the innocents"? What

---

18. See Num 14:18; Ps 103(102):8; Joel 2:13; Nah 1:3; Sir 2:11.

about the torment of mothers and fathers, who had nothing to do with the *hýbris* of Pharaoh? What fault could they have?

Let us try to analyze some passages of Scripture that may guide us in the correct direction. For example, in Psalm 26(25) the psalmist pleads with the Lord as follows: "Gather not my soul with sinners, nor my life with bloody men" (Ps 26(25):9). If such a request is formally submitted to the Lord in a psalm, it means that this possibility exists. That is, the possibility that divine punishment, caused by the abominations of the wicked, will mow down in its fury even the righteous, the innocent.

Do you remember the passage in the book of Ezekiel in which God is angry with the people of Israel and does not allow them to come and question him through the prophet? Well, at this point it is worth reading the conclusion of that chapter, because it will offer us multiple points of reflection.

> Son of man, when the land sinneth against me by trespassing grievously, then will I stretch out mine hand upon it, and will break the staff of the bread thereof, and will send famine upon it, and will cut off man and beast from it: Though these three men, Noah, Daniel, and Job, were in it, they should deliver but their own souls by their righteousness, saith the Lord God. If I cause noisome beasts to pass through the land, and they spoil it, so that it be desolate, that no man may pass through because of the beasts: Though these three men were in it, as I live, saith the Lord God, they shall deliver neither sons nor daughters; they only shall be delivered, but the land shall be desolate. Or if I bring a sword upon that land, and say, Sword, go through the land; so that I cut off man and beast from it: Though these three men were in it, as I live, saith the Lord God, they shall deliver neither sons nor daughters, but they only shall be delivered themselves. Or if I send a pestilence into that land, and pour out my fury upon it in blood, to cut off from it man and beast: Though Noah, Daniel, and Job were in it, as I live, saith the Lord God, they shall deliver neither son nor daughter; they shall but deliver their own souls by their righteousness. For thus saith the Lord God; How much more when I send my four sore judgments upon Jerusalem, the sword, and the famine, and the noisome beast, and the pestilence, to cut off from it man and beast? Yet, behold, therein shall be left a remnant that shall be brought forth, both sons and daughters: behold, they shall come forth unto you, and ye shall see their way and their doings: and ye shall be comforted concerning the evil that I have brought upon Jerusalem, even concerning all that I have brought upon it. And they shall comfort you, when ye see their ways and their doings: and ye shall know that I have not done without cause all that I have done in it, saith the Lord God. (Ezek 14:13-23)

Four times God repeats the same concept. If people sin against him, he will inflict on them the worst calamities, and even if there were among them the three most pious men on earth (Noah, Daniel, and Job), this would not help. All of them would be the object of the divine punishment, except those three, by virtue of their justice. He repeats this four times to reiterate his full conviction in his own words. And if anyone should still have doubts as to whether this chastisement might be too harsh or in some way "unjust," God will provide them with irrefutable proof. After four terrible calamities sent upon Jerusalem, there will be a small group of survivors whom God will spare, not so much because they are not sinners, but rather because they will bear witness to the justice of the divine chastisement. For when the other nations see their behavior and realize the abominations committed by that handful of survivors, they will realize how God did what he did for a just cause.[19]

This is a key point. God does not create evil with no reason (he would be a sadistic God), but if he does, he always does it for a good reason. Our question, however, remains intact: what about the destruction of the innocent? Is it possible that God can tolerate exterminating the wicked along with the righteous, without making too many distinctions?

If we read this other passage from the book of Ezekiel, it would seem so: "Son of man, set thy face toward Jerusalem, and drop thy word toward the holy places, and prophesy against the land of Israel, And say to the land of Israel, Thus saith the Lord; Behold, I am against thee, and will draw forth my sword out of his sheath, and will cut off from thee the righteous and the wicked. Seeing then that I will cut off from thee the righteous and the wicked, therefore shall my sword go forth out of his sheath against all flesh from the south to the north" (Ezek 21:2–4). St. Paul's words come to mind, terrifyingly: "It is a fearful thing to fall into the hands of the living God" (Heb 10:31).

Let us conclude this chapter with Abraham's plea to God: "That be far from thee to do after this manner, to slay the righteous with the wicked: and that the righteous should be as the wicked, that be far from thee: Shall not the Judge of all the earth do right?" (Gen 18:25).

---

19. The Hebrew term used in this passage is the adverb *hinnām* (חִנָּם), indicating an action done without reason.

# 13

# God and the Necessary Evil: the Examples of Noah and Lot

In this chapter, we will look at two iconic examples of evil that came from God.

We begin with the quintessential punishment: the Universal Flood. The story, one of the most fascinating told in the Bible, occupies chapters 6, 7, and 8 of the book of Genesis. The part that interests us most is the initial one, in which God explains the reasons for his decision. In verse 5 of chapter 6, God notes that "the wickedness of man was great in the earth, and that every imagination [*yētsĕr*] of the thoughts of his heart was only evil continually" (Gen 6:5).

The generic concepts of evil and wickedness are rendered by the term *ră'*, while the "imagination" conceived by the hearts of people is rendered by the term *yētsĕr*, the semantic poignancy of which we have already discussed at length. The Hebrew expression literally reads, "every *yētsĕr* of the thoughts of his heart." That is, the form, the structure of the thoughts of the prediluvian people was perverse ("only evil continually"). God sees that there is no remedy for humanity, which has irreparably deviated from his way. So irreparably that, in the following verse, the Lord feels sorrow, almost a sort of repentance, for having created humankind. The Hebrew verb used is *nāhăm* (נָחַם), which indicates the act of deeply inhaling a sigh of sorrow, of disappointment. The decision at this point is unequivocal and irrevocable. Every living thing on the earth will be annihilated. This represents, in the eyes of God, the just punishment—proportionate to the gravity of human conduct. The free will, granted to people by God, has somehow turned against him. The humanity he had created has literally slipped out of his hands. And for this reason, God feels an immense pain for the betrayal that, in the name of free will, people have committed against him. A perverse, irredeemable humanity. The only solution is the annihilation of humanity itself and the creation of a "new humanity," with a real *palingenesis* within Genesis.

Only one person (one in all of humanity!) is in the eyes of God worthy of being spared from punishment: "But Noah found grace in the eyes of the Lord" (Gen 6:8).

These words cannot fail to recall the announcement of the angel Gabriel to Mary: "Fear not, Mary: for thou hast found favour with God" (Luke 1:30). Acquiring divine favor is something that *precedes* any human merits, and it is above all a grace that God grants (and that he would not necessarily be obliged to grant). The grace, which coincides with divine favor, is what in Greek is indicated by the term *cháris* (χάρις). In Hebrew, the connection between Noah and the grace received from God is even more direct, up to a phonetic coincidence. The term used, *hěn* (חֵן) is composed of the two letters *h* (ח) and *n* (נ), which inverted make up precisely the name *Nōăh* (נֹחַ).[1] Noah is the mirror of divine grace.

Only after declaring that Noah found grace in the eyes of the Lord does the text begin to narrate his story, defining Noah as a "just man and perfect in his generations, and Noah walked with God" (Gen 6:9). He walked on the right path following the divine dictates. Not necessarily a saint immune to sin. Simply a person of integrity who, with all the limitations of his human condition, tried with all his might to be pleasing to the Lord. A person, however, who was completely different from the rest of humanity: "The earth also was corrupt before God, and the earth was filled with violence" (Gen 6:11). God announces to Noah that he will bring the Flood[2] on the face of the earth and annihilate every living thing that is not saved in the ark. God announces to Noah that the plan he has prepared for him is that he will bring to safety on the ark (in addition to all the couples of all species of animals) also his wife, and his three sons[3] with their corresponding wives. It is not known whether these seven people (wife, three sons, and three daughters-in-law) had also found grace in the eyes of God. In any case, the practical result is that the grace obtained by Noah somehow acted as a protective shield for them as well. In God's plan, these people were the necessary instruments for the palingenesis, for the creation of a new humanity. If God had saved only Noah, obviously no descendants would have resulted.

We see here one of the distinctive features of God's way of working. The plan that God has for humanity—his will—precedes and is a step above the human understanding of justice. Probably, Noah's wife, sons, and daughters-in-law had not acquired any particular merits before God,[4] but, fortunately for them, they found themselves in the favorable conditions of being necessary to God's plan. The will of God is just by

---

1. Vowels are not part of the Hebrew alphabet. They were introduced later to indicate correct vocalization.

2. Interestingly, the Hebrew term used to indicate God's action in inflicting the Universal Flood is the *hiphil* form of the verb *bô'*, which we have discussed at length in previous chapters. God is the author and prime mover of the Flood. God does not let the flood happen but brings it on and hurls it with nefarious power upon all living creatures.

3. Shem, Ham, and Japheth.

4. Indeed, the Bible repeats that all humankind, except for Noah, was corrupt.

definition, regardless of whether it appears so to human sensibility. Even better: the justice of God coincides with the implementation of his will.

The continuation of the story of Noah is known to all. At the end of the flood, when the waters have receded from the earth, the first thing Noah does is to build an altar to offer holocausts of thanksgiving to the Lord. God is pleased with it and "smelled a sweet savour" (Gen 8:21). As from the "nostrils" of God came out a sigh of sorrow for the perversion in which the prediluvian humanity had fallen, now into the same "nostrils" enters the aroma of the burnt offering of Noah—the sweet scent of gratitude for the grace received from God. God is so pleased with Noah's work that he promises never again to inflict such a devastating punishment on the earth, because—as God himself explains in a gesture of compassion and mercy with respect to human frailty—after all it is true that "the imagination [$y\bar{e}ts\breve{e}r$] of man's heart is evil from his youth" (Gen 8:21). The Hebrew term used to refer to the "imagination" of the heart is always the $y\bar{e}ts\breve{e}r$ we have encountered repeatedly.[5]

One final consideration. If on the one hand, Noah's wife, sons, and daughters-in-law were saved from the greatest punishment inflicted by God on humankind in the history of humankind without having acquired any particular merits in the eyes of God (at least the Bible does not mention any) but simply because they were useful tools for the realization of the divine plan (we could say that they were in the right place at the right time), on the other hand it is difficult to think that every single living being outside of Noah was constantly and irremediably depraved in thoughts, words, and deeds. Even if this were true of every sentient being with reasoning sufficiently developed to discern good from evil, what about all the children and infants? What about the elderly and the sick who were not of sound mind? Were they depraved, too? It makes no sense to think so. Nevertheless, they were all crushed by the tremendous divine chastisement. The same fate struck the firstborn of Egypt, slaughtered by the Lord to punish Pharaoh. They too found themselves, without any fault, in the wrong place at the wrong time. Unfair? Probably so, from a human point of view. But not from the divine point of view. The will of God was to rebuild humanity from scratch. To remake everything. And as such, as implemented divine will, the rebuilding of humanity is just—by definition. Any side effects are irrelevant. Paraphrasing St. Paul, who would dare to argue with a potter who has decided to destroy and throw away the vase he has just made because it is not to his liking? Is not the potter free to make and remake his pot multiple times until it is to his liking?[6]

---

5. There is no contradiction between this passage in Gen 8:21 and the almost similar passage found in Gen 6:5. The fact that the instinct, the $y\bar{e}ts\breve{e}r$ of the heart, is in general inclined to evil does not justify the fact that every single $y\bar{e}ts\breve{e}r$ of the thoughts of the heart, that is, every single choice made by a person, must be evil. God sends the flood not because human instinct is inclined to sin (this is the miserable condition to which humanity is condemned because of original sin), but because prediluvian humanity, although endowed with free will and cognitive abilities to distinguish good from evil, had stubbornly and unilaterally chosen the path of sin.

6. "O house of Israel, cannot I do with you as this potter? saith the Lord. Behold, as the clay is in

A little later, in chapter 18 of Genesis, another story of sin and terrible punishment is told, that of Sodom and Gomorrah, two cities that have become emblematic of the moral depravity people can reach. The outcry against the sins committed in those cities is so great that it reaches the heavens (Gen 18:20–21). God decides to send two angels to verify in person and bring his punishment. It is at this point that Abraham, sensing the Lord's intentions, utters that invocation we saw at the end of the previous chapter, "Wilt thou also destroy the righteous with the wicked?" (Gen 18:23). Abraham, as the defense attorney of those innocents who dwell in Sodom and Gomorrah and who would be unjustly punished, tries in every way to convince the Lord to spare them. The request is not entirely disinterested, since his nephew Lot, son of his brother Haran and with whom he had shared the journey to the Promised Land for years, had made Sodom his home. A sort of bargaining between God and Abraham begins. And as it is done in all bargaining, Abraham begins by raising the asking price, knowing already that in the end he will have to agree on a lower one: "Peradventure there be fifty righteous within the city: wilt thou also destroy and not spare the place for the fifty righteous that are therein?" (Gen 18:24).

Here Abraham is gambling. He is well aware that it is virtually impossible to find fifty righteous people in the cities of Sodom and Gomorrah, but nevertheless he presses the Lord to see if, in the face of this high number, he will budge and agree to spare both cities. God plays along and answers, "If I find in Sodom fifty righteous within the city, then I will spare all the place for their sakes" (Gen 18:26). Abraham, cornered and knowing that he would never be able to find fifty, lowers the price slightly: "Peradventure there shall lack five of the fifty righteous: wilt thou destroy all the city for lack of five?" (Gen 18:28).

God accepts this request as well and confirms that even if only forty-five were found, he would spare the cities. In a game of chance, the same scene is repeated identically four more times, with Abraham backing down, first offering forty, then thirty, then twenty, and finally ten. When God accepts even this last proposal, Abraham does not dare to ask for more, desists, and returns to his home (Gen 18:33). At this point, the fate of the two cities is sealed, and here ends chapter 18 of Genesis.

It is worth noting how perfectly Abraham interprets the sensitivity of the human idea of justice. Destroying the wicked with the righteous would not be correct. If God is truly just, Abraham thinks (but so do we), he cannot allow the innocent, even if they are few, very few, to be punished together with the majority of the wicked. And God, condescending to this sensitivity shown by Abraham, one after another, acquiesces to all his requests, to the point of declaring that if at least ten righteous people can be found in Sodom, for their sake he will refrain from inflicting punishment. Unfortunately for the two cities, not ten, but not even five righteous people can be found. On the contrary, as in the case of the Universal Flood, only one person in the whole city of Sodom, enjoys the divine favor. And this person is Lot, Abraham's nephew.

the potter's hand, so are ye in mine hand, O house of Israel" (Jer 18:6).

It is necessary to emphasize how God's compassionate disposition toward those few righteous people who might dwell in Sodom emerges only as a result of Abraham's somewhat clumsy but insistent prayer. We see here a glimmer of what we will deepen later, that is, the value and power of insistent prayer, which in some way is able to arouse and induce a movement of divine mercy—mercy that is not due *a priori* but given by God in his infinite goodness as an unconditional gift to mortals. And just as the potter is not obliged to explain to his vase why he made it in one way or another, or why he wants to destroy it in order to make it anew if he so desires, in the same way God can make it so that people must demonstrate the necessary humility to explicitly ask for a grace, before he can grant it. As if he were only waiting for this very movement of a person toward himself to move toward him to his rescue.

Once again: grace, by definition, does not spring from human merits, but rather from the divine mercy that allows itself to be moved by the humility of the human soul, that is, by sincere prayer. Otherwise, as St. Paul says, grace would no longer be grace. The idea that a person, just by appearing righteous in God's eyes, should automatically enjoy the luxury of escaping any danger, any calamity, any evil, is pure illusion. As we have seen, God's plan, that is, God's will, precedes the particular needs of the individual.[7] Human beings, aware of this truth, have only one way to hope to navigate unscathed through "this valley of tears": praying—praying insistently that God grant them the grace to be spared from the evil of the world. Evil which, incidentally, as we have seen, may come from God himself, when he decides that humanity needs it in accordance with his plan.

Necessary evil, we could call it. Necessary for the fulfillment of his plan.

The annihilation of all humanity on the face of the earth in the days of the Universal Flood is an atrocious, immense, unrepeatable evil, but at the same time *necessary*. Necessary for the unraveling of the history of divine Providence. The same can be said for the punishment that is about to sweep away Sodom and Gomorrah. And in the face of the immensity of the divine plan, ranging from the beginning to the end of time, people, with their transitory needs, appear small, as invisible, infinitesimal specks of dust[8] in the immense gears of history, unrolled by the wise hand of God.

In the next chapter of Genesis, the narrative takes up the story of the two angels sent by the Lord, who arrive in Sodom at the break of night and meet Lot at the city gate. Lot, recognizing them, prostrates himself before them and invites them to spend the night in his house. Late at night, the shamelessness of the inhabitants of Sodom explodes. Both young and old, intrigued by the presence of the two foreign angels in the city, come knocking on Lot's door asking him to let them out so they can "meet" them.

---

7. If God, before acting in the world, were to consider all the special needs of all righteous people on the face of the earth, his action would be virtually paralyzed.

8. See Gen 18:27: "And Abraham answered and said, Behold now, I have taken upon me to speak unto the Lord, which am but dust and ashes."

Lot, sensing their bad intentions,[9] threatened, surrounded, frightened, and clearly in a state of confusion, in order not to break the laws of hospitality and leave his two guests in the hands of the depraved population of Sodom, offers them a desperate and horrible solution. In exchange for the guests, he offers them his two virgin daughters so that they may do whatever they want with them. The crowd, however, does not accept the indecent proposal, gets even more angry, tries to force the door, but at that point the angels of the Lord intervene and hit them with a blinding glare making them flee.

From now on, the angels of the Lord become the main characters of the plot. They are those who have been materially invested by the Lord with the burden of making sure that his will is done. And the divine will is to annihilate the city of Sodom, but at the same time, going along with Abraham's prayer, to save the only righteous person in the city, that is, Lot together with his family. The angels reveal to Lot that they have been sent by the Lord to destroy the city, that the punishment will fall the next morning, and that in the meantime Lot must warn his wife, his two daughters and their respective future husbands to prepare to flee. Lot hurries to warn his sons-in-law, but they do not take him seriously. At the break of dawn, the angels chase Lot and urge him to take his wife and daughters with him and to get away immediately from the city that is about to be destroyed. It is very interesting to see Lot's reaction, his doubts about the truthfulness of the angels' words, his uncertainty for the future that is to come, his indecision in abandoning his home and the places he loves most to follow what seems to be the divine will: "And while he lingered, the men laid hold upon his hand, and upon the hand of his wife, and upon the hand of his two daughters, by the Lord's great mercy upon him[10]: and they brought him forth, and set him without the city" (Gen 19:16).

This verse is a concentration of mixed emotions and profound concepts. The Hebrew verb used to describe Lot's reluctance is *māhăh* (מָהַהּ), which indicates a denial, a rejection. This verb represents a denominative form of the interrogative adverb *mâ* (מָה), which can introduce questions such as why, how, what, and so forth. The verb implicitly contains all the questions that Lot must have asked the angels, which are not reported in the Bible, but which we can easily imagine: "Why should I leave?" or "How will I live far from my city, my goods, and my property?" or "What will the future hold for me?" Lot, with all his fragility, represents the emblem of human hesitancy when faced with the hard, drastic choice of following God's will by entering territories never explored before, abandoning all the affections and all the material things and blindly entrusting to God's Providence. Lot hesitates, asks questions, asks for explanations, does not understand, sketches a refusal. At that point, something miraculous happens. Although Lot does not seem convinced to follow the divine will, the two angels take him and his family by the hand and literally drag them out of the house, despite their resistance. And this, the Bible says, happens by a great act of divine mercy. We

---

9. The idea of "knowing" implies a perverse sexual interest.
10. The KJV has "the Lord being merciful unto him."

see here the divine grace in action. Lot is a righteous man, but not a sinless saint. He is a man who clearly stands out from the perverted masses that populate Sodom but with all his limitations and frailties (see the indecent proposal to barter guests with the virginity of his two daughters). He is a man who doubts the Lord's will until the very last moment. And yet.

And yet, by a unilateral and unconditional motion on the part of the Lord, Lot receives the blessing, the grace of being saved. Saved from the destruction that is about to befall the cities. The term used to refer to divine mercy is *hĕmlâ* (חֶמְלָה), a noun that appears only twice within the Bible and translates the idea of great compassion and pity. The angels have been tasked with carrying out the divine will, and because of this, whether Lot wants it or not, Lot and his family will have to get to safety. The angels tell Lot to run away and not to stop in the valley but to continue toward the mountains. Again, Lot doubts and explains, addressing God directly, that he does not believe he will be able to escape to the mountain in time. At the same time, however, he finally recognizes that he has been the object of God's saving grace: "Behold now, thy servant hath found grace in thy sight, and thou hast magnified thy mercy, which thou hast shewed unto me in saving my life" (Gen 19:19).

These words are closely reminiscent of Gen 6:8: "But Noah found grace in the eyes of the Lord." Divine mercy is so great that, even in the face of the last doubt, the Lord, condescending, allows Lot to escape not to the mountains but to a small nearby town, which will thus be spared the punishment.[11] We have here in an embryonic state another example of the power of prayer, which seems able to change the divine plan. This is a fundamental concept that we will explore later.

When Lot reaches Zoar, God rains down sulfur and fire from heaven on Sodom and Gomorrah, destroying the whole valley with all the inhabitants of the cities and the vegetation of the ground (Gen 19:24–25). The following verse is of an absolute brevity and strangeness: "But his wife looked back from behind him, and she became a pillar of salt" (Gen 19:26).

Let us leave this verse here for now and move on. The narrative continues as if nothing had happened and describes Abraham contemplating from above the devastation produced by the Lord's punishment. Abraham sees smoke rising from the earth, like smoke from a furnace. The valley of Sodom and Gomorrah is physically and symbolically transformed into the fire of eternal punishment—hell. The conclusion in verse 29 makes clear the connection between Abraham's prayer in chapter 18 and Lot's fate: "And it came to pass, when God destroyed the cities of the plain, that God remembered Abraham, and sent Lot out of the midst of the overthrow, when he overthrew the cities in the which Lot dwelt" (Gen 19:29). Lot was saved not because of

---

11. The city, which will henceforth be called Zoar (צֹעַר), that is, "Insignificant," was part of that group of five cities, including Sodom and Gomorrah, which were to come under divine chastisement. The request, so minimal that Lot called it "insignificant," to spare that city so that he could dwell there, is accepted by God and will name the city itself.

any personal merit, but because of the intercession of Abraham's insistent prayer that aroused divine mercy.

And his wife? As we have seen, a very strange and nefarious fate befalls her. She is transformed by the Lord into a pillar of salt for the mere fact that she has looked back. Let us try to understand. Why does God so quickly and violently withdraw the mercy granted her in making her flee the city? From the Old Testament text, so abrupt and bare, it is difficult to come to a precise conclusion. It will take Jesus himself to explain this passage. He does so in chapter 17 of Luke's Gospel: "Even thus shall it be in the day when the Son of Man is revealed. In that day, he which shall be upon the housetop, and his stuff in the house, let him not come down to take it away: and he that is in the field, let him likewise not return back. Remember Lot's wife. Whosoever shall seek to save his life shall lose it; and whosoever shall lose his life shall preserve it" (Luke 17:30–33).

Jesus is revealing the allegorical interpretation of Scripture. The punishment of Sodom and Gomorrah is not only one of the most interesting stories in the Bible, but, on a higher level, also the symbol of the Universal Judgment that will take place "in the day when the Son of Man is revealed." If this is true, Lot's story then becomes the symbol of salvation from eternal condemnation—from hell, which God, in his infinite mercy, grants to those who are blessed by his grace. Lot's wife, on the other hand, becomes the symbol of those who do not know how to renounce their own stubborn will to submit instead to the divine will. For these, there is no escape, there is no salvation. That "turning back" testifies to the fact that, just as God is leading her to safety, Lot's wife does not have faith in the Lord's will. She wants to see if somehow it is possible to save what can be saved, if there is still a chance to go back to her beloved city. Lot's wife becomes the symbol of those who think they can save themselves with their own hands, who doubt the saving grace of the Lord, and in that doubt reject it, lose it, and condemn themselves ("Whosoever shall seek to save his life shall lose it"). Lot, on the contrary, with all his limitations and hesitations, finally manages to recognize that he has been "pardoned" by the Lord and thus submits to his will, leaving everything behind, recognizing that it is only he who can save and thus conquering salvation ("whosoever shall lose his life shall preserve it"). "Remember Lot's wife," Jesus admonishes his disciples.

And it is no coincidence that in the same passage of Luke's Gospel, where Jesus prophesies the End Times, the other example Christ proposes to his disciples concerns Noah himself: "And as it was in the days of Noe, so shall it be also in the days of the Son of man. They did eat, they drank, they married wives, they were given in marriage, until the day that Noah entered into the ark, and the flood came, and destroyed them all. Likewise also as it was in the days of Lot; they did eat, they drank, they bought, they sold, they planted, they builded; But the same day that Lot went out of Sodom it rained fire and brimstone from heaven, and destroyed them all" (Luke 17:26–29).

Those of Noah and Lot are two portentous stories of the Old Testament, linked by a thin red thread. They are the two stories of damnation and redemption par excellence, allegorical of the Last Judgment, where the wicked will be separated from the righteous[12] and condemned to eternal fire—the necessary evil par excellence. Necessary for the fulfillment of divine justice.

And Lot's daughters? Those who know the story know how it ends (not better than how it had begun). Lot, after having fled to Zoar, continues his way and takes refuge in a cave together with them. The daughters, still virgins, not finding anyone in those lands with whom to lie down, decide to get their father drunk and have incestuous relations with him. From the eldest daughter will be born Moab, from which will descend the lineage of the Moabites. From the younger daughter will be born Ben-Ammi, from which will descend the lineage of the Ammonites. Leaving aside any comment on the moral depravity of such behavior, what we want to emphasize is that we have here confirmation of the fact that Lot's daughters were not saved from punishment for any personal merit. On the contrary. Their behavior and their depraved instincts seem to be in total agreement with the rest of the population of Sodom. They were saved simply because they were in the right place at the right time (like Noah's family). They were most probably worthy of the divine punishment like all the others, but, fortunately for them, they were necessary to the fulfillment of the divine plan in history, in particular for the creation of the two descendants of the Moabites and Ammonites, peoples who will settle along the eastern shores of the Dead Sea and Jordan respectively, and who will be protagonists, as allies, of hard battles against the people of Israel.[13]

If Lot's daughters escaped punishment only because they were useful instruments in God's hands (once again, God's plan precedes and surpasses any human concept of justice), there is no lack of examples in which people, no worse than anyone else, and therefore not with particular demerits, instead meet with an unfortunate fate. They find themselves in the wrong place at the wrong time. And it is interesting that it is Jesus himself who highlights a couple of these episodes, in the Gospel of Luke at the beginning of chapter 13: "There were present at that season some that told him of the Galileans, whose blood Pilate had mingled with their sacrifices. And Jesus answering said unto them, Suppose ye that these Galileans were sinners above all the Galileans, because they suffered such things? I tell you, Nay: but, except ye repent, ye shall all likewise perish. Or those eighteen, upon whom the tower in Siloam fell, and slew them, think ye that they were sinners above all men that dwelt in Jerusalem? I tell you, Nay: but, except ye repent, ye shall all likewise perish" (Luke 13:1–5).

Both events are not reported by any historian, but they must have been well known to the people of the time if they are reported by Luke without further details.

---

12. See Luke 17:34–35: "I tell you, in that night there shall be two men in one bed; the one shall be taken, and the other shall be left. Two women shall be grinding together; the one shall be taken, and the other left."

13. They will both be defeated by King Saul and King David.

From what can be deduced and reconstructed, the first event refers to Pilate's bloody repression of some Galileans while they were offering sacrifices in the Temple.[14] The second event refers to the ruinous collapse of a tower in the city of Siloam, the modern Birket-Silwan. The construction of the tower was undoubtedly part of Pilate's plan to build an aqueduct, which he financed using part of the Temple's treasure. It is likely that the collapse of the tower with the consequent death of eighteen people was seen as a sort of divine punishment for Pilate's sacrilegious act. Both cases (the slaughter of Galileans and the death of the eighteen under the tower of Siloam) are interpreted in the same way by Jesus: those people were no more sinful than others. They were just in the wrong place at the wrong time, we might add. However, Jesus is not ruling out the possibility of divine retribution (he does not say so and therefore we do not know), but that's not the point. The point that Jesus is keen to emphasize is that, even if these episodes were part of a hypothetical divine chastisement for hypothetical human faults, those people who met with an unfortunate fate had no particular demerits and certainly were not "sinners above all men that dwelt in Jerusalem."

With these words, Jesus teaches us of the extreme fragility of human life, constantly subjected to the risk of being broken. Of the unhappy condition in which humanity finds itself, constantly threatened by the evil that pervades the world. With these words, Jesus seeks to overturn our perspective and to make us digest a bitter truth. A truth that emerges clearly from Scripture, but that perhaps it is convenient not to see. It is the same reversal of perspective as the person who looks up at the sky and sees the sun, so big and bright on the horizon, so dazzling that it seems close, that he can almost touch it. But if the same person could hypothetically fly over the surface of the sun and scan the horizon from there, and tried to see the earth, he would see nothing, an infinitesimal dot, faded and blurred, an invisible speck of dust in the immensity of the universe. And the truth is this: God's plan is as large as the vastness of the whole universe, while human life on earth is as ephemeral as the blink of an eye. Somehow insignificant, like that city, Zoar, which was to be destroyed by divine punishment along with Sodom and Gomorrah, but which by Lot's explicit request was spared. In God's eyes, the destruction or salvation of this small village probably appears irrelevant in the grand scheme of his plan.[15] For this, and for this alone, the Lord consents. God is ready to listen to human prayers only if this request is compatible with his plan.

The truth, which is hard to digest, is that throughout the Old Testament, God proves, continuously and explicitly, that he has minimal regard for people's earthly

---

14. These incidents of harsh repression by Roman authorities to maintain public order were quite common at that time. The followers of Judah the Galilean, claimant to the Jewish throne, who gathered in the Zealot sect, were responsible for at least a couple of revolts against the Roman empire in 6 and 7 AD.

15. As Pope benedict XVI explains, "The problem of theodicy is thus resolved. ( . . . ) Evil is necessarily bound up with finitude, and so, from the standpoint of the Infinite, is unreal. Suffering is the pain of limitation, and when it is taken up into the whole, it is abolished" (*In the Beginning*, 89–90).

life. Evil, suffering, death of the body are only accidents, endemic, implicit in the imperfect condition in which humanity has fallen because of the original sin. God nourishes sincere compassion and pity for this unfortunate condition, and for this reason he is ready at any time to run to meet the prayer of the humble, as long as it is functional and compatible with his Providence. In the unfortunate event that it is not, his plan—his will—enjoys unconditional precedence. Human suffering and pain sound like a background echo, faded and distant.

Instead, what counts in the eyes of the Lord, what really makes the difference, is eternal life (or damnation) after earthly life. This is his greatest concern: to save as many souls as possible from the flames of hell. It does not matter if on earth—an imperfect reality by definition—there can be nothing but imperfect justice. The true justice, the divine one, the perfect one, will be made explicit at the moment of earthly death (on a personal level), and then at the moment of the Last Judgement (on a universal level). And so, the evil in which people may incur during their earthly life, besides being simply necessary for the realization of the divine plan, can be at the same time an instrument of trial with which the Lord tempers his chosen ones, to ensure that they are worthy of his favor and, finally, of eternal life. And (surprise!) God, for this kind of evil, can avail himself of none other than the one who represents evil par excellence, that is, Satan—a useful instrument in God's hands.

Who knows better than Job?

# 14

# The Relationship between God and Satan: the Example of Job

"There was a man in the land of Uz, whose name was Job; and that man was perfect and upright, and one that feared God, and eschewed evil" (Job 1:1).

So begins the most inconvenient, most problematic, most fascinating, most painful, and most dramatic book of the entire Old Testament. A unique book, independent of all others, in nature, structure, style, and content—the book of Job. It is written in the form of dialogues within a prose framework. Dialogues that could easily be part of a theatrical drama, through which a truth that is difficult to accept, obscure and incomprehensible at first, but in the end clear and dazzling in its simplicity, unfolds with much effort. It is somehow reminiscent of the style of Platonic dialogues and maintains the strength of the Socratic *ars maieutica*. A book viscerally loved by Kierkegaard, which puts its finger on one of the most painful wounds for the human intellect: the problem of evil. All those questions, so dramatically topical, on why evil, pain, disease exist, and above all on why God causes or, at best, accepts all this, are already contained in the book of Job. These are all questions and issues usually employed to refute the existence of God, which are not only not avoided here, but addressed and even proposed as a legitimate point of view within the Bible, that is, the sacred text that purports to contain the revealed word of God. This is why the story of Job is so disruptive, so powerful—because it resonates powerfully in the human soul of any time and place.

Job was the most powerful man in the East and had everything a person could desire: seven sons and three daughters, a large household, and thousands of head of cattle. He was also morally blameless. He feared God and conscientiously avoided evil. He was so God-fearing that when his sons went out to gobble, he offered holocausts as a sacrifice to the Lord in reparation for their sins (Job 1:5). One day, as God's angels stand before him, including Satan, a very peculiar exchange of banter begins between the two. God asks Satan if in his raids on earth he has noticed his servant Job, perfect in every action and thought. Satan, with his distinctive perverse acumen, points out that, most likely, Job is God-fearing, not so much out of a pure disposition of mind as out of mere personal gain. He may fear losing all his wealth. "Why don't you try touching some of his possessions?" suggests Satan in one of his typical indecent proposals. God considers Satan's suggestion worthy of merit and replies, "Behold, all that he hath is in thy power; only upon himself put not forth thine hand" (Job 1:12). God gives Satan the mandate to attack and destroy Job's possessions, but within very precise limits. Satan will not have the power to extend his destructive hand over Job himself.

In deeming worthy of merit the test to which Satan proposes to subject Job in order to test his true moral worth, God is not abdicating his sovereignty nor is he letting Satan rage on Job without intervening. On the contrary. The decision that Job should undergo the most painful trials is God's (and it could be no one else's).[1] The fact that the inspirer of the trial is Satan does not change the context one iota.[2] Or will we have the audacity to claim that God is a mere puppet that Satan manipulates at his will? The opposite is true. It is Satan, that is, the personification of evil, who is an instrument (one of many) that God can decide to use so that his will be done. And the will of God in this case is that Job should suffer—suffer the unspeakable—until he cannot bear it anymore. Hiding behind a finger, trying to explain that the evil that Job will have to suffer does not come from God, but from Satan, and that God only (only!) allows it, would be like claiming that the crucifixion of Jesus is not Pilate's responsibility, but that of the Roman soldiers who materially nailed him to the cross. If God had not wanted Job to suffer, he could have simply dismissed Satan's insinuation by shutting him up and putting him in his place. Instead, the fact that God follows up Satan's proposal shows that, at that moment, that was his will.

It is important to emphasize these concepts, because too often this precise passage of the Bible has been taken as an example to try to explain in a permissive sense the relationship between God and evil. It is said: evil *seems* to be coming from God, but it actually comes from Satan, to whom God gives permission to harm us. And this passage would demonstrate that. Unfortunately for this argument, this passage instead demonstrates just the opposite. Let us carefully read the dynamics of the dialogue between God and Satan.

> And the Lord said unto Satan, Whence comest thou? Then Satan answered the Lord, and said, From going to and fro in the earth, and from walking up and down in it. And the Lord said unto Satan, Hast thou considered my servant Job, that there is none like him in the earth, a perfect and an upright man, one that feareth God, and escheweth evil? Then Satan answered the Lord, and said,

---

1. Exactly like the fact that the decision for Jesus to be executed is Pilate's and no one else's.
2. Exactly like the fact that the instigators of Jesus' crucifixion were the high priests.

> Doth Job fear God for nought? Hast not thou made an hedge about him, and about his house, and about all that he hath on every side? thou hast blessed the work of his hands, and his substance is increased in the land. But put forth thine hand now, and touch all that he hath, and he will curse thee to thy face. And the Lord said unto Satan, Behold, all that he hath is in thy power; only upon himself put not forth thine hand. So Satan went forth from the presence of the Lord. (Job 1:7–12)

The first fact that jumps out at us is that—contrary to widespread belief—it is not Satan who calls Job's name to the Lord, but rather the opposite. It is God who introduces Job into the conversation, asking Satan for his opinion.

At this point Satan takes the ball, slips into it, and transforms, as only he knows how, doubt into insinuation, and insinuation into concrete possibility. The argument used is subtle. Job would follow the divine dictates only out of convenience, so as not to lose the Lord's protection and blessing. But what if God decided to touch Job's possessions? Would he still be so pious and devout? "But put forth thine hand now, and touch all that he hath, and he will curse thee to thy face," Satan urges (Job 1:11).

The second fact that jumps out at us is that—contrary to widespread belief—Satan does not ask God for permission to torment Job. Satan simply suggests that God take away Job's possessions to see his reaction. Satan is clear about the boundaries within which he can operate. He does not say, "Allow me to put forth my hand," but rather, "put forth thy hand." Satan himself is implicitly admitting that the only one who has the power to give or take away people's wealth is not him, but God. It is only then that God, considering the suggestion to be meritorious, mandates Satan to inflict the painful trial on Job. It is worth noticing that it was by no means a foregone conclusion that God would give Satan the assignment. Nor does Satan specifically request it. In various other Old Testament passages,[3] God inflicts death and calamity through the Destroying Angel, for example. The same angel that put to death all the firstborn of Egypt. The power relationships are clear. Satan could never harm Job if God did not want him to

The third fact that stands out is that—contrary to widespread belief—it is God who places in Satan's hands the power to dispose of Job's possessions (it is not Satan who takes them). And it is still God who sets a clear condition: Job must not be afflicted in his body. A condition that Satan will slavishly respect. Again, the fact that the suggestion comes from Satan is irrelevant. The moment God makes Satan's suggestion his own, this suggestion becomes an integral part of his will.

This interpretation, which is in our opinion the most intellectually honest (although not the most convenient), is usually completely ignored and replaced by the more reassuring permissive view: God is giving Satan permission to test Job. This interpretation cannot be correct. God gives no permission to Satan, simply because

---

3. See 2 Sam 24:15–16; 1 Chr 21:15; 2 Kgs 19:35.

Satan, as seen, asks for no permission. Instead, God instructs Satan to attack Job's wealth. Exactly as Pilate gives orders to his soldiers to crucify Jesus.

Immediately after leaving, Satan begins to rage on Job, first destroying all his livestock and finally collapsing the house where Job's ten sons were eating and drinking, killing them all. Upon receiving the news, Job falls into despair, gets up, tears his clothes, shaves his head, but prostrating himself on the ground he still has the lucidity to keep faith in the Lord: "Naked came I out of my mother's womb, and naked shall I return thither: the Lord gave, and the Lord hath taken away; blessed be the name of the Lord" (Job 1:21).

Job passes the test, and here ends the first chapter. The second takes up the same scene described in the first. God is seated before the host of angels and Satan is also among them. The dialogue between the two is identical. God asks Satan where he is coming from. Satan responds that he has just returned from his raids on earth. God then does not miss the opportunity to bring up Job again: "Hast thou considered my servant Job, that there is none like him in the earth, a perfect and an upright man, one that feareth God, and escheweth evil? and still he holdeth fast his integrity, although thou movedst me against him, to destroy him without cause" (Job 2:3).

God is pleased with Job's integrity but at the same time complains that Satan has persuaded him to test him by causing him untold suffering, for no reason by the way, since Job remained firm in his faith. The Hebrew verb used is *sûth* (סות), which means "to persuade," "to instigate" somebody to do something, especially evil. It is the characteristic activity of the devil: to insinuate doubt in order to persuade to do evil. Satan does not back down. On the contrary, he raises an even greater insinuation: Job has kept the faith only because he has not been materially touched in the body. But would he still be so faithful if a serious illness fell upon him? God, without a moment's thought, considers Satan's objection worthy of merit and gives him a new mandate, even more terrible than the first one: "Behold, he is in thine hand; but save his life" (Job 2:6).

God gives Satan the power to rage on Job's body, with one *caveat*: Job must remain alive. Satan walks away and inflicts Job with a malignant stinging sore that will cover his skin from head to toe. Job, at this point, derelict and devastated, but still whole in his faith, is ridiculed even by his wife. How can he still trust God after all that has happened to him? Job answers with the patience and wisdom of a saint, "What? shall we receive good at the hand of God, and shall we not receive evil?" (Job 2:10).

Job seems to have survived this terrible ordeal unscathed. But in the meantime, three of his friends,[4] who have heard of the misfortunes that have befallen him, decide to visit him to console him. When they see him, so disfigured with grief, they begin to weep, to tear their clothes, to sprinkle their heads with dust, and they lie down beside him for seven days and seven nights without having the courage to speak to him.

---

4. Eliphaz the Temanite, Bildad the Shuhite, and Zophar the Naamathite.

When, after a long silence, Job opens his mouth, it becomes clear that something inside him has changed. The ascetic patience shown at first has vanished. Pain and despair have taken over and Job seems to have lost his faith completely. He curses the day he was born and declares that he would rather have died in his mother's womb (Job 3:11). Like a Romantic hero, he wonders, "Wherefore is light given to him that is in misery, and life unto the bitter in soul?" (Job 3:20).

In chapter 4, a tense, back-and-forth dialogue begins between Job and his three friends. Eliphaz the Temanite is the first to take the floor and, with a total lack of empathy, reminds Job that he has never seen any innocent perish and any righteous person be destroyed (Job 4:7). On the contrary, punishment is reserved for the wicked, who are annihilated by divine wrath. Almost as if to insinuate that Job must necessarily have committed something evil to have received such a punishment. Besides the damage, the mockery. Job should be grateful to God for having corrected him and should learn from his mistakes. Eliphaz speaks from the height of the cold ethical rationalism contained in the so-called "theory of earthly retribution," which has its roots in chapter 28 of Deuteronomy and chapter 26 of Leviticus. If people follow the divine dictates, God will reward them with every kind of blessing. On the contrary, if people turn away from God and lose themselves in sin, God will punish them with every kind of misfortune. It logically follows, according to Eliphaz's reasoning, that if Job was struck down by all these misfortunes, it is because he must have sinned against God. Eliphaz is likely recalling verses 31 to 35 of Deuteronomy chapter 28, which summarize examples of curses with which the Lord threatens the people of Israel:

> Thine ox shall be slain before thine eyes, and thou shalt not eat thereof: thine ass shall be violently taken away from before thy face, and shall not be restored to thee: thy sheep shall be given unto thine enemies, and thou shalt have none to rescue them. Thy sons and thy daughters shall be given unto another people, and thine eyes shall look, and fail with longing for them all the day long; and there shall be no might in thine hand. The fruit of thy land, and all thy labours, shall a nation which thou knowest not eat up; and thou shalt be only oppressed and crushed always: So that thou shalt be mad for the sight of thine eyes which thou shalt see. The Lord shall smite thee in the knees, and in the legs, with a sore botch that cannot be healed, from the sole of thy foot unto the top of thy head. (Deut 28:31–35)

It is no coincidence that when Satan wipes out Job's possessions, he begins by destroying his oxen and asses (Job 1:14–15) and then moves on to his flock of sheep (Job 1:16). He then rages against his sons and daughters (Job 1:18–19), ending by striking Job with a malignant plague that torments him from the soles of his feet to the top of his head (Job 2:7). The rigid and myopic theology of Eliphaz does not consider the fact that these verses of Deuteronomy are the words of the covenant that the Lord ordered Moses to establish with the Israelites (in the land of Moab). They represent a particular case of relationship that God decided to have with the people of Israel, in a well-determined period of history. An alliance, a pact, a sort of contract. The Israelites are warned that, if they break this covenant, they will be punished with those specific curses. But it's not a universal law. It does not always work that way, and the tragic reality of Job confirms that. On the contrary, the fact that the book of Job proposes exactly the kind of calamities that God had announced in Deuteronomy, but in a completely different context and caused by completely different reasons, seems to indicate the precise will of Scripture to show the groundlessness of the "theory of earthly retribution" as a universal principle.

Job, aware that he has now lost all reverential fear of God (Job 6:14), recognizes that his words are bold, but at the same time just and proportionate to the unjust suffering he is undergoing. After all, his life is a breath (Job 7:7), his days are a breath (Job 7:16). He just cannot understand why a God infinitely greater and more powerful than humans pays such maniacal attention to the actions of a poor mortal: "What is man, that thou shouldest magnify him? and that thou shouldest set thine heart upon him? And that thou shouldest examine him every morning, and try him every moment?" (Job 7:17–18).

The verb *pāqǎd* (פָּקַד) is used to indicate the scrutinizing action of God, who every morning reviews every single human being, while the idea of testing is rendered by the verb *bāḥǎn* (בָּחַן), which indicates the action of trying, testing, tempering, especially with reference to precious metals (gold and silver). Job here correctly perceives the sidereal distance between God and mortals, but he uses this distance, which in his eyes seems unbridgeable, to claim the right to be left alone. After all, even if Job had sinned, why would God, who is so superior, take it so hard? Why not simply forgive the sin and forget any wrongdoing committed? (Job 7:20–21).

These are all typical arguments of a person now devoid of faith. Job's reasoning, so firm and lucid at the beginning, has become confused, weakened by the psychophysical suffering to which he is subjected. In some way, he falls into the same error as Eliphaz: he assumes that acting in conformity with divine law automatically and necessarily must generate divine blessing and protection from all evil. Unfortunately for Job (and for all people in general) the postulate "I follow the divine dictates *ergo* God will grant me the grace to escape all evil" is vitiated by a fundamental error: thinking that divine grace springs from human merits. On the contrary, the opposite is true. Acting according to divine dictates springs from the grace granted to people by God to have a heart that knows how to understand and put into practice such dictates. People, with their free will, can certainly put in their own, but in the absence of such grace, it will be virtually impossible for them to continue on the right path. This is why the "theory of earthly retribution," that is, the idea that God rewards the earthly life of a pious person with every kind of blessing, clashes dramatically with the reality of life. Job is the most striking example.

At this point the second friend, Bildad the Shuhite, takes the floor. He too, like Eliphaz, following a strict theological rationalism, tries to explain how Job's complaints have no foundation. If Job's sons and daughters spent the day gobbling, divine punishment is what they deserved: "Doth God pervert judgment? or doth the Almighty pervert justice?" (Job 8:3). Bildad, believing that divine justice is resolved in "earthly retribution," is convinced that the death of Job's sons was due to their sins against God. Nothing could be more mistaken. We know that God, before the dialogue with Satan, had not thought in the least about punishing Job's sons and, even after Satan's intervention, orders their death not as a personal punishment, but as a test of faith for their father Job. Echoed at this point are the words that Jesus used for those who died under the rubble from the collapse of the tower at Siloam: "think ye that they were sinners above all men that dwelt in Jerusalem?" (Luke 13:4). The same words could be used for the sons of Job. It is true that they spent their time guzzling and enjoying their father's wealth, but "think ye that they were sinners above" anyone else? They were simply in the wrong place at the wrong time. Unlike Eliphaz however, Bildad also has wise words of hope for Job: "If thou wouldest seek unto God betimes, and make thy supplication to the Almighty; If thou wert pure and upright; surely now he would awake for thee, and make the habitation of thy righteousness prosperous. Though thy beginning was small, yet thy latter end should greatly increase" (Job 8:5–7).

Job kicks off a sorrowful and heartbreaking harangue. He contemplates divine omnipotence and is distressed that there is such a disparity between God and mortals. How can the mortal claim to be right when confronted with God? Even if the mortal were right, God would have the power and might on his side to do with the mortal what he wants. Even if God does unjust things, he has no one above him to account to and certainly cannot be called to judgment.[5] His rage does not subside and results in blatant blasphemy: "This is one thing, therefore I said it, He destroyeth the perfect and the wicked. If the scourge slay suddenly, he will laugh at the trial of the innocent" (Job 9:22–23).

This passage is reminiscent of the same arguments with which Abraham tried to convince God to spare Sodom and Gomorrah: "That be far from thee to do after this manner, to slay the righteous with the wicked" (Gen 18:25). Job does not understand why suddenly God has become an unfavorable judge (Job 10:2). Again, overwhelmed by despair and pain, he falls into the error of thinking that there must be justice in people's earthly retribution. If, on the other hand, even the righteous are treated like the wicked, what is the point of striving to be whole and follow the Lord's dictates?

At this point, at the height of Job's despair, who invokes upon himself the darkness and the shadow of death (Job 10:21), the third friend, Zophar the Naamathite, intervenes and, scandalized by the audacity of his words, without showing any pity,

---

5. Job's recriminations are exactly those of the clay pot which, seeing itself destroyed by the potter, does not understand the reasons and blames its maker. If thinking of a vase recriminating against its maker seems ridiculous, then Job's arguments must seem ridiculous in God's eyes.

violently attacks him. He tells him to his face that the misfortunes he has received are the result of divine chastisement. Not only that. He should seriously consider the fact that God always demands a little less than the fault committed (Job 11:6). As if to say, God could have punished him more! In the rigidity of his thought, Zophar considers how nothing can escape God, who knows about deceitful people and sees the iniquity in them (Job 11:11), and therefore concludes that God must have seen something really bad in Job's soul to have punished him in that way. But Zophar has an easy solution for Job: "If iniquity be in thine hand, put it far away, and let not wickedness dwell in thy tabernacles. For then shalt thou lift up thy face without spot; yea, thou shalt be stedfast, and shalt not fear" (Job 11:14–15).

Easy, isn't it? Job must stop sinning and everything will work out like magic. The coldness, the obtuseness, the total detachment from reality of this kind of arguments is exactly what Christ will come to flog in the scribes and Pharisees—the hypocrisy of a religion so frozen in the form and in the Law to be dead.[6] Job sends the criticism back to the sender, he beats up the hypocrisy of those who, from the height of their ease, consider the misfortunes of others as just divine punishment, and he has an easy time demonstrating the groundlessness of such conjectures. The reality of the facts proves the contrary: "The tabernacles of robbers prosper, and they that provoke God are secure; into whose hand God bringeth abundantly" (Job 12:6). And this reality is so obvious to those who want to see it, that Job ridicules his interlocutors. Even the animals know this and, if they could speak, would explain it to them: "Who knoweth not in all these that the hand of the Lord hath wrought this? In whose hand is the soul of every living thing, and the breath of all mankind" (Job 12:9–10).

This is one of the most important passages of Job's discourse. If the righteous suffer and the ungodly safely gobble in their golden abodes, it is because God wills it so. And how could it be otherwise? God is in control of everything, and so he is responsible for the evil that falls on the head of the righteous, as well as the secure riches in which the wicked bask. Undoubtedly, in his desperate search for God—a passionate, confused, and at times blasphemous search—Job gets much closer to the mystery of the world's evil than do his three friends. Job contemplates the boundless power of God (Job 12:13–25), recognizes it, accepts it (what else could he do?), but still does not fully comprehend it.

An *ante litteram* Romantic hero, Job says he is ready to challenge God in judgment, sure of his innocence (Job 13:18). But in the depths of his soul, he is still convinced that God is somehow punishing him for some sin he does not understand, or for sins committed in his youth (Job 13:26). Job, like his three interlocutors, is displaced by divine behavior, just as all people are displaced by the sudden evil that seize

---

6. See Matt 23:27–28: "Woe unto you, scribes and Pharisees, hypocrites! for ye are like unto whited sepulchres, which indeed appear beautiful outward, but are within full of dead men's bones, and of all uncleanness. Even so ye also outwardly appear righteous unto men, but within ye are full of hypocrisy and iniquity."

them. He is groping in the dark. The three friends remain firm in their convictions. Job is lost in doubt and desperately searching for a foothold to recover his lost faith. This is probably the same condition in which we would all find ourselves (commentators, scholars, theologians, philosophers, simple readers) if we were asked to explain the drama of Job without knowing the antecedent, that is, the prose framework that describes the dialogue that takes place behind the scenes between God and Satan. A dialogue that is obviously unknown to the protagonists but revealed in the book of Job as the key to a full understanding of the problem of evil in the world.

And then there's chapter 14—the chapter that reaches the highest lyrical heights. A passage that could easily be taken from Leopardi's *Canti*, with God taking the place of stepmotherly Nature. There is the infinite fragility of human beings in front of Creation. There is the desperation for the vanity of their life. There is the drama of death that like a shadow erases them forever. There is the self-pity for an unjust and inexplicable fate. There is the yearning for immortality. There is that sense of impotent rage in front of the impassibility of an inert Creator, insensitive to the cry of pain of his people. When Job declaims, "Man that is born of a woman is of few days and full of trouble. He cometh forth like a flower, and is cut down: he fleeth also as a shadow, and continueth not" (Job 14:1–2); or when he complains, "And surely the mountains falling cometh to nought, and the rock is removed out of his place. The waters wear the stones: thou washest away the things which grow out of the dust of the earth; and thou destroyest the hope of man" (Job 14:18–19); it is impossible not to think of Giacomo Leopardi's famous poem, *Wild Broom*,[7] the flower of the desert that blossoms on Mount Vesuvius just to be erased by the fury of the volcano.

Eliphaz does not retreat, he accuses Job of blasphemy (Job 15:4) and repeats the usual ritual discourse on the "earthly retribution" and on the phantom evils that would haunt the wicked throughout his life (Job 15:20–25). Job is fed up with these theoretical arguments and rebukes his interlocutor with the crude reality of the facts: "God hath delivered me to the ungodly, and turned me over into the hands of the wicked. I was at ease, but he hath broken me asunder: he hath also taken me by my neck, and shaken me to pieces, and set me up for his mark" (Job 16:11–12).

What Job holds against God is the fact that he grabbed him and handed him over, indeed thrown him into evil. The verbs used are *sāgăr* (סָגַר) and *yārăt* (יָרַט). The former indicates the action of "locking up." It is as if God has locked Job in a cage and sold him to his worst enemies. For this, the Septuagint resorts to the verb *paradídōmi*, which we have already encountered before to represent the betrayal of Judas. The latter, used only a couple of times in the Bible, indicates the action of "hurling to the ground." It is a violent verb, which the Septuagint translates as *rhíptō* (ῥίπτω), which gives the idea of a sudden, abrupt motion. God's destructive fury against Job was unleashed from one moment to the next, apparently without reason.

---

7. Leopardi, "La Ginestra," *Canti*, XXXIV.

It should be emphasized that what Job is describing here, although he ignores the reasons, corresponds to the reality of the facts. Job was "quiet," and suddenly God decides to hand him over, to throw him into the hands of Satan, that is, the evil one, the enemy par excellence, so that he may destroy him psychologically and physically. And if on the one hand all this appears to Job as an exercise in unjustified cruelty, on the other hand we know that the divine will was to test Job and his unshakable faith. To quench him as one quenches metals in the crucible. An agonizing test, but one that in the end will prove to be salvific.

The solution to Job's enigma certainly does not lie in resizing divine responsibility by placing the blame for his suffering on Satan (who in the whole of history appears only as a useful instrument in God's hands), but in recognizing and accepting the reasons for God's will that has decided to act this way.

But Job's interlocutors do not want to listen. They go straight ahead, unable to question their granitic certainties. Bildad takes the floor again and what comes out is a photocopy of Eliphaz's speech. The wicked will not get away with it. In the end, they will be crushed by every kind of misfortune. Job, tired of such speeches, contradicts him once again. He is inconsolable: "He hath also kindled his wrath against me, and he counteth me unto him as one of his enemies" (Job 19:11).

He is convinced that God is angry with him for some reason unknown to him. He hypothesizes an unjustified divine wrath against him. But, for the first time, his pain does not turn into mere despair at the idea of death: "And though after my skin worms destroy this body, yet in my flesh shall I see God: Whom I shall see for myself, and mine eyes shall behold, and not another; though my reins be consumed within me" (Job 19:26–27).

Suddenly, Job's mind seems to have a flash of lucidity and, as in a revelation received by divine grace, he perceives the certainty that there will be a future after death. There is all the ineffable emotion at the thought of being able to contemplate God with his own eyes and with his own flesh, even if undone by illness. It is such an enormous expectation that his insides are consumed by the mere thought of it. Here, Job is literally grasping the resurrection of the flesh, a concept that will later be confirmed and explained to his disciples by Christ.

Zophar stubbornly tries to convince Job that the luck of the wicked is only illusory (Job 20:5) and that soon their sins will be poured out on their children (Job 20:10, 22, 28), according to the theory of "collective earthly retribution." According to this theory, it is not so much the individual as the entire collectivity that now enjoys divine favor through the merits of others, now loses it through the demerits of others. In the eyes of his interlocutor, the death of Job's sons seems to be the exemplification of this theory. The terrible sins that Job must have committed to receive such a harsh punishment were poured out on his sons who, inheriting in this way the sins of their father, were annihilated by divine wrath. Again, the book of Job is here to refute even these kinds of arguments. And, if that were not enough, we have chapter 18 of the book of Ezekiel, where God himself explains exactly how it makes no sense to think that the righteous will die because of the wicked or, vice versa, that the wicked will live because of the merits of the righteous. Each will live or die according to his own personal merits (Ezek 18:9–13). But it will take Christ to reveal the deeper meaning of these words. God is not talking about earthly life or death here. He is speaking of eternal life or death. As seen, the earthly life or death of the body matters little in God's eyes. What matters is eternal life or damnation, after the death of the flesh.

It looks like a dialogue between deaf people. Job takes the floor again and tries to demonstrate, data in hand, that the theory that the wicked receive their just punishment eventually is false—tremendously false. It would suffice if they only question those who travel and know about the world (Job 21:29) and they would know that the day of wrath, the *dies irae* that the three interlocutors prophesy for the wicked, not only does not come for them, but often strikes the innocent (Job 21:30). Eliphaz, in response, provokes him heavily. He accuses him of the worst sins (Job 22:5–10) and invites him to repent before God. Only then will he return to enjoy wealth and happiness (Job 22:21). Job, on the contrary, in his desperate search for God (Job 23:9), must surrender before the will of God: "But he is in one mind, and who can turn him? and what his soul desireth, even that he doeth" (Job 23:13).

The dialogue continues with a long defensive harangue on Job's part, which oscillates between bewilderment in front of the divine omnipotence (Job 26:14), maxims of wisdom (Job 28:28), nostalgia for the good old days (Job 29), infinite pain for the present condition (Job 30), and the vindication of his own conduct always whole and correct (Job 31). Faced with this flood of words, the three interlocutors no longer know how to respond. The discussion has reached a dead end.

Then, as in every self-respecting play, a new character intervenes on the scene, Elihu the son of Barachel the Buzite, of the tribe of Ram. Elihu is a young boy and, out of respect for Job and his three older friends, he watched the entire discussion without uttering a word. However, now that Job has declared himself innocent and the three who declared him guilty can find no more arguments to oppose him, Elihu, taken by the indignation toward Job, decides to speak up. His impassioned speech covers six chapters, from 32 to 37. It is full of accusations regarding Job's hypothetical impious conduct (Job 33:27), of clichés (Job 34:20), and of maxims typical of the "theory of earthly retribution."

Elihu falls into the usual misunderstanding into which people typically fall—thinking that the justice of God can be measured by the wealth and well-being obtained by God in proportion to one's own conduct. But then, if God is supremely just, why do the righteous suffer? Elihu, unlike the three older interlocutors, has the intellectual honesty to address this question. His argument starts from the assumption that all people, even those who call themselves "righteous," are basically sinners: "And if they be bound in fetters, and be holden in cords of affliction; Then he sheweth them their work, and their transgressions that they have exceeded. He openeth also their ear to discipline, and commandeth that they return from iniquity. If they obey and serve him, they shall spend their days in prosperity, and their years in pleasures. But if they obey not, they shall perish by the sword, and they shall die without knowledge. But the hypocrites in heart heap up wrath: they cry not when he bindeth them. They die in youth, and their life is among the unclean. He delivereth the poor in his affliction, and openeth their ears in oppression" (Job 36:8–15).

Elihu's "theory of suffering" is based on the idea that God causes people to suffer so that they may understand their errors, recede from their pride, become humble, and turn away from their iniquities. This is the theory of "corrective" suffering. When righteous people tend to deviate from the right path, God makes them suffer so that they understand, opening their eyes and ears, to return to the right path. It is a bit like that electric wire that the shepherd puts at the edge of the field, just before the ravine, to teach his animals how far they can go. If they touch it, the pain makes them back off immediately. The electric shock is minimal. It does not kill but corrects. However, if people do not allow themselves to be corrected by suffering and persist in their iniquitous conduct, they will be terribly punished by the divine wrath, just like that animal that, indifferent to the pain caused by the electric wire, overcomes the imposed boundaries and falls into the ravine. If, on the other hand, they allow themselves to be corrected by the suffering sent by God and return to the right path, their life will be saved. Suffering becomes an instrument useful to God to open people's ears to his dictates.

The Hebrew term that indicates the idea of correction is *mûsār* (מוּסָר), which represents that discipline that parents impart to their children. God would treat us as disobedient children who need to be disciplined every now and then with a few scolds. Elihu is here theorizing the pedagogical function of pain. A theory that, as we will see, will have a lot of followers among scholars and theologians, but that, obviously, is wrongly applied by Elihu to Job. In fact, we know that Job was not only a righteous man (in the sense of an average man). Job was the model of the upright man, perfect in the eyes of God in every respect. He walked on the right path and had the Lord at his side. There was nothing to correct in Job. The pedagogical theory of pain is inapplicable in this case.

Elihu, despite his young age, brings much stronger arguments than the three previous interlocutors, until he touches the key point—a truth as simple as it is hard to accept: "Behold, God is great, and we know him not, neither can the number of his years be searched out" (Job 36:26).

*Ecce Deus vincens scientiam nostram*, will translate the Vulgate. God exceeds our capacity for understanding. Trying to impose on God the rules of human ethics is not only naive, but also harmful. One ends up, like Job, by losing hope and with it—faith. It is at this point, in chapter 37, that Elihu, with a powerful *climax*, finds himself announcing and preparing the entrance of the most important actor in this theatrical work that is the book of Job—the arrival of God himself. *Deus ex machina*. It is a triumphant entrance on the stage. It could fit under a piece of music by Wagner: "In a moment shall they die, and the people shall be troubled at midnight, and pass away: and the mighty shall be taken away without hand" (Job 37:22).

From the swirling clouds a voice is heard. It is God who, tired of listening to vain human discourses, comes to put things back in their place. He first invests Job with a series of rhetorical questions aimed at making him understand how the human claim to be right before him is pure folly. The human perspective is so shortsighted in the face of divine omnipotence: "Where wast thou when I laid the foundations of the earth? declare, if thou hast understanding" (Job 38:4). And then he lists all the natural phenomena that are under his control: the heavens, the stars, the seas, the earth, the physical laws of the universe. He literally buries him with examples of his own omnipotence. When God finishes speaking, Job begins to understand the pettiness of his pride—the pride of having believed that he could not only understand God's reasons, but even judge them. He cups his mouth with his hand and promises never to reply again.

Unfortunately, very often God's answer is reduced to a sort of "non-answer," a long and resounding speech that seems to escape the most provocative questions posed by Job. A solution to the problem of evil that is not a solution, and that does not satisfy the reader. A superficial reading of the passage would seem to give the impression of a God who, far from wanting to explain anything, has an easy time silencing Job. As to say, "Be silent, for I am I, and you are nothing." But on closer inspection, there is more to God's words. Much more.

There is an interesting passage—a passage in which God seems almost to mock poor Job. He challenges him to take up the divine scepter and strike down all the wicked, if he considers himself so good and so just. Let us read: "Hast thou an arm like God? or canst thou thunder with a voice like him? Deck thyself now with majesty and excellency; and array thyself with glory and beauty. Cast abroad the rage of thy wrath: and behold every one that is proud, and abase him. Look on every one that is proud, and bring him low; and tread down the wicked in their place. Hide them in the dust together; and bind their faces in secret. Then will I also confess unto thee that thine own right hand can save thee" (Job 40:9–14).

There is certainly a sarcastic intent in these words. But, in our view, there is more. What God is implicitly saying is that the human idea of divine justice, according to which, if God is just, he should make everything that people may consider "evil" disappear from the face of the earth, is pure utopia, a naive idea, and as such, simply impracticable.

This is the key to understanding the problem of evil in the world. What God is saying is that the elimination *tout court* of evil from the world would be incompatible with the realization of the divine plan. Without evil on earth, God would be deprived of a necessary instrument for his will to triumph. This is an enormous mystery. It is an uncomfortable truth—difficult to accept. But it is a truth that emerges powerfully in all Scripture. And it is a truth that, if not fully understood, will prevent us from getting to the deepest meaning of the Lord's Prayer.

It is at this precise point that Job breaks down. He declares his meanness before God, recognizes that he has spoken without discernment, and bitterly regrets it (Job 42:6). It is a collapse that implies a conversion. When a person lets the wall of his own pride fall before God's omnipotence, the way of conversion—of complete abandonment to God and his will—opens wide before him. This is enough. These few words of sincere repentance are enough for the infinite divine mercy to take over. God has already forgiven Job, and he really wasn't waiting for anything else. Instead, his wrath now pours out against Job's three friends. God reprimands them because they have not said correct things about him (Job 42:7). They—the great holders of the truth and of theological rationalism—denied and unmasked by God himself. On them and on their lack of piety and compassion the divine punishment would be about to pour out, if it were not for Job himself and his prayers: "Therefore take unto you now seven bullocks and seven rams, and go to my servant Job, and offer up for yourselves a burnt offering; and my servant Job shall pray for you: for him will I accept: lest I deal with you after your folly, in that ye have not spoken of me the thing which is right, like my servant Job" (Job 42:8). This is another example of the power of prayer, which can change God's mind,[8] which can prevent the evil inflicted by God on people.

To conclude this long but necessary digression on Job and on the problem of evil, it is of fundamental importance for the continuation of our argumentation to set some very precise boundaries, in order to avoid useless lexical confusions which are, in our opinion, at the basis of the jumble of interpretations, from the most extravagant to the most cerebral, that the sixth petition of the Lord's Prayer has undergone in the course of the centuries.

The first point is that the evil to which Job is subjected is a purely *psychophysical* evil. That is, an evil that aims to wear Job down in flesh and spirit. The mental stress (think of the immense misfortune of the loss of all his ten children and all his possessions) and the physical stress (think of the purulent sores all over his body that tormented him night and day) are of such a high level as to be almost inhuman. In fact, even Job, the most upright person in the East, eventually succumbs to despair and begins to blaspheme God. It is an extremely hard, devastating trial. But at no time during this trial does Satan venture to intervene to try to make Job fall into blasphemy. Satan, throughout the book of Job, serves as a mere executor of divine orders. God has given him a mandate to assault Job with the harshest possible trials for him, but we never see him whispering in Job's ear to behave in one way or another. Job is left alone and free to react to the suffering that has come upon him as his conscience, his intellect, and his free will best advise him. Satan does not trip him up. After having

---

8. This is a deliberately incorrect expression: God does not change his mind. We will see in the next chapters what this means. See Exod 32:14: "And the Lord repented of the evil which he thought to do unto his people."

placed Job in the midst of the most difficult trials, he leaves him alone to see how he will react. Satan is putting Job to the test on God's behalf. But he is not leading him into temptation, according to the meaning of "leading into temptation" as we usually understand it.

Here is one of the fundamental distinctions we must make: testing does not necessarily mean leading into temptation. Putting to the test, however hard the test may be, represents an objective, fair, and honest action. Inducing into temptation, on the other hand, represents the action of spoiling a test—of the perverse attempt to make the one who is facing the test fail. In this sense—and the sense is clear—God puts people to the test (and does so constantly), but he would never dream of leading them into temptation, that is, of acting in such a way that people fail the test that God himself has put before them. That is precisely Satan's distinctive trait: whispering to the heart of people and convincing them with the most subtle techniques so that they choose evil instead of good.

To use a scholastic metaphor, God is like that professor who can propose a difficult exam to his students. But the exam, however difficult, will always be fair. The students have been given by the professor all the means to be able to pass the exam. It is up to them, using their own intellect and knowledge, to answer all the questions correctly. The honest professor will never give his students a rigged exam, that is, one that assumes knowledge that the professor has never given them. What would be the point of such a behavior? The honest professor does not rejoice to see his students fail.[9] Satan, on the other hand, is like that terrible professor assistant who—intelligent but wicked—pretending to help the students, suggests the wrong answers to the most unprincipled.

If God puts people to the test without malice, while Satan induces into temptation with malice (and this is an indisputable fact), in the case of Job we have the representation of an even more complex dynamic. God may use Satan to put people to the test. And this, even if Satan is involved, in no way means that God is leading people into temptation. In other words, Satan can test people with psychophysical evil when he acts on divine command (as in the case of Job), while he can lead people into temptation (confusing their mind and pushing them to sin) when he acts of his own will. Satan too, of angelic nature, is endowed, like human beings, with free will and is left free by God to exercise his own malign influence on humanity. The emblematic example of such activity is found in the passage of the book of Genesis in which the serpent leads Eve into temptation, that is, he deviously convinces her that disobedience to the divine dictates not to eat of the tree of good and evil is not actually a sin. Here, Satan is obviously not acting on a divine mandate; rather, he is using his God-given free will, his perverted intellect, to push Eve into sinning against God.

Much of the confusion around the problem of evil and what God allows Satan to do stems from the fact that in Job's story Satan performs a different task than the

---

9. See Sir 15:12: "Do not say, 'He has led me astray,' for he has no need of a sinner."

one we usually associate the devil with, namely leading one into temptation. To try to understand the meaning of the sixth petition of the Lord's Prayer, the first thing to do is to clear our minds of this cliché. The function of Satan, that is, of evil in the world, is not only and exclusively that of leading people into temptation, but also that of acting as a mere divine instrument. The two functions must necessarily be kept separate, otherwise we risk falling into misinterpretations.

We will see how this confusion between the concept of testing with evil and inducing into temptation (that is, pushing to sin) has ancient roots and is also present in the writings of the church fathers who were the first to attempt to interpret the Lord's Prayer. We will then devote the following chapters to a critique of the church fathers. They were the first to enter the intricate labyrinth of the explanation of the sixth petition of the Lord's Prayer, and we must necessarily begin with them.

The end of Job's story is known to all. God repays Job for all the suffering he has endured by giving him twice his lost possessions. "*[Dio] non turba mai la gioia dei suoi figli se non per prepararne loro una più certa e più grande,*" Alessandro Manzoni would say.[10]

---

10. "[God] never disturbs the joy of his children except to prepare a more certain and greater joy for them" (Manzoni, *I Promessi Sposi*, 8).

# 15

# Critique of the Church Fathers

### TERTULLIAN

Although he is not one of the church fathers in the strict sense of the word and has not been recognized as a saint because of certain positions and conclusions that deviate from modern Catechism, it is not possible to ignore the importance of Tertullian, the first author of a conspicuous series of works that form the basis of Latin Christian literature. It is not by chance that he has been called the father of Latin Christianity and many rightly consider him the founder of Western theology. His thought and writings influenced all the major theologians of the first centuries after Christ. Without him we would probably not have St. Cyprian (a student of Tertullian) or St. Augustine himself. Born in Carthage, in the Roman province of Africa, Tertullian, a lawyer by profession, converted to Christianity at the end of the second century, when he was little more than forty years old, and from there began his prolific production of theological writings. One of his first compositions, dating back to the beginning of the third century, is *De oratione*,[1] in which Tertullian, among other themes, attempts to explain the Lord's Prayer. He is the first Latin author of whom we have evidence who enters the insidious question of the interpretation of the sixth petition of the Lord's Prayer. Since it is the first in history, it is worth reporting it in its entirety, in the original, and discussing it in detail: "*Ne nos inducas in temptationem, id est, ne nos patiaris induci, ab eo utique qui temptat. ceterum absit ut dominus temptare videatur, quasi aut ignoret fidem cuiusque aut deicere sit gestiens: diaboli est et infirmitas et militia.*"[2]

---

1. *On prayer.*
2. "Do not lead us into temptation, that is, do not allow us to be led, obviously by him who tempts. And let it never be that the Lord seems to tempt, as if he were either ignorant of each one's faith or looking forward to destroying it: both ignorance and malice are of the devil" (Tertullian, *De oratione*, 8).

Tertullian is the first author in Latin literature to embrace the permissive interpretation. "Lead us not into temptation" needs to be understood as "do not allow us to be led into temptation." And who leads us into temptation? The one who tempts par excellence, of course (*utique*). That is, the devil. Here then, with a rapid reversal of perspective, an action (that of leading us into temptation) that in the Latin text (as in the Greek one) is clearly referred to God, is instead referred to his opponent, that is, Satan, with God simply standing by and letting him do it. The verb used by Tertullian to render the permissive sense is *patior*, which means "to suffer," "to endure." God would thus be asked not to endure seeing Satan tempt us, but to intervene to deliver us from his clutches.

Tertullian brings a stringent argument to support his thesis. If this were not so, he says, if we really interpreted the passage in the sense of "do not tempt us," then we would be committing heresy, because *temptare* in Latin can have only two meanings: either "to test" or "to induce" to sin. *Aut aut*. But God, Tertullian argues, cannot do either of these things. In fact, whoever puts someone to the test does so to know whether that someone has certain qualities or not. He who puts someone to the test does not know, before the test, whether that someone will pass the test or not. But God knows everything. He is omniscient. And therefore, he does not need to test us to know if we are faithful or not. He already knows. On the other hand, it does not need much explanation to convince us that God cannot induce us to sin. Both cases are then to be rejected. In the first case it would mean that God is not omniscient, in the second case that he is not good. But both ignorance (*infirmitas*) and wickedness (*malitia*) are not characteristics of God—they are of the devil (*diaboli*). The conclusion can only be one: he who tempts us is the devil—not God. And therefore, the only possible interpretation of the passage must be the permissive one.

Tertullian's argument, although it contains logical-interpretive inaccuracies that undermine its soundness, is interesting because it is the first ever attempt to give a definitive interpretation to the sixth petition of the Lord's Prayer, but even more so because it testifies to the fact that the debate on the correct interpretation of this passage was already animating the very first Christian communities.

One of Tertullian's most obvious interpretative errors is that of trying to deny the fact that God can even put people to the test. In his eagerness to demonstrate how God cannot temp (*temptare*) in the sense of inducing to sin, Tertullian is forced to demonstrate that even the neutral meaning of the verb *temptare*, that is, "to test" without malice, is to be rejected as well. And he does so with a very subtle argument. If God is omniscient, he does not need to test anyone. However sharp this argument may seem, it inevitably clashes with the reality of the facts. And the reality of the facts tells us that in the Bible there are countless examples in which God puts people to the test. At a closer look, the entire Old Testament is nothing but a great and prolonged test of faith to which God submits for generations and generations, both individually and collectively, the people of Israel. Trying to deny that God can put people to the test is a desperate task. At least two possibilities (which are not mutually exclusive) may elude Tertullian:

1. the fact that God tests us to know if we are faithful may not necessarily negate divine omniscience;
2. God may be testing people to show them their limitations.[3]

The problem of divine omniscience is not the subject of this essay, nor could it be for purely practical reasons. The deep meaning of this quality of God has been debated by philosophers, theologians, and physicists for centuries, and rivers of ink have been spent in the most intricate and acute logical arguments and counterarguments. It will suffice here simply to point out that the concept of omniscience, understood as a timeless God who knows past, present, and future, is not easily compatible with the concept of free will. Exactly as the concept of omnipotence is not easily compatible with the concept of free will, if it is understood as the ability to make the evil in the world disappear at once.

St. Augustine, reluctant to give up a totemic idea of divine omniscience, will find an interesting solution to the problem. God tests people not because he does not know, but so that people may know.[4] But, even if we take St. Augustine's subtle interpretation at face value, one point is clear: Tertullian's daring attempt to demonstrate how God cannot test people (in whatever sense this verb appears) clashes irremediably with reality. Because God does put people to the test, and this is an undeniable fact.

For example, one of the most emblematic trials to which God subjects a person in the Old Testament is the sacrifice of Isaac, recounted in chapter 22 of the book of Genesis. And how does the narrative open? As follows: "And it came to pass after these things, that God did tempt Abraham" (Gen 22:1).

The verb used to refer to God's action of testing Abraham by asking him to sacrifice his beloved son Isaac is still *nāsâ*. Tertullian does not shy away from the comparison, and indeed he himself raises this example to show how, even when it seems that God is testing a person (as in the case of Abraham), what God does is simply to ascertain, to prove his faith. God does not tempt, or even test. He approves, says Tertullian. In short, he certifies what is already known to him. And why does he do this? So that it may be an example and a lesson to the rest of humanity.[5] However, Scripture speaks very clearly. The original Hebrew uses the verb *nāsâ* which, as we have seen, means "to test." The Septuagint translates with the Greek verb *peirázō* (πειράζω), which still

---

3. Like a professor who already knows that a student will not be able to answer a certain number of questions correctly, but who nevertheless subjects him/her to the exam, not because he rejoices to see his student fail, but so that the student may realize his/her poor level of learning.

4. "*Tentat nos Deus ut scire nos faciat*" (Augustine, *De sermone Domini in monte*, 2.9.31).

5. In the case of Abraham, the divine teaching would be to show that love for God must be even greater than love for one's own children.

means "to test," without any particular connotation of approval.[6] But above all, the Latin Vulgate translates the passage with an eloquent "*Temptavit Deus Abraham.*" It is clear, then, that Tertullian's attempt to explain that when God ordered Abraham to sacrifice Isaac, he did not do so to test his faith ("*non temptandae fidei gratia*"), is a desperate undertaking. If we line up Tertullian's reasoning with the biblical passage in question, we get an unintentionally comical construct: "*Temptavit Deus Abraham non temptandae fidei gratia.*" That is, he tempted him, but not to tempt him. He tested him, but not to test him. There is obviously something that does not add up.

In any case, Tertullian's reasoning is particularly important because it lays the foundations for a reasoned discussion on the concept of trial and temptation, on the difference between *temptare* and *probare*, between *temptatio* and *proba*. All concepts that will be taken up and elaborated by his successors, including St. Cyprian and St. Augustine.

## CYPRIAN

St. Cyprian is the second author on whom we will focus. Born in Carthage, the same place as Tertullian, at the beginning of the third century, he converted to Christianity, just like Tertullian, when he was little more than forty years old, and shortly afterward he was elected bishop of Carthage in 249 AD. He died a martyr nine years later under the persecution of the Roman emperor Valerian, earning his sanctity. He is unquestionably the first Father of the Western Catholic Church, and his many writings occupy the third and fourth volumes of the *Patrologia Latina*. The one that interests us most is *De oratione dominica*,[7] a treatise on the Lord's Prayer. In this work, St. Cyprian gives the Latin version of the Lord's Prayer, which was apparently widespread in the African area of Carthage in the first half of the third century. And the most interesting fact is that the expression that would later become official in the Vulgate ("*ne nos inducas in tentationem*") does not appear, but rather the permissive form that Tertullian had proposed as a possible interpretation a few years earlier: "*Sic, inquit, orate: Pater noster, qui es in caelis, sanctificetur nomen tuum, adveniat regnum tuum, fiat voluntas tua in caelo et in terra, panem nostrum cottidianum da nobis hodie, et dimitte nobis debita nostra, sicut et nos remittimus debitoribus nostris, et ne patiaris nos induci in temptationem, sed libera nos a malo.*"[8]

According to St. Cyprian's writing, the permissive interpretation of the sixth petition of the Lord's Prayer, at least among the early Christian communities in the

---

6. Indeed, there is the verb *dokimázō* (δοκιμάζω), which would have this kind of nuance, but which is not used.

7. *On the Lord's prayer.*

8. "Pray thus," he said, "Our Father, who art in heaven, hallowed be thy name, thy kingdom come, thy will be done in heaven as it is on earth, give us this day our daily bread, and forgive us our trespasses, as we forgive those who trespass against us, and do not allow us to be led into temptation, but deliver us from evil" (Cyprian, *De oratione dominica*, 25).

mid-third century African area of Carthage, had risen to become a true official translation of the Greek originals of Matthew and Luke. It was what the faithful commonly recited. Which testifies to how out of tune that "lead us not into temptation" must have sounded, even at that time. So much so that it was completely censored and replaced with a more acceptable "do not allow us to be led into temptation."

Let us be careful, though. Although the Latin rendering of the sixth petition is identical, there is a great leap in quality between Tertullian's interpretation and that of St. Cyprian. For Tertullian, the one who leads us into temptation is obviously (*utique*) Satan, that is, the tempter par excellence. St. Cyprian, on the other hand, speaks generically of *adversarium* and *malum*: "*Qua in parte ostenditur nihil contra nos adversarium posse, nisi Deus ante permiserit, ut omnis timor noster et devotio atque observatio ad Deum convertatur, quando in temptationibus nihil malo liceat, nisi potestas inde tribuatur.*"[9]

On the one hand, if we consider that the name Satan derives from the Hebrew term *sātān* (שָׂטָן), which means "adversary," and that Satan is also commonly referred to as the Evil One, we understand how the specific choice of the terms *adversarium* and *malum* to indicate that who leads us into temptation immediately refers to the figure of the devil. On the other hand, however, St. Cyprian does not limit himself to a theoretical interpretation of the sixth petition of the Lord's Prayer, but he also offers a series of concrete examples in support of his thesis, from which it is clear that the one who can make us suffer is not only and necessarily Satan. It is any adversary, any enemy who causes us harm. But always within the limits and powers imposed by God. This is a particularly important semantic extension.

The first example he proposes is that of Nebuchadnezzar, king of Babylon, who sacks and destroys Jerusalem, but only because the Lord gave it into his hands ("*dedit eam Dominus in manu eius*"). In the second example, St. Cyprian cites Isa 42:24–25[10] in which God gives the people of Israel into the hands of marauders. In the third example, he cites 1 Kgs 11:14[11] in which God punishes King Solomon for his sins by waving an adversary at him. The fourth example (and it would be impossible for St. Cyprian not to quote it) concerns the events of Job who was tormented by Satan, but only because God had placed him in his hands. The fifth and final example cites a famous New Testament passage from the Gospel of John, when Jesus, in a dramatic

---

9. "In this part it is shown that the enemy can do nothing against us, unless God has previously permitted it, so that all our fear, devotion, and obedience may be turned back to God, since in temptations evil can do nothing, except what God has been given him the power to do" (Cyprian, *De oratione dominica*, 25).

10. "Who gave Jacob for a spoil, and Israel to the robbers? did not the Lord, he against whom we have sinned? for they would not walk in his ways, neither were they obedient unto his law. Therefore, he hath poured upon him the fury of his anger, and the strength of battle: and it hath set him on fire round about, yet he knew not; and it burned him, yet he laid it not to heart" (Isa 42:24–25).

11. "And the Lord stirred up an adversary unto Solomon, Hadad the Edomite: he was of the king's seed in Edom" (1 Kgs 11:14).

confrontation with Pilate, reminds the Roman governor that the power of life and death in his hands was given to him from above.[12]

Nebuchadnezzar, marauders, the Idumean Haddad, Satan, Pilate. The evil that can afflict us can take different shapes and forms. But it is an evil to which God does not give infinite power over us. And that evil can really afflict us only if God tolerates it. In the Lord's Prayer then, says St. Cyprian, we are asking God not to grant evil, that is, our adversaries, the power to torment us. This is a particularly important and far-reaching analysis, which for the first time is able to rise from the mere semantic field of demonic temptation, that is, of Satan's induction to sin. St. Cyprian's lucid argumentation reveals some points that we should hold firmly if we really want to approach the understanding of the sixth petition of the Lord's Prayer:

1. The *tentatio* into which we ask God not to lead us may have nothing to do with the temptation to sin, that is, moral corruption (in none of the five examples cited by St. Cyprian does the one who leads into temptation does so by inducing someone to sin but does so by causing physical harm).
2. The one who leads us into temptation, that is, causes us physical harm, does not do so independently of God. On the contrary, he can do it only because the Lord has given him the power to do so.

By establishing these two simple concepts, Scripture in hand, St. Cyprian comes as close, in our opinion, as few others will, to unraveling the mystery of the Lord's Prayer. Of course, one can find weaknesses in his arguments as well. First of all, the notion that God can empower our enemies to do us harm only in two specific cases: either for punishment when we sin, or for glory when we pass the test ("*vel ad poenam cum delinquimus, vel ad gloriam cum probamur*"). This, in our opinion, is too narrow a view, according to which when we are afflicted by evil, there are only two possibilities: either we are experiencing some sort of divine punishment, or it is God who is instead giving us the opportunity to attain glory if we know how to persevere in the trial that evil inflicts on us. This seems an overly simplistic solution to the problem of evil in the world, but it has the enormous merit of grasping that the great mystery hidden in the sixth petition of the Lord's Prayer cannot be separated from the solution of this problem.

The second weak point of St. Cyprian's interpretation is that he wants at all costs to maintain the permissive construct (*ne patiaris*) in the Latin translation. A permissive construct that, according to St. Cyprian's own reasoning, is unnecessary. For when St. Cyprian judges that evil can do nothing against us except what it has been given the faculty to do, he is implicitly declaring that the sense of the sixth petition cannot be permissive, but causative. If God did not act, if God did not move, if God did not give order, if God did not dispose, not a hair on our head would be wronged. Nebuchadnezzar would never have conquered Jerusalem if God had not put it in his

---

12. "Thou couldest have no power at all against me, except it were given thee from above" (John 19:11).

hands. Satan would never have touched Job's possessions and children if God had not given him provision to do so. St. Cyprian stops just short of concluding that God is the cause of the evil that afflicts us. He says this implicitly but hides it under the shelter of the permissive construct ("*nisi Deus ante permiserit*"). He does not seem ready to admit it yet. Every time St. Cyprian explains how evil receives power and faculty to harm us, the name of God, the one who grants that power and that faculty, fades and disappears, hidden in passive formulas ("*potestas inde tribuatur ( . . . ) potestas vero dupliciter adversus nos datur*"). However, this does not diminish the modernity and scope of St. Cyprian's thought.

## ORIGEN

Let us now move just a little, from Carthage to Alexandria, to pay homage to a great contemporary of St. Cyprian, Origen of Alexandria, known as *Adamantius*, that is, as strong as a diamond. The *corpus* of works produced by Origen, mainly in Greek, is monumental (around 2000 compositions, but they are perhaps even more) and constitutes the foundation of the first great system of Christian philosophy. Raised and educated in the best philosophical schools of Alexandria, he studied the thought of Plato and the Stoics, learned Hebrew, and was influenced by Ammonius Sacca, Plotinus's teacher. Although his relationship with the high ecclesiastical spheres was tumultuous enough to cost him the excommunication for some of his very radical positions, it is undeniable that his refined theological thought is a milestone impossible to ignore.

As far as we are concerned, we will consider one of his *libelli*, *De oratione*, in which Origen tries his hand at commenting on every single verse of the Lord's Prayer. The sixth petition is addressed in chapter 29. Origen is a most valuable source in this regard because he tackles the study of the Gospels in Greek, that is, in the original language. Unlike Tertullian, St. Cyprian, and all the Latin theologians after them, he has the advantage of having Greek as his native language and therefore enjoys a greater sensitivity to the semantic nuances of the New Testament. Let us read the *incipit*: "Unless the Savior teaches us to pray the impossible, it seems to me that it is worth asking ourselves how we should pray not to enter into temptation, when man's life on earth is all about temptation."[13]

Already in this very first sentence we found particularly important concepts. The first impression one gets when reciting the sixth petition in Greek (*mè eisenénkēis eis peirasmón*) is that of a God who leads us, gets us in, that is, exposes us to temptation (*peirasmós*). But what is the point, Origen asks, of praying to God to do something impossible? The very condition of people on earth is, by definition, one of constant temptation. Origen here uses a subtle play on words. If in the text of the Lord's Prayer

---

13. Origen, *De oratione*, 29.

temptation is indicated, as we know, by the term *peirasmós*, the temptation to which people, by their very nature, are subjected on earth for Origen is defined by the term *peiratḗrion* (πειρατήριον). The two terms, which are evidently derived from the same root, have slightly different meanings. *Peirasmós* is the noun associated with the action indicated by the verb *peirázō*, which translates the idea of testing. The *peiratḗrion*, on the other hand, is a term more used in warfare context to indicate the attack of the enemy.[14] Origen sheds new light on the correct interpretation of the term *peirasmós* contained in the Lord's Prayer, associating with it the concept of the danger inherent in the evil that our enemies can cause us.

It is noteworthy that no reference to possible permissive overtones will be found throughout Origen's argument. For Origen, that *mḕ eisenénkēis* poses no interpretive problems. Its meaning is clear. It means that God is leading us to enter somewhere. The point is to understand where and possibly why. Origen, a native Greek speaker, is the first to understand how the only possibility for interpretive freedom lies in the second part of the sixth petition (*eis peirasmón*), and not in the first (*mḕ eisenénkēis*). Origen knows this well, and that is why his efforts are focused on understanding what it means for God to lead us into *peirasmós* (whatever this term means).

Origen elaborates on his reasoning by explaining how human nature is a continuous struggle—a war (*peiratḗrion*) between the *pneûma* (πνεῦμα), that is, the spirit, and the *sárx* (σάρξ), that is, the flesh—the instinct. For Origen, the existence of this dualism (the spirit yearning for God, the flesh struggling against God) makes it impossible to think that the Lord's Prayer teaches how to ask not to be exposed to temptation. After all, the spirit is literally enveloped, surrounded by the flesh, which by definition is itself temptation. Origen deduces that it is unthinkable for people to escape temptation.[15]

However, when it seems evident that Origen is understanding *peirasmós* as an enticement to sin, the two examples he offers to support his argument suddenly overturn these certainties. He says, "That all of man's life on earth is a temptation [*peiratḗrion*] we learn from Job when he said, Perhaps man's life on earth is not a temptation [*peiratḗrion*]? The same idea emerges in Psalm 17: In You I will be delivered from temptation [*peiratḗrion*]."[16]

Origen is quoting Job 7:1 in which Job complains that human life is like a military exercise. Job uses the Hebrew term *tsāvā'* (צָבָא), which indicates a warlike action. One can understand at this point why, to define *peirasmós*, Origen likes to use the warlike term *peiratḗrion*. He has these words of Job in mind. Job, however, when he speaks these words, is not thinking about the struggle between carnal drives and spirit. Instead, he has his own psychophysical sufferings clearly in mind. If the *peirasmós* of

---

14. Hence the term "pirate."

15. Part of the contrasts between Origen and the ecclesiastical hierarchies came from the fact that Origen decided to castrate himself to annihilate the urges of the flesh.

16. Origen, *De oratione*, 29.

the Lord's Prayer were to be intended in the manner of the *peiratḗrion* to which Job refers, one would have to conclude that the temptation of the Lord's Prayer is instead nothing more than the ultimate test of the hardest sufferings. Nothing to do with the weakness of the flesh, understood as the impulse to abandon oneself to sin (of lust, greed, gluttony, and so forth).

The second example cited by Origen goes in the same direction. Verse 30 of Psalm 17 (in the Greek numbering of the Septuagint)—which corresponds to verse 29 of Psalm 18 in the Masoretic numbering—says something different from what Origen would like to imply. What Origen tries to pass off as a deliverance from temptation is, in the verse of the psalm, clearly referring to God's protection in battle. In fact, the original Hebrew psalm reads, "For by thee I have run through a troop; and by my God have I leaped over a wall" (Ps 18(17):29(30)). The metaphor is clearly a warlike one. It speaks of God-given strength to face enemies in battle, thus of physical protection, without any reference to deliverance from moral temptations.

Origen continues by quoting St. Paul and distinguishing between the so-called human temptations (*anthrópinos peirasmós*), that is, those of lesser magnitude and that come from people, and those that derive directly from the prince of darkness and evil spirits, that is, from Satan himself, which are obviously much more subtle and difficult to reject. If our spirit is constantly tempted by the flesh of which we are made, and the world in which we have to live is left in the hands of the devil and his forces of evil, how is it possible, Origen asks, that the Savior tells us to pray that we may not enter into temptation, when in fact, in a certain sense, "God tempts everyone"?[17]

Interestingly, these words—so clear and stark—would have probably scandalized James, who remembers how God cannot be tempted and tempts no one (Jas 1:13). How, then, can we reconcile Origen's "God tempts everyone" with James's "God tempts no one"? It is clear that there is an underlying semantic confusion around the verb *peirázō*. When James says that God does not tempt anyone, he means the verb *peirázō* as the action of leading into moral corruption. On the other hand, when Origen says that God tempts everyone, he understands the verb *peirázō* as the action of subjecting people to (painful) trials. This is testified by all the examples that Origen brings in support of his somewhat scandalous statement. He mentions everything that God did with Abraham, how he put Isaac to the test (*peirázō*), and also how Jacob, when in Mesopotamia of Syria, grazed the sheep of Laban, his mother's brother. Now, Abraham in the Jewish tradition is known to have had to face at least ten trials,[18] each of which tests Abraham's psychophysical endurance (there is no trace of temptations

---

17. "πειράζοντός πως πάντας τοῦ Θεοῦ [*peirázontós pōs pántas toû Theoû*]" (Origen, *De oratione*, 29).

18. 1. God orders him to leave his native land. 2. Once arrived in the Promised Land, a famine breaks out. 3. The Egyptians capture his wife Sarah and take her to Pharaoh. 4. Abraham faces an incredibly adverse fate in the war of the four kings against the five kings. 5. He discovers that his wife Sarah is barren. 6. God commands him to circumcise himself at an advanced age. 7. The king of Gerar captures Sarah 8. God orders him to repudiate his second wife Hagar after having a child with her 9. His son Ishmael abandons him. 10. God asks him to sacrifice his son Isaac.

or enticement to sin). In the same way, Isaac is put to the test by God. He will have to remain a stranger in the land of Gerar, instead of fleeing the famine and taking refuge in Egypt. Isaac will obey and will be rewarded by God with honors, riches, and an endless line of descendants. Less clear is the reference to the events of Jacob, who, however, is rewarded by God for his dedication and honesty when his father-in-law Laban does not want to let him leave: "If he said thus, The speckled shall be thy wages; then all the cattle bare speckled: and if he said thus, The ringstraked shall be thy hire; then bare all the cattle ringstraked" (Gen 31:8).

Finally, Origen quotes the words of King David: "Many are the afflictions of the righteous" (Ps 34(33):19(20)), which are in some way taken up later by St. Paul: "we must through much tribulation enter into the kingdom of God" (Acts 14:22). In both cases, it seems to be understood that *peirasmós* coincides with tribulation, in Greek *thlîpsis* (θλῖψις). *Thlîpsis* is the term used by the Septuagint to translate the original Hebrew *rā'* (רָע), which as we have seen indicates the generic concept of evil, that is, anything that may involve psychophysical suffering. *Thlîpsis* is also the term used by St. Paul to indicate all the sufferings and persecutions that the righteous will have to face to gain the kingdom of heaven. It is curious to note how, in an attempt to demonstrate how Scripture offers multiple examples of how people are constantly subjected to temptation, Origen ends up opening (unintentionally or not, it matters little) a breach in the granitic identification of *peirasmós* with the concept of enticement to moral corruption. Instead, *peirasmós* (or, as Origen likes to say, *peiratḗrion*) seems to be identified with *thlîpsis*, that is, suffering and psychophysical destruction. The expression "God tempts everyone" takes on the meaning of a God who can subject anyone at any time to any kind of psychophysical stress.

And to clear the field of further doubt, Origen explains that asking God not to be exposed to *peirasmós* would be futile and naive. Not even his Apostles were granted this prayer,

> given the myriad things they had to suffer throughout their lives: in many sufferings, in even more cases in prison, in extreme calamities, in even more frequent deaths. And personally Paul "received from the Jews five times forty blows minus one, three times he was beaten with rods, once he was stoned, three times he was shipwrecked, one night and one day he spent on the high seas," a man "afflicted in every way, hesitant, persecuted, landed" and who confesses "until now we are hungry and thirsty, we are naked and we are slapped, we have no stable dwelling and we toil working with our own hands; insulted, we bless; persecuted, we endure; defamed, we exhort."[19]

---

19. Origen, *De oratione*, 29.

Origen has listed here every kind of psychophysical suffering that can affect us: calamities, persecutions, tortures, hunger, cold, death. Nothing that refers to the corruption of the spirit, but to the physical destruction of the body.[20]

So, what is the meaning of the sixth petition? According to Origen there is only one possibility. We are not asking to be exempt from *peirasmós* (which is impossible), but "if tempted, not to succumb to *peirasmós*" ("μὴ ἡττᾶσθαι πειραζομένους"). The Greek verb used by Origen, *hēttáomai* (ἡττάομαι), indicates the idea of not being up to the difficult situation we face. Because (and let us pay attention to this interpretation!) the motion inside the temptation (*eis peirasmón*) implies, according to Origen, automatically falling into the trap of the temptation itself, that is, sin. It is completely different, Origen explains, to be exposed to temptation and to enter into temptation. Exposure implies a struggle but not a fall; entering, on the other hand, already constitutes the failure of the test.

Rivers of ink have been spilled on the correct interpretation of the expression *eis peirasmón*. There is one school of thought[21] that views this expression as a simple exposure to temptation, and another,[22] which sees this motion as yielding to temptation, and thus sinning. To enter into temptation, Origen says, is already to succumb to the temptation itself. Both schools of thought have good arguments to support their thesis, and it would be exhausting (and probably not very useless) to analyze them here.[23]

However, after solving a problem, a bigger one opens up. How can Origen justify the idea of a God who would not only expose us to temptation, but would make us fall into it, would force us into it, would make us succumb to it, and therefore sin without us being able to do much about it? Origen knows this well and is the first to admit the difficulty: "It is worth understanding how we can think that God leads into temptation the one who has not prayed or who is not listened to. Whoever enters into temptation is overcome. Therefore, it is absurd to believe that God leads someone into temptation, because it would be tantamount to exposing him to defeat. And the same aporia remains, however one interprets the words: 'Pray so as not to enter into temptation.' If in fact it is evil to fall into temptation—let us pray that we may not suffer from it—how is it not absurd to think that God, who is good and cannot bear fruits of evil, would throw one into the arms of evil?"[24]

---

20. Here Origen, in order to tie up his argument, is forced to venture into a particularly risky thesis, according to which the physical destruction of the body would be prodromal to moral corruption. Those afflicted by disease and suffering would be more willing to idleness and therefore to sin.

21. See, for instance, Brown, "The Pater Noster as an Eschatological Prayer," 204–8; McCaughey, "Matthew 6:13a," 31–40; Porter, "Mt 6:13 and Lk 11:4," 359–62.

22. See, for instance, Origen, *De oratione*, 29–30; Hilary, *Super psalmos*, 118.aleph.15; Dionysius, *The Gospel according to Luke*, 22.46; Carmignac, *Recherches*, 237–304; Heller, "Die Sechste Bitte des Vaterunser," 85–93; Jeremias, *The Lord's Prayer*, 27.

23. We will have time to expound both schools of thought later.

24. Origen, *De oratione*, 29.

## Eis Peirasmón

A couple of thoughts on this passage. First, when Origen, twice, indicates the action of leading into temptation, he uses the verb *eiságō* (εἰσάγω). This is not, as we know, the exact verb used by the evangelists, who prefer instead *eisphérō* (εἰσφέρω). This is no coincidence. Indeed, it confirms that in the Greek language of the time, when indicating the action of leading a person, the obvious choice would fall on the more common *ágō*. *Eisphérō*, on the other hand, is a very particular lexical choice, which cannot and should not go unnoticed.

Second, far from trying to force a permissive nuance into the original Greek text, Origen very candidly admits that the expression *mḕ eisenénkēis* calls to mind the action of pushing, of forcefully throwing[25] people into *peirasmós*.

To justify the apparent blasphemy of a God who throws us into sin, Origen cites several biblical passages in which it is said that God, angry with the people of Israel for straying from his commandments, abandoned them to the impurity and obstinacy of their hearts. The reader should recall all the time spent in the previous chapters discussing the meaning of this abandonment, the concept of the hardening of human hearts, the predisposition to deviate from the right path. Origen interprets the sixth petition of the Lord's Prayer as a plea to God not to do as he did with the people of Israel, that is, not to throw us into the arms of our most perverse instincts. After spending half of his reasoning inquiring about *peirasmós* as a kind of *thlîpsis*, that is, psychophysical suffering, Origin cannot detach himself from the idea of *peirasmós* as an invitation to moral corruption. But why would God do such a thing? At this point, Origen introduces his theory of free will: "I think that God takes care of each rational soul, aiming at its eternal life; it always has free will and can in itself be in the ideal condition to ascend to the summit of good or to descend in various ways, due to negligence, to this or that abyss of evil."[26]

It may happen then that when one is immersed in sin, God leaves him and abandons him for a while to wallow in his impure passions so that he understands the gravity of his actions. This, according to Origen, may be the solution to the enigma: the usefulness of temptation. This is perhaps the most interesting and enlightened part of Origen's discourse:

> For if, as it is said in Proverbs, "the nets are not unjustly stretched out for the birds," God is right to throw us into the net according to what is written: "Thou didst make me fall into the net"; now if even the most negligible of birds, the sparrow, does not fall into the net without the will of the Father (inasmuch as that which falls into the net falls into it through the misuse of the wings, which were given it to rise), let us pray that we do nothing which according to the right judgment of God is worthy for us to be led into temptation. Into temptation is led everyone who is abandoned by God to impurity in the desires of his heart; everyone who gives himself up to ignominious passions and everyone

---

25. Origen uses the verb *peribállō* (περιβάλλω), which means precisely "to throw around."
26. Origen, *De oratione*, 29.

who is abandoned to his depraved mind, so as to do unseemly things, because he has not proved that he carries God with him.[27]

Origen is perhaps the first to understand that it is not blasphemous to imagine a God who casts us into evil, if that is what we need to convert to him. However, on closer inspection, his reasoning is not precise. Origen had set as a starting point the impossibility of a God who urges us to succumb to temptation, only to end up concluding that God may abandon us to temptation for an indefinite time. The two concepts are not equivalent: leading someone to succumb to temptation is not the same thing as abandoning someone in sin. Origen is right when he says that God can let someone wallow in sin without intervening, but this interpretation does not fit well with the image of a God who urges us, since he is the principal cause, to succumb to temptation itself.[28] Unfortunately, Origen's reasoning is flawed at the very beginning. He quotes a passage from the Old Testament: "Thou broughtest us into the net" (Ps 66(65):12), which has nothing to do with falling into temptation, that is, into moral sin. Instead, the psalmist is talking about falling into the clutches of the enemies, which brings affliction, pain, and shame: "Thou broughtest us into the net; thou laidst affliction upon our loins. Thou hast caused men to ride over our heads; we went through fire and through water: but thou broughtest us out into a wealthy place" (Ps 66(65):11–12).

The image of men "riding over our heads" is typical of Egyptian and Assyrian bas-reliefs, in which the king used to pass with his chariot literally over the bodies of dead and wounded enemies. The expression "going through fire and through water" was also typically used as a metaphor for the most atrocious adversity.

In the conclusion of chapter 29 of his *libellus*, Origen offers two more examples that are supposed to demonstrate the usefulness of temptation: the story of Job and a passage from Deuteronomy.[29] Both examples, far from demonstrating the usefulness of temptation understood as moral corruption, demonstrate once again one thing—that in Origen's mind, *peirasmós* coincides with *peiratērion*, that is, that exhausting struggle, that continuous warlike contention, not between flesh and spirit, but between us and the adversities of life through which God makes us pass.

---

27. Origen, *De oratione*, 29.

28. As we know, the solution is instead the following: God does not push anyone to succumb to temptation, but at most can act on his heart, hardening or softening it, that is, making it more or less impervious to it. The final choice of whether to commit a sin is always the work of our own free will.

29. "Who led thee through that great and terrible wilderness, wherein were fiery serpents, and scorpions, and drought, where there was no water; who brought thee forth water out of the rock of flint; Who fed thee in the wilderness with manna, which thy fathers knew not, that he might humble thee, and that he might prove thee, to do thee good at thy latter end" (Deut 8:15–16).

## DIONYSIUS OF ALEXANDRIA

Contemporary of Origen is Dionysius of Alexandria, called "the Great." After St. Cyprian, he was the most eminent bishop of the third century and is venerated as a saint by the Catholic Church (he is officially considered a church father). St. Dionysius's thought is mainly found collected in the epistles he exchanged with the other bishops of the third century Christian church. His most important writings concern the interpretation of the Gospels of Luke and John as well as the book of Revelation. In his work on the interpretation of the Gospel of Luke, chapter 22 contains an interesting disquisition on the concept of temptation. We will see how most of his arguments are influenced by Origen but with noteworthy variations.

The starting point of St. Dionysius recalls that of Origen. Jesus in the Lord's Prayer cannot have taught us to ask the Father to be spared from temptation, because "it does not seem possible that any man can remain completely without experience of evil."[30] What does Dionysius mean by "evil"? Definitively the psychophysical suffering to which people are constantly subjected. He recalls how Scripture describes in various passages the many tribulations of life, defined as "a valley of tears." "Valley of tears" is also the expression used within one of the most famous invocations to Mary, the *Salve Regina*.[31] It is a remarkably interesting variation on Origen's theme. Remember how Origen argued that it is impossible to escape temptation because our body is made of flesh that naturally tends to sin and struggle against the will of God? Well, St. Dionysius modifies the argument by redefining temptation not as moral corruption, but as psychophysical stress, coming to the same conclusion. We cannot escape from it, because our whole life on earth is a continuous pain—a valley of tears. From this point of view, St. Dionysius is much more consistent than Origen because he aligns his theoretical thought with the practical examples that emerge from Scripture (Job, David, and so forth—the same ones proposed by Origen).

Once he has made this distinction, St. Dionysius continues his reasoning along the same lines. One must distinguish, he explains, between entering into temptation and being tempted. "To tempt" does not mean to cause one to fall into temptation. "To tempt" means to expose to temptation. And that is what God does. God tempts in the sense that he exposes to temptation. But never, ever, could God cause one to enter into temptation. Because entering into temptation, explains Dionysius, following Origen, already means giving in to temptation itself (on this point, the two agree perfectly). But at this point, Dionysius finds himself in a blind alley. If entering into temptation means succumbing to temptation, and if temptation means the tribulations to which people are constantly exposed, the sixth petition of the Lord's Prayer would seem to indicate the possibility that God makes us succumb to evil. But God, Dionysius explains, does not do this. God does not make us succumb to evil. On the contrary. God

---

30. Dionysius, *The Gospel according to Luke*, 22.46.
31. *Ad te suspiramus, gementes et flentes, in hac lacrimarum valle.*

does the opposite. He makes us experience evil to temper us and make us stronger and more worthy of the kingdom of heaven. The one who makes us succumb to evil is the devil, who drags us in with force.

How do we solve this dilemma? Dionysius, after having argued so well, has no other way out than to dredge up the permissive construct. We are not asking God not to expose us to evil (this is impossible because we are naturally exposed to evil on a daily basis); we are not asking God not to make us succumb to evil (this is impossible because God does not make anyone succumb to evil); instead, we are asking God not to *allow* us to succumb to evil.[32] Unfortunately, the logical reasoning of St. Dionysius is vitiated by an insurmountable problem. The idea that the whole life of a person is nothing but a "valley of tears" is obviously a hyperbole. Indeed, human life on earth is not necessarily one of incessant pain and suffering. At least not for anyone. Even for Job, the man tormented by pain par excellence, this is not true. Before and after the hard trial that befell him, Job enjoys prosperity, wealth, and happiness. Therefore, if we abandon the rhetoric of the "valley of tears," one of the fundamental assumptions that support the arguments of St. Dionysius collapses.

## HILARY OF POITIERS

Let us go back to the main thinkers of Latin theology and make a leap to the France of the fourth century to meet Hilary of Poitiers, Roman theologian and bishop, venerated as a saint and patron of the city of Parma, Italy. St. Hilary, considered a doctor of the church, wrote important theological works, among all the *De Trinitate*.[33]

As for us, we will focus on his *Tractatus super psalmos*,[34] a work clearly influenced by Origen where St. Hilary spends some paragraphs on the interpretation of the sixth petition of the Lord's Prayer. More specifically, St. Hilary comments on verse 8 of Psalm 119(118), which in Latin reads, "*Justificationes tuas custodiam; non me derelinquas usquequaque*" (Ps 119(118):8 VUL).

We have previously analyzed some salient passages from Psalm 119(118). One of the main concerns of the psalmist is that God would not abandon him and make him deviate from his commandments. The *incipit* of the psalm in which the verse in question is contained is all an invocation of love to God and a praise for those who are able to follow his commandments and walk in the right path. The psalmist implores God not to abandon him ("*non me derelinquas*"). St. Hilary starts by explaining what this invocation may mean and why there could be the possibility that God abandons us.

His reasoning starts from the fact that when God wants to test us, very often he abandons us in front of temptations ("*nos ab eo ob temptationes derelinqui*"). Pay

---

32. "μὴ ἐάσῃς ἡμᾶς ἐμπεσεῖν εἰς πειρασμὸν [*mè eáseis hēmâs empesein eis peirasmòn*]" = "Do not let us fall into temptation" (Dionysius, *The Gospel according to Luke*, 22.46).
33. *On the Trinity*.
34. *Treatise on the psalms*.

135

attention to the grammatical choice: *ob temptationes* does not indicate a motion, but a position. God leaves us in front of (*ob*) temptations and then "goes away" to see how we fare, so that our faith can be confirmed ("*ut per eas fides nostra probabilis fiat*"). And so, if we know that God, to test us, must necessarily abandon us (temporarily), what sense does the invocation of the psalm make? The key to understanding it, according to St. Hilary, lies in the adverb *usquequaque*. The term *usquequaque* generally indicates an extension that is mostly infinite in space and/or time. Depending on the case, it can be understood as "in every place," or "at all times," or "in all circumstances," and, by extension, it can indicate the totality of the action, that is, "completely," "entirely." The interpretation of St. Hilary is that the psalmist wanted to say, "Do not abandon me *completely*." What does this mean? St. Hilary explains it as follows. On the one hand, we know that God, when he tests us, must abandon us in the face of temptation; on the other hand, we ask God, please, not to abandon us completely, otherwise we would never have the strength to resist temptation. To justify his interpretation, he cites the very sixth petition of the Lord's Prayer: "*Quod et in dominicae orationis ordine continetur, cum dicitur: non nos [derelinquas] in temptatione, quam sufferre non possumus.*"[35]

The first critical point is the use of a static expression (*in temptatione*) instead of a motion (*in temptationem*). Here St. Hilary is consistent with his reasoning (God does not push us into temptation, but rather abandons us in the face of it), but obviously he must alter the original text of the Gospels which, as we know, clearly describe a motion (*eis peirasmón*). The second interesting point is that explanatory addition "*quam sufferre non possumus.*" As if to say, abandon us in all the temptations that you want, but never in those that we would not have the strength to overcome. This, according to St. Hilary, is precisely the meaning of Psalm 119(118) when it says, "do not abandon me *completely*." God would abandon us completely if he left us in the midst of temptations too strong for our possibility of endurance. The third critical point is that St. Hilary cites the explanatory addition not as a gloss, but possibly as an integral part of the prayer recited by the faithful at that time, further confirming the need within the early Christian communities to sweeten and make explicable the apparent scandal of that "*ne nos inducas.*"

In support of his interpretation, St. Hilary quotes the famous phrase of St. Paul contained in the first letter to the Corinthians: "God is faithful, who will not suffer you to be tempted above that ye are able" (1 Cor 10:13). We have already had occasion to analyze this phrase (usually waved by the supporters of the permissive thesis as unquestionable proof of the validity of their interpretation), which for us is clear. God constantly puts people to the test, but he does so honestly, justly, without malice (typical of the devil instead). This is what St. Paul wants to say. God does not play tricks, he does not enjoy seeing us fall, he remains always faithful to us, and for this reason he can never subject us to a test greater than our possibility of endurance. If God were

---

35. "Which is also contained in the verse of the Lord's Prayer when it says: Do not abandon us in the temptation we cannot bear" (Hilary, *Super Psalmos*, 118.aleph.15).

to give a person a test that he already knew that person would not be able to pass, what would be the point of the test itself? It would be a sadistic God, a God without compassion, that is, an evil God.

Does this mean that the sixth petition of the Lord's Prayer should be understood as an invocation to the Father not to abandon us to temptations that are beyond our possibility of endurance? In our opinion it is illogical to think so. Unless, to paraphrase Origen, we are thinking that Jesus is teaching us to pray the impossible. If, as St. Paul explains so well, God is faithful and would never think of putting us before a temptation greater than ourselves, why should we beg him not to do precisely what we already know he will never do? Because if we pray for God not to do something, we are implicitly assuming that there might be a possibility that God may do that something instead. So, Jesus would be teaching us to doubt God's faithfulness? Not only would it be a useless prayer (we would be praying for something we know will never happen), but at the same time blasphemous because it would insinuate the possibility that God might test us with malice, that is, with the sole purpose of seeing us fall.

If we take up again the whole reasoning of St. Hilary, we can see that it does not stand:

1. The sixth petition of the Lord's Prayer should be translated as "do not abandon us in front of temptation."

2. However, we know that in order to be tested, God must necessarily abandon us alone in the face of temptation.

3. So, what the sixth petition of the Lord's Prayer means is "do not abandon us in temptations that we cannot bear."

4. However, we know with certainty (St. Paul tells us) that God will never abandon us in temptations we cannot bear.

A twisted short-circuit of ideas that unfortunately leads nowhere.[36]

In any case, the whole reasoning is vitiated, in our opinion, by an important interpretative problem. That *usquequaque* that St. Hilary interprets as "completely," most likely has another meaning in this context. It indicates the entreaty to God never to abandon us, that is, *under no circumstances*, at no time and for no reason. Translated in this way, verse 8 of Psalm 119(118) makes much more sense. As mentioned, the opening of the psalm is an ode of dispassionate love toward God and his teachings. What the psalmist is asking of God is simply to never abandon him, not to not abandon him completely. Indeed, what would be the point of such an invocation within a declaration of love to God? Think of a lover declaring his love to his beloved. Would

36. The Lord's Prayer is a concise, straightforward, no-nonsense prayer, just as Jesus in the Sermon on the Mount was teaching his disciples to pray—with clear, sharp, unambiguous words. It is impossible to imagine that in order to grasp its profound meaning, one must resort to such convoluted reasoning. The idea that the sixth petition means "do abandon us to temptation, but not completely" goes precisely against that concept of clarity that Jesus is preaching ("Let your saying be: yes yes, no no.").

it make more sense for him to say, "My love, I love you, don't ever leave me!" or "My love, I love you, don't leave me completely"?

This interpretation also corresponds with the original Hebrew text. *Usquequaque* is the Latin translation of the Hebrew adverb ' *ăḏ* (עַד), which has as its first meaning the idea of continuation to infinity in time and space, that is, "always and everywhere." The negation of this adverb indicates the total absence of time and space, that is, it describes an action that does not take place anywhere and at any time, that is, "never and nowhere."

Not to mention the fact that the introduction of the concept of a "static abandonment in temptation" in the translation of the sixth petition of the Lord's Prayer appears as a totally arbitrary—an interpretation that alters the sense of Scripture, which instead, as we know, suggests the idea of a forced motion within the *peirasmós*.

## AMBROSE

A contemporary of St. Hilary is St. Ambrose, bishop by popular acclamation and patron saint of Milan, Italy, whose life covers the last sixty years of the fourth century. A refined theologian, St. Ambrose represents one of the most influential figures within the church of the time and is officially considered a doctor of the church. The *corpus* of his works is impressive. He too, albeit in passing, makes his contribution to the interpretation of the sixth petition of the Lord's Prayer. He does so in *De sacramentis*,[37] in which, blending the interpretations of St. Cyprian and St. Hilary, he warns us to pay attention to the exact words that Jesus said: "*Dicit: ne patiaris nos induci in temptationem, quam ferre non possumus. Non dicit: non inducas in temptationem.*"[38]

It seems paradoxical, but St. Ambrose seems to suggest that the original text of the Gospels does not represent the true words of Jesus. The *Vetus Latina* itself, the official Latin translation of the Bible adopted by the church of Rome at least until the end of the fourth century, as well as the Vulgate that would replace it in the following centuries, contain the well-known expression "*ne nos inducas in tentationem*," that is, precisely what St. Ambrose, in a provocative way, claims that Jesus did *not* say.

Given the importance of St. Ambrose within the church of the fourth century, his position cannot be trivially dismissed, but must be given the necessary consideration. His position bears witness to how, just over three hundred years after Christ's death, the words Christ used in the Lord's Prayer had passed through a process of interpretive rationalization that had not only altered their original meaning, but had even censored them to officially replace them, in the minds of the faithful and in the daily practice of prayer, with the interpretation itself. The interpretation of Scripture not only has the pretension of explaining the texts, but even of replacing them.

---

37. *On the sacraments*.

38. "He says: do not let us be led into temptation that we cannot bear. He does not say: lead us not into temptation" (Ambrose, *De sacramentis*, 5.4.29).

St. Ambrose briefly proposes a comparison that should support his thesis. God trains us with temptation, as one does with an athlete. And a coach obviously has no interest in physically destroying his athlete, but rather in making him progress by giving him difficult, but not impossible, exercises. All correct. However, none of this transpires from the original words of Christ.

For St. Ambrose, as for St. Hilary, it seems necessary to introduce that gloss ("*quam ferre non possumus*") in order to fully explain the petition. A gloss that seems to have become part of the recitation of the Lord's Prayer by the faithful at that time. A gloss which, far from explaining anything, introduces an insurmountable logical problem. If the words of St. Paul (God is faithful and does not allow us to be tempted beyond our possibility of endurance) are correct (and no one has ever doubted that they are), one must logically conclude that it is not possible that Jesus taught us to ask the Father not to allow us to be tempted beyond our possibilities, that is, exactly what St. Paul affirms that God will never do. In conclusion, St. Paul's words in 1 Cor 10:13 are exactly the reason why the sixth petition of the Lord's Prayer cannot be interpreted in this way.

## CHROMATIUS OF AQUILEIA

Now let us move a little further east, while remaining in northern Italy, to meet St. Chromatius, archbishop of Aquileia (he died in 407 AD). One of his most important writings remains the *Tractatus in Evangellium Matthaei*,[39] most likely written in the last years of his life, where St. Chromatius devotes an entire paragraph to discussing the concept of temptation.

The starting point of St. Chromatius is taken up again by Origen. Temptations are necessary and sometimes even useful. There may be different reasons why people are subjected to temptation. Some so that their sins may be repaired ("*ad emendationem*"), others so that their faith may be proven ("*ad fidei probationem*"), others still so that they may attain the glory of the kingdom of heaven ("*ad gloriam*"). If we then understand that temptations are useful, we could never think that Jesus taught us to ask the Father to exempt us from them. Here then is the conclusion: "*Non ergo, ne in toto tentemur, oramus; sed ne, supra quam virtus fidei patitur, tentationi tradamur: quod ipsum in alio libro Evangelii evidenter ostensum est: sic enim scriptum est: Et ne nos inferas in tentationem, quam suffere non possumus.*"[40]

The conclusion is identical to that of St. Ambrose. Since temptations are useful, we are not asking to be exempt from them, but only from those that are too strong for our possibility of endurance. And, to support this conclusion, he quotes the usual

---

39. *Treatise on the Gospel of Matthew.*

40. "Therefore, we do not pray that we may be totally exempted from temptation; but that we may not be delivered to a temptation above what the virtue of our faith can bear: this identical notion is clearly brought out in another book of the Gospel, where it is written: And do not lead us into temptation which we are not able to bear" (Chromatius, *Evangellium Matthaei*, 14.7.1–3).

passage from St. Paul (1 Cor 10:13), without realizing the inconsistency of a prayer that asks the Father not to do something that we already know he will never do. Therefore, if the conclusion is not enlightening, we believe it is nonetheless important to underline two points of St. Chromatius's discourse:

1. St. Chromatius says that in the Gospels it is literally written, "And lead us not into a temptation that we cannot bear." Obviously, St. Chromatius knows that that addition ("that we cannot bear") is posited and does not appear anywhere in the Gospels. Nevertheless, the sensibilities of the time seem to have assimilated that gloss within Scripture, if not formally, certainly in the minds and imaginations of the faithful.

2. St. Chromatius is right when he translates the sixth petition of the Lord's Prayer as "*ne nos inferas.*" Do you remember all the argument around the semantic difference between *phérō* and *ágō* (in Greek) and between *fero* and *duco* (in Latin)? You probably remember that we suggested that a literal translation of the Greek text of the sixth petition of the Lord's Prayer should have used the Latin verb *infero* instead of *induco*. St. Chromatius is confirming that in some Latin translations of the Bible that were circulating at that time there was precisely the wording "*ne nos inferas,*" which in our opinion is the most faithful translation of the original Greek text.

While we cannot agree with the conclusion to which he comes, we must absolutely give credit to St. Chromatius for not having attempted easy loopholes through permissive constructs. On the contrary, St. Chromatius breaks with the tradition of all the main Latin theologians preceding him and proposes the strongest (and truest) translation possible of the original texts ("*ne nos inferas in,*" that is, "do not carry us into") demonstrating great intellectual honesty.

## JEROME

A friend of St. Chromatius of Aquileia is another giant of Latin theology, St. Jerome of Stridon, biblical scholar, translator, theologian, and Roman Christian monk, to whom we owe the entire official translation of the Bible from Hebrew and Greek into Latin, which will become known as the Vulgate, commissioned by Pope Damasio I and that cost him twenty-three years of hard work. To him we owe the Lord's Prayer in Latin, as we know it. Unfortunately, St. Jerome does not offer any kind of commentary on the sixth petition, but a fragment taken from his monumental work *Commentaria in Ezechielem*,[41] written between 410 and 415 AD, is illuminating: "*quotidie in oratione dicentes: Ne inducas nos in tentationem, quam ferre non possumus.*"[42]

41. *Commentary on Ezekiel.*
42. "praying every day and saying, Do not lead us into temptation that we cannot bear" (Jerome, *In Ezechielem*, 14.48.16).

Even though the fragment is taken from a completely different context, St. Jerome confirms to us in this passage (if there were still a need) that the explanatory gloss ("which we cannot bear") had become to all intents and purposes part of the Lord's Prayer that the faithful recited daily. This is the solution that the church fathers adopted in the first centuries after Christ to censure the scandal of that "lead us not into temptation." This solution was so widespread that it became an integral part of the prayer itself.

Unfortunately, however, on closer inspection, it is a solution that solves nothing. The "scandal" is only apparently censored. If it sounds so jarring and almost blasphemous to ask God not to "lead us into temptation," how can it not sound jarring and almost blasphemous to ask God not to "lead us into a temptation that we cannot bear"? For the practical result of the two options is identical: "to lead us into temptation" gives the idea of voluntarily pushing us to sin, while "to lead us into a temptation that we cannot bear" means subjecting us to a temptation that God already knows from the beginning that we will not be able to reject, that is, it means pushing us voluntarily to sin.

## AUGUSTINE

Let us now spend some time with one of the greatest contemporaries of St. Ambrose, St. Chromatius, and St. Jerome—the one who has been considered the greatest church father, the greatest Christian thinker if not one of the greatest geniuses of humanity ever. We are talking about St. Augustine, whose powerful personal story of conversion, philosophy, and theology will forever shape the thinking of the Christian Church. The vastness and importance of the *corpus* of works produced by St. Augustine, steeped in classical culture and a profound connoisseur of Greek and Latin philosophy, is monumental. It is enough to mention his two greatest compositions: *Confessiones*[43] and *De civitate Dei*.[44] Deeply influenced by the preaching of St. Ambrose in Milan, he converted to Christianity at the age of thirty-three and then became Bishop of Hipponia, North Africa, for thirty-five years from 395 AD until his death in 430 AD. After being fascinated by the thought of Manichaeism at an early age, he would break with it because he disagreed with the way the Manichaeans had solved the problem of evil. This problem will remain central in the life and philosophical thought of St. Augustine and will be one of the main reasons that will push him to the Christian faith. The problem of evil in the world and its possible solution within the Christian faith permeate most of his writings. And, having understood by now that it is not possible to fully understand the meaning of the Lord's Prayer if the problem of evil is not fully understood, St. Augustine will prove to be a precious source of inspiration. There are two works in which St. Augustine dwells at length on the interpretation of the sixth

43. *The confessions*.
44. *The city of God*.

petition of the Lord's Prayer: *De sermone Domini in monte*, written in 394 AD, and one of his many sermons,[45] *Sermo LVII*, probably written around 410 AD.

Let us begin with the second book, chapter 9, of *De sermone Domini in monte*. Paragraph 30 is dedicated to the explanation of the sixth petition thus formulated: "*ne nos inferas in tentationem.*" St. Augustine, with great intellectual honesty, starts from the strongly causative interpretation of St. Chromatius, who uses the verb *infero*, equivalent to the original Greek *eisphérō*. He considers it to be the closest Latin translation to the original. However, he admits that some other codes use the expression "*ne nos inducas*" and concludes that the two expressions should be considered equivalent ("*tantundem valere arbitror*"), since they derive from the same original Greek text.[46] But let us read the most interesting passage: "*Multi autem in precando ita dicunt: Ne nos patiaris induci in tentationem, exponentes videlicet, quomodo dictum sit inducas.*"[47]

St. Augustine confirms that the permissive construct had become part of the daily prayer of many of the faithful. Which demonstrates the utter confusion that reigned in those early centuries after Christ about the proper way to declaim the Lord's Prayer. Some used the original causative expression (*ne nos inferas*), others used a substantially equivalent variant (*ne nos inducas*), others a somewhat more arbitrary interpretation (*ne nos derelinquas*), others used the permissive construct (*ne nos patiaris induci*), still others added the explanatory gloss now to the causative expression (*ne nos inducas in tentationem, quam ferre non possumus*), now to the permissive expression (*ne nos patiaris induci in tentationem, quam ferre non possumus*). A *potpourri* of combinations, so that one had essentially the freedom to make Christ say whatever one wanted. St. Augustine, with great lucidity, tries with his writings to put a stop to this interpretative chaos.

First of all, he explains, "*Aliud est autem induci in tentationem, aliud tentari.*"[48] St. Augustine confirms here that the expression "leading into temptation" is perceived in a completely different way from the action of "tempting." In a way that is exactly equivalent to contemporary sensibilities.[49] Since St. Augustine is the first to dispel any kind of ambiguity on this issue (which might seem obvious to us, but clearly was not at that time), from now on we will try to always keep the two expressions distinct. When we speak of "tempting" or "being tempted" we will think of exposing to temptation.

---

45. He composed about 500 of them.

46. The two terms are not exactly equivalent. We have discussed at length the semantic differences between *eisphérō* (*infero*) and *eiságō* (*induco*) in previous chapters.

47. "Many, however, pray thus: Do not allow us to be led into temptation, thus demonstrating how 'lead us not' is to be understood" (Augustine, *De sermone Domini in monte*, 2.9.30).

48. "It is one thing to be led into temptation, quite another to be tempted" (Augustine, *De sermone Domini in monte*, 2.9.30).

49. If I say, "I have been tempted," I am not automatically declaring that I have sinned. I am declaring that I have been exposed to a temptation. But if I say, "I have been led into temptation," I am confessing instead that I have succumbed to temptation and therefore that I have sinned.

When we speak of "leading into temptation" or "being led into temptation," we are thinking of yielding to temptation, that is, of committing a sin.

Having clarified this point, St. Augustine goes on to explain the usefulness of temptation, thus taking up the insights of Origen and in some ways of Tertullian. Temptations, Augustine says, are not useful to God, but to us and to those around us. They allow us to understand how strong our faith is, and the faith of those with whom we come in contact. In fact, he says, "*Deo noti sumus et ante omnes tentationes, qui scit omnia antequam fiant.*"[50]

We had anticipated how St. Augustine would clarify and correct Tertullian's conclusions, but without ever renouncing the concept of divine omniscience. And in order to demonstrate that God does not tempt us because he does not know, but because he wants us to know, St. Augustine devotes the next paragraph to a discussion of that passage from Deuteronomy that we have already analyzed before, in which it says that "the Lord your God tests you, to know whether ye love the Lord your God" (Deut 13:3). His thesis is that this passage should be interpreted differently: "God tempts you to let you know if you love him."[51]

St. Augustine brings two arguments to support his thesis. The first one is that the Bible says "to know" instead of "to make known" because it would be a way of saying commonly used in spoken language ("*in consuetudine loquendi*"). The second argument is more articulated. He cites the episode of the multiplication of the loaves and fishes, in which Jesus, in front of an oceanic crowd, with feigned concern, asks his disciple Philip, "*Unde ememus panes, ut manducent hi?*"[52] (John 6:5). The question seems out of place. How is it possible that Jesus would be concerned about such worldly things as money? It is a rhetorical question, of course, and John hastens to explain: "*Hoc autem dicebat tentans eum: ipse enim sciebat quid esset facturus*"[53] (John 6:6).

St. Augustine quotes this very verse to demonstrate how Jesus tempts (read: tests) Philip, already knowing how Philip would react. St. Augustine then asks himself: if Jesus knows Philip's intentions even before testing him, why does he test him? The conclusion can only be one: so that Philip (not Jesus) would realize his lack of faith.[54]

Having finished this digression on the defense of divine omniscience in the face of free will, in the next paragraph St. Augustine returns to discuss the correct

50. "God knows us even before any temptation, for God knows everything before it happens" (Augustine, *De sermone Domini in monte*, 2.9.30).

51. However, there is not much in the original Hebrew text that may justify such a translation. If the Bible had meant "to make known" instead of "to know," it had every means at its disposal to express such a concept. After all, "make known" represents the causative construct of the verb "to know," and Hebrew, as we know, has a very simple way to conjugate a verb in the causative form—by using the *hiphil* stem. The original Hebrew text, however, does not. The verb *yādāʿ* (יָדַע) is conjugated in the base *qal* form.

52. "Where will we get the money to buy bread to feed all these people?"

53. "He said this to test him: for he of himself knew what he would do."

54. However, to be honest, the passage does not say that Jesus knew what Philip would do, but rather what *ipse*, that is, he himself, that is, Jesus, would do, *independently* of Philip's answer.

interpretation of the sixth petition of the Lord's Prayer. Having ascertained the fact that tempting is a completely different concept from leading into temptation, St. Augustine concludes that in the Lord's Prayer we are not praying not to be tempted, but rather not to be led into temptation (that is, not to sin): "*Non ergo hic oratur ut non tentemur, sed ut non inferamur in tentationem; tamquam si quispiam cui necesse est igne examinari non oret ut igne non contingatur, sed ut non exuratur. Vasa enim figuli probat fornax, et homines iustos tentatio tribulationis.*"[55]

Apart from the usual grammatical reversal (from active to passive) whereby God does not lead us into temptation, but allows us to be led, it is interesting to note how St. Augustine recognizes that, for righteous people, temptation coincides substantially with tribulation. He speaks of "*tentatio tribulationis*," that is, of the trial of psychophysical suffering, which has nothing to do with the seduction of moral corruption.

This overlapping of the two semantic fields (psychophysical suffering and moral corruption), with the consequent confusion that ensues, is clearly fueled by the fact that, until this moment in history, that is, until the end of the fifth century, in both the Greek and Latin languages, no adequate terms had been developed to differentiate the two concepts. Everything is *peirasmós* (in Greek), everything is *temptatio* (in Latin). In the mind of St. Augustine, who had converted to the Christian faith only a few years before, these two types of *temptatio* had not yet been formally distinguished.[56]

He quotes three quite different examples from the Old Testament: Joseph, Susanna, and Job. Joseph, son of Jacob, whose story is told in chapters 37–50 of the book of Genesis, was tempted by the wife of Potiphar, the head of Pharaoh's guard, to whom Joseph had been sold. She wanted to convince him to have an extramarital and therefore sinful relationship with her. Joseph refused and resisted the temptation. He was morally tempted, but not led into temptation, since he did not yield to the seduction of sin. Susanna, whose story is told in the book of Daniel, refuses the indecent proposal of two old servants. Because of this, she will then be falsely accused, arrested, and found guilty of adultery. Only Daniel's intervention will manage to unmask the old servants' deceit and save Susanna. Like Joseph, then, we can say that Susanna was also morally tempted, but not led into temptation, since she did not yield to the seduction of sin.

Job's story should be familiar to the reader at this point. Unlike Joseph and Susanna, Job was never morally tempted. All his temptations were psychophysical. Job is tested in the flesh and in the spirit. He sees all his ten children die in one fell swoop, all his livestock be destroyed, and his body be covered from head to toe with purulent sores that torment him day and night. In other words, Satan's strategy is not to seduce Job into committing even one of the seven deadly sins (lust, gluttony, greed, sloth,

---

55. "For here we pray not that we may not be tempted, but that we may not be led into temptation. Just as one who knows that he will be tested by fire does not pray not to be touched by fire, but not to be burned alive by it. For the potter's vessels are tempered by the furnace, righteous people by the temptation of tribulation" (Augustine, *De sermone Domini in monte*, 2.9.32).

56. St. Augustine's thought will reach this maturity only fifteen years later, when he will theorize the difference between *tentatio* and *probatio* (*Sermo LVII*, 9).

wrath, envy, pride). Satan only wants to weaken Job in flesh and spirit to test how far his faith will go. To find its breaking point, to use an engineering expression. Like a metal that is subjected to increasing stress and strain until it breaks. There is nothing devious, nothing malicious. There is no seduction typical of moral temptation, which appeals to human instinctive attraction to sin. Above all, there is no concept of deception—of snare.[57] Psychophysical suffering, as a test of the faith, is on a completely different level. It does not come in disguise. It is real and natural in all its rawness and in the pain it brings. This is why it is something that people abhor with all their might and would like, if possible, always to avoid. It is the very antithesis of the condition to which a person instinctively yearns on earth—that of a happy and serene life, free of worries. It is the last resource that Satan has in his bow to try to separate people from God—trying them to the point of making them lose their faith. After all, this is what happens to poor Job. After having been "touched" in the flesh by Satan, in the grip of the most unbearable torment, he suddenly loses faith in a just God.

Job, says St. Augustin, is the most striking (*maxime*) example of a person who was tempted, but not led into temptation. We beg to differ on both points. As we have amply described, Job was not tempted, in the malicious sense of the word. That is, he was not subjected to any moral temptation, to any malicious seduction. Instead, Job was tested, in the sense that he was subjected to the most severe psychophysical test imaginable. *Tentatio tribulationis*, to use the expression of St. Augustine. But, even leaving aside this distinction and wanting to consider to all intents and purposes that of Job a "temptation" on a par with the seduction resisted by Joseph and Susanna, how is it possible to conclude that Job was not led into temptation? If to be led into temptation means, as we have seen, to yield to temptation, and if in this case we consider as temptation the psychophysical stress Job had to undergo, how is it possible to conclude that Job did not yield to that stress? Job, unfortunately for him, did give in. He gave in hard and began to blame God, in many cases crossing the line of blasphemy. The fact that, in the end, after the intervention of God, Job asked for forgiveness and was readmitted to enjoy divine favor, does not erase the fact that Job had completely failed the test to which God, through Satan, had subjected him.[58]

And here St. Augustine arrives at the most interesting point of his reflection: "*Fiunt igitur tentationes per satanam non potestate eius sed permissu Domini ad homines aut pro suis peccatis puniendos aut pro Dei misericordia probandos et exercendos.*"[59]

Satan's temptations (which are not in his power though, and only on behalf of God) have two possible purposes. *Aut aut.* Either punitive or educational. Both

57. Recall the widely used metaphor of the snare of temptation, similar to the devices used by hunters to deceive and snare their prey.

58. This is shown by the fact that God, in the beginning, is furious with Job for the way he lost his faith.

59. "There are therefore temptations that take place through Satan (not in Satan's power but permitted by God) either to punish people for their sins or to temper them and confirm their faith according to God's mercy" (Augustine, *De sermone Domini in monte*, 2.9.34).

examples are drawn from the book of Job. Remember the speeches of Elihu, the little boy who could argue more profoundly than the other three elderly friends? He was the one who explained the punitive and pedagogical function of evil. When we stray from his way, God would punish us by "touching" us in the flesh and making us understand that we are going in the wrong direction. On the other hand, Job is the emblem of the fortifying function of temptation. Temptation tempers us. It burns our flesh, it afflicts our spirit, but at the same time it makes us stronger and worthy of the kingdom of heaven ("*ad probandos et exercendos*").

It is useful to highlight how St. Augustine admits that temptations are not in the power of Satan but occur *per satanam*. That is, Satan is the means, the instrument that God has at his disposal to tempt people, that is, to put them to the test. Satan in himself can do nothing ("*non potestate eius'*"). Not a hair on Job's head would have been twisted if God had not wanted it. That "*permissu Domini*" (by divine permission) is a clever euphemism to mask what is however impossible to deny: the temptations given to human beings by God *per satanam* do not happen simply because God *allows* them (almost as if God washed his hands of them), but by precise divine will. *Voluntate Domini*, we should instead say. If the purpose of temptations, as St. Augustine himself declares, is either to punish us for our sins or to make our faith stronger, there is no doubt that the one who wants all this is not Satan, but God. Satan has no interest in punishing us for our sins (he rejoices in them instead) nor does he care about our faith. God does, however, and it is he who wants all these things. Therefore, in our opinion, it is useless to persevere in this permissive misunderstanding. If God did not want it, he would not "allow" it, which means that God did want it. The evil inherent in temptation is part of his will, that is, of divine Providence, that is, of the plan that God has for humanity.

After all, Satan does what is in his nature. He tries in every way to distance people from God. And, like any other being (angelic or human), he tries to get from God what suits him. That is, he tries to conform the divine will to his own will. Is this not what each of us does when we pray? What else is prayer if not a request to God to conform his will to ours? Obviously, not all prayers, not all requests are granted by God. Only those that are conformed to his will have any chance of being answered. What does it mean to be conformed to his will? It means to be compatible with his plan. This is what Jesus teaches us in the third petition of the Lord's Prayer: "Thy will be done." We, as human beings, with our needs and weaknesses, with the short-sightedness that distinguishes us, ask God for a whole series of things that would be useful to us, but we know well that God can consider whether or not to grant them to us only if our requests are compatible with the plan that God has for us and for humankind. This is the power of prayer. God, in his omnipotence, is willing to consider granting people everything they want—he is willing to find a different way for his plan to be realized—provided that they ask him expressly. And the moment God grants a prayer, the will of the one who prays automatically becomes divine will. When we pray to get something from God, we are not asking for permission for that thing to happen. We are asking for God's will for that thing to happen. And when God grants a prayer, he is not granting permission, as if he were granting an exception to the rule. He is confirming that our prayer is in accordance with his will, that is, it is fulfilling his will.

The same is true of Satan. When Satan twice tries to get God to severely test Job's seemingly unshakable faith, he is not asking for permission to torment him. He is asking God that his will be that Job be tormented. Or again, in Luke's Gospel we see Jesus revealing to Peter immediately after the Last Supper that Satan has requested to sift him and all his companions as one would sift wheat: "Simon, Simon, behold, Satan has requested you, that he may sift you as wheat" (Luke 22:31). Jesus is not saying that Satan has asked God's permission to tempt his disciples. He is saying that he has asked that the will of the Father be that the disciples be tempted. So much so that Jesus reveals to Peter that he tried to counter Satan's request with his own prayer before his Father: "But I have prayed for thee, that thy faith fail not" (Luke 22:32).

One of Satan's peculiar characteristics is that he tries to put people in a bad light before God. Not for nothing is he very often referred to as "the Accuser." We saw this in the opening of the story of Job. We also see it on another occasion in chapter 3 of the book of Zechariah, where Satan appears formally as the accuser of the high priest Joshua, who appeared before the Angel of the Lord to be judged (Zech 3:1). In the first case, God consents to Satan's request, and Job will pay the consequences. In the second case, God will be angry with Satan, chase him away with harsh words, and Joshua will be forgiven and cleansed of his sins (Zech 3:2).

Not all temptations that a person faces, however, are imparted by God through Satan, St. Augustine continues. There are temptations into which people fall because of their own human frailty and weakness, without the need for demonic intervention. It is that temptation that St. Paul calls *anthrópinos peirasmós* ("human" temptation), into which a person falls, not because of intrinsic evil, but because of an error of judgment. In fact, St. Augustine quotes the famous passage in 1 Cor 10:13 where St. Paul teaches that God "will not suffer you to be tempted above that ye are able," and concludes that "*non id nobis orandum esse ut non tentemur, sed ne in tentationem inducamur. Inducimur enim, si tales acciderint quas ferre non possumus.*"[60]

This first solution of St. Augustine's aligns with the entire Latin theological tradition preceding him, thus crashing into an irreparable logical short-circuit:

1. The expression "to lead into temptation" does not simply mean "to expose to temptation." In fact, it is equivalent to "to make one fall into the trap of temptation," that is, "to make one commit a sin."

2. However, God cannot—by definition—be the cause of sin.

---

60. "We are not to pray that we may not be tempted, but that we may not be led into temptation. For we are led into temptation if temptations come to us which we are not able to bear" (Augustine, *De sermone Domini in monte*, 2.9.34).

3. Therefore, the petition "lead us not into temptation" must be understood not in a causative sense but in a permissive sense ("do not let us be led into temptation").

4. Also, we know that the one who leads us into temptation is Satan, who tempts us with temptations that we cannot bear (otherwise, if we could bear them, we would not be led into temptation).

5. However, we know (as St. Paul says) that God will never let us be tempted with temptations that we cannot bear.

6. Therefore, praying to ask God not to allow Satan to lead us into temptation is useless.

Pages and pages of sophisticated theological reasoning to conclude that the sixth petition of the Lord's Prayer is useless. But, since we can assume, without risk of being proven wrong, that Christ did not teach us to pray uselessly, there must be something deeply flawed in the reasoning outlined above. One of the most obvious logical errors is, for example, the equation "being led into temptation" = "temptation impossible to endure" ("*inducimur enim, si tales acciderint quas ferre non possumus*"). Because if what St. Paul says is true, then one would have to come to the absurd conclusion that God will never allow us to fall into sin.

So let us try to clarify once and for all what the Apostle means in 1 Cor 10:13. All of St. Paul's reasoning hinges on the phrase "*Deus fidelis*" (God is faithful), of which the expression "he will not suffer you to be tempted above that ye are able" is an explanatory gloss. The fact that God does not allow people to be subjected to temptations that are beyond their ability to bear, does not necessarily mean that we will always be able to overcome all the temptations we face. It simply means that God is faithful to his people and does not lay traps for them. He will never put us in front of temptations that are impossible for us to overcome; that is, in situations where the only way out is through sin.[61] When a person falls into temptation and sins, it is not because God has placed him before a test impossible to overcome, but because, although that person had received from God all the tools to be able to discern good from evil—although that temptation was within his ability to endure—out of his own weakness, out of his own free will, that person has not been able to stand up to it, choosing evil rather than good. How many times do people, even knowing that they are committing a sin, commit it because they are unable to resist temptation? St. Augustine himself admits this in his *Confessiones* when he recalls how, as a boy, he fell into the vice of theft, the intoxication of which overcame the awareness that it was a deplorable act. Was it perhaps that God was allowing him to be tempted beyond his ability to endure? No, he was not. Augustine was perfectly aware that theft was a sin.

---

61. In 1 Cor 10:13, St. Paul concludes, "but will with the temptation also make a way to escape, that ye may be able to bear it."

Therefore, God was giving him all the intellectual tools he needed to be able to make the correct choice.

The responsibility for sin is always ours when we are not able to endure a temptation theoretically possible to endure. It is not God's, who imposed on us a temptation impossible to endure. When St. Paul uses the expression "above that ye are able," he is thinking precisely of temptations that are impossible to bear *in absolute terms*, not of temptations that people are unable to bear due to their own weakness. It follows that trying to explain the sixth petition of the Lord's Prayer (that speaks of "leading into temptation," not of temptations impossible to endure) with St. Paul's phrase in 1 Cor 10:13 produces insurmountable illogicalities.

And in fact, when, fifteen years later, St. Augustine set out to write his *Sermo LVII*, dedicated to the analysis of the Lord's Prayer, he revised part of his reasoning, arriving at a different solution. Let us take a look.

St. Augustine starts from the origins, or rather—if you'll pardon the pun—from Origen. Do you remember how Origen first theorized the impossibility of escaping temptation, given that people are made of flesh and the flesh instinctively struggles against the spirit and against God? To support his thesis, he quoted the famous phrase uttered by Job: "Is not man's whole life on earth a temptation?" (Job 7:1). The original Hebrew term used by Job, as seen, was closer to the concept of war/fight than temptation. The Septuagint translates it very accurately with a specific term used in the military, *peiratĕrion*, which indicates the assault of enemies. Origen, taking advantage of the etymological proximity between *peiratĕrion* and *peirasmós*, considered the two terms essentially interchangeable. Hence, the Latin *tentatio*. If, however, we go and see the official version of the Vulgate, St. Jerome remains faithful to the Hebrew text and translates with *militia*, a term deliberately borrowed from the military sphere. In the best case, the *tentatio* of which Job was complaining was certainly not the struggle of the spirit against the impure instincts of the flesh, that is, against an internal enemy, but rather the constant struggle against the sufferings and miseries of daily life, that is, against an external enemy.

If, however, our whole life is a continuous *tentatio*, "*Quid ergo rogamus?*" asks St. Augustine. What are we asking of God when we recite the sixth petition of the Lord's Prayer? This time, instead of taking his cue from St. Paul (1 Cor 10:13), St. Augustine prefers to pick up the thread of the discourse by starting from the famous epistle of James, which we presented in chapter 1, in which the Apostle declares, "Let no man say when he is tempted, I am tempted of God" (Jas 1:13).

Here, St. Augustine has one of his most powerful insights. He understands that it is necessary—absolutely necessary—if we want to find a reasonable solution to the mystery of the sixth petition—to make a distinction between two types of *tentatio*. On the one hand, the *tentatio* that relies on an enemy that we could define as internal, that is, the human instinct, which is naturally prone to sin, and which is exploited by Satan to confuse, deceive, and seduce people to choose evil rather than good. A *tentatio*, which has its roots in malice, in deception.[62] A *tentatio* that is a trap. This is precisely the temptation of which James speaks, and God has nothing to do with it:[63] "*Est enim alia tentatio, quae appellatur probatio: de ipsa tentatione scriptum est, Tentat vos Dominus Deus vester, ut sciat si diligitis eum.*"[64]

For the first time, a doctor of the church clarifies a concept that had remained utterly confused in the minds of all his predecessors. Using the same term, *tentatio*, both for the temptation that Satan produces with evil intent, and for the test, *probatio*, that God imposes on people with honest intent to test their faith, undermines any reasoning on the sixth petition of the Lord's Prayer.

However, once he has taken this major step, St. Augustine somehow stops and returns to considering only the first type of temptation, the one imparted by Satan, of which James speaks, as the only candidate for the interpretation of the sixth petition. Therefore, he ends up wrapping himself up again in a convoluted interpretation, which follows the one reached by St. Hilary of Poitiers. If the *tentatio* of the sixth petition is the typical temptation of the devil, how is it possible that Christ associated it with God ("*ne nos inferas*")? This is his explanation: "*In illa tentatione qua quisque decipitur et seducitur, neminem tentat Deus: sed plane judicio suo alto et occulto quosdam deserit.*"[65]

That is, while it is true that God does not tempt with evil temptations, it is true, however, that God can abandon some people to them. Why? According to his judgment, which is profound and occult. And when God abandons us, we become Satan's easy prey. Here then is the conclusion: "*Ne deserat ergo nos, ideo dicimus, Ne nos inferas in tentationem.*"[66]

The petition is no longer to not allow us to be tempted with temptations that we cannot bear, but simply not to abandon us to them, not to leave us alone with our (weak) strength to fight against Satan. And here the temptation of which St. Augustine speaks, it is good to clarify, is solely and exclusively the concupiscence of the flesh, and in particular lust. He then quotes St. Paul—not 1 Cor 10:13, but Rom 1:24—in which the Apostle, quoting a passage from the Old Testament, recalls that God delivered his rebellious people to the concupiscence of their hearts. And here is the final gloss: "*Quomodo tradidit? Non cogendo, sed deserendo.*"[67]

---

62. "*Tentationem istam malam dixit, qua quisque decipitur, et daibolo subjugatur; ipsam dixit tentationem*" = "[James] defined this temptation—malicious, by which one is deceived and subjugated by the devil; this he called temptation" (Augustine, *Sermo LVII*, 9).

63. This is demonic territory. God is not responsible for moral evil. Human free will is.

64. "For there is another kind of temptation, which is called a trial: of this temptation it was written, The Lord your God tempts you to know whether you love him" (Augustine, *Sermo LVII*, 9).

65. "God tempts no one with that temptation whereby one is deceived and seduced: he does, however, clearly abandon some to it, according to his deep and occult judgment" (Augustine, *Sermo LVII*, 9).

66. "We therefore say 'Lead us not into temptation,' lest he abandon us" (Augustine, *Sermo LVII*, 9).

67. "How did he deliver them? Not by force, but by abandoning them" (Augustine, *Sermo LVII*, 9).

It is extremely important that St. Augustine clarifies this point. In the action of abandoning, there is nothing coercive ("*non cogendo*"). This clashes irremediably with the verb *infero* (*eisphērō* in Greek), which contains within itself precisely the idea of the forced transportation of a person from one place to another. This interpretation of St. Augustine, like all interpretations that propose a permissive idea of this kind, is vitiated by this insurmountable difficulty, and for this reason cannot be considered satisfactory.

## THOMAS AQUINAS

To conclude this *excursus* among the church fathers, we cannot fail to mention another giant, the one who is considered the greatest theologian in the history of Christian theology, equal to or even superior to St. Augustine, namely St. Thomas Aquinas. It is worth noting that we are in a completely different historical era from that of St. Augustine, in the middle of the thirteenth century. Even the personal history of St. Thomas is completely different.

Born into a noble family and educated from an early age to read Aristotle, he was marked by a strong religious vocation since his adolescence and joined the Dominican order when he was only nineteen years old, against the will of his family. For this reason, he will be torn from the order and kidnapped by his own brother, who will take him back to the family palace, where he will spend a full year imprisoned. Thomas, however, remained faithful to his vocation and was eventually left free to join the Dominican friars. He will spend his life between Rome, Naples, and Paris, where he will teach, strongly opposing the spread of Averroism, and will produce a number of works that will profoundly mark Christian theology to this day. Among all, his *Summa theologiae*[68] will keep him busy for all the years of his life, remaining incomplete. However, it will have the honor of being placed on the altar, during the Council of Trent, next to the Bible. As for us, we will focus on his *Super Evangelium S. Matthei Lectura*,[69] in which St. Thomas comments, one by one, on all the verses of the Lord's Prayer.

Without adding anything extraordinarily new, St. Thomas Aquinas takes up and summarizes the interpretations of St. Augustine and the church fathers, admitting that "*Alia littera: et ne inferas; et alia: et ne nos sinas.*"[70]

St. Thomas, like St. Augustine, confirms that the two versions (causative and permissive) circulated in parallel and were considered substantially equivalent. And what should God not allow? Certainly not to be tempted, because temptations are useful primarily to us and to those around us. But rather not to succumb to them

---

68. *Comprehensive treatise on theology.*
69. *Lesson on the Gospel of St. Matthew.*
70. "Some texts have: And do not lead us; others: And do not allow" (Aquinas, *Super Evangelium S. Matthaei*, 6.3.598).

("*non permittas succumbere*"). And, as usual, he quotes St. Paul in 1 Cor 10:13: God is faithful and will not allow it. These are all concepts that have already been seen and analyzed, and therefore we will not dwell on them further.

Perhaps, the most interesting part of St. Thomas's reasoning is found in the next paragraph, in which he explains how this interpretation of the Lord's Prayer ("do not allow us to succumb to temptation") refutes two gross errors of Pelagianism. Pelagianism was a current of thought, soon declared heretical, which theorized that people, endowed with free will, could, by themselves, without the help of divine grace, fight evil, since it would not be a divine task to alter or influence human will. St. Thomas, on the other hand, replies that the sixth petition of the Lord's Prayer demonstrates just the opposite, that is, that people need divine help to be able to face temptations, because otherwise "*non diceret et ne nos inducas, quod idem est quod: fac nos non consentire; ergo in potestate sua est mutare voluntatem et non mutare, Phil. II, 13: Deus est qui operatur in vobis.*"[71]

A couple of considerations. First, St. Thomas understands how the verb *inducas* has a profoundly causative sense, meaning "to make go in," "to push in." And so, he hypothesizes that the negative adverb associated with a causative verb may be moved onto the base verb. According to this interpretation, "*do not* make us enter into temptation" would be equivalent to "make sure we *do not* enter into temptation." Let us pay attention. This is a rhetorical device that seems innocent, but that completely reverses the hierarchies (in the first case, God is responsible for our entering into temptation, in the second case we are).

However, the two expressions are not, and cannot be, equivalent. The reader may recall an example we presented earlier. If we were climbing a rock face and we said to the person in the rope above us, "Please make sure that I won't fall down," it means that we are asking our partner to take care of us and rescue us in case he sees that we are slipping down. But if we said, "Please do not throw me down!" we would be implicitly blaming him for planning our murder! There is no logical-grammatical basis to support the theory of equivalence of the two expressions.

In fact, every time in the Old Testament God is asked to "make sure that we do not," a negative causative form is *never* used. Instead, a negative imperative (the cohortative imperfect in Hebrew) conjugated in the first-person (singular or plural) is utilized.

Let us consider, for example, Jonah 1:14: "We beseech thee, O Lord, we beseech thee, let us not perish for this man's life." The structure of the invocation ("let us not perish") is identical to some permissive translations of the sixth petition of the Lord's Prayer ("let us not fall into temptation"). However, no *hiphil* stem is used here.

---

71. "He would not say: and do not lead us, which is equivalent to: see to it that we do not yield. So, it is in his power to change or not to change the will, see Phil 2:13: God is the one who works in you" (Aquinas, *Super Evangelium S. Matthaei*, 6.3.598).

Instead, the cohortative imperfect in the first-person plural is utilized. Accordingly, the Septuagint translates with *mḕ apolṓmetha* (μὴ ἀπολώμεθα), which utilizes the aorist middle subjunctive of the verb *apóllymi* (ἀπόλλυμι) conjugated in the first-person plural: "May we not perish!"

In both 2 Sam 24:14 and 1 Chr 21:13, we find an analogous invocation: "let me not fall into the hand of man." Again, the structure of the invocation is identical to some permissive translations of the sixth petition of the Lord's Prayer. However, no *hiphil* stem is used here. Instead, the cohortative imperfect in the first-person singular is utilized. Accordingly, the Septuagint translates with *mḕ empésō* (μὴ ἐμπέσω), which utilizes the aorist subjunctive of the verb *empíptō* (ἐμπίπτω) conjugated in the first-person singular: "May I not fall!"

All these examples indicate that, if Jesus had meant to say, "let us not fall into temptation," or "make sure that we won't fall into temptation," thus asking God for the strength to resist the fatal attraction of temptation, he would have probably used the cohortative imperfect in the first-person plural of the verb "to fall" or "to enter," not the causative stem! And, accordingly, Matthew and Luke would have probably rendered this expression in Greek with the aorist subjunctive of the verb "to enter" by saying something like *mḕ eisélthōmen* (μὴ εἰσέλθωμεν): "May we not enter!"

The fact that both evangelists instead use a direct causative expression ("do not bring us into") is a strong indication that Jesus did use a causative (*hiphil*) form, for which the trick of switching the position of the negative adverb cannot be accepted.

The second consideration about the arguments brought forth by St. Thomas Aquinas concerns the way God works in us to alter our will, that is, the relationship between the divine will and the human free will. Pelagianism maintained a total independence of the two: God does not intervene in the free choices of people. He leaves them completely free to choose good or evil based only on their own strength. It is easy to understand how this line of thought has been officially accused of heresy, given that Scripture offers countless passages in which God clearly works on the heart of people, influencing their will. One out of all is the example of Pharaoh, which we have analyzed at length before, whose heart was hardened by God so much that he disobeyed his orders ten times, bringing upon himself and his people the most pernicious plagues.

We have also explained how God influences the human will by means of the Holy Spirit: the more a heart is permeated by the grace of his Spirit, the more docile it will be to his commandments, and its mind, enlightened, will be more likely to choose good rather than evil. On the contrary, the more a heart is deprived of the grace of the Holy Spirit, the more it will be hardened and deaf to his commandments, and the mind, confused, will be more likely to choose evil instead of good.

It is important to clarify that this kind of relationship between God and free will cannot be a kind of binary categorical variable, that is, all or nothing. If we admit that God does not intervene at all in human choices, we fall into the heresy of Pelagianism.

If, on the other hand, we assume that every single human action is completely determined by the divine will, then we are destroying the concept of free will and we are falling into theological fatalism. And without free will, the concept of temptation, sin, and divine punishment no longer make sense.

It follows that there must necessarily be a gradation of possible intensities by divine intervention on the human heart. So much so that, when the Holy Spirit dwells in the heart of a person and, so to speak, controls it (we could speak of a state of grace), that person's effort in recognizing good and practicing it is null (that is, recognizing and practicing good becomes natural). On the contrary, when God totally abandons a person's heart (we could speak of a state of disgrace), that person's effort in recognizing good and practicing it becomes infinite (that is, recognizing and practicing good becomes virtually impossible).

Here below, for graph lovers, an intuitive schematization.

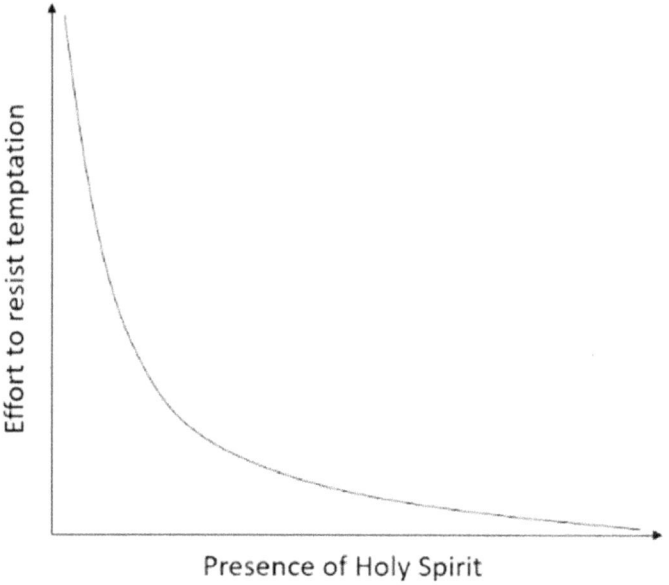

We will conclude this long critique of the church fathers by summarizing the most important lesson we have learned from them. Interpreting *peirasmós* as *mala tentatio*, that is, as a malicious moral temptation on the part of Satan, necessarily leads to insurmountable logical short-circuits:

1. Asking God not to let us fall into *peirasmós* becomes a blasphemous invocation.
2. To remedy this difficulty, there are four alternatives:
   a. We may argue that "to lead into temptation" does not automatically mean "to cause one to fall into temptation," that is, "to sin," but simply "to expose to temptation." However, all the church fathers, especially the Greek-speaking

Origen, agree on the contrary. For if malicious temptation is a trap, to fall into the trap is to yield to temptation, that is, to sin. And in any case, it would make no sense to ask to be exempt from something (moral temptation) to which a person is constantly exposed by his very nature, by the mere fact of being composed of flesh.

b. We may argue that "to lead" does not mean "to lead" but "to abandon." "*Non cogendo, sed deserendo,*" St. Augustine would say. However, both Matthew and Luke chose to use the most causative verb available to them (*eisphérō*). "*Non deserendo, sed cogendo,*" the evangelists seem to respond.

c. We may argue that "to lead" does not mean "to lead" but "to allow us to go." We have spent entire chapters demonstrating how this interpretation is completely arbitrary and has no solid roots in Scripture.

d. We may argue that "to lead into temptation" does not mean "to lead into temptation," but only "to lead into a temptation that we cannot endure." Which is equivalent to point number one, that is, a blasphemous invocation. And in any case, we know (St. Paul says so in 1 Cor 10:13) that God would never do such a thing. Therefore, besides being blasphemous, it would be a useless invocation.

How do we get out of this? In our opinion there is only one possibility. We should stop trying to manipulate—in every possible way—the verb *eisphérō* to make it say what we would like the verb to say (when instead the verb says something very simple: "lead us not"). And above all, we should stop getting stuck on the concept of *peirasmós* as demonic seduction to sin.

In fact, the concept of *peirasmós* in the Old Testament, as we will see in the next chapter, has nothing to do with moral temptation.

# 16

# The Concept of Temptation in the Old Testament

When Jesus declaimed the sixth petition of the Lord's Prayer, the cultural-religious substratum in which he moved, to which his disciples were accustomed, and to which Jesus referred was, of course, that determined by the Scripture of the time, that is, the Old Testament.[1] Therefore, to understand the meaning of the term *peirasmós*, it is essential to understand when and how this word is used in biblical Greek. And quite surprisingly, we find that the term *peirasmós* appears only seven times in the Greek translation of the Hebrew Bible by the Septuagint. There are seven, but we could say that there are only two, because in most cases they appear in the same passages, repeated identically in various parts of the Old Testament.

There are only two specific events, within the entire Hebrew Bible, associated with the Greek term *peirasmós*. The first concerns a famous episode that occurred during the exodus from the land of Egypt, when the people of Israel, exhausted by their wanderings in the desert, rebelled against Moses. Moses had convinced them to leave everything to follow the promise of "his" God. And now where was that God with whom Moses spoke for so long? Why was he not coming to save them from hunger and thirst? Moses, seriously fearing for his life, asks God for help, who promptly answers, "Behold, I will stand before thee there upon the rock in Horeb; and thou shalt smite the rock, and there shall come water out of it, that the people may drink. And Moses did so in the sight of the elders of Israel. And he called the name of the place Massah, and Meribah, because of the chiding of the children of Israel, and because they tempted the Lord, saying, Is the Lord among us, or not?" (Exod 17:6–7).

---

1. It has been calculated that at least 10 percent of all Jesus' phrases in the Gospels are direct quotations from Old Testament passages.

*Peirasmós* is the Greek translation of the place named Massah, in the desert. It is therefore used as a toponym. The Hebrew term *mǎssâ* (מַסָּה) derives from the verb *nāsâ* (נָסָה), which indicates the idea of "putting to the test." The toponym Massah refers to the fact that the Israelites in that place had put the Lord to the test (which the Septuagint translates with the verb *peirázō*). Obviously, in any translation, it is impossible to render exactly the original meaning of this passage. Either preference is given to the signifier, the Hebrew toponym Massah—which however, in any other language, does not carry any specific meaning—or the meaning of the Hebrew term *mǎssâ* is rendered, losing however the correct toponym. This is the choice of the Septuagint which translates the toponym Massah with *Peirasmós*.

From this first example, we have an important indication. In Hebrew *mǎssâ* stands for *nāsâ*, as in Greek *peirasmós* stands for *peirázō*. As in Hebrew *mǎssâ* is the noun that materializes the concept defined by the verb *nāsâ*, so in Greek *peirasmós* is the noun that materializes the concept defined by the verb *peirázō*. If *peirázō* is the natural Greek translation of the Hebrew verb *nāsâ*, it follows that *peirasmós* is the natural Greek translation of the Hebrew noun *mǎssâ*. And *mǎssâ* in this episode of Exodus has nothing to do with demonic moral temptation. Instead, it stands for the proof the Israelites wanted to obtain from God. The proof of his faithfulness. The proof of his presence at Moses' side. What the Israelites were asking for was a sign from heaven. Here *peirasmós* represents a signal, a miracle that would prove the existence of God. *Peirázō* is the act of challenge, of provocation of God: "Is the Lord among us, or not?"

Remember what James said about God? God is "untemptable" (Jas 1:13). And he immediately added, *kakôn* (κακῶν). As if to say, God is not susceptible to evil temptations. It then becomes clear to us how the *peirasmós* of which James speaks can have nothing to do with the *peirasmós* we have just encountered in Exodus. The *peirasmós* of James is the evil temptation that drives to moral corruption, and with this kind of temptation God cannot be tempted. The *peirasmós* that the Israelites impose on God is instead the proof of his existence. And with this kind of proof God may be tempted. Obviously, God will never fall into temptation, and will provide a proof of his existence only if and when he wants to, certainly not in response to human provocation. On the other hand, the action of testing God is clearly a sacrilegious, sinful act that people should avoid at all costs.[2]

This concept is confirmed in three other Old Testament passages. In Deut 6:16, it is recalled how people should never test God as the Israelites tested him at Massah (*Peirasmós*). In Deut 9:22, it is recorded that the people of Israel persevered in testing (*peirázō*) God and provoking him on several occasions, including precisely in the desert of Massah (*Peirasmós*). This passage shows how, when the verb *peirázō* has God as its object, it contains within itself the sense of provocation. To put God to the test means to doubt his existence. It means "playing with fire," testing his patience,

---

2. See Luke 4:12: "And Jesus answering said unto him, It is said, Thou shalt not tempt the Lord thy God."

and potentially provoking his wrath. Finally, in Ps 95(94):8 the listener is implored not to harden his heart "as at Meribah, as on the day of Massah (*peirasmós*) in the wilderness." In this case, the Septuagint opts for the common name *peirasmós* instead of the proper name. The chosen translation is of the type, "as in Meribah, as in the day of temptation in the desert."[3] In any case, at least four of the seven occurrences of the term *peirasmós* in the Hebrew Bible are associated with a specific place in the desert (Massah), where the Israelites tested the Lord.

The other three occurrences of the term *peirasmós* are all found in the book of Deuteronomy and make explicit reference to the plagues of Egypt with which God convinced Pharaoh to let the people of Israel go free. In Deut 4:34, Moses rhetorically asks his people if they have ever seen a God snatch from the clutches of slavery an entire people by means of calamities (*peirasmós*), signs, miracles, wars, and frightening wonders. In Deut 7:19, Moses uses the same expression, reminding his people of the calamities (*peirasmós*), signs, and miracles that God worked and that they saw with their own eyes. Finally, the same expression is found in Deut 29:3, when Moses once again recalls the great calamities (*peirasmós*), the great signs, and miracles that the people of Israel witnessed in Egypt. As we can see in these substantially identical passages, *peirasmós* indicates the trials to which God subjected Pharaoh. They are tremendous and terrible trials, which spread terror and death among the people of Egypt. But at the same time, they are proofs of the greatness and power of God. Nothing to do with the temptations of the flesh.

All seven occurrences of the term *peirasmós* within the Hebrew Bible are the direct translation of the Hebrew noun *mǎssâ* (מַסָּה). It is fair to ask then, are there any other Old Testament passages in which the term *mǎssâ* is used, even if not translated with the Greek *peirasmós*? The answer is yes. There are only two, though. The first one appears in the book of Deuteronomy and indicates again the place (Massah) where the Israelites put God to the test. This time, the Septuagint translates with the term *peîra* (πεῖρα), close relative of *peirasmós*.

The other one occurs in the very book of Job. Do you remember one of Job's moments of greatest despair? He cries out to heaven, "If the scourge slay suddenly, he will laugh at the trial of the innocent" (Job 9:23). It is one of the most dramatic and strongest passages perhaps of all Scripture.[4] The original Hebrew text speaks of a God who laughs at the *mǎssâ* of the innocent. What does this mean? The Septuagint in this case opts for a less literal translation, and simply speaks of "the righteous being mocked." Many different translations have been advanced: "the trial of the innocent," "the despair of the innocent," "the calamity of the innocent," "the suffering of the innocent," and so on. We find "the destruction of the innocents" to be the most apt translation. This *mǎssâ* is definitively much closer to the *mǎssâ* that befell Pharaoh than the *mǎssâ* that the Israelites imposed on God. Job is not simply talking about a harsh trial. He is

---

3. Most likely it would be more appropriate to keep both proper names (Meribah and Massah).
4. St. Jerome will comment, "There is nothing harsher than this passage in the whole book of Job."

talking about a calamity that causes the death of the innocent. Do you remember the slaughter of the innocents perpetrated by the Destroying Angel on divine command as the last and nefarious plague to bend Pharaoh's will? This is the *măssâ* of which Job is speaking. The evil that falls, apparently blind, on humanity, and that mows down both the righteous and the wicked. It would be reductive to translate *măssâ* simply as "trial" or "despair." If one dies mowed down by a speeding car, what trial, what despair are we talking about? The innocent person does not even have time to realize what has happened to him/her. No trial. No despair. Just the scourge of death that comes suddenly. A catastrophe—a destruction indeed.

This passage from Job is illuminating because, if it is true that *peirasmós* is the Greek equivalent of the Hebrew *măssâ*, then we begin to have a much more precise definition of what that *peirasmós* uttered by Jesus in the sixth petition of the Lord's Prayer might mean. And it seems to mean everything but the moral temptation of the flesh. At least according to the Old Testament, from which Jesus drew heavily in his preaching. It seems to be clearly understood instead that, when God is the one who imposes *peirasmós* on people (and not vice versa), the term contains a nefarious concept of catastrophe, calamity, destruction, despair, pain, and death.

Given the scarcity of examples in the Old Testament, it is necessary to try to better define the contours of the noun *peirasmós* by analyzing the verb from which *peirasmós* derives, namely *peirázō*, which is instead used much more frequently. As seen, *peirázō* represents the Greek equivalent of the Hebrew verb *nāsâ*, from which the term *măssâ* derives. Thirty-two of the thirty-six occurrences of the verb *nāsâ* in the Hebrew Bible are precisely translated by the Septuagint with the verb *peirázō*.[5] In the remaining four instances, the verb *nāsâ* is used to give the idea of an attempt. It does not have the meaning of "to put to the test," but of "to try to," "to seek to," "to attempt to," and are therefore translated in Greek in a different way. We can then conclude that, when the verb *nāsâ* means "to test," it has almost a two-way correspondence with the Greek *peirázō*. Let us then briefly see in what contexts the verb *nāsâ* is used in the Old Testament to try to gain further insight into the meaning of *peirasmós*.

The first time the verb *nāsâ* appears in the Bible is in the famous episode of the sacrifice of Isaac, requested by God to Abraham as a proof of his unconditional faith (Gen 22:1). It is an example that we have already had the opportunity to analyze, and that is usually taken as an emblem of the test of faith to which God can subject people. Did God tempt Abraham? He did not, if tempting means trying to make him fall. He certainly did, if tempting means testing. Remember Tertullian trying to show how God did not tempt Abraham (but simply proved his faith), because, as James says, God tempts no one? This kind of explanatory contortions are useless if one admits quite simply that God does tempt, in the sense that he tests. What kind of test did Abraham have to pass? Without any doubt, the test of his unwavering faith in God. Total abandonment to his will—even when this will seems inadequate, unjust, even

---

5. Or with its synonym *ekpeirázō* (ἐκπειράζω).

horrible, such as the request to murder his dearest son. It is a request, that of God, so audacious and scandalous, that it would probably have crushed the faith of anyone. Not Abraham's, who assures himself of divine favor for the rest of his life. It is not an ordinary test that Abraham is subjected to. It is a test that tests his psychophysical resistance to levels that not even Abraham could have imagined. Let us keep this concept in mind and proceed.

The second episode in which we encounter the verb *nāsâ* is found in the book of Exodus and tells of how God, on an occasion similar to that of Massah, gave Moses the power to make the water near Marah drinkable by throwing in a stick. After that, he put his people to the test (*nāsâ*) by saying, "If thou wilt diligently hearken to the voice of the Lord thy God, and wilt do that which is right in his sight, and wilt give ear to his commandments, and keep all his statutes, I will put none of these diseases upon thee, which I have brought upon the Egyptians: for I am the Lord that healeth thee" (Exod 15:26).

This is a passage that we have already analyzed previously. God "confesses" that it was he who inflicted all the calamities that befell Pharaoh and his people (no permissive sense). But he promises the Israelites that he will not do the same to them—but only if they keep all his commandments. Is God tempting them? No, he is simply putting them to the test. A very delicate test, with enormous risks. A very sharp sword of Damocles hangs over the Israelites. Following all the commandments of the Lord is not an easy task, especially under the pressure of being punished with horrible calamities in case of failure. It is very interesting to note that in this *peirasmós* that God proposes to his people there lurks another (quite explicit) *peirasmós*, the *măssâ* of the calamities that rained down on the people of Egypt, and that could also rain down on the people of Israel if they do not obey. Let us continue.

In the following chapter of Exodus, we are told of the famous episode of the manna raining down from heaven. Once again, we find the people of Israel complaining to Moses because they are starving. God, anticipating Moses, decides to grant them the coveted bread, but under extremely specific conditions. They will have to collect every day the necessary ration for that day, not one gram more. On the sixth day they will have to collect the necessary ration for two days, since on the seventh day they will have to rest, and no one will have to leave the camp. All this, says the Lord, so that "I may test[6] [*nāsâ*] them, whether they will walk in my law, or no" (Exod 16:4).

Here is another test that God imposes on the Israelites: the test of unconditional obedience to his dictates. Destroyed by their seemingly aimless wandering in the midst of the hostile deserts of the Arabian peninsula, literally dying of hunger and thirst, they will have to know how to keep faith with the divine conditions, without indiscriminately pouncing on the manna raining from heaven. Is God tempting them? Certainly not in the sense of pushing them to disobey his orders. The test is arduous

---

6. The KJV generally translates *nāsâ* with "to prove." We consider "to test" to be more appropriate.

but without tricks or deception. The rules of the game are well understood by all. God is instead tempering them, testing their psychophysical resistance.

In the next chapter of Exodus, the verb *nāsâ* appears twice more. The episode is the one already described when the Israelites, exhausted by thirst, tested God by asking him for a sign of his presence in the desert of Massah (Exod 17:2, 7). Similarly, in Deut 33:8 and in Pss 78(77):18, 41, 56; 95(94):9; 106(105):14, there is a reminder of all the times the Israelites tested the Lord's patience, provoked him, and rebelled against him. In all these cases, the verb *nāsâ* indicates the act of provocation of God by people.

Chapter 20 of Exodus is one of the most important passages in the Bible. It is where God delivers to Moses the Ten Commandments. The setting of the event is dramatic. The Lord descends on Mount Sinai in a dense cloud of fire and smoke, among thunder, lightning, and loud trumpet blasts. The earth trembles. The people of Israel camped on the slopes of the mountain are shaken by fear: "And mount Sinai was altogether on a smoke, because the Lord descended upon it in fire: and the smoke thereof ascended as the smoke of a furnace, and the whole mount quaked greatly. And when the voice of the trumpet sounded long, and waxed louder and louder, Moses spake, and God answered him by a voice" (Exod 19:18–19).

It is at this point that God declares his commandments. When Moses comes down from Sinai, the Israelites are terrified. Moses reassures them with these words: "Fear not: for God is come to test [*nāsâ*] you, and that his fear may be before your faces, that ye sin not" (Exod 20:20).

Once again, the *peirasmós* to which the Israelites are subjected is a psychophysical stress. The prodigious signs their eyes witness are obviously not a temptation, but a test. Proof of divine power, but at the same time trial that fills their souls with terror and makes them tremble like leaves. It is evidence of the fear of God, which keeps people from sin.

In Num 14:22, after the umpteenth disobedience of the Israelites to the divine dictates, Moses finds himself once again before God, imploring his forgiveness. God, "longsuffering, and of great mercy, forgiving iniquity and transgression, and by no means clearing the guilty" (Num 14:18), decides to stop his hand which is ready to strike, but at the same time promises that, whoever has put him to the test (*nāsâ*) disobeying him already ten times, will not see the Promised Land. Further confirmation that, when the verb *nāsâ* has God as object, it indicates the act of provocation toward him. The same is true for the two occurrences of the verb *nāsâ* in Deut 6:16. In chapter 8 of the book of Deuteronomy, Moses returns to speak to his people:

> And thou shalt remember all the way which the Lord thy God led thee these forty years in the wilderness, to humble thee, and to test [*nāsâ*] thee, to know what was in thine heart, whether thou wouldest keep his commandments, or no. And he humbled thee, and suffered thee to hunger, and fed thee with manna, which thou knewest not, neither did thy fathers know; that he might make thee know that man doth not live by bread only, but by every word that

proceedeth out of the mouth of the Lord doth man live. Thy raiment waxed not old upon thee, neither did thy foot swell, these forty years. Thou shalt also consider in thine heart, that, as a man chasteneth his son, so the Lord thy God chasteneth thee. (Deut 8:2–5)

And again: "Who fed thee in the wilderness with manna, which thy fathers knew not, that he might humble thee, and that he might test [*nāsâ*] thee, to do thee good at thy latter end" (Deut 8:16).

These passages directly recall Exod 16:4 and define its contours even more clearly. God tested the people of Israel by making them suffer thirst and hunger for forty years in the desert before reaching the Promised Land. He tested them in the sense that he tried them, physically and psychically. He wore them out, literally. He disciplined them as a strict father does with his children. He tempered them in the crucible of psychophysical suffering (*tentatio tribulationis*). He humiliated them, that is, he purified their hearts of any dross of pride and *hýbris*, thus making them docile to his dictates. What we are talking about here is a *purifying peirasmós*, an extremely hard, anguished *peirasmós*, but necessary in order to be worthy of divine favor.

We have already spoken at length about the passage in Deut 13:3 where it says that "the Lord your God tests you (*nāsâ*) to know whether you love the Lord your God with all your heart and with all your soul." Aside from the (interesting) disquisition on the meaning of that "to know,"[7] this phrase is again linked to the purifying action of a God who tempers his people until they are worthy to enter the Promised Land, a prophetic anticipation of the kingdom of heaven promised by Christ.

In the second chapter of the book of Judges, God, angry with his own people, decides to put them to the test by leaving them at the mercy of the enemy nations: "And the anger of the Lord was hot against Israel; and he said, Because that this people hath transgressed my covenant which I commanded their fathers, and have not hearkened unto my voice; I also will not henceforth drive out any from before them of the nations which Joshua left when he died: That through them I may test [*nāsâ*] Israel, whether they will keep the way of the Lord to walk therein, as their fathers did keep it, or not" (Judg 2:20–22).

Here, we are in the presence of a *pedagogical peirasmós*. The people of Israel demonstrated by their disobedience the need to be disciplined. Just as their fathers had been disciplined. Discipline necessarily passes through a painful process of purification. Painful in the sense that it entails psychophysical suffering aimed at humiliating the people themselves, at wrenching from their hearts every residue of pride. And God uses the enemy nations of Israel to humiliate his people, to test them (*nāsâ*), and to make them docile to his commandments (the same exact concept is reiterated in Judg 3:1–4).

---

7. Does it mean that God does not know before the test, or does it mean that God wants people to know?

In chapter 7 of the book of Isaiah, Ahaz (the son of Jotham, the son of Uzziah, king of Judah) is concerned because Jerusalem is under siege. God speaks to Ahaz, and he volunteers to provide the people of Israel with a sign of his protection. Ahaz only has to ask for it to get it. Here of course God is not inciting Ahaz to tempt him, but rather to ask him for a favor, through prayer. God is ready to help him, but only if Ahaz will explicitly ask for help. We find here explained in a few words the mystery of the power of prayer, on which we have previously dwelt. The divine Providence is constructed in such a way as to grant people every possible request that conforms to the divine will, but only if this request is made explicit through prayer. Ahaz is confused by the words of the Lord, he thinks it is a sort of trap, he screens himself saying, "I will not ask, neither will I tempt [*nāsâ*] the Lord" (Isa 7:12).

Ahaz's answer, paradoxically and ironically, tests the Lord's patience! It will take Isaiah to unravel the skein and explain that God will send a sign.[8]

The last occurrence of the verb *nāsâ* which has God as subject and human beings as object is found in Ps 26(25) in which King David, so sure of his own moral integrity, asks God, "Examine me, O Lord, and test [*nāsâ*] me; try my reins and my heart" (Ps 26(25):2).

We left this example for last because it contains in one line all the possible nuances of "test" to which God can subject people. In Hebrew, there are basically three ways to express the idea of "testing." One is the one we have analyzed so far, rendered by the verb *nāsâ*, which corresponds to the Greek *peirázō*. It is the highest form, if we can say so, of test. The one that pushes human beings beyond their limits. It is a mostly painful and terrible test that tests their psychophysical resistance. At times it has a purifying, pedagogical intent (see the people of Israel). Some other times, it has a purely punitive intent, whereby the divine will manifests itself in all its destructive power (see the plagues of Egypt).

The second way to express the concept of "putting to the test" is through the verb *bāhăn* (בָּחַן). This is the first verb with which David addresses the Lord in Ps 26(25):2. "Examine me!" implores David. The verb *bāhăn*, in most cases, indicates the action of "checking," "examining," "scrutinizing," and by extension—"judging." The trial that the verb *bāhăn* implies is not necessarily one that subjects people to any psychophysical stress. It is not a test that necessarily pushes human beings beyond their limits. Most importantly, it is not a test that intends to punish them. It is simply a test that merely tests their moral quality without necessarily presupposing any effort on the part of the people tested. The burden of proof, so we might say, lies with the one who examines, rather than with the one who is examined. When David asks God to "examine him" (*bāhăn*), he is not asking to subject him to any test. He is simply asking God to thoroughly examine his heart to check that it is completely pure.

---

8. And, incidentally, the sign that God will send is the famous prophecy of Jesus' birth, found in Isa 7:14: "Behold, a virgin shall conceive, and bear a son, and shall call his name Immanuel."

The verb *bāhăn* is usually translated into Greek with the verb *dokimázō* (δοκιμάζω) and corresponds to the Latin *probare* of which St. Augustine spoke. *Dokimázō*, as well as *probare*, refers to a proof that corresponds to a demonstration, to an examination.

It is not, just to make it clear, the kind of test to which Abraham was subjected during the sacrifice of Isaac. Now we have all the tools to understand this. Abraham's test was not simply a demonstration of his faith. It was a test of his faith that tested his mental and physical fitness. It was a test that Abraham could have failed, if only his faith had wavered for a moment. The request to sacrifice his beloved son is something Abraham most likely never expected to hear from his God. God did not simply scrutinize (*bāhăn*) Abraham's heart for integrity. Instead, he subjected him to a most severe test. He placed between himself and Abraham a seemingly insurmountable obstacle—the sacrifice of his son. It was up to Abraham to climb that mountain, to go beyond his own limits, and reach the Lord who was waiting for him on the other side. Scripture rightly speaks of a God who tests Abraham. He tests him in the sense of *nāsâ*, in the sense of *peirázō*. The *peirasmós* of the sixth petition of the Lord's Prayer cannot be a mere *proba*, that is, a verification, or approval of human faith. It must be something else—something much stronger and more terrible.

Beyond *bāhăn* and *nāsâ*, there is another nuance of testing, which is defined by the verb *tsārăph* (צָרַף). This verb literally indicates the action of the craftsman who works the metal by smelting and refining it. God, in many passages of the Bible, is represented metaphorically as the goldsmith who melts the gold or silver in the crucible of the furnace to refine it and remove all dross of impurities. It generally corresponds to the Greek *pyróō* (πυρόω), which, as indicated by the root of the verb, contains the concept of purifying fire. It is metaphorically used in the sense of "tempering," "purifying." Sometimes it is closer to the semantic field defined by *bāhăn* (that is, metaphorically melting human heart to test its purity). Some other times, it is closer to the semantic field defined by *nāsâ* (that is, metaphorically making people pass through the crucible of tribulation, either to purify them, or to push them beyond their limits, or to punish them for their sins). At other times the two semantic fields overlap.[9]

For example, in chapter 48 of the book of Isaiah, God addresses the people of Israel with these words: "Behold, I have refined [*tsārăph*] thee, but not with silver; I have chosen thee in the furnace of affliction ['*ônî*]" (Isa 48:10). The verb *tsārăph* contains in this case a purifying sense. God tempers and refines people in the "crucible of affliction." In the furnace of misery. The metaphor is all too eloquent. God is here revealing the cathartic function of suffering. The *tentatio tribulationis* of St. Augustine. Which has nothing to do with moral temptation, and much to do with the psychophysical pain of the flesh. The Hebrew term '*ônî* (עֳנִי), with which the concept of affliction is translated, comes from the root of the verb '*ānâ* (עָנָה), which means "to oppress," "to

---

9. See Zech 13:9: "And I will bring the third part through the fire, and will refine [*tsārăph*] them as silver is refined, and will try [*bāhăn*] them as gold is tried: they shall call on my name, and I will hear them: I will say, It is my people: and they shall say, The Lord is my God."

afflict," "to humiliate." The verb *tsārăph* is also the verb used by David in Ps 26(25):2 when he asks God to examine him, test him, and temper his mind and heart with fire. *Bāhăn*, *tsārăph*, and *nāsâ*—all three gradations of "test" present in a single invocation! Although the semantic fields defined by these three verbs are sometimes overlapping, there is no doubt that in general the couple *nāsâ*/*măssâ* (*peirázō*/*peirasmós* in Greek) is at the top of the hierarchical scale, indicating the hardest kind of test possible for human beings.

In any case, it is evident that none of these "tests" ever has any relation to temptation understood in the common sense of the term, that is, as a seduction to moral sin. And even when the verb *nāsâ* does not involve God, but has as subject and object only human beings, it always simply indicates a test and never a temptation to commit a sin. For example, in 1 Kgs 10:1 and in 2 Chr 9:1, it is told how the Queen of Sheba, having heard about the fame of Solomon and his proverbial wisdom, came to test him (*nāsâ*) with riddles and difficult questions. An arduous examination, but definitely not a temptation to sin. Or, in the first chapter of the book of Daniel, it is told how Daniel, not wanting to be contaminated with the food of the king and with the wine of his banquets, asked the head of the officials to put him to the test (*nāsâ*), and to give him to eat only legumes for ten days. After testing (*nāsâ*) Daniel, the overseer found that after ten days his face was more beautiful and more florid than that of all the other young men who ate the king's food (Dan 1:15). Again, this is a test of physical endurance and definitely not a temptation to sin.

And then comes the book of Sirach.

As we have already had occasion to say, the book of Sirach is considered apocryphal and for this reason excluded from the Hebrew Bible, while it is part to all intents and purposes of the canon of the Catholic Bible. It is a wonderful text, which is part of the sapiential writings, composed by the Jewish scribe Ben Sira at the beginning of the second century BC and translated into Greek by his nephew toward the end of the same century. The original Hebrew text has been found, only in part and in different historical periods, since the late 1800s. In the text of Sirach, the concept of "test" is found in multiple passages. The Greek verb *peirázō* is used at least four times. Chapter 39, for example, praises the behavior of a wise person, who "travels among foreign peoples, investigating [*peirázō*] good and evil among men" (Sir 39:4). Here, *peirázō* translates the concept of investigation and experience. He is wise who investigates by experiencing good and evil.

In chapter 34, this concept is explained even better: "He who has not been tested [*peirázō*], knows little; he who has traveled has increased shrewdness" (Sir 34:10). Also in this case, *peirázō* indicates the experience that the wise people acquire by traveling the world and experiencing new customs and habits. Unfortunately, the Hebrew text of these two passages has not (yet) been found, so we cannot compare them with the original.

## Eis Peirasmón

Let us read a verse for which we have the original Hebrew text: "Son, in your life test [*peirázō*] yourself" (Sir 37:27). This is an exhortation to put oneself to the test, to test one's limits in order to expand one's knowledge of oneself and of the world.[10] The original Hebrew text uses the verb *nāsâ* in this case, confirming its perfect correspondence with the Greek *peirázō*.

Another fragment of which the original in Hebrew has been found appears in chapter 4. This passage is interesting because the Greek text seems to deviate from the original in a significant way. The sense of the passage in the two idioms is similar, but it is clear that we are not in the presence of a literal translation. Let us begin with the Greek text where the verb *peirázō* appears: "At first, he will lead him through tortuous places, instill fear and dread in him, and torment him with her discipline, until he can trust him, and has proved [*peirázō*] him by his decrees; but then he will lead him back to the straight path and manifest to him his own secrets. If he treads a false path, he will let him go and abandon him at the mercy of his fate" (Sir 4:17–19).

Of whom is the text of Sirach speaking? At first glance one might say that this is the perfect description of how God approaches people. How he disciplines them. How he tests them with fear, sacrifice, and suffering. How he manifests his secrets to them if they walk on the right path, and how he abandons them to the obstinacy of their hearts if they do not want to obey his teachings. But it does not. At least, apparently. The subject of this passage is Wisdom. All of the above works logically even if we replace God with Wisdom. And this is obviously no accident. Wisdom—the one inspired by the Holy Spirit—coincides with the divine will. And the divine will is to temper people and make them docile to his commandments. How? By means of psychophysical stress. The divine discipline is not a walk in the park: "He will lead him through tortuous places, he will instill fear and dread in him, he will torment him with his discipline." It is a *peirasmós* that implies pain, affliction, humiliation, fear. Certainly not seduction nor deception.

Let us turn now to the original Hebrew text: "He will go with him secretly, and first he will examine [*bāhăr*] him in trials; he will instill in him fear and dread, and he will torment him with his discipline until he keeps it in his thoughts, and he can trust him. Then he will return to him and give him strength, make him happy, reveal to him his mysteries, and grant him knowledge and discernment of what is right. But if he deviates from the high road, he will reject him and deliver him into the hands of those who will destroy him."

Similar, but not identical. Let us dwell particularly on the passage where it says that Wisdom will examine people in trials. The Hebrew verb used is *bāhăr* (בָּחַר), which is commonly translated as "to choose." To choose as a result of a test. People are indeed chosen because they have passed the test. But the literal (though less usual) meaning of the verb *bāhăr* is "to examine," "to try," "to test." The exact Hebrew

---

10. It recalls that *gnôthi seautón* (γνῶθι σεαυτόν) engraved on the door of the temple of Apollo at Delphi, Greece.

expression is as follows (from right to left): "יבחרנו בנסיונות"[11] (Sir 4:17). The imperfect verbal form *ybhrnû*, where we discern the root of the verb *bāhăr*, is associated with the static preposition *b-* (-בְּ), which indicates the place where the person will be tested. And the place is defined by the term *nisyônôth* (נִסְיוֹנוֹת), which represents the plural (feminine) of the noun *nissāyôn* (נִסָּיוֹן). Notice anything? The term *nissāyôn* comes from the same root as the verb *nāsâ*, and is the noun associated with it. It is the equivalent of the Greek *peirasmós*! We discover that there is another Hebrew term, in addition to *măssâ*, which is in direct correspondence with the Greek *peirasmós*. The terms *măssâ* and *nissāyôn* are in fact synonymous.

It is important to note, however, that the term *nissāyôn* never appears within the Hebrew Bible. To find the term *nissāyôn*, one must look in the book of Sirach which, as mentioned is part of the canonical texts of the Catholic Church but is considered apocryphal by Jewish tradition. And, surprisingly enough, we find numerous examples there. Do you remember how the term *peirasmós* in the translation of the Septuagint appears only seven times in the entire Hebrew Scripture? Well, in the Greek translation of the book of Sirach alone, it appears six times! In only three of these cases, we can compare the Greek translation with the original Hebrew fragments found. Let us begin with the three for which we do not have the original Hebrew text.

Let us read the *incipit* of chapter 2 according to the translation of the Italian Episcopal Conference (CEI): "*Figlio, se ti presenti per servire il Signore, prepàrati alla tentazione. Abbi un cuore retto e sii costante, non ti smarrire nel tempo della seduzione*"[12] (Sir 2:1–2 CEI).

Temptation. Seduction. So, does *peirasmós* really mean malicious inducement to sin? No, it does not. This translation, as well as many others, is unfortunately invalidated by a legacy that has been consolidated over the centuries, probably impossible to overcome by now, so that the term *peirasmós* within the Christian culture cannot have any other meaning than "seduction of the flesh." If, instead, we read the Greek text, everything makes sense again: "Son, if you intend to serve the Lord, prepare your spirit for trial [*peirasmós*]. Keep a righteous heart and be persevering, do not be impulsive in the time of affliction" (Sir 2:1–2).

How do we know that this is the correct translation? For two specific reasons. First, the Greek term that the CEI translates as "seduction" is *epagōgḗ* (ἐπαγωγή). Do you remember it? *Orgḗ, ekdíkēsis, epagōgḗ*. Wrath, chastisement, calamity. These are the three basic steps of how divine justice develops. The Septuagint uses the term *epagōgḗ* to indicate calamity, scourge, physical destruction. In short, everything that produces affliction, oppression, tribulation, psychophysical suffering. Certainly not to indicate the concept of malicious seduction to sin. Second, if we just go on reading a couple more verses, all doubt disappears: "Accept everything that happens to you,

---

11. "*ybhrnû b-nsyônôth*" = "He shall examine him in trials."

12. "Son, if you present yourself to serve the Lord, prepare yourself for temptation. Have a righteous heart and be constant, do not go astray in the time of seduction."

endure patiently in painful events, for in the fire is tested gold, and people well accepted in the crucible of pain" (Sir 2:4–5).

Endure patiently. Painful, humiliating, miserable events. The crucible of pain. The *tentatio tribulationis*. We always go back there. The *peirasmós* spoken of in the *incipit* of chapter 2 of Sirach is all of this. No moral seduction. Only material suffering of the flesh. Which is what the Greek text call *tapeinōsis* (ταπείνωσις), that is, everything that oppresses people to the point of crushing them, humiliating them in the literal sense of the term—lowering them to the level of the earth (*humus*) in a miserable condition.

In chapter 27 of Sirach, the usual metaphor of the furnace is used again, but this time to simply indicate the test of a person's quality. The term *peirasmós* is used twice with this meaning: "The furnace proves [*dokimázō*] the objects of the potter, the proof [*peirasmós*] of man is in his conversation. The fruit shows how the tree is cultivated, so speech reveals man's feeling. Do not praise a man before he has spoken, for this is the proof [*peirasmós*] of men" (Sir 27:5–7).

This is a type of proof that, according to what was said earlier, would best align with the semantic field defined by the verb *dokimázō*, which is used at the beginning of verse 5. Unfortunately, we do not have the original Hebrew text to help us. In any case, even if the term *peirasmós* seems to be used here in a broad sense (that is, not as a psychophysical proof, but as a generic demonstration), it is certainly not a matter of evil temptation.

Much more interesting instead is to analyze those three passages of which the original Hebrew text has been preserved. For example, in chapter 6 of Sirach we read the wise words: "If you want to make a friend, get him in the test [*peirasmós*]" (Sir 6:7). It is in difficult situations that one can discern who is a loyal friend and who is not. The term *peirasmós* thus indicates here the moment of need, that is, a moment of adversity and suffering, certainly not of moral temptation. The fragment in Sir 6:7 found in manuscript A (MS. A) uses the term *nyssyn* (ניסין), a variation of the *nissāyôn* encountered earlier, confirming its perfect correspondence with the Greek *peirasmós*.

In chapter 44 of Sirach, the term *peirasmós* is once again associated with the episode of the sacrifice of Isaac by Abraham: "Abraham was the great ancestor of many peoples; no one was like him in glory. He kept the law of the Most High and entered into covenant with him. He established this covenant in his own flesh, and in the test [*peirasmós*] he was found faithful" (Sir 44:19–20).

What is the text of Sirach telling us? That the test, the *peirasmós* to which Abraham was subjected and which Abraham brilliantly overcame by demonstrating the integrity of his faith, was a test that touched him in the flesh. The covenant between God and Abraham passed through a process that left an indelible mark on his flesh. That is, it caused him a psychophysical stress that was almost impossible to bear—choosing between obeying God and murdering his beloved son. Again, the text of Sirach is associating *peirasmós* with a material suffering of the flesh. And the original

Hebrew text found in manuscript B (MS. B) uses the term *nyssûy* (ניסוי), close relative of the *nissāyôn* encountered earlier.

It is interesting to note that the exact same expression associated with Abraham ("in the trial [*peirasmós*] he was found faithful") is found in the first book of Maccabees. The first two books of Maccabees, like Sirach, are also deuterocanonical texts (they are not part of the Hebrew Bible), but have been incorporated into the Christian Bible. Only a Greek version composed at the beginning of the first century BC has remained. The original Hebrew text has been lost. The Hebrew *translation* of the Greek text reads (from right to left): "נוסה במסה"[13] (1 Macc 2:52), which literally means "was tested in the trial." Notice something? Obviously, the use of the verb *nāsâ* associated this time with *măssâ*! Another confirmation that *măssâ* and *nissāyôn* (or variants) are essentially synonyms derived from the root of the same verb (*nāsâ*) and both corresponding to the Greek *peirasmós*.

Finally, let us analyze the last occurrence of the term *peirasmós* in the book of Sirach. It is found at the beginning of chapter 33: "Whoever fears the Lord will incur no evil, but in the trial [*peirasmós*] he will be delivered once and again" (Sir 33:1).

What "evil" is being talked about? What "trial" is being talked about? Is reference being made to moral evil and temptation? The Greek text does not help because it speaks generally of *kakón* (κακόν) and *peirasmós*. Fortunately, there are no less than three manuscripts (MS. B, MS. E, and MS. F) in which this fragment was found, so it is possible to reconstruct exactly the original Hebrew text. The evil of which it speaks is the famous *răʿ* (רַע), which we have already met, and which represents the most generic term possible in the Hebrew language to indicate everything that causes pain, destruction, misery, unhappiness. The verb associated with it is *pāḡăʿ* (פֶּגַע) which indicates the action of bumping into something. Whoever is God-fearing can then enjoy the certainty of not being crushed by any evil that comes between his head and neck. Why? Because God, in the midst of the trial, that is, of the suffering caused by evil, will be ready every time to come to our aid to pull us out. The verb used in the Greek text is *exairéō* (ἐξαιρέω), which indicates the action of snatching away. God literally drags us out of the *peirasmós*, if only we implore his help. The original Hebrew verb is *mālăṭ* (מָלַט), which indicates the idea of wriggling, of slipping out. God can get us through the midst of the most terrible *peirasmós* unscathed, without harm coming to us. It will be good to keep this verse from Sirach in mind, for it will be one of the keys to unhinging the correct meaning of the sixth petition of the Lord's Prayer.

The Hebrew term corresponding to *peirasmós* that appears in Sir 33:1 is still *nyssûy* (ניסוי), the same one used to indicate the trial that befell Abraham (Sir 44:20). The concept that "the one who fears the Lord will incur no evil" (Sir 33:1) will be taken up and elevated in Solomon's book of Wisdom, another deuterocanonical text, the last of the Old Testament. At the beginning of chapter 3 we read: "The souls of the righteous are in the hand of God, and no torment will touch them" (Wis 3:1).

---

13. "*nûssâ b-măssâ*" = "He was tested in the trial."

Here the author of the book of Wisdom is probably referring to eternal post-mortem torment, that is, hell. The Greek term used is *básanos* (βάσανος), which literally means an instrument of torture, something that produces excruciating physical pain. The concept around which this passage revolves is that of the afterlife retribution. Although on earth the righteous suffer and seem to die in misery as if they had been punished by God, their reward in the kingdom of heaven is great. Earthly sufferings and the very death of the flesh are little because "God tested [*peirázō*] them and found them worthy" (Wis 3:5).

A final consideration. In Sir 6:7; 33:1; 44:20, the Greek text uses the expression *en peirasmôi* (ἐν πειρασμῷ), that is, "in the trial." No motion. It indicates the condition of being in the midst of the trial. If, however, the trial is to be understood as a temptation, that is, as a deception, as a trap that hides the mortal sin, to fall into this trap, to find oneself *in* it, would mean, as already stated several times, to be metaphorically already dead, that is, to have succumbed to sin. Like an animal that has fallen into the hunter's net, it is an animal destined for death. To be trapped, *en peirasmôi*, means to be already doomed. However, in all these passages, *en peirasmôi* indicates the condition of being subjected to a psychophysical stress. A tribulation from which a person can still escape (*mālăt*), thanks to the help of God.

The end. Of all the Old Testament occurrences of the term *peirasmós*, not even one refers, not even remotely, to the modern idea of temptation as an incitement to moral sin. Not one. That must mean something.

Does this mean that in the Old Testament the idea of temptation as we understand it today had not yet developed? Obviously not. The idea of the temptation to disobey divine dictates permeates the entire Old Testament. We need only mention perhaps the most famous episode in the entire Bible: the temptation of Eve by the serpent, narrated in chapter 3 of the book of Genesis. The Temptation par excellence, we might say. The serpent confuses Eve's mind by making her believe that eating of the tree of good and evil is not a sin. And when God comes to demand an account of her disobedience, how does Eve justify herself? Let us read: "The serpent beguiled me, and I did eat" (Gen 3:13).

It does not say, "The serpent tempted me." In fact, the verb *nāsâ* never appears in the entire text of Genesis. Instead, Eve uses another verb, *nāshā'* (נָשָׁא), which means "to seduce," "to beguile," "to confuse," "to deceive." Doesn't all of this correspond to an evil temptation? *Nāsâ* and *nāshā'* —two verbs, coincidentally, so phonetically similar, but deriving from different roots. The first always indicates the act of testing someone in a harsh but honest way, without any shadow of malice. The second, on the other hand, which contains the idea of deception, seduction, and moral corruption. But *nāshā'* is not the only one. There are others. The Hebrew biblical text often uses the verbs *sûth* (סוּת) and *pātâ* (פָּתָה), for example, to indicate the idea of seduction and deceptive persuasion to perform a sinful act.

In conclusion, when Jesus declaims the sixth petition of the Lord's Prayer and uses a Hebrew (or Aramaic) term corresponding to the Greek *peirasmós* reported by the Gospels of Matthew and Luke, he must necessarily have had recourse to either the noun *mǎssâ* or the noun *nissāyôn*, both derived from the root of the verb *nāsâ*. These are the only terms, as seen, that stand in correspondence with the Greek *peirasmós* in the entire Old Testament of the Septuagint.[14] And if Jesus used language drawn directly from—or at least profoundly influenced by—the sacred texts, it would be very curious, not to say impossible, to think that he used *mǎssâ* or *nissāyôn* with a completely different sense from that with which these terms appear in the Old Testament. This simple reasoning would be enough to convince us that the chances that Jesus, when he spoke of *peirasmós* in the sixth petition of the Lord's Prayer, is referring to a malicious temptation to sin are to be considered practically nil.

Unfortunately, however, nothing is as straightforward as it seems. It is precisely when we get into the New Testament that things apparently start changing. It is precisely in this passage from the Old to the New, from ante- to post-Christ, that the Greek term *peirasmós* evolves and expands its semantic field, thus literally giving way to centuries of lexical confusion.

Let us see how.

---

14. We are speaking here of the Hellenistic Greek of the *koinḗ* (κοινή), commonly spoken in the last three centuries before the birth of Christ.

# 17

# The Concept of Temptation According to the Evangelists

Let us begin with a simple consideration. The term *peirasmós* appears only nine times in the four Gospels. One in Mark, two in Matthew, six in Luke. Never in John, who prudently keeps away from it. And if we consider the Gospels of Mark, Matthew, and Luke from a synoptic point of view, we can say that there are only five distinct occurrences of this term. Moreover, of the nine times that the term *peirasmós* appears in the Gospels, eight times it is "pronounced" by Jesus.[1] It is a term used almost exclusively by Christ, and one with which the evangelists (all except perhaps Luke) seem to have little confidence. This clear disproportion between the *peirasmós* pronounced by Jesus and those (only one!) used in the prose of the four Gospels is already in itself a very strong indication that the presence of this Greek term is mainly due to the need to render a specific word (probably *măssâ* or *nissāyôn*), apparently common in the lexicon used by Jesus.

Indeed, it seems to be understood that it is Jesus himself who, through his preaching and exhortations, wants to educate his disciples in the correct use and meaning of this term. Six of the eight *peirasmós* pronounced by Jesus can be traced back to the exact same expression used in the sixth petition of the Lord's Prayer. Two occurrences are found in the Lord's Prayer reported by both Matthew and Luke. The other four all refer to the exhortation that Jesus makes to his three disciples (Peter, James, and John) in the garden on the Mount of Olives: "pray that you do not enter into *peirasmós*." There is an urgency on Jesus' part for his disciples to understand the *gravitas* of this petition. On the other hand, if for a moment we leave out these six *peirasmós*, all of

---

1. When we speak of Jesus "pronouncing" the term *peirasmós*, we are obviously referring to the Greek term that the evangelists use to render the Aramaic term (unknown) used by Jesus. It is not clear if Jesus knew Greek, but for obvious reasons his preaching was certainly not in Greek.

which can be traced back to the same expression that we are trying to interpret, we can see that there are only three occurrences left within the four Gospels that may suggest the correct interpretative key. Very few. The field of available examples widens if we consider the occurrences of the verb *peirázō* and analyze the other New Testament writings, in particular the letters of St. Paul. Unfortunately, however, with them the semantic field that *peirasmós* covers also widens, perhaps making its decipherment even more complicated. But let us proceed step by step.

## MARK

Let us begin with what is now generally considered by scholars to be the earliest Gospel in circulation—that of Mark. The only occurrence of the term *peirasmós* in this Gospel is in the garden on the Mount of Olives, when Jesus, as mentioned, in the midst of his agony implores Peter, James, and John to pray not to enter *eis peirasmón* (Mark 14:38). This expression is substantially identical to the sixth petition of the Lord's Prayer and adds little—from a purely grammatical point of view— to our analysis.[2] Mark, on the other hand, uses the verb *peirázō* more casually. We find it in Mark 1:13 when it is narrated that Jesus remained in the desert for forty days *peirazómenos hypò toû Satanâ* (πειραζόμενος ὑπὸ τοῦ Σατανᾶ), that is, "while he was tempted by Satan." This can be considered for all intents and purposes the first ever occurrence within Scripture of the verb *peirázō* explicitly associated with Satan's tempting action. This is an important qualitative leap. The very fact that *peirázō* has Satan as its subject implicitly gives the verb a malicious, misleading, deceptive meaning. All characteristics that, as we have seen, were not present in the Old Testament *nāsâ*. Mark does not explain to us what kind of temptations Satan used (to find out we have to read the same passage in the other synoptic Gospels). That *peirazómenos* remains suspended in the semantic field of "testing" (implicitly with malice, given that we are dealing with Satan), but without further specification.

An especially important clarification that the evangelist makes is the fact that Jesus does not go of his own free will into the desert to be tempted by Satan, but is led there by the Holy Spirit, immediately after his baptism in the Jordan by John the Baptist. This is a passage not to be underestimated: "And immediately the spirit driveth him into the wilderness" (Mark 1:12).

The term used by Mark to render the scene is remarkable. It is the verb *ekbállō* (ἐκβάλλω), which is composed of the preposition *ek* (ἐκ) and the verb *bállō* (βάλλω), which means "to throw," "to cast." The preposition *ek* gives the verb an even rougher, almost violent connotation. It gives the idea of "throwing out," of "dragging out." The Holy Spirit takes Jesus, newly baptized, drags him out and away from all traces of civilization, and throws him among the rocks of the desert. Let us see how the other

---

2. We will devote a separate chapter to the agony of Jesus where we will try to interpret the exact meaning of these words.

evangelists describe the same scene. Matthew in the beginning of chapter 4 writes, "Then was Jesus led up of the Spirit into the wilderness to be tempted [*peirázō*] of the devil" (Matt 4:1).

The verb that Matthew uses is *anágō* (ἀνάγω), a compound of the verb *ágō* (ἄγω), which as we know indicates the idea of leading. Matthew confirms that it is not Jesus by himself who goes into the desert. He goes by the will of the Father, brought about through the work of the Holy Spirit. If there was any doubt, Matthew also specifies the precise reason why the Holy Spirit leads Jesus into the desert, using an infinitive construct: so that he would be tempted by the devil. Satan does not just happen to walk by. Satan does not target Jesus. Instead, it is the Father who leads the Son directly to be tempted by Satan. Luke uses similar words: "And Jesus being full of the Holy Ghost returned from Jordan, and was led in the Spirit[3] into the wilderness, Being forty days tempted [*peirázō*] of the devil. And in those days he did eat nothing: and when they were ended, he afterward hungered" (Luke 4:1–2).

Luke's image is even more precise. Not only is Jesus led by the Spirit, but he is led *in the Spirit*. What Luke is telling us is that the Holy Spirit has taken complete control of Jesus-man, has become one with him. The Holy Spirit is within him, leading him in the desert to his encounter with Satan.

Do not these images recall the same one that is suggested by the verb *eisphérō* in the sixth petition of the Lord's Prayer? Is not the Holy Spirit (that is, God) here forcefully and decisively leading his Son to be tempted? Is he not literally leading him into temptation? Of course, he is. But only if the expression "leading into temptation" is not to be understood in an *idiomatic* sense, but in a literal sense: leading to be tempted. Understood: by Satan.

These simple passages from the three evangelists would be enough to sweep away rivers and rivers of ink poured out to defend an improbable permissive interpretation of the sixth petition of the Lord's Prayer. If God did not simply allow his Son to be tempted by Satan, but led him there of his own precise will, why should we have all these problems to think of a God who brings us (miserable human beings) into the clutches of the devil, to put us to the test? Why all this modesty in sweetening that *mḕ eisenénkēis* with permissive formulas ("do not allow," "do not forsake us"), when the evangelists themselves have shown no fear in using explicitly causative verbs?

## THE IDIOMATIC INTERPRETATION

The answer lies in the idiomatic interpretation of the sixth petition of the Lord's Prayer. "To lead into temptation" has always been understood, almost unanimously, by the church fathers as being equivalent to "to cause to fall into sin." And it is obvious that, in this case, God does not cause anyone to fall into sin. *Ergo*, the need for permissive

---

3. The KJV has "by the Spirit."

constructs that avoid the scandal of a God who would otherwise seem to cause people to fall into sin.

Now, the disquisition on whether the expression used by Jesus in the sixth petition of the Lord's Prayer is to be understood in a literal sense ("lead us not into temptation," that is, "do not lead us to be tempted by Satan as you God led your Son to be tempted by Satan") or in an idiomatic sense ("do not make us fall into sin") is undoubtedly interesting, but, in our opinion, risks to lose sight of much of the profound meaning contained in the petition. Therefore, we will try to briefly demonstrate below how the problem lies not in the diatribe between literal and idiomatic interpretation of the sixth petition (both of which present insurmountable logical problems), but in the interpretation of that *peirasmós* as a "sin trap."

We will proceed by reduction *ad absurdum*, assuming that *peirasmós* is precisely the trap of moral temptation to sin, and we will show how both literal and idiomatic interpretations are, in this case, unsatisfactory. We have already discussed sufficiently the "scandal" of the idiomatic interpretation that depicts a God who would urge us to sin. As we have seen, practically all the church fathers had reached this conclusion, both those of Greek mother tongue (Origen and Dionysius of Alexandria) and those of Latin tradition, above all St. Augustine. It is one thing to say one has been tempted. It is another to say one has entered (fallen) into temptation, that is, have yielded to temptation itself. There can be no shadow of doubt about this. And to resolve this "scandal" one must force the text to say something it does not say, that is, introduce permissive constructs ("do not allow that," "do not suffer that") or add explanatory glosses that create more issues than they solve ("that we are tempted beyond what we can bear").

Another major problem of the idiomatic interpretation is the following. If "to enter into temptation" is a Greek way of saying (later taken up in the Latin world and finally entered into our everyday language) to mean "to fall into sin," we must assume that there was an identical way of saying in Aramaic. Otherwise, we would be faced with the (unfortunate) situation of Gospels that, instead of reporting (in Greek) the exact words of Jesus (in Aramaic), interpret and render them in Greek with idiomatic expressions, which are specific to an idiom, but difficult to translate (and easily misunderstood) in other languages. This is not credible. And the possibility that Jesus wanted to use (in Aramaic) an idiomatic expression is almost nil. For two very precise reasons.

First. In the whole Bible there are no idiomatic expressions containing the Hebrew verb *bô'* (to enter). This verb always indicates concrete entry into a physical place. The only examples that could be understood in a figurative sense (figurative, not idiomatic!) are found in the book of Job (Job 14:3; 22:4) and the book of Ecclesiastes (Eccl 11:9; 12:14), where the expressions "to enter judgment against someone" and "to bring someone/something to judgment" are used in the legal/forensic sense of "to impose a sentence," "to judge." When we say that God "enters judgment against someone" or "brings someone to judgment" it means that he subjects them to his judgment. It is a figurative motion (judgment is not a physical place), but the meaning is clear. There are no obscure semantic leaps. On the other hand, when one interprets the expression "entering into temptation" not as "being subjected to temptation," but as "falling into sin," there is a non-obvious semantic leap involved ("temptation" and "sin" are two different concepts). And only those accustomed to the idiomatic use of this expression could understand it.

The second reason is that if Jesus had really wanted to say, "do not let us fall into sin," he could have said it explicitly, without using idiomatic expressions. Again: why, immediately after having admonished his disciples so that their speech would be clear ("yes yes, no no"), would Jesus have had to contradict himself? In fact, there is not a single case in the entire Bible where, in order to indicate the fact that someone has committed a sin (or that someone has led someone else to commit a sin), it is said that that someone has "gone into sin" (or that that someone "led someone else into sin"). One simply uses the verb "to sin," or the causative (*hiphil*) form of the verb "to sin" ("to cause to sin").

Where, then, does the idiomatic expression "to enter/lead into temptation" understood in the sense of "to commit a sin" come from? It is very likely that it all begins with a passage used by St. Paul in his first letter to Timothy in which he says, "But they that will be rich fall into temptation [*eis peirasmón*] and a snare, and into many foolish and hurtful lusts, which drown men in destruction and perdition" (1 Tim 6:9).

The verb used by St. Paul is *empíptō* (ἐμπίπτω) which means "to fall in." Why does he use this verb with the same expression used in the Lord's Prayer (*eis peirasmón*)? The answer lies in the following image of the "trap." Do you remember how the metaphor of the net that the hunter uses to catch animals is abundantly used in the Bible to indicate the trap of temptation to sin? Well, here St. Paul picks it up again using the specific term *pagís* (παγίς), which we have encountered before, in conjunction with *peirasmós*. St. Paul speaks of falling *eis peirasmòn kaì pagída* (εἰς πειρασμὸν καὶ παγίδα). Literally: into temptation and a trap. That is, when one falls into *peirasmós*, one automatically falls into a trap (εἰς παγίδα). The pair could be better translated as "the trap of temptation."[4] St. Paul is clearly speaking here of the snare of moral temptation—specifically, of avarice. Those who live to enrich themselves are not only tempted by money, but they have already fallen into the trap of temptation, they have already succumbed to it, and thus have already committed sin. And precisely because *peirasmós* is understood as a *pagís*, a trap that necessarily leads "to ruin and perdition," "to fall/enter into temptation" is to be understood as surrendering oneself to the death of sin. It is likely, then, that the expression *empíptein eis peirasmòn kai pagída* ("to fall into the trap of temptation") evolved into the simpler truncated formula *empíptein eis peirasmón* ("to fall into temptation"), where the meaning of "trap" remains implicit. In any case, it is worth noting that this kind of linguistic evolution is a post-Christ phenomenon.

4. It is typical in Greek to juxtapose two similar terms (or synonyms) to reinforce their meaning.

## TEMPTATION ACCORDING TO JESUS

Jesus, when he wants to talk about a real enticement to sin, does it without too many turns of phrase, locutions, or idiomatic expressions. In fact, he casually and abundantly uses verbs such as *skandalízō* (σκανδαλίζω) and *planáō/apoplanáō* (πλανάω/ἀποπλανάω), which contain all the typical concepts of temptation. *Skandalízō* is derived from the noun *skándalon* (σκάνδαλον), which indicates the stumbling stone. The verb *skandalízō* indicates the idea of placing a stumbling stone in someone's path to make them fall. It means to create a propitious occasion for sin. In short, it means to induce someone to commit a sin. It means to lead him into temptation. Think of the famous passage in the Sermon on the Mount where Jesus explains, "And if thy right eye is an occasion of sin [*skandalízō*] for thee,[5] pluck it out, and cast it from thee: for it is profitable for thee that one of thy members should perish, and not that thy whole body should be cast into hell. And if thy right hand is an occasion of sin [*skandalízō*] for thee, cut it off, and cast it from thee: for it is profitable for thee that one of thy members should perish, and not that thy whole body should be cast into hell" (Matt 5:29–30; see also Mark 9:43–48).

Or think of another very harsh passage in Jesus' preaching about anyone corrupting the innocence of children:

> But whoso shall be an occasion of sin [*skandalízō*] for one of these little ones which believe in me, it were better for him that a millstone were hanged about his neck, and that he were drowned in the depth of the sea. Woe unto the world because of occasions of sin [*skándalon*]! for it must needs be that occasions of sin [*skándalon*] come; but woe to that man by whom the occasion of sin [*skándalon*] cometh! Wherefore if thy hand or thy foot are an occasion of sin [*skandalízō*] for thee, cut them off, and cast them from thee: it is better for thee to enter into life halt or maimed, rather than having two hands or two feet to be cast into everlasting fire. And if thine eye is an occasion of sin [*skandalízō*] for thee, pluck it out, and cast it from thee: it is better for thee to enter into life with one eye, rather than having two eyes to be cast into hell fire. (Matt 18:6–9; see also Mark 9:42 and Luke 17:1–2)

When Jesus prophesied to his disciples that he would have to suffer and die at the hands of the high priests and the scribes before being resurrected on the third day, Peter, shaken by the master's words, took Jesus aside and tried to convince him, consoling him, that this would never happen. At that point, Jesus' reaction is, to say the least, irritated—probably ungenerous. He apostrophizes Peter with these words: "Peter, Get thee behind me, Satan: thou art a temptation[6] [*skándalon*] unto me: for thou savourest not the things that be of God, but those that be of men!" (Matt 16:23).

---

5. The KJV has "offend thee."
6. The KJV has "an offence."

Why such harsh words? Why does he go so far as to affix to Peter the epithet of Satan? Because Peter, unconsciously and with good intentions, is in some way placing an obstacle, a *skándalon*, between Jesus and the will of his Father. He is tempting him just as Satan might have done. The typical temptation of Satan is that of convincing people not to do the will of God. If Jesus had wanted to avoid persecution by the high priests, he could have easily done so. He could have stayed away from Jerusalem and preached elsewhere. He could have stopped his ministry and devoted himself to a private life. But, of course, this was not the will of his Father. Peter's inappropriate but naive words insinuate the idea that Jesus could somehow escape the Father's will. They are a real (involuntary) satanic temptation.

And so, in one of the clearest passages where Jesus is talking about the ultimate temptation of Satan, where he could have revealed once and for all the hidden meaning of the term *peirasmós*, he decides instead to use a different term. He does not tell Peter that he is a *peirasmós* for him, but a *skándalon*, that is, a stumbling block, that is, an occasion of sin, that is, a temptation in the evil sense of the term. Why? Because what Peter is hoping for (that Jesus will escape death) is something that goes against the ultimate purpose of Jesus' very presence on earth—to save people from divine wrath by immolating himself in their place. Suggesting to Jesus to escape from his destiny of sacrificial lamb (but Peter could not understand this yet) means to destroy the whole plan of redemption that God had prepared for the salvation of humanity.[7] It is an infinitely destructive temptation, which would take away from the whole of humanity the last chance of redemption. Nothing good can come from such a temptation. For this reason, Jesus sees in these words a satanic temptation—a *skándalon*, not a *peirasmós*. And he rejects it with all his might, "Get thee behind me, Satan."

Or when Jesus explains the parable of the weeds in the field, he speaks of the end of the world in these terms: "The Son of man shall send forth his angels, and they shall gather out of his kingdom all those that are an occasion of sin [*skándalon*], and them which do iniquity; And shall cast them into a furnace of fire: there shall be wailing and gnashing of teeth" (Matt 13:41–42).

Jesus is speaking of the wicked, the workers of iniquity, that is, those who wallow in sin and are destined for hell. Not only that. The same fate will also befall those who are occasions of sin. That is, those who incite to sin (not by sinning themselves materially) and are for others an evil temptation. And even in this case Jesus does not use the term *peirasmós* but *skándalon*.

It should be clear from all these examples that Jesus, when he wants to express the concept of temptation to moral/mortal sin, uses the couple *skandalízō/skándalon*, and not *peirázō/peirasmós*. Upon closer inspection, Jesus uses the verb *peirázō* only once in all four Gospels. The episode is reported by both Matthew and Mark. When the Pharisees send their disciples ahead to ask Jesus whether it is lawful to pay taxes to

---

7. See John 12:27: "Now is my soul troubled; and what shall I say? Father, save me from this hour: but for this cause came I unto this hour."

the Roman emperor, Jesus, knowing their sly motives, replies, "Why tempt [*peirázō*] ye me, ye hypocrites?" (Matt 22:18; see also Mark 12:15).

The one occasion when Jesus uses the verb *peirázō* has nothing to do with inducing people into temptation, as we commonly understand it. The disciples of the Pharisees are not trying to goad Jesus into committing any sin. They are simply asking a trick question to see if Jesus could somehow contradict himself, and thus catch him in error in his speeches, and then discredit him before the eyes of his disciples. They are not even talking about Scripture or divine commandments. They are pushing him to talk about politics!

And although it is a question asked with malice, for Jesus it is a *peirasmós* to all intents and purposes, because it pushes him beyond his "limits" (if we can speak of "limits"[8]) and to find a way to get out of the corner in which the Pharisees had driven him. Jesus, as we know, comes out brilliantly with the famous maxim, "Render therefore unto Caesar the things which are Caesar's; and unto God the things that are God's" (Matt 22:21). As if to say, do not confuse the law of God with the law of people. Test passed.

The same is true of the other two occurrences of the verb *peirázō* in Mark. In Mark 8:11, for example, we always find the Pharisees asking Jesus for a proof of his divine nature (see also Matt 16:1). This test is similar to the one which the Israelites asked for in the desert of Massah. It is the test to which people tend to subject God because they doubt his existence. In Mark 10:2, the same Pharisees put Jesus to the test (*peirázō*) again with thorny questions concerning divorce: "Is it lawful for a man to put away his wife for every cause" (Matt 19:3). Once again Jesus seems to be cornered. The Mosaic law provided the possibility for a husband to repudiate his wife. But once again, he comes out brilliantly explaining how Moses had given them that law "because of the hardness of their hearts" and concluding with the famous phrase, "What therefore God hath joined together, let not man put asunder" (Mark 10:9).

It is worth noticing at this point how, in general, the verb *peirázō* is much more widely used, both within the New Testament and the Old, than the corresponding noun, *peirasmós*. For example, in the Hebrew Bible the verb *nāsâ* appears thirty-six times, while the noun *măssâ* only nine. In the New Testament, *peirázō* appears thirty-nine times, while *peirasmós* only twenty-one. On the other hand, when we consider only the words pronounced by Jesus, this ratio is reversed: the occurrences of *peirázō* are only two, while those of *peirasmós* are eight. This cannot be a coincidence, at least from a purely statistical point of view. As mentioned, Jesus seems to want to put a lot of emphasis on this noun; certainly, much more than on the corresponding verb *peirázō*, used only on the occasion mentioned above and in a context that has nothing to do with temptation understood as seduction to moral sin. He seems to want to tell us that the noun *peirasmós* is much more than just the effect produced by the action

---

8. "Limits" in the sense that Jesus came to explain the divine law and fulfill the prophecies contained in Scripture, certainly not to delve into thorny political diatribes.

described by the verb *peirázō*. *Peirázō* cannot be equivalent to "*eisphérō eis peirasmón.*" Otherwise, Jesus would not have used a locution, but a simple verb. *Peirasmós* is a term characterized by an enormous semantic poignancy (necessary, given the brevity of the Lord's Prayer), which goes beyond the simple, generic "trial" (or "temptation," whatever we want to call it), and that it is up to the faithful to discover, contemplating its mystery.

If, with the expression "lead us not into temptation," Jesus had wanted to indicate the action of pushing one to sin, he could have used *planáō* (πλανάω), a verb which would have been much clearer and easier to understand. It is a term we have encountered before and literally describes the action of sending someone astray. It is an intrinsically causative verb, which is used metaphorically very often to indicate the action of pushing someone to do something wrong, to commit a mistake, a sin. *Planáō* would be the most appropriate Greek verb to translate the concept of leading into temptation!

The only expression in the entire Vulgate that matches the expression used in the sixth petition of the Lord's Prayer is found in chapter 24 of the Gospel of Matthew: "*ita ut in errorem inducantur (si fieri potest) etiam electi.*"[9] (Matt 24:24 VUL)

*Inducere in errorem*. That is, to lead into error. That is, to deceive. This is the Latin translation of the Greek verb *planáō*. And why then, despite having this simple verb at his disposal,[10] should Jesus have adopted an obscure idiomatic expression, foreign to the Hebrew (or Aramaic) language, to express the same idea? This is neither reasonable nor credible. Not even justifying it with undefined needs of metrics. As if Jesus himself was reciting a poem and needed "more words" to complete the verse. That the Lord's Prayer in Aramaic has a cadence, a melody and a rhythm that are essentially irreproducible in other idioms is undoubtedly true. But from here to claim that Jesus had to use poetic and idiomatic expressions (not necessarily used in everyday speech) simply to adapt to the metric of the verse is a long way off.

## THE LITERAL INTERPRETATION

Now what? If the idiomatic interpretation is not tenable, is it the literal one that can unhinge the mystery of the sixth petition? "Lead us not into temptation" in the sense of "do not lead us to be tempted (by Satan)"? This is undoubtedly a much more acceptable interpretation and one that adheres to the original Greek text of the Gospels. But an interpretation that is at the same time not robust and still unsatisfactory. For a specific logical reason. When the Spirit drags him into the desert, Jesus lets himself be docilely transported by the will of his Father. He does not resist. He does not kneel to pray to the Father to spare him that trial, that *peirasmós*. He courageously submits to it

---

9. Insomuch that, if it were possible, they shall deceive the very elect.

10. In Hebrew, Jesus would have even had the choice between two synonyms, *shāgâ* (שָׁגָה) and *tāʻâ* (תָּעָה).

and apparently overcomes it without any particular effort. He considers it a necessary, unavoidable *peirasmós*, preparatory to the beginning of his preaching ministry. Satan's temptation is indeed a temptation (we will see this clearly later on), but, before being a temptation, it is first and foremost a great *peirasmós* to which the Father subjects the Son—a veritable rite of initiation, where Satan acts only as an extra, a useful instrument of the divine will.

Given these premises, how is it possible to think that the same Jesus, who submitted himself without batting an eyelid to the will of the Father and accepted to be dragged by the Holy Spirit in the desert to be tempted by Satan, then teaches his disciples to implore the Father not to do the same with them? And if God has not even granted his Son the grace of being able to escape the temptations of the devil, what hope could we miserable mortals have? And finally, on closer inspection, the temptations with which Satan tries to make Jesus fall have little or nothing to do with the temptations to which a person may be subjected. In fact, the temptations in the desert are temptations explicitly designed and conceived for a God-man, not for a simple mortal. They are similar to the temptations with which the Israelites tried to test God in the desert of Massah. And perhaps it is no coincidence that the two types of temptation both occur in the same desolate setting. The parallelism between the episode in Massah in which the Israelites tested the Lord and the temptations of Christ by Satan is evident.

We can read the details in the Gospel of Matthew, chapter 4: "And when the tempter [*peirázō*] came to him, he said, If thou be the Son of God, command that these stones be made bread" (Matt 4:3). For the first time in the Bible, Satan is identified with this epithet: *ho Peirázōn* (ὁ πειράζων), or "the Tempter." The most common epithet until then for Satan had been "the Accuser," that is, the one who accuses us falsely, and tries maliciously to convince God to condemn us to hell.[11] We are in the presence of a notable semantic evolution, unknown to the Old Testament. This confirms that already within the very first Christian communities, the verb *peirázō* had to all intents and purposes encompassed the malignant sense of "to tempt," that is, of "attempting to bring down." So much so that the devil is defined as "he who tempts."

Now, what kind of temptations does the Tempter address to Jesus? We have seen the first one. If Jesus is truly the Son of God (as he claims), he will have no difficulty in turning stones into bread. This is a clear reminiscence of the miracle performed by God in the desert, when he made it rain manna from heaven for the hungry Israelites. It is the same kind of test to which the people of Israel submitted the Lord in the desert. If God was really with them, he had to prove it by providing them with food and drink.

---

11. It is no coincidence that "devil" comes from the Greek word *diábolos* (διάβολος), which contains the same root as the verb *diabállō* (διαβάλλω), which means "to accuse." The devil is literally "the Accuser."

The second temptation is along the same lines as the first. Satan takes Jesus to the pinnacle of the Temple of Jerusalem and incites him to throw himself down. If Jesus is really the Son of God (as he claims), his Father will have no difficulty in ordering the angels to support him. To which Jesus replies, "It is written again, Thou shalt not tempt [*peirázō*] the Lord thy God" (Matt 4:7). Satan is trying (*peirázō*) to convince the Son of God to put the Father to the test (*peirázō*).

The third temptation represents Satan's last (desperate) attempt to overturn the power relations between himself and God, to subject the Son of God (that is, God) to his evil will, exploiting his human weakness. He promises him dominion over all the kingdoms of the earth: "All these things will I give thee, if thou wilt fall down and worship me" (Matt 4:9).

Satan's forbidden dream is to substitute himself for God. Satan (who has power in the earthly world, but not in the heavenly one) makes, so to speak, an indecent proposal to the Son of God. He proposes an exchange. God will have dominion over the earth, but Satan will have dominion over him. The attempt is obviously unsuccessful, and Satan has to withdraw admitting defeat (Matt 4:11).

The first point that we must absolutely clarify is that these three "trials" to which Satan subjects Jesus are to all intents and purposes "temptations," in the evil sense of the term. Satan is not simply testing the Son of God. He is deviously trying to convince him to do something profoundly wrong. He is trying to make him fall. He is tempting him, in the common sense of the term. At the same time, however, these are temptations that are part of a great trial (this one conceived without malice), of a great *peirasmós* to which the Father subjects the Son. It is, as we have said, a great rite of initiation, necessary for the Son of Man to demonstrate, first of all to himself, that he is immune to evil. It is a *peirasmós* that intimately relates to the mystery of the double nature, human and divine, present in Christ. Jesus-God does not need to overcome any *peirasmós*. He does not need to overcome any limit (God has no limits by definition). Jesus-man, however, does. Jesus-man is afflicted by all the doubts and all the anxieties typical of mortals. Jesus-man can indeed be put to the test. On the contrary, it is necessary that he be put to the test, to be able to carry out the plan that the Father has in store for him.

These considerations lead us to the second crucial point. These temptations to which Jesus is subjected are temptations that make sense only for a God-man. "If indeed you are the Son of God," Satan says to introduce his temptations. The devious attempt is to separate the Jesus-man from the Jesus-God. To make Jesus-man doubt Jesus-God. This is perhaps one of the greatest mysteries contained in the Gospels. Human fragility coexists, indeed coincides with, divine perfection in the person of Christ. It is this fragility that Satan attacks.

If this is true, then the parallelism proposed by the literal interpretation of the sixth petition of the Lord's Prayer does not stand. The Father brings his Son, through the Holy Spirit, to be tempted by Satan with a very precise purpose—that of testing the fragility of his human nature in relation to his divine nature. There is no other passage in the Old or New Testament where God literally leads someone into Satan's lair to be tempted by him. He does so only with his Son. And only because his Son is God, but also man. And since the condition of God-man does not pertain to mortals, there is no need for the Father to lead us to be specially tempted by Satan, as he did with his Son. In fact, for people to be tempted by Satan (with temptations proper to mortals), God does not need to lead us anywhere. Satan already does everything himself. If he wants to, he comes after us. If he wants to, he comes to tempt us. If he wants to, he tries to infiltrate our heart to make it dry, hard, and impermeable to the divine Spirit.

If he wants to. This is another concept to keep in mind. Angels (even the fallen ones—Satan and his demons) enjoy, like all beings created by God, *free will*. They have rational capacity and decision-making ability. If they did not have it, Satan and his court of demons would never have decided of their own free will to disobey God and turn against him. And this free will is maintained over time, even after the fall from heaven. Satan has free will to decide which souls to attack and morally tempt, to try to corrupt them and thus drag them to hell. With those souls whose hearts are hard and deaf to divine grace, Satan has an easy job. A little temptation is enough to make them fall into sin immediately. With those souls whose hearts are permeated by divine grace, Satan must fight fiercely to succeed in corrupting them and dragging them to himself. We are talking about moral corruption—incitement to mortal sin. This is in some way the task, the mission, the daily occupation of the devil, who wanders the world in search of souls to make fall (1 Pet 5:8).[12] What sense would there be in Jesus teaching us to ask the Father not to lead us to be tempted by Satan? Satan already does this of his own accord! Satan comes after us, without the Father needing to bring us to him.

Nor can Waetjen's position on this matter be considered acceptable. Herman C. Waetjen, professor emeritus of New Testament at San Francisco Theological Seminary, after analyzing Jesus' temptations in the desert and following E. Schweizer,[13] argues that this type of dynamics (God leading us to be tempted by Satan) is what the sixth petition of the Lord's Prayer would be referring to.[14] To support his conclusion, Waetjen explains that God, through Jesus, established a new hierarchy, according to which we are no longer children of God. We have "come of age," and God does not need to put our faith to the test anymore, as he did in the Old Testament with the Israelites. While God may not test us anymore though, he may lead us to be tested by Satan. This is because God wants to engage us in his ultimate battle against the power of evil. In this sense, Jesus was led by the Father to be tempted by Satan to kick off this

---

12. Worthy of note, above all, is the famous prayer *Oratio ad Sanctum Michael* that Pope Leo XIII composed in 1884 after having a vision of the terrible battle taking place between Satan and the church. The archangel Michael is asked to defend us in the daily battle against "Satan and all the evil spirits, who prowl about the world seeking the ruin of souls" ("*Satanam aliosque spiritus malignos, qui ad perditionem animarum pervagantur in mundo*").

13. Schweizer, *The Good News*, 62.

14. Waetjen, *Praying the Lord's Prayer*, 93–104.

battle against the Evil One—a battle to which all Jesus' disciples are called. However—this is Waetjen's conclusion—since the idea of engaging in a fight with the devil is a "terrifying prospect," we should pray God, if possible, not to put us in this terrifying situation. Hence, the sixth petition of the Lord's Prayer.

Several steps in Waetjen's argument sound glaringly contradictory. First, if God's goal for Jesus' disciples—for us— is to participate in a conflict with the power of evil, why would Jesus teach his disciples exactly the opposite, that is, to ask God to be spared from that conflict? If anything, we know for a fact that Jesus never taught his disciples to ask to be spared from the conflict with Satan. Instead, he acknowledged that this fight is inevitable, and he prayed that their faith would not fail.[15] Second, if indeed God, according to this "new moral order" established by Jesus, does not need to put our faith to the test anymore, why would he delegate the testing to Satan? Does God still need to test us or does he not? And if not, why is God leading us to be tested (by Satan)? Just to pick up a fight with him? Having us tested by Satan sounds like an odd way of engaging us in a battle against him. In fact, if this is the case, it would appear as if God and Satan are on the same team—against us (as in Job's case). Third, if indeed God, under this "new moral order" established in the New Testament, does not need to put our faith to the test anymore, what are we going to do with all those passages in the New Testament that explicitly or implicitly say that God is still the one doing the testing?[16] Finally, Waetjen considers the expression "Do not lead us into being tried!" equivalent to "Prevent us from being tested!"[17] In other words, he is assuming that "prohibition" equals "prevention." However, the two concepts cannot be superimposed: "prohibition" implies causation, "prevention" implies permission. And we have already demonstrated that interpreting causation permissively is an unsustainable position.[18]

If, as we hope to have demonstrated, both the literal and the idiomatic interpretations are largely unsatisfactory, the problem must lie elsewhere, namely in the identification of *peirasmós* with the temptation to sin. If one persists in considering the *peirasmós* of which Jesus speaks in the sixth petition of the Lord's Prayer as the moral temptation, one necessarily finds oneself in logical contradictions from which it is impossible to escape, if not by making havoc on the original texts.

---

15. See Luke 22:31–32: "Simon, Simon, behold, Satan hath desired to have you, that he may sift you as wheat: But I have prayed for thee, that thy faith fail not"; John 17:15: "I pray not that thou shouldest take them out of the world, but that thou shouldest keep them from the evil." Jesus is not asking the Father to spare his disciples form the battle against the Evil One, but to give them strength so that they may remain firm in their faith.

16. See, for example, Luke 8:13 (cf. Mark 4:6); 1 Cor 3:13; 1 Thess 2:4; Rev 3:10.

17. Waetjen, *Praying the Lord's Prayer*, 93.

18. Otherwise, according to this logic, asking somebody, "Please, don't kill me" would be equivalent to asking, "Please, prevent me from dying," and vice versa. The two expressions are obviously different, and trying to make them equivalent produces absurd results. In the first, we are asking somebody that has the power to kill us and is about to do so, to instead spare our life. In the second, we are asking somebody that has the power to save us from an external threat, to indeed come help us.

## MATTHEW

In addition to the episode of the temptations in the desert, Matthew uses the verb *peirázō* four other times, and always to indicate the Pharisees' attempt to make Jesus contradict himself. We have already seen three of these occurrences in identical episodes narrated by Mark (Matt 16:1; 19:3; 22:18). Finally, in Matt 22:35 a doctor of the law questions Jesus, testing him (*peirázō*), about which the greatest commandment would be. Jesus responds brilliantly (Matt 22:37–40). In all these cases, *peirázō* has nothing to do with the idea of trying to induce someone to sin. On the other hand, Matthew uses the noun *peirasmós* in only two passages of his Gospel: one within the sixth petition of the Lord's Prayer and the other in the garden on the Mount of Olives.

If we summarize the two Gospels now unanimously considered by scholars as the earliest ones in chronological order, we see how the noun *peirasmós* is never used by the evangelists, except to translate two specific expressions used by Jesus: "lead us not *eis peirasmón*" (Matt 6:13), and "pray that you do not enter *eis peirasmón*" (Mark 14:28; Matt 26:41). As mentioned, the two expressions are grammatically similar, and thus the latter helps little in the interpretation of the former. This confirms the fact that *peirasmós* is the Greek word used by the evangelists only to render a specific Aramaic term used by Jesus. On the other hand, Matthew and Mark seem much more comfortable with the verb *peirázō* (four times in Mark, six times in Matthew). Three of these ten *peirázō* pertain to the temptations of Jesus in the desert by Satan. The remaining seven describe the trials (not temptations) to which the Pharisees subjected Jesus.

## LUKE

We must turn our gaze to Luke's Gospel to try to get a broader perspective on the possible meanings of the noun *peirasmós*. It is interesting to note that Luke is much more familiar with this term than all the other evangelists. He uses it as many as six times. At the same time, the verb *peirázō* appears only twice in his Gospel, in episodes already extensively analyzed: once to describe the tempting action of Satan in the desert (Luke 4:2) and once to indicate the request by the Pharisees for a sign demonstrating the divine nature of Christ (Luke 11:16).

Of the six occurrences of the noun *peirasmós* in Luke's Gospel, one appears in the sixth petition of the Lord's Prayer and as many as two in the garden on the Mount of Olives (the same expression "pray that you do not enter *eis peirasmón*" is repeated in both Luke 22:40 and Luke 22:46.). There remain, then, only three, used in different grammatical contexts, which can point us in the right direction.

One of these appears at the end of the episode of the temptations in the desert: "And when the devil had ended all the temptation [*peirasmós*], he departed from him for a season" (Luke 4:13).

## Eis Peirasmón

Luke speaks of *pánta peirasmón* (πάντα πειρασμόν), that is, of every possible kind of temptation. It is indeed, as we have seen, a temptation (because Satan subtly tries in every way to make Jesus fall), but it is a very particular temptation, a desperate attempt to leverage the weakness of Christ's human nature to destroy his divine nature as well. As we have seen, the *peirasmós* to which Jesus is subjected in the desert has little to do with the temptations of the flesh—with the deadly sins that lead people to moral destruction. Instead, it has to do with the specific divine nature of Christ.

The other two occurrences of the term *peirasmós* are much more interesting. Why? Because they are the only two (besides the Lord's Prayer and the episode in the garden on the Mount of Olives) in which Jesus himself uses this term. They are the milestones from which we must necessarily start in order to understand what kind of meaning Jesus—not the evangelists, nor any other disciple or Apostle—gave to this term.

The first appears in chapter 8, where Luke relates one of Jesus' most famous parables, that of the sower. It is necessary to read the entire passage to have a complete vision: "A sower went out to sow his seed: and as he sowed, some fell by the way side; and it was trodden down, and the fowls of the air devoured it. And some fell upon a rock; and as soon as it was sprung up, it withered away, because it lacked moisture. And some fell among thorns; and the thorns sprang up with it, and choked it" (Luke 8:5–7).

So, there are four *mutually exclusive* scenarios that Jesus presents:

1. the seed that falls on the road and is crushed and devoured;
2. the seed that falls on the rocky ground and dies for lack of water;
3. the seed that falls among the brambles and is smothered;
4. the seed that falls on good soil and sprouts and produces fruit.

Faced with the doubts of the disciples who do not seem to understand the metaphor, Jesus explains:

> Now the parable is this: The seed is the word of God. Those by the way side are they that hear; then cometh the devil, and taketh away the word out of their hearts, lest they should believe and be saved. They on the rock are they, which, when they hear, receive the word with joy; and these have no root, which for a while believe, and in the time of *peirasmós*[19] fall away. And that which fell among thorns are they, which, when they have heard, go forth, and are choked with cares and riches and pleasures of this life, and bring no fruit to perfection. But that on the good ground are they, which in an honest and good heart, having heard the word, keep it, and bring forth fruit with patience. (Luke 8:11–15)

---

19. The KJV has "temptation."

This is a most precious passage because not only is Jesus using the term *peirasmós* in a parable, but he is also explaining it! So, let us see what meaning he attributes to it. Better yet, let us start from what meanings he does *not* attribute to it.

The first scenario is that of the seed that falls on the road. Jesus teaches us that these are those who have been exposed to God's teachings, but since their hearts are completely hard and their ears are completely deaf to such dictates, Satan has an easy time sneaking into their hearts and making them lose their way. This first group is particularly subject to satanic temptations. As soon as Satan makes them doubt the truthfulness of the word of God, they fall for it and immediately stop believing, losing their only chance of salvation. We find here the description of the typical temptation that Satan tends to people. And for this type of temptation Jesus does *not* use the term *peirasmós*.

Let us move on to the third scenario, that of the seed falling among the thorns. What do the thorns represent? Jesus tells us they are the worries, wealth, and pleasures of life. They are the daily temptations! The ones that suffocate our good will and that appeal to human frailty, to the lust of the flesh.[20] And even in this case, Jesus does *not* use the term *peirasmós*.

However, in the second scenario, where neither Satan with his diabolical temptations nor the flesh with its daily temptations appear, Jesus *does* speak of *peirasmós*! Curious, isn't it? Just a coincidence? In our opinion, it is not. Rather, this is one of the proofs (if not the ultimate proof) that *peirasmós* is something—in Jesus' mind—that goes far beyond the concept of mere temptation (whether daily or satanic). It is something else. It is something more. The second scenario refers to the seeds that fall on the rock, take root, but then find themselves without water and die. These are those who welcome the word of God in good spirit, but then, when the *peirasmós* comes, they fail. *En kairôi peirasmoû* (ἐν καιρῷ πειρασμοῦ), Luke says. At the critical moment of *peirasmós*.[21] Sibylline expression. What does it mean? Well, we already know what it does not mean in this parable: neither satanic temptation, nor daily temptation. What, then, is this *peirasmós* that brings down people of little faith?

To understand this, we must go and read the same parable narrated in the other two synoptic Gospels of Mark (Mark 4:1–20) and Matthew (Matt 13:1–23), which add valuable details. First of all, they tell us that this plant with its roots sunk into the rock is burned as a result of the sunrise: "But when the sun was up, it was scorched; and because it had no root, it withered away" (Mark 4:6; see also Matt 13:6).

---

20. See Gal 5:19–21: "Now the works of the flesh are manifest, which are these; Adultery, fornication, uncleanness, lasciviousness, Idolatry, witchcraft, hatred, variance, emulations, wrath, strife, seditions, heresies, Envyings, murders, drunkenness, revellings, and such like: of the which I tell you before, as I have also told you in time past, that they which do such things shall not inherit the kingdom of God."

21. *Kairós* (καιρός) in Greek does not simply indicate a moment in time. It represents a *critical* moment.

The rising of the sun is thus the metaphor for *peirasmós*. The moment the sun rises and its rays begin to burn, *en kairôi peirasmoû*, the roots burn and the shoots die. And how does Jesus explain this passage, according to Matthew and Mark's account? He does not use the sibylline term *peirasmós* reported by Luke, but he explicitly describes what this critical moment consists of using a clear example: "when affliction or persecution ariseth for the word's sake, immediately they faint"[22] (Mark 4:17).

Like a litmus test, after superimposing the passages of the three synoptic Gospels that report the same episode, a clear fact is revealed before us. Affliction, *thlîpsis* (θλῖψις). Persecution, *diōgmós* (διωγμός). This is what Jesus means here by *peirasmós*. It is that combination of mental and physical suffering that can break down the faith of those who do not have sufficiently deep roots. Nothing to do with the devil's devious moral temptations. It's about psychophysical pain—bodily suffering and anguish of the soul. The ardor of the sun's rays burning the rootless shoots is precisely the metaphor of the pain that burns the flesh and the anguish that pierces the soul.

The power of the synoptic Gospels, which make it possible to examine the same episode, the same phrase, the same expression, from two or even three (slightly) different angles, is revealed in this passage. What theoretically could have remained obscure in the Gospel of Luke is masterfully revealed in the Gospels of Mark and Matthew.

But what were the exact words of Jesus, one might ask? The more cryptic ones reported by Luke, who speaks of a generic moment of *peirasmós*, or the illustrative ones reported by both Mark and Matthew? It is impossible to know, but one can speculate about it. It would seem likely, in our opinion, that Jesus used both expressions, first the more cryptic *en kairôi peirasmoû*, followed by the examples of tribulation or persecution, so that the meaning could not be misunderstood. Let us not forget that here Jesus is not simply telling a parable to his disciples. He is explaining it privately to the Apostles. It is a grace, that of receiving the exact explanation of the word of God, which is not granted to everyone—indeed, only to a restricted group of the chosen ones. It is likely that Jesus wanted to use the examples of tribulation and persecution to make the meaning of that *peirasmós* clear. Mark and Matthew who, as we have seen, do not seem very familiar with the use of the term *peirasmós*, probably decided to report only the explanatory examples. Luke, on the other hand, who seems to use the term *peirasmós* much more casually, considers those examples not strictly necessary for understanding the passage and leaves them out.

When Jesus tells this parable, he probably has at least a couple of Old Testament passages in his head. The first is found in the book of Jeremiah in chapter 17: "Blessed is the man that trusteth in the Lord, and whose hope the Lord is. For he shall be as a tree planted by the waters, and that spreadeth out her roots by the river, and shall not fear when scorching heat cometh, but her leaf shall be green; and shall not worry in the year of drought, neither shall cease from yielding fruit" (Jer 17:7–8).

---

22. The KJV has "they are offended."

The Septuagint translates "scorching heat" as *kaûma* (καῦμα), which represents the burning fire that comes from the sun and brings drought (see also Rev 7:16; 16:9). The second is found in the book of Proverbs in chapter 24: "If thou faint in the day of adversity, thy strength is small" (Prov 24:10).

The Hebrew text presents a beautiful *paronomasia* (almost impossible to reproduce in English) between the noun *tsārâ* (צָרָה), which indicates distress understood as suffering, and the adjective *tsăr* (צַר), which indicates the narrowness of a place. The *tsārâ* thus represents affliction, adversity, psychophysical stress, anguish, suffering, tribulation, *thlîpsis*. The Septuagint translates with the expression *en hēmérai thlípseōs* (ἐν ἡμέρᾳ θλίψεως). In the moment of *thlîpsis*. In the time of *tsārâ*. In the year of the drought. *En kairôi peirasmoû*. In the time of tribulation.

One final consideration. Who is responsible for the *peirasmós* mentioned by Luke? From whom does it come? From the rising of the sun. And who causes the sun to rise? Certainly not Satan. Remember when, looking for examples of implicit causative verbs, we came across (Matt 5:45) the expression "he maketh his sun to rise on the evil and on the good"? We had observed how this example clearly demonstrated the causative (not permissive) function of the verb *anatéllō*, "to make the sun rise." It may be a coincidence (or perhaps it is not) that at the moment in which Jesus makes explicit reference to *peirasmós*, the one who causes the *peirasmós* is not Satan, but God himself (who makes the sun rise).

The last occurrence of the term *peirasmós* in Luke's Gospel is found in chapter 22, right during the Last Supper. Jesus has just instituted the mystery of the Eucharist and announced that one of the Twelve will betray him. Jesus addresses his disciples as follows: "Ye are they which have continued with me in my trials [*peirasmós*]"[23] (Luke 22:28).

The term *peirasmós* is used here in the plural and with the definite article, *en toîs peirasmoîs* (ἐν τοῖς πειρασμοῖς). This is not a generic *peirasmós*, but rather the trials that the disciples are familiar with, since Jesus faced them alongside them, and they persevered with him. Of what *peirasmós* is Jesus speaking in this case? Perhaps the temptations to which he was subjected by the devil in the desert? Obviously not. At that time, Jesus had not yet begun his preaching ministry and the Twelve had yet to be chosen. Is he speaking then of moral temptations to which both he and the disciples would have been subjected? There are no episodes of this kind in the Gospels. What then? It is impossible to say with absolute certainty, but it is likely that Jesus is referring to the "persecution" suffered by the Pharisees, the high priests, and the doctors of the law. The greatest trials that Jesus had to endure during his three years of preaching came from the religious elite of the time. And it's not just the trick questions they asked him from time to time to test him. It's the physical threats. Several times and in several passages of the Gospels it is told how the high priests tried to kill Jesus, but never succeeded. In the Gospel of Luke, it is narrated that after Jesus had spoken in

---

23. The KJV has "in my temptations."

the synagogue of Nazareth, they "rose up, and thrust him out of the city, and led him unto the brow of the hill whereon their city was built, that they might cast him down headlong. But he passing through the midst of them went his way" (Luke 4:29–30). In the Gospel of John, it is explained that "the Jews sought the more to kill him, because he not only had broken the sabbath, but said also that God was his Father, making himself equal with God" (John 5:18). In another passage, it is narrated that the Jews "took up stones to cast at him: but Jesus hid himself, and went out of the temple, going through the midst of them, and so passed by" (John 8:59). Or that "the Jews took up stones again to stone him" (John 10:31). And then again, "they sought again to take him: but he escaped out of their hand" (John 10:39). Not to mention the anathema hurled against him by the high priest Caiaphas: "Then from that day forth they took counsel together for to put him to death" (John 11:53). If we combine all these episodes of attempted murder (the plan to eliminate Jesus had already been underway for some time) with the situation in which those words are pronounced (only a few hours before being finally arrested, summarily tried, barbarously tortured, and crucified), it is plausible to think that the *peirasmós* to which Jesus is thinking represents precisely the persecution (both psychological and material) suffered in all those years by the high priests. His disciples, even though they saw that the highest religious authorities of the time were plotting the elimination of their master, had up to that moment remained at his side without giving in to the fear of suffering the same persecution. Here again, Jesus uses the term *peirasmós* to indicate that psychophysical stress which makes the flesh suffer and throws the soul into anguish.

While it is true that this is the last occurrence of the term *peirasmós* in the Gospel of Luke, it is also true that it is not the last time Luke uses this term in his writings. Luke is also the author of the book of the Acts of the Apostles, which recounts the events of the Apostles immediately following the death and resurrection of Christ. Most of the chapters in Acts are devoted to describing St. Paul's evangelization journeys in Greece and throughout Asia Minor. During one of these journeys, Paul arrives in Miletus and from there has the elders of the church called to Ephesus for a final farewell before returning to Jerusalem. It is a very emotional moment—somehow similar to Jesus' last farewell to his disciples during the Last Supper: "Serving the Lord with all humility of mind, and with many tears, and trials [*peirasmós*], which befell me by the lying in wait of the Jews: And how I kept back nothing that was profitable unto you, but have shewed you, and have taught you publicly, and from house to house, Testifying both to the Jews, and also to the Greeks, repentance toward God, and faith toward our Lord Jesus Christ. And now, behold, I go bound in the spirit unto Jerusalem, not knowing the things that shall befall me there: Save that the Holy Ghost witnesseth in every city, saying that bonds and afflictions abide me" (Acts 20:19–23).

Just as the highest religious authorities of the Jews had tried in every way to put Jesus to death, so the Jews themselves were trying to stop the process of St. Paul's evangelization among the communities of the so-called Gentiles, that is, the people of non-Jewish origin. And as Jesus initially escaped all the snares set for him by the high priests, in the same way the plots of the Jews to eliminate St. Paul could not stop his wanderings (Acts 20:3). And just as Jesus during the Last Supper reminded his disciples of all the anguish he endured, so St. Paul, with tears in his eyes, recalls all the suffering and anguish he suffered at the hands of the Jews. Not only that. Just as Jesus foretold the Twelve that he will return to Jerusalem to be put to death, so St. Paul foreshadows to them all the persecutions and tribulations that await him in every city to which he will go. The terms St. Paul uses are *desmá* (δεσμά), which indicates chains, that is, captivity, and the usual *thlîpsis* (θλῖψις), which indicates the most acute tribulation. Again, as in the parable of the sower, the term *peirasmós* is explicitly associated with the concept of persecution and tribulation. Certainly not temptation to sin.

Luke, in the rest of the book of Acts, uses the verb *peirázō* five times. In three of them (Acts 9:26; 16:7; 24:6), the verb is used with an infinitive construct and simply indicates an attempt to perform an action. In the other two instances (Acts 5:9; 15:10), the verb is used to indicate the nefarious tendency of people to test God.

## JOHN

To conclude with the evangelists, we must point out that in the Gospel of John the term *peirasmós* never appears. Only the verb *peirázō* appears, and only a couple of times. The first occurs in John 6:6, which we have already analyzed. Jesus tests Philip's faith by asking him how they can raise enough money to feed all the people who came. The second occurrence is found in John 8:6 where the famous episode of the adulteress brought before Jesus by the scribes and Pharisees is narrated.[24] The Mosaic law prescribed stoning in cases of open adultery. What will Jesus say about this? Will he violate the Mosaic law, or will he support the stoning? Here Jesus is put to the test, again in a corner from which it is apparently impossible to escape. Jesus, however, as we know, will come out of it brilliantly: "He that is without sin among you, let him first cast a stone at her" (John 8:7).

We have to read the last book of the New Testament to find the only occurrence of the term *peirasmós* in St. John's writings. The evangelist reports the prophecies that Jesus Christ himself revealed to him through his seven angels, and the messages to be sent to the seven churches respectively.[25] To the church of Philadelphia Jesus prophesies, "Because thou hast kept the word of my patience, I also will keep thee from the hour of trial [*peirasmós*], which shall come upon all the world, to try them that dwell upon the earth" (Rev 3:10).

---

24. All modern scholars agree that the pericope of the adulteress did not exist in the original text of John's Gospel and was only a later addition. None of the oldest papyri containing the Gospel of John record this passage. None of the church fathers who commented on John's Gospel mention it. It appears for the first time in the *Codex Bezae*, a fifth-century Greek and Latin text.

25. Ephesus, Smyrna, Pergamum, Thyatira, Sardis, Philadelphia, and Laodicea.

Since this passage appears in the book of Revelation, commentators generally believe it to be a reference to the second coming of Christ, the one that will take place at the End Times to perform the Last Judgment. Before the second coming of the Son of Man, the biblical tradition taught that there would be a period of great tribulation. The great tribulation of the End Times. The eschatological test. *Ho peirasmós* (ὁ πειρασμός). The *Peirasmós* with a capital P and preceded by the definite article. Not just any test, but the Test, the final Test.

We will have the opportunity to deepen the eschatological interpretation of the term *peirasmós* in a dedicated chapter. It will be sufficient here to underline how, even if at a higher eschatological level, *Peirasmós* with a capital P coincides with *Thlîpsis*, that is, with the Tribulation with a capital T. Wars, pestilence, famine, earthquakes, portentous signs, pains, tortures, persecutions, fratricidal fights, hatred, death. This is the *Thlîpsis*. This is the *summa* of the *Peirasmós*. Does not this language evoke the great plagues of Egypt? Do you remember that *măssâ* (*peirasmós* in Greek)—those calamities with which God had tried in every way to snatch the people of Israel from the clutches of Pharaoh? (Deut 4:34; 7:19; 29:3). The *Peirasmós* of the End Times takes up all these concepts.

In the message of the Angel of the Lord to the church of Smyrna, which appears in chapter 2 of Revelation, we find further confirmation of what we have just seen. The term *peirasmós* does not appear explicitly, but the verb *peirázō* does appear, associated twice with *thlîpsis*, that is, the persecution that hangs over that community: "I know thy works, and tribulation [*thlîpsis*], and poverty, (but thou art rich) and I know the blasphemy of them which say they are Jews, and are not, but are the synagogue of Satan. Fear none of those things which thou shalt suffer: behold, the devil shall cast some of you into prison, that ye may be tried [*peirázō*]; and ye shall have tribulation [*thlîpsis*] ten days: be thou faithful unto death, and I will give thee a crown of life" (Rev 2:9–10).

The persecution spoken of here is not the eschatological test of the End Times. It is more simply the persecution to which the church of Smyrna will be subjected by the Jews, defined as "a synagogue of Satan." The Jews (this is the prophecy), incited and led by Satan, will inflict all sorts of pain on this community. They will be put in prison for ten days and suffer. It will be a most severe trial. It will be a *peirasmós*, indeed. But if they can remain firm in the faith until martyrdom, they will obtain "the crown of life," that is, the kingdom of heaven. Once again, there is no trace of moral temptations, but rather of very painful psychophysical trials.

The last occurrence of the verb *peirázō* in the writings of St. John is found at the beginning of chapter 2 of Revelation, in the message of the Angel of the Lord to the church of Ephesus. It praises the fact that this community does not endure the wicked and has tested (*peirázō*) and exposed the false apostles (Rev 2:2). The verb *peirázō* has no evil connotation here, quite the contrary. It represents the test that unmasks those who falsely declare themselves to be apostles of Christ and disseminate false teachings.

In conclusion, in the circle of the four evangelists, the semantic field defined by the terms *peirasmós/peirázō* clearly overlaps with (and is identified with) the semantic field defined by the term *thlîpsis*, that is, tribulation, that is, psychophysical suffering. *Tentatio tribulationis*, as St. Augustine would define it. And this fits perfectly into the biblical tradition of the term *măssâ*, the Hebrew equivalent of the Greek *peirasmós*, used exclusively to indicate the calamities inflicted by God on Pharaoh and his people, or the misfortunes inflicted by God, through Satan (*per satanam*), on Job. The only case in which the terms *peirasmós/peirázō* indicate the tempting action of the devil is the very particular temptation of Christ in the desert. Temptation which, as we have seen, has little to do with human temptation to sin, and much to do with the test of the dual human and divine nature of the Son of Man.

# 18

# The Big Misunderstanding

Let us expand our analysis to the rest of the New Testament, and see how the remaining three Apostles (Peter, James, and Paul) use the terms *peirasmós/peirázō*.

## PETER

We will begin with Peter, the person closest to Christ during the years of his preaching and to whom Christ gives the honor and the task of taking the reins of his church after his death. Peter, despite being a simple unlettered fisherman, demonstrates, unlike any other disciple, that he is the one who understands with great clarity the divine nature of Jesus (Matt 16:16). The connection, the human relationship between Christ and Peter is such that his words offer an inevitably privileged point of view. We note that Peter, in the two epistles attributed to him, never uses the verb *peirázō*. On the contrary, he uses the term *peirasmós* three times.

Indeed, the concept of *peirasmós* is the first concept introduced by Peter in his first epistle to the faithful. After a brief introduction and praise of the Lord and his mercy, Peter explains, "Wherein ye greatly rejoice, though now for a season, if need be, ye are in heaviness through manifold trials [*peirasmós*]: That the trial of your faith, being much more precious than of gold that perisheth, though it be tried [*dokimázō*] with fire, might be found unto praise and honour and glory at the appearing of Jesus Christ" (1 Pet 1:6–7).

The *peirasmós* of which Peter speaks here is the test of faith, *to dokímion tês písteōs* (τὸ δοκίμιον τῆς πίστεως). It is the test of suffering,[1] which implies persecution, the *thlîpsis*, which tests the faith, purifies it, and strengthens it. Peter takes up the biblical

---

1. Peter uses the verb *lypéō* (λυπέω), which indicates the idea of affliction, pain, psychophysical suffering.

tradition of the metaphor of the precious metal, passed to the crucible so that it loses its impurities. It is not by chance that, in verse 7, Peter includes in the semantic field of *peirasmós* that of *dokimázō*, more used in the case of metals. If for precious metals (but in any case, less precious than human faith) one speaks of *dokimásia* (read: purification), for people one speaks instead of *peirasmós*, which is something even higher, more noble and, at the same time, more arduous and painful.

The pain and suffering which a believer must be able to endure, in communion with the sufferings endured by Christ, are a central theme of Peter's first epistle. Enduring unjust persecutions results in obtaining grace with God (1 Pet 2:20), "because Christ also suffered for us, leaving us an example, that ye should follow his steps" (1 Pet 2:21).

Similarly, Peter argues, if the will of God is that we should suffer, then it is better to suffer for doing good than for doing evil (1 Pet 3:17). If the will of God wills it,[2] says Peter. Blatant admission of how the suffering that afflicts us is always in accordance with the divine will. And above all, the extreme sacrifice of Christ must be for the Christian a model to keep always in mind: "For Christ also hath once suffered for sins, the just for the unjust, that he might bring us to God, being put to death in the flesh, but quickened by the Spirit" (1 Pet 3:18).

We find here the contrast between the suffering of the flesh, transient and mortal, the *sárx* (σάρξ), and the exaltation of the spirit, the *pneûma* (πνεῦμα), which enjoys eternal life. Let us pay attention though. The *sárx* here is not to indicate, as in other passages, the concupiscence of the most depraved human instincts. The *sárx*, as opposed to the *pneûma*, is simply the weakest part of the human being, because it is subject to physical pain, death, and material corruption. This physical disintegration is nothing compared to the spirit, to the soul, which, immortal, can live forever in divine glory. Not only that. The physical suffering of the flesh can be preparatory to its humiliation, and thus serve as a deterrent to its possible moral corruption: "Forasmuch then as Christ hath suffered for us in the flesh, arm yourselves likewise with the same mind: for he that hath suffered in the flesh hath ceased from sin; That he no longer should live the rest of his time in the flesh to the lusts of men, but to the will of God" (1 Pet 4:1–2).

The flesh, the *sárx*, becomes the physical vehicle through which the suffering inflicted on people by God with the *peirasmós* is made possible and manifested. If people were not made of mortal flesh subject to pain (both material and psychological), the *peirasmós* would lose much of its force. There is no *peirasmós* without physical pain of the flesh. There is no physical pain of the flesh without *peirasmós*.[3] Here is Peter's conclusion, in which the second occurrence of the term *peirasmós* appears:

---

2. "εἰ θέλοι τὸ θέλημα τοῦ θεοῦ [*ei théloi tò thélēma toû theoû*]."

3. By physical pain is meant here psychophysical pain, that is, anything that can bring material suffering and psychological anguish to a person.

> Beloved, think it not strange concerning the fiery trial which is to try [*peirasmós*] you, as though some strange thing happened unto you: But rejoice, inasmuch as ye are partakers of Christ's sufferings; that, when his glory shall be revealed, ye may be glad also with exceeding joy. If ye be reproached for the name of Christ, happy are ye; for the spirit of glory and of God resteth upon you: on their part he is evil spoken of, but on your part he is glorified. But let none of you suffer as a murderer, or as a thief, or as an evildoer, or as a busybody in other men's matters. Yet if any man suffer as a Christian, let him not be ashamed; but let him glorify God on this behalf. (1 Pet 4:12–16)

The fiery trial of which Peter speaks is indicated by the term *pýrōsis* (πύρωσις), which derives from the root of the verb *pyróō* (πυρόω) already encountered earlier. It is the verb that in the biblical tradition is used to indicate the action of the goldsmith who passes to the crucible the precious metals to purify them from their impurities. This metaphorical purifying fire takes place *pròs peirasmón* (πρὸς πειρασμόν), Peter says. That is, for a specific purpose—to test the believer. And it represents, we might well say, the fiery test of suffering. If the Christian can persevere in affliction and persecution, in *thlîpsis*, he will obtain the kingdom of heaven.

There is one final occurrence of the term *peirasmós* in Peter's writings, and it is found in the second chapter of his second epistle. The passage in which it appears is so important (and in our opinion crucial to understanding the proper meaning of the sixth petition of the Lord's Prayer) that it is good to report it in its entirety. The passage (and the reasoning that unravels in it) may be convoluted, and so we will try to elucidate it as much as possible. Let us read.

> But there were false prophets also among the people, even as there shall be false teachers among you, who privily shall bring in damnable heresies, even denying the Lord that bought them, and bring upon themselves swift destruction. And many shall follow their pernicious ways; by reason of whom the way of truth shall be evil spoken of. And through covetousness shall they with feigned words make merchandise of you: whose judgment now of a long time lingereth not, and their damnation slumbereth not. For if God spared not the angels that sinned, but cast them down to hell, and delivered them into chains of darkness, to be reserved unto judgment; And spared not the old world, but saved Noah the eighth person, a preacher of righteousness, bringing in the flood upon the world of the ungodly; And turning the cities of Sodom and Gomorrha into ashes condemned them with an overthrow, making them an ensample unto those that after should live ungodly; And delivered just Lot, vexed with the filthy conversation of the wicked: (For that righteous man dwelling among them, in seeing and hearing, vexed his righteous soul from day to day with their unlawful deeds;) The Lord knoweth how to deliver the godly out of *peirasmós*, and to reserve the unjust unto the day of judgment to be punished. (2 Pet 2:1–9)

The passage takes its cue from the false prophets who put "damnable heresies" into the world. These sinners harass and exploit righteous people for their own personal gain. Why does God allow all this? Why does he not come to the aid of the righteous? In other words, why does evil exist in the world? Why does suffering exist? And above all, where is God when the just suffer? This is a very modern question, one that the faithful probably often asked Peter, and to which Peter here seeks to give an adequate answer. Peter's words then are words of hope. Peter does not deny the fact that the righteous are very often subjected to all kinds of humiliation, but at the same time he reminds the faithful that God is not insensitive to the righteous' cry for help. In particular, the wicked will be subjected to a "swift destruction," which will not be delayed. This is the conviction that must give strength to the righteous: not only is God close to the innocent who suffer, but he will at the same time know how to properly punish those who sin. And the punishment of the wicked will not be long in coming.

Peter gives three examples: the angels who had turned against God punished and relegated to the underworld, the Universal Flood, and the destruction of Sodom and Gomorrah. These are the three most striking examples of divine punishment. Punishment that does not delay, that comes from heaven and sweeps away sinners, locking them up in the underworld waiting for the Last Judgement. On the other hand, Noah and Lot represent righteous people in a world of depraved evildoers. And for this very reason God spared them and protected them from his wrath. All these examples, Peter concludes, demonstrate how God knows how to deliver the righteous from *peirasmós*. But what does this mean? There are at least three interpretive levels. Let us look at them one by one.

The first one is the most trivial and, in our opinion, the most erroneous. When God sends the Flood on the world but spares Noah, when he sends fire and flames on Sodom but spares Lot, what he is doing is removing them from the influence of worldly temptations. *Peirasmós* would be understood as moral corruption in which both Noah and Lot could have fallen if God had not intervened. There are several arguments against this type of interpretation. First, it does not appear from the biblical passages in question that either Noah or Lot were under the influence of moral temptation, that is, that they were somehow struggling not to fall into temptation. Both Noah and Lot are presented as righteous men, as opposed to the rest of the population, who were sinful and depraved. There is no mention of any struggle or difficulty in resisting the temptations of the world around them. On the contrary, they were righteous people precisely because they had always rejected those depraved customs and lived according to divine dictates. If the point was to save Noah and Lot from the possibility that they might fall into temptation, there does not really seem to be any reason to do so. Neither Noah nor Lot needed to be saved from any temptation. They were people of integrity and, thanks to the grace they received from God, they were able to maintain the right path in a world of sinners. Second, even supposing that God had really wanted to save Lot from the moral temptations of the inhabitants of Sodom, fearing for his integrity, if that really was the divine intention, there was no need to wipe out the rest of the population. He could have simply sent one of his angels to command Lot to move away from there and find a more suitable place to live. Moreover, if Lot really needed to be saved from the temptations of the inhabitants of Sodom, he could have, of his own accord, moved away from that city and found a more suitable place to live. He certainly did not need the Lord's destructive intervention to cut his roots with that depraved world.

The second interpretative level is certainly more robust, but still unsatisfactory. Indeed, one might understand *peirasmós* as that state of continuous vexation to which Lot is subjected. We know that Lot is terrified of what his fellow villagers might do. He is aware of their depravity and stays away from them. We see this in the biblical passage that we discussed earlier, when the citizens of Sodom flock to the door of Lot's house, curious about the visitors (the angels of the Lord). They order him to let them out so that they can "know" them. Lot, sensing their perverse intentions, is reluctant to open the door. He does not want to let them in. Faced with their fury and fearing for his life and for the fate of his guests, he even offers them his own daughters to satisfy their passions. Such was the level of harassment and psychophysical stress to which he was subjected. Peter explains it well. Lot was oppressed by their dissolute conduct and his righteous soul was tormented. The term he uses to indicate the oppression Lot endured is the verb *kataponéō* (καταπονέω), composed of the preposition *katá* (κατά), which indicates downward movement, and the root noun *pónos* (πόνος), which indicates fatigue resulting from exhausting work, and thus by extension, suffering, affliction, and psychophysical stress. Peter is telling us that Lot was harassed, oppressed (literally compressed downward), exhausted by the impudence and intrusiveness of his fellow citizens. He did not fear for his moral integrity. He feared for his physical integrity! And because of this, his soul was in a state of continuous anguish, in endless torment. Peter uses the verb *basanízō* (βασανίζω), which indicates the action of torturing, of inflicting psychophysical torment. God, leading Lot out of the city of Sodom, about to be annihilated, would save him once and for all from this stress—from this *peirasmós*. It is an interpretation that seems to us to be very robust, one that is in line with the meaning of the term *peirasmós* encountered so far in Scripture, and that well explains the emphasis placed by Peter on the state of oppression to which Lot was subjected. An interpretation, therefore, that fits the example of Lot like a glove.

But what about the example of Noah? Can we interpret the episode of the Universal Flood in the same way? Can the *peirasmós* from which God saves Noah be assimilated to that from which he saves Lot? For if *peirasmós* is in this case to be understood as psychophysical anguish, from what anguish was Noah freed? Unfortunately, it is not known. It does not appear that Noah was either harassed or distressed. Yes, the whole world around him was permeated with injustice and violence (Gen 6:11). So, we can imagine that Noah in some way suffered and perhaps experienced the threats. But we must admit that, in the case of Noah, this interpretation seems weak, and much less convincing.

And here we come to the third and final interpretive level. *Peirasmós* not understood as temptation to sin. *Peirasmós* not so much (or rather: not only) understood as psychophysical suffering. Rather, *peirasmós* understood as the manifestation of divine wrath. It is certainly not a novelty or a surprise. The first appearance of the term *peirasmós* in the Bible occurs in Deut 4:34 and indicates precisely those calamities inflicted by God on the people of Egypt, as a punishment for Pharaoh's *hýbris*—a portentous demonstration of divine wrath. To arrive at this type of interpretation, it is necessary to pay attention to the verbs used by Peter, to the analogies and the contrasts. In the first example, that of the angels who fell into disgrace with God for having rebelled against him, Peter says of them that the Lord did not spare them. Peter uses the verb *pheídomai* (φείδομαι), which indicates the action of sparing someone a due punishment. The same verb is used in the example of Noah. God did not spare the ancient world. On the contrary, he protected Noah. Peter uses here the verb *phylássō* (φυλάσσω), which indicates the action of preserving someone from misfortune, suffering, violence, calamity, and so on. *Phylássō* is the equivalent of *pheídomai*. If on the one hand God is supremely just and does not spare (*pheídomai*) the punishment to the wicked, at the same time he knows how to protect (*phylássō*) the righteous from the devastating effects of the punishment itself. In fact, God did not spare Noah from temptation. He did not spare Noah even from supposed suffering inflicted on him by the wicked. He spared him from the *peirasmós* of the Universal Flood. In the same way, while God condemned Sodom and Gomorrah to destruction by reducing them to ashes, at the same time he saved Lot by rescuing him from a certain destiny of death. The term Peter uses in this case is the verb *rhýomai* (ῥύομαι), which indicates the action of saving someone by dragging him out of imminent danger.[4] God did not save Lot from temptation (he did not need it). Yes, he did save Lot from the sufferings inflicted on him by the wicked. But above all, he saved him from the *peirasmós* of the destructive fire that was about to fall on his city.

And in any case, without too much philosophizing, if one were to ask anyone the simple question, "What do Noah and Lot have in common?" with the following options:

1. both were saved from temptation,
2. both were saved from oppression,
3. both were saved from divine punishment,

there is no doubt that the last option would be the most popular. Noah and Lot are indeed famous for being spared from the *peirasmós* of divine wrath. In this simple

---

4. It is no accident that the verb *rhýomai* is the same one that appears in the last petition of the Lord's Prayer ("but deliver us from evil"). We will have the opportunity to explore this aspect in more detail later.

consideration lies the answer to our question. And in this regard, it is good to note the elegance with which Peter describes God's protective/salvific action. He does not say, "If all this is true, then it means that God will deliver the righteous from *peirasmós*." He says, "If all this is true, then it means that God *knows how* to deliver the righteous from *peirasmós*." He knows the way (2 Pet 2:9), and he is able to do it. But knowing how to do something does not necessarily mean that that thing will be done. The fact that a craftsman knows how to fix a clay vase, which came out of the lathe defective, does not mean that he will waste time fixing it. In fact, it will probably take him less time to destroy it and do it again. Likewise, saying that God knows how to save the righteous from *peirasmós* necessarily implies that there is a possibility that God, for several reasons, would *not* want to do so. This is a subtle, but clear concept.

We have seen numerous Old Testament examples where God inflicts *peirasmós* on both the wicked and the righteous. Indeed, if you recall, the entire Lot episode revolves around this dynamic. Does it make sense for a supremely just God to wipe out the righteous along with the wicked? (Gen 18:25). Peter is implicitly telling us that, for the righteous, escaping divine wrath is not a given. We have seen that Lot, for example, was saved through an extraordinary act of mercy by God (Gen 19:16) and through the intercession of Abraham's insistent prayer (Gen 19:29). It was not a foregone conclusion that Lot would be spared. But, in this case, God willed it. Corollary: in other cases, it may be that God does not will it, and the righteous is annihilated along with the wicked.[5]

One final consideration. Divine punishment is aroused by the blasphemous conduct of the ungodly and is aimed at annihilating sinners, who not only wallow in blasphemy but also corrupt those around them. Peter has very harsh words for them. He defines them as "natural brute beasts, made to be taken and destroyed" (2 Pet 2:12), "beguiling unstable souls" and "cursed children" (2 Pet 2:14). They are those who follow the most perverse instincts of the flesh (*sárx*) and seek to make the weakest souls fall into their perversions. They lead them into temptation, in short. And how does Peter describe the act of moral corruption? With the expression *eisphérō eis peirasmón*? No, he does not. He uses the simple verb *deleázō* (δελεάζω), which literally indicates the action of capturing a prey with a bait. We are back to the idea of temptation as a trap (*pagís*) to which the prey takes the bait. The verb *deleázō* derives from the same root as the noun *dólos* (δόλος), which indicates malice, deception, trickery, fraud. Temptation is a deception, and the one who tempts deceives us, lures us.

---

5. As already pointed out extensively, there is nothing "unjust" about this. Divine justice is not measured by the human yardstick. The righteous, though vexed and torn on earth by all manner of misfortune, will enjoy his true reward in the kingdom of heaven.

## JAMES

Let us now analyze the writings of another apostle, usually identified with James the Just, also known as "the brother of the Lord."[6] He was one of the most influential personalities of the mid-first century and head of the church in Jerusalem after the death of Christ. To him is attributed an epistle that is part of the canon of the New Testament. We have already mentioned his epistle at the beginning of our essay because it represents one of the fundamental passages in the correct interpretation of the meaning of the sixth petition of the Lord's Prayer. The *incipit* of the letter of James is one of the milestones—one of those passages that is always necessarily quoted when discussing temptation and *peirasmós*. And so, it is worth reading it all, slowly.

> James, a servant of God and of the Lord Jesus Christ, to the twelve tribes which are scattered abroad, greeting. My brethren, count it all joy when ye are subjected to any type of trial [*peirasmós*];[7] Knowing this, that the trying [*dokímion*] of your faith worketh patience. But let patience have her perfect work, that ye may be perfect and entire, wanting nothing. If any of you lack wisdom, let him ask of God, that giveth to all men liberally, and upbraideth not; and it shall be given him. But let him ask in faith, nothing wavering. For he that wavereth is like a wave of the sea driven with the wind and tossed. For let not that man think that he shall receive any thing of the Lord. A double minded man is unstable in all his ways. Let the brother of low degree rejoice in that he is exalted: But the rich, in that he is made low: because as the flower of the grass he shall pass away. For the sun is no sooner risen with a burning heat, but it withereth the grass, and the flower thereof falleth, and the grace of the fashion of it perisheth: so also shall the rich man fade away in his ways. Blessed is the man that endureth trial [*peirasmós*]: for when he is tried [*dókimos*], he shall receive the crown of life, which the Lord hath promised to them that love him. Let no man say when he is tempted [*peirázō*], I am tempted [*peirázō*] of God: for God cannot be tempted with evil, neither tempteth [*peirázō*] he any man: But every man is tempted [*peirázō*], when he is drawn away of his own lust, and enticed [*deleázō*]. Then when lust hath conceived, it bringeth forth sin: and sin, when it is finished, bringeth forth death. (Jas 1:1–15)

Let us take it slow. In just a few verses the term *peirasmós* appears two times and the verb *peirázō* four times. An undoubtedly significant concentration, indicating that James was anxious to explain these terms exactly. In verses 2 and 3 we find the same expressions used by Peter in the *incipit* of his first epistle:

1. *peirasmoîs poikílois* (πειρασμοῖς ποικίλοις) = "manifold trials" (Jas 1:2; 1 Pet 1:6);

---

6. In the traditional Catholic interpretation, James the Just is identified with the apostle James, son of Alphaeus, also known as "the Lesser."
7. The KJV has "fall into divers temptations."

2. *tò dokímion hymôn tês písteōs* (τὸ δοκίμιον ὑμῶν τῆς πίστεως) = "the proof of your faith" (Jas 1:3; 1 Pet 1:7).

This is obviously no accident. Both Peter and James are addressing the faithful recognizing all the difficulties that the early Christian communities were facing at that time.[8] Just as Peter encouraged the faithful to rejoice in the many trials, in the same way James explains how being subjected to all sorts of trials should be cause for immense joy. Comparing the opening of Peter's first epistle with the opening of James's epistle allows us to fully understand what James is talking about. He is alluding to the whole series of persecutions (*thlîpsis*) that the first Christians had to endure at the hands of the ungodly. And the test of suffering automatically becomes the test of faith. Those who know how to remain steadfast in their faith even amid the harshest adversity will receive "the crown of life" (Jas 1:12; 1 Pet 5:4).

The two occurrences of the term *peirasmós* in James in verse 2 and verse 12 refer once again to the same concept: the test of faith through the test of suffering. No reference, either explicitly or implicitly, to the temptations of the flesh. This is demonstrated by the verb used by James, *hypoménō* (ὑπομένω), composed of the preposition *hypó* (ὑπό), which indicates a subordinate position, and the verb *ménō* (μένω), which indicates the action of continuing, of persevering. The expression *hypoménō peirasmón* indicates the action of remaining steadfast even when crushed under the weight of *peirasmós*. It indicates the strength and psychophysical endurance of any kind of adversity that may fall on our heads. It is a verb that is used for the endurance of psychophysical stress, not for resistance to a perverse instinct. Temptations of the flesh do not crush us. They do not weigh on our shoulders and our heads. Simply because they go straight to the heart, the seat of our instincts. They do not strike us from above, but from within. They seduce us, they lure us, but they do not make us suffer. On the contrary, it is usually the opposite. Temptations appeal to the pleasure—not to the suffering—of the flesh. And in fact, every occurrence of the verb *hypoménō* within the New Testament has to do with the endurance of pain, never with the resistance to worldly temptations.

To clear the field of any doubt, James, *ex abrupto*, in verse 13 launches his famous warning: "Let no man say when he is tempted, I am tempted of God; for God cannot be tempted with evil, neither tempteth he any man." In a single verse, the verb *peirázō* is presented three times, not counting the adjective *apeírastos* (ἀπείραστος), which comes from the root of the same verb. An unprecedented concentration, and one that cannot be accidental. James's urgency to clarify a lexical confusion that must have spread among the very first Christian communities is felt most strongly. Is *peirázō* a verb that can be attached to God? James's answer is clear. It cannot, if *peirázō* is understood as testing with malice, tempting with evil. It can, if *peirázō* is understood as testing without

---

8. The recognition of such difficulties by both Peter and James at the very beginning of their epistles can be read as a rhetorical device, a *captatio benevolentiae*, to show empathy for those Christian communities.

malice.[9] If in the very first Christian communities, following the Gospel of Matthew, the devil was identified as the Tempter (or *ho Peirázōn*), it is understandable how the verb *peirázō* had assumed, in the common feeling, also a possible negative connotation. It is understandable how the sixth petition of the Lord's Prayer, which asks God literally not to take us into *peirasmós*, could create confusion among the faithful. If the verb *peirázō* was commonly used to indicate Satan's malignant tempting action, how is it possible to think that God would take us into something (*peirasmós*) that shares with *peirázō* the same etymological root? It is possible that these doubts circulated among the early believers, and that James with this letter seeks to sweep them away.

If one reads the letter of James well, one can come to only one conclusion. The *peirasmós* of the sixth petition of the Lord's Prayer cannot have anything to do with the temptations of the flesh. Let us see why.

James is telling us that *peirázō*, when understood in a malicious sense, cannot be attached to God in any way: "Let no man say" (Jas 1:13). Why? Because God has nothing to do with mischievous things. God does not test with (moral) evil, nor can he be tested with (moral) evil. God does not take anyone into (moral) evil, nor can he be brought into it. In short, in any circumstance in which *peirázō*/*peirasmós* is understood in a malicious sense, there God cannot be. Rather, the blame for the fact that we are led into mischievous temptations is ours alone, James explains. It is our perverse, disordered instincts, that is, the concupiscence of the flesh, what James calls *epithymía* (ἐπιθυμία), which leads us into temptation in two ways: by enticing us and by seducing us. The two terms James uses are illuminating: one is *deleázō* (δελεάζω), which we have just encountered in Peter's writings, and the other is *exélkō* (εξέλκω). Both verbs literally indicate the way the hunter catches a prey with a trap, just as the fisherman catches a fish with a disguised bait. This is the moral temptation. And God has nothing to do with this kind of temptation.

Now, with all that cleared up, there are only two possible ways to proceed:

1. We can assume that the *peirasmós* of the sixth petition of the Lord's Prayer is the *epithymía*, that is, the concupiscence of the flesh, that is, that temptation that comes from the perverse instincts of our heart and with which James teaches us that God has nothing to do, and then proceed backward forcing the text of the Gospels with circumlocutions that make God appear as extraneous to it ("do not let us fall into temptation," "do not allow us to be led into temptation," "do not abandon us to temptation").

2. Or we can follow James's teachings simply and straightforwardly and conclude that, if the Lord's Prayer teaches us that there can be the possibility of God leading us into *peirasmós*, then, by definition, that *peirasmós* cannot take on any malicious meaning, and therefore cannot mean moral temptation.

---

9. It is impossible to think that James is not aware of Scripture and ignores, for example, the fact that in the Old Testament it is explicitly stated that God tested (*peirázō*) Abraham (Gen 22:1).

Let the reader judge which of the two ways is logically more rigorous and intellectually honest.

Now that we have exhausted the analysis of the texts related to the circle of evangelists (Mark, Matthew, Luke, John) and the apostles closest to Jesus (Peter and James), it is particularly useful to visually summarize the distribution of the term *peirasmós* by semantic field in a table.

| Author | Moral Temptation | Temptations of Christ | Psychophysical Suffering | Lord's Prayer or Garden of Olives |
|---|---|---|---|---|
| Mark | 0 | 0 | 0 | 1 |
| Matthew | 0 | 0 | 0 | 2 |
| Luke | 0 | 1 | 3 | 3 |
| John | 0 | 0 | 1 | 0 |
| Peter | 0 | 0 | 3 | 0 |
| James | 0 | 0 | 2 | 0 |
| Total | 0 | 1 | 9 | 6 |

Out of the sixteen total occurrences, *none* has any connection with moral temptation, one refers to the temptation of the Son of God by Satan, nine fall into the semantic realm of psychophysical suffering (tribulation, persecution, divine punishment, and so forth), and six (found in the Lord's Prayer or in the episode of the garden on the Mount of Olives) remain, for now, outstanding, because they represent the very expression we are trying to make sense of. This shows that, in the minds of the evangelists and apostles close to Jesus, it is much more likely, at least from a purely statistical point of view, that the term *peirasmós* evoked the concept of the trial of psychophysical suffering.

For the sake of completeness, we also present a summary table of the distribution of the verb *peirázō* by semantic field.[10]

| Author | Moral Temptation | Temptation of Christ | Psycho-physical Suffering | Pharisees' Tests | Man Testing God | Generic Test |
|---|---|---|---|---|---|---|
| Mark | 0 | 1 | 0 | 3 | 0 | 0 |
| Matthew | 0 | 2 | 0 | 4 | 0 | 0 |
| Luke | 0 | 1 | 0 | 1 | 2 | 3 |
| John | 0 | 0 | 2 | 2 | 0 | 1 |

---

10. Although it is necessary, for obvious reasons, to consider the analysis of the occurrences and the respective meanings of the verb *peirázō*, such an analysis cannot be put on the same level or have the same value as the analysis of the noun *peirasmós*. This is one of the main procedural errors in the interpretation of the sixth petition of the Lord's Prayer: throwing *peirasmós* and *peirázō* into the same cauldron and treating them as if they were interchangeable terms. They are not. St. Augustine was the first to understand lucidly that tempting is not the same thing as leading into temptation. And in the sixth petition of the Lord's Prayer, the noun appears, not the verb. Although they share the same etymological root, it is not surprising to think that, in everyday speech, the noun was used predominantly only for a specific semantic field, while the verb with a wider semantic spectrum.

| Peter | 0 | 0 | 0 | 0 | 0 | 0 |
| James | 4 | 0 | 0 | 0 | 0 | 0 |
| Total | 4 | 4 | 2 | 10 | 2 | 4 |

We see immediately that the distribution of the verb *peirázō* is much more varied than that of the noun *peirasmós*. The verb is primarily used to describe the questions with which the Pharisees were trying to catch Jesus off guard. In several instances it is used either to indicate Christ's temptations in the wilderness, or to indicate attempts and generic trials. A couple of times to indicate either the trials to which people try to subject God or the sufferings with which people are tried. The only four occurrences where it is used explicitly to indicate moral corruption appear in a couple of verses in James, as we have just seen (Jas 1:13–14), as a demonstration that it is wrong to associate *peirázō* (but only in the evil sense of the term) with God.

## PAUL

It is time to turn our attention to the one who is commonly referred to by the church fathers as "the Apostle," without having been technically a disciple of Jesus. We are talking about Saul of Tarsus, called Paul, whose letters and preaching occupy a large part of the New Testament and lay the foundations of all Catholic doctrine. A Hellenized Jew of Roman citizenship, with a great proficiency in Greek and knowledge of Hebrew, St. Paul initially dedicated himself to the fierce persecution of the first Christians, only to convert in the dramatic episode of his journey to Damascus. From that moment on, he became the most influential ambassador of the gospel among the Gentiles, that is, the pagans—Greeks and Romans. His many travels are documented by Luke in the Acts of the Apostles. He died a martyr in Rome in 67 AD, beheaded during the persecution of Christians by the emperor Nero.

Paul uses the terms *peirasmós* and *peirázō* with great familiarity, and we will see that it is to him that we owe, for the first time in the Greek language, the extension of the semantic field defined by the noun *peirasmós* to that of moral temptation. He is the one who, perhaps more than anyone else, contributed—unintentionally of course—to the lexical confusion between "trial" and "temptation" that persists today. But let us go slowly.

The first occurrences of the terms *peirasmós* and *peirázō* in St. Paul's writings are found in the first letter to the Corinthians. The passage is incredibly famous. We have already encountered and analyzed it previously. It is quoted by virtually every theologian who has ventured to interpret the Lord's Prayer. Let us read it once again: "There hath no temptation [*peirasmós*] taken you but such as is common to man: but God is faithful, who will not suffer you to be tempted [*peirázō*] above that ye are able; but will with the temptation [*peirasmós*] also make a way to escape, that ye may be able to bear it. Wherefore, my dearly beloved, flee from idolatry" (1 Cor 10:13–14).

## Eis Peirasmón

First of all, we must frame the context correctly. At the end of the previous chapter, Paul confesses to conducting works of bodily mortification: "But I keep under my body, and bring it into subjection: lest that by any means, when I have preached to others, I myself should be a castaway" (1 Cor 9:27). He is clearly speaking of mortification of the flesh, of the *sárx* understood as the origin of *epithymía*, that is, of the disordered and perverse instincts that drag us to mortal sin (Jas 1:14–15). This statement introduces the main theme set out in the next chapter. It is not enough to be Christians and believers to be immune to temptation. On the contrary, as soon as one relaxes or believes oneself to be immune (thus sinning in *hýbris*), that is the moment in which one falls most precipitously (1 Cor 10:12). In this regard, Paul cites the best-known biblical example. The Israelites on their way to the Promised Land were all guided by the Lord. His divine words and dictates had been revealed to them all by Moses. They all ate and drank from the same spiritual food, but many of them gave themselves over to temptation and sinned: "But with many of them God was not well pleased: for they were overthrown in the wilderness" (1 Cor 10:5).

What kinds of temptations and sins is St. Paul referring to? First, idolatry. In chapter 32 of the book of Exodus that Paul cites, Moses catches the Israelites feasting and dancing around a golden calf. Why is idolatry at the top of St. Paul's list of concerns? It's quickly stated. St. Paul is preaching to Greek communities living within a deeply pagan context. Greece is a land physically sprinkled capillary with temples dedicated to the Olympian gods, part of a developed mythology with centuries-old roots. The confusion in recognizing that those gods adored until yesterday, represented everywhere by masterfully executed sculptures and sung by the *aoidoi*, are only plastic idols, useless and harmful, to be thrown away and replaced with the true God of whom St. Paul speaks, is enormous. The temptation to remain somehow anchored in mythological tradition is great. Giving up all those centuries-old rituals of sacrifice is undoubtedly arduous. St. Paul knows this well, and that is why the main objective of his evangelization process is to convince those non-Jewish ("uncircumcised") communities to completely abandon the dross of those pagan customs and traditions.

Therefore, idolatry is at the top of the list of sins to be avoided at all costs. Renouncing idolatry is the *condicio sine qua non* the Christian faith cannot flourish and develop. The main reason is that, if one remains anchored to gods known to be corrupted by every kind of human vice[11]—if they are the term of comparison—everything, on a human level, becomes licit (1 Cor 10:23). Idolatry inevitably falls into adultery and immorality. The two go hand in hand.

Paul refers to the episode narrated in chapter 25 of the book of Numbers, in which it is said that some of the Israelites indulged in immoral relations with the daughters of Moab, which at the same time led them to offer sacrifices to their gods

---

11. Let us just think of Zeus and all the incestuous relationships attributed to him in Greek mythology.

and to join the cult of Baalpeor (Num 25:1–3). This is a striking example of how idolatry and adultery are understood as two sides of the same coin.

With idolatry and adultery, the third great sin to be avoided according to St. Paul is rebellion against God, which manifests itself when one doubts him and puts him to the test. St. Paul makes explicit reference to two episodes narrated again in the book of Numbers, in chapter 21 and 17 respectively, when the Israelites tested the Lord's patience with their complaints. God punished them with various calamities: poisonous serpents (Num 21:6) and a scourge brought by the Destroying Angel (Num 17:14).

Hence Paul's conclusion: all these episodes of immorality with consequent punitive atonement are nothing more than examples to keep in mind so as not to fall into the same errors. It is precisely at this point that we encounter the passage where St. Paul explains God's faithfulness, which is manifested in the fact that he does not allow us to be tempted beyond what we can bear (1 Cor 10:13). Let us analyze one sentence at a time.

First of all, St. Paul acknowledges that the community of Corinth had so far been able to resist the kinds of temptations described before—idolatry, fornication, and rebellion against God. He does so by implicitly theorizing, for the first time ever, that there must be at least two kinds of *peirasmós*: one that Paul calls *anthrópinos* (ἀνθρώπινος), that is, typical of humans, and one that is not. What does this mean? The commonly accepted interpretation of this expression concerns the fact that there may be temptations that are induced by our own human nature (fragile and fallible) and others that are induced by something more powerful and perverse, by Satan's army of evil, that is, by demonic spirits. These types of temptations are of a higher degree than those typically human and aim directly at people's moral destruction and spiritual death.

St. Augustine, taking up St. Paul's reasoning, will give an enlightening example to understand the difference between one type and another of temptation: "And it is very important to understand what kind of temptation one can fall into. For Judas, who sold the Lord, did not fall into the same temptation into which Peter fell, who was terrified and denied the Lord. In fact, there are also human temptations, I believe, when one, in good faith, falls into an error of judgment because of human frailty, or becomes angry with a brother to correct him, going a little beyond what Christian tranquility requires. In this regard, the Apostle says: No temptation, except a human one, has seized you."[12]

The principal characteristic of the *peirasmòs anthrópinos* is identified by St. Augustine in the "good faith" ("*bono animo*"). If one falls into error through human

---

12. "*Et interest plurimum, in qualem quisque tentationem incidat. Non enim in talem incidit Iudas, qui vendidit Dominum, in qualem incidit Petrus, cum territus Dominum negavit. Sunt etiam humanae tentationes, credo, cum bono quisque animo, secundum humanam tamen fragilitatem in aliquo consilio labitur, aut irritatur in fratrem studio corrigendi, paulo tamen amplius quam christiana tranquillitas postulat. De quibus Apostolus dicit: Tentatio vos non apprehendat nisi humana*" (Augustine, *De sermone Domini in monte*, 2.9.34).

frailty, but without malice, without malevolent intent, then he will have fallen into a "human" temptation. This is the case of Peter who, with all possible good faith, had sworn to Jesus that he was ready to suffer all kinds of persecution in his name (Mark 14:29; Luke 22:33; John 13:37), only to deny him three times at the thought of suffering the same fate. What *peirasmòs anthrópinos* had seized Peter? The fear of being arrested and being put to death. The fear of dying—a human instinct for self-preservation. There was no malice in Peter. On the contrary, Judas, with his obscure plot to sell the Son of Man for thirty *denarii*, had exposed himself to demonic temptation and had himself become an instrument of Satan.[13]

Also interesting is the term chosen by Paul to indicate that the Corinthians had not fallen until then into any of these demonic temptations. He uses the verb *lambánō* (λαμβάνω), which is not a simple "to take," but rather "to take with force," therefore "to seize," "to capture." It conveys the idea of an external force, the *peirasmós*, grabbing us and pulling us into sin. Like a snare that springs out suddenly to catch the prey. It is a use of the term *peirasmós* never seen before. Non-existent before Paul.[14]

It is at this point that St. Paul explains why the Corinthians were able to resist such demonic temptations. It depends on the fact that God is *pistós* (πιστός), that is, faithful, honest with people. What does it mean? Pay attention to the exact grammatical construction used by Paul. It means that "God will not allow you to be tempted above what you can bear."

First consideration: the permissive construct. Paul uses an explicit permissive construct through the verb *eáō* (ἐάω). He does not say, "God will not tempt you," assuming the reader will grasp the permissive meaning. How could he? James has already clearly explained that God does not tempt anyone with malice. Demonstration of how the Greek language has all the tools necessary to make the permissive sense clear, without hiding it in ambiguous direct causative constructs. But, because it is so convenient, it is taken for granted that here Paul is explicitly explaining what would be implicitly contained in the sixth petition of the Lord's Prayer. In our opinion, however, there is nothing to suggest that this is St. Paul's intention here.

What St. Paul is explaining to an audience of recently converted pagans is not how to pray, but how the demonic temptation works, intimately linked to the worship of pagan idolatry. Paul is explaining to them that not only are pagan gods not the true God, but they are also intimately tied to demonic spirits, that is, Satan's army. How then does one defend oneself against these spirits? Why does the true God allow their very existence? These are the doubts of the community of Corinth, which St. Paul tries to dispel with this letter.

---

13. Not coincidentally, John reports that Judas completed the betrayal of Christ only after Satan entered him (John 13:27).

14. The *peirasmós* of the Old Testament, of the evangelists, and of the other apostles, as seen, is primarily an external force that weighs on our heads and inflicts a psychophysical stress on us: a suffering, a persecution, a disaster, a calamity, and so on.

Second consideration: the passive construct. The one who carries out the tempting action cannot be God, who simply allows it. It is understood that demonic (not "human") temptation is, by definition, carried out by demonic spirits.

Third consideration: the upper limit of temptation. God is not the cause of an evil temptation, but he allows it and even draws its limits. Why? Because God is *pistós*. He does not make pitfalls for us. He does not enjoy seeing us commit sins. If he were to allow satanic spirits to "tempt us beyond what we can bear," he would be implicitly condemning us to sin, without us being able to do anything about it (even if we tried our best, we would not be able to resist). Our sin at that point would immediately lose its meaning, with God assuming, *de facto*, the complete responsibility for it.

St. Paul is explaining what is obvious. To think that God could allow Satan and his followers to drag us into mortal sin without us having any kind of possibility to oppose them would immediately make the whole Christian theology collapse. But what is obvious to us was not obvious to the "non-circumcised." The gods of Olympus were anything but "faithful." They were cruel, spoiled, adulterous, deceitful, envious, malicious, wrathful, vindictive. Paul's proclamation that the God of Christians is *pistós* must have sounded revolutionary to their ears! But on closer inspection, Paul's is a tautology to all intents and purposes, and like all tautologies it cannot add any useful information to the discussion. It can only reiterate what is already known. Thinking of obtaining valuable information about the meaning of the sixth petition of the Lord's Prayer from a tautology is pure illusion. And in fact, all attempts to apply Paul's "interpretation" to the sixth petition of the Lord's Prayer have had grotesque results.

We have already seen this, but it is worth repeating. Thinking that Jesus, when he taught his disciples to implore the Father not to bring us into *peirasmós*, meant to teach us to say, "Do not allow us to be tempted beyond what we can bear," does not make any sense. It would be equivalent to imploring God to remain faithful to us, as if there were any possibility that God could deceive us (as if he were in league with Satan to bring us down!), when the opposite is obviously true. It is we who must remain faithful to him. Jesus could never have thought of teaching something like this—a bold, if not blasphemous, prayer. The fact that God is faithful is not a possibility. It is a fact. It is a distinctive feature of God. And it is unimaginable for the Son of God to teach us to question this truth.

Let us be clear. St. Paul is not saying anything bad. On the contrary, his argument is theologically perfect. It is those who try to use his words to explain the sixth petition of the Lord's Prayer who fall into a gross interpretive error. St. Paul is simply explaining to us that, just as God leaves us free and allows us, through our free will, to choose between good and evil, and thus also to sin (if that is our will), so too he leaves the same faculty to Satan and his army of evil spirits (to seek to corrupt us, if that is their will). The permissive construct chosen by St. Paul fits like a glove in this case. God does not nurture moral evil but allows it through the free will granted to living beings, whether human or angelic. At the same time, however, he remains faithful to us, and gives us all the necessary tools, if we wish, to resist temptations. He always leaves a way out open to us, and he is there waiting for us. It is up to us to escape the demonic temptations, taking advantage of that escape route that the Lord grants us. The concepts that St. Paul expresses in this passage represent milestones in Christian doctrine, but they have little to do with the sixth petition of the Lord's Prayer.

St. Paul concludes his reasoning as follows: "Wherefore, my dearly beloved, flee from idolatry" (1 Cor 10:14). What connection is there between idolatry and satanic temptations? He explains it clearly in the second part of the same chapter. Being a Christian and at the same time sacrificing meat to the gods is a horror in the eyes of God. Just as eating the Eucharist means entering into communion with God, eating meat sacrificed to the gods means entering into communion with evil spirits (1 Cor 10:20–21). Again, the whole argument always ends there. St. Paul is not explaining the Lord's Prayer. He is simply trying to convince the Corinthian community to reject any remnant of pagan customs and traditions.

The third occurrence of the term *peirasmós* in St. Paul's writings appears in the epistle to the Galatians. The Apostle describes a personal episode, of which there are no further details: "Ye know how through infirmity of the flesh I preached the gospel unto you at the first. And the test [*peirasmós*] of you in my flesh[15] ye despised not, nor rejected; but received me as an angel of God, even as Christ Jesus" (Gal 4:13–14).

It seems to be understood that Paul had been suffering from a physical illness for some time and that this fact somehow prompted him to preach the gospel for the first time to this community. The fact that Paul was ill could have been a reason for the Galatians to reject or despise him, but they did not. On the contrary, they had welcomed him warmly. Paul's physical suffering became in effect a test, a *peirasmós*, for the Galatians, and they had passed it brilliantly.

The fourth occurrence of the term *peirasmós* is found in the first epistle to Timothy, which we considered earlier. Those who live to enrich themselves fall into the trap (*pagís*) of temptation (*peirasmós*) (1 Tim 6:9). Without further ado, let us recall that *peirasmós* is here associated with the concept of a trap, and thus to fall into *peirasmós* is to fall into a trap, that is, to commit sin. This is the passage that probably establishes the idiomatic expression that still survives in our day—"to fall into temptation," that is, to sin after having been exposed to a temptation. An idiomatic expression of which, it is worth repeating, there is no trace in the biblical texts, and of which it is very unlikely that Jesus had any notion when he declaimed the Lord's Prayer.

The last occurrence of the term *peirasmós* is found in the epistle to the Hebrews, in which St. Paul quotes the famous verse of Psalm 95(94), which recalls how the Israelites tested the Lord in the desert of Massah (*Peirasmós*).

In conclusion, what is important to point out is that in Paul's writings the term *peirasmós* is used for the first time in the Bible explicitly to denote temptation as we commonly understand it today, that is, the snare of moral corruption. We

---

15. The KJV has "my temptation which was in my flesh."

can—without any great doubt—affirm that it is from here onward (and only from here onwards—from St. Paul's epistles around the middle of the first century) that the term *peirasmós* within Christian doctrine expands its semantic field to include precisely moral temptation, satanic temptation. Indeed, the concepts of moral temptation, mortal sin, and satanic forces are so prominent in Paul's writings that in all subsequent doctrine, which has its roots in Paul, the term *peirasmós* will take on the primary meaning of "moral temptation" and, only marginally, that of "trial." We thus observe a clear, and at the same time rapid, evolution of the term *peirasmós* exactly in the transition from the Old to the New Testament. What was a semantic field still *in nuce* until the first half of the first century blows up, starting from the second half of the first century, and becomes essentially the main—if not the only—semantic field associated with the term *peirasmós*. Such semantic field is adopted *in toto* by the Latin term *tentatio*.

And for the sake of completeness, let us briefly present the ways in which St. Paul instead uses the verb *peirázō* in his writings. This term appears as many as fourteen times, five of which are explicitly associated with the enticement to sin (1 Cor 7:5; 10:13; Gal 6:1; 1 Thess 3:5). Three times it is used to recall how the Israelites had tested God (1 Cor 10:9 [*ekpeirázō*]; Heb 3:9). Three times to indicate the test of suffering (Heb 2:18; 11:37). Once to recall the test God imposed on Abraham (Heb 11:17), once to recall the temptations of Christ (Heb 4:15), and once to exhort the faithful to test themselves in order to know themselves better (2 Cor 13:5). It is interesting to note the difference in Paul's communicative register depending on the audience. All occurrences of the verb *peirázō*, understood as enticement to sin, are found in the epistles addressed to the Gentiles (Corinthians, Galatians, Thessalonians). On the other hand, all occurrences of the verb *peirázō*, understood in the "pre-Pauline" manner, are found in the epistle addressed to the Jews, that is, to a Judeo-Christian community. This cannot be a coincidence.[16] It is instead, in our opinion, a very strong indication of how the evolution of the semantic field defined by the couple *peirázō/peirasmós* to encompass (and then to concur with) the idea of moral temptation is a phenomenon purely linked to the spread of Christianity in the pagan world. Within the Jewish communities that had just converted to Christianity, the couple *peirázō/peirasmós* substantially maintained its Old Testament meaning. And Jesus, when he declaimed the Lord's Prayer, was to all intents and purposes part of the Jewish tradition, with roots firmly planted in the Old Testament.

One can understand at this point what could be defined as "the big misunderstanding," that is, the attempt to interpret a term (*peirasmós*), which is the Greek equivalent of the Hebrew terms *mǎssâ* and *nissāyôn*—which belong mainly to the Old Testament tradition and which have no relation to the temptation to sin—with

---

16. The difference in register is so striking that the canonicity of the epistle to the Hebrews was debated for centuries before it officially became part of the New Testament, to such an extent that the attribution to St. Paul is still considered uncertain by some scholars.

hindsight, that is, in the light of the meanings that have been stratified on that term in the course of time. It would be a bit like trying to understand how the ancient Romans built roads, by analyzing the tar used today. Nothing plausible can be deduced from this. Instead, it is necessary to remove the layers of tar, dig, and discover the original stones that the Romans had cut and laid. Likewise, one cannot try to interpret the sixth petition of the Lord's Prayer from the meaning that *peirasmós* has taken on over time. Instead, it is necessary to dig and remove those "semantic layers" that were not contemporary to Jesus, to be able to get to the deep meaning of that prayer.

Let us turn our attention once again to the Old Testament, Jesus' main source of inspiration. And, if it is true that God may take us into *peirasmós*, let us then try to understand what this *peirasmós* might be.

# 19

## Lead Us Not into *Peirasmós*

If God does not lead into moral temptation, where may he lead us? Well, the Old Testament provides a vast array of examples that clearly indicate how, if God never brings us into moral evil, he can instead bring us into psychophysical evil. Let us look at some of them.

Chapter 26 of the book of Leviticus reads, "And ye shall perish among the heathen, and the land of your enemies shall eat you up. And they that are left of you shall pine away in their iniquity in your enemies' lands; and also in the iniquities of their fathers shall they pine away with them. If they shall confess their iniquity, and the iniquity of their fathers, with their trespass which they trespassed against me, and that also they have walked contrary unto me; And that I also have walked contrary unto them, and have brought them into the land of their enemies; if then their uncircumcised hearts be humbled, and they then accept of the punishment of their iniquity" (Lev 26:38–41).

The meaning is clear and terrible. God punished the sinful people by taking them "into the land of their enemies" so that they would be humiliated, killed, destroyed as atonement for their sins. It is interesting to see how the Vulgate renders the same passage: "*Ambulabo igitur et ego contra eos, et inducam illos in terram hostilem.*"[1]

The verb *induco* that St. Jerome uses is the same as in the sixth petition of the Lord's Prayer. The grammatical construction is remarkably similar ("*ne nos inducas in tentationem*"). God "induces" his people into a hostile land. That is, he brings them to the place of suffering—the place of punishment.

In chapter 14 of the book of Numbers, the Israelites, having just come out of the land of Egypt and terrified of perishing at the hands of some hostile people, rebel against their leaders: "And all the children of Israel murmured against Moses and against

---

1. "I will also therefore move against them and bring them into hostile territory."

Aaron: and the whole congregation said unto them, Would God that we had died in the land of Egypt! or would God we had died in this wilderness! And wherefore hath the Lord brought us unto this land, to fall by the sword, that our wives and our children should be a prey? were it not better for us to return into Egypt?" (Num 14:2–3).

The Israelites tremble. They cannot conceive how God could lead them to die after having saved them from Pharaoh. The Latin version is again enlightening, "*et non inducat nos Dominus in terram istam*,"[2] which seems almost a parallel to the sixth petition ("*et ne nos inducas in tentationem*"). Here too, God "induces" his people into a hostile land. He brings them to the place of suffering—to the potential place of death.[3]

Let us continue with a passage from the book of Zechariah, which we have encountered before: "And it shall come to pass, that in all the land, saith the Lord, two parts therein shall be cut off and die; but the third shall be left therein. And I will bring the third part through the fire, and will refine them as silver is refined, and will try them as gold is tried" (Zech 13:8–9).

Here the movement is *through* a place more than a movement *to* a place. The fire, the furnace, the crucible through which God will bring part of his people (the chosen ones, the ones not exterminated because of their sins) is not the end, but the means to arrive at the goal, purified of all waste and impurities.

It is impossible not to read in these words a vivid metaphor of the dynamics of hell and purgatory. Two great types of *peirasmós*. On the one hand, the *peirasmós* that annihilates and condemns to death, that is, to eternal fire, most of humanity. On the other, the *peirasmós* that burns, that causes fierce burns, that punishes but does not kill, that purifies, that purges the elected humanity, to make it worthy to enter the kingdom of heaven: "They shall call on my name, and I will hear them: I will say, It is my people: and they shall say, The Lord is my God" (Zech 13:9).

It is the same concept repeated in Psalm 66(65), which we have already had the opportunity to analyze: "For thou, O God, hast proved [*dokimázō*] us: thou hast tried [*pyróō*] us, as silver is tried [*pyróō*]. Thou broughtest us into the net [*pagís*]; thou laidst affliction upon our loins. Thou hast caused men to ride over our heads; we went through fire and through water: but thou broughtest us out into a wealthy place" (Ps 66(65):10–12).

So many concepts condensed in a couple of verses. God tests, in the sense that he purifies through pain, suffering, psychophysical stress. God leads us into hostile territory, where we are subject to ambushes and traps (that is, *pagís/peirasmós*). But they are traps that have nothing to do with moral temptation. They are traps that

---

2. "May the Lord not bring us into this land!"

3. This concept is echoed a little later in chapter 20 of Numbers. The people of Israel accuse Moses and Aaron, without explicitly mentioning God, but the meaning is identical: "And why have ye brought up the congregation of the Lord into this wilderness, that we and our cattle should die there? And wherefore have ye made us to come up out of Egypt, to bring us in unto this evil place? It is no place of seed, or of figs, or of vines, or of pomegranates; neither is there any water to drink" (Num 20:4–5).

humiliate the flesh and the spirit, to eliminate from us any residue of *hýbris*. One sees, clearly, the dynamic of a God who "brings into" and "brings out of" the *peirasmós*. The two Hebrew verbs used are the causative (*hiphil*) form of *bô'* (בּוֹא), which indicates the idea of "leading into," and its opposite, the causative (*hiphil*) form of *yātsā'* (יָצָא), which indicates the idea of "bringing out," of "redeeming." God first brings us into the *peirasmós* to suffer and purify ourselves, then, once we are purified, he releases us from the *peirasmós* itself, and brings us out of it, giving us a new life.

But in addition to this type of *purifying peirasmós* into which God can bring us, there is also the one used to punish us and condemn us to eternal death. We find this second type of *peirasmós* in two passages of the book of Ezekiel:

> And in the morning came the word of the Lord unto me, saying, Son of man, hath not the house of Israel, the rebellious house, said unto thee, What doest thou? Say thou unto them, Thus saith the Lord God; This burden concerneth the prince in Jerusalem, and all the house of Israel that are among them. Say, I am your sign: like as I have done, so shall it be done unto them: they shall be removed and go into captivity. And the prince that is among them shall bear upon his shoulder in the twilight, and shall go forth: they shall dig through the wall to carry out thereby: he shall cover his face, that he see not the ground with his eyes. My net also will I spread upon him, and he shall be taken in my snare: and I will bring him to Babylon to the land of the Chaldeans; yet shall he not see it, though he shall die there. And I will scatter toward every wind all that are about him to help him, and all his bands; and I will draw out the sword after them. And they shall know that I am the Lord, when I shall scatter them among the nations, and disperse them in the countries. But I will leave a few men of them from the sword, from the famine, and from the pestilence; that they may declare all their abominations among the heathen whither they come; and they shall know that I am the Lord. (Ezek 12:8–16)

> Therefore thus saith the Lord God; As I live, surely mine oath that he hath despised, and my covenant that he hath broken, even it will I recompense upon his own head. And I will spread my net upon him, and he shall be taken in my snare, and I will bring him to Babylon, and will plead with him there for his trespass that he hath trespassed against me. And all his fugitives with all his bands shall fall by the sword, and they that remain shall be scattered toward all winds: and ye shall know that I the Lord have spoken it. (Ezek 17:19–21)

The net, the trap that in this case God prepares for people, does not have a cathartic end, but it is a *punitive peirasmós* because of their wicked conduct. At the end of the *peirasmós* there is not a new life, but death (eternal).

And the action of "leading" a sinner into *punitive peirasmós* also works in reverse. God can inflict a *peirasmós* upon a sinner. The dynamic is relative. The concept is identical. Countless are the examples of God "inducing" (in the Latin sense of the term), that is, inflicting all sorts of evil upon those who deserve it. It is not possible to cite them all. They range from the locusts inflicted as a plague on Pharaoh (Exod 10:4: "*Ecce ego inducam cras locustam in fines tuos*"), to the "sword" (*gladium*) as a metaphor of death at the hands of the enemy (Ezek 5:17: "*gladium inducam super te*"; Ezek 6:3: "*Ecce ego inducam super vos gladium*"; Ezek 11:8: "*Gladium metuistis, et gladium inducam super vos*"), to simple terror (Jer 49:5: "*Ecce ego inducam super te terrorem*"), to affliction (Jer 19:3: "*Ecce ego inducam afflictionem super locum istum*"), to generic evils (Kgs 14:10: "*Ego inducam mala super domum Jeroboam*"; 1 Kgs 21:21: "*Ecce ego inducam super te malum*"; 1 Kgs 21:29: "*inferam malum domui ejus*"; 2 Kgs 21:12: "*Ecce ego inducam mala super Jerusalem et Judam*"; 2 Chr 34:24: "*Ecce ego inducam mala super locum istum*"; Jer 11:23: "*inducam enim malum super viros Anathoth*"), up to universal evils (Jer 19:15: "*Ecce ego inducam super civitatem hanc, et super omnes urbes ejus, universa mala*").

God can even induce on a person, if he wants, a *peirasmós*, from which the person has no chance of escape: "I will bring evil upon them, which they shall not be able to escape; and though they shall cry unto me, I will not hearken unto them" (Jer 11:11). "*Ecce ego inducam super eos mala de quibus exire non poterunt*," says the Vulgate. "*De quibus exire non poterunt*": from which they will not be able to get out.

This verse from Jeremiah illuminates even better the understanding we have gained up to this point of the concept of *peirasmós*. Specifically, what are the limits of *peirasmós*? We know (St. Paul teaches us in 1 Cor 10:13) that God is faithful to us, that is, he does not allow us to be tempted beyond our means, and that, with *peirasmós*, he always gives us an opportunity, always provides a way out. How then does this passage from St. Paul reconcile with what we have just read in Jeremiah? Does God do or do not provide us with an escape in the midst of *peirasmós*? The answer is: it depends. It depends on what kind of *peirasmós* we are talking about. If *peirasmós* is understood as temptation to moral evil, then yes: God could never put us in a situation where the only way out is sin. It would make no sense; we have already discussed this. If, on the other hand, *peirasmós* is understood with punitive intent, then no: it is not said that God will provide us with a way to escape it. It would make no sense. The punitive function would be lost. On the contrary, God clearly specifies that, in this case, the prayer to be freed from *peirasmós* might not be successful ("I will not hearken unto them"). If this were not the case, the very meaning of divine justice would be lost.

It would be literally impossible to cite all the examples in the Old Testament (there are hundreds) in which God, with punitive intent, delivers the unfortunate into the hands of his enemies. That is, he inflicts *peirasmós* by means of a third party. The term normally used in Hebrew is the verb *nāthăn* (נְתַן), which we have encountered before, which indicates the idea of "putting in." God can literally put us in the hands of our enemies so that we receive the proper punishment for our sins. For example, in the first book of Kings we read:

> If they sin against thee, (for there is no man that sinneth not,) and thou be angry with them, and deliver them to the enemy, so that they carry them away captives unto the land of the enemy, far or near; Yet if they shall bethink themselves in the land whither they were carried captives, and repent, and make supplication unto thee in the land of them that carried them captives, saying, We have sinned, and have done perversely, we have committed wickedness; And so return unto thee with all their heart, and with all their soul, in the land of their enemies, which led them away captive, and pray unto thee toward their land, which thou gavest unto their fathers, the city which thou hast chosen, and the house which I have built for thy name: Then hear thou their prayer and their supplication in heaven thy dwelling place, and maintain their cause, And forgive thy people that have sinned against thee, and all their transgressions wherein they have transgressed against thee, and give them compassion before them who carried them captive, that they may have compassion on them: For they be thy people, and thine inheritance, which thou broughtest forth out of Egypt, from the midst of the furnace of iron. (1 Kgs 8:46–51)

The Greek verb normally used by the Septuagint to render the idea of a God who delivers us into the hands of our enemies is *paradídōmi* (παραδίδωμι), the verb that indicates the betrayal of Jesus by Judas—his delivery into the hands of his enemies. The delivery into the enemy's hands translates into the deportation of the unfortunates to a hostile land. *In terram hostilem*. Therefore, whether God brings us materially or delivers us to our enemies, the punitive result is the same. We are given at the mercy of those who will make us suffer for our sins.

That this entire passage in the first book of Kings revolves around the concept of *peirasmós* is evident from the explicit reference to the furnace. We know well that this is the metaphor par excellence of purifying *peirasmós*. The Israelites' prayer to God is the following. If you God have freed us from the purifying *peirasmós* that we had to endure in the land of Egypt, forgive us also the sins that we will commit in the future (because no one is immune to sins), and, in your infinite mercy, deliver us from the punitive *peirasmós* that you will inflict on us by delivering us into the hands of our enemies. Let us keep this passage well in mind because it represents one of the many pieces of the puzzle we are trying to put together.

In the book of Lamentations, we find another illuminating passage: "The yoke of my transgressions is bound by his hand: they are wreathed, and come up upon my neck: he hath made my strength to fall, the Lord hath delivered me into their hands, from whom I am not able to rise up" (Lam 1:14). The Hebrew term used here is the verb *qûm* (קום), which indicates the idea of standing up. God put the unfortunate man in the hands of enemies so strong that it is not even possible for him to stand up and face them. The intent is obviously punitive, as can be deduced from the reference to the yoke of guilt. This passage confirms the previous intuition. When *peirasmós* has a punitive intent, the limits of which St. Paul speaks in 1 Cor 10:13 no longer apply. In fact, it is clearly stated how God has placed him in the hands of enemies that are too strong for him—strong beyond his ability to resist.

The expression "deliver into the hands of enemies" is used dozens of times in the Old Testament[4] and represents the most natural form by which God punishes people for their sins. There are three psalms that speak of this type of punishment.

In the first one God is implored as follows: "Deliver me not over unto the will of mine enemies" (Ps 27(26):12). The translation of the Septuagint is noteworthy: "μὴ παραδῷς με εἰς ψυχὰς θλιβόντων με,"[5] because it follows exactly the sixth petition of the Lord's Prayer, where the generic *peirasmós* represents here the will of those who afflict the unfortunate. *Thlibóntōn*: those who inflict *thlîpsis*, that is, tribulation, persecution, psychophysical suffering. If *peirasmós* is identifiable with *thlîpsis* and if the idea of delivering (*paradídōmi*) is assimilated to the action of leading (*eisphérō*), what this verse is saying is nothing less than "*mḕ eisenénkēis me eis peirasmón*"!

Psalm 125(124) concludes with this curse: "As for such as turn aside unto their crooked ways, the Lord shall lead them forth with the workers of iniquity" (Ps 125(124):5). The idea of leading is in this case rendered by the causative (*hiphil*) form of the verb *hālăk* (הָלַךְ), which indicates the generic action of walking. God will make those who deviate from his precepts "walk" along with the wicked. In this expression we can read, quite clearly, a punitive intent. God will consider those who deviate from his way as the wicked, and their fate will be similar.

In Psalm 124(123), on the other hand, the Lord is thanked in this way: "Blessed be the Lord, who hath not given us as a prey to their teeth" (Ps 124(123):6). Again, noteworthy is the translation of the Septuagint: "οὐκ ἔδωκεν ἡμᾶς εἰς θήραν,"[6] which traces the sixth petition of the Lord's Prayer. Prey, a term used in the original Hebrew text, is interpreted by the Septuagint from the point of view of the hunter. If there is a prey, there is a trap, a *thḗra* (θήρα), a term we have already seen used by St. Paul in Rom 11:9 in combination with *pagís*. And we know perfectly well how *peirasmós* is generally interpreted as a trap (a *pagís*) into which, whoever falls into it, finds death. A trap, in this case, which produces psychophysical suffering, not moral temptation. If *peirasmós* is identifiable with *pagís*, that is, with *thḗra*, and if the idea of delivering (*paradídōmi*) is identifiable with the action of leading (*eisphérō*), what we are doing with this verse is simply thanking the Lord for not having led us into *peirasmós*!

And to make the concept even better, the psalm concludes with the same metaphor: "Our soul is escaped as a bird out of the snare [*pagís*] of the fowlers: the snare [*pagís*] is broken, and we are escaped" (Ps 124(123):7). The net—the trap—is precisely

---

4. Some examples can be found in Gen 14:20; Lev 26:25; 2 Kgs 17:20; 21:14; 1 Chr 14:10; Judg 3:28; 6:1; Josh 10:19.

5. "*mḕ paradôis me eis psychàs thlibóntōn me*" = "Do not give me up to the will of those who afflict me."

6. "*ouk édōken hemâs eis thḗran*" = "He has not delivered us to the snare."

the *pagís* and from that trap the Lord freed them. We find again the same dynamic of "bringing in" as opposed to "bringing out." God can bring us into *peirasmós* to punish us, but, if he wants, thanks to his infinite mercy, he can take us out of it. Let us keep this passage in mind as well because it represents another key piece of the puzzle.

When God leads us into the trap and places us in the hands of our enemies to punish or humiliate us, the consequence of this is abandonment. God abandons us there, in the trap, in the middle of the *peirasmós*. It is at that point that it is up to us to turn to God, with all the faith we can muster, asking him to take us out, to rescue us from the *peirasmós* into which he has cast us. God, in accordance with his will and according to his infinite mercy, will decide if and when to deliver us from *peirasmós*. This concept is, for example, expressed in a passage in the book of Judges in which Gideon addresses the Angel of the Lord with these words: "Oh my Lord, if the Lord be with us, why then is all this befallen us? and where be all his miracles which our fathers told us of, saying, Did not the Lord bring us up from Egypt? but now the Lord hath forsaken us, and delivered us into the hands of the Midianites" (Judg 6:13).

Abandonment is not something independent of the action of bringing in. God brings us into the *peirasmós* and then abandons us within it. It is not a permissive abandonment. He does not let us into the *peirasmós* in the sense of allowing. He brings us right into it of his own volition. He does not abandon us in the *peirasmós*, in the sense of turning away as we enter into it. He abandons us, after he has created the *peirasmós* and brought us into it and leaves us there alone for a specific will and purpose.

In the psalm tradition, there are numerous songs in which, in the moment of anguish and suffering, we rhetorically ask God why he has abandoned us and why he does not come to redeem us.

In Psalm 10(9) we read: "Why standest thou afar off, O Lord? why hidest thou thyself in times of trouble?" (Ps 10(9):1(22)). The Hebrew term used to indicate distress is *tsārâ* (צָרָה), a noun that indicates all that produces difficulty, worry, suffering, psychophysical stress, affliction, adversity, distress, tribulation, and so forth. The Septuagint translates with the expression *en thlípsei* (ἐν θλίψει), in tribulation.

In an analogous way, in Psalm 13(12), it is asked, "How long shall I take counsel in my soul, having sorrow in my heart daily? how long shall mine enemy be exalted over me? Consider and hear me, O Lord my God: lighten mine eyes, lest I sleep the sleep of death?" (Ps 13(12):2–3). The psychophysical stress is evident: on the one hand anguish, anxiety, sadness in the heart (psychological stress), on the other hand oppression by enemies (physical stress).[7]

In several other psalms, this estrangement of God from his people is explicitly associated with wrath—with divine disdain for them. For example, in Psalm 60(59), it is said, "O God, thou hast cast us off, thou hast scattered us, thou hast been displeased; O turn thyself to us again. Thou hast made the earth to tremble; thou hast broken it:

---

7. See Pss 42(41):9(10); 43(42):2; 44(43):23–24(24–25).

heal the breaches thereof; for it shaketh. Thou hast shewed thy people hard things: thou hast made us to drink the wine of astonishment" (Ps 60(59):1–3(3–5)).

We understand that the abandonment by the Lord is not a simple "turning away." Instead, it is a full-fledged rejection. It is a casting off from himself, disgusted with human conduct. The harsh trials that God makes his people experience are what is referred to in Hebrew as *qāshĕh* (קָשֶׁה). The adjective *qāshĕh* is the counterpart of the Greek word *sklērós* (σκληρός), which means "hard." It indicates any situation that is hard, difficult for a person—hard in the sense of cruel, severe, violent. In the same vein are the pleas found in Ps 74(73):1 ("O God, why hast thou cast us off for ever? why doth thine anger smoke against the sheep of thy pasture?") and Ps 88(87):14(15) ("Lord, why castest thou off my soul? why hidest thou thy face from me?"). In Psalm 102(101) we can perceive the psalmist's despair: "Mine enemies reproach me all the day; and they that are mad against me are sworn against me. For I have eaten ashes like bread, and mingled my drink with weeping. Because of thine indignation and thy wrath: for thou hast lifted me up, and cast me down" (Ps 102(101):8–10(9–11)).

Thou hast lifted me up and cast me down. It is not a forsaking in the sense of "letting go." It is an abandonment in the sense of violently taking and throwing away! Nothing permissive in it. When we speak of punitive *peirasmós*, which implies indignation and wrath on the part of the Lord, we are faced with the most extreme form of direct causation. The sublimation of this concept occurs in the so-called "Psalm of the Cross," in which David, prophesying the crucifixion of Christ, cries out to heaven, "My God, my God, why hast thou forsaken me?" (Ps 22(21):1(2)).

One of the enemies into whose hands God can throw us is the Adversary par excellence, namely Satan. As outrageous as this statement may seem, it is what shines through clearly in Scripture, particularly the New Testament, this time around. Of course, in the Old Testament we have the grandiose example of Job, delivered by God into the hands of Satan so that he might suffer the harshest possible *peirasmós*, which, in the end (but only in the end), makes Job rediscover, in a new light, the greatness of God. In the New Testament, on the other hand, we find at least three examples where it is expressly stated that an unfortunate person was delivered into the hands of Satan with punitive/humiliating intent.

In the first chapter of the first epistle to Timothy, St. Paul mentions Hymen and Alexander, who apparently had strayed from the faith and indulged in blasphemous practices. Of them St. Paul says, "I have delivered [them] unto Satan, that they may learn not to blaspheme" (1 Tim 1:20).

These are seemingly problematic, scandalous words. St. Paul delivering people into the hands of Satan? And yet it is so. The apostles, including St. Paul, were apparently known to have power, like Christ, over demonic spirits (see Mark 6:7). And among these powers was that of "using" demonic spirits to subject those who deserved it to the necessary punishment. Was St. Paul leading Hymen and Alexander into temptation? No, he was not. He was leading them into a punitive *peirasmós*, inflicted through Satan (*per satanam*). Nothing to do with temptation to sin. Quite the contrary: psychophysical suffering as punishment and expiation for their blasphemous conduct ("they may learn not to blaspheme").

This is not an isolated case. In chapter 5 of the first epistle to the Corinthians, St. Paul hurls the same anathema against a man who had been guilty of a hateful impure act (he was living with his father's wife): "In the name of our Lord Jesus Christ, when ye are gathered together, and my spirit, with the power of our Lord Jesus Christ, To deliver such an one unto Satan for the destruction of the flesh, that the spirit may be saved in the day of the Lord Jesus" (1 Cor 5:4–5).

Here, the dynamic is even clearer. The power that St. Paul has to throw an unfortunate person into the hands of Satan comes directly from Christ. And the intent of this action is bodily humiliation, the ruin of the flesh (*sárx*), leading to a conversion that can ultimately save the soul. Is St. Paul leading this wretch into temptation? No, he is not. He is again leading him into a punitive/purifying *peirasmós*, inflicted through Satan (*per satanam*).

Incredibly, St. Paul confesses, in the second epistle to the Corinthians, that he himself was given into the hands of Satan, so that he would not sin of *hýbris*. He, to whom the gospel had been made known not by direct transmission, but revealed by divine grace, confesses, "And lest I should be exalted above measure through the abundance of the revelations, there was given to me a thorn in the flesh, the messenger of Satan to buffet me, lest I should be exalted above measure. For this thing I besought the Lord thrice, that it might depart from me. And he said unto me, My grace is sufficient for thee: for my strength is made perfect in weakness" (2 Cor 12:7–9).

God inflicted this *peirasmós* on St. Paul to humble his flesh with a constant torment so that his *hýbris* would not grow. A psychophysical torment that St. Paul understands, accepts, but which, of course, he tries, if possible, to shake off. This is why he implores God, not once but "three times," to remove this thorn from him. He is begging him, in short, to deliver him from *peirasmós*. But the prayer is unsuccessful. God explains to him that his grace (that is, the strength granted to him by the Holy Spirit) will be sufficient to endure the *peirasmós* that has befallen him.

We thus discover, if we can say so, an unusual face of Satan, a prerogative that the devil is not usually associated with in common feeling—that of acting as a pure instrument of humiliation for mortals. Humiliation wanted by God, *per satanam*. Humiliation resulting from the suffering of the flesh—of the *sárx*. Physical humiliation, not moral temptation. After all, this should not sound surprising since the demonic spirits that appear several times in the Gospels are always associated with psychophysical torments: infirmity, diseases, blindness, mutism, epilepsy, madness, deformities, and so forth.[8]

---

8. See Mark 3:10–11; 5:2–5; 7:25; 9:17–22, 25; Matt 8:16; 10:1; Luke 6:17–18; 7:21; 8:2, 26–29; 9:38–42; 13:11.

On the other hand, Jesus comes into the world, among other things, to demonstrate to the world precisely the merciful face of God the Father, who can not only bring us into *peirasmós*, but more importantly can deliver us from it. As Peter says in chapter 10 of the Acts of the Apostles, "That word, I say, ye know, which was published throughout all Judaea, and began from Galilee, after the baptism which John preached; How God anointed Jesus of Nazareth with the Holy Ghost and with power: who went about doing good, and healing all that were oppressed of the devil; for God was with him" (Acts 10:37–38).

The devil is depicted here primarily not as the one who tempts, but as the one who oppresses, who torments physically. *Katadynasteúō* (καταδυναστεύω) is the verb chosen by Luke to render the expression used by Peter, which indicates the exercise of a severe, harsh, oppressive power, bordering on torture, over someone.

Even from this kind of *peirasmós* Jesus came to deliver us.

# 20

# But Deliver Us from Evil

A key point on which we have not yet dwelt is the different form that the Lord's Prayer takes in Luke's Gospel, which appears to our eyes today as a reduced version of the Lord's Prayer that we all know, the one found in Matthew's Gospel. What is most striking is the ending. Matthew concludes with the well-known formula "but deliver us from evil" (the seventh petition), while Luke does not. In Luke, the sixth petition is also the last: "and lead us not into temptation." The end.

Why? There are several theories about this, all more or less reasonable. It may be that Jesus himself, during his preaching, had used two slightly different versions. It may be, as Joachim Jeremias argues, that Matthew's version is an extension of Luke's version, which should be considered to be the original.[1] The seventh petition that appears in Matthew would be a sort of gloss—a conclusion added in Judeo-Christian circles to eliminate the roughness of such a sudden conclusion. It would have been unthinkable in those circles, as Jeremias explains, to end a prayer with the term "temptation." Luke, on the other hand, who is addressing communities of Gentiles, would not have had this kind of concern. Nevertheless (this is not the point we wish to make here), the indisputable fact is that, within the first Christian communities of the first century, two slightly different versions of the Lord's Prayer circulated. One containing a seventh petition, one not.

From this simple fact we could already conclude that the seventh petition in Matthew's version cannot be completely independent of the others. On the contrary, it must be a sort of "redundant" petition, whose content is in some way already contained in the preceding ones and whose removal does not entail drastic mutilations to the overall sense of the prayer. This is also the perception that practically all the church fathers had. The seventh petition in Matthew is not a new petition, different

---

1. Jeremias, *The Lord's Prayer*, 10–14.

from the previous ones. It would simply be an explanation of the sixth petition. A way to make the sixth petition more digestible. The sixth and seventh petition of the Lord's Prayer would be two sides of the same coin. They sound different, but they say the same thing. They would be, in good substance, a single petition.

This was, for example, what St. Augustine thought: "It may be that 'deliver us from evil' is part of the same sentence. And in fact, so that we understand that it is one sentence, he says, 'Lead us not into temptation, but deliver us from evil.' He added that 'but' to show how it was all part of one sentence, 'Lead us not into temptation but deliver us from evil.' In what way? I will offer it as a single phrase. Lead us not into temptation but deliver us from evil. He does not lead us into temptation when he delivers us from evil. He delivers us from evil when he does not lead us into temptation."[2]

In St. Augustine's mind, the two petitions are identical, one the exemplification of the other. A real tautology. There are countless clues that suggest how the conclusion St. Augustine arrives at is reasonable.[3] First, the absence of the seventh petition in Luke's version. Second, the use, in its own unnatural way, of that "but" to introduce it (it is the only one that begins with an adversative conjunction). We add a third one: the complete grammatical parallelism between the sixth and seventh petition. Let us visualize it in the original Greek language:

| Sixth Petition | And | do not | lead | us | into | temptation, |
|---|---|---|---|---|---|---|
| | kaì | mḕ | eisenénkēis | hēmâs | eis | peirasmón |
| | καὶ | μὴ | εἰσενέγκῃς | ἡμᾶς | εἰς | πειρασμόν |
| Seventh Petition | ἀλλὰ | | ῥῦσαι | ἡμᾶς | ἀπὸ | τοῦ πονηροῦ |
| | allà | | rhŷsai | hēmâs | apò | toû ponēroû |
| | but | | deliver | us | from | evil. |

It is evident that, like two sides of the same coin, the seventh petition "mimics" the sixth, in some way proposing the same concept, but from a different point of view. The seventh petition uses a positive form (while the sixth is presented in the negative

---

2. "*Libera nos a malo; potest ad eamdem ipsam sententiam pertinere. Ideo sic est, ut intellegas unam sententiam, Ne nos inferas in tentationem; sed libera nos a malo. Ideo addidit sed: ut ostenderet hoc totum ad unam sententiam pertinere, ne nos inferas in tentationem; sed libera nos a malo. Quomodo? Singula illam proponam: Ne nos inferas in tentationem, sed libera nos a malo. Liberando nos a malo, non nos infert in tentationem: non nos inferendo in tentationem, libera nos a malo*" (Augustine, *Sermo LVII*, 10). See also Cyril of Alexandria: "*Habent autem haec dicta plurimam connexionem: est enim consectaneum ut si in tentationem non ingredimur, malo liberemur. Imo si quis dicat, liberari idem esse ac non ingredi in tentationem, a veritate non abludet*" (*In Lucam*, 11.4).

3. Calvin is a strong supporter of this thesis: "Some people have split this petition into two. This is wrong: for the nature of the subject makes it manifest, that it is one and the same petition. The connection of the words also shows it: for the word *but*, which is placed between, connects the two clauses together, as Augustine judiciously explains. The sentence ought to be resolved thus, *That we may not be led into temptation, deliver us from evil*" (Calvin, *Commentary on Matthew*, https://www.ccel.org/ccel/calvin/calcom31.ix.liv.html).

form). *Allá* (adversative conjunction) is the opposite of *kaí* (copulative conjunction). *Eisenénkēis* ("to bring into") is the opposite of *rhŷsai* ("to bring out"). *Eis* (motion into) is the opposite of *apó* (motion away from). The object of the action is identical: *hēmâs* ("us"). From which it follows that the *peirasmós* of the sixth petition and the *ponērón*[4] of the seventh must be intimately related, if not even the same thing.

This is not a foregone conclusion. It opens up an immense opportunity for us to understand even better what Jesus is referring to when he speaks of *peirasmós*. If the *ponērón* from which God is supposed to deliver us is identifiable with the *peirasmós* into which we ask that he not bring us, it will then be sufficient to explore everything from which God, throughout history, has delivered (and has promised that he would deliver) his people, in order to gain an insider's perspective on the meaning of the term *peirasmós*.

Let us begin then with the term "deliver." The Greek verb used by Matthew is *rhŷsai* (ῥῦσαι), the aorist imperative of *rhýomai* (ῥύομαι), which indicates the idea of "dragging out," "dragging toward oneself." *Rhýomai* is a deponent verb analogous to *rhéō* (ῥέω), which indicates a flowing, a sliding, thus a dragging.[5] It is, from a semantic point of view, a verb opposite to *eisphérō*, which retains, however, all the strength of *eisphérō*. If *eisphérō*, as we have emphasized on several occasions, is a verb that does not simply mean "to lead into," but more precisely "to carry inside with force," in the same way *rhýomai* does not simply indicate the action of "delivering from," but more precisely of "pulling out," of "dragging out," of "wrenching away" from an imminent danger, or from a situation that has become unbearable for those who are delivered. Like he who, enveloped by the waves, is about to be swept away by the current, but instead a friendly hand comes to his rescue to snatch him away from certain death and bring him to shore. This is the image we need to keep in mind when we come across the verb *rhýomai*.

There is another verb in Greek which is generally used as a synonym for *rhýomai*, and which retains its force. It is *exairéō* (ἐξαιρέω), a compound of the verb *hairéō* (αἱρέω), which indicates the idea of grasping. *Exairéō* therefore means "to draw out," "to pull out," "to snatch away." Matthew uses this verb on only two occasions, both related to the same sentence pronounced by Jesus, which we have already analyzed: "If your (right) eye is an occasion of sin, pluck it out [*exairéō*] and throw it away from you" (Matt 5:29; 18:9).

Finally, there is a third verb in Greek to indicate the generic action of delivering. It is the verb *sózō* (σόζω), which simply means "to save."

---

4. We will discuss later whether this term should be understood in the masculine (the Evil One, that is, Satan), or in the neuter (evil in general).

5. The reader may recall the famous Heraclitus's motto *pánta rheî* (πάντα ῥεῖ), that is, "everything flows."

The three verbs *rhýomai*, *exairéō* and *sōzō* are the three verbs associated with the liberating action of God. In a couple of passages of the psalms, we find all three together:

> But the salvation of the righteous is of the Lord: he is their strength in the time of trouble. And the Lord shall help them, and deliver [*rhýomai*] them: he shall deliver [*exairéō*] them from the wicked, and save [*sōzō*] them, because they trust in him. (Ps 37(36):39-40)

> Deliver [*rhýomai*] me in thy righteousness, and cause me to escape [*exairéō*]: incline thine ear unto me, and save [*sōzō*] me. ( . . . ) Deliver [*rhýomai*] me, O my God, out of the hand of the wicked, out of the hand of the unrighteous and cruel man. (Ps 71(70):2, 4)

These three verbs, in the Septuagint, are clearly used as synonyms. The corresponding three Hebrew verbs are *nātsăl* (נָצַל), *pālăt* (פָּלַט), and *yāshă'* (יָשַׁע).

*Nātsăl* literally means "to grasp by carrying away," "to snatch away," and is thus generally used to denote the action of rescuing someone in danger: the Septuagint translates it with either *rhýomai* or *exairéō*.

*Pālăt* literally means "to be smooth and agile," and is therefore indicated to render the idea of "slipping out," that is, escaping a danger without suffering any damage: the Septuagint translates it almost always with *rhýomai*.

*Yāshă'* literally means "to be wide": in Hebrew the breadth of space is associated with the concept of freedom, the narrowness instead with a condition of slavery, oppression, suffering, restriction. The causative (*hiphil*) form of *yāshă'* therefore indicates the action of making someone free, that is, saving: the Septuagint translates it almost always with the verb *sōzō*. Not surprisingly, the name Jesus derives from the Greek *Iēsoûs* (Ἰησοῦς), which corresponds to the Hebrew name *Yēshû'ă* (יֵשׁוּעַ), which derives from the root of the verb *yāshă'*, "to save." Jesus is the one who saves: "And she [Mary] shall bring forth a son, and thou shalt call his name Jesus: for he shall save his people from their sins" (Matt 1:21).

In Hebrew there are three other verbs that are associated with the concept of liberation: *mālăt* (מָלַט), *hālăts* (חָלַץ), and *gā' ăl* (גָּאַל).

*Mālăt* is a synonym of *pālăt* and indicates the action of slipping someone unharmed out of a dangerous situation: the Septuagint generally translates it either with *rhýomai* or with *sōzō*.

The verb *hālăts* literally means "to pull out," "to extract," and is for this reason generally rendered by the Septuagint with either *rhýomai* or *exairéō*.

Finally, *gā' ăl* indicates the action of freeing someone, but upon a ransom. Hence the sense of "redeeming." It is not by chance that this verb becomes an appellative of Jesus Christ. Christ is the Redeemer to the extent that he redeems humanity by the sacrifice of his death on the cross. The Greek verb that the Septuagint uses in this case is generally *lytróō* (λυτρόω).

Summing up, in the semantic field of "delivering," we find mainly six verbs in Hebrew, translated with four verbs in Greek, connected in the following way:

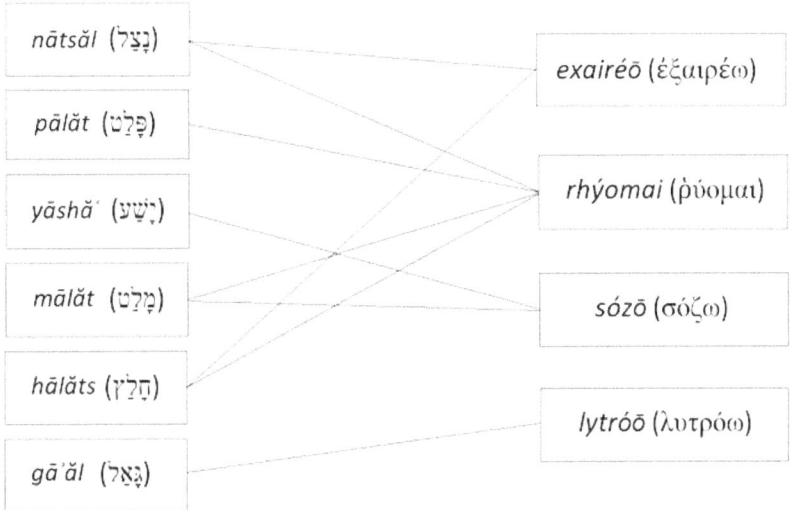

But from what, exactly, does God deliver us? To understand this, we must, once again, turn back to analyze the Old Testament and, for completeness of analysis, explore all the occurrences of the six Hebrew verbs mentioned, because they represent all the ways in which God can come to our aid. All six are in some way synonymous with (or otherwise relatable to) the *rhýomai* used in the seventh petition of the Lord's Prayer.

In total, there are over 250 occurrences of these six verbs which refer to the saving intervention of God. We will not bore the reader with each of them but will analyze only those passages that are most representative, and finally summarize the results of this analysis.

Let us begin with the verb *nātsăl*. The first occurrence of this verb with the meaning of "to deliver" is found in chapter 32 of the book of Genesis. Jacob is hunted by his brother Esau, who is marching against him at the head of an army of four hundred men. Jacob is desperate and relies on divine protection imploring, "Deliver [*exairéō*] me, I pray thee, from the hand of my brother, from the hand of Esau: for I fear him, lest he will come and smite me, and the mother with the children" (Gen 32:11). The scene is clear. Jacob is in a state of anguish, fearing for his life and the life of his family. He is praying to God to save him from the hand that could inflict death on him.

Another typical example that recurs throughout the Old Testament concerns the liberation of the people of Israel from slavery in Egypt. For example, in the book of Exodus, we read: "I am the Lord, and I will bring you out from under the burdens of the Egyptians, and I will rid [*rhýomai*] you out of their bondage, and I will redeem [*lytróō*] you with a stretched out arm, and with great chastisements"[6] (Exod 6:6).

It is interesting to note that "I will bring you out" is rendered by the causative (*hiphil*) form of the Hebrew verb *yātsā'* (יָצָא), which we have already met, and which indicates the action of "bringing out." It is rendered by the Septuagint by the verb *exágō* (ἐξάγω), which represents, from a grammatical point of view, the opposite of the verb *eisphérō*. The *ponērón*, the evil from which God saves the Israelites, represents not a temptation, but a terribly tight and heavy yoke (that of Pharaoh), a psychophysical oppression. How does liberation come about? By means of "great chastisements." The Hebrew term used here comes from the verb *shāphăt* (שָׁפַט), which means "to judge." The punishment, the calamities inflicted on Pharaoh are the expression of the divine judgment—the sentence of condemnation in accordance with his justice.

We thus begin to glimpse what kind of relationship there may be between the *peirasmós* of the sixth petition and the *ponērón* of the seventh. The *peirasmós* inflicted on Pharaoh and his people[7] becomes a picklock to redeem the Israelites from the *ponērón* that oppresses them. The verb *nātsăl* is used many times to indicate the liberation of Israel from the yoke of Pharaoh.[8]

The people of Egypt were not the only ones who put Israel into slavery. Another threat that would constantly hang over Jerusalem was the expansionist aims of the king of Assyria.[9] So much so that the Israelites had even thought of signing a treaty of alliance with Pharaoh so that he would put them under his protective wing and defend them from the Assyrians. God, of course, did not like this choice. Instead of asking him for protection, his people were thinking of putting themselves in the hands of the pagans. We find this account in the book of Isaiah. God is angry and threatens the Israelites so that they may desist from their intentions and promises to come to their aid: "As birds flying, so will the Lord of hosts defend Jerusalem; defending also he will deliver [*exairéō*] it; and passing over he will preserve [*sózō*] it" (Isa 31:5).

The promise of the Lord is to come to the aid of his people with destructive power. It is enlightening to read the whole passage:

> Behold, the name of the Lord cometh from far, burning with his anger, and the burden thereof is heavy: his lips are full of indignation, and his tongue as a devouring fire: And his breath, as an overflowing stream, shall reach to the midst of the neck, to sift the nations with the sieve of vanity: and there shall be a bridle in the jaws of the people, causing them to err. Ye shall have a song, as in the night when a holy solemnity is kept; and gladness of heart, as when

---

6. The KJV has "judgments."
7. See Deut 4:34; 7:19; 29:3 (LXX).
8. See Exod 3:8; 18:4, 8; Judg 6:9; 1 Sam 10:18; Isa 19:20.
9. The verb *nātsăl* is used a total of eighteen times to indicate deliverance from the king of Assyria (2 Kgs 18:30; 20:6; 2 Chr 32:11–17; Isa 31:5; 36:15–20; 38:6) and three times for deliverance from the Philistines (1 Sam 7:3, 14, 37). See also Josh 24:10; 1 Sam 14:48; Jer 1:19; 39:17; 42:11.

one goeth with a pipe to come into the mountain of the Lord, to the mighty One of Israel. And the Lord shall cause his glorious voice to be heard, and shall shew the lighting down of his arm, with the indignation of his anger, and with the flame of a devouring fire, with scattering, and tempest, and hailstones. For through the voice of the Lord shall the Assyrian be beaten down, which smote with a rod. And in every place where the grounded staff shall pass, which the Lord shall lay upon him, it shall be with tabrets and harps: and in battles of shaking will he fight with it. (Isa 30:27–32)

The divine *orgé* has flared up and is about to spill over all of Assyria. The people of Israel have been threatened and those who have threatened them (the king of Assyria) will suffer a terrible *peirasmós*. We see the same dynamic in action. The *peirasmós* resulting from divine wrath acts as a pick to free the oppressed from the *ponērón* inflicted by the oppressor. And how does God deliver the oppressed? By having him escape the *peirasmós* itself—by sparing him from his wrath. The Hebrew verb used here is *pāsăh* (פָּסַח), which means "to pass over." It is an important verb, perhaps the most important in the Judaic tradition. It is the verb which gives name to the Passover, and which recalls how God freed the people of Israel from the yoke of Pharaoh. The Destroying Angel, passing house by house, had slaughtered all the firstborn, but spared those of the people of Israel.[10] He had passed over. If we read the passage in the book of Exodus where this episode is narrated, we find all these concepts again: "It is the sacrifice of the Lord's passover, who passed over [*pāsăh*] the houses of the children of Israel in Egypt, when he smote the Egyptians, and delivered [*rhýomai*] our houses" (Exod 12:27).

*Rhýomai* is a liberation from oppression, from suffering, from tribulation, but at the same time it coincides with protection from *peirasmós*. They are two sides of the same coin. God frees the Israelites from the *ponērón* that weighs down on them (because of the slavery imposed by Pharaoh), sparing them from the punitive *peirasmós* that befalls the land of Egypt.

Deliverance from the enemy, that is, from anyone attacking the people of Israel, is a recurring theme—probably the theme par excellence of the Old Testament. The verb *nātsăl* is used numerous times to indicate the liberating action of God from the violent hands of the enemies.[11] Among these, we will cite Psalm 18(17): "Then the channels of waters were seen, and the foundations of the world were discovered at thy rebuke, O Lord, at the blast of the breath of thy nostrils [*orgé*]. He sent from above, he took me, he drew me out of great waters. He delivered [*rhýomai*] me from my strong enemy, and from them which hated me: for they were too strong for me. They

---

10. See Exod 12:13, 23.

11. See Deut 23:14; Judg 8:34; 1 Sam 12:10–11; 17:37; 2 Sam 12:7; 22:1, 18, 49; 1 Chr 16:35; 2 Chr 25:15; 2 Kgs 17:39; Ezra 8:31; Neh 9:28; Mic 4:10; Pss 18(17):1, 17(18), 48(49); 31(30):15(16); 40(39):13(14); 51(50):14(16); 59(58):1–2(2–3); 70(69):1(2); 71(70):2; 72(71):12; 82(81):4; 97(96):10; 143(142):9; Ezek 13:21–23; 34:27; Zech 11:6; Jer 15:20–21; 20:13; 21:12.

prevented me in the day of my calamity: but the Lord was my stay. He brought [*exágō*] me forth also into a large place; he delivered [*rhýomai*] me, because he delighted in me" (Ps 18(17):15–19(16–20)).

We find here various concepts already explored, such as the divine wrath (*orgḗ*) that produces *peirasmós* that befalls the enemies who oppress the righteous. The oppression is always psychophysical: yoke, slavery, sword, death. The metaphor of the "great waters": the righteous oppressed by the wicked is like someone who is at the mercy of the current that sweeps him away and drowns him. From this certain death, God comes to the rescue and with his hand literally snatches, that is, drags away the righteous from the *ponērón* that oppresses him, takes him out (*exágō*) of it, and restores him to freedom.[12]

Psalms 69(68) and 144(143) take up the metaphor of the great waters that represent the threat of those who want to harm us: "Deliver [*sózō*] me out of the mire, and let me not sink: let me be delivered [*rhýomai*] from them that hate me, and out of the deep waters" (Ps 69(68):14(15)); "Send thine hand from above; rid [*exairéō*] me, and deliver [*rhýomai*] me out of great waters, from the hand of foreigners"[13] (Ps 144(143):7).

The yoke of the enemy—the slavery in which the people of Israel found themselves very often in the course of their history—is a condition which not only involves physical suffering, but also, and above all, psychological suffering. The humiliation of being at the mercy of the enemy's violence is a terrible shame to bear in front of other nations. Liberation from the enemy also becomes liberation from shame: "O keep my soul,[14] and deliver [*rhýomai*] me: let me not be ashamed; for I put my trust in thee" (Ps 25(24):20).

In fact, one of the main concerns of the Israelites was that of not being put to shame in front of other nations, of not feeling that they were the laughingstock of the enemy. And so, one of the most common prayers was to ask God to spare them the shame of falling into slavery, the shame of being deprived of their freedom. This is true both on a collective level and on an individual level, as long as shame and humiliation may come from evildoers. Several times in the psalms the verb *nātsăl* is used to indicate a deliverance from those who spread false rumors about the psalmist (Pss 109(108):21; 120(119):2; 144(143):11).

Finally, Psalm 106(105) offers us a slightly different view, where God is angry with his own people and, as a punishment, gives them to his enemies without rushing to their aid: "Therefore was the wrath of the Lord kindled against his people,

---

12. An identical passage is found in 2 Sam 22:18.

13. The KJV has an improbable "from the hand of strange children."

14. Here the Hebrew term *nĕphĕsh* (נֶפֶשׁ) does not have a spiritual sense, even though it is translated as "soul." Instead, it needs to be understood as "life." The psalmist's concern (it is clear from the context) is to not fall victim to his enemies, of whom there are many and who hate him with violent hatred (Ps 25(24):19).

insomuch that he abhorred his own inheritance. And he gave [*paradídōmi*] them into the hand of the heathen; and they that hated them ruled over them. Their enemies also oppressed them, and they were brought into subjection under their hand. Many times did he deliver [*rhýomai*] them; but they provoked him with their counsel, and were brought low for their iniquity" (Ps 106(105):40–43).

The Lord's indignation is in this case a real disgust. The conduct of his people is so abominable that God can do nothing but reject it. It is only when the *peirasmós* reaches its climax that God is moved to compassion: "Nevertheless he regarded their affliction,[15] when he heard their cry: And he remembered for them his covenant, and repented according to the multitude of his mercies" (Ps 106(105):44–45).

There is no human abomination that can surpass divine mercy in magnitude. God hears the cry for help, sees (that is, realizes) how much his people are suffering, forgives, and, by forgiving, saves them (Ps 86(85):13). The suffering is all psychophysical. The flesh (*sárx*) is beaten, scourged by the hand of the enemies.

Many other times the verb *nātsăl* indicates a liberation from a generic condition of psychophysical suffering, of tribulation,[16] which can take the form of persecution,[17] calamity,[18] and finally death[19] procured by an enemy or an adverse event.

But it is also true that—and here we begin to approach the most interesting part of the discourse—the one who can inflict this condition of suffering from which we ask God to free us is not necessarily an enemy, but God himself. Emblematic is this passage from Ezekiel:

> Son of man, when the land sinneth against me by trespassing grievously, then will I stretch out mine hand upon it, and will break the staff of the bread thereof, and will send famine upon it, and will cut off man and beast from it: Though these three men, Noah, Daniel, and Job, were in it, they should deliver [*sózō*] but their own souls by their righteousness, saith the Lord God. If I cause noisome beasts to pass through the land, and they spoil it, so that it be desolate, that no man may pass through because of the beasts: Though these three men were in it, as I live, saith the Lord God, they shall deliver [*sózō*] neither sons nor daughters; they only shall be delivered [*sózō*], but the land shall be desolate. Or if I bring a sword upon that land, and say, Sword, go through the land; so that I cut off man and beast from it: Though these three men were in it, as I live, saith the Lord God, they shall deliver [*sózō*] neither sons nor daughters, but they only shall be delivered [*sózō*] themselves. Or if I send a pestilence into that land, and pour out my fury upon it in blood, to cut

---

15. The Septuagint uses the verb *thlíbō* (θλίβω), from which the noun *thlipsis*, tribulation, is derived.

16. 1 Sam 26:24; Job 5:19; Ezek 34:10–12; Jonah 4:6; Pss 22(21):8(9); 34(33):4(5), 17(18), 19(20); 54(53):7(9); 107(106):6.

17. Pss 7:1(2); 119(118):170; 142(141):6(7).

18. Hab 2:9; Ps 91(90):3.

19. Pss 33(32):19; 56(55):13(14).

off from it man and beast: Though Noah, Daniel, and Job were in it, as I live, saith the Lord God, they shall deliver [*sózō*] neither son nor daughter; they shall but deliver [*sózō*] their own souls by their righteousness. (Ezek 14:13–20)

It is clear that sin (particularly that of idolatry) unleashes divine wrath, from which it is impossible to escape.[20] How, then, to remedy a sin committed? The only way to escape the divine wrath is to implore his mercy. In a couple of psalms,[21] the verb *nātsăl* indicates the liberation from sin. And how does God free us from sin? Through his forgiveness, which comes from his infinite mercy.

Let us be careful. Liberation from sin has nothing to do with liberation from temptation to sin. Deliverance from sins amounts to nothing more than forgiveness of those sins (once committed). Deliverance from temptation to sin (before sin is committed) is a concept that does not emerge in the Old Testament. There is perhaps only one passage where such an idea can be discerned. It is found in the second chapter of Proverbs: "Discretion shall preserve thee, understanding shall keep thee: To deliver [*rhýomai*] thee from the way of the evil man, from the man that speaketh froward things; Who leave the paths of uprightness, to walk in the ways of darkness; Who rejoice to do evil, and delight in the frowardness of the wicked; Whose ways are crooked, and they froward in their paths: To deliver thee from the foreign woman, even from the stranger which flattereth with her words; Which forsaketh the guide of her youth, and forgetteth the covenant of her God" (Prov 2:11–17).

The semantic distribution observed so far for the verb *nātsăl* is repeated almost identically for all the other five Hebrew verbs mentioned before and associated with the concept of liberation, and therefore we will not dwell further. In any case, the passage from the book of Proverbs just quoted will remain the only one where a deliverance from temptation is explicitly mentioned. Let us then present a small chart that summarizes the semantic distribution of all six Hebrew verbs used as synonyms of delivering.

---

20. See Judg 10:15; Ezek 7:19; Zeph 1:18; 2 Kgs 18:33; Job 10:7.
21. Pss 39(38):8(9); 79(78):9.

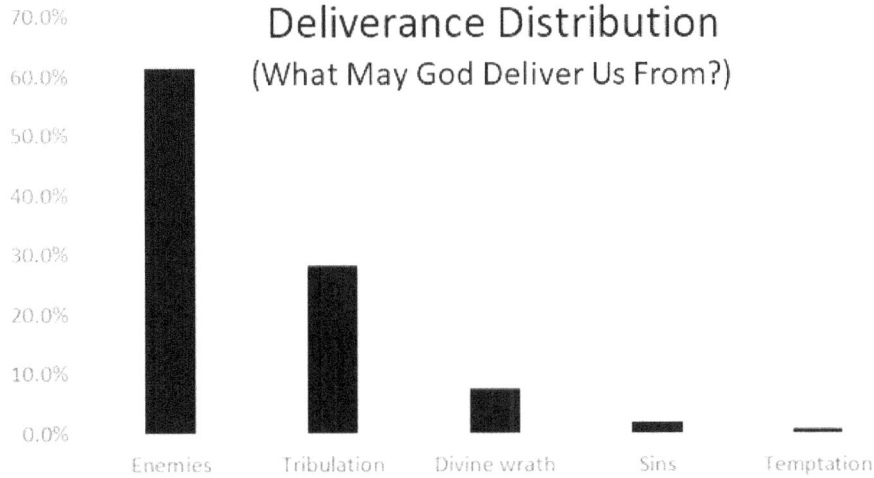

In the Old Testament, the concept of salvation is almost always (~90 percent) associated with the idea of liberation from psychophysical suffering (oppression by enemies, tribulation). Suffering that in some cases (~8 percent) is a direct consequence of divine wrath, unleashed by sins (~2 percent). The deliverance from moral temptation described in the book of Proverbs is an exceptional case and represents less than 1 percent out of a total of more than 250 occurrences.

Therefore, if we are to follow the logic that the *peirasmós* of the sixth petition represents that *ponērón* from which one asks to be freed in the seventh, we again arrive at the same unambiguous conclusion. The probability that the *peirasmós* of the sixth petition means moral temptation is practically nil.

To conclude this analysis, we would like to propose another couple of passages that we find particularly illuminating. The first is found again in the book of Proverbs: "If thou faint in the day of adversity, thy strength is small. If thou forbear to deliver [*rhýomai*] them that are drawn [*ágō*] unto death, and those that are ready to be slain" (Prov 24:10–11).

After reading this passage again, one cannot help but be reminded of the parable of the sower that we have already analyzed previously (Mark 4:1–20; Matt 13:3–23; Luke 8:4–14). Jesus explains that one who faint on the day of *peirasmós* is like a plant without roots, where *peirasmós* is to be understood as some tribulation or persecution. The Septuagint underscores this concept with a redundant expression: "on the unfortunate day [*kakós*] and on the day of tribulation [*thlîpsis*]." Interestingly enough, immediately after this more or less explicit reference to *peirasmós*, the following verse speaks of a deliverance from death and slaughter, where the verb "to deliver" is rendered by the very same *rhýomai* used in the seventh petition. This is, on closer inspection, a structure somewhat reminiscent of that of the Lord's Prayer. Who is asked to be delivered and saved? He who is led to death, to slaughter. Here the reference to eternal death, to destruction, to infernal torment is clear. Note the use of the verb "to lead," rendered by the verb *ágō*, which recalls the *eisphérō* used in the Lord's Prayer. The *peirasmós* is here identified, at a level that we could define as earthly, as a tribulation, and at the same time, at a transcendent level, as the ultimate suffering, eternal death.

We will conclude our analysis regarding the Old Testament reading a passage from the book of Sirach that we analyzed earlier: "He who fears the Lord incurs no evil, but in the trial [*peirasmós*] will be delivered [*exairéō*] once and again" (Sir 33:1).

We have already discussed at length how this passage refers to the liberating action of God who comes to the aid of the righteous in the moment in which he is afflicted, crushed almost, by *peirasmós*, that is, by all that can cause pain, destruction, misery, unhappiness. We find illuminating the Latin translation of the Vulgate: "*Timenti Dominum non occurrent mala: sed in tentatione Deus illum conservabit, et liberabit a malis.*"

This is another clear example in which the concept of *tentatio* and deliverance from evil are intimately connected, literally merged in the same verse, as if it were one. It is impossible not to notice a striking similarity with the sixth and seventh petition of the Lord's Prayer, in which practically the same words appear: "*ne nos inducas in tentationem, sed libera nos a malo.*"

If the evil from which God delivers us in Sir 33:1 is an entirely psychophysical evil, and if this evil coincides with the *tentatio* of the sixth petition, we must conclude once again that *peirasmós* is to be understood precisely as tribulation and suffering, and not as moral temptation.

Let us turn our attention at this point to the New Testament. It is essential to understand what the evangelists and the apostles meant by the concept of "deliverance from evil." Let us begin with a statistical consideration. The verb *rhýomai* in the seventh petition of the Lord's Prayer appears sixteen times outside the context of the Lord's Prayer itself. Interestingly, however, only two of these sixteen occurrences appear in the four Gospels. All others are found in the letters of the apostles Peter and Paul.

And even more curiously, these two occurrences appear one at the beginning (of Luke's Gospel) and the other at the end (of Matthew's Gospel), as if to seal the entire earthly parable of Jesus. The first one is found when Zacharias, having regained the use of speech, under the inspiration of the Holy Spirit, glorifies God for the unexpected birth of his son, John the Baptist, and prophesies,

> Blessed be the Lord God of Israel; for he hath visited and redeemed his people, And hath raised up an horn of salvation for us in the house of his servant David; As he spake by the mouth of his holy prophets, which have been since the world began: That we should be saved from our enemies, and from the hand of all that hate us; To perform the mercy promised to our fathers, and to remember his holy covenant; The oath which he sware to our father Abraham, That he would grant unto us, that we being delivered [*rhýomai*] out of the

hand of our enemies might serve him without fear, In holiness and righteousness before him, all the days of our life. (Luke 1:68–75)

The liberation for which Zacharias thanks God is, as usual, from the hands of the enemies and their violent hatred. Nothing new.

The second one is found during Jesus' agony on the cross: "Likewise also the chief priests mocking him, with the scribes and elders, said, he saved others; himself he cannot save. If he be the King of Israel, let him now come down from the cross, and we will believe him. he trusted in God; let him deliver [*rhýomai*] him now, if he will have him: for he said, I am the Son of God" (Matt 27:41–43). The sarcastic words of the high priests refer to a liberation from the agony of the cross, the emblem of psychophysical suffering.

The Apostle Paul uses the verb *rhýomai* several times. In his second letter to the Thessalonians, we read: "And [pray] that we may be delivered [*rhýomai*] from unreasonable and wicked men: for all men have not faith. But the Lord is faithful, who shall stablish you, and keep you from evil" (2 Thess 3:2–3).

It is clear from the context that the evil from which God will preserve the righteous is not the Evil One (as we read in many translations[22]), but the evil that "unreasonable and wicked men" can bring upon the righteous. We are once again within the realm of a liberation from the violent enemy.

Similarly, in his second letter to Timothy, Paul speaks of all the persecutions and sufferings he had to endure at the hands of the pagans and from which God always delivered him (2 Tim 3:10–11).

The same concept is reiterated in the next chapter in which Paul recalls how he was brought before the courts at the hands of the Gentiles and, by the grace of God, managed to come out unscathed: "At my first answer no man stood with me, but all men forsook me: I pray God that it may not be laid to their charge. Notwithstanding the Lord stood with me, and strengthened me; that by me the preaching might be fully known, and that all the Gentiles might hear: and I was delivered [*rhýomai*] out of the mouth of the lion. And the Lord shall deliver [*rhýomai*] me from every evil work, and will preserve me unto his heavenly kingdom: to whom be glory for ever and ever. Amen" (2 Tim 4:16–18).

Paul here makes explicit reference to the tribulation suffered by Daniel, who was thrown into the lions' den. But, as in the case of Daniel, the Lord intervened to free him and will continue in the future to free him "from every evil work."[23] Although obvious, it is good to clarify at this point that the evil deeds of which Paul speaks are not those that he himself might commit in the future, but those that his enemies might commit against him. Let us continue.

---

22. NIV, NLT, ESV, BSB, NKJV, NASB, CSB, ASV, GNT, ISV, NAB, NET, NRSV, NHEB, WEB.

23. "ἀπὸ παντὸς ἔργου πονηροῦ [*apò pantòs érgou ponēroú*]."

## Eis Peirasmón

In chapter 15 of his letter to the Romans, Paul urges them to pray that he "be delivered from them that do not believe in Judaea" (Rom 15:31). Again, Paul's concern is the persecution that he might suffer from the ungodly and that might hinder him in his evangelizing journeys. In the same letter, a few chapters earlier, Paul goes into a very intimate reasoning about the inner struggle between the will to do good and the instinct to commit evil. Let us read the entire passage because it is very interesting:

> For we know that the law is spiritual: but I am carnal, sold under sin. For that which I do I allow not: for what I would, that do I not; but what I hate, that do I. If then I do that which I would not, I consent unto the law that it is good. Now then it is no more I that do it, but sin that dwelleth in me. For I know that in me (that is, in my flesh,) dwelleth no good thing: for to will is present with me; but how to perform that which is good I find not. For the good that I would I do not: but the evil which I would not, that I do. Now if I do that I would not, it is no more I that do it, but sin that dwelleth in me. I find then a law, that, when I would do good, evil is present with me. For I delight in the law of God after the inward man: But I see another law in my members, warring against the law of my mind, and bringing me into captivity to the law of sin which is in my members. O wretched man that I am! who shall deliver [*rhýomai*] me from this body devoted to death? I thank God through Jesus Christ our Lord. So then with the mind I myself serve the law of God; but with the flesh the law of sin. (Rom 7:14–25)

Here Paul elaborates on the theme of the inexhaustible struggle between the flesh (*sárx*), instinctively and naturally inclined to sin and eager to abandon itself to every kind of temptation, and the mind—the reason, the free will, which would like to follow divine dictates, but has a hard time and often yields to the baser instincts of the flesh. It is an open confession, in Augustinian style, of his total fragility. Paul despairs of this condition, which devours him internally, but understands and admits that this is the condition in which human beings find themselves living. The condition that has been given to them and from which it is not possible to escape. And for this reason, he cries out, "who shall deliver me from this body devoted to death?" The question is obviously rhetorical, because as long as the soul is "trapped" in the body, this is the state in which people have to live. No one, not even God, could free him from this eternal conflict. Here then, in the very passage in which Paul laments the impossibility of not being exposed to temptation and the extreme difficulty of resisting it, Paul does not ask God to free him, but by asking rhetorically, "who will free me?" he confesses that his own will, which always has the last word on the decision to do good rather than evil, is at this moment too weak to prevail: "So then with the mind I myself serve the law of God; but with the flesh the law of sin."

At the beginning of the second letter to the Corinthians, Paul mentions the persecutions he received during his travels in Asia Minor: "For we would not, brethren, have you ignorant of our trouble [*thlîpsis*] which came to us in Asia, that we were pressed out of measure, above strength, insomuch that we despaired even of life: But we had the sentence of death in ourselves, that we should not trust in ourselves, but in God which raiseth the dead: Who delivered [*rhýomai*] us from so great a death, and doth deliver [*rhýomai*]: in whom we trust that he will yet deliver [*rhýomai*] us; Ye also helping together by prayer for us, that for the gift bestowed upon us by the means of many persons thanks may be given by many on our behalf" (2 Cor 1:8–11).

The verb *rhýomai* appears three times here and recounts the divine saving intervention that, just as it saved Paul once from a death sentence, will do so again in the future (see Sir 33:1). The liberation is once again from a psychophysical tribulation (*thlîpsis*). Most importantly, St. Paul, the same one who in his first letter to the Corinthians reminded us of how God is faithful and does not allow us to be tempted "above our strength," has no hesitation here in his second letter in recalling that the tribulation which came to them in Asia pressed them "out of measure," that is, above their strength. This is further evidence that, when *peirasmós* is to be understood as *thlîpsis* and not as moral temptation, the limits outlined by St. Paul in 1 Cor 10:13 no longer apply.

It is in the first chapter of another letter, the first to the Thessalonians, that the verb *rhýomai* appears once more: "And to wait for his Son from heaven, whom he raised from the dead, even Jesus, which delivered [*rhýomai*] us from the wrath to come" (1 Thess 1:10).

St. Paul introduces a fundamental theme for our discussion. Jesus is explicitly identified as the one who, through his sacrifice on the cross, rescues us from the impending divine wrath (see also Rom 5:8–11). We will have the opportunity to examine this aspect (which is the basis of Christian theology) in the next chapters. For now, it will suffice to observe that this type of liberation (from divine wrath) represents nothing new and falls to all intents and purposes into the Old Testament canon.

This is why, in the last occurrence of the verb *rhýomai* in the Pauline letters, at the beginning of the first letter to the Thessalonians, Paul can say, "Who hath delivered [*rhýomai*] us from the power of darkness, and hath translated us into the kingdom of his dear Son: In whom we have redemption through his blood, even the forgiveness of sins" (Col 1:13–14).

Jesus' sacrifice on the cross represents the picklock with which the divine wrath is avoided and the doors of heaven, closed and inaccessible to people since the expulsion of Adam and Eve from the garden of Eden, are indeed opened. The power of darkness (that is, death, the eternal one, which separates mortals from God) is vanquished. Jesus, with his sacrifice, reconciles humanity with God and, literally, transfers us from the darkness of eternal death to the light of eternal life in the kingdom of God. The verb used by Paul is a very intense one, *methístēmi* (μεθίστημι). It is composed of the preposition *metá* (μετά) which indicates a sequence, a temporal or spatial succession, and the verb *hístēmi* (ἵστημι) which means "to place." *Methístēmi* thus gives the idea of taking something from one place and transferring it to another. Deliverance from eternal death occurs through Jesus, who literally takes us from the darkness into which we would have fallen after earthly death (without his sacrifice on the cross) and transfers us into the kingdom of God to enjoy eternal life.

Let us keep this dynamic in mind and continue by analyzing the two occurrences of the verb *rhýomai* in the letters of the apostle Peter. The passage in which these two occurrences appear should be familiar because it has been analyzed previously. It is found in the second chapter of the second epistle, in which Peter recalls three emblematic episodes of divine wrath: the fall of the rebellious angels, the Universal Flood, and the destruction of Sodom and Gomorrah. Let us read it again:

> For if God spared not the angels that sinned, but cast them down to Hell, and delivered them into chains of darkness, to be reserved unto judgment; And spared not the old world, but saved Noah the eighth person, a preacher of righteousness, bringing in the flood upon the world of the ungodly; And turning the cities of Sodom and Gomorrha into ashes condemned them with an overthrow, making them an ensample unto those that after should live ungodly; And delivered [*rhýomai*] just Lot, vexed with the filthy conversation of the wicked: For that righteous man dwelling among them, in seeing and hearing, vexed his righteous soul from day to day with their unlawful deeds. (2 Pet 2:4–8)

Without repeating here all the considerations set forth before, we will emphasize how, in the light of our entire analysis of the concept of deliverance and salvation within Scripture, the picture now appears clear. The very moment the divine wrath is unleashed and the just divine punishment falls upon the world, God brings to safety the righteous and condemns the wicked. God saved Noah but destroyed the rest of sinful humanity. God saved Lot but destroyed the rest of the inhabitants of Sodom and Gomorrah. That is why Peter concludes, "The Lord knoweth how to deliver [*rhýomai*] the godly out of *peirasmós*, and to reserve the unjust unto the day of judgment to be punished" (2 Pet 2:9).

This verse is fundamental to our research. It is the only passage in the New Testament in which the two concepts, that of *peirasmós*, found in the sixth petition, and that of deliverance (*rhýomai*), found in the seventh petition, are condensed into a single expression. This cannot be accidental. Peter is here explaining to us the profound meaning of the concluding distich of the Lord's Prayer, explicitly confirming that the evil from which we ask God to free us (*rhýomai*) in the seventh petition coincides with the *peirasmós* in which we ask that God not drag us (*eisphérō*) in the sixth.

In conclusion of our analysis, we can say with certainty that the verb *rhýomai* represents a deliverance from two types of evil:

1. the iniquities, injustices, persecutions, physical and psychological violence committed against us by evil people;

2. the just punishment, a direct consequence of the divine wrath unleashed by our sins, in which we should incur, but from which we may be spared by virtue of the infinite divine mercy.

With an explanatory gloss not to be underestimated: the two possibilities just described are often superimposable. That is, the just punishment is often expressed for people in becoming the object of iniquity, injustice, persecution, and so forth.

Never is it about deliverance from moral temptation. As if God could somehow either shield us completely from temptation or prevent us from committing evil when we are tempted. Both cases are illogical. The first, because, as Paul explains, people are made of flesh and by their very nature are constantly inclined to evil and subject to the most abject instincts. For God to shield us completely from temptation, he would have to literally tear off our flesh, which is obviously impossible in this earthly life. Or he would have to "inundate" us with the Holy Spirit to take total control over us—a grace which, however desirable, God simply does not grant (except in very exceptional cases and circumstances). Second, because it would be incompatible with the concept of free will, which leaves people free to fall or not to fall into the temptation to sin. The ultimate decision to yield or not to sin is always and only our responsibility—a decision in which God does not intervene. Never is it about deliverance from the Evil One's attempt to make us fall into temptation.

And yet. Yet everything is tremendously more complicated than that. If we go and look at the term used by Matthew and Luke to render the evil of the seventh petition of the Lord's Prayer, we discover that the genitive *toû ponēroû* (τοῦ πονηροῦ)—in the expression *apò toû ponēroû* ("from evil")—is compatible with both the neuter gender, *tó ponērón* (τό πονηρόν), which indicates evil in general, and with the masculine gender, *ho ponērós* (ὁ πονηρός), which indicates instead the evil person and, in our case, more specifically, the Evil One.

And if the expression *apò toû ponēroû* with which the Lord's Prayer ends is to be understood not simply as a generic "deliver us from evil," but more specifically as "deliver us from the Evil One" (as many scholars, with good reason, believe), then the hypothesis that the *peirasmós* of the sixth petition means "moral temptation" (the Evil One being the Tempter par excellence) gains traction once again.

Or does it?

# 21

# Is It *Ponērós* or *Ponērón*?

The fact that the masculine genitive *toû ponēroû* (τοῦ πονηροῦ) is in Greek identical to the neuter genitive *toû ponēroû* (τοῦ πονηροῦ) is a case that we could call unfortunate because it introduces further freedom of interpretation (and there was honestly no need for it). Nor does the Latin translation of the Vulgate (*libera nos a malo*) help, for the same reason (the masculine adjective *malus* and the neuter *malum* are indistinguishable in the ablative case). And even though the official translation adopted by the Catholic Church today is the generic "deliver us from evil," scholars have been struggling for centuries to try to understand whether Jesus, in the last verse of the Lord's Prayer, meant evil in the neuter or the Evil One in the masculine. Since it is not our intention to enter such a long-standing debate (and unfortunately useless because, at the end of the day, there is no way of knowing with absolute certainty whether *toû ponēroû* is to be understood as masculine or neuter), we will try to expound the reasons (both extremely valid) of the two sides in order to try, if possible, to arrive at a synthesis.

Let us read, as an example, what Daniel Baird Wallace, American Professor of New Testament Studies at Dallas Theological Seminary, has to say about this: "Although the KJV renders this 'deliver us from evil,' the presence of the article indicates not evil in general, but the evil one himself. In the context of Matthew's Gospel, such deliverance from the devil seems to be linked to Jesus' temptation in 4:1–10: Because the Spirit led him into temptation by the evil one, believers now participate in his victory."[1]

Wallace places emphasis on the fact that the Greek expression explicitly contains the article *toû* (τοῦ), implying that, if Jesus had meant evil in general, he would have simply said *apò ponēroû* (ἀπὸ πονηροῦ). However, the argument of the presence of the article that would lean toward the masculine interpretation (the Evil One) is *not* convincing. The use of the article in Greek does not follow the same rules as in English.

---

1. Wallace, "Greek Grammar, Beyond the Basics," 233.

The presence of the article in Greek does not necessarily imply a determination of the object under consideration.[2] The neuter expression *tó ponēron* (τό πονηρόν) does not necessarily mean "this specific evil," but it can easily mean evil in general. There are a variety of examples that demonstrate this.

In chapter 6 of Luke's Gospel, we find both the masculine and the neuter expression: "A good man out of the good treasure of his heart bringeth forth that which is good; and an evil man [*ho ponērós*] out of the evil treasure of his heart bringeth forth that which is evil [*tó ponēron*]: for of the abundance of the heart his mouth speaketh" (Luke 6:45). As we can see, the article, used in both the masculine and the neuter, does not indicate a specific person or a specific evil in either case.

Similarly, in his epistle to the Romans, Paul exhorts them as follows: "Let love be without dissimulation. Abhor that which is evil [*tò ponēron*]; cleave to that which is good [*tò agathón*]" (Rom 12:9). Again, we find the neuter article associated with the generic concept of evil (and of good too).

Likewise, in the third epistle of John, we read: "Beloved, follow not that which is evil [*tò kakòn*], but that which is good [*tò agathón*]" (3 John 1:11). Here, we find *kakón* instead of *ponērón*, but the concept is the same.[3]

Indeed, if we look closely, within the New Testament there are no cases in which, when the generic concept of evil is translated with the neutral singular term *ponērón*, the article is *not* used![4]

However, it is necessary to point out that, indeed, whenever one wants to indicate a specific evil person and, in particular, the Evil One, the article is used. The expression *ho ponērós* (ὁ πονεηρός) is used several times within the New Testament to unequivocally indicate the devil.[5]

For example, in the parable of the sower narrated in the Gospel of Matthew it is said, "When any one heareth the word of the kingdom, and understandeth it not, then cometh the wicked one [*ho ponērós*], and catcheth away that which was sown in his heart. This is he which received seed by the way side" (Matt 13:19). That Jesus is referring to the Evil One is already clear enough from the context, but comparing the text with that of Mark, we are certain of it: "And these are they by the way side, where the word is sown; but when they have heard, Satan cometh immediately, and taketh away the word that was sown in their hearts" (Mark 4:15).

The same can be said of another parable (that of the tares) that Jesus, in the Gospel of Matthew, tells immediately after that of the sower and that, at the precise

---

2. The same is true of Aramaic, the original language of the Lord's Prayer.

3. See Rom 2:9; 7:21; 12:21; 13:4; 16:19; 1 Cor 13:5.

4. More frequent, however, is the use of the neuter plural *ponērá* (πονηρά) without an article, equivalent to "evil things." This does not mean that in Greek the generic concept of evil can never be translated by the simple term *ponērón* (anarthrous). One example out of all is found in Gen 3:5 (LXX): "God knows that when you eat of it, your eyes will be opened and you will become like God, knowing good and evil [γινώσκοντες καλὸν καὶ πονηρόν]."

5. Whereas *ho kakós* (ὁ κακός) is never associated with Satan.

request of his disciples, he explains as follows: "The field is the world; the good seed are the children of the kingdom; but the tares are the children of the wicked one [*toû ponēroú*]; The enemy that sowed them is the devil [*diábolos*]; the harvest is the end of the world; and the reapers are the angels" (Matt 13:38–39). Since it is the devil who has sown the tares, the devil is its father, and the tares represent its children.

In the first epistle of John, we read: "I write unto you, young men, because ye have overcome the wicked one [*tòn ponērón*]" (1 John 2:13). It is not possible to interpret it otherwise. The article *tón* is masculine (not neuter) and must indicate a person. But who can this person be if not the Evil One?

The same reasoning must be done for a passage contained in the same letter: "We know that whosoever is born of God sinneth not; but he that is begotten of God[6] keepeth himself, and that the wicked one [*ho ponērós*] toucheth him not. And we know that we are of God, and the whole world lieth in wickedness [*en tôi ponērôi*]" (1 John 5:18–19). For the different interpretations of this passage, we refer to the footnote. In any case, whether protection from the Evil One derives directly from Jesus Christ ("the one born of God") or simply from the fact of being born of God (that is, believing in Jesus Christ, the Son of God), it is unequivocal that *ho ponērós* indicates here not simply a generic evil person but precisely the Evil One.

At this point, it will be good to pause and try to properly understand the theology that St. John is expounding here, because it is of fundamental importance for the

---

6. The meaning of this expression is a matter of debate. The Greek text reads *ho gennētheís* (ὁ γεννηθεὶς), aorist participle of the verb *gennáō* (γεννάω), which means "to give birth," "to generate." Literally, *ho gennētheís* means "the one who was begotten." Many believe that John is referring here precisely to Jesus Christ, "the only begotten Son of God." According to this interpretation it is Jesus himself who protects from the Evil One all those who are begotten of God, *pâs ho gegennēménos* (πᾶς ὁ γεγεννημένος), that is, all those who, by baptizing and believing in Jesus Christ, renounce Satan and become "sons of God" (John 3:4–5). The grammatical distinction between "all who are begotten of God" at the beginning of verse 18 and "the one who was begotten of God" is usually emphasized as evidence that the former are to be understood as those who are converted to the gospel and the latter is instead the only begotten Son of God. *Gegennēménos* is a perfect participle indicating a continuous action ("those who continue to be born of God"), while *gennētheís* is an aorist participle indicating a finite action accomplished in time ("the one who was begotten of God," that is, Jesus Christ). It should also be considered that the expression *ho gennētheís* is used, among all of John's writings, only in this passage. Normally, the perfect participle is preferred (John 3:8; 1 John 3:9). Others, however, believe that the two expressions simply have the same meaning, notwithstanding the slight grammatical distinction. "He who was begotten of God" would not be understood as Jesus Christ, but simply as all those who, being born of God, have become his legitimate children. *Ho gennētheís* would simply be a restatement of the same concept introduced just before by *ho gegennēménos*. The whole sentence would be understood as follows: "We know that whoever is born of God does not sin: and whoever is born of God preserves himself, and the Evil One does not touch him." One difficulty with this type of translation is the use of the reflexive "himself," which does not appear in the original Greek text. Some (including Calvin) read the personal pronoun *autòn* (αὐτὸν), meaning "him," in the reflexive sense *heautòn* (ἑαυτὸν), meaning "himself," but it seems more of an unwarranted stretch. St. Jerome, author of the Latin translation of the Vulgate, adopts a third interpretive way, one that does not require the reflexive forcing, but retains the meaning. *Ho gennētheís* would be interpreted emphatically as a *nominativus pendens*: "he who was begotten of God, (this fact) protects him and the Evil One does not touch him." St. Jerome uses the expression *generatio Dei conservat eum*, that is, "the fact of having been generated by God protects him."

continuation of our reasoning. What does it mean that "whosoever is born of God sinneth not"? And what does it mean that he who is born of God cannot be touched by the Evil One?

Let us take a brief step back. In the opening of his first epistle, John elaborates on the relationship between the believer and sin as follows:

> This then is the message which we have heard of him, and declare unto you, that God is light, and in him is no darkness at all. If we say that we have fellowship with him, and walk in darkness, we lie, and do not the truth: But if we walk in the light, as he is in the light, we have fellowship one with another, and the blood of Jesus Christ his Son cleanseth us from all sin. If we say that we have no sin, we deceive ourselves, and the truth is not in us. If we confess our sins, he is faithful and just to forgive us our sins, and to cleanse us from all unrighteousness. If we say that we have not sinned, we make him a liar, and his word is not in us. (1 John 1:5–10)

And again:

> My little children, these things write I unto you, that ye sin not. And if any man sin, we have an advocate with the Father, Jesus Christ the righteous: And he is the propitiation for our sins: and not for ours only, but also for the sins of the whole world. And hereby we do know that we know him, if we keep his commandments. He that saith, I know him, and keepeth not his commandments, is a liar, and the truth is not in him. But whoso keepeth his word, in him verily is the love of God perfected: hereby know we that we are in him. He that saith he abideth in him ought himself also so to walk, even as he walked. (1 John 2:1–6)

How can this passage be reconciled with the definitive ruling we just read that "whosoever is born of God sinneth not"? To understand this, we must get to the end of the first epistle: "If any man see his brother sin a sin which is not unto death, he shall ask, and he shall give him life for them that sin not unto death. There is a sin unto death: I do not say that he shall pray for it. All unrighteousness is sin: and there is a sin not unto death" (1 John 5:16–17).

Putting together the *incipit* and the conclusion of the first epistle, we understand how John is talking about the "sin unto death," the mortal sin, that is, the serious sin committed in full conscience and conviction. Whoever is born of God does not commit this kind of sin, otherwise we would be lying to ourselves. But we would be lying (and we would not be true children of God) even if we said that we do not commit any (venial) sin. But for these sins, the sacrifice of Jesus Christ on the cross is sufficient—his blood erases them. It is enough to acknowledge them.

For John, being without (mortal) sin and being children of God (in Christ) are two identical concepts. It is an axiom. If one falls, so does the other. Therefore, to commit (mortal) sin is not to be children of God, but of the Evil One. And vice versa, "Whosoever abideth in him sinneth not: whosoever sinneth hath not seen him, neither known him. ( . . . ) He that committeth sin is of the devil; for the devil sinneth from the beginning. For this purpose the Son of God was manifested, that he might destroy the works of the devil. Whosoever is born of God doth not commit sin; for his seed remaineth in him: and he cannot sin, because he is born of God" (1 John 3:6; 8–9).

Johannine theology does not allow for nuance. The distinction between light (Christ) and darkness (the kingdom of the Evil One—the world) is absolute. Where light ends, darkness begins. And vice versa. Either we are in the light, or we are in the darkness. Whoever is in the darkness, whoever is of the world, that is, has not believed in Christ, is automatically a child of the Evil One and is in mortal sin (and vice versa). On the other hand, he who is in the light, that is, who believed in Christ and automatically became a child of God, does not commit mortal sin (and vice versa). And the Evil One cannot "touch" him. Why? Because there is a clear separation between light and darkness. The Evil One lives and dwells in the darkness and cannot enter the light. Whoever dwells in the light is automatically safe from the Evil One. And what makes us dwell in the light? The unshakable faith in Christ.

We see, then, that the whole debate about whether those who are born of God are protected from the Evil One by virtue of their status as children of God or by virtue of Christ's saving intervention is probably a matter of hairsplitting. After all, on closer inspection, the two concepts converge.

Similar considerations are also found in the sixth chapter of the epistle to the Ephesians, where St. Paul urges them to confront the Evil One and his legion of evil spirits with the inexhaustible power of faith:

> Put on the whole armour of God, that ye may be able to stand against the wiles of the devil [*toû diabólou*]. For we wrestle not against flesh and blood, but against principalities, against powers, against the rulers of the darkness of this world, against spiritual wickedness in high places. Wherefore take unto you the whole armour of God, that ye may be able to withstand in the evil day, and having done all, to stand. Stand therefore, having your loins girt about with truth, and having on the breastplate of righteousness; And your feet shod with the preparation of the gospel of peace; Above all, taking the shield of faith, wherewith ye shall be able to quench all the fiery darts of the wicked [*toû ponēroû*]. (Eph 6:11–16)

Again, given the context, the fiery darts are unequivocally from the Evil One, and not from a generic evil. The "fiery darts of the wicked [*toû ponēroû*]" in verse 15 correspond to the "wiles of the devil [*toû diabólou*]" in verse 11. Paul uses a very particular term here to refer to the wiles of the Evil One, *methodeías* (μεθοδείας). It is a term that appears only twice within the New Testament and both times in the same letter to the Ephesians. In chapter 4, we read: "That we henceforth be no more children, tossed to and fro, and carried about with every wind of doctrine, by the sleight of men, and cunning craftiness, whereby they lie in wait to deceive [*methodeía*]" (Eph 4:14).

"Sleight," "craftiness," "lie," "deceive." In an emphatic crescendo of synonyms, Paul is here alluding to those false prophets who in the pagan Greek world, with the counterfeit art of eloquence, used sophistry and rhetorical tricks to corrupt the message of the gospel. We understand at this point what these "fiery darts" and snares are that are designed by the Evil One himself. They are the false doctrines, which, mixing orthodoxy and heresies, tended to spread in pagan circles and to confuse and mislead "the children of God" to make them return under the dominion of darkness, from which they had come out by divine grace. In these false doctrines Paul clearly sees the hand of the Evil One. This is why Paul admonishes the Ephesians, reminding them that the battle at this point is no longer against mere people, made of flesh and blood, but precisely against those satanic powers that, using people, will devise every kind of trick and trap to crack the armor of the faith of the children of God and bring them back under their control.

Putting together the writings of John and Paul on this subject, we have at this point a clear view of their thinking. Before Christ, people find themselves in a condition of subjection to the Evil One, because they dwell in the world, which, by definition, is the kingdom of darkness (the Evil One is also called "the Prince of the world"). World, darkness, subjection to the Evil One—these are three expressions that define the condition of the absence of God. When Christ enters the world, he brings a light for the first time, a light that creates a gash in the darkness (John 1:9). Whoever among the people of the world recognizes and believes in Jesus Christ, accepts the light he brings and, in this way, escapes the dominion of the Evil One. He passes from the world of darkness into light. The fact that the message of Christ is revealed to the heart of a person and that person is converted and believes is, however, only divine merit. It is a grace granted by God and that has nothing to do with any earthly merits (good works) of the person (Eph 2:8–10). Once, by divine grace, people transit from darkness to light, they are born again of God and become to all intents and purposes his children. And as long as they remain in the light, the Evil One no longer has any power over them.

Does this mean that the Evil One is resigned and can no longer do anything? Absolutely not. The Evil One will try in every way, with his tricks and snares, to bring those people back under his rule, until the last moment of their life. Therefore, all believers, to remain firm in the light, will have to gird themselves with the armor of faith, which will protect them from every possible vicious attempt of the Evil One. It is the constant battle, of which Paul speaks, against the satanic forces that every believer will have to fight daily. It is that battle of which, as we have already mentioned, Pope Leo XIII had a clear vision in 1884, following which he composed the famous *Oratio ad Sanctum Michael*,[7] in which he asks the archangel to cast into hell "Satan and all the evil spirits that prowl about the world seeking the ruin of souls."

People can win this battle by means of two elements:

---

7. *Prayer to St. Michael.*

1. the armor of God, as Paul defines it, that is, the protection of the Holy Spirit, which people must continually ask the Father to send into their heart to make them steadfast in faith;

2. one's own strength of will, strengthened by faith, which drives people to ultimately choose good over evil.

At this point it is necessary to return to a passage to which we have previously alluded. It is found in Luke's Gospel in chapter 22 where the Last Supper is recounted. Jesus reveals to his disciples one of his greatest concerns now that he is about to leave the world. The Evil One will target them, trying to sap their faith: "And the Lord said, Simon, Simon, behold, Satan hath requested[8] to have you, that he may sift you as wheat: But I have prayed for thee, that thy faith fail not: and you, in turn,[9] strengthen thy brethren. And he said unto him, Lord, I am ready to go with thee, both into prison, and to death. And he said, I tell thee, Peter, the cock shall not crow this day, before that thou shalt thrice deny that thou knowest me" (Luke 22:31–34).

Let us analyze this passage slowly because we can draw interesting insights from it. The opening reads, "Simon, Simon." The repetition of the vocative is not accidental. It is reminiscent of the expression used by Jesus to reprimand Martha: "Martha, Martha, you worry and fret about many things, but only one thing is needed. Mary has chosen the best part, which will not be taken away from her" (Luke 10:41–42). It is a good-natured way of expressing a reproach, but also a grave concern. Just as the use of the name Simon, instead of Peter, is not accidental. Jesus wants to highlight all his human weakness, in contrast with the naive bravado of his disciple, obviously unaware of the power of the Evil One. Jesus reveals to Simon Peter that Satan has requested him and the other apostles to sift them like wheat.

We have already had occasion to comment on this prayer of Satan (to God). The verb used by Luke is very particular: *exaitéō* (ἐξαιτέω) indicates the action of forcefully asking, of claiming for oneself with evil intentions. Satan insistently prayed to God that his will was that the Apostles be sifted, that is, harassed by him, as one does with wheat. The verb *siniázō* (σινιάζω) indicates the action of sifting, which implies a mighty agitation that overturns the grains of wheat. Jesus is here prophesying the extreme persecutions and tribulations to which each of them will be subjected by the forces of evil (most of them will die martyrs). Will their faith be strong enough to withstand the attacks of the Evil One? For this reason, Jesus reveals to Peter that he has prayed for him, so that his faith will not waver.

It is interesting to note how Jesus, even though the Evil One's aims are directed at all the Apostles ("Satan has requested you [*plural*]"), says that he has prayed specifically for Peter ("but I have prayed for you [*singular*]"). Some interpret this detail as an allusion to the fact that Peter, of all the Apostles, will be the one who will fall most

---

8. The KJV has "desired."
9. The KJV has "when thou art converted."

thunderously (when he denies Jesus three times), and therefore the most in need of prayer. This explanation is not convincing, for several reasons.

First, if so, it would mean that Jesus' prayer was unsuccessful. Although Jesus prayed for him, Peter fell at the first occasion. Is it possible that Jesus' prayer before the Father was completely ignored, when instead Satan's prayer seems to have been answered? Hard to believe.

Second, the temptation into which Peter falls when he denies Jesus has little to do with Satan and much to do with Peter's own human weakness. And how can we be so sure? Well, do you remember the passage in which St. Augustine explained that not all temptations are performed by the devil, but that there are also temptations that are, so to speak, "human," that is, due to human frailty and weakness? The example St. Augustine gave to illustrate a temptation that is not satanic is precisely the episode in which Peter denied the Lord, not because he was attacked by Satan, but because he was simply terrified at that moment.[10]

Third, Peter immediately senses that Jesus is prophesying something serious (and not a harmless question from a servant of the high priest) and swears he is "ready to go to prison and to death." Jesus, almost touched by the naivety of his disciple, replies with the prophecy of the rooster that will not crow before Peter has denied him three times. As if to say, you tell me that you are ready to die for me, as if you did not even need my prayer, but I tell you that at the first trivial occasion, you will fall thunderously. Not once, but three times. And just as I have prayed for you, you, in turn,[11] give strength to the others to stand firm in the faith.

This prayer of Jesus that Peter's faith may not waver, reported by Luke, is probably the same as the one John speaks of in chapter 17 of his Gospel, in which Jesus, addressing the Father directly during the Last Supper, asks him to maintain his disciples out of the influence of the Evil One: "I have given them thy word; and the world hath hated them, because they are not of the world, even as I am not of the world. I pray not that thou shouldest take them out of the world, but that thou shouldest keep them from the evil [*ek toû ponēroû*]. They are not of the world, even as I am not of the world" (John 17:14–16).

We find here the fundamental concept of Johannine theology: the world, depicted as the kingdom of darkness of which the Evil One is the undisputed prince, as opposed to the light of Christ and his disciples. Jesus specifically asks the Father not to "take them out of the world," that is, not to shorten their life on earth (with all its sufferings), but to give them the strength to remain upright in the faith in the face of every type of persecution to which the world, which "hated them," led by the Evil

---

10. Augustine, *De sermone Domini in monte*, 2.9.34.

11. We believe that the expression "in turn" is a more logical translation of the participle *epistrépsas* (ἐπιστρέψας), which literally means "returned," than translations such as "once converted," or "once repentant." It is unclear what Peter is supposed to be converted from or repented of. For having repudiated him? Christ is simply outlining a line of succession. Christ is praying to protect Peter, the head of the church, who *in turn* will be responsible for protecting the church itself (see John 21:15–17).

One, will subject them. Persecutions that, it is good to remember, are the precise will of the Father. In fact, Jesus does not pray that his disciples be spared from this kind of *peirasmós* ("I pray not that thou shouldest take them out of the world") but that, once in *peirasmós*, they keep the faith by remaining in the light without transitioning back to the darkness ("but that thou shouldest keep them from the evil"). Jesus' prayer is that the Apostles remain "in the world" to suffer and bear testimony of their faith (as light in the darkness), but at the same time be maintained "out of" (*ek toû*) the evil of the world.[12] This implies that Satan's pressing request to God to persecute the Apostles (all scholars agree on this) seems to have been granted, thus making it a precise will of the Father.

At this point, we have gathered enough material[13] to be able to make the following statements:

1. The use of the article *toû* in front of the adjective *ponēroû* does not necessarily imply that Jesus is referring to the Evil One.

2. When *ponēroû* simply means a generic evil, it is more common to find the article than not.

3. If Jesus had meant the Evil One, the expression *apò toû ponēroû* is exactly what we would expect to encounter.

4. If Jesus had meant evil in general, the expression *apò toû ponēroû* is very likely what we would expect to encounter.

5. In all those cases where, from a purely grammatical point of view, the declension of the neuter of the adjective *ponērós* is indistinguishable from that of the masculine, the context, most of the times, indicates that *ponērós* is to be understood as the Evil One.[14] Why should the case of the Lord's Prayer be an exception?

6. Whenever the verb *rhýomai* is associated with deliverance from evil, the Evil One never appears. Why should the case of the Lord's Prayer be an exception?

As we can see, both positions have their good reasons for supporting one or the other thesis. Which one of the two is more likely? It is hard to say. Nor is it possible to

---

12. It is important to notice here that the expression "keep them from the evil" is substantially different from the seventh petition of the Lord's Prayer. The verb *tēréō* (τηρέω) means "to keep," "to maintain." It does not have any connotation of "deliverance," implied by the *rhýomai* of the seventh petition. *Tēréō* is a static verb, while *rhýomai* is dynamic. *Tēréō* refers to the continuation of the *status quo*. The apostles are "in the light," and God is asked to give them strength *to remain* "in the light." He is not asked to "deliver them from evil" (*apò toû ponēroû*). He is asked to "maintain them out of evil" (*ek toû ponēroû*), that is, "out the darkness," that is, "in the light." Hence, it would be incorrect to use John 17:15 to explain the seventh petition of the Lord's Prayer.

13. There are other passages in which the term *ponēroû* appears. In 1 John 3:2 it obviously refers to the Evil One (based on context); in 2 Thess 3:3 it obviously refers to evil and perverse people (based on context); in Matt 5:37 it is not clear: it could refer to both.

14. This is a purely statistical figure, collected on a small sample, so it should be taken with caution.

dismiss the debate by claiming that in the end, since the Evil One is the prince of evil, evil and Evil One coincide. For if it is true that, by definition, every work of the Evil One is evil, the reverse is not true. Not every evil that happens to a person is the work of the Evil One. On the basis of this simple consideration alone, it would be reductive, in the absence of absolute certainty as to how *apò toû ponēroû* should be interpreted, to render the seventh petition as "but deliver us from the Evil One." If only because we would run the risk of leaving out an important slice of the possible meaning of this expression. And so, it seems to us that the official translation "but deliver us from evil" is also the more reasonable one, because it is the more conservative (it includes both possibilities).

In conclusion, we believe that the most honest position is to consider the expression *apò toû ponēroû* as a request for deliverance from evil, which also includes deliverance from the clutches of the Evil One—but not only, and not necessarily. And in order to get the full picture, we will list below the main types of evil from which we may ask, in theory, to be delivered:

1. Evil in the sense of temptation to sin (moral *peirasmós*), that is, induction to moral evil (concupiscence of the flesh, avarice, hatred, selfishness, envy, and so forth). This type of evil is inherent in our flesh (Gal 5:19–21) and is used by the Evil One, who leverages our perverse instincts to make us fall into temptation. This is a type of *peirasmós* that does not come from God,[15] but from the free will of Satan, who, with the freedom granted to him by God, wanders the world in search of souls to devour (1 Pet 5:8).

2. Evil in the sense of psychophysical tribulation (psychophysical *peirasmós*). This kind of evil may come from God. And it may (but not necessarily) be imparted by means of Satan, who would act in this case as a mere instrument executor of the divine will, for varied reasons and in different ways. It seems to us that we can identify at least five different types of psychophysical *peirasmós*:

    a. *Fortifying psychophysical peirasmós*: this is the evil that God sends to temper the faith of believers. If the believer remains firm in faith, he will obtain the "crown of life" (Rev 2:10; Jas 1:12).

    b. *Purifying psychophysical peirasmós*: this is the evil that God sends to forge the souls of those believers who still have too much dross in their souls, to prepare them for the encounter with God.

    c. *Pedagogic psychophysical peirasmós*: this is the evil that God sends to humiliate the souls that he still wants to save, but that sin in pride and have turned away from him. Humiliation is the last opportunity that God gives

---

15. God has nothing to do with moral evil and, the Evil One, in order to impart this kind of evil, does not need to pray to God to be granted the faculty to do so.

to that soul to realize that it has deviated from the right path and thus return to him.

d. *Expiatory psychophysical peirasmós*: it is the evil that God sends to the souls that are dearest to him, so that they may share, without being responsible for any specific fault, the sufferings of Christ on the cross and thus collaborate (in an infinitesimal way compared to Christ, but still significant in God's eyes) in the atonement for the sins committed by past, present and future sinners. It is the ultimate expression of divine mercy.[16]

e. *Punitive psychophysical peirasmós*: this is the evil that God sends as just punishment for the sins we commit. It is the ultimate expression of divine justice.

This list, while not claiming to be exhaustive, paints a general picture that encompasses most of the evils that can befall people. As we can see, the different types are not necessarily mutually exclusive and do not necessarily imply the intervention of the Evil One. So, there we have it. If, at this point in our analysis, it is still premature to try to figure out what exact type of *peirasmós* Jesus is talking about in the sixth petition of the Lord's Prayer, one concept should be clear by now. Of all the possible types of *peirasmós* listed above, the one we feel certain to exclude is the first (the moral one). For the rest, we still have to dig deeper.

And yet. Yet, the supporters of the thesis that the *ponērón* in the seventh petition cannot refer to anything other than the Evil One (*ergo* the *peirasmós* in the sixth petition must coincide with moral temptation) do not give up. They try to reduce the Lord's Prayer to a sort of exorcism that would keep every evil spirit away from us.[17] And they try to prove their thesis by shifting attention to an unprecedented archaeological discovery, dating back to the middle of the last century when, almost by accident, some Bedouins of the Desert of Judea found in the Caves of Qumran (on the northwestern shore of the Dead Sea) several texts containing the oldest copy of the Hebrew Bible known so far, along with hundreds of other extra-biblical, apocryphal, and pseudo-epigraphic documents. These manuscripts date back to a period that covers more than three centuries (from the third century BC to the first century AD), exactly the time span preceding and contemporary to Jesus Christ. For this reason, they can give a valuable insight into the religious-cultural *humus* in which Jesus was born and grew up.

They are known as the Dead Sea Scrolls.

---

16. We will elaborate on this theme in later chapters.

17. See, for example, Boice, *The Sermon on the Mount*, 205: "Keep us from wandering into paths where we will be tempted by the devil; but if he comes, keep us out of his clutches."

# 22

# The Dead Sea Scrolls and the Extra-Biblical Tradition

In a time span of about ten years, from 1946 to 1956, researchers were able to collect from eleven of the twelve Qumran Caves something like 981 manuscripts, most of which unfortunately, damaged by time and man, contain only a few fragments of text.[1] Only a dozen scrolls have been preserved almost intact. Scholars believe that several of these manuscripts were written by the Jewish sects (perhaps the Essenes) that formed the community of Qumran. They represent the religious literature that circulated abundantly in Judea from the third century BC to the first century AD. Most of the scrolls are made from animal skins and are written in Hebrew (about 90–95 percent). Only a few texts are written in Aramaic and Greek. About 40 percent of the texts are Hebrew copies of Scripture and, as mentioned, represent the most ancient version of the Hebrew Bible known today. About 30 percent of the texts, on the other hand, contain apocryphal material, which was never officially canonized within Hebrew Scripture. These include some apocryphal psalms, which we will have a chance to analyze. The rest represents a composition of rules, beliefs, and habits specific to the Qumran sects.

So, let us come to the point. What would be these original texts within the 981 manuscripts of the Dead Sea Scrolls that would demonstrate how the sixth and seventh petition of the Lord's Prayer are essentially a prayer of deliverance from evil spirits?

Let us read, for example, what Dr. Bradford Humes Young, Professor of Biblical Literature at the Center for Judaeo-Christian Studies at Oral Roberts University in Oklahoma, writes about this: "The basic sense of the Hebrew word נִסָּיוֹן (ni-sa-YON, temptation) is 'test' or 'trial.' ( . . . ) In the Lord's Prayer, the word 'temptation' seems

---

1. About 90 percent of the texts were found in Cave 4 alone, where something like 15,000 fragments were collected.

to be related to man's inclination to sin. ( . . . ) 'Deliver us from evil,' the second part of the parallelism, goes beyond the idea of trial and introduces a plea for deliverance from the forces of evil. Jewish prayers from Jesus' time exhibit an awareness of the power of evil which has the potential to overpower an individual. Prayers appealing to God for deliverance from this power have been found in the Dead Sea Scrolls."[2]

Although it is admitted that the basic meaning of the term *nissāyôn* is not "moral temptation" but "trial," for some mysterious reason, in the Lord's Prayer this term must nevertheless be associated with "man's inclination to sin," that is, with what we defined in the previous chapter as moral *peirasmós*. And from what is this inferred? From the fact that the seventh petition represents "a plea for deliverance from the forces of evil." And what would demonstrate this? "Jewish prayers from Jesus' time" found in the Dead Sea Scrolls. Well, let us read these prayers immediately, then!

Actually, all this buzz and excitement revolves around not multiple, undefined "prayers," but only around a couple of verses. Not a couple of prayers: a couple of verses. Among the thousands that have been found in the Scrolls.

The first verse is found in Psalm 155 (apocryphal) discovered in Qumran Cave 11, in which we read: "Remember me and don't forget me, and don't lead me into situations [too] difficult for me" (11QPs[a] xxiv.11).

The similarity with the sixth petition of the Lord's Prayer is obvious. First of all, the predicate: "don't lead me into." In the text of the Scrolls, one finds the causative (*hiphil*) form of the Hebrew verb *bô'* (בוֹא), which means "to enter." The same form that most likely underlies the *eisphérō* found in the Lord's Prayer texts of Matthew and Luke. And where do we ask that God not lead us? Into temptation? No, simply "into difficult situations." The Hebrew term used is the feminine plural of the adjective *qāshĕh* (קָשֶׁה), which has all of the following meanings: hard, difficult, painful, laborious, heavy, severe, serious, intense, cruel, vehement, and so forth.

If we were to, simply from this verse (taken out of context), decide whether this is a prayer for deliverance from tribulation or from satanic temptation, we would have no doubt about it. But, for intellectual honesty, let us read all the apocryphal Psalm 155.[3]

> 1. XXIV O Lord, I have called to Thee, hear me.
> 2. I have spread out my hands towards Thy holy dwelling-place.
> 3. Turn Thine ear and grant me my request,
> 4. and do not withhold my plea from me.
> 5. Construct my soul and do not cast it away,
> 6. and do not leave it alone before the wicked.
> 7. May the true judge turn away from me the rewards of evil.
> 8. Lord, do not judge me according to my sins, for no living man is righteous before Thee.
> 9. Lord, cause me to understand Thy Law and teach me Thy judgements.

2. Young, *Jewish Background*, 31–32.
3. For the translation of the Scrolls, we will follow Vermes, *Dead Sea Scrolls in English*.

10. And the multitude shall hear of Thy deeds, and peoples shall honour Thy glory.

11. Remember me and forget me not, and bring me not to unbearable hardships.

12. Put away from me the sin of my youth, and may my sins not be remembered against me.

13. Lord, cleanse me from the evil plague, and let it not return to me.

14. Dry up its roots within me, and permit not its leaves to flourish in me.

15. Lord, Thou art glory; therefore my plea is fulfilled before Thee.

16. 6 To whom shall I cry so that he will grant it to me? What more can the po[wer] of the sons of men do?

17. From before Thee, O Lord, comes my trust. I cried to the Lord and he answered me; he healed the brokenness of my heart.

18. 8 I was sleepy [and I] slept; I dreamt and also [I awoke].

19. [Lord, Thou didst support me when my heart was stricken, and I called upon the Lor]d [my saviour].

20. Now I will see their shame; I have relied on Thee, and I will not be ashamed. (Render glory for ever and ever.)

21. Redeem Israel, Thy pious one, O Lord, and the house of Jacob, Thine elect.[4]
($11QPs^a$ xxiv.1–21)

Is this all? And this would be a prayer that contains a plea for deliverance from the forces of evil? No evil spirit and no Evil One is ever mentioned by chance. On the contrary, there is always the usual insistent request to make sure that God does not leave us alone in the hands (not of the Evil One), but of the wicked. On the other hand, there are several requests for God to forgive all the sins committed, among which there is the request not to be led by God in situations that are difficult for us, that is, hard, painful, distressing, and so forth (G. Vermes translates with "unbearable hardships"). This is clearly referring to a punitive psychophysical *peirasmós* (as we defined it in the previous chapter). In other words, the request is as follows: "God, please, forgive my sins, and do not punish me too severely."

Interesting, indeed. We started with the hypothesis that this psalm (apocryphal, by the way) demonstrated that the sixth petition of the Lord's Prayer may allude to a moral *peirasmós*, and we must conclude that it supports instead the idea of a punitive psychophysical *peirasmós*.

Let us then turn to the other verse, to see if it has more substance. It is found in the so-called *Plea for Deliverance*, a poetic composition written in a biblical psalm style, discovered in Qumran Cave 11 as well: "Let neither Satan nor an unclean spirit rule over me; let neither pain nor an evil instinct take possession of my bones" ($11QPs^a$ xix.15–16).

---

4. Vermes, *Dead Sea Scrolls in English*, 360–61.

Here we go. Satan has finally appeared. But not alone. He is associated with the impure spirits, that is, the army of evil spirits under his command. Also interesting is the second part of the verse in which, in addition to Satan and his army of evil, reference is made to (physical) pain and perverse instinct (remember the famous *yētsĕr*?). So, we find—condensed into a couple of verses—various kinds of "evil," internal and external, physical and moral. All mixed together. With the hope/request that God will see to it that none of these take possession of us.

So what? What is this short verse—extrapolated from an apocryphal composition—supposed to prove? That the Lord's Prayer is a prayer of deliverance from evil spirits? The conclusion seems to us, to be benevolent, far-fetched. Do we really need to bother with a verse from an apocryphal psalm of a minor sect that lived on the shores of the Dead Sea? Is it possible to draw any logical connection between the beliefs of this sect and the teachings of Jesus? We doubt it.

Especially when we consider that a similar—almost identical—verse is found in a *canonical* psalm. It is Psalm 119(118). In verse 133, we read: "Order my steps in thy word: and let not any iniquity have dominion over me" (Ps 119(118):133).

The construction is identical, both grammatically and syntactically. Let us compare the two texts (from right to left):

| | | | | |
|---|---|---|---|---|
| Ps 119(118):133 | כָּל אָוֶן | בִּי | תַּשְׁלֶט | אַל |
| | any iniquity | over me | have dominion | Let not |
| 11QPs$^a$ xix.15 | שטן | בי | תשלט | אל |
| | Satan | over me | have dominion | Let not |

The verb used is also the same: *shālăt* (שָׁלַט), which means "to rule," "to dominate," "to have power over something or someone."[5] The only difference is in the subject of the action. In the apocryphal psalm, reference is made to Satan. The term used in the canonical text, on the other hand, is 'āwĕn (אָוֶן), which indicates a generic evil action, an injustice. But what kind of injustice? An injustice committed *by us* or *against us*? Are we asking God not to be oppressed by our injustice or by the injustice others commit against us?

To understand this, we need only broaden our vision a bit and read the context in which verse 133 appears within Psalm 119(118):

> I hate vain thoughts: but thy law do I love. Thou art my hiding place and my shield: I hope in thy word. Depart from me, ye evildoers: for I will keep the commandments of my God. Uphold me according unto thy word, that I may live: and let me not be ashamed of my hope. Hold thou me up, and I shall be safe: and I will have respect unto thy statutes continually. Thou hast trodden down all them that err from thy statutes: for their deceit is falsehood. Thou puttest away all the wicked of the earth like dross: therefore I love thy

---

5. From a related Arabic root comes the term "sultan."

testimonies. My flesh trembleth for fear of thee; and I am afraid of thy judgments. I have done judgment and justice: leave me not to mine oppressors. Be surety for thy servant for good: let not the proud oppress me. Mine eyes fail for thy salvation, and for the word of thy righteousness. Deal with thy servant according unto thy mercy, and teach me thy statutes. I am thy servant; give me understanding, that I may know thy testimonies. It is time for thee, Lord, to work: for they have made void thy law. Therefore I love thy commandments above gold; yea, above fine gold. Therefore I esteem all thy precepts concerning all things to be right; and I hate every false way. Thy testimonies are wonderful: therefore doth my soul keep them. The entrance of thy words giveth light; it giveth understanding unto the simple. I opened my mouth, and panted: for I longed for thy commandments. Look thou upon me, and be merciful unto me, as thou usest to do unto those that love thy name. Order my steps in thy word: and let not any iniquity have dominion over me. Deliver me from the oppression of man: so will I keep thy precepts. Make thy face to shine upon thy servant; and teach me thy statutes. Rivers of waters run down mine eyes, because they keep not thy law. (Ps 119(118):113–136)

Depart from me, ye evildoers. Leave me not to mine oppressors. Let not the proud oppress me. Let not any iniquity have dominion over me. Deliver me from the oppression of man. Is there any doubt left? It is clear *from the context* that the injustices spoken of are those perpetrated by the ungodly, the wicked, the proud, the oppressors, against us. Our sins are not being spoken of. So, we find that the canonical verse, corresponding to the apocryphal verse, contains a plea for deliverance not from Satan, not from moral temptations, but from the oppression of the proud. Who are the proud? The Hebrew term denoting them is zēdîm (זֵדִים), which literally means "inflated." They are the insolent, the arrogant, those who sin in *hýbris*, that is, those who refuse God's help believing themselves invincible and above God himself. They are the idolaters, the pagans, those who have no fear of God and of his punishments, who have no moral restraint and have no qualms about tormenting and persecuting the God-fearing. Hence, the plea for deliverance. As long as I am oppressed (physically and psychologically) by them, says the psalmist, I will not be free to follow your precepts. But if you, God, deliver me, then I will be able to obey you fully.[6]

6. Although the context is clear, a large number of interpreters and scholars nevertheless prefer to see in this verse a deliverance not from an external enemy (the proud), but from an internal enemy, namely our sinful instincts. They cite in this regard a similar passage found in Ps 19(18):13(14), which the KJV translates as follows: "Keep back thy servant also from presumptuous sins; let them not have dominion over me: then shall I be upright, and I shall be innocent from the great transgression." This translation has an underlying ineliminable weakness. What is rendered by "presumptuous sins" is actually the very term zēdîm (זֵדִים), which, as we have seen, denotes "the proud." This noun appears thirteen times in the Old Testament, and all the times it means nothing more than "the proud." Insolent people made of flesh. Nothing to do with "presumptuous sins." This translation, in addition to being obviously forced, is, on closer inspection, completely unnecessary. In fact, the straightforward translation is also the one that makes the most sense: "Protect your servant even from the proud; let them not rule over me. Then I shall be spotless and cleansed from great sin." As we can see, the request

## Eis Peirasmón

Once this concept is clarified, let us return to the apocryphal composition containing Satan. Even if we pretend not to know that this verse is part of a canonical psalm in which neither Satan nor evil spirits are mentioned at all, are we sure that what has been called *Plea for Deliverance* is really a request for liberation from the Evil One? To understand it, it is enough to widen our vision and take just a couple of minutes to read all the apocryphal text:

> For no worm thanks Thee, nor a maggot recounts Thy lovingkindness.
> 
> Only the living thank Thee, all they whose feet totter, thank Thee, when Thou makest known to them Thy loving-kindness, and causest them to understand Thy righteousness.
> 
> For the soul of all the living is in Thy hand; Thou hast given breath to all flesh.
> 
> O Lord, do towards us according to Thy goodness, according to the greatness of Thy mercies, and according to the greatness of Thy righteous deeds.
> 
> The Lord listens to the voice of all who love his name and does not permit his loving-kindness to depart from them.
> 
> Blessed be the Lord, doer of righteous deeds, who crowns his pious ones with loving-kindness and mercies.
> 
> My soul shouts to praise Thy name, to praise with jubilation Thy mercies, to announce Thy faithfulness; there is no limit to Thy praises.
> 
> I belonged to death because of my sins, and my iniquities had sold me to Sheol.
> 
> But Thou didst save me, O Lord, according to the greatness of Thy mercies, according to the greatness of Thy righteous deeds.
> 
> I, too, have loved Thy name, and have taken refuge in Thy shadow.
> 
> When I remember Thy power, my heart is strengthened and I rely on Thy mercies.
> 
> Forgive my sins, O Lord, and purify me of my iniquity.
> 
> Grant me a spirit of faithfulness and knowledge; let me not be dishonoured in ruin.
> 
> Let not Belial[7] dominate me, nor an unclean spirit; let pain and the evil inclination not possess my bones.
> 
> For Thou, O Lord, art my praise, and I hope in Thee every day. My brethren rejoice with me and the house of my father is astounded by Thy graciousness.
> 
> ( . . . ) for ever I will rejoice in Thee.[8]
> 
> (11QPs^a xix.1–18)

---

is always the same: deliverance from the oppression of the wicked, who by their violence do not allow the righteous to follow the divine dictates. Interesting to note the translation of the Septuagint, which renders *zēdîm* with *allótrioi* (ἀλλότριοι), that is, the foreigners, the pagans, the idolaters (although the Septuagint may have confused זָרִים, foreigners, with זֵדִים, proud).

7. Vermes decided to translate *sātān* (שטן) with Belial, the demon of wickedness.

8. Vermes, *Dead Sea Scrolls in English*, 361–62.

The first thing to notice is how the composition is almost perfectly divided into two *stanzas* of nine verses each. The first one contains a series of praises, which, if they were not addressed to God, we could define as "rapturous" and redundant, to the goodness and mercy of God. In a rhetorical *crescendo*, entire phrases or expressions are repeated multiple times ("according to Thy goodness, according to the greatness of Thy mercies, and according to the greatness of Thy righteous deeds"). All this is done to prepare for the second *stanza*, in which the reason for so much gratitude on the part of the psalmist is finally explained. And the key passage is certainly not the one containing Satan and evil spirits (which are counted among the different types of evil that can afflict people) but the following, which is located right in the middle of the psalm: "I belonged to death because of my sins, and my iniquities had sold me to Sheol[9]. But Thou didst save me, O Lord, according to the greatness of Thy mercies, according to the greatness of Thy righteous deeds."

And, if it is not clear enough, the psalmist goes on to say, "Forgive my sins, O Lord, and purify me of my iniquity." We understand then that the real plea is for deliverance from the consequences of sin, rather than the causes. The psalmist delves into that series of repetitive praises because, he admits, he was in a situation of mortal sin—he had by then one foot in hell—but, despite that, the divine mercy intervened, purified him by forgiving all his sins, and saved him from eternal condemnation. It is not by chance that God's saving action is mentioned in verse 10 (where the idea of hell appears) and not in verse 15 (where Satan appears). The psalmist is so grateful for God's loving mercy because he is fully aware that God could have easily punished (and not forgiven) him if he had wanted to. He could have made him an object of ridicule because of his sins ("dishonoured in ruin"). He could have given him into the hands of Satan or some evil spirit to torment him and make him suffer (this is the meaning of verse 15). But he did not. God, from the height of his infinite mercy, wanted to give him another chance and forgave his sins. And the psalmist, in this prayer, begs God to continue to forgive him in the future, to save him once and for all from (eternal) death.

On closer inspection, the two apocryphal texts that we have just analyzed, Psalm 155 and the *Plea for Deliverance*, ask for the same thing: the forgiveness of sins through the cancellation of the just punishment that should follow. Those "difficult situations" mentioned in Psalm 155 correspond precisely to that dishonor "in ruin" mentioned in the *Plea*.

But why, at this point, do we want to focus only on a couple of verses among the thousands found in the Scrolls? Wouldn't it be more honest to take an overall view in order to understand what the Scrolls tell us about the concept of deliverance? For, if we really want to continue with the game of extrapolating a verse from a couple of

---

9. Given the explicit reference to the sins and iniquities committed, Sheol, which was usually identified as the abode of the dead in the Jewish tradition, is here to be understood as a place of punishment, meant for the wicked dead.

apocryphal compositions to make the Lord's Prayer say whatever interests us most, then let us play along.

Why don't we read another apocryphal psalm? For example, Psalm 154, which is found in the Scrolls just before Psalm 155:

> 16 Behold the eyes of the Lord have compassion on the good,
> 17 and his mercy is great over those who glorify him; from an evil time he saves [their] souls.
> 18 [Bless] the Lord who redeems the humble from the hand of str[angers] [and deliv]ers [the perfect from the hand of the wicked;][10]
> (11QPs$^a$ xviii.16–18)

Always the same concept: God's mercy has compassion on the oppressed and will deliver them from all their sufferings.[11]

In Qumran Cave 4, fragments of a purification ritual were found where we read: "And he will bless there [the God of Israel. Answering, he will say: Blessed art Thou, God of Israel. And I stand] before Thee on the feas[t] ( . . . ) Thou hast ( . . . ) me for purity ( . . . ) and his burnt-offering and he will bless. Answering he will say: Blessed art Thou, [God of Israel, who hast delivered me from al]l my sins and purified me from impure indecency and hast atoned so that I come ( . . . ) purification and the blood of the burnt-offering of Thy goodwill and the pleasing memorial"[12] (4Q512 29–32 vii). Here, we find the divine mercy that delivers from the sins committed and, forgiving the faults through expiation, cancels the just punishment.

Again, in Qumran Cave 4, about fifty fragments of a sapiential poetic composition were found, which was given the title of *Beatitudes* because of its similarity to the Sermon on the Mount narrated in Matt 5:3–11—fragments dating, according to the paleographic method, to about the second half of the first century BC. Fragment 14 reads, "your feet will [walk] in an open place and you will advance on the high grou[nd of] your [e]nemy. [You will love God with all your heart and with all] your soul, and He will deliver you from all evil. Terror will not come upon you"[13] (4Q525 14 ii). It is interesting to note how the first commandment ("You will love God with all your heart and with all your soul") is intimately associated with the concept of deliverance from evil. As usual, evil is understood as an enemy that oppresses and instills terror.

Again, in Qumran Cave 4, fragments of a poetic composition renamed *Bless, My Soul* were found. Fragment 1 reads,

---

10. Vermes, *Dead Sea Scrolls in English*, 360.

11. Note how the wicked (רְשָׁעִים) are identified with the foreigners (זָרִים), that is, the pagans who threaten and oppress the people of Israel. From this point of view, the Septuagint translation of Ps 19(18):13(14) is to be considered completely legitimate (see previous footnotes).

12. Vermes, *Dead Sea Scrolls in English*, 456.

13. Vermes, *Dead Sea Scrolls in English*, 514.

Bless, my soul, the Lord for all His marvels for ever,
and may His name be blessed.
For He has delivered the soul of the poor,
and has not despised the humble,
and has not forgotten the misery of the deprived.
He has opened His eyes towards the distressed,
and has heard the cry of the fatherless,
and has turned His ears towards their crying.
( . . . )
He has not forsaken them amid the multitude of their misery,
neither has He handed them over to the violent,
nor has He judged them together with the wicked.
[He has] not [directed] His anger against them,
neither did he annihilate them in His wrath.
While all His furious wrath was not growing weary,
He has not judged them in the fire of His ardour,
but He has judged them in the greatness of His mercy.
The judgements of His eyes were to try them,
and He has brought His many mercies among the nations,
[and from the hand of] men He has delivered them.
He has not judged them (amid) the mass of nations,
and in the midst of peoples He has not judged [them].
But He hid them in [His] ( . . . )
He has turned darkness into light before them,
and crooked places into level ground,
( . . . )
He sent and covered them and commanded that no plague [should affect them]. His angel fixed his camp around them;
He guarded them lest [the enemy?] destroy them.[14]
(4Q434 1.i)

This passage is full of important concepts, some already known, others newer, that will come in handy for our reasoning:

1. God, based on his infinite mercy, does not abandon the oppressed into the hands of their oppressors, but delivers them from them.
2. God, based on his infinite mercy, does not judge the oppressed in the heap of the ungodly, but knows how to distinguish between oppressed and oppressor.
3. God, based on his infinite mercy, directs his wrath toward the oppressors, but knows how to spare the oppressed.

---

14. Vermes, *Dead Sea Scrolls in English*, 502–3.

4. God, based on his infinite mercy, protects the oppressed from every evil: enemies, tribulations, plagues, calamities, chastisements.

And then there are all the *Thanksgiving Hymns* found in Qumran Cave 1, which offer multiple examples of deliverance from evil.

In the first hymn, deliverance is understood as forgiveness of sins:

> Thou forgivest transgression, iniquity, and sin,
> and pardonest rebellion and unfaithfulness.
> For the bases of the mountains shall melt
> and fire shall consume the deep places of Hell,
> but Thou wilt deliver
> all those that are corrected by Thy judgements
> ( . . . )
> Thou wilt keep Thine oath
> and wilt pardon their transgression;
> Thou wilt cast away all their sins.[15]
> (1QH[a] iv, Hymn 1)

In the eighth hymn we find themes that should be familiar by now. Deliverance is understood as liberation from the wickedness of the ungodly—from shame, humiliation, derision, and so forth:

> I thank Thee, O Lord,
> for Thou hast [fastened] Thine eye upon me.
> Thou hast saved me from the zeal
> of lying interpreters,
> and from the congregation of those
> who seek smooth things.
> Thou hast redeemed the soul of the poor one
> whom they planned to destroy
> by spilling his blood because he served Thee.
> ( . . . )
> Thou, O my God, hast succoured
> the soul of the poor and the needy
> against one stronger than he;
> Thou hast redeemed my soul
> from the hand of the mighty.
> Thou hast not permitted their insults to dismay me
> so that I forsook Thy service
> for fear of the wickedness of the [ungodly],
> or bartered my steadfast heart for folly.[16]

---

15. Vermes, *Dead Sea Scrolls in English*, 296.
16. Vermes, *Dead Sea Scrolls in English*, 311.

(1QH$^a$ x, Hymn 8)

The effects of the oppression of the ungodly are explained in detail here. Oppression is not only violence and physical persecution (see the plans of murder for those who do not follow their idolatries), but also and above all psychological persecution. Those who do not follow their idolatrous practices are humiliated, mocked, made objects of shame. This is a fundamental point. The feeling of shame—the fear of being mocked and humiliated—is what might not allow a righteous person to fully follow the divine dictates. Here is how the dynamic works: the deliverance from the psychophysical oppression of the wicked allows the oppressed, finally, to serve God with all their strength and without any fear.

The tenth hymn recalls the *Plea for Deliverance*, when it says that God has saved his servant from hell, from eternal death: "I thank Thee, O Lord, for Thou hast redeemed my soul from the Pit, and from the hell of Abaddon. Thou hast raised me up to everlasting height"[17] (1QH$^a$ xi, Hymn 10).

The thirteenth hymn goes back to the concept of deliverance from both hell and the psychophysical tribulations and persecutions inflicted by the wicked (we even find the metaphor of the net!):

> [Thou hast not] judged me
> according to my guilt,
> nor hast Thou abandoned me
> because of the designs of my inclination;
> but Thou hast saved my life from the Pit.
> Thou hast brought [Thy servant deliverance]
> in the midst of lions destined for the guilty,
> and of lionesses which crush the bones of the mighty
> and drink the blood of the brave.
> ( . . . )
> The wicked and fierce have stormed against me
> with their afflictions;
> they have pounded my soul all day.
> But Thou, O my God,
> hast changed the tempest to a breeze;
> Thou hast delivered the soul of the poor one
> like [a bird from the net
> and like] prey from the mouth of lions.[18]
> (1QH$^a$ xiii, Hymn 13)

The fifteenth hymn insists on the concept of liberation from hell, identified as "the Pit of no forgiveness":

---

17. Vermes, *Dead Sea Scrolls in English*, 313.
18. Vermes, *Dead Sea Scrolls in English*, 320–21.

## Eis Peirasmón

> I have no fleshly refuge,
> [and Thy servant has] no righteous deeds
> to deliver him from the [Pit of no] forgiveness.
> But I lean on the [abundance of Thy mercies]
> and hope [for the greatness] of Thy grace.[19]
> (1QH$^a$ xv, Hymn 15)

The eighteenth hymn presents the concept of deliverance from the plots of the ungodly and forgiveness of sins:

> For Thou art my refuge, my high mountain,
> my stout rock and my fortress;
> in Thee will I shelter
> from all the [designs of ungodliness,
> for Thou wilt succour me] with eternal deliverance.
> ( . . . )
> Thy just rebuke accompanies my [faults]
> and Thy safeguarding peace delivers my soul.
> The abundance of (Thy) forgiveness is with my steps
> and infinite mercy accompanies Thy judgement of me.[20]
> (1QH$^a$ xvii, Hymn 18)

The twenty-second hymn speaks of deliverance from calamities and physical distress in accordance with divine mercy:

> Thou freed me from my calamities
> in accordance with Thy forgiveness;
> and in my distress Thou hast comforted me
> for I have leaned on Thy mercy.[21]
> (1QH$^a$ xix, Hymn 22)

Finally, the twenty-fourth hymn makes explicit reference to deliverance from a judgment of condemnation (again the metaphor of the snare!), which inflicts eternal death:

> Thou hast [caused the perverse heart to enter]
> into a Covenant with Thee,
> and hast uncovered the heart of dust
> that it may be preserved from evil
> and saved from the snares of Judgement
> in accordance with Thy mercies.[22]

---

19. Vermes, *Dead Sea Scrolls in English*, 330.
20. Vermes, *Dead Sea Scrolls in English*, 338–39.
21. Vermes, *Dead Sea Scrolls in English*, 345.
22. Vermes, *Dead Sea Scrolls in English*, 349.

(1QHᵃ xxi, Hymn 24)

Enough. We started from the hypothesis that the Dead Sea Scrolls contained original material which would demonstrate that the sixth and seventh petitions of the Lord's Prayer were nothing more than a plea for deliverance from the (moral) temptations of the Evil One, like a sort of exorcism that would keep evil spirits at bay, and instead we discover a whole series of songs, psalms, hymns, and apocryphal compositions that not only largely (if not completely) align with canonical theology, but also confirm that when deliverance from God is mentioned in Scripture, it is always understood as deliverance from a psychophysical, not a moral, *peirasmós*.

And yet. Yet there is one final objection to be discussed, which does not come from any verse in the Dead Sea Scrolls, but from a Jewish prayer of rabbinic origin, to be recited in the evening, before going to sleep (and a similar one, to be recited in the morning as soon as one wakes up). The evening prayer goes as follows:

> May Your will, O Lord my God,
> be that You make me lie down in peace and that You give me my portion in Your Law (Torah),
> accustom me to (Your) commandments, and do not accustom me to transgression,
> lead me not into sin, nor into injustice, nor into temptation, nor into anything shameful.
> May the good instincts rule over me
> And may the bad instincts not rule over me.
> Save me from bad accident and bad disease.
> Let no nightmares or worries disturb me.
> Let my bed be perfect in Your eyes, so that my offspring need not be imperfect.
> Enlighten my eyes in the morning that I may not sleep the sleep of death, never to awaken again.
> Blessed are You, O Lord, who gives light to all the world in its glory.[23]

Have you noticed anything? The sixth petition of the Lord's Prayer seems to be incorporated into the fourth verse! "Lead me not into temptation." Exactly the same. The verbal construction is also the same. "Lead me not into temptation" is rendered precisely by the causative (*hiphil*) form of the verb *bô'*, which Matthew and Luke render with the Greek verb *eisphérō* and which we have had occasion to discuss at length. Joachim Jeremias, German Lutheran theologian, one of the greatest New Testament scholars of the twentieth century and supporter of the permissive interpretation of the sixth petition of the Lord's Prayer, writes in this regard:

> How the verb [*eisphérō*] is really to be construed is shown by a very ancient Jewish evening prayer, which Jesus could have known and with which he perhaps makes a direct point of contact. The pertinent part (which recurs, incidentally, almost identically worded in the morning prayer) runs as follows:

---

23. Berakhot, 60ᵇ.

# Eis Peirasmón

> Lead my foot not into the power of sin,
> And bring me not into the power of iniquity,
> And not into the power of temptation,
> And not into the power of anything shameful.

> The juxtaposition of "sin," "iniquity," "temptation," and "anything shameful," as well as the expression "bring into the power of," show that this Jewish evening prayer has in view not an unmediated action of God but his permission which allows something to happen. (To put it in technical grammatical terms: the causative forms which are here translated "lead" and "bring" have a permissive nuance.) The meaning therefore is, "Do not permit that I fall into the hands of sin, iniquity, temptation, and anything shameful." This evening prayer thus prays for preservation from succumbing in temptation.[24]

Let us summarize Jeremias's reasoning:

1. The sixth petition of the Lord's Prayer is incorporated into this Hebrew evening prayer.

2. This Hebrew evening prayer is very ancient and probably known to Jesus.

3. Jesus in the Lord's Prayer is quoting this very Hebrew evening prayer.

4. This Hebrew evening prayer, besides asking God not to lead us into temptation, also asks him not to lead us into sin, injustice, and anything shameful.

5. But since God would never lead us to do such things, the meaning of that "leading" must necessarily be permissive, "Do not allow me to fall into sin, injustice, temptation, and so forth."

6. Conclusion: the sixth petition of the Lord's Prayer must be interpreted in the same way, "do not allow us to fall into temptation."

Another great contemporary scholar of biblical studies, Joseph Augustine Fitzmyer, a Catholic priest of the Society of Jesus and professor emeritus at Catholic University of America (Washington, DC), takes up and comments on this Hebrew evening prayer:

> From this late period comes also an interesting parallel in a Jewish evening prayer, preserved in the Babylonian Talmud:
>
> ולא תרגילני לידי עבירה ולא תביאני לידי חטא
> ולא לידי עון ולא לידי נסיון ולא לידי בזיון

---

24. Jeremias, *The Lord's Prayer*, 27.

"Accustom me not to transgression, and lead me not into sin, and not into iniquity, and not into temptation, and not into contempt" (*b. Berakoth* 60b).

> In contrast to the late Christian reformulations of the sixth petition, the Jewish prayer preserves the protological thinking of the OT [Old Testament], because it is a prayer addressed to God, asking him not to lead one into such situations. The parallel reveals that the Matthean sixth petition would be at home in a Jewish context.[25]

Fitzmyer comes to the same conclusion as Jeremias. Since it is a prayer directed to God, he is asked not to lead us into such situations. However, Jesus meant, "Do not allow us to get into such situations." This is what Fitzmyer calls "protological thinking." It is the theory (which we described earlier) that, in the Old Testament, a permissive sensibility in relation to God's action had not yet developed. Since everything that happens is in some way considered to be the work of God (both good and evil), God becomes the cause of both the good and the evil that happens to a person and that a person accomplishes. And therefore, apparently, God becomes, according to this protological thought, also the cause of the sins of people—the cause of their temptations. Which is obviously inconceivable. Therefore, the only solution is to introduce a more mature permissive sense to the (apparently) causative verbs, which would restore once and for all God's reputation, undermined by the somewhat primitive (this is what "protological" means) way of speaking of the Old Testament.

Since we have already abundantly refuted all these permissive interpretations, we will not dwell further on this point. We will only quote Fitzmyer's vitriolic conclusion because it is very interesting: "It is puzzling, however, why so many commentators on the sixth petition cite this parallel as if it were already part of the contemporary Jewish background of Jesus' prayer, when it is attested only in a fifth-sixth century talmud, and coming, not from Jesus' homeland, but from far off Babylon. Since there is no evidence that the prayer already existed in pre-Christian Palestinian Judaism, it has little relevance for the interpretation of the sixth petition of the PN [*Pater Noster*] beyond being an interesting parallel of the same protological formulation of later date."[26]

Fitzmyer points out that the Jewish prayer itself appears only 500–600 years after Christ and it is therefore absolutely improbable that Jesus knew it (or at least there are no elements to support this hypothesis) and even less that he had it in mind when he composed the Lord's Prayer.

Now, leaving aside the incoherence of the "protological thinking" hypothesis (as if Jesus, Son of God, did not yet know how to express himself in exact terms regarding the Father), Fitzmyer gives a mortal blow to any interpretation of the Lord's Prayer that is based on a prayer that appeared half a millennium later. And we could end the matter here.

25. Fitzmyer, "And Lead Us Not into Temptation," 267–68.
26. Fitzmyer, "And Lead Us Not into Temptation," 268.

But since we want to remove all doubt, we will pretend to think that Jesus really knew that prayer and that, perhaps, that prayer was part of the prayers he recited every night before going to sleep. Does that "lead me not into sin, nor into unrighteousness, nor into temptation, nor into anything shameful" really mean what it seems to mean?

Let us take a step back. Let us start with the previous verse, "Accustom me to (Your) commandments and do not accustom me to transgression." What does that mean? Is it imaginable a God who accustoms us to transgression and trains us to commit sins? Is this, again, a "protological" expression? We believe it is not. And the whole misunderstanding lies, again, in confusing the object with the subject of transgression.

Can God accustom us to transgress his commandments? No, that would be a logical absurdity. Instead, can God accustom us to the transgressions of those who transgress his commandments? Sure. How? By putting us in the hands of the wicked and abandoning us to their will. All the requests for deliverance read in the Dead Sea Scrolls go along these lines. "Do not accustom me to transgression" therefore means "do not accustom me to be the *object* of transgression." In other words, "come and deliver me from those who transgress against me." Just as "lead us not into temptation" implies "deliver us from evil" (and vice versa).

Likewise, "do not lead me into sin" does not mean "do not make me sin" (blasphemy!), but rather "do not make me the object of sin," and so, "deliver me from the oppression of those who sin against me." Likewise, "do not lead me into unrighteousness" does not mean "do not make me do unrighteous things" (blasphemy!), but rather "do not make me the object of unrighteousness," and so, "deliver me from the oppression of those who perform unrighteous things against me." Likewise, "do not lead me into temptation" does not mean "do not try to make me fall" (blasphemy!), but rather "do not make me the object of *peirasmós* (*nissāyôn*, in Hebrew)," and so, "deliver me from psychophysical oppression." Likewise, "do not lead me into anything shameful" does not mean "do not make me act shamefully" (blasphemy!), but "do not make me the object of shame," and so, "deliver me from those who mock and humiliate me."

There are several reasons that support our interpretation:

1. If we were truly the subject of the four evils that are listed (sins, injustices, temptations, and shameful actions), the verse would have an obvious logical inconsistency. Let us try to expand the "active" interpretation: "Do not lead me to commit sins, nor to commit injustices, nor to commit temptations, nor to commit shameful deeds." Commit temptations? That would make little sense.[27] In order for the verse to make sense, we are forced to give a "passive" interpretation to the third evil, but only to this one: "Do not lead me to commit sins, nor to commit injustices, nor to *undergo* temptations, nor to commit shameful deeds." If, on the other hand,

---

27. Jeffrey B. Gibson would probably argue that "committing temptation" would mean committing the same sin the Israelites committed at Massah, when they put God to the test. We will dedicate the next chapter to Gibson's active interpretation of the term *peirasmós*, showing how it causes more issues than it solves.

we assume that we are not the subject, but rather the object of the four evils that are listed, every logical inconsistency evaporates: "Do not lead me to be subjected to sin, nor to be subjected to injustice, nor to be subjected to temptation, nor to be subjected to shame." In fact, the Hebrew text of the prayer does not simply say "do not lead me into sin," but precisely "do not lead me *into the hands of* sin." The preposition *lîdê* (לִידֵי) literally means "into the hands of," indicating subjugation. And how many times have we read in the psalms (canonical and apocryphal) the direct prayer to God to deliver us "from the hands of the enemies," "from the hands of the wicked," "from the hands of the ungodly," "from the hands of the unjust," "from the hands of the violent," and so forth?

2. Another logical inconsistency concerns the types of evil into which God should not lead us. The first, second and fourth (sin, injustice, shameful actions) fall into the semantic field of a completed and consummated crime. The third (temptation) falls instead into the semantic field of sin not yet committed. The breaking of the semantic symmetry of the verse would be jarring. Moreover, what sense would it make to ask first not to be led into sin, and then not to be led into temptation, when obviously temptation precedes sin? The logical *consecutio* of evils is shaky.

3. What Jeremias translates as "anything shameful" is a stretch. The text, given in Berakhot 60ᵇ, presents the noun *bizzāyôn* (בִּזָּיוֹן) from the root verb *bāzâ* (בָּזָה), which means "to despise." The term *bizzāyôn* therefore means "contempt," "shame," "disgrace," "humiliation." And contempt, shame, disgrace, and humiliation are not something that one "commits," but rather they represent a (miserable) state in which one may find oneself. Remember all the prayers to God to keep us from being the object of humiliation and falling into a state of ruin and disgrace?[28] Here is where the "passive" interpretation presented earlier takes on an even more fulfilled sense: "Do not lead me to be subjected to sin, nor to be subjected to injustice, nor to be subjected to temptation, nor to be subjected to humiliation."

4. What both Jeremias and Fitzmyer translate as "temptation" does not mean moral temptation by the Evil One. The text, reported in Berakhot 60ᵃ, presents the term *nissāyôn* (נִסָּיוֹן), which we have already encountered multiple times and which, as we know, has the neutral meaning of "test," without necessarily any malicious overtones. And it may also be the term used by Jesus in the sixth petition of the Lord's Prayer. Now, to understand the exact meaning of this term within the evening prayer, we need to put the whole verse together. Because, clearly, the verse is emphatically constructed, with a rhetorical use of repetition: neither into sin, nor into unrighteousness, nor into temptation, nor into contempt. Four

---

28. See Job 8:22; 17:2, 6; 30:9–10; Pss 1:1; 25(24):2, 20; 31(30):1(2); 39(38):8(9); 44(43):10–17(11–18); 69(68):7–12(8–13); 70(69):3(4); 73(72):8; 79(78):4; 80(79):6(7); 109(108):25; 119(118):22; 123(122):3–4; Isa 54:4; 59:18; Jer 18:16; 24:9; Ezek 36:2–4, 15.

examples of evil. But if we look closely, there is an obvious substructure. The first two evils, sin and unrighteousness, are synonymous, almost interchangeable, and thus form a closed pair. The last two types of evil (temptation and contempt) are connected by a clear poetic alliteration—*nissāyôn* and *bizzāyôn* sound almost identical. The choice of the term *bizzāyôn* cannot be accidental: *bizzāyôn* is a rare noun, used only once in the entire Old Testament (Esth 1:18). It is likely that it was chosen to close the rhyming verse and, by symmetry, create a closed pair with *nissāyôn* (just as sin and injustice create a semantic pair of their own). If this is true, *nissāyôn* and *bizzāyôn* must be illustrations of the same concept. And if the expression "in the hands of contempt" is to be understood as the humiliation, the shame that our enemies, those who persecute us, inflict on us, then *nissāyôn* must mean a trial involving a kind of humiliation, shame, contempt. Psychophysical affliction, we could say. In Greek, *peirasmós*.

5. The term *nissāyôn* appears only one other time within the Berakhot treatise, where the evening and morning prayers are reported. It is a very curious passage, but also a significant one, which is worth analyzing briefly. Indeed, it is narrated that Rabbi Bar Kappara (late third and early fourth century AD) turned to Rabbi Yehuda HaNasi to interpret some of his dreams. In particular, Bar Kappara recounts that in one of his dreams it was prophesied that he would die in the month of Adar and that he would not see the month of Nisan.[29] Rabbi Yehuda HaNasi gives the following interpretation of the dream: "He said to him: 'You will die in glory and you will not be led into *nissāyôn*.'"[30] To understand the meaning of this answer, we need to explain the wordplay. The name of the month of ʾădār (אֲדָר) has the same root as the term ʾădrûthāʾ (אַדְרוּתָא), which means "glory," "magnificence." Similarly, the name of the month of *Nîsān* (נִיסָן) sounds similar to the term *nissāyôn* (נִסָּיוֹן). What is the rabbi telling him then? That he will die "in glory" and not "in temptation"? It does not make much sense, honestly. It is clear from the context that *nissāyôn* in this case must mean something antithetical to glory and magnificence. And the opposite of glory and magnificence is certainly not temptation. The opposite of glory and magnificence is shame, humiliation, disgrace, ruin, and so on. The rabbi is simply telling him that he will die "in glory" and not "in ruin." So, we have found, in a completely different context, the exact same image: "to be led into *nissāyôn*" means here "to be led into ruin," "to be subjected to the worst psychophysical afflictions."

---

29. *Adar* is the last month of the Jewish ecclesiastical calendar (corresponding to the February–March period of the Gregorian calendar). *Nisan*, on the other hand, is the first month of the Jewish ecclesiastical calendar (corresponding to the March–April period of the Gregorian calendar).

30. Berakhot, 56[b].

The last objection we will address[31] concerns another Jewish prayer—a prayer for the morning this time (but different from those just analyzed), which is part of the Talmudic tradition. This prayer is reported in the Berakhot treatise too:

> May Your will, Lord our God and God of our fathers,
> be that Thou save us from arrogant men and arrogance in general,
> from bad men and a bad accident,
> from a bad instinct, from a bad companion,
> from a bad neighbor, from Satan the Destroyer,
> from a difficult legal trial and from a stern plaintiff,
> whether a member of the covenant, a Jew,
> or not a member of the covenant.[32]

Now, why this prayer should have any bearing on the Lord's Prayer is beyond our understanding. There are dozens of prayers in the rabbinic tradition that contain requests concerning anything. This one mentions a long list of evils from which God is asked to deliver us. These include Satan the Destroyer. So what? The prayer also mentions deliverance from a "stern plaintiff." Should we conclude that Jesus also had "stern plaintiffs" in mind when he recited the Lord's Prayer? And, in any case, according to Talmudic tradition, this prayer is attributed to Rabbi Yehudah ha-Nasi, the one who compiled the *Mishnah*.[33] Now, this rabbi lived in the second half of the second century AD. Why should a prayer composed by a rabbi almost two hundred years after Christ have any relevance to the interpretation of the Lord's Prayer? Why should we go poking around in the rabbinic tradition of a period later than Christ? That same rabbinic tradition that, by definition, had rejected Christ and his message and was in the wake of the Pharisaic tradition whose teachings Christ had so violently flogged?

This way of proceeding, piling up short quotations (always taken out of context) taken from compositions, either apocryphal or extra-biblical, that have nothing to do with each other, coming from completely disparate places and periods, just to support an interpretation given *a priori*, is not only unfair, but contributes to throw smoke and increase confusion around the sixth petition of the Lord's Prayer.

But since, by playing along, as we have seen, we always "risk" learning something new, we will also welcome another idea found in the same article by Dr. Young. It is a quotation extrapolated from another Talmudic treatise (*Sanhedrin*) in which it is narrated the (extra-biblical) tradition according to which King David asked God of his own free will to put him to the test. And as a result, he failed resoundingly (he became guilty of adultery and murder). It is reported that Rav, a disciple of Rabbi Yehudah

---

31. See Young, *The Jewish Background*, 32–34.
32. Berakhot, 16ᵇ.
33. The Mishnah is the earliest written collection of texts from the Jewish oral tradition (Oral Torah).

ha-Nasi (third century AD), commented, "One should never put himself to the test as David, king of Israel, put himself to the test and failed."[34]

The expression "to put to the test" is rendered by the same construct we encountered in the Hebrew evening prayer: "to lead (causative form of *bô'*, to enter) into the hands of (*lîdê*) the test (*nissāyôn*)." We thus find that, at least in the speech pattern of the Second Generation Amoraic era (250–290 AD), the expression "to lead into *nissāyôn*" (the equivalent of the Greek expression "to lead into *peirasmós*" of the sixth petition) was not understood as an idiomatic way of saying "to make fall into temptation," as we understand it today. Which (albeit indirectly) supports the idea that when we ask God not to lead us into *peirasmós*, we are not asking that he not cause us to fall into sin, but that he not submit us to a certain kind of trial. This should be clear by now.

But what kind of test? What kind of *peirasmós*? The debate among scholars rages furiously.

---

34. Sanhedrin, 107[a].

# 23

# The Active Interpretation

In this chapter, we would like to present one of the most original interpretations of the sixth petition, which, although most likely incorrect, has the merit of at least overturning the schemes and seeking an alternative solution to those presented throughout the centuries, all more or less aligned on the permissive interpretation according to which one would ask God not to let Satan tempt us. It was recently presented by the scholar Jeffrey B. Gibson, who argues that the sixth petition should be interpreted as follows: "In telling his disciples to pray 'and do not lead us into temptation,' Jesus was telling them to pray, 'prevent us, God, from testing your faithfulness.'"[1]

Interesting point of view. Almost disorienting. Gibson flips the perspective and hypothesizes that the *peirasmós* of the sixth petition has not a passive valence ("to be subjected to *peirasmós*"), but an active valence ("to commit the sin of *peirasmós*"). We would not be the object of the *peirasmós* anymore, rather the subject. But what is this sin of *peirasmós*? It is the sin that people commit when they do not trust God and put him to the test.

The strength of Gibson's argument is based on the examples of *peirasmós* in the Old Testament. Remember how the Hebrew term corresponding to the Greek *peirasmós* within the Old Testament is *mǎssâ* (מַסָּה)? And how this term appears only nine times in the entire Hebrew Bible? Five times to indicate the physical place (Massah) where the Israelites had put God to the test.[2] Three times to indicate the plagues of Egypt.[3] Once in the book of Job[4] to indicate the disgrace that afflicts the innocent. If instead we expand the search to the verb *nāsâ* (נָסָה), from whose root the noun *mǎssâ*

---

1. Gibson, *The Disciples' Prayer*, 146. See also Gibson's unpublished paper, "Testing Temptation: The Meaning of Q 11:4b."
2. Exod 17:7; Deut 6:16, 22; 33:8; Ps 95(94):8.
3. Deut 4:34; 7:19; 29:3.
4. Job 9:23.

derives and which appears thirty-six times within the Old Testament, we discover that the percentage of times this verb indicates a test of a person by God is exactly equal to the percentage of times this verb indicates a test of God by a person. From a purely statistical standpoint, then, Gibson can argue that the hypothesis of an "active" interpretation of *peirasmós* is exactly as likely as a "passive" interpretation.

Gibson's hypothesis is noteworthy because indeed the idea that people can tempt God is a recurring theme of the Old Testament. Gibson starts with the following question: what is the one thing that people should shun at all costs? If we can answer this question, we will probably also be well on our way to correctly interpreting the sixth petition. This is a type of approach to the problem that we consider extremely valid. The sixth petition is the only one in the Lord's Prayer to appear in the negative form, and so it must have a special significance. Whatever the *peirasmós*, into which we ask God not to lead us, is, it must be something repugnant, to be avoided at all costs.

Gibson speculates that the sin to be avoided is precisely that of rebellion against God, and thus interprets the *peirasmós* of the sixth petition as the temptation aimed at God.

To support his conclusion, he start from the fact that the expression "to lead into" (in Greek, *eisphérō eis*) is the causative form of the expression "to go into," which in Greek is translated with the verb *eisérchomai* (εἰσέρχομαι). And in Greek, the expression "to go into (*eisérchomai eis*) something," Gibson argues, is very often used to indicate the action of *engaging in* something. If the non-causative form "to go into *peirasmós*" means "to engage in the act of *peirasmós*," the sixth petition must be interpreted in the active causative form along the following lines: "Do not lead us to commit the *peirasmós*," that is, "Do not lead us to test you." Ingenious, no doubt.

Gibson cites the passage in Psalm 143(142), in which we plead with God not to judge us: "And enter not into judgment [*eis krísin*] with thy servant: for in thy sight shall no man living be justified"[5] (Ps 143(142):2). The expression "enter into judgment" is rendered by the Septuagint with the verb *eisérchomai*: *eisérchomai eis krísin* (εἰσέρχομαι εἰς κρίσιν). Gibson notes that "to enter into judgment" means in this case nothing more than "to engage in judging," in the active sense.

However, if we try to generalize this "rule," we find that in other cases the expression "*eisérchomai eis*" has a passive, not an active, sense. For example, in the Gospel of John we find this famous phrase of Jesus: "Verily, verily, I say unto you, He that heareth my word, and believeth on him that sent me, hath everlasting life, and shall not come into condemnation [*eis krísin*]; but is passed from death unto life"[6] (John 5:24).

---

5. "μὴ εἰσέλθῃς εἰς κρίσιν μετὰ τοῦ δούλου σου [*mḕ eisélthēis eis krísin metà toû doúlou sou*]."

6. "λέγω ὑμῖν ὅτι ὁ τὸν λόγον μου ἀκούων καὶ πιστεύων τῷ πέμψαντί με ἔχει ζωὴν αἰώνιον, καὶ εἰς κρίσιν οὐκ ἔρχεται [*légō hymîn hóti ho tòn lógon mou akoúōn kaì pisteúōn tôi pémpsantí me échei zōḕn aiṓnion, kaì eis krísin ouk érchetai*]."

The expression "come into condemnation" is identical to the one just seen, with the only difference in the use of the verb *érchomai* (ἔρχομαι) instead of *eisérchomai*.[7] In this case, however, *érchomai eis krísin* (ἔρχομαι εἰς κρίσιν) does not mean "to engage in judging," but "to be judged," "to be condemned."

Similarly, in the Acts of the Apostles, we read: "Not only is there a danger of our business to enter into contempt"[8] (Acts 19:27). The expression "to enter into contempt" is again rendered by the use of the verb *érchomai* (ἔρχομαι) followed by the preposition *eis* (εἰς). Again, the sense here is clearly passive: "to enter into contempt" does not mean "to despise," but rather "to be despised." This argument of Gibson's thus comes across as unconvincing.[9]

However, curiously enough, Gibson cites another expression, appearing twice in the first book of Samuel,[10] where David is about to go and punish Nabal and his men for his rudeness. Only the intervention of Abigail, Nabal's wife, convinces David to desist from his murderous plans. The image of preventing David from "shedding Nabal's blood" is rendered by the Septuagint with the expression *eltheîn eis haîma* (ἐλθεῖν εἰς αἷμα), literally "to go into blood." Here, we may agree with Gibson that the sense is active: "to go into blood" means "to engage in a bloodshed." However, the expression is to be interpreted as a figurative way of saying, "to get to the point of shedding blood."[11] A sort of figurative motion to an extreme situation.

In any case, what is most striking about this passage is that in both 1 Sam 25:26 and 1 Sam 25:33, when the Septuagint wants to translate the idea of "prohibition," or "prevention," it never thinks for a moment about using the causative form of *eisérchomai*. In fact, in 1 Sam 25:26, Abigail does not say, "the Lord did not *lead* you into blood." She explicitly uses a prohibitive construct through the verb *kōlýō* (κωλύω), which means "to prevent," and she says, "the Lord hath withholden thee from coming to shed blood." Similarly, in 1 Sam 25:33, David does not say, "you did not *lead*

---

7. *Eisérchomai eis* is equivalent to *érchomai eis*.

8. "οὐ μόνον δὲ τοῦτο κινδυνεύει ἡμῖν τὸ μέρος εἰς ἀπελεγμὸν ἐλθεῖν [*ou mónon dè toûto kindyneúei hēmîn tò méros eis apelegmòn eltheîn*]." The KJV has "to be set at nought."

9. Other examples cited by Gibson (Jer 16:5; Josh 23:7; Dan 3:2) appear forced. Jer 16:5 simply states, "not to go to their funeral banquet." It does not talk about engaging into mourning. It is a simple motion into a physical place, that is, the house where the funeral banquet is taking place. Josh 23:7 simply states, "not to go into these nations that remain among you." It does not talk about engaging in idolatrous practices. It is a simple motion into a physical place, that is, the land of the idolatrous. Dan 3:2 simply states that "Nebuchadnezzar the king sent to gather together the princes, the governors, and the captains, the judges, the treasurers, the counsellors, the sheriffs, and all the rulers of the provinces, to come to the dedication of the image which Nebuchadnezzar the king had set up." In fact, "coming to the dedication" simply refers to a motion to the place where the dedication of the statue was to be performed. Satraps, prefects, governors, advisers, treasurers, judges, magistrates are not "engaging in" anything other than going to the place where the king told them to go. They are not performing the dedication themselves. They are just going there to attend the ceremony.

10. 1 Sam 25:26, 33.

11. Similar to the English expression "to come to blows," which means "to get to the point of fighting, after disagreeing verbally."

me into blood." He explicitly uses a prohibitive construct through the verb *apokōlýō* (ἀποκωλύω), which again means "to prevent," and he says, "blessed be thou, which hast kept me this day from coming to shed blood."

So, the only thing that this example proposed by Gibson proves is that the Greek language knows exactly when and how to use an *explicit* prohibitive construct to convey the idea of "prohibition," of "prevention." If such a construct is *not* used (as in the Lord's Prayer), this is strong indication that no "prohibition" nuance has to be found. Again, both Hebrew and Greek agree on this. When a permissive (or prohibitive) nuance is meant, both languages always make it explicit by means of explicit verbs that mean "to allow" (or "to prevent"). This is precisely why Gibson's idea of interpreting "do not lead" as "prevent us from" has no exegetical nor grammatical support (as any other permissive interpretations), and as such cannot be accepted.

The last argument concerns the fact that the seventh petition (interpreted as deliverance from the Evil One) fits perfectly with the idea of people testing God. We remember how, during Jesus' temptations in the desert, Satan tried to make Jesus test God. And since the devil's favorite activity is to induce us to doubt God, the sixth petition, Gibson concludes, must reflect this idea. And by the way, he continues, even if the *ponērón* of the seventh petition simply meant a generic evil and not the Evil One, it would still work: we would be asking God to prevent us from committing anything evil.

Now, as original and worthy of consideration as this hypothesis can be, it seems scarcely credible, for a long list of reasons:

1. As already explained, the following argument,
    a. "to lead into temptation" is the causative form of "to enter into temptation,"
    b. "to enter into something" in Greek means "to engage in something,"
    c. therefore, "lead us not into temptation" means "do not lead us to tempt you,"
    is based on a very weak point (assumption b.).
2. Moreover, even if this were the case, it would be completely illogical to ask God not to lead us to do something that offends him to the utmost power. For we know that there is nothing that inflames the wrath of God more than the little faith of his people. How could God ever lead us to do such a thing? The answer to this objection is always the same: the prohibitive nuance. In fact, we would be asking God to *prevent* us from testing him. It is curious to notice how Gibson, even though perfectly aware of the strong causative meaning of the verb *eisphérō*, after arguing that it would be wrong to attach any permissive nuance to the expression, ends up adopting a permissive construct himself! In fact, "to prevent" means nothing more than not "to allow." Again, in Gibson's solution, it is not God that leads us somewhere. Instead, God would simply prevent us from doing

something, that is, would not allow us to do something. A permissive (prohibitive) interpretation that we have already rejected and refuted extensively.

3. Gibson's argument is flawed at the very beginning. In fact, in order to be able to convert "do not lead us into" into "prevent us from," he needs to assume that the verb *eisphérō* refers to a movement from one place to another, *but not into it*. We have extensively proved that the opposite is true. In the New Testament, the expression "*eisphérō eis*," with the emphatic redundance of the preposition *eis*, always refers to a movement from one place *into*, and not, notably, only up to, another.

4. One of Gibson's main arguments is that, when Jesus finds his disciples asleep in the garden on the Mount of Olives and tells them to pray so that they may not enter *eis peirasmón*, he is doing so because his disciples would be about to put God to the test, that is, to commit the same sin the Israelites committed at Massah. Now, it is not clear why Jesus, in the middle of his agony, would feel the urgency to spur his disciples not to commit the sin of Massah. At Massah, by quarrelling with Moses, the Israelites had rebelled against God. Was Jesus sensing that his disciples would soon do the same? Quarrelling with him or rebelling against him? There is nothing in the Gospels that could even remotely suggest anything like this.

Yes, Jesus had predicted Peter would deny him three times (Matt 26:34). But his denial (Matt 26:69–75) will be a result of Peter's weakness, not of Peter's rebellion to Jesus/God. Similarly, Jesus had predicted that all the disciples would abandon him that very night (Matt 26:31). But their desertion (Matt 26:56) will be a result of their weakness, of their fear to be arrested and put to death, not of their rebellion to Jesus/God. When the sheep flee because they see their shepherd being attacked and killed by wolves, they do it not because they are rebelling against their shepherd or because they do not trust him anymore, but simply because they are scared! When the disciples run away after Jesus is arrested, they are not repeating the sin of Massah. They are not putting God to the test. They are not asking for a sign from him to prove his existence or his favor or his power. They are not doubting his existence. They have not lost their faith in him. They are not rejecting him. They are simply—humanly scared. And they run for their life. Yes, it is a weakness on their part. But it is completely understandable—it is not an act of rebellion.

The act of "putting God to the test" is not about a simple human weakness. It is the most serious offense against God. It is a defiant attitude toward God. It is not reasonable to think that we are putting God to the test anytime we stumble in our own weaknesses. In fact, when Jesus prophesizes that that very night all his disciples would abandon him, he uses the verb *skandalízomai* (σκανδαλίζομαι), which means "to fall away." He does not prophesize that they will put God to the test (*peirázō*), but simply that they will desert him. The idea that the disciples were somehow one inch away from putting God to the test appears to be—at a minimum—a stretch on Gibson's part, somehow in need to find support for his thesis.

5. Gibson points out that Jesus' admonition to pray so that they may not enter *eis peirasmón* would be a way for the disciples to ask God's help not to put him to the test. Now, if this interpretation may work in theory in the context of the garden on the Mount of Olives (where no causative verb/construct is used), it does not in the context of the Lord's Prayer. In fact, all the reformulations of the sixth petition of the Lord's Prayer along the lines of "give us the strength not to," "help us not to," "make sure that we do not" cannot be accepted.

   Curiously enough, Gibson himself first argues against the practice of deliberately moving the negative particle from the subject of the causative construct onto the object (from "*do not cause* us to enter" to "cause us *not to enter*"), and then he ends up using this trick himself! The sixth petition cannot be interpreted as "give us the strength not to fall into," or "help us not to enter," or "prevent us from entering," simply because this is not what the verb *eisphérō* is about. When we pray the sixth petition, we are asking God *not to do something to us*. We are *not* asking God to help us not to do something. The subject of the action is God, not us. We are just the object, in God's hands.

6. After arguing (*contra* J. Carmignac et al.) about how wrong it would be to interpret the sixth petition as a plea not to succumb to temptation, that is, a plea to prevent us from sinning, Gibson's solution ends up being a plea to prevent us from sinning (the sin of Massah).

7. Another major problem with Gibson's argument is that he is assuming that the expression "enter into *peirasmós*" is an idiomatic way of saying "putting to the test." Guess what? There is not one single example in all the Septuagint Bible where, in order to say that somebody put God (or somebody else) to the test (and the examples are many), it is said that somebody "entered into *peirasmós*." Scripture simply uses the verb *peirázō*. Therefore, we can safely argue that if Jesus meant to tell his disciples to pray so that they may not put God to the test, he would have simply used the verb *peirázō*. He would not have said to pray "μὴ εἰσέλθητε εἰς πειρασμόν," but simply "μὴ πειράσητε τόν Θεόν."

   And, as we pointed out previously, if "enter into *peirasmós*" really were a Greek way of saying "to put to the test," we must conclude that there was an identical way of saying in Aramaic. And guess what? There is not one single example in all the Hebrew Bible where, in order to say that somebody put God (or somebody else) to the test (and the examples are many), it is said that somebody "entered into *măssâ*." Scripture simply uses the verb *nāsâ*, which corresponds, as we know, to the Greek *peirázō*. As previously explained, any idiomatic interpretation of the sixth petition is not tenable.

8. The *common* noun *peirasmós* never appears in Scripture with the generic meaning of "temptation aimed at God."[12] It becomes difficult to think that in the Lord's Prayer, without any precise context that might help to decipher the term, it would precisely acquire this meaning. Moreover, as pointed out by Nijay K. Gupta,[13] if Jesus had wanted to intend the temptation *of God*, to avoid any misunderstanding he could have added a simple objective genitive (God being the object of temptation): μὴ εἰσενέγκῃς ἡμᾶς εἰς πειρασμόν σου ("lead us not into temptation *of you*"). The absence of such a genitive is a strong indication against Gibson's argument.

9. As Gupta himself points out, no theologian in the entire history of Patristics, including especially the Greek church fathers, while debating all the different interpretative nuances, has ever questioned the fact that *peirasmós* is to be understood in the passive sense ("to undergo" *peirasmós*, and not "to engage in" *peirasmós*). It is illogical to think that no one has ever grasped this total reversal of meaning if it were so obvious in the Greek language.

10. The interpretation of the seventh petition in light of Gibson's argument must necessarily include the Evil One, on the basis that the Evil One is indeed the one who is known to try to make a person lose faith in God and put him to the test. Otherwise, the intimate connection between the sixth and the seventh petition would be lost. In fact, if we consider the seventh petition to refer to evil in general, in the active sense, as Gibson understands it, it will read, "Deliver us from doing evil." This conclusion is not acceptable. We know for a fact that, throughout the entire Bible, God always delivers people from the evil that people suffer. He does not deliver (in the sense of "preventing") people from the evil that they might commit in the future.[14] There can be no doubt about this.

---

12. At most, it appears capitalized, *Peirasmós*, as a toponym to indicate the *proper* name of the place where the Israelites put God to the test (Massah). One may argue that Ps 95(94):8 (also quoted by Paul in Heb 3:8) talks about "the day of the temptation in the wilderness," and not about "the day of Massah in the wilderness." This is how the Septuagint interprets it. However, the appearance of the proper name Meribah in the previous verse makes it highly probable that this *mǎssâ* too refers to a proper name, Massah (Meribah and Massah are usually cited together as the places where the Israelites put God to the test). In any case, even assuming that *peirasmós* in Ps 95(94):8 is indeed a *common* noun, it is not referring to the generic act of putting God to the test, but to the specific episode occurred in Massah.

13. Gupta, "Lead Us Not Into Temptation," 138.

14. At most as deliverance from evil committed (or to be committed) in the future, understood as forgiveness of sins. The concept of deliverance from evil, understood as prevention from committing evil, does not exist in Scripture.

# 24

# The Eschatological Interpretation and the Unsolved Problem

Let us now analyze a much more robust hypothesis, advanced and explored by a significant number of scholars for decades.[1] This is the so-called eschatological interpretation of the Lord's Prayer as a prayer concerning the End Times.[2] Prophecies concerning the end of the world have their roots in the Old Testament, particularly in the book of Daniel, but the details of the signs that will precede it are explained by Jesus himself a few days before being put to death. The narrative of the End Times made by Jesus, probably one of his most important discourses, is narrated in all three synoptic Gospels, with minimal variations, which help to interpret the more sibylline passages. The most complete text is found in chapter 24 of Matthew's Gospel. We will follow his account, using Mark and Luke as additional explanatory sources. It is necessary to understand the picture that Jesus is painting in order to correctly judge the eschatological interpretation of the Lord's Prayer.

After Jesus has triumphantly entered Jerusalem, in the days immediately preceding the Passover in which he knows he will be immolated as a sacrificial lamb, Jesus spends his days teaching in the temple. In the evenings, he retires with his disciples to the Mount of Olives, just outside the walls of Jerusalem. On one of those evenings, as he is leaving the temple, the disciples point out to him the beauty of the building. Jesus then takes the opportunity to make his first prophecy about the beginning of the End Times: "See ye not all these things? verily I say unto you, There shall not be left here one stone upon another, that shall not be thrown down" (Matt 24:2).

---

1. Ernst Lohmeyer, Henry Van den Bussche, Heinz Schürmann, Donald A. Hagner, Joachim Jeremias, C. F. W. Smith, Raymond E. Brown et al.

2. The term "eschatological" is derived from the Greek adjective *éschatos* (ἔσχατος), meaning "last."

The disciples are amazed by this prophecy and, once arrived on the Mount of Olives, they ask Jesus when all these things will come to pass. But, in addition to the specific question about the destruction of the temple in Jerusalem, the disciples also expressly ask about the second coming of Christ and the end of the world: "Tell us, when shall these things be? and what shall be the sign of thy coming, and of the end of the world?" (Matt 24:3). At this point, Jesus' speech begins.

But let us be careful. It is crucial to distinguish, during the narrative, which of these three questions (destruction of Jerusalem, signs of the second coming of Christ, end of the world) Jesus is answering. Otherwise, it is easy to get confused and lose the logical and chronological sense of the events. Jesus seems to be speaking off the cuff, often introducing flashbacks and flashforwards that can be difficult to understand. It is obviously not a written and prepared speech. In Jesus' mind, the destruction of Jerusalem as an example of divine wrath somehow overlaps with the destruction of the last days, in which divine wrath will be poured out on the wicked.

First, Jesus decides to answer the question about his return (flashforward). It is a point that is particularly close to his heart. And then he warns the disciples against the false prophets who will announce the second coming of Christ. They must not be deceived. Christ will not casually appear in a house or in the desert. Christ's second coming will be something astonishing, like a thunderbolt in the sky, which no one will be able to locate precisely.

But before entering the details of his coming, Jesus prophesies to the disciples that there will be wars, famines, earthquakes (flashback). All of this, however, will only be "the beginning of sorrows" (Matt 24:8). This is a crucial clarification. Jesus is here prophesying the beginning of a period of tribulation, characterized by all kinds of affliction and suffering: "For nation shall rise against nation, and kingdom against kingdom: and there shall be famines, and pestilences, and earthquakes, in divers places" (Matt 24:7).

The destruction of Jerusalem fits precisely into this description, as the cornerstone of the beginning of the sorrows. It is interesting to note the term used by Matthew, *ōdînes* (ὠδῖνες), which indicates the excruciating pains of childbirth. Jesus is speaking not of an instantaneous, momentary pain, but of a pain protracted in time, of which the devastation of Jerusalem will mark only the beginning. And wars, famines and earthquakes will not be the worst of it! Jesus warns the disciples to think of themselves (Mark 13:9), for they will suffer endless persecution, in the synagogues and before pagan courts. Then—and here Jesus returns to where he started from—false prophets will appear who will try to confuse the faithful. Injustice and evil will be rampant and because of this many will lose faith. "But he that shall endure unto the end, the same shall be saved" (Matt 24:13). Finally, the gospel must be proclaimed to all the peoples of the earth. Only then will the end come (Matt 24:14).

Jesus sets clear stakes at the beginning and at the end of the great period of tribulation that awaits the world. Only when all these things have taken place will there be the second coming of Christ, the so-called *parousía* (παρουσία).

Jesus goes back to describe the beginning of the tribulation (flashback) in detail. In Matthew and Mark, he does so with a sibylline allusion to a passage in the book of Daniel (see Dan 9:27; 11:31; 12:11): "When ye therefore shall see the abomination of desolation, spoken of by Daniel the prophet, stand in the holy place, (whoso readeth, let him understand)" (Matt 24:15). Luke dispels all doubt and explains, "And when ye shall see Jerusalem compassed with armies, then know that the desolation thereof is nigh" (Luke 21:20).

This is precisely the prophecy of the siege and destruction of Jerusalem and of the profanation and destruction of the Temple by the army of the Roman emperor Titus, which will take place in 70 AD, not even forty years after the death of Christ. The Temple, from that moment, would never be rebuilt. The prophecy is devastating. The ferocity of the Roman army will fall on Jerusalem with such a violence that it will cause a great tribulation, a *thlîpsis megálē* (θλῖψις μεγάλη), "such as was not since the beginning of the world to this time, no, nor ever shall be" (Matt 24:21). A prophecy that will be fulfilled precisely.[3]

Luke also explains the reason for this destruction: "For these be the days of vengeance, that all things which are written may be fulfilled" (Luke 21:22). These are the days of divine vengeance. It is the punitive *peirasmós* sent by God upon the city that had rejected and killed his son.

After this bloody prophecy, Jesus returns to speak of the following events: the false christs (*pseudóchristoi*) and false prophets (*pseudoprophêtai*) who will try to deceive even the elect. But, as anticipated, his coming will be sudden and unidentifiable *a priori* (flashforward): "For as the lightning cometh out of the east, and shineth even unto the west; so shall also the coming of the Son of man be" (Matt 24:27).

At this point, Jesus again steps back (flashback) to explain the events and signs that will precede "the coming of the Son of Man." "Immediately after the tribulation of those days," Matthew reports, "shall the sun be darkened, and the moon shall not give her light, and the stars shall fall from heaven, and the powers of the heavens shall

---

3. The Jewish historian Josephus, a direct witness to the siege of Jerusalem, describes it as follows: "But when they went in numbers into the lanes of the city with their swords drawn, they slew those whom they overtook without and set fire to the houses whither the Jews were fled, and burnt every soul in them, and laid waste a great many of the rest; and when they were come to the houses to plunder them, they found in them entire families of dead men, and the upper rooms full of dead corpses, that is, of such as died by the famine; they then stood in a horror at this sight, and went out without touching any thing. But although they had this commiseration for such as were destroyed in that manner, yet had they not the same for those that were still alive, but they ran every one through whom they met with, and obstructed the very lanes with their dead bodies, and made the whole city run down with blood, to such a degree indeed that the fire of many of the houses was quenched with these men's blood." (Josephus, *De bello judaico*, 6.8.5).

be shaken" (Matt 24:29).[4] It will be a period of great terror: "Men's hearts failing them for fear, and for looking after those things which are coming on the earth" (Luke 21:26). The collapse of the stars in the sky will be the signal of the imminent coming of Christ: "And then shall appear the sign of the Son of man in heaven: and then shall all the tribes of the earth mourn, and they shall see the Son of man coming in the clouds of heaven with power and great glory. And he shall send his angels with a great sound of a trumpet, and they shall gather together his elect from the four winds, from one end of heaven to the other" (Matt 24:30–31).

Having said this, Jesus, with a quick flashback, returns to the present time and tells the disciples the parable of the fig tree, "Now learn a parable of the fig tree; When his branch is yet tender, and putteth forth leaves, ye know that summer is nigh: So likewise ye, when ye shall see all these things, know that it is near, even at the doors" (Matt 24:32–33). What are "all these things"[5] that Jesus is talking about here? They are evidently "all those things" of which the disciples were asking at the beginning, that is, the destruction of Jerusalem. And in fact, he adds, "Verily I say unto you, This generation shall not pass, till all these things be fulfilled"[6] (Matt 24:34).

Then, with a quick flashforward, Jesus relates the destruction of Jerusalem to the end of the world: "Heaven and earth shall pass away, but my words shall not pass away. But of that day and hour knoweth no man, no, not the angels of heaven, but my Father only" (Matt 24:35–36). With a clear parallelism between the destruction of Jerusalem and the divine wrath that will be poured out upon the world at the End Times, Jesus

---

4. That "immediately after" has been the subject of much debate among scholars, between those who argue that Jesus' prophecy was not fulfilled (Christ has not yet manifested himself after 2000 years) and those who instead attempt to explain that human time does not correspond to divine time (a blink of an eye for God can correspond to millennia for us). Either explanation does not seem to be correct. Jesus has already explained that wars, famines, and earthquakes are only the beginning of the sorrows. And that this period of tribulation will last at least until the gospel is proclaimed to all the nations scattered throughout the world. Immediately after this time of tribulation, the end will come, that is, the *parousía* of Christ. But the time of the tribulation is not, as Jesus clearly explained, an isolated episode in time, but rather a period that will unfold throughout history, throughout the centuries, "until the times of the Gentiles be fulfilled" (Luke 21:24).

5. "ταῦτα πάντα [*taûta pánta*]."

6. Again, this expression has been the subject of numerous debates among scholars, between those who argue that Jesus' prophecy did not come true (the end of the world has not yet occurred after 2000 years) and those who instead try to imaginatively interpret "this generation," as all future generations of Christians. The truth as usual lies in the middle and is found in the simplest interpretation. Unless Jesus really thought that, within a generation (30–40 years), his gospel would be proclaimed to all the peoples of the world, with all the false prophets, persecutions, world wars, famines, earthquakes, all condensed into the span of a few decades, or more simply Jesus is prophesying that "all these things," referring specifically to the destruction of the Temple the disciples were asking about at the beginning, will happen within 30–40 years, which actually happened. Otherwise, the Gospel of Luke, written, according to most, after 80 AD (that is, when the Temple had already been destroyed, "this generation" had already ended, and the end of the world not yet happened), would have been automatically invalidated. As proof of this fact, Jesus specifies that, if the destruction of Jerusalem is a historical event whose timing he knows (it will happen within the next 30–40 years), the exact moment of the end of the world is not known, not even to him.

compares its dynamics to the Universal Flood that destroyed all humanity in the time of Noah and to the fire that suddenly fell from heaven and incinerated Sodom and Gomorrah. It is not by chance that Jesus cites the two most emblematic examples of punitive *peirasmós* in the Old Testament. The punishment that will fall on Jerusalem will be a sinister premonition of the greater punishment that will fall on the world at the End Times: "Then shall two be in the field; the one shall be taken, and the other left. Two women shall be grinding at the mill; the one shall be taken, and the other left" (Matt 24:40–41).

The separation between the elect, who will be gathered from all parts of the world and "taken" by the angels to enjoy eternal life, and the wicked, who will be "abandoned" to a destiny of eternal death, is clear. Hence, the conclusion of Jesus' discourse: since no one (except the Father) knows when the second coming of Christ will take place, people will do well to be ever alert, "for in such an hour as ye think not the Son of man cometh" (Matt 24:44). The recommendation is clear and repeated several times. Luke sums it up best of all: "And take heed to yourselves, lest at any time your hearts be overcharged with surfeiting, and drunkenness, and cares of this life, and so that day come upon you unawares. For as a snare shall it come on all them that dwell on the face of the whole earth. Watch ye therefore, and pray always, that ye may be accounted worthy to escape all these things that shall come to pass, and to stand before the Son of man" (Luke 21:34–36).

The *parousía*, the second coming of Christ, is associated with the terrible fate that will fall on the heads of those who are not ready. Those who do not resist before the Last Judgment will be punished with immense severity, and "there shall be weeping and gnashing of teeth" (Matt 24:51).

Here ends Jesus' account of "the things that are to happen," soon and at the End Times. Jesus has answered the disciples' questions, but without going into detail. He has given them a sketch—a glimpse of the events to come, but he has left much unsaid.

To complete the apocalyptic picture, it is necessary to read other passages of the New Testament, in particular the second letter of St. Paul to the Thessalonians and, obviously, the book of Revelation of St. John.

Let us start with St. Paul. Let us read from the second chapter:

> Now we beseech you, brethren, by the coming of our Lord Jesus Christ, and by our gathering together unto him, That ye be not soon shaken in mind, or be troubled, neither by spirit, nor by word, nor by letter as from us, as that the day of Christ is at hand. Let no man deceive you by any means: for that day shall not come, except there come apostasy first, and that man of sin be revealed, the son of perdition; Who opposeth and exalteth himself above all that is called God, or that is worshipped; so that he as God sitteth in the temple of God, shewing himself that he is God. Remember ye not, that, when I was yet with you, I told you these things? And now ye know what withholdeth that he might be revealed in his time. For the mystery of iniquity doth

already work: only he who now letteth will let, until he be taken out of the way. And then shall that Wicked be revealed, whom the Lord shall consume with the spirit of his mouth, and shall destroy with the brightness of his coming [*parousía*]: Even him, whose coming [*parousía*] is after the working of Satan with all power and signs and lying wonders, And with all deceivableness of unrighteousness in them that perish; because they received not the love of the truth, that they might be saved And for this cause God shall send them strong delusion, that they should believe a lie: That they all might be damned who believed not the truth, but had pleasure in unrighteousness. But we are bound to give thanks always to God for you, brethren beloved of the Lord, because God hath from the beginning chosen you to salvation through sanctification of the Spirit and belief of the truth: Whereunto he called you by our gospel, to the obtaining of the glory of our Lord Jesus Christ. (2 Thess 2:1–14)

First of all, Paul makes one thing clear. He says, get it out of your head that the *parousía* of Christ is imminent. Why? Because first there are other events that must occur, in particular *apostasy* (ἀποστασία), that is, the mass renunciation of the Christian faith. Paul is here developing the expression used by Jesus in Matt 24:12: "because iniquity shall abound, the love of many shall wax cold." Most importantly, Paul is explaining the meaning of those pseudo-christs (those false christs) of whom Jesus had spoken. At the appropriate time, before the coming of Christ, the Antichrist must be revealed. The *parousía* of Christ will be preceded by the *parousía* of the Antichrist, who will rise above God and reign on earth making himself worshipped as a god.[7] The *parousía* of Christ will be the necessary response to the *parousía* of the Antichrist, so that the kingdom of the Antichrist will be destroyed, and the kingdom of God will be established.

But the most interesting idea related to the *parousía* of the Antichrist lies in those "power," "signs," "lying wonders," and "all deceivableness of unrighteousness" that will take place concomitantly. It will be a kind of global deception into which all those who have refused to accept the gospel will fall. And from whom does this global deception come? From Satan? From the Antichrist? No, from God!

Paul is clear on this. Again, we find a recurring concept. Satan (or whoever for him: the Antichrist) is just a tool in God's hands, which God uses to punish and destroy those whom God has already decided to destroy (because of their ungodliness). To such an extent that it seems that it is God himself who "deceives" the ungodly and "leads them into temptation." But this kind of "leading into temptation" is not a whim of God, who would enjoy seeing people fall. It does not go against the axiom that God does not lead anyone into temptation. Instead, it is an integral part of how his justice works. The wicked who rejected his word have already condemned themselves with their own hands. They are, as Paul calls them, *apollyménoi* (ἀπολλυμένοι), that is,

---

7. As undefined as the figure of the Antichrist is, scholars agree that it must be not Satan himself, but a person, ruled and used by Satan to establish his reign of evil on earth.

literally, "in the process of being destroyed." They are people destined to ruin, to eternal death.[8] And God, through the deception of the Antichrist, simply "facilitates" their miserable end. It is a deception that resembles little to a moral temptation and much to a terrible punishment (punitive *peirasmós*). And in fact, Paul concludes, those who have accepted God's word and remained faithful to it have nothing to fear. God "has chosen them to salvation."

Let us move on to analyze St. John's book of Revelation to gather further elements that may clarify the picture of the End Times. The book of Revelation, because of its distinctive visionary-prophetic character, is one of the most complex and difficult to interpret books of the New Testament.[9] Since a discussion about the entire book goes far beyond the scope of this analysis, we will limit ourselves to listing below the salient points that interest us.

The formal beginning of the Apocalypse, understood as the revelation[10] of the mystery of evil and the final victory of good, occurs with the opening of the seals of the book of life, where the names of the saved are written. The only one deemed worthy to open the seals is the immolated lamb, that is, Christ, who makes his triumphant appearance in Rev 5:7.

A mighty event is associated with the opening of each of the seven seals. At the opening of the seventh and final seal, seven angels appear, each with a trumpet. To each trumpet blast of the seven angels corresponds a tremendous calamity, which falls on the earth and on people. Worthy of note is the fifth trumpet blast which corresponds to the opening of the Abyss (read hell), from which comes a host of giant locusts that take to torment people who do not have the seal of God on their foreheads. The seventh and last trumpet blast marks the beginning of the ultimate battle between the army of good, led by the archangel Michael, and of evil, led by Satan. Michael prevails and Satan and his angels are thrown on the earth, where they establish the kingdom of evil. Whoever on earth worships the Beast will receive the mark on his forehead and will eventually be the object of God's wrath.

It is at this point that the *dies irae* is unleashed. Seven angels pour on the earth the seven bowls of God's wrath, which inflict plagues, calamity, and destruction. Satan is thrown back into the Abyss and chained there for a thousand years. But it is not over yet. After a thousand years, Satan is freed from the Abyss and left free to return to earth to seduce nations and gather followers for the last, desperate battle. A battle that, obviously, he will lose. Satan is driven back to hell forever, where he will be tormented for eternity. Only then, the books will be opened, and the Universal Judgement will

---

8. Contrast this with the *sōizoménoi* (σῳζομένοι), that is, those who are destined to be saved.

9. According to the famous Greek historian Eusebius (fourth century AD), Dyonisus of Alexandria would very candidly admit about the book of Revelation: "It is beyond my comprehension" (Eusebius Caesariensis, *Historia ecclesiastica*, 25.4).

10. The term "revelation" is derived from the Greek verb *apokalýptō* (ἀποκαλύπτω), which literally means "to unveil that which is hidden."

take place, where everyone will be rewarded according to their works: the righteous with eternal life, the wicked thrown into the pool of fire.

Now, let us take a deep breath and try to put the pieces together. As we have seen, the story is very confusing, full of allegories and twists. However, the concepts that interest us are only a couple. The Revelation is the story of the ultimate battle between Satan and Christ and of the divine wrath that flares up on the earth, annihilating and relegating all the ungodly to eternal fire. We can summarize schematically all that we have learned so far in the following chart.

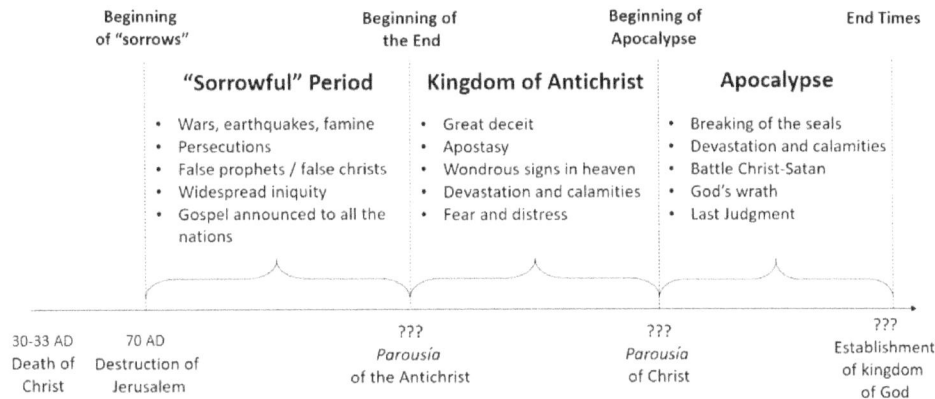

Now, with all that in mind, let us try to get back to the original question: what would the Lord's Prayer have to do with any of this? In other words, what does the eschatological interpretation of the Lord's Prayer consist of?

First of all, we must point out that there are a considerable number of scholars who support this hypothesis. Not all of them necessarily agree on the details of how the sixth petition should be interpreted, but they all agree that it has an eschatological character. That is, when we ask God to "lead us not into temptation" we are asking for something pertaining to the End Times. We will follow, in this regard, two schools of thought (in some way similar and complementary): that of Joachim Jeremias on the one hand and of Raymond E. Brown on the other.

We have already had occasion to analyze Jeremias's thought in relation to the Jewish evening prayer in which the expression "lead us not into the hands of *peirasmós*" appears. Although we disagree with the conclusion Jeremias arrives at in his specific interpretation of the sixth petition, we must nevertheless recognize the immense value of his research on the Lord's Prayer in general, which uncovers an important and hitherto too neglected point of view. The Lord's Prayer understood as a prayer that rises above the mere material needs of people and that goes beyond, with a clear tension to the transcendent. Indeed, says Jeremias, the Lord's Prayer has little to do with daily prayer. It is, to all intents and purposes, an eschatological prayer, totally focused on the End Times.

His argumentation starts from the consideration that the first three petitions ("Hallowed be Thy name," "Thy kingdom come," "Thy will be done") emerge from a clear Hebrew substratum, visible in an ancient Aramaic prayer, the *Qaddish*,[11] still one of the most used prayers in the Jewish culture:

> Exalted and sanctified be Thy great name
> In the world which He has created according to His will.
> May His kingdom reign
> Throughout our life and in your days
> and for all the life of the whole House of Israel,
> quickly and soon. And say, Amen![12]

Although it is impossible to trace the exact period when this prayer began to circulate in Jewish circles, the clear similarity to the beginning of the Lord's Prayer suggests that Jesus knew it very well.[13] Jeremias explains that the sanctification of God's name takes the form of the establishment of his kingdom on earth. And the *Qaddish* is a prayer for this to happen "quickly and soon." It is, Jeremias concludes, an eschatological prayer. From which it would be deduced that the first three petitions of the Lord's Prayer are also eschatological in nature. To ask for God's kingdom to come on earth would be equivalent to asking for Christ's *parousía* to defeat evil forever.

The rest of the Lord's Prayer, Jeremias continues, is also all about the End Times. "Give us this day our daily bread" would be a request for final communion with the bread of life, that is, Christ. So, it would be another way of asking for the same thing—the reunion of the faithful with Christ at the End Times. Jeremias prefers to translate "daily" with "of tomorrow."[14] "Give us today the Bread of tomorrow." The request would be to anticipate the times and to ensure that the bread of life that has been promised to us "tomorrow" be given to us already today, "quickly and soon." The forgiveness of sins is obviously a prayer for mercy—mercy promised by Christ at the End Times, but requested in the Lord's Prayer "already here, already today." Here we come to the last two petitions. Jeremias explains,

> the concluding petition of the Lord's Prayer does not request that he who prays might be spared temptation, but that God might help him to overcome it.

11. The Aramaic term *qaddish* (קדיש) means "holy."

12. *Qaddish* (original form).

13. Obviously, the two prayers are not the same and do not say the same things, but the fact that the first three verses of the *Qaddish* contain exactly the first three themes of the Lord's Prayer (name of God, kingdom of God, will of God) cannot be a coincidence.

14. The Greek term *epioúsion* (ἐπιούσιον), commonly translated as "daily," is of obscure interpretation and the subject of unresolved debate. Origen reports finding no example of the use of this term in any other Greek writer (*De oratione*, 27.7). St. Jerome, the extender of the Vulgate, had no small amount of trouble finding the appropriate Latin term. In the end, he decided on *supersubstantialem*, literally "bread above substance," that is, "transcendent bread." Jerome also reports that, during his research, he had found in the (Aramaic) Gospel of the Nazarenes (now lost), the term *māhār* (מָחָר), meaning "tomorrow." Hence the idea of "tomorrow's bread."

All this becomes fully clear when we ask, secondly, what the word "temptation" means. This word (*peirasmós* in Greek) does not mean the little temptations or testings of every life, but the final great Testing which stands at the door and will extend over the whole earth — the disclosure of the mystery of evil, the revelation of the Antichrist the abomination of desolation (when Satan stands in God's place), the final persecution and testing of God's saints by pseudo-prophets and false saviors. The final trial at the end is — apostasy! Who can escape?

The concluding petition of the Lord's Prayer therefore says, "O Lord, preserve us from falling away, from apostasy."[15]

If up to this point, we have followed Jeremias's reasoning (and largely agreed with him), the conclusion he reaches regarding the sixth petition must be pondered carefully, given the number of themes that are introduced to justify it. Let us break it down.

1. Jeremias belongs to the group of scholars who maintain that the sixth petition indicates a request not for protection from temptation, but rather for help so that we do not succumb to temptation. The problem with this kind of interpretation is always the same: it requires a very "creative" paraphrase of the original Greek text. As explained and demonstrated repeatedly, "leading into temptation" in the Greek text is not a figure of speech equivalent to "making fall into temptation." It simply means what it literally means: "to lead into the place of temptation," that is, to bring one to be the object of *peirasmós* (whatever *peirasmós* means). This interpretation of Jeremias has another substantial problem. It twists the strongly causative sense of the verb *eisenénkēis* to introduce an unacceptable permissive sense ("Do not allow us to succumb to temptation").

2. Jeremias hypothesizes that *peirasmós* does not mean the little trials/temptations of everyday life, but rather the final trial, which awaits humanity at the End Times. We agree with the first part, less so with the second. That *peirasmós* does not mean the little trials/temptations of everyday life we have amply demonstrated during our analysis. However, the idea that *peirasmós* means the eschatological test—the one related to the battle against the Antichrist—is a conclusion (very fascinating to tell the truth) that has no support in the Gospels, for several reasons:

    a. When Jesus, during the Sermon on the Mount, teaches his disciples to pray, he is still at the beginning of his public ministry. Up to that time there had been no hint of the End Times, let alone an ultimate battle against the Antichrist. If this was truly the meaning Jesus wanted to convey, it is hard to see why he did not take the time to explain this (at least) to his closest Apostles (as he would explain them the various parables). It was impossible that the disciples, with the information they had at that time,

15. Jeremias, *The Lord's Prayer*, 28.

could even imagine that *peirasmós* meant the eschatological test—the one concerning the battle against the Antichrist. The most obvious hypothesis is instead that *peirasmós* meant something immediately comprehensible to his listeners.

b. Even assuming that Jesus wanted, for some reason, to conceal this truth initially so that it would be revealed only later, it is necessary to note that Jesus never specifically speaks of a final test that includes a battle against the Antichrist. Jesus only speaks generically of "false prophets" and "false christs" (plural!) who, in the course of history, will try to mislead and deceive possibly even the chosen ones. No reference to a specific event in time. And above all, these "false prophets" and "false christs" are mentioned together, *en passant*, with other types of trials (wars, calamities, persecutions, and so forth) that humanity will have to face during "the time of travail," in an unspecified time before his *parousía*. It does not seem to be the final trial, but simply one of many.

c. The only passage in the entire New Testament that can support Jeremias's hypothesis is found in the passage from St. Paul's second letter to the Thessalonians that we analyzed before: "Let no man deceive you by any means: for that day shall not come, except there come a falling away first, and that man of sin be revealed, the son of perdition; Who opposeth and exalteth himself above all that is called God, or that is worshipped; so that he as God sitteth in the temple of God, shewing himself that he is God" (2 Thess 2:3–4). This is precisely the passage that Jeremias, while not specifically quoting it, has in mind.[16] Now, thinking that the correct interpretation of the sixth petition of the Lord's Prayer is hidden in a couple of verses of a letter of St. Paul, written at least twenty years after the death of Christ, seems at least difficult to believe. And even if we take for granted what Paul prophesies, namely the apostasy[17] related to the appearance of the son of perdition,[18] the details regarding that event are so sparse and confusing that it is difficult, if not impossible, to find a logical connection with the Lord's Prayer. The concept of the Antichrist is, to tell the truth, still the subject of debate within the church itself. There are multiple interpretations of it, differing in when and how this Antichrist should appear. The idea that it

---

16. John briefly mentions that "the Antichrist must come," but without any reference to mass apostasy (1 John 2:18). John speaks of the coming of the Antichrist more as a useful signal to identify the End Times than as a concrete threat to the faith. At least, not more threatening than the various false prophets and false christs that John says had already appeared in his days.

17. The term "apostasy," understood as renunciation of the faith because of the Antichrist, does not appear in any other passage of the New Testament.

18. The exact same epithet, ὁ υἱὸς τῆς ἀπωλείας [*ho huiòs tês apōleías*], had been used by Jesus for Judas (John 17:12).

is precisely this very controversial issue the key to understanding the sixth petition of the Lord's Prayer seems objectively far-fetched.

d. Jeremias, in order to link the prophecy of Christ to the apostasy prophesied by St. Paul, interprets the "abomination of desolation" mentioned in Matt 24:15 as the establishment of the kingdom of the Antichrist. This interpretation, fascinating as it sounds, must be rejected. For at least a couple of reasons:

1. While Matthew and Mark keep the expression in abeyance, leaving the reader with the challenging task of interpreting the prophecy ("whoso readeth, let him understand"), Luke explains it explicitly: "when ye shall see Jerusalem compassed with armies, then know that the desolation thereof is nigh" (Luke 21:20). The abomination of desolation is nothing more than the destruction of the Temple in Jerusalem by the Roman army. Nothing to do with the Antichrist.

2. Not only does Luke interpret it this way. Jesus himself interprets it that way! In fact, he says, "Then let them which be in Judaea flee into the mountains" (Matt 24:16). The reference is specifically to a threat hanging over Judea, not the whole earth. It cannot therefore have anything to do with a phantom Antichrist, whom Jesus does not even think of mentioning.

3. "Who can escape the test of the Antichrist?" asks Jeremias. Well, if we read what St. Paul says, the answer is easy: all those who have accepted the love of the truth. St. Paul explains that the final test, as Jeremias defines it—the temptation of the Antichrist—is a power of deception sent by God to destroy definitively "those who are destined for destruction" because they have rejected the love of the truth (2 Thess 2:10–12). It is not a test intended for all humanity. It is a punishment for those who have already rejected the word of God.[19] Those who have accepted Christ have nothing to fear from the temptation of the Antichrist (2 Thess 2:13). It does not seem so irresistible a test, to be honest.

4. The conclusion of Jeremias's argument is as follows: the seventh petition of the Lord's Prayer, because of the interpretation of the sixth, is to be understood as a prayer of prevention from apostasy. This interpretation is to be rejected for the same reasons that Gibson's interpretation is to be rejected. Gibson says, "Prevent us from committing the sin of Massah." Jeremias says, "Prevent us from committing the sin of apostasy." Both say, "Deliver us from doing evil." This thesis, as we have seen, is unacceptable.

---

19. In the rare cases (Jdt 9:23–24; 1 Sam 16:14–16; 18:10) in which, on a superficial reading, it might seem that God is the instigator of a "moral temptation," it turns out instead that God is simply exercising his justice: *Quos Deus vult perdere, prius dementat*.

God always delivers from the evil that people suffer, not from the evil that people might commit. Again, there can be no doubt about this.

5. And finally, the Achilles heel of any eschatological interpretation: the fact that the Lord's Prayer is being reduced to a prayer for the few. If one is really asking God to have the strength to resist the temptation of the Antichrist, it means that the only ones who really need to recite the sixth petition of the Lord's Prayer are those who will be living on earth at the very moment of the Antichrist's appearance. A tiny, if not insignificant, percentage compared to all of humanity that ever existed in the previous millennia. Can we really think that Jesus was teaching the disciples to recite a prayer that would obviously make no sense for them to recite?[20]

We now turn to analyze Raymond E. Brown's eschatological arguments, which are somewhat complementary, but not identical, to Jeremias's.

While the reasoning around the eschatological character of the first part of the Lord's Prayer closely follows Jeremias's arguments, it is in the specific interpretation of the sixth and seventh petitions that we see some interesting divergence. First of all, Brown never mentions the coming of the Antichrist, nor the apostasy associated with it. He simply speaks of the "terrible obstacle that separates the Christian from that triumph, namely, the titanic struggle between God and Satan which must introduce the last days."[21] Now, the final battle between God and Satan, as seen in our reconstruction of Revelation, is part of the *post-parousía* of Christ, when the Antichrist has already been destroyed by Christ (2 Thess 2:8). It seems to be understood, then, that Brown, who with Jeremias shares the same idea of the Lord's Prayer as an eschatological prayer, has a very different idea of what this last *peirasmós* should be. It is no longer the deception of the Antichrist and the false prophets and the apostasy that would result, but rather the tribulations that people at the End Times will have to endure while God and Satan struggle furiously.

Another interesting divergence is the fact that Brown, unlike Jeremias, categorically rejects any permissive interpretation of the sixth petition, calling it with great intellectual honesty a "desperate explanation." It follows that Brown, unlike Jeremias, considers the sixth petition not a request that we not succumb to *peirasmós*, but rather a request that we be spared *peirasmós*. Brown explains, "The word for 'trial, temptation' here is *peirasmos*. While this word can refer to ordinary temptation, it also has a specialized reference to the final onslaught of Satan."[22]

Unfortunately, this assertion has no foundation. Indeed, there is not a single instance in Scripture where the term *peirasmós* is associated with the "final onslaught of Satan." From what then does Brown deduce his conclusion? From a passage that

---

20. It was obvious that the Antichrist would not appear before the end of that generation.
21. Brown, "The Pater Noster," 204.
22. Brown, "The Pater Noster," 205.

appears in the book of Revelation and is almost always cited by proponents of the eschatological interpretation as evidence that *peirasmós* means the test of the End Times. Indeed, Brown says, "Ap 3:10 contains a promise of Christ: Because you have kept my command and stood fast, I will keep you from the hour of trial (*peirasmos*) which is coming on the whole world, to try those who dwell on earth."[23] Sounds very apocalyptic, doesn't it? Unfortunately, the mere fact that the term *peirasmós* appears in the book of Revelation does not mean that it must be interpreted in eschatological terms. And in fact, if we widen our range of action for a moment and avoid, as usual, taking a verse out of context in order to give it the meaning that suits us best, we realize many interesting things.

It may sound paradoxical but the beginning of the book of Revelation does not correspond to the beginning of the Apocalypse. The first three chapters of the book of Revelation contain what we could call a prologue, which has only a very distant relation to the actual Apocalypse. The apostle John tells that, while he was on the island of Patmos during one of his evangelization trips, he had a revelation (different from— and previous to—the other revelation in which he will see the Apocalypse). Christ himself spoke to him and told him to send specific messages to the seven churches of Asia Minor (Ephesus, Smyrna, Pergamum, Thyatira, Sardis, Philadelphia, and Laodicea).[24]

Now, it is interesting to briefly read the content of these seven messages:

1. Jesus reproaches the church of Ephesus for having abandoned the love of old. Hence, the warning to repent, otherwise "I will come unto thee quickly, and will remove thy candlestick out of his place, except thou repent" (Rev 2:5). In other words, a threat of punitive *peirasmós*.

2. For the church of Smyrna, Jesus professes his closeness in the tribulation (read: persecution) it is undergoing and will undergo in the near future: "Fear none of those things which thou shalt suffer: behold, the devil shall cast some of you into prison, that ye may be tried [*peirázō*]; and ye shall have tribulation [*thlîpsis*] ten days: be thou faithful unto death, and I will give thee a crown of life" (Rev 2:10). As always, we find the concept of *peirasmós* associated with that of *thlîpsis*, that is, affliction, persecution, tribulation. The one who performs the *peirasmós* is in this case Satan himself, which closely resembles the *peirasmós* suffered by Job. This is

---

23. Brown, "The Pater Noster," 205.

24. The seven churches listed in the book of Revelation do not represent all the Christian churches in Asia Minor at that time, but they were probably chosen because their different characteristics exemplified different attitudes (some good, many bad) recurring within the early Christian communities. The order in which they appear is also not random. From south to north along the western coast of present-day Turkey: Ephesus, Smyrna, Pergamum. From north to south inland: Thyatira, Sardis, Philadelphia, and Laodicea. Like a sort of inverted U, probably following the evangelization journey made by John in Asia Minor.

the psychophysical fortifying *peirasmós*, as we defined it earlier, the one sent by God to test the faith of believers. Whoever endures it will have eternal life.

3. To the church of Pergamum, as to that of Ephesus, Jesus recognizes merits, but reproaches it for having welcomed into its community idolaters and heretics (the Nicolaitans). Hence the warning, "Repent; or else I will come unto thee quickly, and will fight against them with the sword of my mouth" (Rev 2:16). In other words, a threat of punitive psychophysical *peirasmós*.

4. To the church of Thyatira, Jesus, while recognizing some of its qualities, reproaches the fact of having allowed itself to be deceived by a false prophetess, a certain Jezebel, who led them to idolatry and fornication. Hence, the terrible warning: "Behold, I will cast her into a bed, and them that commit adultery with her into great tribulation [*thlîpsis megálē*], except they repent of their deeds. And I will kill her children with death; and all the churches shall know that I am he which searcheth the reins and hearts: and I will give unto every one of you according to your works" (Rev 2:22–23). The expression used by Christ is particularly strong. The threat of punitive psychophysical *peirasmós* is evident and chilling. The *thlîpsis megálē*, the great tribulation to which Jesus here alludes, is reminiscent of the *thlîpsis megálē* that he prophesied would fall on Jerusalem.[25]

5. To the church of Sardis, Jesus sends a stinging message. On the surface, it looks like a healthy community, but in reality, it is "dead." Hence, the warning: "Be watchful, and strengthen the things which remain, that are ready to die: for I have not found thy works perfect before God. Remember therefore how thou hast received and heard, and hold fast, and repent. If therefore thou shalt not watch, I will come on thee as a thief, and thou shalt not know what hour I will come upon thee" (Rev 3:2–3). The threat is a clear reference to the passage in Matt 24:42–44: "Watch therefore: for ye know not what hour your Lord doth come. But know this, that if the goodman of the house had known in what watch the thief would come, he would have watched, and would not have suffered his house to be broken up. Therefore be ye also ready: for in such an hour as ye think not the Son of man cometh." As we know, the coming of the Son of Man for those who are found "asleep" is synonymous with chastisement and ruin: punitive psychophysical *peirasmós*.

6. To the church of Philadelphia,[26] Jesus dedicates only praises. Hence the famous promise, quoted by Brown: "Because thou hast kept the word of my patience, I also will keep thee from the hour of the *peirasmós*, which shall come upon all the world, to try them that dwell upon the earth. Behold, I come quickly: hold that

---

25. The verbal violence contained here ("βάλλω αὐτὴν εἰς θλῖψιν μεγάλην" = "I will throw her into great tribulation") provides an interesting parallel to the sixth petition of the Lord's Prayer ("μὴ εἰσενέγκῃς ἡμᾶς εἰς πειρασμόν" = "do not bring us into *peirasmós*").

26. The modern Alaşehir (Turkey).

fast which thou hast, that no man take thy crown" (Rev 3:10–11). Although it is not very clear what this "*peirasmós* that is about to come upon the whole world" consists of, from the fact that the church of Philadelphia will be spared by virtue of its righteous conduct, one can safely conclude that it is a punitive *peirasmós* that will affect those who have *not* remained faithful to the word of God.

7. To the church of Laodicea, Jesus expresses all his disdain for the "lukewarmness" of its faith, which is something that kindles divine wrath, even more than the absence of faith itself. Hence, the very harsh warning: "I will spue thee out of my mouth" (Rev 3:16). But he adds, "As many as I love, I rebuke and chasten" (Rev 3:19). In other words, a threat of pedagogical psychophysical *peirasmós*. Christ uses the term *paideúō* (παιδεύω), which means "to educate with discipline and strictness."

We have discovered that the "*peirasmós*, which shall come upon all the world" is part of a very particular message that Christ wants to send to one of the first Christian communities in Asia Minor (the church of Philadelphia), which distinguished itself by its irreproachable conduct. Also, all the other messages to the other churches contain extremely specific historical references in place and time (the persecution of some believers of the church of Smyrna thrown in jail for ten days, the sect of the Nicolaitans, the false prophetess Jezebel, and so forth) that have nothing to do with the End Times. They are just messages that have value within the historical context of that time (first century AD). Thinking that Christ is telling the church of Philadelphia that he will spare it "the final battle between God and Satan" makes no logical sense. Simply because it is a fact that the final battle between God and Satan is yet to come, but the church of Philadelphia has been extinct since quite some time.

So, what is Christ referring to when he speaks of "*peirasmós*, which shall come upon all the world"? To some calamity? To some plague? To some enemy invasion? Unfortunately, not much is known about the history of the church of Philadelphia.[27] The most honest answer is therefore: we do not know, and probably we will never know. Trying to attribute eschatological connotations to this passage is, as Brown himself would say, a "desperate explanation." But Brown tries anyway and explains, "As Christ himself admitted, if the Lord had not shortened the days of this tribulation, no human being would be saved. But He added by way of encouragement that the days have been shortened for the sake of the elect (Mk 13:19–20). And the text of Ap 3:10 [Rev 3:10], cited above, shows Christ promising to keep His faithful Christians from the trial. Therefore, asking for preservation from the final diabolic onslaught is simply following Christ's directions."[28]

---

27. One thing is known, however, and quite curious: it was the last of the seven churches mentioned in Revelation to survive.

28. Brown, "The Pater Noster," 206.

Now, this argument contains so many hasty logical connections, and for this reason it cannot be accepted. Christ did "admit" that, "if the Lord did not shorten the days of this tribulation, no human being would be saved." However, he was clearly talking about the destruction of Jerusalem, not about Satan's final attack. The text in Rev 3:10 does show Christ "promising to preserve His faithful Christians from trial." However, he was referring specifically to the faithful of a small first-century community in Asia Minor. There is no logical reason to believe, as explained, that the trial of which Christ speaks has anything to do with the ultimate battle between God and Satan.

It is at this point, then, that Brown plays the famous card of the Dead Sea Scrolls, which would prove how the cultural substrate of that time was obsessed with the influence of the forces of evil. We have already extensively analyzed the contents of those Scrolls, which most likely belonged to a Jewish sect settled along the shores of the Dead Sea, the Essenes. Brown observes, "The Christian community had an eschatological outlook not too far from that of the Essenes."[29] A conclusion that is far-fetched, to say the least. And even if it were, what would it prove? That Jesus had been influenced by the beliefs of this sect? Unimaginable. In any case, the simple observation that the two communities had similar beliefs (a fact that has yet to be proven[30]) does not imply any causal relationship between the two. This is, therefore, an argument without any explanatory power.

Another technical subtlety, which argues for the rejection of the eschatological hypothesis of the sixth petition as proposed by Jeremias and Brown, is the fact that the term *peirasmós* appears without any article within the Lord's Prayer. The passage in Rev 3:10, on the other hand, is one of the few in the New Testament in which the term *peirasmós* appears with the article (*toû peirasmoû*). If the term *peirasmós* in Rev 3:10 is precisely the final trial, the one that precedes the establishment of the kingdom of God at the End Times, and if it appears with the article precisely to emphasize that it is not a generic trial, but the final one, it is not clear why the article does not appear in the sixth petition of the Lord's Prayer. If the *peirasmós* of the Lord's Prayer referred to a specific episode, determined in time—that will happen in the future and will affect the inhabitants of the earth of that specific future time—why did Jesus omit the article? Why leave it so indeterminate? Why not give any precise details about the Antichrist, and expect that, without any kind of concrete information about it, the disciples (those very disciples who could not even understand the simplest parables!) could understand that this generic *peirasmós* meant the eschatological test *with* the article?

To conclude this digression on the various aspects of the eschatological interpretation of the sixth petition of the Lord's Prayer, we would like to make at least a couple of concepts clear:

---

29. Brown, "The Pater Noster," 206.

30. Indeed, many of the rules of the Essenes' community found in the Scrolls blatantly clash with Christ's message.

1. What we are debating and refuting here is not the fact that the Lord's Prayer contains, in general, eschatological connotations. On the contrary, we are in complete agreement with Jeremias et al. that it is undeniable that the Lord's Prayer also has a clear eschatological dimension. The request that the kingdom of God be established "on earth as it is in heaven" vibrates with a clear eschatological tension. In the same way, the request for "daily" bread cannot be interpreted merely as a trivial request to stock up the larder so as not to starve. Certainly, this need is also legitimate, but Jesus expressly taught that "man shall not live by bread alone" (Matt 4:4) and explained to his disciples (just a few moments after he had recited the Lord's Prayer in front of them!) not to worry about what they will eat or drink, because God will provide for their every need (Matt 6:25). It is reasonable to think that the reference to the daily bread is also a reference to the Eucharist, to the bread of life that Jesus promised them—a not too hidden reminiscence of the *manna* given by God to the Israelites in the desert.

2. But, if all this is true, the attempt to connote also the sixth (and seventh) petition of the eschatological sense proposed by Jeremias et al. appears totally forced (the reasons for which we have abundantly explained). Let us be careful, though. We are not saying that even the sixth and the seventh petitions of the Lord's Prayer cannot be interpreted in an eschatological sense. We are saying that, if we want to interpret them in that sense, it must be a much more immediate sense, much more obvious, much simpler to understand, rather than a not well-defined apostasy concerning a not well-defined Antichrist, or a confused final battle between God and Satan of which Christ has told us little and nothing.

We conclude by presenting the point of view of another scholar in line with the eschatological interpretation of the sixth petition of the Lord's Prayer because it introduces an important detail. C. F. W. Smith, in his essay "The Lord's Prayer,"[31] explains that while praying to be exempt from the "trial" on earth, understood as anticipation of the final judgment, is contradictory, because it is indeed part of what a good Christian should expect (*peirasmós* on earth would indeed be healthy), praying to be exempt from the test of the End Times makes sense. After all, think of the Antichrist, Satan unleashing his demons, and so forth. "Who wouldn't want to be exempt from such a trial?" wonders Smith. The *peirasmós*, he concludes, must be a test that seems to be insuperable. Only the final test of the End Times seems to fit this description.

Now, again, the idea that the *peirasmós* of the sixth petition of the Lord's Prayer is not merely a temptation of daily life, but must be something truly terrible, to be shunned, if possible, with all our might, is something we agree on and that we are strongly convinced of. This is not the point. The point is to see in that *peirasmós* the Antichrist. The point is to see in that *peirasmós* Satan unleashing his demons on the

---

31. Smith, "The Lord's Prayer," 157.

humanity of the future—of the End Times. All this appears to us as an unnecessary forcing, and in any case difficult to justify.

But there is an interesting point that Smith raises. Praying to be exempt from *peirasmós* on earth is contradictory, because *peirasmós* on earth is actually healthy. Leaving aside the fact (this indeed is contradictory) that the *peirasmós* as understood by Smith et al. is for all intents and purposes an earthly *peirasmós*[32] (and therefore, according to Smith's own reasoning, healthy) the question is: is it legitimate to think that any earthly *peirasmós* is healthy? This is a profound question, one that touches on the age-old problem of the mystery of evil in the world, and one that has no simple answer.

Ceslas Spicq, in his "Theological Lexicon of the New Testament," defines *peirasmós* as "a trial of virtue by means of affliction or adversity, or even by Satan's intervention."[33] He points out that "Matthew 6:13a involves not the possibility of a 'wicked solicitation' but rather 'a difficult or painful trial.'"[34] In summary, it is a test of a believer's faith, a tribulation that can occur in various forms at any time in the believer's life, which "demonstrates not only the sincerity and the moral resources of the believer, but is also for the believer a means of perfection because he has to suffer in order to remain faithful to his resolves and his decision for God; he emerges from the trial purified and more convinced than ever to serve his Lord, whose sovereignty over him he thus confesses to be total."[35]

We must say that Spicq hits the mark and gives perhaps the most lucid definition of the term *peirasmós* that we have ever read. But the problem raised by Smith remains. If all this is part of divine Providence, if *peirasmós*, even the most painful, is for good, carried out for our purification and perfection, why would Jesus have taught us to ask to be exempt from it? If, with this kind of *peirasmós*, the believer who remains steadfast in faith gains "the crown of life," why would the believer ask God to be exempt from this incredible opportunity?[36]

It is what C. F. D. Moule calls "the unsolved problem."[37] Why should a person pray to be exempt from the trial? If *peirasmós* is the inevitable trial that must be faced by believers, then asking for its exemption is absurd, illogical. Moule sketches a possible explanation based on psychology. From a purely human point of view, praying to be exempt from the trial might make sense as far as praying for the opposite (that is, to be put to the test) would constitute a blatant form of *hýbris*. There are, however, at least a couple of arguments that make this explanation shaky. One is proposed by Moule

32. The Antichrist will not magically appear in the sky but will stay with his feet firmly planted on the ground, mixed with people.

33. Spicq, *Theological Lexicon of the New Testament*, 3:82.

34. Spicq, *Theological Lexicon of the New Testament*, 3:86.

35. Spicq, *Theological Lexicon of the New Testament*, 3:83.

36. As Calvin puts it, "It would be foolish to ask, that God would keep us free from every thing which makes trial of our faith" (Calvin, *Commentary on Matthew*, https://www.ccel.org/ccel/calvin/calcom31.ix.liv.html).

37. Moule, "An Unsolved Problem," 33.

himself: "all the rest of the traditions of Jesus' teaching emphasizes the inevitability of suffering, and do not bid the disciples [to] pray for escape."[38] But above all, if asking to be put to the test certainly sounds out of tune, like an act of gratuitous *hýbris*, this does not justify the fact that we are legitimized to ask the opposite, that is, not to be tested, which would be instead a blatant form of false humility.

So let us take a step back and try to understand whether *peirasmós* is really the inevitable test that every believer must face sooner or later in order to obtain the crown of life.

Let us consider, for example, Psalm 26(25), in which David, certain of his moral integrity, with a request bordering on *hýbris*,[39] asks the Lord to examine his heart and put him to the test: "Examine me, O Lord, and test me; try my reins and my heart" (Ps 26(25):2).

Or let us recall how Peter, in his first epistle, encourages the faithful afflicted by persecution with these words:

> Beloved, think it not strange concerning the fiery trial which is to try you, as though some strange thing happened unto you: But rejoice, inasmuch as ye are partakers of Christ's sufferings; that, when his glory shall be revealed, ye may be glad also with exceeding joy. If ye be reproached for the name of Christ, happy are ye; for the spirit of glory and of God resteth upon you: on their part he is evil spoken of, but on your part he is glorified. But let none of you suffer as a murderer, or as a thief, or as an evildoer, or as a busybody in other men's matters. Yet if any man suffer as a Christian, let him not be ashamed; but let him glorify God on this behalf. For the time is come that judgment must begin at the house of God: and if it first begin at us, what shall the end be of them that obey not the gospel of God? And if the righteous scarcely be saved, where shall the ungodly and the sinner appear? Wherefore let them that suffer according to the will of God commit the keeping of their souls to him in well doing, as unto a faithful Creator. (1 Pet 4:12–19)

*Peirasmós*, understood as *thlîpsis*, as psychophysical affliction, Peter says, is something to be accepted heartily by Christians. Indeed, a good Christian should rejoice in suffering, since he or she "shares in the sufferings of Christ." Of the same tenor is the message that Paul sends to the Romans: "And not only so, but we glory in tribulations also: knowing that tribulation worketh patience; And patience, experience; and experience, hope" (Rom 5:3–4). *Peirasmós*, understood as *thlîpsis*, as psychophysical affliction, Paul says, is a valuable opportunity to grow in such foundational virtues as patience and hope.

And again, do you remember Christ's message to the church at Smyrna in Rev 2:10? Jesus himself encourages the faithful of that community not to fear the

---

38. Moule, "An Unsolved Problem," 75.

39. Cyril of Alexandria explains, "It is necessary not to dare too much in temptations, but rather to consider the weakness of our mind" (*In Lucam*, 11.4).

persecution they are about to face: "Fear none of those things which thou shalt suffer: behold, the devil shall cast some of you into prison, that ye may be tried [*peirázō*]; and ye shall have tribulation [*thlîpsis*] ten days: be thou faithful unto death, and I will give thee a crown of life."

Finally, how can we fail to recall the famous verse from the book of Sirach that says, "Son, if you present yourself to serve the Lord, prepare your spirit for *peirasmós*" (Sir 2:1). The *peirasmós*, whatever that means, seems to be really understood as an integral, inevitable part of the life of a true believer.

St. Paul, soon after being stoned almost to death, explicitly says, "we must through much tribulation enter into the kingdom of God" (Acts 14:22).

We will also quote a famous *non-canonical* saying attributed to Jesus himself and quoted by Tertullian: "*Neminem intemptatum regna celestia consecuturum.*"[40]

Is this *peirasmós* inevitable then? And if so, why would Jesus teach us to petition to avoid it? Is the sixth petition a null, useless petition? How do we solve Moule's "unsolved problem"? In our opinion, there is only one way. To go back, more or less 2000 years, to the night that, willingly or not, changed the course of history, forever.

The night in the garden of *Gethsēmaní*.

---

40. "No one, unless he has been tested, can obtain the kingdom of heaven" (Tertullian, *De baptismo*, 20.2).

# 25

# The Lord's Prayer in the *Gethsēmaní* and the Problem of Trivialization

*Gethsēmaní* is the Grecized name of the garden where Jesus withdrew to pray after the Last Supper, on the so-called Mount of Olives. The name derives from the Hebrew construct *Găth-Shēmānê*, which literally means "oil press," an obscure omen, perhaps, of the extreme suffering endured by Jesus, crushed, shattered, smashed by excruciating psychophysical pain. What is commonly called "the agony of Christ in the *Gethsēmaní*" is narrated by all three synoptic Gospels.[1] The accounts of Mark and Matthew are almost identical, with minimal lexical and syntactical variations. Luke's account agrees with the other evangelists, but it is shorter, drier, and contains some original details.

Let us follow the narrative step by step. Immediately after the end of the Last Supper, Jesus sets out with the eleven Apostles,[2] as was his custom, toward the Mount of Olives. Once he has reached this garden called *Gethsēmaní*, he stops, takes with him his three favorite disciples, Peter, John and James—the same ones who, not by chance, he had chosen to witness his transfiguration—and orders the others to wait for him outside. With the three, he enters the garden, and, at this point, the agony begins.

Jesus begins to experience feelings of sadness, anguish, and fear. Matthew and Mark use three specific verbs. *Lypéomai* (λυπέομαι) indicates a state of sadness, grief, sorrow, and psychological suffering. *Adēmonéō* (ἀδημονέω) indicates a state of psychic heaviness, distress, almost depression. *Ekthambéō* (ἐκθαμβέω) indicates a state of frightening terror. Jesus confesses this to his disciples, "My soul is exceeding sorrowful, even unto death: tarry ye here, and watch with me" (Matt 26:38).

---

1. There is only a vague hint of this in John (John 12:27).
2. Judas, possessed by Satan, already left to call the guards of the high priests to arrest Jesus.

Imagine the three of them. Never before had they seen their master in such a condition. They had always seen him spiritually strong, always in control of the situation. A fearless leader, at whose command they had sworn that they could even meet death (Matt 26:35; Mark 14:31). But now it is different. Suddenly, Jesus' soul is about to collapse in a state of affliction never felt before. In the total darkness of the night, among the black shadows of the olive trees, in the solitary silence of the mountain, Jesus begins to appear terrified. A new terror, so frightening to take his breath away. The change of register is as violent as it is sudden.

Jesus is about to reveal to his closest disciples—and only to them—the deepest mystery of his human nature (complementary to his divine nature). It will be a painful, deeply humiliating spectacle, and Jesus feels the need (an all-too-human need) to feel the support of his most trusted friends. But it is not mere psychological support that Jesus needs at this moment. He needs them to see, to be spectators of the mystery that is about to be revealed before their eyes, and to understand. That is why he recommends to them, "tarry ye here and watch with me."

The idea of keeping watch, of being alert and ready, is not new. Jesus had already instructed his disciples on the importance of keeping watch so that they would be prepared when the Son of Man returns (Matt 24:42–44; Mark 13:33–37; Luke 21:34–36). And here, in the garden of *Gethsēmaní*, Jesus' first concern is that his disciples keep watch with him—an indication that the disciples, overcome by fatigue and sleep and probably unable to grasp the exceptional nature of the events that were unfolding before their eyes, will blatantly disregard.

Jesus moves away from the three, but not by much, and throwing himself face down on the ground begins to pray. The situation is the following. Jesus, prostrated in the thick of the garden; a little further back Peter with John and James; further down at the entrance to the garden, perhaps now out of sight, all the other eight apostles, waiting. But Jesus is no longer with them. He is immersed in an intense and heartbreaking dialogue with the Father. And he prays. He prays desperately. The three disciples can clearly hear his words. And what he prays is none other than the prayer that he himself had taught them—the Lord's Prayer. Admittedly, not in the same two schematic forms that he had codified in Matt 6:9–13 or Luke 11:2–4. But the salient concepts and expressions are unmistakable.

A sort of "third Our Father," we could call it, hidden between the lines and reinterpreted by the author himself, which becomes, to all intents and purposes, a "My Father." And it is with this expression that Jesus begins his prayer in Matt 26:39.[3] Mark even gives us the exact expression in Aramaic, Jesus' *ipsissima vox*: "Abba!" he shouts, face to the ground. *Abba* is the Greek transliteration of the Aramaic term ' *ăbbā*' (אַבָּא), about whose exact meaning scholars have long debated. Many point to the fact that ' *ăbbā*' represents the loving way in which children address their parent in childhood—a kind of "daddy." In this sense, this term, which Mark wanted to bring

---

3. "Πάτερ μου [*Páter mou*]" = "My Father."

back into Aramaic so that its original meaning would not be lost, would represent all the typically familial intimacy between God the Father and God the Son.

While this is certainly true, to reduce Jesus' 'ăbbā' invocation to a simple and colloquial sort of "daddy" would be wrong and we would risk losing sight of a fundamental aspect. From a semantic point of view, 'ăbbā' indicates not only an affective relationship between the two, but above all a relationship of complete dependence, trust, and obedience of the son toward his father. It is a term that reaffirms the authority of the father over the son. Authority to which the son surrenders himself completely. It is an informal and formal term at the same time, probably untranslatable. It is reminiscent of that tragic "Father!" pronounced by Isaac in Gen 22:7, after having, unaware of everything, followed his father Abraham in silence to the place where his sacrifice was to take place. In the same way, now that the Father is asking his Son for the ultimate sacrifice, the Son turns to him with that very sorrowful invocation, 'ăbbā', to signify a last desperate request for help, but at the same time a submission to the authority and will of the Father: "O my Father, if it be possible, let this cup pass from me: nevertheless not as I will, but as thou wilt" (Matt 26:39).

Let us pause to analyze this prayer. *Ei dynatón estin* (εἰ δυνατόν ἐστιν): if it be possible. Every request to God is subject to this precondition. God cannot guarantee anything that is not compatible with his providential plan. If the human request, whatever it may be, becomes an insurmountable obstacle to the implementation of divine Providence, the prayer immediately becomes null and void, inadmissible. This does not mean that every human request, which is not an insurmountable obstacle to the implementation of divine Providence, must be automatically granted. The divine will to modify the ways and times of the implementation of his providential plan to meet the human request is part of the infinite mercy of God, and is not guaranteed *a priori*, but proceeds from a special grace granted by God himself. What counts is the ultimate goal—the realization of Providence. The ways and times in which it will be realized are secondary and can be modified at the discretion of the Father. Hence the great mystery of the power of human prayer, which we have already had occasion to explore.

Let us think, for example, of the episode of the miracle of the wedding feast of Cana, in which Jesus changes water into wine. This is perhaps one of the most famous miracles of Jesus, also because it was the first one in absolute. It is an episode narrated only in the Gospel of John (John 2:1–11), when Jesus was not yet known publicly, and few disciples followed him. Present at the wedding is Mary, the mother of Jesus, who realizes a problem: the bride and groom have run out of wine for the party. It is not a simple whim, nor is it a minor problem. The reputation of the bride and groom themselves is at stake, which Mary seems to be particularly worried about. Mary understands the only way to solve the situation is to ask her son for a miracle. But Mary does not even ask for a miracle. She simply explains him the problem: "They have no wine" (John 2:3). Hence Jesus' famous answer: "And what's that got to do with me and you, woman? mine hour is not yet come" (John 2:4).

The reply, objectively abrupt,[4] shows how the request has somehow displaced him. He probably didn't expect it: "It's not my time yet," he tells her. But the look of understanding between mother and son says something else: her son will grant her the request. "Do whatever he tells you," Mary tells the disciples. The prayer has already been answered. Even though his hour has not come yet.

It is a critical passage. Jesus reveals to his mother a fleeting flash of what the Father's providential plan is. And, according to the terms of that plan, the hour to publicly reveal himself to the world with a miracle has not yet arrived. It is not yet the appropriate historical moment for Jesus to reveal his divine nature. "How can you ask me such a thing?" Jesus seems to say to his mother, "My Father's plan does not contemplate me revealing myself right now!"

And yet. Yet the mother's request to her son wins out. The request of a small human being (Mary), however perfect she may be, is able to convince God to modify the timing of his providential plan for humanity. The water will be turned into wine and from that moment, anticipated with respect to the original plan, "manifested forth his glory; and his disciples believed on him" (John 2:11). This is a mystery of devastating significance. God is willing, in his infinite mercy, to make even the smallest, infinitesimal human will (such as that of preventing an embarrassment at a wedding party) become his will, provided that this human will is compatible with the ultimate implementation of divine Providence.

We are now ready to fully understand that "if it be possible," pronounced by Jesus in the prayer in the garden of *Gethsēmaní*. Jesus asks the Father, if possible, that "this cup" be removed from him. The verb used is *parérchomai* (παρέρχομαι), which indicates the idea of passing away, from the point of view of both time and space. "Let this cup pass away from me!" one might translate. The image is that of God the Father handing the Son a chalice to drink. A chalice containing a drink with a terrible taste. Almost like a father who invites his son to drink a very bitter medicine, and the son who, with his hand, tries in vain to push the cup away from his mouth and to convince his father that, perhaps, it is not so necessary for him to drink it. And just as a son who knows that sooner or later he will have to drink that bitter medicine enters into a state of agitation and sadness at the mere thought of having to swallow such a disgusting drink, so the mere thought of having to drink from the cup that the Father has offered him plunged Jesus into the most extreme terror. So much so that he cries out, "*Abba*, if it be possible, take this cup away from me!"

---

4. The term "woman," *gýnai* (γύναι), though it has been the subject of endless discussions between Protestants and Catholics, cannot have the same derogatory sense with which it is understood today. It is, for example, the same term with which Jesus will address his mother from the cross (John 19:26), when he recommends her to take his beloved disciple (John) with her.

But what is so disgusting about this cup to drink? Just the excruciating physical suffering (see scourging and crucifixion) he is about to undergo? That is possible, but not entirely convincing. Jesus was fully aware of the fate of physical suffering that awaited him. He had anticipated it repeatedly to his disciples (Matt 16:21; Mark 8:31; Luke 9:22; 17:25). There was nothing unexpected about it. He knew that soon he would die, and he had carefully prepared his departure. Lucidly. He had dined for the last time with his Apostles and had given them the gift of the Eucharist. Everything had been prepared in the smallest detail. But now, suddenly, the sight of that cup offered by the Father had brought darkness down upon his soul. What terrible concoction was the Father asking him to drink?

To understand this, we must understand what is behind the image of the chalice. The Greek term is *potḗrion* (ποτήριον), which corresponds to the Hebrew *kôs* (כּוֹס). Well, in the Old Testament, *kôs*, the cup from which God makes people drink is always associated with the concept of *orgḗ* (ὀργή), that is, of wrath and divine punishment. Let us look at some examples.

In Psalm 11(10) the idea of the cup is associated with the devastating punishment of the wicked: "Upon the wicked he shall rain snares, fire and brimstone, and an horrible tempest: this shall be the portion of their cup" (Ps 11(10):6).

The same concept is repeated in Psalm 75(74): "But God is the judge: he putteth down one, and setteth up another. For in the hand of the Lord there is a cup, and the wine is red; it is full of mixture; and he poureth out of the same: but the dregs thereof, all the wicked of the earth shall wring them out, and drink them" (Ps 75(74):7–8(8–9)).

The passage in chapter 51 of the book of Isaiah is emblematic:

> Awake, awake, stand up, O Jerusalem, which hast drunk at the hand of the Lord the cup of his fury; thou hast drunken the dregs of the cup of trembling, and wrung them out. There is none to guide her among all the sons whom she hath brought forth; neither is there any that taketh her by the hand of all the sons that she hath brought up. These two things are come unto thee; who shall be sorry for thee? desolation, and destruction, and the famine, and the sword: by whom shall I comfort thee? Thy sons have fainted, they lie at the head of all the streets, as a wild bull in a net: they are full of the fury of the Lord, the rebuke of thy God. Therefore hear now this, thou afflicted, and drunken, but not with wine: Thus saith thy Lord the Lord, and thy God that pleadeth the cause of his people, Behold, I have taken out of thine hand the cup of trembling, even the dregs of the cup of my fury; thou shalt no more drink it again. (Isa 51:17–22)

Of the same tone is the passage in chapter 23 of the book of Ezekiel, in which God speaks metaphorically to the "two sisters," Samaria and Jerusalem, both prostituted to idolatry: "Thus saith the Lord God; Thou shalt drink of thy sister's cup deep and large: thou shalt be laughed to scorn and had in derision; it containeth much. Thou shalt be filled with drunkenness and sorrow, with the cup of astonishment and desolation, with the cup of thy sister Samaria. Thou shalt even drink it and suck it out, and thou shalt break the sherds thereof, and pluck off thine own breasts: for I have spoken it, saith the Lord God" (Ezek 23:32–34).

In chapter 25 of the book of Jeremiah, God spreads his fury on all rebellious nations: "For thus saith the Lord God of Israel unto me; Take the wine cup of this fury at my hand, and cause all the nations, to whom I send thee, to drink it. And they shall drink, and be moved, and be mad, because of the sword that I will send among them. Then took I the cup at the Lord's hand, and made all the nations to drink, unto whom the Lord had sent me: To wit, Jerusalem, and the cities of Judah, and the kings thereof, and the princes thereof, to make them a desolation, an astonishment, an hissing, and a curse; as it is this day" (Jer 25:15–18).

Later, in chapter 49 of the same book, we find the same image in a prophecy about the Edomites: "For thus saith the Lord; Behold, they whose judgment was not to drink of the cup have assuredly drunken; and art thou he that shall altogether go unpunished? thou shalt not go unpunished, but thou shalt surely drink of it. For I have sworn by myself, saith the Lord, that Bozrah shall become a desolation, a reproach, a waste, and a curse; and all the cities thereof shall be perpetual wastes" (Jer 49:12–13).

Finally, in the second chapter of the book of Habakkuk, we find a prophecy against the oppressors: "Thou art filled with shame for glory: drink thou also, and let thy foreskin be uncovered: the cup of the Lord's right hand shall be turned unto thee, and shameful spewing shall be on thy glory" (Hab 2:16).

In chapter 20 of Matthew and chapter 10 of Mark, a very particular episode is recounted. James and John have a request, so to speak, brazen. They ask Jesus to allow them to sit one at his right and the other at his left in the kingdom of heaven.[5] Jesus' answer is a clear prophecy of his agony in the *Gethsēmaní*: "Ye know not what ye ask. Are ye able to drink of the cup that I shall drink of?" (Matt 20:22; see also Mark 10:38).

Also in John, who skips over the description of Jesus' agony, we find an explicit reference to drinking from the bitter cup. We are already at the moment of Jesus' arrest, when Peter had cut off the ear of Malchus, a servant of the high priest, with a blow of the sword: "Then said Jesus unto Peter, Put up thy sword into the sheath: the cup which my Father hath given me, shall I not drink it?" (John 18:11).

Finally, the noun *potērion* appears three more times, all in the book of Revelation. In chapter 14, three angels appear announcing God's judgment:

> And I saw another angel fly in the midst of heaven, having the everlasting gospel to preach unto them that dwell on the earth, and to every nation, and kindred, and tongue, and people, Saying with a loud voice, Fear God, and give glory to him; for the hour of his judgment is come: and worship him that made heaven, and earth, and the sea, and the fountains of waters. And there followed another angel, saying, Babylon is fallen, is fallen, that great city,

---

5. Curiously, in Matthew the request does not come directly from the brothers, but from their mother.

because she made all nations drink of the wine of the wrath of her fornication. And the third angel followed them, saying with a loud voice, If any man worship the beast and his image, and receive his mark in his forehead, or in his hand, The same shall drink of the wine of the wrath of God, which is poured out without mixture into the cup [*potērion*] of his indignation; and he shall be tormented with fire and brimstone in the presence of the holy angels, and in the presence of the Lamb. (Rev 14:6–10)

In the next chapter, seven angels appear, charged with pouring out the seven chalices of God's wrath on the world:

And I saw another sign in heaven, great and marvelous, seven angels having the seven last plagues; for in them is filled up the wrath of God. ( . . . ) And after that I looked, and, behold, the temple of the tabernacle of the testimony in heaven was opened: And the seven angels came out of the temple, having the seven plagues, clothed in pure and white linen, and having their breasts girded with golden girdles. And one of the four beasts gave unto the seven angels seven golden vials [*potērion*] full of the wrath of God, who liveth for ever and ever. And the temple was filled with smoke from the glory of God, and from his power; and no man was able to enter into the temple, till the seven plagues of the seven angels were fulfilled. (Rev 15:1, 5–8)

And in the very next chapter the last of the seven scourges is described:

And the seventh angel poured out his vial into the air; and there came a great voice out of the temple of heaven, from the throne, saying, It is done. And there were voices, and thunders, and lightnings; and there was a great earthquake, such as was not since men were upon the earth, so mighty an earthquake, and so great. And the great city was divided into three parts, and the cities of the nations fell: and great Babylon came in remembrance before God, to give unto her the cup [*potērion*] of the wine of the fierceness of his wrath. And every island fled away, and the mountains were not found. And there fell upon men a great hail out of heaven, every stone about the weight of a talent: and men blasphemed God because of the plague of the hail; for the plague thereof was exceeding great. (Rev 16:17–21)

We are finally able to fully understand the meaning of Jesus' prayer in the *Gethsēmaní*. That chalice that Jesus asks the Father to remove from his mouth is not just any chalice. It is a chalice filled with his wrath—his steaming anger for humanity.

And, at this point, we must necessarily approach the mystery of the divine incarnation. A mystery that too often is left in the background. A mystery that may seem inappropriate to highlight, because it does not align with the easy and reassuring idea, so fashionable, of a God who is pure love and nothing else. Certainly, God's infinite love for humankind is one of the pillars of faith, but it is only one of the two sides of the coin. If we do not understand what this infinite love consists of, we end up running into contradictions and paradoxes that are devastating for the faith itself. One cannot understand why there is evil in the world, for example. If God is infinite love, why should he allow so many evils to afflict humanity? This is one of the basic arguments of atheism. God does not exist, because if he existed, he would be infinitely good and would not allow wars, famines, diseases, calamities to happen, not only on sinners, but also on innocents.

The importance of Christ's coming into the world is generally associated with his resurrection. Jesus demonstrated by his death and resurrection that the righteous will indeed be resurrected after death. Which is undoubtedly true. An extremely reassuring message. But it is a partial view. For if we reduce Christ's incarnation to a simple demonstration of God's power (when the Father resurrects the Son), again we are losing sight of the real reason for the mystery of the incarnation. It means focusing on the consequences, but not on the causes. Christ's resurrection is the consequence of his incarnation, the consequence of the infinite divine love. But the cause of that incarnation is another. And here we come to the inconvenient mystery.

The reason for the incarnation of Christ is to be found in the other, equally infinite, divine quality: his justice. Love (read: mercy) and justice are the two most important attributes of God. And in continuous competition with each other. In the immutable divine unity, there is a continuous tension between them. One (justice) claims the necessity of punishment for every sin committed. The other (mercy) claims the necessity of forgiveness for every sin committed. The concept of infinity in relation to these two attributes must be understood in the following way. There is no sin (however venial) that can go unpunished, but at the same time there is no sin (however horrible) that cannot be forgiven. When the measure of tolerance of human *hýbris* is full and justice wins over mercy, here is that the divine wrath is unleashed violent and devastating. On the contrary, when mercy has the upper hand in the face of sincere human contrition, God's love spreads to forgive even the most terrible faults. They are two infinities that tend to cancel each other out. And if one does not fully understand this inner tension of the divine, one will not be able to understand the mystery of the incarnation, and with it the meaning of the Lord's Prayer.

When it is said that Jesus came to free us from our sins, too often it is not properly explained what this liberation consists of. It certainly does not mean that, by virtue of Christ's death and resurrection, all our sins (past, present, and future) are automatically forgotten by God. Nor does it mean that the mere coming of Christ makes us immune to temptation and therefore incapable of sinning. What, then, does Christ free us from?

God the Son immolated himself as a sacrificial lamb on the altar of the cross to appease the wrath of God the Father—wrath that was ready to explode and pour out on the whole of humanity but was held back by virtue of Christ's sacrifice (Rom 5:8–11).

However inconvenient, or ancestral, this mystery of the incarnation may appear,[6] it is necessary that it be emphasized, highlighted, brought to light in all its disruptive power. Otherwise, it is not possible to make sense of Christian theology. Otherwise, it is not possible to make sense of the Lord's Prayer.

We are now in the ideal conditions to understand what Jesus meant when he warned his disciples, "And fear not them which kill the body, but are not able to kill the soul: but rather fear him which is able to destroy both soul and body in hell" (Matt 10:28). That is, God the Father.[7] We are also able to understand in its full scope St. Paul's dire warning contained in his letter to the Hebrews: "It is a fearful thing to fall into the hands of the living God" (Heb 10:31).

Not for nothing, just before entering the garden of *Gethsēmaní*, Luke relates that Jesus uttered, "For I say unto you, that this that is written must yet be accomplished in me, And he was reckoned among the transgressors: for the things concerning me have an end" (Luke 22:37). What does it mean?

Jesus is quoting the last verse of chapter 53 of the book of Isaiah. It is necessary to read this chapter in its entirety, because it represents probably the most stunning prophecy of the Old Testament, which will find its full fulfillment in the passion and death of Christ:

> Who hath believed our report? and to whom is the arm of the Lord revealed? For he shall grow up before him as a tender plant, and as a root out of a dry ground: he hath no form nor comeliness; and when we shall see him, there is no beauty that we should desire him. He is despised and rejected of men; a man of sorrows, and acquainted with grief: and we hid as it were our faces from him; he was despised, and we esteemed him not. Surely he hath borne our griefs, and carried our sorrows: yet we did esteem him stricken, smitten of God, and afflicted. But he was wounded for our transgressions, he was bruised for our iniquities: the chastisement of our peace was upon him; and with his stripes we are healed. All we like sheep have gone astray; we have turned every one to his own way; and the Lord hath laid on him the iniquity of us all. He was oppressed, and he was afflicted, yet he opened not his mouth: he is brought as a lamb to the slaughter, and as a sheep before her shearers is dumb, so he openeth not his mouth. He was taken from prison and from judgment: and who shall declare his generation? for he was cut off out of the land of the living: for the transgression of my people was he stricken. And he made his grave with the wicked, and with the rich in his death; because he had done no violence, neither was any deceit in his mouth. Yet it pleased the Lord to bruise him; he hath put him to grief: when thou shalt make his soul an offering for

---

6. The ethical problem of the idea that God's infinite wrath toward mortals can be appeased only by means of a human sacrifice of infinite value, that is, the sacrifice of the God-man Jesus, is the object of heated debate among theologians and academics.

7. Obviously, this does not refer to Satan, but to God. Satan has no power to condemn anyone to hell, God does.

> sin, he shall see his seed, he shall prolong his days, and the pleasure of the Lord shall prosper in his hand. He shall see of the travail of his soul, and shall be satisfied: by his knowledge shall my righteous servant justify many; for he shall bear their iniquities. Therefore will I divide him a portion with the great, and he shall divide the spoil with the strong; because he hath poured out his soul unto death: and he was numbered with the transgressors; and he bare the sin of many, and made intercession for the transgressors. (Isa 53:1–12)

The truth of a God who chastises and prostrates people with pain because of their sins, is too often sweetened, almost hushed up, mentioned *en passant*.[8] Forgetting the fact that, if the profound motive of the sacrifice of Christ is sweetened, the sacrifice of Christ totally loses its meaning and its strength.

If God is "all love" and that's all, the sacrifice of Christ has no sense. If the Christian God is "all love" and nothing else, Christianity has no sense. If we start from the (erroneous) assumption that God is "all love" and nothing else, we will never understand the meaning of the sixth petition of the Lord's Prayer.

We are now in the ideal conditions to understand the reason for so much (initial) reluctance on the part of Jesus in accepting the bitter chalice that the Father is offering him in the *Gethsēmaní*. That chalice overflows with the most nefarious divine anger. That chalice contains the sum of the divine anger for all the sins committed from the beginning of creation until the end. Who can drink it if not a man who is also God?

But just because he is (also) a man, Jesus lays down on the ground and cries desperately to the Father, if possible, to see if his plan of redemption of humanity may not contemplate his atrocious sacrifice. This is a legitimate request, from a purely human point of view. God the Son is asking God the Father, if possible, to find an alternative solution. And we have learned that God can contemplate alternative solutions to his providential plan if alternative solutions exist. And Jesus knows this very well. That's why he ends the prayer with "but not as I will, but as You will." Thy will be done. Jesus is here clearly paraphrasing the third petition of the Lord's Prayer[9]. The possibility of a modification of the divine plan can only occur if that modification is a precise divine will. And in this specific case, God the Father will not grant the Son's prayer. The redemption of humanity can only take place through the supreme sacrifice of God the Son.

---

8. As Pope Benedict XVI explains, "we had long ago actually halved Jesus' message. ( . . . ) We speak a great deal—and like to speak—about evangelization and the good news in such a way as to make Christianity attractive to people. But hardly anyone ( . . . ) dares nowadays to proclaim the prophetic message: Repent! Hardly anyone dares to make to our age this elementary evangelical appeal, with which the Lord wants to induce us to acknowledge our sinfulness, to do penance, and to become other than what we are. ( . . . ) Sin has become almost everywhere today one of those subjects that are not spoken about. Religious education of whatever kind does its best to evade it" (*In the Beginning*, 61–2).

9. Some scholars even argue that Matthew's Lord's Prayer had been expanded based on these very words of Jesus in the *Gethsēmaní*, which would explain why the "Thy will be done" petition is not present in Luke's version (see, for example, Neumann, "Thy Will Be Done," 161–82).

Jesus immediately perceives the rejection of his prayer by the Father (this can be understood from a detail that we will analyze shortly). Luke tells us, and he is the only one among the evangelists to do so, that in that precise moment—in his moment of greatest human despair—an angel from heaven comes to comfort him: "And being in an agony he prayed more earnestly: and his sweat was as it were great drops of blood falling down to the ground" (Luke 22:44).

*En agōníai* (ἐν ἀγωνίᾳ), says Luke. In agony. This is a noun used uniquely in this verse throughout the New Testament. To understand the exact meaning of this psychophysical state, it is helpful to read the only other passage in which the term *agōnía* appears in Scripture, in the second book of Maccabees: "Whoever looked at the appearance of the high priest brought back a heartbreak, for the face and the change of color showed his inner torment [*agōnía*]. His whole person was immersed in a fear and in a trembling of the body from which appeared manifest, to the observer, the anguish that he had in his heart" (2 Macc 3:16–17).

The episode concerns an event that has nothing to do with the agony of Christ, but the accurate description of the high priest in agony gives us the measure of what Luke is trying to describe. *Agōnía* is a state of psychophysical torment that is so profound that it causes a psychosomatic alteration in those who experience it. The face of the high priest in question is disfigured, so disfigured that it changes color. Similarly, the psychophysical tension to which Jesus is subjected in the *Gethsēmaní* causes him to break into a cold sweat, so disruptive, so powerful, that he throws blood from his skin pores. This situation of agony is to all intents and purposes an extreme example of psychophysical *peirasmós*. The greatest of the entire earthly experience of Jesus. So shocking that Satan's *peirasmós* in the wilderness appears as "child's play."

The agonizing terror of Jesus cannot be explained by a "simple" satanic *peirasmós* (Jesus had already gone through a satanic *peirasmós* in the desert and had passed it with ease).

Jesus' cry of despair, "Father, take this cup away from me!", becomes the cry of despair of all humanity.

And so, the first thought of Jesus is to go to his beloved disciples. Where does this urgency come from? What does he have that is so important to tell them? With what little strength he has left, drenched in sweat and blood, he barely lifts himself off the ground. The weight of people's sins has literally crushed him, smashed him, just as in that garden every day olives are smashed in the press. He takes a few steps and, instead of finding them gathered in prayer as he had asked them to do, in the supreme hour of his earthly *peirasmós*, he finds them asleep. Hence, all his disappointment: "What, could ye not watch with me one hour?" (Matt 26:40). Jesus needs them to stay awake so that they may see his humiliation—so that they may understand. But how can they understand such a great mystery? And so, he gives them his most important teaching:[10]

---

10. In Luke's Gospel this exhortation even appears twice, once at the entrance into the *Gethsēmaní* (Luke 22:40), the other at the climax of the agony (Luke 22:46).

# Eis Peirasmón

"Watch and pray, that ye enter not into temptation [*eis peirasmón*]" (Matt 26:41; see also Mark 14:38; Luke 22:46).

Does this remind us of anything? Jesus, in his hour of most excruciating pain, at the height of his psychophysical *peirasmós*, interrupts his own prayer with God the Father, in which the plan of redemption of humanity is being decided, to go and remind his disciples to recite the sixth petition of the Lord's Prayer! Isn't this incredible?

And that this indication of Jesus to pray "not to enter into temptation" is just a rephrasing of the sixth petition of the Lord's Prayer is quite evident without need of too much exegesis. The only difference between the sixth petition of the Lord's Prayer and the prayer of the *Gethsēmaní* is in the verbal form: causative in the Lord's Prayer, intransitive in the *Gethsēmaní*. But the basic verb is identical. The Greek verb "to lead," *eisphérō* (εἰσφέρω), used in the sixth petition, represents the causative of the verb "to enter," *eisérchomai* (εἰσέρχομαι), used in the *Gethsēmaní*. And since Jesus was speaking to the disciples in Aramaic—where the base form and the causative form of a verb are not represented by two distinct verbs but are just two different conjugations of the same verb—the connection between the two expressions had to sound even more obvious.

In Aramaic, the verb "to lead into," *hăn'ēl* (הַנְעֵל), is nothing more than the causative form (commonly called *haphel* in Aramaic) of the verb "to enter," "to go in," *'ălăl* (עֲלַל). And even assuming that Jesus, for some reason, expressed himself at that moment in Hebrew, the result would not change. In Hebrew, the verb "to lead into," *hēvî'* (הֵבִיא), is nothing but the causative form (commonly called *hiphil* in Hebrew) of the verb "to enter," "to go in," *bô'* (בּוֹא). In Greek, *eisphérō* stands for *eisérchomai* as *hăn'ēl* stands for *'ălăl* in Aramaic (or as *hēvî'* stands for *bô'* in Hebrew). But while in Greek *eisphérō* and *eisérchomai* are two completely distinct verbs, not so in Semitic languages (*hăn'ēl* and *'ălăl*, as well as *hēvî'* and *bô'*, are two conjugations of the same verb).

Once we understand that, without any doubt, Matt 26:41, Mark 14:38, and Luke 22:46 are only a non-causal reformulation of the sixth petition of the Lord's Prayer, we have in our hands a particularly important key to deciphering the meaning of that petition. For if the two Our Father's, those codified in Matt 6 and Luke 11, are theoretical prayers, decontextualized and therefore more difficult to interpret, the "third" Our Father, that of the *Gethsēmaní*, is a prayer that is put into practice in a particular context, in the midst of a psychophysical agony. Understanding this context will be of enormous help to us in understanding the petition itself.

Let us return to Jesus who, in the midst of the most extreme psychophysical affliction, feels the need to interrupt his dialogue with the Father in order to go and tell the disciples to pray that they "do not enter into *peirasmós*" (if we understand this passage, we have also deciphered the sixth petition of the Lord's Prayer).

What might Jesus have meant by this expression? Let us look at the different hypotheses on the table.

1. One of the most trivial and incoherent interpretations that has been put forward is that the *peirasmós* of which Jesus speaks would be "the temptation to fall asleep." Jesus would be reproaching the disciples for the fact that they had fallen asleep and would be ordering them to stay awake and pray that . . . they stay awake. This explanation is so illogical in its self-referentiality that it is not even worth going into further detail. Why would Jesus interrupt his close dialogue with the Father to go and say something so illogical? And why, if he really wanted to exhort them to stay awake, did he not simply tell them to . . . stay awake? What was the point of bringing up that verse from the Lord's Prayer? As if the Lord's Prayer had anything to do with the temptation to yield to sleep.

2. Another interpretation, advanced, as seen, by Gibson, views the *peirasmós* not as a temptation that the disciples might suffer, but for which the disciples might be responsible to God. "Pray that you may not tempt God," would be the meaning of the expression. This interpretation is decidedly original, but it has no textual support. There is no example in Scripture that suggests that the expression "enter into temptation" is an idiomatic construct meaning "to tempt," in the active sense. And in any case, the concept of "tempting God" seems to have nothing to do with the context of the *Gethsēmaní*. The reason why Jesus, so out of nowhere, feels the need to urge the disciples to pray not to tempt God, honestly escapes us. Not to mention the fact that praying to God that he does not cause us to tempt God does not seem to make any logical sense.

3. Another interpretation is the eschatological one, to which we have dedicated an entire chapter. Jesus would be reminding the disciples to prepare for the End Times and the ultimate battle with Satan and the Antichrist. We have already explained how this hypothesis appears to be a stretch, for a whole series of reasons, so we will not dwell further. We will only mention the fact that Jesus, before that moment, had never spoken to the disciples explicitly about an ultimate battle with Satan, let alone with a specific Antichrist (he had simply warned them against false prophets and false christs). But if this were indeed the case, it would have been objectively impossible for the three to understand that Jesus was referring precisely to the end-time battle. Why would Jesus have spoken to them in such an occult way? Again, this expression ("not to enter into *peirasmós*") had to have an immediately understandable meaning for the disciples. It is not conceivable that it was a cryptic allusion to something of which they were completely unaware.

4. Another interpretation sees in that *peirasmós* an explicit reference to the temptation that Peter will undergo shortly thereafter—that of denying him. The prayer would be either to avoid this situation of embarrassment for Peter or in any case to have the strength to resist this temptation (depending on whether "enter" is interpreted as a simple exposition to temptation or a fall in the face of temptation). This explanation is not convincing, for at least two reasons:

a. Jesus' invitation to pray is not addressed specifically to Peter, but to all three Apostles ("watch and pray," in the plural form);

b. Jesus has already predicted not only that Peter would be tempted in a few hours, but also that he would fall thunderously into that temptation, not once but three times. Is Jesus inviting them to pray so that a prophecy that he himself had taken for granted a few minutes before would not come true?

5. Another interpretation sees in that *peirasmós* a reference to the future persecutions that the disciples will suffer. The prayer would thus be to avoid such afflictions.[11] This is one of the explanations that we consider most worthy of attention, because it remains faithful to the profound meaning of *peirasmós*, which, as we know, is intrinsically connected to the concept of *thlîpsis*, that is, of psychophysical tribulation. Nevertheless, for intellectual honesty, we must point out that even this interpretation has at least a couple of weak points:

    a. Jesus has already foretold to the disciples, and in particular to Peter, that they will have to undergo many tribulations. He himself prayed for Peter, but, if you remember, he did not pray that Peter would be spared such tribulations, but that his faith would not waver, thus taking for granted that Peter would have to go through those tribulations sooner or later. Also, according to this interpretation, Jesus would be inviting them to pray that a prophecy that he himself had taken for granted a few minutes earlier would not come true.

    b. Jesus, immediately after admonishing the disciples to stay awake and pray so as not to enter *peirasmós*, by way of explanation adds, "The spirit, on the one hand, is ready, but the flesh, on the other hand, is weak." What is he referring to? The expression is clearly defined by the use of the correlative construct *mèn* (μὲν) ... *dè* (δὲ), on the one hand ... on the other, sandwiched between article and noun (τὸ μὲν πνεῦμα ... ἡ δὲ σὰρξ), indicating a sharp contrast between the two concepts. On the one hand the *pneûma*, that is, the spirit, the soul, the transcendent component of human beings; on the other hand, the *sárx*, that is, the flesh, the instinct, the material component of human beings. This is a well-known contrast that we have had the opportunity to analyze many times. Remember how Paul complained of being trapped in the flesh, subject to the most perverse instincts? The *pneûma* represents the tension toward God, the *sárx* the tension toward sin. And the sin typically associated with the flesh is concupiscence, which includes all those disordered instincts

---

11. See, for example, what R. T. France has to say: "[The prayer] relates rather to the texting experiences which are the normal lot of disciples who try to live according to the principles of the kingdom of God in a world which does not share those values. The sort of persecution envisaged in [Matt] 5:11–12 comes to mind. In [Matt] 26:41 Jesus will again exhort his disciples to pray from deliverance from *peirasmos*, with reference to the immediate danger rather than an eschatological threat" (*Gospel of Matthew*, 252).

tending to libertinism, debauchery, avarice, violence, gluttony, and so forth. The weakness of the *sárx* is rarely associated with the concept of weakness in the face of persecution. This gloss on prayer cannot—and should not—be ignored. Here, Jesus is clearly referring not so much to persecution, but to disordered instincts, which are a natural component of human beings, and to all the sins that result from them. So, what do we do? Do we return to the original hypothesis that "entering into *peirasmós*" really means falling into (moral) temptation? Actually, even this interpretation, which would seem to be supported by Jesus' explanatory gloss, does not convince us at all. We will explain why right now.

6. The commonly accepted interpretation is that the *peirasmós* of which Jesus speaks in the *Gethsēmaní* is precisely the moral temptation to sin. Hence, the commonly adopted translation: "Watch and pray so that you will not fall into temptation." Leaving aside the fact that the Greek text does not speak of "falling" (*empíptō*), but simply of "entering" (*eisérchomai*), this explanation supposes that Jesus, in the most excruciating hour of his agony, at the height of his psychophysical suffering, felt the sudden urge to interrupt his prayer in order to deliver to his chosen disciples a teaching that, it seems, could not be postponed—to pray (imagine that!) not to fall into temptation. Now, the fact that the disciples were simple fishermen, completely unlettered, of humble origins, and probably of not very refined intellect, is something known and accepted (Jesus had to explain to them even the most obvious parables). But thinking that up until that moment they had neither understood nor ever heard that it is good and just not to fall into temptation is perhaps a bit too much. All this urgency to tell the disciples something so trivial is not justified, nor justifiable. This is one of the main reasons why we believe that reducing the sixth petition of the Lord's Prayer to a simple request to have the strength to resist daily temptations risks being an unacceptable trivialization of the text given to us by Jesus.

The *problem of the trivialization* of the concept of *peirasmós* is in our opinion the main problem—and, incidentally, the reason for us writing this essay.

The only thing to do at this point, if we want to try to unravel all this skein that seems inextricable (every interpretation exposed above seems to have insurmountable flaws), is to focus on the expression *eisérchomai eis peirasmón*, "enter into temptation." It is commonly assumed that this expression has idiomatic value, just as today we understand "to enter into temptation" in the same way as "to commit a sin." But really, in the Greek of that time, could the verb *eisérchomai* be used in an idiomatic form? The answer is simple: no, it could not.

First, let us present a simple demonstration by *reductio ad absurdum*. Let us assume that "*eisérchomai eis peirasmón*" really means "to fall into temptation," in the way we understand it today, that is, "to commit a sin." Then, since the analogous expression in the sixth petition of the Lord's Prayer, "*eisphérō eis peirasmón,*" is the causative form of "*eisérchomai eis peirasmón,*" we must infer that "*eisphérō eis peirasmón*" must mean "to cause one to fall into temptation," that is, "to commit a sin." We are back where we started. In the sixth petition of the Lord's Prayer, we would be asking God not to be the cause of our sins. Since this conclusion is unacceptable, we must necessarily reject the initial hypothesis as well: "*eisérchomai eis peirasmón*" cannot mean "to fall into temptation" in the way we understand it today.

Let us try to restrict the problem. If a solution exists to this dilemma, it must be one that makes sense in both cases—both in the intransitive form, "to enter into *peirasmós*" (as used in the *Gethsēmaní*), and in the causative form "to cause to enter, to lead into *peirasmós*" (as used in the Lord's Prayer). We have just shown that interpreting *peirasmós* as moral temptation can explain the intransitive expression (it makes sense to think that people can by themselves fall into temptation), but not the causative one (it makes no sense to think that God is the cause of our falling into temptation). On the other hand, even if "entering into *peirasmós*" were understood as a simple exposure to moral temptation, we would (perhaps) be able to explain the causative expression (it might make sense to think that God is the cause of our exposure to temptation, perhaps to see if we are able to overcome it), but not the intransitive one (as practically all the church fathers have emphasized, it would be useless to pray not to be exposed to moral temptation, which is an intrinsic, ineradicable part of the human being, born with instincts inclined to sin). How do we solve the problem then?

The verb *eisérchomai* is a particularly common verb in the Greek language and is used 198 times within the New Testament (194 if we exclude the four times it appears in the synoptic Gospels in the *Gethsēmaní* episode). In none of them is *eisérchomai* used in idiomatic form to mean something other than the literal text. *Eisérchomai* is almost always used to denote the physical entrance into a place. Typically, this place is a city, a house, a temple, a concrete place that can be seen and touched. Other times, however, it is an abstract place. Now, since *peirasmós* can be interpreted in many ways, but certainly not as a concrete place, if we want to have some minimal chance of understanding what the expression "*eisérchomai eis peirasmón*" means, it will be good to go and see all those examples where *eisérchomai* indicates the entrance into an abstract place.

We can then narrow it down further. Whatever *peirasmós* means, it is certainly not something palatable, nor is it good. If we are asking God not to take us into *peirasmós*, that *peirasmós* must be something negative, unpleasant, terrible. It is not a place where we would want to be. We can then leave out all the occurrences in which *eisérchomai* indicates entry into something abstract that produces feelings of psychophysical pleasure. For example, *eisérchomai* is used many times to indicate the entry into the kingdom of heaven,[12] or the entry into glory,[13] or the entry into (eternal) life,[14] or the entry into the rest, into the consolation provided by Christ.[15] All of these are examples of entry into something abstract, but which obviously have no relation to the concept of *peirasmós*. What is left? Just one example, but one that might put us on the right track.

It is found in chapter 7 of the Gospel of Matthew, and it is always part of the same Sermon on the Mount in which, shortly before, Jesus had declaimed the Lord's Prayer. It says, "Enter [*eisérchomai*] ye in at the strait gate: for wide is the gate, and broad is the way, that leadeth to destruction [*apóleia*], and many there be which go in [*eisérchomai*] thereat: Because strait is the gate, and narrow is the way, which leadeth unto life [*zōē*], and few there be that find it" (Matt 7:13–14).

The image is that, on the one hand, of a narrow street, almost impassable and desolate, at the end of which an equally narrow door allows entry into eternal life, into the kingdom of heaven.[16] On the other hand, we are presented with a wide and spacious street, easy to travel and crowded with people, at the end of which a door, equally wide, leads to eternal death. The term used here is *apóleia* (ἀπώλεια), which is probably derived from the root verb *apóllymi* (ἀπόλλυμι), meaning "to perish," "to destroy," "to go to ruin." The *apóleia* is therefore the eternal death, understood as God's punishment for unrepentant souls. This meaning is evident, since it is contrasted with life, *zōē* (ζωή), which appears in verse 14. The wide door represents the entrance *eis tēn apóleian* (εἰς τὴν ἀπώλειαν), that is, into eternal death. The narrow door, on the other hand, represents the entrance *eis tēn zōēn* (εἰς τὴν ζωήν), that is, into eternal life. We find here, then, a passage which, though indirectly (there is a door in between), associates *eisérchomai* with the entrance *eis tēn apóleian*, into the destruction of body and soul.

Of course, this example is too little to draw any conclusions. What is left, for what it may be worth, are the synonyms for *eisérchomai*.

The verb *érchomai* (ἔρχομαι), for example, simply means "to go" or "to come," but followed by a motion introduced by the preposition *eis* (εἰς), it becomes to all intents and purposes a synonym for *eisérchomai*, "to enter." A couple of examples are noteworthy.

In chapter 16 of Luke's Gospel, Jesus tells the parable of the beggar who, in life, lived off the crumbs that fell from the rich man's table. After death, the poor man rests in "Abraham's bosom," while the rich man is tormented in the fires of hell. The

---

12. Matt 5:20; 18:3; 19:23; 23:13; Mark 9:47; 10:15, 23–25; Luke 11:52; 18:17, 24–25; John 3:5; Acts 14:22.

13. Matt 25:21–23; Luke 24:26.

14. Matt 18:8–9; 19:17; Mark 9:43, 45.

15. Heb 3:11, 18; 4:1–11.

16. The idea of the narrowness of the door that allows entry into the kingdom of heaven will be reiterated in Matt 19:24: "And again I say unto you, It is easier for a camel to go through the eye of a needle, than for a rich man to enter into the kingdom of God."

rich man begs Abraham for mercy, asking him to let the poor man come and dip his lips in water. Abraham refuses the request: neither would it be right nor allowed. The rich man, in despair, thinking of his brothers who are still alive and destined for hell because of their dissolute conduct, replies, "I pray thee therefore, father, that thou wouldest send him to my father's house: For I have five brethren; that he may testify unto them, lest they also come [*érchomai*] into this place of torment" (Luke 16:27–28).

The term *básanos* (βάσανος) literally means an instrument of torture, which was used to convince the unfortunate to tell the truth. It is the same term used by Matthew to refer to the torments suffered by the sick people that Jesus cured every day.

In John chapter 5, we find another example. Jesus is revealing how the Father has given him the power to judge: "Verily, verily, I say unto you, He that heareth my word, and believeth on him that sent me, hath everlasting life, and shall not come [*érchomai*] into condemnation; but is passed from death unto life" (John 5:24). Literally: he shall not enter into judgment, *eis krísin* (εἰς κρίσιν). Jesus is obviously not saying that those who believe his word will not be subjected to the Last Judgment—all will have to be subjected to it (John 5:29). He is saying that those who believe his word will not suffer a sentence of condemnation (it is clear from the conclusion of the verse: they will pass from death to eternal life). *Érchomai eis krísin* therefore means, in this case, "to be condemned."

We have gathered at least three passages in which the entry into an abstract place (with its negative consequences) is linked to the concept of eternal condemnation to hell. Let us continue. There are other verbs, also close "relatives" of *eisérchomai*, constructed from the verb *érchomai* with the initial addition of a preposition.

For example, *synérchomai* (συνέρχομαι), constructed with the preposition *sýn* (σύν) meaning "with," indicates "going together." Followed by the preposition of motion to place *eis* (εἰς), it becomes a synonym for "*eisérchomai*," when not one but several persons enter a certain place together. In chapter 11 of the first letter to the Corinthians, Paul admonishes the faithful not to mistake the celebration of the Eucharist as a kind of feast where one eats and drinks to excess:

> Wherefore whosoever shall eat this bread, and drink this cup of the Lord, unworthily, shall be guilty of the body and blood of the Lord. But let a man examine himself, and so let him eat of that bread, and drink of that cup. For he that eateth and drinketh unworthily, eateth and drinketh damnation to himself, not discerning the Lord's body. For this cause many are weak and sickly among you, and many have died. For if we would judge ourselves, we should not be judged. But when we are judged, we are chastened of the Lord, that we should not be condemned with the world. Wherefore, my brethren, when ye come together to eat, tarry one for another. And if any man hunger, let him eat at home; that ye come not together [*synérchomai*] unto condemnation. And the rest will I set in order when I come. (1 Cor 11:27–34)

This "coming together into condemnation" is so reminiscent of the passage just seen in John 5:24. But here it is not necessarily about eternal condemnation. Paul explains that the reason so many among them are sick or even dead is because, by their unworthy conduct, they have drawn divine condemnation upon themselves, what we have called the punitive psychophysical *peirasmós*.

Another verb, *apérchomai* (ἀπέρχομαι), constructed with the preposition *apó* (ἀπό) meaning "away from," indicates "leaving." It is a verb that in many cases is used as an intensive, emphatic form of the verb *érchomai*. For example, in chapter 25 of Matthew's Gospel, Jesus is talking about the Last Judgment: "And these shall go away [*apérchomai*] into everlasting punishment: but the righteous into life eternal" (Matt 25:46).

In chapter 8 of Luke's Gospel, the episode is described in which a pack of demons, which Jesus has just brought out of an unfortunate man, are terrified by his presence: "And they besought him that he would not command them to go out [*apérchomai*] into the deep" (Luke 8:31). Jesus, having power over demons, could have decided to relegate them to hell.

But the most significant example is, in our opinion, the one found in chapter 9 of Mark, where the verb *apérchomai* is placed in close correlation with the verb *eisérchomai*:

> And if thy hand is an occasion of sin for thee, cut it off: it is better for thee to enter [*eisérchomai*] into life maimed, than having two hands to go into [*apérchomai*] hell, into the fire that never shall be quenched: Where their worm dieth not, and the fire is not quenched. And if thy foot is an occasion of sin for thee, cut it off: it is better for thee to enter [*eisérchomai*] halt into life, than having two feet to be cast into hell, into the fire that never shall be quenched: Where their worm dieth not, and the fire is not quenched. And if thine eye are an occasion of sin for thee, pluck it out: it is better for thee to enter [*eisérchomai*] into the kingdom of God with one eye, than having two eyes to be cast into hell fire: Where their worm dieth not, and the fire is not quenched. (Mark 9:43–48)

The triple emphatic repetition of the same concept allows us to appreciate an important detail. On the one hand, if one avoids sin, one enters (*eisérchomai*) into eternal life. On the other, if one yields to sin, one enters (*apérchomai*) hell, or is cast into it. The verb, used in the passive, is *bállō* (βάλλω), which means precisely "to throw," "to cast," "to hurl." The symmetry with which the passage is constructed allows us to conclude that "entering hell" or "being thrown into it" are two identical concepts, considered from two different points of view, the human and the divine. People enter hell to the extent that they yield to sin and submit to God's just condemnation. People are thrown into hell to the extent that God inflicts upon them a sentence of condemnation for their sins. They are two sides of the same coin.

If we then want to further expand the field of research and focus our attention on synonyms of *eisérchomai* not derived from the same root (πορεύομαι, ὑπάγω, and so forth), we can do so: the result is identical.[17] It may be a coincidence, but every time the expression "to enter into something unpleasant" is used, we systematically come across the ruin, the condemnation that God inflicts on us for our sins.

Let us go back to the original question: how do we solve the problem of trivializing the concept of *peirasmós*? In our opinion there is only one way: by interpreting it as punitive *peirasmós*.

We need to imagine the context. Jesus has just been offered by the Father the chalice of his wrath, full of the punitive *peirasmós* ready to fall on humanity.

Taking strength, he gets up and returns to his most beloved disciples. He has something particularly important to tell them. There is not much time left. The guards of the high priests, led by Judas, are already on their way to arrest him. He finds them asleep. Discouragement envelops him. Simon! Are you asleep? Have you not been able to keep watch for one hour? (Mark 14:7). "But watch to do what?" the three seem to say with their eyes.

Watch and pray that you do not enter the punitive *peirasmós* sent by my Father.

This is the meaning, and it cannot be otherwise. The spirit—the *pneûma*—is ready, but the flesh—the *sárx*—is weak. Being subject, constantly, to sin is a peculiar characteristic of the human condition. Being a sinner is not a possibility, but a certainty.[18] Praying not to commit sins is a prayer that is likely to be short-lived.[19] Our only hope is to entrust ourselves to his infinite mercy.

It cannot be a coincidence that when St. Paul, explaining the duality between *pneûma* and *sárx*, admonishes, "For if ye live after the flesh [*sárx*], ye shall die: but if ye through the Spirit [*pneûma*] do mortify the deeds of the body, ye shall live" (Rom 8:13). Yielding to the sinful flesh is the perfect recipe for entering the torments of the eternal death: *eisérchomai eis peirasmón*. And that this passage is, in Paul's mind, intimately related to the Lord's Prayer and in particular to the prayer in the *Gethsēmaní*, is demonstrated by the fact that, a couple of verses later, he explicitly recalls, "For ye have not received the spirit of bondage again to fear; but ye have received the Spirit of adoption, whereby we cry, Abba, Father" (Rom 8:15).

This is the important message—the last one—that Jesus leaves to his beloved disciples. It is necessary to pray, unceasingly, at every useful moment, so that the infinite mercy of God may have the better of his infinite justice.

It is impossible not to notice the similarity between Jesus' exhortation to the disciples in the *Gethsēmaní* and the words with which Jesus concludes his digression on the End Times in Luke's Gospel: "And take heed to yourselves, lest at any time your hearts be overcharged with surfeiting, and drunkenness, and cares of this life, and so

---

17. See Matt 25:41: "Πορεύεσθε ἀπ' ἐμοῦ [οἱ] κατηραμένοι εἰς τὸ πῦρ τὸ αἰώνιον τὸ ἡτοιμασμένον τῷ διαβόλῳ καὶ τοῖς ἀγγέλοις αὐτοῦ" = "Go away, away from me, ye cursed, into everlasting fire, prepared for the devil and his angels"; Rev 13:10; 17:8, 11.

18. See 1 Kgs 8:46: "there is no man that sinneth not."

19. See Ps 51(50):5(7): "Behold, I was shapen in iniquity; and in sin did my mother conceive me."

that day come upon you unawares. For as a snare [*pagís*] shall it come on all them that dwell on the face of the whole earth. Watch ye therefore, and pray always, that ye may be accounted worthy to escape all these things that shall come to pass, and to stand before the Son of man" (Luke 21:34–36).

It is, in some ways, the prose version of the dry exhortation in the *Gethsēmaní*. Here Jesus was talking about the final condemnation, that of the Last Judgment, which will come upon the world as an unexpected snare. Remember? Snare, *pagís*, is used often as a metaphor for *peirasmós*. Of punitive *peirasmós*, in this case. And so, we must pray that that *peirasmós*, that snare sent by God as a just punishment for our sins, does not seize us and take us away forever, to eternal condemnation.

But there is no more time to explain further. The time for recommendations is over. Jesus retraces his steps. He throws himself back on the ground: "O my Father, if this cup may not pass away from me, except I drink it, thy will be done" (Matt 26:42).

These sound like the same words as before, but they are not. If the previous prayer began with "if it be possible," now the prayer begins with "if it may not." Jesus has become fully aware that the Father is not willing to remove that cup from his mouth. And so, he concludes with the third petition of the Lord's Prayer: "Thy will be done." Jesus accepts his own sacrifice. He accepts it by abandoning himself totally to the will of the Father.

At this point a heartbreaking "ballet" begins. Jesus returns to his disciples. Same scene. He would like to speak to them, perhaps explain further, but they have fallen asleep again. Obviously, they did not understand. But how could they have even perceived the mystery of his agony? They are embarrassed, they do not know what to say (Mark 14:40). Jesus returns to pray for the third time, continuing to repeat the same words (Matt 26:44). And for the third time, he returns to the disciples.[20] Same scene.

But there is no more time for reproaches or exhortations. The footsteps of the guards can be heard in the distance. They better rest for what little time remains. The Son of Man is ready to be immolated. Just like the lamb that the Jews, that same day, used to slaughter for the Passover celebration.

---

20. The threefold repetition of the same scene has high symbolic value and denotes the solemnity of the moment.

# 26

## *Agnus Dei*

The Passover was celebrated every year on the 14th of the month of Nisan (between March and April), as solemnly established by the Lord in Lev 23:5 as a commemoration of the liberation of Israel from the slavery of Egypt, which lasted 430 years. We have already had the opportunity to analyze the terrifying sequence of calamities inflicted by God on Pharaoh. The Passover commemorated the last and most tragic of those scourges, namely the extermination of all the firstborn, including Pharaoh's own son (it will be the blow that will definitively break all resistance and will ensure that the Israelites will be set free). More specifically, Passover celebrated the fact that the Lord did not allow his Destroying Angel to enter the homes of the Israelites to strike down their firstborn sons. The protection of their families had been guaranteed by God himself, who had commanded them to immolate a lamb at sunset and with its blood to sprinkle the jambs and vaults of their doors. This would be the signal for the Destroying Angel not to enter those houses, but to *pass over*.

The lamb, and its blood in particular, in Jewish symbolism, were understood as the instrument by which the Israelites were delivered from evil (the yoke of Pharaoh) and at the same time spared from the punitive *peirasmós* that had fallen on the wicked. We can speak in this case without a shadow of a doubt of *peirasmós* because this is precisely the term with which the Septuagint translates *măssâ* (מַסָּה), the Hebrew term that indicates the ten calamities inflicted on the Egyptians by God.[1]

These calamities are the result of the furious explosion of the divine *orgḗ* against Pharaoh. God had warned the Israelites. His wrath, provoked by Pharaoh's *hýbris*, could not wait a minute longer. They would have to eat the flesh of the lamb quickly, before midnight, to allow the Destroying Angel to impart the nefarious condemnation: "And thus shall ye eat it; with your loins girded, your shoes on your feet, and

---

1. Deut 4:34; 7:19; 29:3.

your staff in your hand; and ye shall eat it in haste: it is the Lord's passover. For I will pass through the land of Egypt this night, and will smite all the firstborn in the land of Egypt, both man and beast; and against all the gods of Egypt I will execute judgment: I am the Lord. And the blood shall be to you for a token upon the houses where ye are: and when I see the blood, I will pass over you, and the plague shall not be upon you to destroy you, when I smite the land of Egypt" (Exod 12:11–13).

At exactly midnight, the scourge comes down on Pharaoh and his people: "And it came to pass, that at midnight the Lord smote all the firstborn in the land of Egypt, from the firstborn of Pharaoh that sat on his throne unto the firstborn of the captive that was in the dungeon; and all the firstborn of cattle. And Pharaoh rose up in the night, he, and all his servants, and all the Egyptians; and there was a great cry in Egypt; for there was not a house where there was not one dead" (Exod 12:29–30).

The devastation is total, despair is rampant. The terrifying punitive *peirasmós*, clamored for by the infinite divine justice, is accomplished. But the blood of the sacrificial lamb has protected the Israelites and delivered them from the fury of divine wrath. This dynamic, somewhat obscure and certainly singular, of "passing over" every house sprinkled with the blood of the lamb, will find full clarification and fulfillment in the figure of Christ who, as a new sacrificial lamb—a lamb without blemish (Exod 12:5)—will be immolated precisely on the day of the celebration of the Passover to save humanity from the imminent[2] fury of the divine *orgḗ*.

If we do not understand this passage, if we do not always keep it in mind, it is not possible to understand the agony in the *Gethsēmaní*, nor is it possible to understand the meaning of the Lord's Prayer, which is recited over and over again in that very garden.

Jesus had made it clear: "Ye know that after two days is the feast of the Passover, and the Son of man is betrayed to be crucified" (Matt 26:2). The sacrifice of the paschal lamb overlaps with the sacrifice of the Son of God. The consecration will take place precisely during the Last Supper. It is the dinner during which Christ *immolates himself*: "And as they were eating, Jesus took bread, and blessed it, and brake it, and gave it to the disciples, and said, Take, eat; this is my body. And he took the cup, and gave thanks, and gave it to them, saying, Drink ye all of it; For this is my blood of the new covenant, which is shed for many for the remission of sins" (Matt 26:26–28).

His death represents the ultimate sacrifice, offered on the altar of the cross, to appease the Father's wrath, brought about by human *hýbris*. His blood, like that of the lamb slaughtered in the Exodus, consecrated at the Last Supper, will literally be poured out in the garden of *Gethsēmaní*, then spilled in rivers under the blows of the scourging ordered by Pilate, will then drip from his thorn-perforated temples, sprinkle the streets of Jerusalem, from the Praetorium up to Calvary, and finally impregnate the wood of the altar on which Christ is nailed. As the blood of the lamb slaughtered

---

2. See Matt 3:4–11; 1 Thess 1:10.

in the Exodus and sprinkled on the houses of the Israelites had delivered them from the destructive fury of God.

Only by keeping this dynamic in mind is it possible to understand the cry that Jesus utters from the cross: ʼ ēlî, ʼ ēlî, lāmâ shəvāqtănî (יְנַתְקְבֹּשׁ הָמָל יְלֵא יְלֵא). "My God, my God, why have you forsaken me?"[3] Not only does Jesus publicly reveal himself as the one of whom David sang in Psalm 22(21) (and thus as the fulfillment of Scripture). But, at the same time, he describes with an excruciating cry the terrifying misfortune of us humans, who, morally dead in sin, dig an unbridgeable chasm between ourselves and God, and bring about the definitive estrangement of divine mercy. Through the compassion with which the Father looks upon the naked body of the Son on the cross, the Father's anger toward humanity vanishes. And humanity is finally saved. The Son, by making himself a perfect sacrifice in the eyes of the Father, has thus redeemed a humanity destined for destruction.

> *Libera nos a malo.*
> *Agnus Dei, qui tollis peccata mundi, miserere nobis.*[4]

This is the great mystery on which Christianity is founded, and without which Christianity and all its doctrine lose their meaning. People, in their lowest nothingness, in their tragic moral corruption, draw upon themselves, every moment, the indignation of God the Father. Their only anchor of salvation is to appeal to his mercy. To clamor for his mercy. As Jesus taught his disciples in the *Gethsēmaní*: watch and pray that you do not run into *peirasmós*.

This mystery, as great as it is terrible in its rawness, has always been present in the church for almost two thousand years. But if we go and read the text of the Traditional Latin Mass (the Tridentine Mass), renamed by Pope Benedict XVI as the Extraordinary Form, based on the Roman Missal published in 1962, it is striking to note the emphasis with which, repetitively—almost obsessively—the celebrant asks, prays, and implores the Father to grant the faithful forgiveness for their sins. From the beginning to the very end of the Mass.

The Tridentine Mass begins with the sprinkling of holy water, the symbol of divine mercy that descends upon people and cleanses them of their sins. If the rite of sprinkling takes place outside the Easter season, an antiphon taken from Psalm 51(50) is sung: "*Asperges me, Domine, hyssopo et mundabor. Lavabis me, et super nivem dealbabor. Miserere mei, Deus, secundum magnam misericordiam tuam.*"[5]

Psalm 51(50) is not chosen at random. It is the heartbreaking psalm in which David, immediately after committing adultery, collapses under the remorse of the sin he has committed, admits all his faults, and implores God to grant him his mercy.

---

3. Mark 15:34; Matt 27:46.

4. Lamb of God, who takes away the sins of the world, have mercy on us.

5. "You will sprinkle me, Lord, with hyssop, and I will be pure. You will wash me, and I will be more resplendent than snow. Have mercy on me, God, according to your great mercy."

During the Easter season, however, another antiphon is sung, partly taken from Ezek 47:1 and partly from Psalm 118(117), but always centered on the theme of purification and mercy: "*Vidi aquam egredientem de templo, a latere dextro, alleluia: Et omnes ad quos pervenit aqua ista, salvi facti sun. Et dicent: alleluia, alleluia. Confitemini Domino quoniam bonus: quoniam in saeculum misericordia eius.*"[6]

Immediately following the rite of sprinkling, the celebrant recites a few verses, to which the assembly responds, "*Ostende nobis, Domine, misericordiam tuam.*"[7]

At this point the proper Mass begins with the choir intoning the *Introibo ad altare Dei*[8] from Psalm 43(42), in which the following is requested: "*Judica me, Deus, et discerne causam meam de gente non sancta: ab homine iniquo, et doloso erue me.*"[9]

Let us pay attention to the type of request. Deliverance from evil—from the unrighteous and false people—can only come about through a just judgment, which knows how to distinguish the cause of the righteous from that of the wicked. The main concern is that the fury of the divine *orgḗ*, stirred up by the sins of the wicked, will wipe out the righteous as well. This is something not given *a priori*. That is why it is necessary, again, to appeal to divine mercy.

The Mass continues with the celebrant reciting the *Confiteor*, the prayer of admission of one's sins, to which the assembly of the faithful responds with a request for mercy: "*Misereatur tui omnipotens Deus, et dimissis peccatis tuis, perducat te ad vitam aeternam.*"[10]

In turn, the celebrant responds to the assembly with the same request for mercy. He then continues, "*Indulgentiam, absolutionem, et remissionem peccatorum nostrorum tribuat nobis omnipotens et misericors Dominus.*"[11]

A little further on, the celebrant repeats the same formula pronounced previously ("*Ostende nobis, Domine, misericordiam tuam*"), to which the assembly replies, "*Et salutare tuum da nobis.*"[12]

This introductory part of the Mass ends with a twofold request for remission of sins: "*Aufer a nobis, quaesumus, Domine, iniquitates nostras: ut ad Sancta sanctorum puris mereamur mentibus introire. Per Christum Dominum nostrum. Amen. Oramus

---

6. "I saw water gushing from the Temple, from the right side, Alleluia. And all those to whom this water came were saved. And they shall say, Alleluia, Alleluia. Celebrate the Lord, for he is good; for eternal is his mercy."

7. "Show us, O Lord, your mercy."

8. James Joyce opens his celebrated novel "Ulysses" with a parody of the entrance in the Tridentine Mass, in which Buck Mulligan, holding a bowl "on which were laid, crossed, a mirror and a razor," intones this very formula in Latin.

9. "Judge me, God, and distinguish my cause from that of the unholy folk: deliver me from the iniquitous and false man."

10. "May Almighty God have mercy on you, forgive you and your sins, and lead you to eternal life."

11. "May the almighty and merciful Lord grant us indulgence, absolution, and remission of our sins."

12. "And grant us your salvation."

*te, Domine, per merita Sanctorum tuorum, quorum reliquiae hic sunt, et omnium Sanctorum: ut indulgere digneris omnia peccata mea. Amen.*"[13]

The choir follows by singing the *Kýrie Eléison*, in which the plea for mercy is made nine times (first three times to the Lord, then three times to Christ, then three times again to the Lord). After the *Kýrie*, the *Gloria* is sung, in which the Lamb of God is implored, again, three times, to accept the plea for mercy: "*Domine Fili unigenite, Jesu Christe, Domine Deus, Agnus Dei, Filius Patris, qui tollis peccata mundi, miserere nobis; qui tollis peccata mundi, suscipe deprecationem nostram. Qui sedes ad dexteram Patris, miserere nobis.*"[14]

The Mass continues with the usual sequence: readings, homily, Creed.

At this point the second part of the Mass begins, in which the sacrifice of the Lamb of God is celebrated. The antiphon of the offertory explicitly asks God to accept the sacrifice of the immaculate host in remission of sins: "*Suscipe, sancte Pater, omnipotens aeterne Deus, hanc immaculatam hostiam, quam ego indignus famulus tuus offero tibi Deo meo vivo et vero, pro innumerabilibus peccatis, et offensionibus, et negligentiis meis, et pro omnibus circumstantibus et pro omnibus fidelibus christianis vivis atque defunctis: ut mihi et illis proficiat ad salutem in vitam aeternam. Amen.*"[15]

The celebrant, with the deacon, continues with the offering of the chalice, in which clemency is expressly implored, by virtue of the sweet odor that, from the shed blood of the lamb, ascends to the nostrils of God: "*Offerimus tibi, Domine, calicem salutaris, tuam deprecantes clementiam: ut in conspectu divinae majestatis tuae, pro nostra et totius mundi salute, cum odore suavitatis ascendat. Amen.*"[16] Then, a humble plea for acceptance of the sacrifice: "*In spiritu humilitatis, et in animo contrito suscipiamur a te, Domine: et sic fiat sacrificium nostrum in conspectu tuo hodie, ut placeat tibi, Domine Deus.*"[17]

---

13. "Remove from us, we ask you, Lord, our sins, so that we may be worthy to enter the *Sancta Santorum* with a pure mind. Through Christ our Lord. Amen. We beseech thee, Lord, by the merits of thy saints whose relics are here, and of all the saints, that Thou deignest to forgive all my sins. Amen."

14. "Lord Only Begotten Son, Jesus Christ, Lord God, Lamb of God, Son of the Father, who takes away the sins of the world, have mercy on us. You who take away the sins of the world, receive our prayer. You who sit at the right hand of the Father, have mercy on us."

15. "Accept, holy Father, almighty and eternal God, this immaculate host, which I, an unworthy servant, offer to you, my living and true God, for my innumerable sins, offenses, and negligence, and for all those gathered here and for all the faithful Christians living and dead, that I may obtain for myself and for them salvation in eternal life. Amen."

16. "We offer you, Lord, the chalice of salvation, imploring your clemency, so that it may ascend, with sweet odor, into the presence of your divine majesty, for our salvation and that of the whole world."

17. "With a spirit of humility and a contrite soul, we implore you, Lord, that our sacrifice may be pleasing to you today, Lord God."

The blessing of the offerings concludes with yet another request for mercy, accompanied by the pleasant smell of incense, which propitiates divine favor: "*Incensum istud a te benedictum, ascendat ad te, Domine: et descendat super nos misericordia tua.*"[18]

The celebrant, standing on the right side of the altar, washes his hands as a gesture of purification before the sacrifice, and recites a prayer, taken from Psalm 26(25), in which we find themes already met previously: "*Ne perdas cum impiis, Deus: animam meam, et cum viris sanguinum vitam meam. In quorum manibus iniquitates sunt: dextera eorum repleta est muneribus. Ego autem in innocentia mea ingressus sum: redime me, et miserere mei.*"[19] The concern that the divine punitive *peirasmós* will destroy the righteous along with the wicked triggers yet another plea for mercy.

At this point begins a long section in which the celebrant implores, again, through the intercession of all the saints, that God deigns to accept the sacrifice about to be made on the altar. The most salient passage reads, "*Hanc igitur oblationem servitutis nostrae, sed et cunctae familiae tuae, quaesumus, Domine, ut placatus accipias: diesque nostros in tua pace disponas, atque ab aeterna damnatione nos eripi, et in electorum tuorum jubeas grege numerari.*"[20]

We find here the participle *placatus*, which indicates the idea of a God who, *appeased* in his wrath by virtue of the sacrifice about to be celebrated, extends his mercy over humankind and spares us eternal damnation. The Latin verb *eripio* does not simply indicate the action of "saving," but precisely that of "snatching," of "subtracting with force" from eternal death. It would be an appropriate translation of the verb *rhýomai* (ῥύομαι), which appears in the seventh petition of the Lord's Prayer.

This part is followed by the traditional consecration of the Eucharist. But it is expressly juxtaposed with the sacrifices that Abel, Abraham, and the high priest Melchizedek had offered to God: "*Supra quae propitio ac sereno vultu respicere digneris: et accepta habere, sicuti accepta habere dignatus es munera pueri tui justi Abel, et sacrificium Patriarchae nostri Abrahae: et quod tibi obtulit summus sacerdos tuus Melchisedech, sanctum sacrificium, immaculatam hostiam.*"[21]

The canon of the Mass concludes with a prayer in a low voice by the celebrant who once again reiterates the hope of the faithful in divine mercy ("*de multitudine miserationum tuarum sperantibus*"). This request is followed by the recitation of the

---

18. "May this incense, blessed by you, ascend to you, Lord, and may your mercy descend upon us."

19. "Destroy not with the wicked, O God, my soul, nor my life with that of murderers. Their hands are dripping with iniquity: their right hand is full of misdeeds. But I stand in my innocence: save me and have mercy on me."

20. "Therefore, we ask that you, O Lord, in your appeasement, accept this oblation of service not only from us but also from your whole family, that you dispose our days in your peace, and command that we be saved from eternal damnation and included in the flock of your chosen ones."

21. "Deign to look upon these offerings with an auspicious and serene countenance and accept them, as you deigned to accept the offerings of your righteous servant Abel, the sacrifice of our patriarch Abraham, and the holy sacrifice offered to you by your high priest Melchizedek, an immaculate victim."

Lord's Prayer, at the end of which the last petition is resumed and expanded to ask for deliverance from every evil (present, past, and future) and, more specifically deliverance from every sin (in the sense of "forgiveness of sins") and from every tribulation: "*ut ope misericordiae tuae adjuti, et a peccato simus semper liberi, et ab omni perturbatione securi.*"[22]

Then, it is the turn of the choir to sing the *Agnus Dei*, a prayer in which the Lamb of God is implored three times to have mercy on us: "*Agnus Dei, qui tollis peccata mundi, miserere nobis. Agnus Dei, qui tollis peccata mundi, miserere nobis. Agnus Dei, qui tollis peccata mundi, dona nobis pacem.*"[23]

Immediately after the exchange of the sign of peace, a new request for liberation (in the sense of forgiveness) from all sins committed is found, by virtue of the sacrifice of the body and blood of Christ: "*libera me per hoc sacrosanctum Corpus et Sanguinem tuum ab omnibus iniquitatibus meis, et universis malis.*"[24] But, if it wasn't clear yet, the prayer concludes with the following formula: "*Perceptio Corporis tui, Domine Jesu Christe, quod ego indignus sumere praesumo, non mihi proveniat in judicium et condemnationem: sed pro tua pietate prosit mihi ad tutamentum mentis et corporis, et ad medelam percipiendam.*"[25] The communion with the body of Christ—this is the prayer—acts as a shield for the faithful, as a passport against any possible sentence of condemnation for their sins.

At this point, the celebrant, until then facing the altar with his back to the assembly, turns, shows the consecrated host to the faithful, and announces, "*Ecce Agnus Dei, ecce qui tollit peccata mundi.*"[26]

After distributing Communion, the celebrant returns to the altar and, while cleansing the chalice and ciborium, recites the following formula: "*Corpus tuum, Domine, quod sumpsi, et Sanguis, quem potavi, adhaereat visceribus meis: et praesta; ut in me non remaneat scelerum macula, quem pura et sancta refecerunt sacramenta.*"[27]

The image is that of the blood and flesh of Christ, which by combining with the blood and flesh of the believer, cleanses him or her of every stain of sin. It is not simply a spiritual communion. It is a communion, we might say, *biological*, which guarantees the remission of sins. It is the final act of the Mass. But before giving the final blessing,

---

22. "So that, with the help of your mercy, we may always be free from sin and secure from all distress."

23. "Lamb of God, who takes away the sins of the world, have mercy on us. Lamb of God, who takes away the sins of the world, have mercy on us. Lamb of God, who takes away the sins of the world, grant us peace."

24. "Deliver me, through this your sacrosanct Body and Blood, from all my sins and all evil."

25. "May your Body, Lord Jesus Christ, which I unworthily am about to consume, not bring me to judgment and condemnation, but through your mercy serve me as a protection of mind and body, and a remedy of healing."

26. "Behold the Lamb of God, behold him who takes away the sins of the world."

27. "May your Body, Lord, which I have consumed, and your Blood, which I have drunk, adhere to my bowels; and may it be that no stain of sin remains in me, whom the pure and holy sacraments have made new."

the celebrant reiterates one last time, in a sort of summary gloss, the meaning of the sacrifice just celebrated: "*Placeat tibi, sancta Trinitas, obsequium servitutis meae: et praesta; ut sacrificium, quod oculis tuae majestatis in indignus obtuli, tibi sit acceptabile, mihique, et omnibus, pro quibus illud obtuli, sit, te miserante, propitiabile.*"[28]

The Mass is over. The celebrant imparts the blessing, but before leaving there is still time for the reading of the *incipit* of the Gospel of John, the climax of which is reached when the following words are pronounced: "*Et verbum caro factum est.*"[29]

The celebrant genuflects at the reading of this passage, again emphasizing the mystery of the incarnation that made it possible to save humanity by virtue of Christ's sacrifice. Three Hail Mary's. A prayer to St. Michael the archangel to lock Satan in hell, and then the final supplication. A triple invocation to the mercy of the Most Sacred Heart of Jesus: "*Cor Iesu Sacratissimum, miserere nobis. Cor Iesu Sacratissimum, miserere nobis. Cor Iesu Sacratissimum, miserere nobis.*"[30]

That's it.

Literally, from beginning to end, the Traditional Latin Mass revolves around a continuous, repeated, obsessive supplication to God the Father to grant to those present his mercy, the remission of sins, and the consequent salvation from a sentence of eternal condemnation. This deliverance is obtained only by virtue of God the Son, present in the consecrated host and offered by the celebrant on the altar to God the Father as a sacrificial lamb.

It is amazing to see how the church had everything clear from the beginning. How it perfectly understood the meaning of Jesus' exhortation to the three chosen disciples in the garden of *Gethsēmaní*: "watch and pray so that you do not enter into *peirasmós*." And the Latin Mass had codified exactly what this *peirasmós* consists of.

But then, thanks also to a literal but ambiguous Latin translation of the sixth petition of the Lord's Prayer, for two thousand years it has not been able to move away from that "*ne nos inducas in tentationem*," where "*tentatio*" is always and only understood as a moral temptation.

There is not, throughout the entire Traditional Latin Mass, a single supplication for deliverance from moral temptation, as commonly understood. Instead, there is a continuous supplication for deliverance from the punitive *peirasmós* that a sinful humanity deserves, but from which it is spared by virtue of the infinite divine mercy, embodied in the Son and poured out in his sacrifice on the cross.

---

28. "May the offering of my service please you, Holy Trinity, and may the sacrifice which I, unworthy, have offered before the eyes of your majesty be acceptable to you, and may it be, according to your mercy, an atonement for me and for all those for whom I offered it."

29. "And the word became flesh."

30. "Most Sacred Heart of Jesus, have mercy on us."

# 27

# The Meaning of *Peirasmós* in the Sixth Petition

The time has come to pull the strings of our argument. We will structure it in ten points, as follows:

1. There is no logical/grammatical reason to manipulate the meaning of the verb *eisphérō* in the sixth petition of the Lord's Prayer in a permissive sense:

    a. Even assuming that *eisphérō* is a literal translation of a causative form of an Aramaic verb (probably ' *ălăl*, עֲלַל), the causative stem in Semitic languages always indicates only the *cause* of the action itself, and never implies a permissive sense (except in a few very rare cases, which however can be traced back to a causative sense).

    b. If Semitic languages want to give a permissive sense to a sentence, they have at their disposal explicit permissive constructs introduced by verbs that mean "to allow," "to let," and so forth.

    c. Assuming that the use of the causative instead of the explicit permissive construct is a not quite "mature" way of understanding God's action in the world (see Fitzmyer's "protological thinking" hypothesis) is unacceptable. First, because there is no need for it. When it is said that God is the cause of the evil that befalls people, it simply means that God is the cause of the evil that befalls people. Whether we like it or not. God creates both good and evil and disposes of them as he sees fit. Second, thinking that the Son of God would express himself in a language "not yet mature" with respect to the work of God is, to say the least, unimaginable.

    d. In Greek, as in most non-Semitic languages, there is no causative conjugation. If one wants to give a causative sense, one needs to use a causative construct, or a verb that has itself a causative meaning. On the other hand, if one wants to give a permissive sense, one simply uses a permissive construct. Both Matthew and Luke decide to translate the verb used by Jesus with "the most causative verb" existing in Greek to indicate the action of "leading into," *eisphérō*, which is usually not even used for people, but for the transportation of things and animals.

    e. When *eisphérō* is associated with the transportation of people, it always indicates the fact that those people would not go where they are led, if there was not a force, superior to them, that causes their movement and leads them where they would not or could not go. *Eisphérō* indicates a forced, compulsory transportation, often against the will of those who are transported. If Jesus had indeed given a permissive sense to the sixth petition of the Lord's Prayer, it would mean that both Matthew and Luke chose the worst possible verb to render that permissive sense. It would mean that both Matthew and Luke are very mediocre, if not unreliable, reporters of Christ's message.

2. *Eisphérō* simply means what *eisphérō* always means in the Greek language: "to bring into."

3. The Greek term *peirasmós* is the translation that both Matthew and Luke adopt of either the term *măssâ* (מַסָּה) or the term *nissāyôn* (נִסָּיוֹן), which never, within the Old Testament, indicate moral temptation.

4. When Jesus speaks of *peirasmós* in the New Testament, he *never* means moral temptation. When Jesus means moral temptation, he always speaks of *skándalon*.

5. If *eisphérō* means "to lead into," in the sense of "making us fall into," then it is blasphemous to think of a God who makes us fall within moral temptation: *peirasmós* cannot mean moral temptation.

6. If *eisphérō* means "to lead into," but only in the sense of "exposing to," then it makes no sense to pray to God not to expose us to moral temptation.

    If moral temptation is understood as the internal temptation of the flesh, of the *sárx*, of the disordered instincts that inhabit the bowels of people, then people, materially made of flesh, are *already* constantly exposed to moral temptation. They do not need God to expose them to it: *peirasmós* cannot mean carnal moral temptation.

    But even if moral temptation were understood as the external temptation exercised by Satan, which infiltrates our hardened heart and leverages the weakness of our *sárx* to make us fall into sin, still there is no need for God to expose us to it. Simply because Satan already does it himself, without needing to ask God's permission. He comes after us whenever and however he wants, based on his own free will (1 Pet 5:8). In Scripture, God has never led anyone to be morally tempted by Satan, except his Son, God-man. And for a specific reason—to test

Jesus's double nature (human and divine). God, who is by definition *apeírastos* ("untemptable"), could not, in theory, be tempted by Satan. But in order to make this happen (and this must happen, so that the plan of redemption for humanity can be brought to completion), God voluntarily decides to submit himself, in the person of God the Son, to Satan's temptation. For this reason, he has the Holy Spirit lead Jesus to be tempted. To be physically brought to be tempted by Satan is a "privilege" that God reserves only for . . . himself. But, as we can see, this does not apply to ordinary mortals: *peirasmós* cannot mean Satanic moral temptation.

7. If *eisphérō* means "to lead into," *peirasmós* cannot even mean temptation toward God (as Gibson speculates). Praying to God that he does not lead us to tempt him, that is, that he does not push us to tempt him, is illogical in its self-referentiality. Why would he do such a thing? And any prohibitive reformulations along the lines of "prevent us from" is to be rejected for the same reason as any permissive interpretation has no reason to subsist.

8. The Greek term *peirasmós* always indicates, both in the Old Testament and on the lips of Jesus in the New Testament, acute psychophysical suffering. It is synonymous with *thlîpsis*, tribulation, affliction, pain, torment.

9. Once the fundamental meaning of the term *peirasmós* (trying psychophysical tribulation) is understood, any difficulty in interpreting the verb *eisphérō* vanishes. Does it make sense to think of a God who leads us into psychophysical tribulation? Yes, it does. Like it or not, the Old Testament is a long narrative of all the psychophysical tribulations inflicted by God on his people because of their many sins and deviations from the divine precepts.

10. Once the fundamental meaning of the term *peirasmós* is understood, the discussion of whether *eisphérō* indicates a simple exposure to psychophysical tribulation or an actual succumbing to psychophysical tribulation also loses its importance. God can do both. He can test us with psychophysical tribulation (for example, to test our faith) or inflict psychophysical tribulation that we cannot escape (for example, to punish us for our sins).

The only question that remains is the following: into what kind of *peirasmós* (read: psychophysical tribulation) does it make sense to pray to God that he not take us? Let us examine all possible options.

1. Does it make sense to pray to God that he does not lead us into what we have called fortifying psychophysical *peirasmós*? That is, that tribulation that God sends to test and temper the faith of believers? No, it does not, because we would be excluding ourselves from a unique opportunity to prove ourselves worthy before the Lord and thus earn the "crown of life."

2. Does it make sense to pray to God that he does not lead us into what we have called purifying psychophysical *peirasmós*? That is, that tribulation that God

sends to forge the souls of those believers who still have too much dross in their souls, to prepare them for the encounter with God? No, it does not, because we would be excluding ourselves from a unique opportunity to meet the Lord and be worthy of accessing his kingdom.

3. Does it make sense to pray to God that he does not lead us into what we have called pedagogical psychophysical *peirasmós*? That is, that tribulation that God sends to humble the souls he still wants to save, but who sin in pride and have turned away from him? No, it does not, because we would be excluding ourselves from the last opportunity that God gives us to realize that we have deviated from the right path and thus return to him.

4. Does it make sense to pray to God that he does not lead us into what we have called expiatory psychophysical *peirasmós*? That is to say, the tribulation that God sends to the souls dearest to him, so that they may share, without having committed any specific fault, the sufferings of Christ on the cross and thus collaborate (in an infinitesimal way with respect to Christ, but nevertheless significant in the eyes of God) in atonement for the sins committed by past, present and future sinners?[1] No, it does not, because we would be excluding ourselves from a precise divine will, which wants us to be instruments of redemption of sinful souls.

5. Does it make sense to pray to God that he does not lead us into the eschatological *peirasmós*? That is, that tribulation that is supposed to be falling upon the earth at the End Times and that has to do with the Antichrist and the ultimate battle between God and the devil? The answer to this question might be yes. Generally speaking, it would be better, from a purely human point of view, not to be witnessing such a battle, with the risk of being crushed in it. But does it make sense to think that this is what the Lord's Prayer is trying to say? The answer to this question is: no, it does not. For multiple reasons. It would be a highly cryptic and completely unintelligible message to the disciples, who had no means of reaching this conclusion. It would be a confusing/contradictory request. Are we asking God to let us die before the end of the world comes? Are we asking God to do us a favor and postpone the coming of his kingdom, after having asked in the second petition that his kingdom come soon instead? Or are we asking, should we find ourselves witnessing the End Times, to survive the calamities that will befall the earth at that point? It would be an incredibly sectarian prayer—one that would only apply to the small percentage of humans (compared to all of humanity who have lived throughout history) who will inhabit the earth at the End Times. In fact, *peirasmós* does not appear in the sixth petition with the article, indicating

---

1. So many saints are witnesses to this type of *peirasmós*. We will explore, in this regard, the Diary of St. Maria Faustina Kowalska in the next chapter. See Matt 16:24: "If any man will come after me, let him deny himself, and take up his cross, and follow me."

that that *peirasmós* cannot be understood as a specific kind of tribulation that will happen only in a particular place and in a pre-established time, but rather a generic *peirasmós* that can happen in any place and time in history.

6. Does it make sense to pray to God that he does not lead us into what we have called punitive psychophysical *peirasmós*? That is, that tribulation that God sends as a just punishment and reparation for the sins committed? Tribulation that, in the most extreme case, can coincide with the condemnation to eternal torment, that is, to hell? Our answer is: yes, it does! And now we will explain why (also because it is, probably, the only option that remains).

First, is it legitimate to understand *peirasmós*, which in general indicates a "test," in a punitive sense? Can a "test" be also a sort of "punishment"? Or vice versa, can a "punishment" be understood as a "test"? This is, perhaps, the most critical passage of our argument. So, we will be extremely careful in making our point here.[2]

The idea that the *peirasmós* in the Lord's Prayer may be understood in a punitive sense ("*afflictio punitiva*") had been proposed by a couple of German scholars, Adolf von Harnack and K. Knoke, more than one century ago.[3] In our opinion, they are the only two scholars who have grasped the correct meaning of the sixth petition so far. However, their hypothesis never got the attention it deserved and was quickly dismissed, probably because they were quoting passages in the New Testament (Mark 4:17; Acts 20:19; 1 Peter 1:6; Heb 11:37) that would support the very opposite point they were trying to make, that is, the idea of a *peirasmós* understood instead as a proof of faithfulness ("*afflictio temptativa*").[4]

However, considering all the evidence we have gathered so far, we would like to explain here why not only is it legitimate to understand *peirasmós* in a punitive sense, but it is also the only true meaning that the *peirasmós* in the Lord's Prayer may be given. Let us see why.

1. The punitive meaning is the only meaning *peirasmós* had in the Old Testament. *Peirasmós* is the Greek term by which the Septuagint translates the term *mǎssâ*

---

2. For example, Gibson (*Temptations of Jesus*, 53–60) argues that *peirasmós*, in all of its known instances before 150 AD, has never been used with a punitive meaning, but only as a "proof of integrity or faithfulness." See also Dahms, "Lead Us Not Into Temptation," 223–30 and Seesemann, "πεῖρα, κτλ.," 23–36.

3. Harnack, "Bitte des Vaterunser," 942–47; Knoke, "Der urspr. Sinn d. 6. Bitte," 200–220.

4. More recently, Cameron ("Lead Us Not into Temptation," 299–301) fell short of getting to the same conclusion as Knoke and Harnack, by proposing to interpret *peirasmós* as a "trial" in the forensic sense of the word. Cameron understands the sixth petition as "Do not judge us according to our deserts, do not bring us into open court where the verdict would be inevitable." Cameron's interpretation cannot be accepted for three main reasons. First, there are no instances in which the term *peirasmós* (or the verb *peirázō*) maintains a forensic meaning of "trial." If this were the meaning, Jesus would have probably used the word *krísis* (κρίσις) instead. Second, asking God not to bring us to judgment would be useless, since God is expected to judge everyone at the Last Judgment. Third, asking God not to bring us to trial otherwise "the verdict would be inevitable," would mean to second-guess God and to distrust his infinite mercy. Who are we to anticipate God's judgment?

(מַסָּה) when it denotes the plagues inflicted by God on Pharaoh to punish him for his *hýbris* (Deut 4:34; 7:19; 29:3). This kind of *peirasmós* is no doubt punitive in nature. It retains almost nothing of its original "testing" meaning.[5] By inflicting *peirasmós* on Pharaoh, God is not really testing him (in any possible sense that a "test" can be thought of). He is not, as Gibson instead believes, putting Pharaoh to the "proof of integrity or faithfulness." God does not care about either the integrity or the faithfulness of Pharaoh. He cares about his elect people, the Israelites. God already knows that Pharaoh has no integrity at all. He is the symbol of evil, of the wicked mighty, of the liars, of the ungodly arrogant that God despises. What kind of test of integrity would this be? For the same reasons, God has no interest in Pharaoh to be faithful to him either. God already knows that Pharaoh is a pagan, that he has no faith. What kind of test of the faith would this be then? God does not want to convert Pharaoh. He just wants to destroy his *hýbris* so that Pharaoh may send his people free. He is retaliating against him for his stubbornness. He is killing his first-born son! Divine justice, by chastising his *hýbris*, is giving Pharaoh the just retribution for his bad choices. It is a type of *peirasmós* that has little to do with God testing Pharaoh and a lot with God unleashing his wrath on him and his people. Let us read what Psalm 78(77) has to say about this: "He cast upon them the fierceness of his anger, wrath, and indignation, and trouble, by sending evil angels among them. He made a way to his anger; he spared not their soul from death, but gave their life over to the pestilence; And smote all the firstborn in Egypt; the chief of their strength in the tabernacles of Ham" (Ps 78(77):49–51).

If anybody had any residual doubt about this, please go ahead and read these passages from the book of Exodus: "Wherefore say unto the children of Israel, I am the Lord, and I will bring you out from under the burdens of the Egyptians, and I will rid you out of their bondage, and I will redeem you with a stretched out arm, and with great chastisements" (Exod 6:6); "I may lay my hand upon Egypt, and bring forth mine armies, and my people the children of Israel, out of the land of Egypt by great chastisements" (Exod 7:4). The Hebrew word used here for chastisement is *shĕphĕt* (שֶׁפֶט), which comes from the root of the verb *shāphăt* (שָׁפַט), which means "to judge," "to pronounce a sentence." A sentence that can be either for or against somebody. In this case, the sentence is clearly against. Hence, the meaning of "punishment," "chastisement." God did not free his people by casually inflicting generic ordeals. That ordeal—that *peirasmós*—was the consequence of a precise judgment pronounced by God against Egypt. It was indeed a "punishment." And on top of being "just" a punishment, *măssâ* is a "test" because it becomes the demonstration—the proof—of God's power and justice. It is no coincidence that in all these passages where *măssâ* appears, this term is always associated with the image of "wonders," "miracles," and "great signs." By inflicting all these extraordinary calamities on Egypt, God is not only

---

5. See Seesemann, "πεῖρα, κτλ.," 29: "The element of temptation is not ruled out, but it should not be automatically included wherever the word [*peirasmós*] occurs."

punishing Pharaoh but also demonstrating his justice, to which nobody can resist. In fact, the verb *nāsâ* (נָסָה), from which *măssâ* is derived, may have a connection with the term *nēs* (נֵס), which represents a "flag," a "pole," a "banner" that is raised up high, a "sign" indeed, which, if performed by God, becomes a "miracle," a tremendous "sign" of his power.

But there is one more example that is usually neglected. In the book of Job, the term *măssâ* occurs again: "This is one thing, therefore I said it, He destroyeth the perfect and the wicked. If the scourge slay suddenly, he will laugh at the trial [*măssâ*] of the innocent" (Job 9:23). The Septuagint does not translate it with *peirasmós* this time. Actually, it does not even translate the Hebrew verse literally. It has a sort of paraphrasis ("For the wicked die in glory, but the innocents are ridiculed"). In any case, whatever the reason is for the Septuagint to deviate from the Hebrew, we cannot conclude that *măssâ* is not to be understood as *peirasmós* here. Instead, if *măssâ* is the term that Jesus had in mind when he recited the Lord's Prayer, this passage in the book of Job is absolutely relevant (no matter how the Septuagint decides to translate it). And what this passage is saying is that Job understands *măssâ* to be the calamities with which God afflicts not only the wicked, but also the innocent (Job 9:22). Even in this case, *măssâ* retains almost nothing of its original "testing" meaning. There is no testing going on "when a scourge brings sudden death." Death does not concede any second chance. Therefore, it *cannot* be a test of the innocent's faith and/or integrity. When death strikes, there is only destruction, ruin, disgrace, catastrophe, annihilation. That's the end of it. In fact, Job, unaware of the agreement between God and Satan, cannot understand why this is happening at all. He cannot wrap his mind around the fact that divine justice can inflict a *măssâ*, that is, a punitive *peirasmós*, on an innocent person like him. He is confusing the fortifying *peirasmós* with which God is testing him, with the punitive *peirasmós* with which God usually afflicts the wicked.

All the other four occurrences of the word *peirasmós* in the Greek translation of the Hebrew Bible by the Septuagint refer to a toponym, the proper noun of the place in the desert where the Israelites put God to the test.[6] It is a *Peirasmós* that corresponds to the name of the city (Massah). It is not used to denote the generic act of putting God to the test. This is not something that should be overlooked. There is not one single example in Scripture where the word *peirasmós* (with lower case "p") is casually used to indicate the act of testing God. When it is used, it is always used to refer to the city of Massah (or the *specific* episode of rebellion occurred in Massah). Instead, the act of testing God is always rendered by the use of the verb *peirázō*. So, we see that, when Gibson argues that *peirasmós* has ever been used only as a "proof of integrity or faithfulness," he is saying something highly imprecise. In fact, the *common* noun (not the *proper* noun!) *peirasmós* is virtually never applied to God (the verb *peirázō* is).

In any case, in all the (few) occurrences of the term *măssâ* in the Hebrew Bible (when used as a *common* noun like in the Lord's Prayer), we can always find, clearly,

---

6. Exod 17:7; Deut 6:16, 22; Ps 95(94):8.

a punitive intent. In fact, even though *măssâ* is the noun derived from the same root of the verb *nāsâ* ("to test")—exactly as *peirasmós* is the noun derived from the same root of the verb *peirázō* ("to test")—its meaning in Scripture has very little to do with the idea of "testing" and a lot with the idea of "punishment," "ruin," "destruction," "calamity," "death."

In fact, Job 9:22 talks about a God that "destroyeth the perfect and the wicked." The Hebrew verb used here is *kālâ* (כָּלָה), which means "to put to an end." God, by sending the *măssâ*, is not simply "testing." He is destroying, exterminating, annihilating. In conclusion, interpreting the term *măssâ* (and its only legitimate corresponding Greek translation, *peirasmós*) in a punitive sense is not only permissible, but it is the only way to recover the original meaning it had in the Old Testament.

2. The punitive meaning of *peirasmós* was recognized by Peter, the Apostle to whom Jesus entrusted the church. We have already seen how, in his second epistle, Peter associates the *peirasmós* with the divine punishment which fell first upon the rebellious angels, then upon humankind at the time of Noah, and finally upon the cities of Sodom and Gomorrah:

> For if God spared not the angels that sinned, but cast them down to Hell, and delivered them into chains of darkness, to be reserved unto judgment; And spared not the old world, but saved Noah the eighth person, a preacher of righteousness, bringing in the flood upon the world of the ungodly; And turning the cities of Sodom and Gomorrha into ashes condemned them with an overthrow, making them an ensample unto those that after should live ungodly; And delivered just Lot, vexed with the filthy conversation of the wicked: (For that righteous man dwelling among them, in seeing and hearing, vexed his righteous soul from day to day with their unlawful deeds;) The Lord knoweth how to deliver the godly out of *peirasmós*, and to reserve the unjust unto the day of judgment to be punished. (2 Pet 2:4–9)

Do not be afraid, says Peter. Do not despair, as Job did. The Lord, when he sends the punitive *peirasmós*, knows how to distinguish between the righteous and the wicked. The former he saves, the latter he condemns to destruction. Well, one could argue back, what about the other two occurrences of the same term *peirasmós* in 1 Pet 1:6 and 1 Pet 4:12? In these two passages, no punitive intent is to be found! Why would 2 Pet 2:9 be more relevant than these two passages? Fair question, but the answer is easy. It is more relevant because in 2 Pet 2:9 there is an obvious reference to the Lord's Prayer: "The Lord knoweth how to deliver [*rhýomai*] the godly out of *peirasmós*." Peter is quoting the seventh petition (the verb *rhýomai*, "to deliver," is the same) and replacing "evil" with *peirasmós*. He is somehow condensing the sixth and the seventh petition in one! Therefore, the *peirasmós* Peter is talking about here must be the same *peirasmós* Jesus was talking about in the Lord's Prayer.[7] Even in this case,

---

7. The passages in 1 Pet 1:6 and 1 Pet 4:12, which are talking about a different type of *peirasmós*

we can rule out the possibility that *peirasmós* means "putting to the proof of integrity or faithfulness." If it were so, why would Peter reassure his audience that God will be able to deliver them from it? If this were a test of their integrity, of their faithfulness, God would not need to deliver them. He would just need to stand and watch if/how the faithful would pass the test. Otherwise, it would not be a test of the faith anymore. So much so that, when Peter understands *peirasmós* as a "proof of integrity or faithfulness," he never tells his audience to pray or hope for God's deliverance. Instead, he tells them to rejoice!

> Wherein ye greatly rejoice, though now for a season, if need be, ye are in heaviness through manifold trials [*peirasmós*]. That the trial of your faith, being much more precious than of gold that perisheth, though it be tried with fire, might be found unto praise and honour and glory at the appearing of Jesus Christ. (1 Pet 1:6–7)

> Beloved, think it not strange concerning the fiery trial which is to try [*peirasmós*] you, as though some strange thing happened unto you: But rejoice, inasmuch as ye are partakers of Christ's sufferings; that, when his glory shall be revealed, ye may be glad also with exceeding joy. (1 Pet 4:12–13)

By reassuring his audience that God knows how to deliver them from the *peirasmós*, Peter is making it clear that the *peirasmós* Jesus is talking about in the Lord's Prayer cannot be the "proof of integrity or faithfulness."

3. The punitive meaning of *peirasmós* was in the mind of Jesus himself in his revelation to St. John. As we have seen, the *peirasmós* that appear in Rev 3:10 and that is usually cited to support the eschatological interpretation of the sixth petition, far from having any eschatological implications, is nothing more than a clear (threat of) punitive *peirasmós*. When Jesus sends the following message to the church of Philadelphia, "Because thou hast kept the word of my patience, I also will keep thee from the hour of trial [*peirasmós*], which shall come upon all the world, to try [*peirázō*] them that dwell upon the earth," he is not talking about the test of "integrity or faithfulness." This becomes clear if we consider the following facts:

a. Jesus explicitly says that the church of Philadelphia will be spared the *peirasmós* that is about to fall on the earth because it remained faithful to Jesus' word. Hence, we can deduce that the rest of the world had not remained faithful to Jesus' word. Why would Jesus send on the rest of the world a test of their "integrity or faithfulness," when he already knows that they are unfaithful? Imposing a test of faithfulness on people that have already proved to be unfaithful makes no sense.

b. If we compare this message to the one that Jesus sends to the church of Smyrna in Rev 2:10 ("Fear none of those things which thou shalt suffer: behold, the devil shall cast some of you into prison, that ye may be tried [*peirázō*]; and ye shall have

---

(fortifying psychophysical *peirasmós*), have no clear connection with the Lord's Prayer.

tribulation ten days: be thou faithful unto death, and I will give thee a crown of life."), we can clearly see a different approach. Jesus is not telling the church of Smyrna that he will spare them the suffering that is about to hit them. So, why such a disparity of treatment? Why is the church of Philadelphia spared the *peirasmós*, while the church of Smyrna is not? Is Jesus discriminating? Of course, he is not. The answer is that we are in front of two distinct types of *peirasmós*. Jesus is not promising to spare the church of Smyrna the *peirasmós* inflicted *per satanam* simply because this is indeed a test of their "integrity or faithfulness." Sparing them this test would mean to deprive them of an incredible opportunity to obtain the "crown of life." On the other hand, Jesus is promising the church of Philadelphia that he will spare them the *peirasmós* that is about to fall on the earth, because this is a different kind of *peirasmós*! It is a punitive *peirasmós*, to punish those that have been unfaithful.

4. The punitive meaning of *peirasmós* appears in at least a couple of passages of the book of Sirach. We have already seen how in the book of Sirach there is an unusual concentration of occurrences (six) of the term *peirasmós*. For this reason, the book of Sirach represents a precious source of information for the understanding of this term. In Sir 2:1, we find the famous admonishment: "Son, if you present yourself to serve the Lord, prepare your spirit for *peirasmós*." The next verse explains how we can prepare ourselves: "Keep a righteous heart and be persevering, do not be impulsive in the time of affliction" (Sir 2:2). *En kairôi epagōgês* (ἐν καιρῷ ἐπαγωγῆς). In the time of *epagōgḗ*. This is what our spirit needs to be ready for. There is a clear connection here between *peirasmós* and *epagōgḗ*. And we all recall how *epagōgḗ* is the term that refers to the calamities that God inflicts on the world because of the *hýbris* of the evildoers. So, the point the book of Sirach seems to be making here is that, if we really want to follow God, we need to be able to know how to handle the afflictions, the tribulations, the calamities that God may inflict upon the world (as a punishment for evildoers' sins). This is indeed a recurring theme: the evil that God sends upon the world as a chastisement may affect and cause pain to the innocent too. And so, how should somebody that want to serve the Lord react in this case? By falling into despair and acting impulsively, maybe accusing God of being unfair (as Job did)? Of course not, says the book of Sirach. Instead, we should persevere with enduring patience, knowing that, as St. Peter would say, "the Lord knows how to deliver the godly out of *peirasmós*."

How do we know this is the correct interpretation of Sir 2:1? It is sufficient to read a little further in the same chapter: "For the Lord is benevolent and merciful and remits sins and delivers in the time of tribulation" (Sir 2:11). *En kairôi thlípseōs* (ἐν καιρῷ θλίψεως). In the time of *thlîpsis*. Sir 2:11 uses the same expression as in Sir 2:2, by replacing *epagōgḗ* with *thlîpsis*. But the *thlîpsis* in Sir 2:11 is clearly the result of the sins of evildoers (see the explicit reference to God being merciful and remitting sins). So, all the pieces of the puzzles fit together perfectly. The *thlîpsis* in Sir 2:11 is the tribulation that God sends upon the world because of our sins, and it is a perfect synonym with *epagōgḗ* in Sir 2:2. *Peirasmós, epagōgḗ, thlîpsis*. A clear thread connects these terms and shows that the *peirasmós* in Sir 2:1 needs to be understood in a punitive sense. And that is precisely why Sir 2:11 says that the Lord will deliver those who serve him faithfully from this kind of *peirasmós*—because he is merciful and remits sins (and the punishment inflicted because of them). As we know, God has no interest in delivering someone from the test of faith, otherwise the test would be immediately invalidated.

In Sir 33:1 ("He who fears the Lord incurs no evil, but in the trial [*peirasmós*] will be delivered once and again"), we find the concept of deliverance once again. The situation is the same as described in chapter 2. The faithful have nothing to fear because no harm can come to them, but if it does, God will always deliver them. As we know very well (see chapter 19 for details), God deliverance is always either from the evil our enemies can inflict on us or from the evil that God sends on earth because of his wrath against people. And we also know that these two options may often overlap: the evil our enemies inflict on us may represent the means by which God punishes us for our sins. God never delivers from the test of "integrity or faithfulness." However, God knows very well how to deliver people from the punitive *peirasmós* (by exercising his mercy) that gets unleashed upon the earth.

5. The punitive meaning of *peirasmós* was recognized by St. Cyprian, St. Chromatius, and St. Augustine, who distinguish between two types of *peirasmós* (*tentatio*, in Latin), the punitive one and the fortifying one:

> *Fiunt igitur tentationes per satanam non potestate eius sed permissu Domini ad homines aut pro suis peccatis puniendos aut pro Dei misericordia probandos et exercendos.*[8]

> *vel ad poenam cum delinquimus, vel ad gloriam cum probamur.*[9]

> *aliis per peccatum tentatio infertur ad emendationem, aliis ad fidei probationem, aliis infertur ad gloriam.*[10]

Interestingly enough, although the idea that *peirasmós* (*tentatio*) might have a punitive sense was perfectly clear from the first centuries after Christ (St. Cyprian, St. Chromatius, and St. Augustine demonstrate this), this interpretation was never taken seriously in the exegesis of the sixth petition of the Lord's Prayer.

6. The term *peirasmós* defines a semantic field that is often overlapping with that of "snare," *pagís* (παγίς) in Greek. In fact, "temptation" is always understood as a

---

8. "There are therefore temptations imparted through Satan (not in Satan's power but permitted by God) either to punish people for their sins or to test and temper them according to God's mercy" (Augustine, *De sermone Domini in monte*, 2.9.34).

9. "or for punishment when we sin, or for glory when we pass the test" (Cyprian, *De oratione dominica*, 25).

10. "Temptation is imparted to some to repair for their sin, to some other to test their faith, and to some other for their glory" (Chromatius, *Tractatus in Evangellium Matthaei*, 14.7.1).

"trap."[11] The trap, the snare of temptation, is maliciously set by Satan to make people fall into moral destruction. However, when the *pagís* is set by God is always set with a punitive intent. The snare becomes the means by which God leads the wicked to their *physical* destruction (eternal death). This is the typical snare, the typical *peirasmós* that we should ask God to be spared from. We would like to cite, as an example among all, what to us represents the "Plea for Deliverance" par excellence, that is, Psalm 91(90). Let us read it all.

> He that dwelleth in the secret place of the most High shall abide under the shadow of the Almighty. I will say of the Lord, He is my refuge and my fortress: my God; in him will I trust. Surely he shall deliver thee from the snare [*pagís*] of the fowler, and from the noisome pestilence. He shall cover thee with his feathers, and under his wings shalt thou trust: his truth shall be thy shield and buckler. Thou shalt not be afraid for the terror by night; nor for the arrow that flieth by day; Nor for the pestilence that walketh in darkness; nor for the destruction that wasteth at noonday. A thousand shall fall at thy side, and ten thousand at thy right hand; but it shall not come nigh thee. Only with thine eyes shalt thou behold and see the reward of the wicked. Because thou hast made the Lord, which is my refuge, even the most High, thy habitation; There shall no evil befall thee, neither shall any plague come nigh thy dwelling. For he shall give his angels charge over thee, to keep thee in all thy ways. They shall bear thee up in their hands, lest thou dash thy foot against a stone. Thou shalt tread upon the lion and adder: the young lion and the dragon shalt thou trample under feet. Because he hath set his love upon me, therefore will I deliver him: I will set him on high, because he hath known my name. He shall call upon me, and I will answer him: I will be with him in trouble; I will deliver him, and honour him. With long life will I satisfy him, and shew him my salvation. (Ps 91(90):1–16)

The deliverance of the righteous, of which God speaks, is from the calamities that afflict the ungodly, from the *pagís*, the snare of the plague, of the extermination, of the pestilence, and so forth. It is a deliverance from the punitive *peirasmós* that comes upon the world because of the sins of humanity, as a retribution, as a "reward of the wicked."

The same image appears in Psalm 11(10), where the metaphor of the snare is associated with that of the cup of the divine wrath that befalls the wicked: "Upon the wicked he shall rain snares [*pagís*], fire and brimstone, and an horrible tempest: this shall be the portion of their cup" (Ps 11(10):6).

Therefore, interpreting the term *peirasmós* in a punitive sense is not only legitimate, but also recovers the original concept of "trial," in the sense of "trap," of *pagís*, which, when set by God, refers not to moral temptation, but to divine chastisement.

---

11. See 1 Tim 6:9: "But they that will be rich fall into temptation [*peirasmós*] and a snare [*pagís*]."

# Eis Peirasmón

7. The term *peirasmós* defines a semantic field that is often overlapping with that of "psychophysical tribulation," *thlîpsis* (θλῖψις) in Greek. Any "tribulation," any "suffering," any "affliction" is perceived as a "trial" by people. However, not every "trial," not every "tribulation," not every "affliction" that befalls us occurs because God (or anybody else) is putting us to the test. After all, even in modern English, the term "trial," which comes from the same root of the verb "to try," that is, "to test," may define a semantic field that retains little of the original idea of "test" and conveys instead the idea of "hardship," "distress," "psychophysical stress," *thlîpsis* indeed. The exact reason for the *thlîpsis* that falls upon a person may not be clear to that person at all. We saw how Job understood the *thlîpsis* that hit him as a punitive tribulation, when we know that it was in fact a tribulation sent by God to test his faith (the opposite may also occur). The exact reason for human suffering is known to God, and to God alone. And, in most cases, it is either to test our faith or to punish us for our sins. Therefore, interpreting the term *peirasmós* in a punitive sense is not only legitimate, but also recovers the original concept of "trial," in the sense of "psychophysical tribulation," of *thlîpsis*, which is sent by God as divine chastisement.

8. Once clarified that the semantic field defined by *peirasmós* is often overlapping with the semantic fields defined by *thlîpsis* and/or *pagís*, we can get even more detailed by presenting the following Venn diagram:

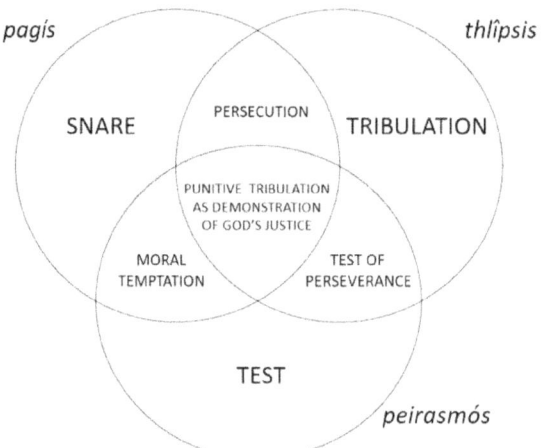

A *pagís* that is not a *thlîpsis* nor a *peirasmós* is simply a snare (like the one set by the fowler). A *thlîpsis* that is not a *pagís* nor a *peirasmós* is simply a tribulation that occurs as inevitable consequence of living in an imperfect world (like accidents, illness, and so forth). A *peirasmós* that is not a *pagís* nor a *thlîpsis* is simply a test. A *peirasmós* that is also a *pagís* but not a *thlîpsis* is a moral temptation by Satan. A *pagís* that is also a *thlîpsis* but not a *peirasmós* is a persecution that the innocent may have to undergo as an inevitable consequence of living in an imperfect world ruled by evildoers. A *thlîpsis* that is also a *peirasmós* but not a *pagís* is a tribulation sent by God to test our perseverance and our faith. Finally, a *peirasmós* that is also a *pagís* and a *thlîpsis* at the same time represents that destructive *tribulation* sent by God as a *snare* to annihilate the wicked and as a *proof* of his justice. This is the punitive *peirasmós* we are talking about.

But how can we be sure that this is the picture Jesus had in mind when he declaimed the Lord's Prayer? Well, that Jesus (and all the Old Testament tradition) always intended *peirasmós* as a psychophysical tribulation, that is, a *thlípsis*, we have demonstrated sufficiently. That *peirasmós* in the Lord's Prayer and in the *Gethsēmaní* is specifically understood also as a snare, that is, a *pagís*, is demonstrated by the use of very clear verbs of movement, *eisphérō* and *eisérchomai*, always followed by the preposition *eis* to precisely indicate the entrance *into* something. And this something that we enter or that we are led into cannot be anything other than something that is going to catch us and inflict us that psychophysical tribulation as described by the semantic field defined by the term *thlîpsis*. In other words, it must be a trap, a snare, a *pagís* that causes our destruction.

We understand this even better if we follow Luke account of the Passover. At the very end of his speech about the End Times and just before the start of the feast of the Unleavened Bread, Jesus specifically warns his disciples about the risk of not being prepared for the second coming of the Son of Man. And what kind of metaphor does Jesus use?

> And take heed to yourselves, lest at any time your hearts be overcharged with surfeiting, and drunkenness, and cares of this life, and so that day come upon you unawares. For as a snare [*pagís*] shall it come on all them that dwell on the face of the whole earth. (Luke 21:34–35)

The Last Judgment will fall upon the earth *hōs pagís* (ὡς παγίς), like a snare. Suddenly and destructively. Hence the admonishment: "Watch ye therefore, and pray always, that ye may be accounted worthy to escape all these things that shall come to pass, and to stand before the Son of man" (Luke 21:36).

As we have already mentioned, it would be impossible not to observe the connection between these words and the analogous words that Jesus will speak soon after in the *Gethsēmaní*: "Watch and pray, that ye enter not into *peirasmós*" (Matt 26:41). If we put together the exhortation in Luke 21:36 to "watch and pray ( . . . ) to stand before the Son of man," because that day will befall humanity "as a snare," with the exhortation in the *Gethsēmaní* to "watch and pray not to enter into *peirasmós*," after considering the intimate semantic connection between *pagís* and *peirasmós*, we must conclude that the *peirasmós* into which the disciples are asked to pray not to enter can only be that destructive snare, that terrible condemnation, that dreadful *orgḗ* experienced by Jesus in the garden, that tremendous punitive *peirasmós* that will catch by surprise those that are found unprepared, "asleep," and that let the weakness of their *sárx* overcome the readiness of their *pneûma*.

9. In Greek, there is a verb that is synonymous with *peirázō*, from whose root a noun is derived, which is synonymous with *peirasmós*. We are talking about the verb *etázō* (ἐτάζω) and the noun associated with it, *etasmós* (ἐτασμός). Like *peirázō*, *etázō* has the basic meaning of "to test." Like *peirasmós*, *etasmós* has the basic meaning of "test." We find, for example, both (verb and noun) in the Septuagint translation of this passage in Genesis: "And the Lord plagued [*etázō*] Pharaoh with evil [*ponērós*] plagues [*etasmós*]" (Gen 12:17). Although these calamities that God inflicts on Pharaoh have nothing to do with the famous plagues of Egypt (these occur much earlier), the concept is the same. It is a punitive *peirasmós*, or we would do better to say, a punitive *etasmós*. The term that the Septuagint translates with *etasmós* is *négăʿ* (נֶגַע), which indicates a "blow." Similarly, the term that the Septuagint translates with *etázō* is *năgăʿ* (נָגַע), which indicates the act of "striking." An affliction, a chastisement, a "blow" inflicted by God is perceived by the Septuagint as a "test." Interesting to note also that this *etasmós* is defined with the adjective *ponērós* (that is, evil), the same used in the seventh petition of the Lord's Prayer. Also in this case, a term (*etasmós*) that has "test" as a basic meaning retains almost nothing of this original sense. By inflicting *etasmós* on Pharaoh, God is not really testing him (in any possible sense that a "test" can be thought of). Instead, he is chastising him with "evil plagues."

The term *etasmós* also appears in the second book of Maccabees, used as a synonym for "scourges," an expression of divine chastisement:

> But thou, O sacrilegious and most wicked of all men, exalt thyself not in vain, waving secret hopes, while thou liftest up thy hand against the children of heaven; for thou art not yet safe from the judgment of the almighty God, who seeth all things. Even now our brethren who have endured brief torment have received from God the inheritance of eternal life. But you, by the judgment of God, will suffer the just punishment of your pride. I too, like my brothers, sacrifice my body and my life for the laws of the land, begging God to show his people that he will soon be appeased, and that you, in the midst of hard trials [*etasmós*] and scourges, will confess that he alone is God; but may the wrath of the Almighty, justly drawn upon all our race, stop with me and my brothers. (2 Macc 7:34–38)

By itself, this consideration would be no proof that *peirasmós* could/should be understood with a punitive sense. However, when put together with all the rest of the evidence collected so far, it provides strong support to our argument.

10. *Peirasmós* is derived from the same root as the noun *peîra* (πεῖρα), which has, again, as its basic meaning that of "test."[12] In Wisdom of Solomon, there is an enlightening passage in which the term *peîra* is used twice: "The trial [*peîra*] of death struck even the righteous, and in the wilderness there was slaughter of many; but the wrath

---

12. In fact, the connection between *peîra* and *peirasmós* appears even more evident if we think that in Deut 33:8 the Septuagint translates the proper noun *măssâ* (Massah), usually translated with *Peirasmós*, precisely with *Peîra*.

[*orgḗ*] did not last long ( . . . ) Faced with this the exterminator recoiled, he was afraid, for one trial [*peîra*] of wrath [*orgḗ*] was sufficient" (Wis 18:20, 25). As already pointed out for the passage in Job 9:23, death has nothing to do with the idea of "testing"—it is a capital punishment. Yet, it is so defined (*peîra*). Similarly, in verse 25, the idea of "trial" (*peîra*) is explicitly associated with the punishment resulting from God's wrath, from the divine *orgḗ*—even though God's wrath has little to do with a "test" and a lot with divine chastisement.

At this point, we hope we have managed to convince even the most skeptical reader not that the true meaning of the *peirasmós* appearing in the sixth petition of the Lord's must be understood in a punitive sense, but at least that this option may legitimately be taken into consideration and cannot be quickly dismissed as lacking any basis.

Now, to summarize what we know about the use of *peirasmós* in Scripture (Septuagint and New Testament), we observe that this term appears thirty-five times, to which we would add those two cases where the Hebrew *măssâ* is not translated as *peirasmós* (Deut 33:8; Job 9:23). Out of all these thirty-seven occurrences of the couple *măssâ*/*peirasmós*, we counted seven occurrences (Deut 4:34; 7:19; 29:3; Job 9:23; Sir 2:1; 33:1; Rev 3:10) bearing a punitive meaning; seven occurrences (Sir 44:20; 1 Macc 2:52; Luke 8:13; Jas 1:1, 12; 1 Pet 1:6; 1 Pet 4:12) indicating "the test of the faith"; four occurrences (Exod 17:7; Deut 6:16; 9:22; 33:8) indicating the toponym "Massah"; one occurrence (Ps 95(94):8), quoted also in Heb 3:8, referring to either the toponym "Massah" or to the temptation aimed at God at Massah (subject to interpretation); four occurrences (Sir 6:7; 27:5, 7; Gal 4:14) indicating a generic "test of integrity" (not from God though); three occurrences (Luke 4:13; 1 Cor 10:13; 1 Tim 6:9) indicating "temptation to sin"; two occurrences (Luke 22:28; Acts 20:19) indicating generic persecutions by the Jews; six occurrences either in the Lord's Prayer or in the *Gethsēmaní* (Matt 6:13; 26:41; Mark 14:38; Luke 11:4; 22:40, 46), whose meaning we are trying to unveil.

Based on these dry statistics, one should already conclude that the hypothesis of a punitive *peirasmós* is, at least, as valid as any other option. At the same time, Gibson's argument claiming that *peirasmós* has ever been used only as a "proof of integrity or faithfulness," appears, at best, inaccurate. In fact, if it is true that the test of the faith always implies some sort of psychophysical suffering (*thlîpsis*), it would be unreasonable to think that any psychophysical suffering we may experience is coming from God to test our faith. At a minimum, there is also psychophysical suffering (*thlîpsis*) that comes from God to punish people's sins (punitive *peirasmós*): this is undeniable.

But even worse than being inaccurate, the claim that the term *peirasmós* cannot have any punitive connotations whatsoever is uselessly detrimental, because it forces us into a corner (choosing *peirasmós* to be either a "test of the faith"—eschatological or earthly—or an "enticement to sin," or an "act of rebellion against God"), from which it is *impossible* to escape without crashing into insurmountable logical, theological, and exegetical dilemmas.

And the impossibility of escaping is due to the fact that *all* these interpretations eventually boil down to the same plea, which goes along these lines, "God, give us the strength not to sin against you." Whatever the reason is for this sin to be committed—either due to us yielding to internal or external temptations, or to us rebelling against God, or to us failing the test of the faith and falling away from God—the result is always the same: the sixth petition would be a prayer to prevent us from sinning. Which clashes thunderously with the image, clearly pictured by the verb *eisphérō*, of a God that drags us into *peirasmós*.

Again, the sixth petition of the Lord's Prayer is not about us doing something, but about *God doing something to us*. There is no way out from here.

# 28

# The Meaning of the Sixth Petition

Now, if the reader is willing to give the punitive *peirasmós* a chance, we will show how this interpretation is able to solve all the interpretative dilemmas at once.

But before doing that, some might still ask how it is possible to reconcile the idea of a God who is "infinite love," but who, at the same time, has no qualms about unleashing all his destructive fury on those who do wrong. For those who still have doubts about this, we recommend reading Psalm 78(77):

> They remembered not his hand, nor the day when he delivered them from the enemy. How he had wrought his signs in Egypt, and his wonders in the field of Zoan. And had turned their rivers into blood; and their floods, that they could not drink. He sent divers sorts of flies among them, which devoured them; and frogs, which destroyed them. He gave also their increase unto the caterpiller, and their labour unto the locust. He destroyed their vines with hail, and their sycomore trees with frost. He gave up their cattle also to the hail, and their flocks to hot thunderbolts. He cast upon them the fierceness of his anger, wrath, and indignation, and trouble, by sending evil angels among them. He made a way to his anger; he spared not their soul from death, but gave their life over to the pestilence. ( . . . ) And delivered his strength into captivity, and his glory into the enemy's hand. He gave his people over also unto the sword; and was wroth with his inheritance. The fire consumed their young men; and their maidens were not given to marriage. Their priests fell by the sword; and their widows made no lamentation. (Ps 78(77):42–50, 61–64)

Or Psalm 90(89): "For we are consumed by thine anger, and by thy wrath are we troubled. Thou hast set our iniquities before thee, our secret sins in the light of thy countenance. For all our days are passed away in thy wrath: we spend our years as a tale that is told. The days of our years are threescore years and ten; and if by reason of strength they be fourscore years, yet is their strength labour and sorrow; for it is soon cut off, and we fly away. Who knoweth the power of thine anger? even according to thy fear, so is thy wrath" (Ps 90(89):7–11).

Or that verse of Malachi against the unfaithful priests: "Behold, I will corrupt your seed, and spread dung upon your faces, even the dung of your solemn feasts; and one shall take you away with it" (Mal 2:3).

We have already explained this. God is the creator of both good and evil (Isa 45:7), and he dispenses of them to each according to his merits and faults, without having to account for them to anyone. The idea of a God who is "infinite love" and who therefore always closes his eyes to human *hýbris* has nothing to do with Scripture. It is a somewhat naive optical illusion. Nothing more than that.

And that from the terrible divine punishment one must pray to be spared by appealing to divine mercy is a truly clear and developed concept in Scripture. We find a very enlightening passage in chapter 3 of the book of Tobi (included in the Catholic and Orthodox canon, but not in the Jewish):

> Now, Lord, remember me and look upon me. Do not punish me for my sins and for the mistakes of me and my fathers. Violating your commands, we have sinned before you. You have abandoned us to depredation, to captivity, to death, and to being the fable, the mockery, the scorn of all nations, among whom you have scattered us. Now in dealing with me according to the faults of me and of my fathers, true are all thy judgments, because we have not observed thy decrees, walking before thee in truth. Act now as it pleases you; give order that my life be taken, so that I may be taken from the earth and become earth, for death is preferable to life for me. The reproaches I have to hear arouse great pain in me. Lord, command me to be removed from this affliction; let me depart to the eternal home; Lord, do not turn your face away from me. For it is better for me to die than to see this great distress in front of me, so that I may no longer be insulted. (Tob 3:3–6)

Tobi weeps and begs the Lord not to punish him for his sins and those of his fathers. God, as a punitive *peirasmós*, has inflicted on them a whole series of misfortunes, including the contempt of all nations—a supreme ignominy! Now Tobi, while acknowledging that the divine punishment is just, appeals to divine mercy so that he may be freed from all these evils. The request is emphatic, but at the same time real and desperate. Tobi asks God to give him death, because death is in any case more desirable than the afflictions and pain he is suffering. Another important detail is the collective dimension of sin and of its consequences. The request is to be spared from punishment due to the sins of the fathers. There is a clear concern that the divine wrath, when it is unleashed, may drag with it even the "innocent," that is, those who are not personally responsible for that wrath. It is a well-founded, real concern.

It is found, for example, in Psalm 26(25), which we have already found quoted in the Tridentine Mass: "Gather not my soul with sinners, nor my life with bloody men"

(Ps 26(25):9). We find the same plea in Psalm 28(27): "Draw me not away with the wicked, and with the workers of iniquity" (Ps 28(27):3).

This point is crucial. Let us not forget that the Lord's Prayer is not a personal prayer, but a communal one. Jesus teaches us to pray in the plural, together. It is not only necessary to pray for the remission of personal sins, but for the whole community. It is not only necessary to pray so that the divine punishment for our personal sins does not reach us, but also so that we are spared from the divine punishment that could reach us because of the sins committed by the community itself.

In the same book of Tobi, later in chapter 11, his son Tobias, by divine grace, cures his father Tobi of his blindness. Tobi thanks God, recognizing that it was he who inflicted the punishment according to his justice, but that it is always he who healed him according to his mercy: "Blessed be God! Blessed is his great name! Blessed are all his holy angels! Blessed is his great name upon us, and blessed are his angels for ever and ever. For he chastised me, but then he had mercy on me, and behold, now I contemplate my son Tobias" (Tob 11:14).

In chapter 13, Tobi's song of exultation is more elaborate:

> Blessed is God, who lives forever; his kingdom endures for ever and ever; He chastises and uses mercy, He brings down the depths of the earth, He brings up from the Great Perdition, and nothing escapes his hand. Praise him, children of Israel, before the nations; He has scattered you among them to proclaim his greatness. Exalt him before every living person; he is the Lord, our God, he is our Father, the God for ever and ever. He chastises you for your iniquities, but he will use mercy on all of you. He gathers you from all the nations among which you have been scattered. Repent to him with all your heart and with all your soul, to do righteousness before him, then he will repent to you and will not hide his face from you. (Tob 13:2–6)

God is portrayed as the one who "causes people to go down" but also "causes people to go up." The verbs used are *katágō* (κατάγω) and *anágō* (ἀνάγω), which are compounds of *ágō* (synonymous with *phérō*) and literally mean "bring down" and "bring up." The duality between the two main attributes of God is here made explicit: his justice, which tends to punish people for their sins by throwing them into hell, and his mercy, which tends to bring people up from the abyss, where they would deserve to be abandoned. But the hope is that in the end his mercy will prevail, as Isaiah prophesies: "Moreover the light of the moon shall be as the light of the sun, and the light of the sun shall be sevenfold, as the light of seven days, in the day that the Lord bindeth up the breach of his people, and healeth the stroke of their wound" (Isa 30:26).

The same concept is expressed by St. Paul in his first letter to the Thessalonians: "For God hath not appointed us to wrath [*orgḗ*], but to obtain salvation by our Lord Jesus Christ" (1 Thess 5:9).

At this point it is necessary to address a particularly critical issue: the forgiveness of sins does not coincide with the annulment of the penalty for the sins committed.

It is easy to superimpose these two concepts, considering them equivalent, when in fact they are not. The forgiveness of sins is only the *initial* part of the process of God's reconciliation with his people. However, this does not mean that the just punishment the sinners deserve for their sins has also been forgotten. Sin creates a wound, a rift between humans and God. This rift must be recomposed, the wound must be repaired. Divine justice demands it. The punishment for the sins committed is the *final* act of God's reconciliation with his people.

This is why, for example, immediately after the sacrament of Reconciliation, at the end of which the priest recites the formula "I absolve you of your sins, in the name of the Father, and of the Son, and of the Holy Spirit," the person who has just confessed must perform the penance decided by the priest. Absolution from sins does not imply the cancellation of the penance necessary to make reparation for those sins.

King David discovered this dramatical reality on his own skin when, after committing adultery and having a child from the illicit relationship with Bathsheba and after having Uriah, her husband, killed, he obtained from God the forgiveness of those horrible sins. But the terrible punishment for those sins did not take long to arrive:

> And David said unto Nathan, I have sinned against the Lord. And Nathan said unto David, The Lord also hath put away thy sin; thou shalt not die. Howbeit, because by this deed thou hast given great occasion to the enemies of the Lord to blaspheme, the child also that is born unto thee shall surely die. And Nathan departed unto his house. And the Lord struck the child that Uriah's wife bare unto David, and it was very sick. David therefore besought God for the child; and David fasted, and went in, and lay all night upon the earth. And the elders of his house arose, and went to him, to raise him up from the earth: but he would not, neither did he eat bread with them. And it came to pass on the seventh day, that the child died. (2 Sam 12:13–18)

David's sin is all the more serious because it was committed by a chosen one of the Lord. The fall of a chosen one gives occasion to the wicked to insult God even more. And God cannot tolerate this. The son born from the illicit relationship must die. At that point, David's pleas for mercy and acts of penitence are worth nothing. Divine justice has the better of divine mercy. This concept is reiterated in the *incipit* of the book of Nahum: "The Lord is slow to anger, and great in power, and will not at all acquit the wicked" (Nah 1:3).

And so, when divine mercy prevails over justice, this event must be a cause for exultation and joy: "Sing, O daughter of Zion; shout, O Israel; be glad and rejoice with all the heart, O daughter of Jerusalem. The Lord hath taken away thy judgments, he hath cast out thine enemy: the king of Israel, even the Lord, is in the midst of thee: thou shalt not see evil any more" (Zeph 3:14–15). The Lord finally delivered Israel from the punishment for their sins. The Lord has heard the plea for mercy: *libera nos a malo*.

We can at this point, as a logical conclusion to our entire argument, come to make the following statement:

*The term peirasmós, which appears in the sixth petition of the Lord's Prayer, has nothing to do with temptation to sin. It has nothing to do with the temptations of Satan. Instead, it has everything to do with God's wrath and its consequence—the just punishment that God may inflict on us because of our sins. Such punishment may be inflicted by means of torments and psychophysical tribulations during our life on earth but may also result in the eternal punishment of hell in case we die in a state of mortal sin.*

Once we are willing to interpret the term *peirasmós* of the sixth petition of the Lord's Prayer in this way and are willing to give up the idea that the Lord's Prayer is a plea for protection from Satan,[1] all exegetical difficulties evaporate at once:

1. We finally understand why Matthew and Luke choose a verb with such a strong causative sense (*eisphérō*), rarely used with persons and, if used at all, used to indicate forcible transportation—often against the will of the person being transported. Who would want to be brought to be the subject of God's wrath?

2. We finally understand the emphatic use of the preposition *eis*, which appears both in the verb (*eisphérō*) and before the place where the movement ends (*eis peirasmón*). When God punishes us for our sins, he drags us *into* that ordeal of tribulations from which, by our own strength alone, we could certainly not escape. He throws us *into* the snare (*pagís*) of *punitive peirasmós*. A snare from which we can only hope to be freed by appealing to the infinite mercy of God.

3. We finally understand why the sixth petition is the only one in which we ask God *not* to do something. Asking God not to punish us for our sins not only makes sense from the human point of view (obvious), but also from the divine point of view. It means asking that God's infinite mercy get the better of his infinite justice. It is a legitimate request. Indeed, it is the request par excellence, the one codified in the canon of the Mass.

4. We finally understand why the sixth petition comes *after* the fifth. It seems trivial, but no one has ever posed the problem of the logical *consecutio* of the petitions in the Lord's Prayer. As if the petitions were somehow independent of each other and could have been rearranged in a different order without altering their meaning. Why would Jesus teach to pray *first* for the forgiveness of sins and *then* for the strength not to fall into temptation? By definition, temptation to sin comes before sin, not after. The logical sequence should be exactly the opposite. First, we should be praying for the strength not to fall into temptation, then, in case we

---

1. In the whole of the very long Sermon on the Mount in which the recitation of the Lord's Prayer is inserted, there is not a single explicit reference to Satan and his power to tempt us and/or make us fall into temptation.

have fallen into temptation, we should be praying for the forgiveness of the sins committed. If Jesus puts the sixth petition after the fifth (and not before), it is because he has in mind what might happen *after* a sin has been committed, and even after a sin has been forgiven—the just punishment for that sin! The sixth petition has nothing to do with the causes of sin, but with its consequences.

5. We finally understand why Jesus never feels the need to explain the sixth petition, nor do the disciples ever feel the need to ask for clarification (the same disciples who were not ashamed even to have the simplest parables explained to them). The only solution to this dilemma is to think that the meaning of that petition was something obvious to understand! And the possibility of God dragging us into his chastisement as a consequence of our sins is something quite easy to grasp. Almost natural to expect. Especially if in the preceding petition we are specifically asking God to forgive the sins we have committed.

6. We finally understand why Jesus, when he finishes reciting the Lord's Prayer, returns to reiterate the importance of . . . the fifth petition,[2] skipping the sixth and the seventh. But this is only an optical illusion. There is no logical leap. The fifth, sixth, and seventh petitions can be brought together in a single petition, because they all speak of the same thing: the process of reconciliation between a person and God. A process that begins with our forgiveness of the sins committed against us, continues with God's forgiveness of our sins committed against him, and ends with the annulment of the punishment we deserve to suffer for those sins, or with the deliverance from that punishment (if God has decided to inflict it on us). The seventh and sixth petitions are meaningless unless we pray the fifth first. It all starts with our willingness to forgive others. If we are not willing to forgive the sins committed against us, there is no hope that God will forgive the sins we commit against others. And what's more, there is no hope he will grant us the grace to spare us the just punishment.

The same dynamics can be observed, for instance, in Psalm 85(84): "Lord, thou hast been favourable unto thy land: thou hast brought back the captivity of Jacob. Thou hast forgiven the iniquity of thy people, thou hast covered all their sin. Selah. Thou hast taken away all thy wrath: thou hast turned thyself from the fierceness of thine anger. Turn us, O God of our salvation, and cause thine anger toward us to cease. Wilt thou be angry with us for ever? wilt thou draw out thine anger to all generations? Wilt thou not revive us again: that thy people may rejoice in thee? Shew us thy mercy, O Lord, and grant us thy salvation" (Ps 85(84):1–7(1–8)).

The reconciliation process between God and a person starts with the forgiveness of sins (fifth petition of the Lord's Prayer; Ps 85(84):2(3)), and ends with

---

2. "For if ye forgive men their trespasses, your heavenly Father will also forgive you: But if ye forgive not men their trespasses, neither will your Father forgive your trespasses" (Matt 6:14–15).

the exhaustion of God's anger (sixth petition of the Lord's Prayer; Ps 85(84):3(4)) and with the outpouring of God's mercy through a salvific deliverance (seventh petition of the Lord's Prayer; Ps 85(84):7(8)).[3]

In Psalm 32(31), we find the same concepts: "I acknowledge my sin unto thee, and mine iniquity have I not hid. I said, I will confess my transgressions unto the Lord; and thou forgavest the iniquity of my sin. Selah. For this shall every one that is godly pray unto thee in a time when thou mayest be found: surely in the floods of great waters they shall not come nigh unto him. Thou art my hiding place; thou shalt preserve me from trouble; thou shalt compass me about with songs of deliverance" (Ps 32(31):5–7).

The forgiveness of sins (fifth petition of the Lord's Prayer; Ps 32(31):5) is the *condicio sine qua non* so that God's wrath may not reach us (sixth petition of the Lord's Prayer; Ps 32(31):6)[4] and he may instead deliver us from trouble (seventh petition of the Lord's Prayer; Ps 32(31):7). The list of examples could go on forever.[5]

7. We finally understand the anarthrous use of the term *peirasmós* (without the definite article). Punitive *peirasmós*, in contrast to the idea of eschatological *peirasmós*, does not require the article. Divine punishment can occur *at any time* here on earth, as it can refer to the extreme punishment of hell. This interpretation fits very well with the structure of the Lord's Prayer which, as we have already noted, is all played out on a double level: earthly and otherworldly. On earth, as it is in heaven. Thus, every petition can have a double interpretation—immanent and transcendent. The debts we incur on earth among people correspond to the sins we "incur" with God in heaven. The daily bread indicates a request for bodily sustenance, but also, and above all, a request for Eucharistic communion

---

3. The term used here for "salvation" is *yēshă'* (יֵשַׁע), almost identical to the Hebrew name for "Jesus." The plea may be read by Christians as, "give us your Jesus," where Jesus represents the incarnation of God's mercy that provides the ultimate salvation from the punishment that would be required to repair our sins.

4. Notice the reference to "the rising of the mighty waters," clear allusion to the chastisement of the Universal Flood.

5. See, for example, Ps 25(24):17–18: "The troubles of my heart are enlarged: O bring thou me out of my distresses. Look upon mine affliction and my pain; and forgive all my sins"; Ps 38(37):1–3, 21–22(2–4, 22–23): "Lord, do not O Lord, rebuke me not in thy wrath: neither chasten me in thy hot displeasure. For thine arrows stick fast in me, and thy hand presseth me sore. There is no soundness in my flesh because of thine anger; neither is there any rest in my bones because of my sin. ( . . . ) Forsake me not, O Lord: O my God, be not far from me. Make haste to help me, O Lord my salvation"; Ps 78(77):38–39: "But he, being full of compassion, forgave their iniquity, and destroyed them not: yea, many a time turned he his anger away, and did not stir up all his wrath. For he remembered that they were but flesh; a wind that passeth away, and cometh not again"; Ps 79(78):8–9: "O remember not against us former iniquities: let thy tender mercies speedily prevent us: for we are brought very low. Help us, O God of our salvation, for the glory of thy name: and deliver us, and purge away our sins, for thy name's sake"; Ps 103(102):3–4: "Who forgiveth all thine iniquities; who healeth all thy diseases; Who redeemeth thy life from destruction; who crowneth thee with lovingkindness and tender mercies."

with God ("man does not live by bread alone"). In the same way, *peirasmós* can mean, from an earthly point of view, those tribulations that God inflicts on us to punish us for our sins, but, at a higher level, the eternal, otherworldly torment in the flames of Gehenna.

8. We finally understand the urgency that Jesus feels in the garden of *Gethsēmaní* to go and wake up his most beloved disciples to tell them to recite the sixth petition of the Lord's Prayer, immediately after having experienced the *orgḗ* of the Father toward humanity.

9. We finally understand the expression used in the *Gethsēmaní*: *eisérchomai eis peirasmón*, that is, "to enter into *peirasmós*." The verb *eisérchomai* (and similar derivatives of *érchomai*) is often used figuratively to indicate the movement of going to meet the sentence of condemnation (*krísis*), destruction (*apṓleia*), and ultimately entering hell (*Géenna*). The expression *eisérchomai eis peirasmón*, otherwise difficult to interpret, fits very well within this range of expressions that indicate the idea of being subjected to God's wrath.

10. We finally understand how it is possible that the prayer in the *Gethsēmaní* is presented in the intransitive form (pray that you do not enter the *peirasmós*), while in the Lord's Prayer is presented in the causative form (lead us not into the *peirasmós*). They are two sides of the same coin: the one who sins can run into the punitive *peirasmós* to the extent that he/she is led there by the one who inflicts that *peirasmós*, that is, God. The point of view is different, but the meaning remains unchanged in both cases.

11. We finally understand why Jesus, in the *Gethsēmaní*, right after admonishing the disciples to pray not to enter into *peirasmós*, explains, "The spirit indeed is willing, but the flesh is weak" (Matt 26:41). The *peirasmós* into which we need to pray not to enter is the direct consequence of the weakness of our flesh: "For if ye live after the flesh, ye shall die" (Rom 8:13).

12. We finally understand the meaning of the seventh petition: the evil from which we ask to be delivered and spared, is the just punishment we deserve for our sins—chastisement that goes from simple temporary, earthly suffering to the extreme tribulation, that is, the eternal torment in the flames of hell.

13. We finally understand the intimate connection—the complementarity—between the sixth and the seventh petition. They both appeal to the two main attributes of God: justice and mercy. The sixth appeals to God's justice; the seventh to God's mercy.[6]

14. We finally understand why in the sixth petition we are asking God not to bring us into *peirasmós* and in the seventh petition we are indeed asking God to deliver us from such evil. This is a legitimate request because what the Lord's Prayer is

---

6. We will elaborate on this concept in the next chapter.

about is not the *peirasmós* understood as the test of our faith, much needed to make us worth of the kingdom of heaven. It is the *peirasmós* understood as the punitive chastisement, much needed to satisfy God's justice. Moule's unsolved problem is finally solved.

Not convinced yet? Consider this, then. Remember that we mentioned how the meaning of the sixth petition should be something immediately understandable given the fact that the disciples never felt the urgency for an explanation? This statement is not entirely correct. The disciples never asked for an explanation probably because Jesus, indirectly, gave them the explanation himself!

Let us go read from chapter 18 in Matthew's Gospel, where Jesus gives his disciples another sermon similar to—but shorter than—the Sermon on the Mount. Suddenly, Peter intervenes asking Jesus how many times he is supposed to forgive if his brother trespasses against him. The reference to the fifth petition of the Lord's Prayer ("forgive our trespasses, as we forgive those who trespass against us") is obvious. We do not really know why, all of a sudden, such a question pops up in Peter's mind. Likely it's because Jesus had been speaking about how to deal with somebody who sins against you and refuses to admit his guilt (Matt 18:15–17). Peter's mind must have made an instinctive connection with the fifth petition of the Lord's Prayer, as to say, "Jesus, you have taught us that we should forgive whoever sins against us in order to obtain forgiveness from the Father, but how many times, exactly, are we supposed to forgive? Is there a limit? Maybe seven times?" It may sound like a naive question, but it is very human. The idea of forgiving different people that sin against us is certainly "digestible," but what about somebody that keeps sinning against us? Does it make sense to keep forgiving the same person repeatedly?

Jesus responds by telling Peter the parable of the merciful king who forgives his servant a huge debt (ten thousand talents). The first part of the parable is the exemplification of the first part of the fifth petition, "forgive our trespasses." The second part of the parable focuses instead on the lack of mercy of the same servant, who had himself small claim (a hundred pence) on a fellow-servant. The wicked servant refuses to forgive his fellow-servant the small debt and throws him into prison. This second part of the parable is the (antithetical) exemplification of the second part of the fifth petition: "as we forgive those who trespass against us."

How does the parable end? The king, after realizing what his wicked servant did, gets furious. The adjective used by Matthew is illuminating: *orgistheís* (ὀργισθείς), that is, full of *orgḗ*, full of wrath. The king—the metaphor for God—unleashes his wrath upon the servant and delivers him into the hands of those who will be torturing him—the metaphor for the devils in hell/purgatory—until the very last penny of his debt is paid off. Jesus is explaining what would happen to us in the unfortunate case we do not forgive whoever trespasses against us—in case we do not show the same infinite mercy that our Father in heaven shows us: "So likewise shall my heavenly

Father do also unto you, if ye from your hearts forgive not every one his brother their trespasses" (Matt 18:35).

Jesus is explaining what would happen to us in case we fail to comply with the fifth petition of the Lord's Prayer. He is explaining what may happen after the fifth petition. He is explaining the sixth petition! God may do with us exactly what that merciful king did with the wicked servant. He may throw us into the midst of terrible torments. He may lead us into *peirasmós*, indeed.

Once the fundamental meaning of the sixth petition has been ascertained, trying to find a "more correct" or "less misleading" translation of that "lead us not into temptation" becomes more of a stylistic exercise than anything else. A necessary exercise though, because the expression "to lead into temptation" has by now entered modern language as a synonym for "to entice to sin," and thus it gives a terribly wrong idea of what the sixth petition is trying to get us to say.

The sixth petition is not a request to God to give us the strength not to fall into temptation (sure, it could be, but on a secondary level, as a sort of corollary). Nor is it a request to God that he not allow Satan to tempt us.

The sixth petition is a desperate plea to God, as desperate as that prayer of Jesus in the *Gethsēmaní*, that he would not subject us to his legitimate wrath against us. It is an unconditional plea for mercy, lest he punish us for our sins with earthly and/or eternal torment.

Similarly, the seventh petition is not a request to God to give us the strength not to sin. Nor is it a request to God to protect us from Satan. It is a desperate plea for him to deliver us from the chastisement that comes upon the ungodly and sinners and that might sweep us away with them. And if we were the sinners in question, it is a desperate plea that he would have mercy on us and reverse the sentence of condemnation that he has inflicted upon us.

With these concepts in mind, we can sketch feasible alternative translations. First of all, it is ironic to note that, although everyone has more or less tried to hammer the verb *eisphérō*, distorting its meaning in every possible and imaginable way, in a desperate attempt to blunt its very obvious causative meaning ("do not allow us to fall," "do not let us enter," "do not abandon us," "prevent us from experiencing," "preserve us from succumbing," and so forth), the solution to this dilemma was simply to leave that *eisphérō* alone and focus instead on grasping the correct idea behind the term *peirasmós*, which, as we have seen, has nothing to do with the concept of temptation, as we commonly understand it.

The verb *eisphérō* should then be translated literally: "to lead." Period. No more, no less. Variations on the theme could be considered ("to bring," "to push," "to drag"), but there seems to be no need. In Latin we would prefer the verb *infero* (instead of *induco*) because it maintains, even phonetically, a perfect adherence to the Greek *eisphérō*.

The term *peirasmós* on the other hand, if we do not want to use periphrases that would stray too far from the original text, must be translated with nouns that render the idea of a punishment implying psychophysical suffering, possibly both earthly and otherworldly—which the term "temptation" does not describe at all. "Trial" could be a nice candidate because it contains both the idea of "trying," in the sense of "testing," and of "suffering." But it still does not capture the idea of punishment fully. Affliction, tribulation, pain, suffering, could all be valid options. But none of them contains the explicit idea of punishment, which is ultimately the most important concept to bring out. We were not able to find a word in English that would condense all these ideas in one term (we are open to suggestions). However, since the most important concept in the sixth petition is the idea of eternal punitive *peirasmós*, it seems to us that a term like "damnation" would do nicely. It also maintains a certain phonetic adherence to the word "temptation," which we are all accustomed to. Equally valid options could include "destruction," which would remind of eternal death, or "torment," which would recall the psychophysical suffering in hell.

In Latin instead, we have a term, *supplicium*, which we find accurate because it contains the idea of both intense pain and punishment, both earthly and eternal. It also has the support of the Vulgate: "*Et ibunt hi in supplicium aeternum: justi autem in vitam aeternam*"[7] (Matt 25:46 VUL).

The verb *rhýomai* in the seventh petition, translated with a too elegant and delicate "to deliver," does not render its strength, its impetus. We would prefer "to rescue," which better renders the idea of the merciful hand of God that comes to seize us when we are already lost, weakened, tried by punishment, to give us the grace of salvation. The verb "rescue" maintains, even phonetically, a nice adherence to the Greek *rhýomai*. In Latin, the verb *eruo* would work very well, meaning precisely "to pull out," "to tear out," and which maintains, even phonetically, a perfect adherence to the Greek *rhýomai*.

Here then is our proposal for a revised translation of the last petitions of the Lord's Prayer (in both Latin and English):

> *Et ne nos inferas in supplicium, sed erue nos a malo.*[8]
> And lead us not into damnation, but rescue us from evil.

Our analysis may end here.

However, in the next two chapters, we will present additional material that, although not strictly necessary to the demonstration of our argument, we believe corroborates its credibility. We are aware of the fact that this material may resonate only with a strictly Catholic reader, but we also hope that it may raise interest and be thought-provoking for a much broader audience.

---

7. "And these will go to eternal torment: the righteous, on the other hand, to eternal life."
8. Similarly, Tertullian: "*sed erue nos a maligno*" (*De fuga in persecutione*, 2).

We will first take a leap of nearly two thousand years to the Poland of the first half of the twentieth century, on the brink of World War II, to discover the thought of one of the minds that produced some of the most original theological thinking of the twentieth century. We are talking about Helena Kowalska, known as St. Faustina, canonized by Pope John Paul II on April 30, 2000. Then, we will move to Portugal, in the midst of World War I, to rediscover the message that Our Lady of Fatima gave to three shepherd children: Lúcia, Francisco, and Jacinta.

What does all this have to do with the sixth petition of the Lord's Prayer? In our opinion, it has everything to do with it.

# 29

# The Secretary of Divine Mercy

Helena Kowalska was born on August 25, 1905, in a small village in the heart of Poland and her life was to be an incredible adventure.

The third of ten children in a poor peasant family, she feels called to religious life at the age of seven. Her parents do not give her permission and so she finds herself working as a janitor to support her family.

At the age of nineteen, when the idea of a vocation is now a distant memory, during a party with her peers in a park in a small town near her home, right in the middle of the dancing, Helena suddenly freezes. The expression on her face from jovial becomes pale. She sits down with an excuse. Then she abandons her sister and her friends and starts running away, without being noticed. She won't stop running until she reaches the city's cathedral. There, she throws herself face down in front of the exposed Blessed Sacrament. Immediately afterward, she goes home and, without telling her parents and without taking even a change of clothes with her, she rushes to the station and takes the first train to Warsaw. Arriving in the capital after a couple of hours of travel, she goes to a nearby village, where she finds a makeshift accommodation.

The next day, early in the morning, she goes to the first church she finds and, after attending mass, asks the priest for help, who recommends a home where she can stay temporarily. It is only after several weeks spent in vain asking to enter various religious institutes that she is finally accepted at the convent of *Zgromadzenie Sióstr Matki Bożej Miłosierdzia*,[1] not as a novice but as an orderly. It is only a year later that she is officially admitted to religious life. And so, at the age of 20, Helena would take her vows under the name Sister Maria Faustina.

What had Helena seen during that party to make her suddenly abandon her home and family and take the first train to Warsaw without any idea of how or where

---

1. Congregation of the Sisters of Our Lady of Mercy.

# Eis Peirasmón

she would find lodging? She herself will reveal this in her diary, written during her short life:

> Once I was at a dance [probably in Lodz] with one of my sisters. While everybody was having a good time, my soul was experiencing deep torments. As I began to dance, I suddenly saw Jesus at my side, Jesus racked with pain, stripped of his clothing, all covered with wounds, who spoke these words to me: How long shall I put up with you and how long will you keep putting Me off? At that moment the charming music stopped, [and] the company I was with vanished from my sight; there remained Jesus and I. I took a seat by my dear sister pretending to have a headache in order to cover up what took place in my soul. After a while I slipped out unnoticed, leaving my sister and all my companions behind and made my way to the Cathedral of St. Stanislaus Kostka. It was almost twilight; there were only a few people in the cathedral. Paying no attention to what was happening around me, I fell prostrate before the Blessed Sacrament and begged the Lord to be good enough to give me to understand what I should do next. Then I heard these words: Go at once to Warsaw; you will enter a convent there. I rose from prayer, came home, and took care of things that needed to be settled. As best I could, I confided to my sister what took place within my soul. I told her to say good-bye to our parents, and thus, in my one dress, with no other belonging, I arrived in Warsaw.[2]

From that moment and throughout the rest of her troubled life, Sister Faustina will continue to have vivid visions of Jesus, who will speak to her and guide her spiritually. Above all, he will order her to write—to write incessantly all that he has to say to her, all that he needs the world to know. Hence, the Diary of St. Faustina entitled "Divine Mercy in My Soul" is born. Hundreds of pages written on an almost daily basis, containing her experience of life in the convent, her sufferings due to her illness (probably tuberculosis), which would prove to be painful until the very end, and her very personal relationship with Jesus.

The great message that Jesus seems to want to make known explicitly to the world through Sister Faustina is the mystery of his infinite mercy. And Faustina, as perhaps no one ever before in the history of the church, fully and clearly understood this mystery and described it in detail in the pages of her diary. That is why Jesus himself would call her the "secretary of divine mercy."

St. Faustina will be the first to clearly explain the theological mystery of the dynamic between divine justice and mercy—of that tension, all internal to God, which we mentioned in the previous chapters. And because of her profound, original theological arguments, in October 2001 several cardinals and bishops signed a petition to the then Pope Benedict XVI for St. Faustina to be awarded the prestigious title of doctor of the church—a title granted in the entire history of the Catholic Church to

---

2. Kowalska, *Diary*, 9–10.

only thirty-three men and four women, among whom are names of the caliber of St. Ambrose, St. Augustine, St. Jerome, and St. Thomas Aquinas.

We will now try to summarize the salient passages of the teachings that Jesus revealed to St. Faustina. For, we shall see, they are in direct relation to everything we have said about the sixth petition of the Lord's Prayer.

One of Sister Faustina's first visions concerns the suffering of souls in purgatory. The commonly held idea of purgatory is a place of temporary purification, before one can enter heaven. Not necessarily a place of atrocious suffering. Sister Faustina, on the other hand, describes it as a "place full of smoke and fire with a great number of suffering souls," a "prison of pain." Sister Faustina says she heard an inner voice (of Jesus) explain, "My mercy does not want this, but justice demands it."[3]

Purgatory, as a physical place where sins committed in life are repaired, becomes a place of terrible punitive *peirasmós*, certainly not eternal, but very painful. The flames burn the flesh and the distance from God causes excruciating spiritual pain. This is a mystery that Sister Faustina understood clearly: purgatory is the place of the highest psychophysical suffering and is comparable to hell, if not in duration, certainly in intensity.[4]

What is the reason for purgatory? Jesus explains it in no uncertain terms: to satisfy divine justice. No sin can go unpunished. Sister Faustina will understand this clearly only a few months before her death: "I understood the great justice of God, how each one had to pay off the debt to the last cent."[5]

It is not by chance that, in the Sermon on the Mount, just before reciting the Lord's Prayer, Jesus had recalled, "Agree with thine adversary quickly, whiles thou art in the way with him; lest at any time the adversary deliver thee to the judge, and the judge deliver thee to the officer, and thou be cast into prison. Verily I say unto thee, Thou shalt by no means come out thence, till thou hast paid the uttermost farthing" (Matt 5:25–26; see also Luke 12:58–59).

Purgatory is the prison where divine justice has, for a certain period of time, the better of his mercy. And as such it is a place where we would not want to spend a single minute, if possible. But is it possible? Yes, it is. Divine mercy is willing to shorten the time of the *peirasmós* of souls in purgatory in exchange for the prayers and expiatory pain of those still alive.

This is another mystery that St. Faustina would experience on her skin. Jesus would explicitly ask her to offer all her physical suffering due to tuberculosis as atonement for the souls in purgatory. This is an example of what we have called expiatory

---

3. Kowalska, *Diary*, 20.

4. In Sister Faustina's visions, purgatory appears as a kind of hell limited in time: "And although it seems to me that this soul is not damned, its torments are nevertheless in no way different from the torments of hell; there is only this difference: that, one day, they will end" (*Diary*, 426). In another vision Sister Faustina will see the souls in purgatory, atoning for their sins and surrounded by "many demons" (*Diary*, 412).

5. Kowalska, *Diary*, 1375.

psychophysical *peirasmós*, that is, the *peirasmós* inflicted by God on the souls dearest to him, capable of replacing and therefore reducing, if not cancelling, the punitive psychophysical *peirasmós* inflicted on sinners: "Great persecutions and sufferings are in store for you, but be comforted by the thought that many souls will be saved and sanctified by this work."[6]

Jesus explains this clearly: "When I was dying on the cross, I was not thinking about Myself, but about poor sinners, and I prayed for them to My Father. I want your last moments to be completely similar to Mine on the cross. There is but one price at which souls are brought, and that is suffering united to My suffering on the cross."[7]

Every soul, even the most wicked, can be saved through the expiatory suffering of other righteous souls. This is another aspect of the great mystery of divine mercy. And St. Faustina fully embraces this expiatory *peirasmós* because she understands its redemptive power: "It would be a very ugly thing for a religious to seek relief from suffering."[8]

St. Faustina is implicitly explaining to us here that the *peirasmós* of the sixth petition of the Lord's Prayer cannot refer to expiatory *peirasmós*. Instead, this type of *peirasmós* is to be embraced with all strength as a mark of divine mercy: "Suffering is a great grace; through suffering the soul becomes like the Savior."[9]

The expiatory *peirasmós* allows one to participate in Christ's expiatory sacrifice, through which so many souls are saved from the punitive *peirasmós*.

We thus understand another aspect, implicit in the sixth petition of the Lord's Prayer. When we are asking God not to lead us into *peirasmós*, that is, not to condemn us to the just torment for our sins, we are not only asking God not to throw us into hell, but also, according to his infinite mercy, to shorten as much as possible that punitive *peirasmós* in purgatory (a *peirasmós* in all respects comparable to that of hell in terms of intensity of suffering), through which we may have to pass anyway before we can access heaven.

In another vision, Jesus specifically asks Sister Faustina to offer every bit of suffering and indulgence for the souls in purgatory: "Today bring to Me the souls who are in the prison of Purgatory, and immerse them in the abyss of My mercy. Let the torrents of My Blood cool down their scorching flames. All these souls are greatly loved by Me. They are making retribution to My justice. It is in your power to bring them relief. Draw all the indulgences from the treasury of My Church and offer them on their behalf. Oh, if you only knew the torments they suffer, you would continually offer for them the alms of the spirit and pay off their debt to My justice."[10]

---

6. Kowalska, *Diary*, 966.
7. Kowalska, *Diary*, 324.
8. Kowalska, *Diary*, 387.
9. Kowalska, *Diary*, 57.
10. Kowalska, *Diary*, 1226.

Here, Jesus is describing purgatory as the place where souls repay all debts (read: sins) incurred with God during their earthly lives. He is describing purgatory as a (temporary) place of punitive *peirasmós*. And he is trying to make Sister Faustina understand how terrible the torments suffered by these souls are, how terrible the idea of having to repay the debts contracted with God is.

We understand even more deeply the connection, which we have already mentioned in the previous chapter, between the fifth, sixth, and seventh petitions of the Lord's Prayer. They are all essentially one great request that God "forgive us our trespasses," that is, "not bring us to suffer the torment" of reparation, but "free us from this punishment" as soon as possible, by the grace of his infinite mercy. All this corroborates the idea that it is not only reasonable that Jesus taught us to ask the Father not to inflict this kind of punitive *peirasmós* on us, but necessary. Necessary, because there is always a way of escaping divine justice— by means of his mercy.

One year before her death, St. Faustina recounts having had a vision in which the Virgin Mary addresses these words to all the sisters of the Congregation: "Everyone who perseveres zealously till death in My Congregation will be spared the fire of Purgatory."[11] Even the Mother of God teaches us to do everything possible to avoid the punitive *peirasmós*.

We see how St. Faustina is clear from the beginning about the continuous tension between two of God's greatest attributes: justice and mercy. But Faustina is certain: "I understood that the greatest attribute is love and mercy."[12]

Here we come to the nodal point of the theological revelation given to St. Faustina. The Son of God became incarnate for a specific reason—to protect humanity from the Father's just punishment. Faustina expresses this concept repeatedly: "O my God, I am conscious of my mission in the Holy Church. It is my constant endeavor to plead for mercy for the world. I unite myself closely with Jesus and stand before him as an atoning sacrifice on behalf of the world. God will refuse me nothing when I entreat him with the voice of his son. My sacrifice is nothing in itself, but when I join it to the sacrifice of Jesus Christ, it becomes all-powerful and has the power to appease divine wrath. God loves us in his Son; the painful Passion of the Son of God constantly turns aside the wrath of God."[13]

Not for nothing do most of Sister Faustina's revelations revolve around Jesus' experience in the *Gethsēmaní*. In one in particular, Jesus makes an implicit reference to his agony: "There are souls who despise My graces as well as all the proofs of My love. They do not wish to hear My call, but proceed into the abyss of Hell. The loss of these souls plunges Me into deadly sorrow."[14]

---

11. Kowalska, *Diary*, 1244.
12. Kowalska, *Diary*, 180.
13. Kowalska, *Diary*, 482.
14. Kowalska, *Diary*, 580.

The reference to "deadly sorrow" closely recalls Mark 14:34: "My soul is exceeding sorrowful unto death: tarry ye here, and watch." We have confirmation that much of Jesus' agony in the *Gethsēmaní* lies in realizing the horror of divine punishment toward those souls who stubbornly reject his mercy and proceed speedily toward their destruction. They proceed into the abyss of hell. Sister Faustina uses the verb *iść*, which means "to go" in Polish. Just like that *eisérchomai* pronounced in the *Gethsēmaní*: watch and pray lest you go into *peirasmós*.

Jesus will make this reference explicit in a later vision: "Today bring to Me souls who have become lukewarm, and immerse them in the abyss of My mercy. These souls wound My Heart most painfully. My soul suffered the most dreadful loathing in the Garden of Olives because of lukewarm souls. They were the reason I cried out: 'Father, take this cup away from Me, if it be Your will.' For them, the last hope of salvation is to flee to My mercy."[15]

The greatest pain suffered by Jesus in the *Gethsēmaní* was precisely that of seeing how people who were not bad, but simply "lukewarm," that is, armed with a weak, almost dormant faith, with the concrete possibility of being able to save themselves, proceed instead unaware, because of their lack of will, toward the abyss of hell. This is the main reason Jesus felt that irrepressible need to interrupt his desperate prayer to the Father to go and motivate his beloved disciples. He absolutely did not want them to come to that horrible end. Watch and pray that you do not go into *peirasmós*.

Jesus thus reveals that, thanks to his passion, the ultimate example of divine mercy, the Father's wrath is banished from the earth. St. Faustina will receive an impressive revelation in this regard: "Towards the end of the litany I saw a great radiance and, in the midst of it, God the Father. Between this radiance and the earth I saw Jesus, nailed to the Cross in such a way that when God wanted to look at the earth, He had to look through the wounds of Jesus. And I understood that it was for the sake of Jesus that God blesses the earth."[16]

It is a stunning viewpoint that St. Faustina offers us. God looks at the earth, but he can only look at it through the wounds of Jesus on the cross. It is Christ who shields the earth, literally, with his arms stretched out on the cross, and protects it from the Father's wrath.

The Son becomes the person of the Trinity who personifies mercy, while the Father becomes the person of the Trinity who personifies justice. The tension between justice and mercy within God corresponds to the continuous tension between the Father and the Son—the same tension that is narrated in the Gospels during the Passion ("Father, take this cup away from me," "My God, my God, why have you forsaken me?). This is not a contrast, nor a disagreement. It is an "impossible" coexistence of infinities.

---

15. Kowalska, *Diary*, 1228.
16. Kowalska, *Diary*, 60.

This concept is repeated on multiple occasions and found throughout the Diary. For example, Jesus recalls how the blood and water that flowed from his side pierced by the spear of the centurion on the cross are like two rays that "shield souls from the wrath of My Father. Happy is the one who will dwell in their shelter, for the just hand of God shall not lay hold of him."[17] Those who trust in God's mercy will be protected from his justice.

In one of the last revelations, Jesus will confess to her, "My daughter, tell souls that I am giving them My mercy as a defense. I Myself am fighting for them and am bearing the just anger of My Father."[18]

However—and this is another fundamental concept that emerges in St. Faustina's revelations—this tension between the Father and the Son will not last forever. It will last only until the *parousía*, the second coming of Christ, when the Father will finally grant the Son the power to judge. At that point, and only at that point, will there be complete overlap between mercy and justice. If Christ came for the first time as the prince of mercy to announce this incredible opportunity of redemption for humanity, when he returns, he will come instead as a judge. But, at that point, time will be over. Jesus anticipates this to Faustina: "Write this: before I come as the Just Judge, I am coming first as the King of mercy."[19]

Then, the Mother of God reveals to her, "You have to speak to the world about his great mercy and prepare the world for the Second Coming of him who will come, not as a merciful Savior, but as a just Judge. Oh, how terrible is that day! Determined is the day of justice, the day of divine wrath. The angels tremble before it. Speak to souls about this great mercy while it is still the time for [granting] mercy."[20]

Jesus himself confirms, "Speak to the world about My mercy; let all mankind recognize My unfathomable mercy. It is a sign for the end times; after it will come the day of justice. While there is still time, let them have recourse to the fount of My mercy."[21]

And that day—the Day of Judgment—will be a terrible day for those who have not drawn with full hands from the grace of divine mercy: "God's floodgates have been opened for us. Let us want to take advantage of them before the day of God's justice arrives. And that will be a dreadful day!"[22]

We find confirmation of how the entire agony of the *Gethsēmaní* is directly connected to the Last Judgment, in which the wrath of God will be poured out on all humanity—that bitter cup from which Jesus had to drink in order to save many souls. The plea to God's mercy that prevents God's justice from being unleashed is one of the recurring motifs of St. Faustina's revelations: "Today, the Lord gave me knowledge of

17. Kowalska, *Diary*, 299.
18. Kowalska, *Diary*, 1516.
19. Kowalska, *Diary*, 83.
20. Kowalska, *Diary*, 635.
21. Kowalska, *Diary*, 848.
22. Kowalska, *Diary*, 1159.

his anger toward mankind which deserves to have its days shortened because of its sins."[23]

Hence, the request for mercy to the Son: "O my Jesus, I implore You by the goodness of Your most sweet Heart, let Your anger diminish and show us Your mercy. May Your wounds be our shield against Your Father's justice."[24]

The Son is the one who prevents the Father from carrying out the just punishment: "Out of love for you all, I will avert any punishments which are rightly meted out by My Father's justice."[25]

Jesus, through his "secretary," will also establish the first Sunday after Easter as the day of the feast of divine mercy, with this precise promise: "whoever approaches the Fount of Life on this day will be granted complete remission of sins and punishment."[26]

Notice how, in addition to the remission of sins, Jesus also specifically speaks of the remission of punishment. The two concepts, as we have explained, do not coincide. The remission of sins does not imply the remission of the punishment necessary to repair the sins themselves. This explains why, after the fifth petition in which we ask for the remission of sins, it is necessary to pray the sixth as well—to ask for the remission of the punishment!

And the crucial moment in which it is necessary to pray is at the point of death. That is our last chance to draw on the mercy of the Son. Here is the famous prayer of St. Faustina: "O merciful Jesus, stretched on the cross, be mindful of the hour of our death. O most merciful Heart of Jesus, opened with a lance, shelter me at the last moment of my life. O Blood and Water, which gushed forth from the Heart of Jesus as a fount of unfathomable mercy for me at the hour of my death, O dying Jesus, Hostage of mercy, avert the divine wrath at the hour of my death."[27]

Without the shield of his mercy, our soul would be naked before the Father's wrath because of all the sins committed in life: "O human souls, where are you going to hide on the day of God's anger? Take refuge now in the fount of God's mercy."[28]

And again: "Souls who spread the honor of My mercy I shield through their entire lives as a tender mother her infant, and at the hour of death I will not be a Judge for them, but the merciful Savior. At that last hour, a soul has nothing with which to defend itself except My mercy. Happy is the soul that during its lifetime immersed itself in the Fountain of mercy, because justice will have no hold on it."[29] For the soul that has no shield, there is the ominous fate of the eternal flames of hell.

---

23. Kowalska, *Diary*, 1434.
24. Kowalska, *Diary*, 611.
25. Kowalska, *Diary*, 570.
26. Kowalska, *Diary*, 300.
27. Kowalska, *Diary*, 813.
28. Kowalska, *Diary*, 848.
29. Kowalska, *Diary*, 1075.

One of the most impressive revelations granted to St. Faustina is precisely that of the vision of hell. It is good to read the whole description that St. Faustina gives of it, because we will have full vision of what we are really asking for when we recite the sixth petition of the Lord's Prayer:

> Today, I was led by an Angel to the chasms of Hell. It is a place of great torture; how awesomely large and extensive it is! The kinds of tortures I saw: the first torture that constitutes Hell is the loss of God; the second is perpetual remorse of conscience; the third is that one's condition will never change; (160) the fourth is the fire that will penetrate the soul without destroying it—a terrible suffering, since it is purely spiritual fire, lit by God's anger; the fifth torture is continual darkness and a terrible suffocating smell, and despite the darkness, the devils and the souls of the damned see each other and all the evil, both of others and their own; the sixth torture is the constant company of Satan; the seventh torture is horrible despair, hatred of God, vile words, curses and blasphemies. These are the tortures suffered by all the damned together, but that is not the end of the sufferings. There are special tortures destined for particular souls. These are the torments of the senses. Each soul undergoes terrible and indescribable sufferings, related to the manner in which it has sinned. There are caverns and pits of torture where one form of agony differs from another. ( . . . ) What I have written is but a pale shadow of the things I saw. But I noticed one thing: that most of the souls there are those who disbelieved that there is a Hell.[30]

Hell, in the words of St. Faustina, appears as the apotheosis of psychophysical torment, of that punitive *peirasmós* from which we ask to be spared when we recite the Lord's Prayer. And if we are still not convinced that this is the profound meaning of the last petitions of the Lord's Prayer, let us read the dialogue that St. Faustina reports between Jesus and a soul on the verge of despair:

> Jesus (interrupting): Do not be absorbed in your misery—you are still too weak to speak of it—but, rather; gaze on My Heart filled with goodness, and be imbued with My sentiments. Strive for meekness and humility; be merciful to others, as I am to you; and, when you feel your strength failing, if you come to the fountain of mercy to fortify your soul, you will not grow weary on your journey.
> Soul: Now I understand Your mercy, which protects me, and like a brilliant star, leads me into the home of my Father, protecting me from the horrors of Hell that I have deserved, not once, but a thousand times.[31]

We find here the fifth, sixth, and seventh petitions all together! "Be merciful to others, as I am to you" echoes the "forgive us our trespasses, as we forgive those who

---

30. Kowalska, *Diary*, 741.
31. Kowalska, *Diary*, 1486.

trespass against us" of the fifth petition. "Your mercy leads me into the home of my Father" echoes (antithetically) the "lead us not into *peirasmós*" of the sixth. And "protecting me from the horrors of Hell" echoes that "deliver us from evil" of the seventh.

Finally, all the pieces of the puzzle seem to fit together perfectly. The duality between the Father and the Son translates into the duality between justice and mercy, which in turn translates into the duality between the sixth and seventh petition of the Lord's Prayer:

1. The sixth petition is a plea to divine justice, lest it take its course and lead us to suffer the just torment we would deserve.

2. The seventh petition, complementary to the sixth, is a plea to divine mercy, that it may shield us from justice and deliver us from the just torment we deserve.

The sixth petition is about damnation; the seventh about redemption. God's justice would lead us into *peirasmós*, but God's mercy delivers us from it.

Sister Maria Faustina Kowalska, the saint who, perhaps more than anyone else, understood the profound mystery of the relationship between divine mercy and divine justice, ended her brief life in Krakow, amidst atrocious sufferings due to her illness, on October 5, 1938. Just at the age—what a coincidence—of 33.

Shortly before her death, she had implored the sisters of the Congregation to pray for Poland because, she said, "there will be a war, a terrible, terrible war." Exactly 365 days after her death, on October 6, 1939, the German army would end its occupation of Poland, which would kick off World War II—the most terrible war humanity has ever witnessed to date.

# 30

# The Lord's Prayer, Corrected

A few months before St. Faustina's death, on the night of January 25, 1938, the sky above Europe was lit up with shining streaks of green and red due to an extraordinary Aurora Borealis—a storm of light never seen or documented in Europe since at least 1709. A young nun, then in her early thirties, who had taken her vows only four years earlier under the name of Sister Mary of Sorrows, looking at that sky from the window of her convent in Tui, Spain, just across the northern border with Portugal, could not help but recall that July 13$^{th}$ of twenty-one years earlier, in the middle of World War I, when, still a child—she was just over ten years old—she had the most terrifying mystical experience of her entire life.

At that time, Lúcia de Jesus Rosa dos Santos—this is her real name at the time of her birth—was just a poor shepherdess from a very small town north of Lisbon (Fatima), who spent her days taking care of the flock together with her two best friends, her cousins Jacinta and Francisco.

On May 13$^{th}$ of that year (1917), they had the first of what would become perhaps the best known and most important Marian apparitions in history. A lady "all dressed in white, brighter than the sun" appeared to the three *pastorinhos*, asking them if they would be willing to return to the same place every 13 of the month for the following five months (until October 13, 1917). She had also predicted to them that she would take all three of them to heaven, but that Francisco would first have to "pray many rosaries." The apparition ended with this dialogue between the lady and the three children, which Lúcia reports in detail in her *Memoirs*:

> "Are you willing to offer yourselves to God to bear all the sufferings He wills to send you, as an act of reparation for the sins by which He is offended, and of supplication for the conversion of sinners?"
> "Yes, we are willing," was our reply.

"Then, you are going to have much to suffer, but the grace of God will be your comfort."[1]

This message, which seems so unusual when addressed to children of a few years of age, is the same message that Jesus confided, as we have seen, to Sister Faustina: reparation for the sins of the world through personal suffering.

The lady "all dressed in white" asks them if they are willing to accept the sacrifice of expiatory *peirasmós*, necessary so that God would grant the grace to many sinners to be able to convert and not end up in hell. The shepherd children respond enthusiastically. And from that day on, as Sister Lúcia recounts, they try to find any excuse to make small acts of sacrifice in order to save as many souls as possible.

In the next apparition, on June 13, 1917, the Lady predicts to the three cousins that she would take Jacinta and Francisco to heaven very soon, while she would leave Lúcia on earth for many years, so that she could fulfill the plan that God had in store for her.[2]

In the third apparition, the most frightening of all, on July 13, 1917, the three shepherd children are waiting as usual, kneeling in front of the holm oak tree on which the lady had appeared to them the first two times. A large crowd of faithful and curious people surround them. Suddenly, the signal—a sudden light. The lady appears, and without ever explicitly revealing her identity, simply asks the three to continue reciting the rosary daily, imploring for world peace and an end to the war. But then, just before disappearing "towards the East," as she had done the other times, the lady opens her arms and

> we saw as it were a sea of fire. Plunged in this fire were demons and souls in human form, like transparent burning embers, all blackened or burnished bronze, floating about in the conflagration, now raised into the air by the flames that issued from within themselves together with great clouds of smoke now falling back on every side like sparks in huge fires, without weight or equilibrium, amid shrieks and groans of pain and despair, which horrified us and made us tremble with fear. (It must have been this sight which caused me to cry out, as people say they heard me). The demons could be distinguished by their terrifying and repellent likeness to frightful and unknown animals, black and transparent like burning coals. Terrified and as if to plead for succor, we looked up at Our Lady, who said to us, so kindly and so sadly: You have seen hell where the souls of poor sinners go.[3]

---

1. Lucia, *Memoirs*, 82–83.

2. Francisco would die only a few months after the apparitions, on April 4, 1918, at the age of not even ten, after being struck by the violent epidemic of "Spanish Flu." Jacinta would die not even two years later, on February 20, 1920, also not even ten years old, after a long and painful illness. Lúcia will die on February 13, 2005, at the age of almost ninety-seven.

3. Lucia, *Memoirs*, 178.

It is a terrifying vision, which will impress the three children so much that they will increase the number of voluntary sacrifices in reparation for the sins committed in the world. The lady explains to the children that if the world is not converted, another and more terrible war will ravage the earth: "When you see a night illumined by an unknown light, know that this is the great sign given you by God that he is about to punish the world for its crimes, by means of war, famine, and persecutions of the Church and of the Holy Father."[4]

For the rest of her life, Sister Maria Lúcia would remain convinced that the extraordinary Aurora Borealis that swept over the entire world on the night of January 25, 1938, was precisely the sign that the lady had foretold to her—the ominous sign of the beginning of World War II, which would break out the following year. This vision of hell is in line with the description given by St. Faustina in her Diary.

But why would the lady have had the urgency to show the horrors of hell to three little shepherds? To understand this, we must connect a few clues.

From the first apparition, the only insistent request that the lady continues to make to the three little cousins is to recite the rosary incessantly. This is why she will be formally known as Our Lady of the Holy Rosary of Fatima. And why is the rosary so important? Because it could have prevented the coming war, that is, that punitive *peirasmós* that, according to the words of the lady, would soon befall the earth, as punishment for the crimes of humanity.

We understand that Our Lady of Fatima is explicitly associating the recitation of the rosary, and therefore of the Lord's Prayer, with a prayer of protection from the punitive *peirasmós*!

Most likely, what Our Lady of the Holy Rosary is trying to explain is that the combination of the fifth, sixth, and seventh petitions of the Lord's Prayer with the supplication to the Mother of God to intercede "for us sinners, now and in the hour of our death" is the most powerful combination possible to appease God's wrath and obtain his mercy.

But there is much more. The lady, after having shown the children a cross-section of hell, does not limit herself this time to encouraging them to recite the rosary. She expressly tells them to add a specific prayer at the end of each mystery—a short, dry prayer, made up of three simple petitions (in the original Portuguese):

> *Ó meu Jesus, perdoai-nos*
> *e livrai-nos do fogo do Inferno,*
> *levai as almas todas para o Céu, e socorrei principalmente as que mais precisarem.*[5]

Forgive us. Lead us to heaven. Deliver us from the fire of hell.

Forgive us our trespasses. Lead us not into *peirasmós*. Deliver us from evil.

---

4. Lucia, *Memoirs*, 179.

5. O my Jesus, forgive us and deliver us from the fire of hell, lead all souls to heaven, especially those who need it most.

The similarities between the three petitions of the Fatima prayer and the last three petitions of the Lord's Prayer are striking. Indeed, the Fatima prayer is, to all intents and purposes, an obvious reformulation of the last three petitions of the Lord's Prayer. Even the verb "*levar*," which indicates carrying (not simply leading) a person, seems to be the Portuguese counterpart of the original *eisphérō* of the sixth petition of the Lord's Prayer.

After all, there are only two places where God can take us eventually: eternal life or eternal death. Asking that God not take us into eternal death is evidently equivalent to asking that he take us into eternal life instead.

And if that were not clear enough, here goes the explicit request, "deliver us from the fire of hell." To indicate that the "evil" of the seventh petition of the Lord's Prayer, from which we ask to be delivered, must be understood, in its most extreme meaning, as the extreme punitive *peirasmós*, that is, the eternal torment in the flames of hell.

It seems to us that this message of Fatima, which despite being part of the so-called "private revelations" has been considered by the Catholic Church, after interminable investigations and meticulous "interrogations," to be "worthy of faith" and therefore true, is a powerful confirmation of the conclusion we arrived at in our analysis of the Lord's Prayer.

Indeed, it seems to us that Our Lady of the Rosary wanted, with this addition, to "correct" the common translation and interpretation of the sixth petition. For why would she have instructed the three shepherd children to add these three petitions after each mystery of the rosary?

There are only two possibilities. Either because these petitions were somehow new—original to what was already contained in the Lord's Prayer. Or because these petitions represented a sort of explanatory gloss to what was already contained in the Lord's Prayer, but to which the Portuguese translation did not do justice.

We do not deem the first option reasonable. First, it seems impossible to think that the mother of Jesus would teach the little shepherds a "new" piece of the Lord's Prayer, as if the Lord's Prayer that Jesus left to his disciples was somehow stumped. Second, the first petition of the Fatima prayer (that simple "forgive us") is nothing new, nothing original. It is already all contained in the fifth petition of the Lord's Prayer. Why then should Our Lady include it again? Simple redundancy? It is not credible.

The only sensible explanation, in our opinion, is that the first petition of the Fatima prayer is an explicit reference to the fifth petition of the Lord's Prayer. As if to say to the little shepherds, "after reciting the Lord's Prayer in the manner you were taught,[6] start this prayer again from the fifth petition, but change the sixth and seventh according to my reformulation." Reformulation that brings to light the true

---

6. All the various versions of the Lord's Prayer in Portuguese contain either the permissive formulation ("*Não nos deixeis cair em tentação*"), or the idea of inducing ("*E não nos induzas a tentação*"), or exposing to temptation ("*E naon nos metas em tentazaon*," João Ferreira de Almeida, 1753).

# THE LORD'S PRAYER, CORRECTED

meaning of those petitions. A meaning which, in the version of the Lord's Prayer you were taught, would remain totally hidden.

We like to think then that at Fatima the mother of God wanted to reveal the world not only the famous three secrets, but above all the true meaning of the sixth petition of the Lord's Prayer.

In fact, asking God not to send us to hell, but to lead us to eternal life should be the prayer par excellence of every Christian. Everything else—temptations, sins, sufferings, tribulations of life—take a back seat.

What counts for Christians is, in the end, only what God will decide to do with them, regardless of the more or less good works done in life: either to exercise his mercy by forgiving all their sins and granting them the grace to enter his presence, or to exercise his justice by punishing them to eternal fire. And it is unthinkable that such a fundamental request for a faithful would not find a place in the prayer that Jesus left us as a prototype.

After all, isn't this what is recited every day in every church in the world when, at the very beginning of Mass, the celebrant (unconsciously?) rephrases the last three petitions of the Lord's Prayer?

> May almighty God have mercy on us [seventh petition],
> forgive us our sins [fifth petition],
> and lead us to everlasting life [that is, lead us not into damnation: sixth petition].
> Amen.

# Appendix

## NUMBERING OF PSALMS

| Masoretic Text (MT) | Septuagint (LXX) | Verse Shift |
|---|---|---|
| 1–2 | 1–2 | None |
| 3 | 3 | MT 3:1 = LXX 3:1–2 |
| 4 | 4 | MT 4:1 = LXX 4:1–2 |
| 5 | 5 | MT 5:1 = LXX 5:1–2 |
| 6 | 6 | MT 6:1 = LXX 6:1–2 |
| 7 | 7 | MT 7:1 = LXX 7:1–2 |
| 8 | 8 | MT 8:1 = LXX 8:1–2 |
| 9:1–20 | 9:1–21 | MT 9:1 = LXX 9:1–2 |
| 10:1–18 | 9:22–39 | None |
| 11 | 10 | None |
| 12 | 11 | MT 12:1 = LXX 11:1–2 |
| 13–17 | 12–16 | None |
| 18 | 17 | MT 18:1 = LXX 17:1–2 |
| 19 | 18 | MT 19:1 = LXX 18:1–2 |
| 20 | 19 | MT 20:1 = LXX 19:1–2 |
| 21 | 20 | MT 21:1 = LXX 20:1–2 |
| 22 | 21 | MT 22:1 = LXX 21:1–2 |
| 23–29 | 22–28 | None |
| 30 | 29 | MT 30:1 = LXX 29:1–2 |
| 31 | 30 | MT 31:1 = LXX 30:1–2 |
| 32–33 | 31–32 | None |
| 34 | 33 | MT 34:1 = LXX 33:1–2 |
| 35 | 34 | None |
| 36 | 35 | MT 36:1 = LXX 35:1–2 |
| 37 | 36 | None |
| 38 | 37 | MT 38:1 = LXX 37:1–2 |

| | | |
|---|---|---|
| 39 | 38 | MT 39:1 = LXX 38:1-2 |
| 40 | 39 | MT 40:1 = LXX 39:1-2 |
| 41 | 40 | MT 41:1 = LXX 40:1-2 |
| 42 | 41 | MT 42:1 = LXX 41:1-2 |
| 43 | 42 | None |
| 44 | 43 | MT 44:1 = LXX 43:1-2 |
| 45 | 44 | MT 45:1 = LXX 44:1-2 |
| 46 | 45 | MT 46:1 = LXX 45:1-2 |
| 47 | 46 | MT 47:1 = LXX 46:1-2 |
| 48 | 47 | MT 48:1 = LXX 47:1-2 |
| 49 | 48 | MT 49:1 = LXX 48:1-2 |
| 50 | 49 | None |
| 51 | 50 | MT 51:1 = LXX 50:1-3 |
| 52 | 51 | MT 52:1 = LXX 51:1-3 |
| 53 | 52 | MT 53:1 = LXX 52:1-2 |
| 54 | 53 | MT 54:1 = LXX 53:1-3 |
| 55 | 54 | MT 55:1 = LXX 54:1-2 |
| 56 | 55 | MT 56:1 = LXX 55:1-2 |
| 57 | 56 | MT 57:1 = LXX 56:1-2 |
| 58 | 57 | MT 58:1 = LXX 57:1-2 |
| 59 | 58 | MT 59:1 = LXX 58:1-2 |
| 60 | 59 | MT 60:1 = LXX 59:1-3 |
| 61 | 60 | MT 61:1 = LXX 60:1-2 |
| 62 | 61 | MT 62:1 = LXX 61:1-2 |
| 63 | 62 | MT 63:1 = LXX 62:1-2 |
| 64 | 63 | MT 64:1 = LXX 63:1-2 |
| 65 | 64 | MT 65:1 = LXX 64:1-2 |
| 66 | 65 | None |
| 67 | 66 | MT 67:1 = LXX 66:1-2 |
| 68 | 67 | MT 68:1 = LXX 67:1-2 |
| 69 | 68 | MT 69:1 = LXX 68:1-2 |
| 70 | 69 | MT 70:1 = LXX 69:1-2 |
| 71-74 | 70-73 | None |
| 75 | 74 | MT 75:1 = LXX 74:1-2 |
| 76 | 75 | MT 76:1 = LXX 75:1-2 |
| 77 | 76 | MT 77:1 = LXX 76:1-2 |
| 78-79 | 77-78 | None |
| 80 | 79 | MT 80:1 = LXX 79:1-2 |
| 81 | 80 | MT 81:1 = LXX 80:1-2 |
| 82 | 81 | None |
| 83 | 82 | MT 83:1 = LXX 82:1-2 |

| | | |
|---|---|---|
| 84 | 83 | MT 84:1 = LXX 83:1-2 |
| 85 | 84 | MT 85:1 = LXX 84:1-2 |
| 86-87 | 85-86 | None |
| 88 | 87 | MT 88:1 = LXX 87:1-2 |
| 89 | 88 | MT 89:1 = LXX 88:1-2 |
| 90-91 | 89-90 | None |
| 92 | 91 | MT 92:1 = LXX 91:1-2 |
| 93-101 | 92-100 | None |
| 102 | 101 | MT 102:1 = LXX 101:1-2 |
| 103-107 | 102-106 | None |
| 108 | 107 | MT 108:1 = LXX 107:1-2 |
| 109-113 | 108-112 | None |
| 114:1-8 | 113:1-8 | None |
| 115:1-18 | 113:9-26 | None |
| 116:1-9 | 114:1-9 | None |
| 116:10-19 | 115:1-10 | None |
| 117-139 | 116-138 | None |
| 140 | 139 | MT 140:1 = LXX 139:1-2 |
| 141 | 140 | None |
| 142 | 141 | MT 142:1 = LXX 141:1-2 |
| 143-146 | 142-145 | None |
| 147:1-11 | 146:1-11 | None |
| 147:12-20 | 147:1-9 | None |
| 148-150 | 148-150 | None |

APPENDIX

# WORLDWIDE TRANSLATIONS

| Idiom | Semantic field of "to carry" (phérō) | Semantic field of "to lead" (ágō) | Semantic field of "to let" |
|---|---|---|---|
| Afrikaans | | | Let us not enter into temptation |
| Albanese | Do not drag us into temptation | | |
| Arab | | Do not expose us to temptation | |
| Armen | | Lead us not into temptation | |
| Basque | Do not carry us into temptation | | |
| Bosnian | Do not introduce us into temptation | | |
| Bulgari | Do not introduce us into temptation | | |
| Chinese | | | Let us not fall into temptation |
| Creole (Haiti) | | | Let us not fall into temptation |
| Croatian | Do not introduce us into temptation | | |
| Czech | | Lead us not into temptation | |
| Danish | | Lead us not into temptation | |
| English | | Lead us not into temptation | |
| Estonian | | Lead us not into temptation | |
| Finnish | | Lead us not into temptation | |
| French | Do not submit us to temptation (until 2017) | | Let us not enter into temptation |
| Gaelic (Scotland) | | | Let us not enter into temptation |
| German | | Lead us not into temptation | |
| Greek | Do not introduce us into temptation | | |
| Hawaiian | | | Let us not enter into temptation |
| Icelandic | | Lead us not into temptation | |

# APPENDIX

|  | | | |
|---|---|---|---|
| Irish | | | Let us not fall into temptation |
| Italian | | Do not induce us to temptation (until 2020) | Do not abandon us to temptation |
| Japanese | | | Let us not fall into temptation |
| Korean | | | Let us not fall into temptation |
| Latvian | | Lead us not into temptation | |
| Lithuanian | | | Do not permit us to be tempted |
| Macedonian | Do not introduce us into temptation | | |
| Malaysian | | | Let us not lose our faith when we are tempted |
| Norwegian | | | Let us not enter into temptation |
| Polish | | Lead us not into temptation | |
| Portuguese | | | Let us not fall into temptation |
| Romanian | | Lead us not into temptation | |
| Russian | Do not introduce us into temptation | | |
| Serbian | Do not introduce us into temptation | | |
| Slovenian | Do not introduce us into temptation | | |
| Spanish | | | Let us not fall into temptation |
| Swedish | | Lead us not into temptation | |
| Turkish | | Lead us not into temptation | |
| Ukrainian | | | Let us not fall into temptation |
| Uzbek | | Do not expose us to temptation | |
| Welsh | | | Let us not fall when we are tested |

377

# Bibliography

Ambrose. "*De sacramentis.*" In *Patrologia Latina*, edited by Jacques P. Migne, 16:1–6. Paris: 1844–1864.

Aquinas, Thomas. *Super Evangelium S. Matthaei Lectura*. Turin: Marietti, 1951.

Augustine. "*De sermone Domini in monte.*" In *Patrologia Latina*, edited by Jacques P. Migne, 34:1229–1308. Paris: 1844–1864.

———. "*Sermo LVII.*" In *Patrologia Latina*, edited by Jacques P. Migne, 38:326–93. Paris: 1844–1864.

Beentjes, Pancratius C. *The Book of Ben Sira in Hebrew*. Supplements to Vetus Testamentum 68. Atlanta, GA: Society of Biblical Literature, 2006.

Betz, Hans D. *The Sermon on the Mount: A Commentary on the Sermon on the Mount, Including the Sermon on the Plain*. Minneapolis, MN: Fortress, 1995.

Blomberg, Craig L. *Matthew: An Exegetical and Theological Exposition of Holy Scripture*. The New American Commentary, Volume 22. Nashville, TN: Broadman, 1992.

Bock, Darrell L. *Luke, Volume 2: 9:51–24:53*. Baker Exegetical Commentary on the New Testament. Grand Rapids, MI: Baker, 1996.

Boice, James M. *The Sermon on the Mount: Matthew 5–7*. Grand Rapids, MI: Baker, 2006.

Brown, Raymond E. "The Pater Noster as an Eschatological Prayer." In *New Testament Essays*, edited by Raymond E. Brown. Milwaukee, WI: Bruce, 1965.

Bussche, Henry van den. *Understanding the Lord's Prayer*. London: Sheed and Ward, 1963.

Calvin, John. *Commentary on Matthew, Mark, Luke*. Volume 1.

Cameron, Peter S. "Lead Us Not into Temptation." *Expository Times* 101 (1989) 299–301.

Carmignac, Jean. *Recherches sur le Notre Père*. Paris: Letouzey & Ané, 1969.

Charlesworth, James H. "The Beth Essentiae and the Permissive Hipel (Aphel)." In H. Attridge, J. J. Collins and T. Tobins (eds.), "Of Scribes and Scrolls: Studies on the Hebrew Bible, Intertestamental Judaism, and Christian Origins." *College Theological Society Resources in Religion* 5, 67–78. New York and London: Lanham, 1991.

———. "Jewish Prayers in the Time of Jesus." *Princeton Seminary Bulletin* 13 (1992) 36–55.

Chromatius. "*Tractatus in Evangellium Matthaei.*" In *Patrologia Latina*, edited by Jacques P. Migne, 20:328–68. Paris: 1844–1864.

Cullmann, Oscar. *Prayer in the New Testament*. Translated by John J. Bowden. First North American Edition: Augsburg Fortress, 1995.

Cyprian. "*De oratione dominica.*" In *Patrologia Latina*, edited by Jacques P. Migne, 4:535–60. Paris: 1844–1864.

Cyril of Alexandria. "*Commentarius in Lucam.*" In *Patrologia Graeca*, edited by Jacques P. Migne, 72:695–96. Paris: 1844–1864.

# BIBLIOGRAPHY

Dahms, J. V. "Lead Us Not into Temptation." *Journal of the Evangelical Theological Society* 17 (1974) 223-30.

Davies, W. D., and Dale C. Allison. "Matthew." *International Critical Commentary*. Edinburgh: T. & T. Clark, 1985.

Dionysius of Alexandria. *The Gospel According to Luke*. Exegetical fragment 22:42-48.

Dunn, James D. G. "Prayer." *Dictionary of Jesus and the Gospels*, 619-25. Illinois: InterVarsity, 1992.

Evans, C. F. *The Lord's Prayer*. London: SCM, 1997.

Fitzmyer, Joseph A. "And Lead Us Not into Temptation." *Biblica* Vol. 84 (2003) 259-273.

———. "The Gospel According to Luke." *The Anchor Bible*. New York: Doubleday, 1970-1985.

France, R. T. *The Gospel of Matthew*. The New International Commentary on the New Testament. Grand Rapids, MI: Eerdmans, 2007.

———. *Matthew: An Introduction and Commentary*. Tyndale New Testament Commentaries. Downers Grove, IL: InterVarsity, 1985.

Garland, David E. "The Lord's Prayer in the Gospel of Matthew." *Review & Expositor* 89 (1992) 215-28.

———. *Reading Matthew: A Literary and Theological Commentary on the First Gospel*. Reading the New Testament. Macon, GA: Smith & Helwys, 2001.

Gibson Jeffrey B. *The Disciples' Prayer: The Prayer Jesus Taught in Its Historical Setting*. Minneapolis, MN: Fortress, 2015.

———. *The Temptation of Jesus in Early Christianity*. Edinburgh: T. & T. Clark, 2004.

———. "Testing Temptation: the Meaning of Q 11:4b" (unpublished paper presented at the Annual Meeting of the Society of Biblical Literature). Orlando, FL: 1998.

Guelich, Robert A. "Interpreting the Sermon on the Mount." *Interpretation* 41 (2) (1987) 117-130.

Gupta, Nijay K. "Lead Us Not into Temptation, Deliver Us from Evil." In *The Lord's Prayer*. Smyth & Helwys Bible Commentary. Macon: Smyth & Helwys, 2017.

Hagner, Donald A. *Matthew*. Word Biblical Commentary, 33A. Nashville, TN: Thomas Nelson, 1995.

Harnack, Adolf von. *Marcion: The Gospel of the Alien God*. Translated by J. E. Steely and L. D. Bierma. Durham, NC: Labyrinth, 1990.

———. "Zwei Worte Jesu. 1. Zur 6. Bitte des Vaterunser (Matt 6:13 = Luke 11:4)." *Sitzungsberichte der Preussischen Akademie der Wissenschalften zu Berlin* (1907) 942-47.

Heller, Johannes. "Die Sechste Bitte des Vaterunser." *Zeitscrift fur katholische Theologie* 25 (1901) 85-93.

Higgins, A. J. B. "Lead Us Not into Temptation: Some Latin Variants." *Journal of Theological Studies* 46 (1945) 179-83.

Hilary of Poitiers. "*Tractatus super psalmos*." In *Patrologia Latina*, edited by Jacques P. Migne, 9:231-889. Paris: 1844-1864.

Hoare, J. N. "Lead Us Not into Temptation." *Expository Times* 50 (1938-39) 333.

Jeremias, Joachim. *The Lord's Prayer*. Translated by J. Reumann. Philadelphia, PA: Fortress, 1964.

———. *The Sermon on the Mount*. Translated by N. Perrin. Philadelphia, PA: Fortress, 1963.

Jerome. "*Commentaria in Ezechielem*." In *Patrologia Latina*, edited by Jacques P. Migne, 25:15-490. Paris: 1844-1864.

Josephus, Flavius. *De bello judaico*. Translated by William Whiston (1737).

Knoke, K. "Der ursprüngliche Sinn der sechsten Bitte." *Neue kirchliche Zeitschrift* 18 (1907) 200–220.

Korn, Joachim H. *Πειρασμός: Die Versuchung des Gläubigen in der griechischen Bibel.* Stuttgart: Kohlhammer, 1937.

Kowalska, Maria Faustina. *Diary: Divine Mercy in My Soul.* Stockbridge, MA: Marian, 2005.

Lohmeyer, Ernst. *Das Vater-Unser.* Göttingen: Vandenhoeck & Ruprecht, 1952 [*Our Father: An Introduction.* Translated by John Bowden. New York: Harper & Row, 1965].

Lowe, John. *The Lord's Prayer.* Oxford: Clarendon, 1962.

Luz, Ulrich. *Matthew 1–7: A Commentary.* Minneapolis, MN: Augsburg, 1989.

Manson, T. W. "The Lord's Prayer." *Bulletin of the John Rylands Library.* Manchester, XXXVIII (1955–56) 99–113.

Manzoni, Alessandro. *The Betrothed: I Promessi Sposi.* New York: Penguin (1984).

Marshall, Howard I. *The Gospel of Luke: A Commentary on the Greek Text.* New International Greek Testament Commentary. Exeter, UK: Paternoster, 1978.

———. "Jesus—Example and Teacher of Prayer in the Synoptic Gospels." In *Into God's Presence: Prayer and the New Testament*, edited by Richard N. Longenecker, 113–31. Grand Rapids, MI: Eerdmans, 2001.

McCaughey, Davis J. "Matthew 6:13a: The Sixth Petition in the Lord's Prayer." *Australian Biblical Review* 33 (1985) 31–40.

Moor, Johannes C. de. *The Reconstruction of the Aramaic Original of the Lord's Prayer.* Structural Analysis of Biblical and Canaanite Poetry. Sheffield: Journal for the Study of the Old Testament, 1988.

Moore, E. "Lead Us Not into Temptation." *Expository Times* 102 (1991) 171–72.

Moule, C. F. D. "An Unsolved Problem in the Temptation Clause in the Lord's Prayer." *Reformed Theological Review* 33 (1974).

Neumann, James N. "Thy Will Be Done: Jesus's Passion in the Lord's Prayer." *Journal of Biblical Literature* 138, No. 1 (2019) 161–82.

Nolland, John. *The Gospel of Matthew: A Commentary on the Greek Text.* The New International Greek Testament Commentary. Grand Rapids, MI: Eerdmans, 2005.

———. *Luke 9:21–18:34.* Word Biblical Commentary 35B. Dallas, TX: Word, Incorporated, 2002.

Origen. "*De oratione.*" In *Patrologia Graeca*, edited by Jacques P. Migne, 11:415–560. Paris: 1844–1864.

Pitre, Brant. *Jesus, the Tribulation, and the End of the Exile.* Grand Rapids, MI: Baker Academic, 2006.

Porter, Stanley E. "Mt 6:13 and Lk 11:4, Lead Us Not into Temptation." *Expository Times* 101 (1990) 359–62.

Powell, W. "Lead Us Not into Temptation." *Expository Times* 67 (1955–56) 177–78.

Ratzinger, Joseph (Pope Benedict XVI). *"In the Beginning..." A Catholic Understanding of the Story of Creation and the Fall.* Grand Rapids, MI: Eerdmans, 1995.

———. *Jesus of Nazareth: From the Baptism in the Jordan to the Transfiguration.* New York: Doubleday, 2007.

Richards, C. L. "Lead Us Not into Temptation." *Expository Times* 59 (1947–48) 24–25.

Schürmann, Heinz. *Praying with Christ: The "Our Father" for Today.* New York: Herder and Herder, 1964.

Schweizer, Eduard. *The Good News According to Matthew.* Atlanta: John Knox, 1975.

Seesemann, H. "πεῖρα, κτλ." In *Theological Dictionary of the New Testament (TDNT)* 6:23–36.

Smith, C. F. W. "The Lord's Prayer." In *Interpreter's Dictionary of the Bible (IDB)* Volume 3, 157. Nashville, TN: Abingdon, 1962.

Spicq, Ceslas. *Theological Lexicon of the New Testament*. Translated by J. D. Ernest. Carol Stream, IL: Tyndale House, 1995.

Sykes, M. H. "And Do Not Bring Us to the Test." *Expository Times* 73 (1961–1962) 189–90.

Tertullian. "*De baptismo*." In *Patrologia Latina*, edited by Jacques P. Migne, 1:1197–1224. Paris: 1844–1864.

———. "*De fuga in persecutione*." In *Patrologia Latina*, edited by Jacques P. Migne, 2:101–20. Paris: 1844–1864.

———. "*De oratione*." In *Patrologia Latina*, edited by Jacques P. Migne, 1:1144–96. Paris: 1844–1864.

Verity, G. B. "Lead Us Not into Temptation, but . . ." *Expository Times* 58 (1946–47) 221–22.

Vermes, Geza. *The Complete Dead Sea Scrolls in English*. London: Penguin, 2004.

Waetjen, Herman C. *Praying the Lord's Prayer: An Ageless Prayer for Today*. London: Bloomsbury, 1999.

Walker, M. B. "Lead Us Not into Temptation." *Expository Times* 73 (1961–62) 287.

Wallace, Daniel B. *Greek Grammar Beyond the Basics: An Exegetical Syntax of the New Testament*. Grand Rapids, MI: Zondervan, 1996.

Willimon, William H., and Stanley Hauerwas. *Lord, Teach Us: The Lord's Prayer & the Christian Life*. Nashville, TN: Abingdon, 2002.

Willis, G. G. "Lead Us Not into Temptation." *Downside Review* 93 (1975) 281–88.

Young, Bradford H. *The Jewish Background to the Lord's Prayer*. Tulsa, OK: Gospel Research Foundation, 1984.

www.ingramcontent.com/pod-product-compliance
Lightning Source LLC
Chambersburg PA
CBHW080406300426
44113CB00015B/2411